A GEN[?]
AND PERS[?]NAL HISTORY
OF
BUCKS COUNTY,
PENNSYLVANIA

By William W. H. Davis

Edited by

WARREN S. ELY
and
John W. Jordan

CLEARFIELD

Originally prepared
under the editorial supervision of
Warren S. Ely and John W. Jordan and
Published as Volume III of
History of Bucks County Pennsylvania,
second edition, New York and Chicago,
1905

Reprinted
Genealogical Publishing Company, Inc.
Baltimore, Maryland, 1975

Reprinted in Two Parts for
Clearfield Company, Inc. by
Genealogical Publishing Co., Inc.
Baltimore, Maryland
1992, 1994, 1999, 2002

International Standard Book Number: 0-8063-4863-1
Set Number 0-8063-0641-6

Library of Congress Cataloging in Publication Data
Davis, William Watts Hart, 1820-1910.
    History of Bucks County, Pennsylvania from the discovery of the
Delaware to the present time.
    Reprint of v. 3 of the 1905 ed. published by Lewis Pub. Co.,
New York.
    1. Bucks Co., Pa.—Genealogy. I. Title.
F157.B8D32   1975   929'.1'0974821   74-18311

The publisher gratefully acknowledges
the loan of the original volume from the
Maryland Historical Society
Baltimore, Maryland

Made in the United States of America

PART I

INTRODUCTORY

The present volume forms a fitting supplement to the ample historical narrative from the pen of General W. W. H. Davis. For its preparation especial thanks are due to Mr. Warren S. Ely, of more than merely local fame as a genealogist and historian. Out of his abundant store of material and through familiarity with the official records of Bucks and adjoining counties, he has been enabled to write with care and intelligence the genealogical history of various branches of leading families in Bucks county, and his sketches will be readily identified by all who are familiar with the methods which he has observed so successfully in making investigations into ancestral fields in response to many exacting requisitions by individuals and family associations. He has also, in this work, dealt largely with the personal history of leading men of affairs in his native county, and his facile pen can be readily traced by the great mass of readers in that region who for years have been familiar with his clear and cogent writings along the lines which he has pursued with that genuine enthusiasm becoming to one who holds in proper appreciation the sturdy race from whom he sprang and among whom he was reared, and who possesses the ability of rightly weighing their lives and achievements.

An earnest effort has been made to give an authentic history of most of the early settlers, as well as of those who later found homes in this historic county, and their descendants down to the present time, giving special attention to the part taken by them in its history and development. It has been impossible, however, to give as full an account of some of the old families as might have been desired, by reason of the paucity of data furnished, many families of more or less prominence in the affairs of the county, at different periods, being without exact records of their family line, and it being, of course, impracticable in a work of this general character for the publishers to undertake extensive and expensive researches in untrodden paths. Neither was it possible for Mr. Ely to revise and verify all the data furnished by the representatives of the families treated of in the work. It can be said, however, with reference to the biographical matter contained in this volume that in its preparation the publishers have observed the utmost care as to accuracy and authenticity, so far as lay in their power. In all cases the sketches have been submitted to the subject, or present representative of the family, for correction and revision, and the publishers believe that they are placing before the public, in the contents of this volume, a valuable adjunct to the narrative history of the events in this historic county, to which General Davis has devoted nearly a lifetime of painstaking and intelligent research, by giving some authentic account of most of the families that have participated in those events, and following these genealogical and historical sketches with some account of the present generation, on whom and their descendants the grand old county must depend for the maintenance of the high standard of citizenship that has characterized her in the past. An effort has also been made to give some account of the descendants of Bucks county ancestry who have wandered from their alma mater and distinguished themselves in the various walks of life in other sections. We believe, therefore, that we have rendered a lasting service to posterity in gathering together and placing in enduring form much valuable information that would otherwise soon have been irretrievably lost through the passing away of many custodians of family and other records, and the consequent dispersion of such matter.

The publishers desire to express their appreciation of the assistance rendered them and their editors in the preparation of this work, by various persons who have placed at their disposal the result of valuable researches made on genealogical and historical lines for private purposes. As stated therein, much of the data in reference to the Holland families who were the first actual settlers on the Neshaminy in Northampton, Southampton and adjoining parts of Warminster, Bensalem, Middletown and Bristol townships, is the result of more than twenty years of research conducted on these lines by R. Winder Johnson, of Philadelphia, very little if any of which has been heretofore published. Again, much of the data in reference to the early German settlers in upper Bucks, whose part in the history of the county has probably never received proper recognition, is the result of exhaustive researches made by Mr. Ely, in which he was materially aided by the Rev. A. J. Fretz, of Milton, New Jersey, who has devoted years of unselfish work to these lines. Many others have contributed more or less to the value of the work by giving us the benefit of their valuable researches.

                                                      THE PUBLISHERS.

INDEX

BUCKS COUNTY.

THE PEMBERTON FAMILY. Four miles south of Morrisville, Bucks county, Pennsylvania, on the mainland, near the Delaware river, opposite Biles' Island, there is an old family graveyard, dating back to the ninth decade of the seventeenth century. It is one of the oldest graveyards in the county, if not in the state. Within its walls, measuring two rods square, lies the remains of four generations of one family, all of whom died in the short space of fifteen years. There rest the five young children of Phineas and Phebe (Harrison) Pemberton, as well as both the parents of these children. Near them also repose their grandparents, Ralph Pemberton, and James Harrison and Anne his wife; and adjoining lies the remains of their great-grandmother, Agnes Harrison, born in one of the last years of the reign of Queen Elizabeth. Not often, even in a well settled and long established country, is found such a number of generations, encompassed by one enclosure. The early history of the family that lies buried in this ancient burying ground is so closely interwoven with the history of the founding of Penn's colony on the Delaware and the causes that led up to that event, and so typical of that of most of the early families that formed the van guard of the Quaker emigrants to Pennsylvania,—explaining, as it does, the motive that led these early settlers to leave the land of their birth and seek homes in an unknown wilderness—that we wish to preface a brief account of the family with some account of the early sufferings of the Society of Friends, of which they were representative members. Let us take a glance at the condition of the Friends in England, prior to Penn's establishment of his colony in America.

The development of Quakerism in England under, let us say, the reign of Henry VIII, would have been an impossibility; but the growth of popular government and freedom of thought which were so firmly established by the genius and power of Oliver Cromwell, rendered possible that which would have been entirely impossible a century earlier. All the force of government, however, and all the power of the church were thrown against the Society of Friends, and no means were spared to persecute them and subject them to ignomy and contempt. No class of life or society was spared in these persecutions. Many of the early converts to Quakerism were of noble birth or people of power and influence in the realm. William Penn was "the companion of princes and the dispenser of royal favors." Thomas Elwood was of gentle birth, being nearly related through his mother to Lady Wenman. George Barclay was of good stock and a fine classical scholar. Yet all these men, because of their religious convictions, were frequently imprisoned, sometimes herded with the lowest felons and vilest prostitutes—"nasty sluts indeed they were," says Elwood in his autobiography. "Remember," said Phineas Pemberton, in an epistle that was intended as a preface to the "Book of Minutes of the Yearly Meeting of Friends," on the setting up of that body at Burlington, New Jersey; "Remember, we were a despised people in our native land, accounted by the world scarce worthy to have a name or place therein; daily liable to their spoil; under great sufferings, by long and tedious imprisonments, sometimes to the loss of life—banishment, spoil of goods, beatings, mockings, and ill treatings; so that we had not been a people at this day had not the Lord stood by us and preserved us." (Friends' Miscellany, vol. vii, p. 42.) His description is not overdrawn: "Come out," they cried before Phineas Pemberton's door in 1678; "Come out, thou Papist dog, thou Jesuit, thou devil, come out." He was several times imprisoned in Chester and Lancaster castles, being confined in the latter prison in 1669, nineteen weeks and five days, and this, too, before he was twenty-one years of age.

James Harrison, who lies buried beside Phineas Pemberton and who was his father-in-law, was very active as a minister among Friends and was imprisoned in 1660, in Burgas-gate prison for nearly two months; in 1663 in the county jail of Worcester; in 1664, 1665 and 1666 in Chester castle: "But none of these things," says Phineas. were done unto us because of our evil deeds, but because of the exercise of our tender consciences towards our God." Nor were these cases exceptional; to such a pitch of nervousness had the government been wrought by the various plots, and so great was the fear of Catholic ascendency among the people at that time, that later in 1686, when James II issued the general pardon to all who were in prison on account of conscientious dissent, over twelve hundred Quakers—perfectly inoffensive and harmless subjects as they were —were released, "many having been immured in prison, some of them twelve or fifteen years and upwards, for no crime but endeavoring to keep a good conscience towards God."

It was from this English barbarism and English oppression that William Penn invited his fellow Friends to join him in what he called his "Holy Experiment" in America. Accordingly, on the 5th of the 7th month (September), 1682, the Pembertons and Harrisons, with other families, sailed from Liverpool in the ship "Submission" for Pennsylvania. As it may be of interest to their descendants we give below the list of passengers on the "Submission." This list is taken from James Pemberton Parke's mss. account of the Pemberton family, 1825. It is from this manuscript that the account of the family published in the Friends' miscellany, vol. vii, is drawn. The latter, however, contains only a partial list of the passengers given below. Our list also contains some particulars not included in the list given in the "Sailing of the Ship Submission" in vol. i, no. 1, of the "Publications of the Genealogical Society of Pennsylvania," Philadelphia, 1895.

Passengers on board the ship "Submission."

Ralph Pemberton, Bolton, Lancashire, age 72; servants, Joseph Mather, Elizabeth Bradbury.

Phineas Pemberton, Bolton, Lancashire, age 33; servants, William Smith, servant of Phineas Pemberton, came in Friends' Adventure, arrived 7th mo. 28, 1682.

Phebe Pemberton, wife of Phineas, daughter of James Harrison, age 23

Abigail Pemberton, daughter of Phineas, age 3 years.

Joseph Pemberton, son of same, aged one year.

James Harrison, Bolton, Lancashire, age 57 years; servants, Joseph Steward, Allis Dickerson, Jane Lyon.

Agnes Harrison, Bolton, Lancashire, mother of James, age 81.

Ann Harrison, his wife, Bolton, Lancashire, age 61.

Robert Bond, son of Thomas Bond, of Waddicar Hall, near Garstang, Lancashire, age 16; being left by his father to the tuition of sd. James Harrison.

Lydia Wharmsby, of Bolton afsd., age 42.

Randolph Blackshaw, Hollingee, in the Co. of Chester, servants, Sarah Bradbury, Roger Bradbury, and Elinor his wife and their children Hager, Jacob, Joseph, Martha, and Sarah.

Alice Blackshaw, his wife, and their children, Phebe, Sarah, Jacob, Mary, Nehemiah, Martha and Abraham, the latter died at sea, 8 mo. 2d, 1682.

Ellis Jones, and Jane his wife, County of Denby or Flint, in Wales, and their children, Barbara, Dorothy, Mary and Isaac Jones. "Servants of the Governor Penn these came."

Jane Mode and Margery Mode of Wales, daughters of Thomas Winn, and the wife of sd. Thomas Winn; servants, Hareclif Hodges, servant of Thomas Winn.

James Clayton, of Middlewitch, Chester, blacksmith, and Jane his wife, and children James, Sarah, John, Mary, Joshua and Lydia.

The list conforms to the account given in the original "Book of Arrivals" in the handwriting of Phineas Pemberton, now in possession of the Bucks County Historical Society. The list given in the Publications of the Genealogical Society, above referred to, gives, in addition to the above, "Richard Radclif, of Lancashire, aged 21," and Ellen Holland, whose name adjoins that of Hareclif Jones; "Joseph Clayton, aged 5," and omits Joshua Jones; and gives age of Barbara Jones as 13, gives "Margery and Jane *Mede*, aged 11 1-2 and 15, respectively. It also gives "Rebeckah Winn, 20 years," but omits the name of —— Winn, wife of Thomas. In re, Winn and Mode, see "Penna. Magazine of History and Biography," vol. ix, p 231, also "Genealogy of Fisher Family, 1896, pp. 15, 199, and "Ancestry of Dr. Thomas Wynne," 1904.

James Settle, captain of the ship "Submission," was by the terms of his agreement to proceed with the ship to the "Delaware River or elsewhere in Pennsylvania, to the best convenience of the freighters," but through his dishonesty they were taken into Maryland, to their very great disadvantage where after a severe storm they had encountered at sea, on 8 mo. 2, 1682, they arrived in the Patuxent river, on the 30th of October, and unloaded their goods at Choptank. Here James Harrison and Phineas Pemberton, his son-in-law, left their respective families, at the house of William Dickenson, and proceeded overland to the place of their original destination, the "falls of the Delaware," in Bucks county. William Penn, who had arrived on October 24, was at that time in New York; Harrison and Pemberton had hoped to meet him at New Castle. When they arrived at the present site of Philadelphia they could not procure entertainment for their horses, and so "spancelled" them and turned them into the woods. The next morning they sought for them in vain they having strayed so far in the woods that one of them was not found until the following January. After two days searching they were obliged to proceed up the river in a boat. Philadelphia was not then founded, and the country was a wilderness.

James Harrison had received grants of 5,000 acres of land of Penn, when in Eng-

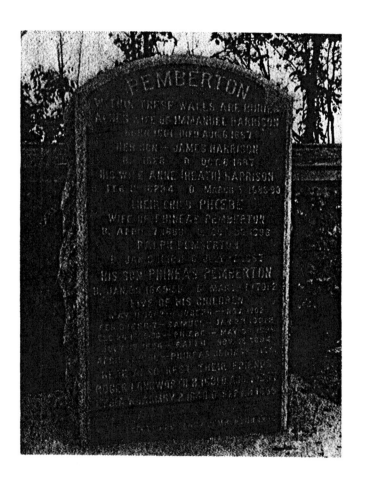

land, a short time before his departure, for America. Most of this land was subsequently located in Bucks county. In the following spring, 1683, Harrison and Pemberton brought their families and household goods from Maryland to this county, Harrison stopping at Upland, now Chester, on the way south, to attend the first Assembly, to which he had been elected. Until Phineas could erect a house in Bucks county, he and his family stayed at the house of Lyonel Brittian, who had arrived in Bucks, 4 mo. (June) 1680. On 11 mo. 17, 1683, Phineas Pemberton purchased a tract of 500 acres on the Delaware, opposite Oreclan's (later Biles') Island and built a house there. It must have been a satisfaction to him, after the storms at sea and wanderings on land, to have his family at last under his own roof-tree. This plantation he called "Grove Place." He appears, however, at first to have called it "Sapasse," since letters to him from friends in England in 1684 were addressed "Sapasse, Bucks County." It was part of a tract of over 8,000 acres of land, purchased by Penn from an old Indian king, and had once been a royalty called "Sepessain." (On Peter Lindstrom's map of 1654, in Sharp and Westcott's "History of Philadelphia," vol. i, p. 75, the name appears as "Sipaessing Land"). The old burying ground before referred to was located on this tract. Being desirous of erecting a more comfortable home for his family, Phineas Pemberton finished one in 1687. On the lintel of the door was this inscription:

P.
"P.   P. 7 D. 2 mo. 1687."

The initials signifying Phineas and Phebe Pemberton. This lintel is now in the possession of the Historical Society of Pennsylvania, Philadelphia. This house Pemberton moved after his second marriage to another tract of land five miles distant and more in the interior. It was taken down in 1802 by his grandson, James Pemberton. In the year 1687 a great deal of sickness prevailed in the colony, and Phineas Pemberton lost his father, Ralph Pemberton, and his father-in-law, James Harrison. Agnes Harrison, the mother of James, also died. Three years later Anne (Heath) Harrison, the widow of James died; and in 1696 Phineas lost his wife Phebe, who died 8 mo. 30, 1696, exactly fourteen years after her arrival in Patuxent river, Maryland.

On the 18th day of May, 1699, Phineas Pemberton married, at the Meeting House at Falls, Alice Hodgson, "of Burlington, in the Province of West Jersey, spinster, daughter of Robert Hodgson, late of Rhode Island, deceased." The following names, as witnesses appear on the marriage certificate:

Alice Dickerson,   Joseph Borden,
Martha Drake,   John Borradaill,

Ann Elett,
Ann Jennings,
Elenor Hoopes,
Mary Baker,
Abigail Sidwell,
Eliz. Browdon,
Sarah Surket,
Mary Webster,
Phebe Kirkbride,
Sarah Jennings,
Grace Lloyd,
Mary Badcoke,
Elizabeth Badok,
Ann Borden,
Elizabeth Stacy,
Sarah Stacy,
William Croasdell,
George Browne,
John Surket, Junr.,
Joseph Large,
Peter Webster,
Seth Hill,
Edwd. Penington,
Tho. Brock,
Joseph Kirkbride,
John Jones,
Jeremiah Langhorn
William Ellett,
John Biles,

Saml. Beakes,
Arthur Cooke,
John Simcocke,
Saml. Jennings,
Thos. Duckett,
Jos. Growdon,
Mahlon Stacy,
Henry Baker,
Richard Hough,
Will. Dunkin,
Isaac Mariott,
Peter Worrall,
Edward Lucas,
Abraham Anthony,
John Cooke,
John Sidwell,
Robert Hodgson,
Philip England,
Mary Yardley,
Abell Janney,
Jos. Janney,
Mary Williams,
Abigail Pemberton,
Eliz. Janney,
Joseph Pemberton,
Israel Pemberton,
Thomas Yardley,
Rand'l Blackshaw,
Joseph Mather.

The original certificate is in the possession of a descendant, Mr. Henry Pemberton, of Philadelphia. Phineas had no children by his second wife. After his death she married, in 1704, Thomas Bradford, being also his second wife. She died August 28, 1711.

James Harrison was at an early date the friend and confidant of Penn. "He was," says Proud, "one of the Proprietor's first Commissioners of Property, was divers years in great esteem with him, and his agent at Pennsbury, being a man of good education and a preacher among the Quakers." In the library of the Historical Society of Pennsylvania at Thirteenth and Locust streets, Philadelphia, (Penn mss. Domestic Letters) there are many original letters from Penn to Harrison, some of them written before Penn left England. They undoubtedly belong to the collection of Pemberton mss.* now owned by the His-

*This collection, mounted in about one hundred volumes, extends over a period of about two hundred years from a date before the birth of Penn to within modern times. It was presented to the Society in 1891 by Henry Pemberton, of Philadelphia, and comprises mss. of the Pemberton, Harrison, Galloway, Rawle, Shoemaker, Clifford and other families. Two volumes of letters now in the "Etting Collection" of the same Society, belonged originally to this collection as they are docketed on the outside in the handwriting of James Pemberton. Harrison was a member of the first provincial council, which met in Philadelphia on the tenth day of the first month, 1682-3. In the same year he was a member of the committee to draw up the charter of the colony. In 1685 he was appointed by Penn as chief justice of the supreme court, but declined to serve: but the following year he accepted the position of associate justice. He was Penn's steward and agent in Pennsylvania until his death, on October 6, 1687. His daughter Phebe married Phineas Pemberton, the 1st day of 11 mo. (January) 1676-7, at the house of John Haydock, in Coppull, near Standish, Lancashire, England, under the supervision of Hardshaw Monthly Meeting of Friends.

torical Society, since they contain an index drawn in the handwriting of Phineas Pemberton. Many of these letters from Penn are interesting in that they contain reference to matters current in the earliest days of the colony, and also occasionally give a picture of political life in England.

Phineas Pemberton took an active part in the public affairs of the colony as well as of Bucks county. He was a member of provincial council in 1685-7, 1695, and 1697-9; was a member of assembly 1689, 1694, 1698 (the latter year he was speaker), and in 1700, and a member of Penn's council of state in 1701. But it was in the affairs of Bucks county, where he lived, that his activity and usefulness was the greatest and his work of the most value. He was beyond doubt the most prominent man of his time in the county and the most efficient, as shown by the mass of records he has left behind him in his own handwriting, and by the number of official positions he filled. In addition to filling the local positions of register of wills, recorder, and clerk of all the courts, he held for a time the positions of master of the rolls, register general, and recorder of proprietary quit-rents for the province; and the records of the county up to the time of his fatal illness are entirely in his handwriting, and are models worthy of imitation by officials of our day. The records of the different courts left by him are invaluable to the historian, and greatly superior to those of his successors in office in the matter of lucidity and completeness. Many of our historians have noticed and acknowledged this fact, which is apparent to all that have had access to them. Buck, in his "History of Bucks County," referring to the records left by Pemberton, says, "they comprise the earliest records of Bucks county offices, and, though they have been referred to by different writers, comparatively little has been heretofore published from them. To us they have rendered valuable aid and we must acknowledge our indebtedness for information that could, possibly, from no other source have been obtained." In like manner Battle, in his "History of Bucks County," writing on the same subject, states, "From that period (i. e. 1683) until disabled by a fatal illness, save an unimportant interval, the records of the county were written wholly by his hand; and in them he has left a memorial of himself that will not be lost so long as the history of the commonwealth which he helped to establish shall be read."[*]

Phineas Pemberton died March 1, 1701-2, at the age of fifty-two years, and was

buried in the old graveyard above referred to. "Poor Phineas," wrote Penn to Logan on September 8, 1701, "is a dying man, and was not at the election, though he crept, (as I may say) to Meeting yesterday. I am grieved at it; for he has not his fellow, and without him this is a poor country indeed." Again, in a letter from London to Logan in 1702, Penn writes, "I mourn for poor Phineas Pemberton, the ablest as well as one of the best men in the Province. My dear love to his widow and sons and daughters." Samuel Carpenter, in a letter to Penn, quoted in J. Pemberton Parke's mss., writes, "Phineas Pemberton died the 1st mo. last, and will be greatly missed, having left few or none in these parts or adjacent, like him for wisdom, integrity, and general service, and he was a true friend to thee and the government. It is a matter of sorrow when I call to mind and consider that the best of our men are taken away, and how many are gone and how few to supply their places."

Of the nine children of Phineas and Phebe (Harrison) Pemberton, but three survived him for any length of time: Abigail, who married, November 14, 1704, Stephen Jenkins, and settled in Abington township—her descendants being the founders of Jenkintown—Priscilla, married, 1708-9, Isaac Waterman, and settled at Holmesburg; and Israel, the only son, who lived to manhood, married 2 mo. 12, 1710, Rachel Read, daughter of Charles Read, a provincial councillor. He was an active and influential Friend, and for nineteen consecutive years a member of colonial assembly. He left three sons: Israel Jr., born 1715; James, born 1723; and John, born 1727. Of these, John, who was a prominent preacher among Friends, left no issue, and James left only daughters, one of whom married Dr. Parke, and another Anthony Morris. Israel Jr. married Sarah Kirkbride of Bucks county, and had two daughters, and one son, Joseph, who married Ann Galloway of Maryland, first cousin of Joseph Galloway, the Bucks county loyalist, and died at the early age of thirty-six, leaving a large family, of whom John Pemberton, born in 1783, was in 1812 the only male representative of the family in America. He married Rebecca Clifford, and left a large family, of whom Henry Pemberton, of Philadelphia, referred to in this sketch, was the fifth. A complete genealogy of the descendants of Phineas Pemberton will be found in Glenn's "Genealogy of the Lloyd, Pemberton and Parke Families," Phila., 1898. Isreal, James and John, the sons of Israel and grandsons of Phineas, were prominent in the religious, political, social and business life of Phliadelphia, where their descendants are still found.

Further accounts of the Pemberton Family, may be found in Appleton's "Cyclopaedia of American Biography," vol. iv, p. 706; Westcott's "Historic Mansions of

---

[*]The Records of Arrivals " published in vol. ix. of Penna. Mag. of History and Biography, was compiled by Phineas Pemberton, although through an editorial oversight it is not accredited to him therein. This record has proved very valuable in genealogical and historical research. The original Record of Arrivals in Bucks County in Pemberton's handwriting is in possession of the Bucks County Historical Society, while that of Philadelphia and elsewhere is in the possession of the Historical Society of Pennsylvania.

Philadelphia," p. 494; Sarah E. Titcomb's "Early New England People," p. 52; "Glenn's Genealogy;" and "Friends' Miscellany," vol. vii, both before referred to.

RICHARD HOUGH AND SOME OF HIS DESCENDANTS.

Richard Hough, Provincial Councillor from Bucks county, for many years one of the most prominent figures in the Provincial Assembly, as well as in all the affairs of the Province and Bucks county, justice of the county court, etc., was a native of Macclesfield, in the county of Chester, England, and came to Pennsylvania in the "Endeavor" of London, arriving in the Delaware river 7th mo. 29, 1683 (O. S.), bringing with him four servants or dependents—Francis Hough, (probably a younger brother or nephew), Thomas Wood (or Woodhouse) and Mary his wife, and James Sutton. He settled at once in Bucks county on land doubtless previously purchased, though patented later. This land consisted of two tracts fronting on the Delaware in Makefield township, one of them in what became later Upper Makefield and covered the present site of Taylorsville, and the other lying along the original (but not the present) line of Falls township in Lower Makefield. On the lower tract fronting on the river about one-fourth of a mile and extending inland about three miles, Richard Hough made his home and erected his first and only Bucks county home, a stone house, (one of the earliest to be erected of that material) from a quarry on his plantation which Penn considered of so much importance that he ordered a memorandum be entered in the land-office, "that ye great quarry in Richard Hough's and Abel Janney's lands be reserved when they come to be confirmed, being for ye public good of ye county." On this plantation lived six generations of the eldest male branch of the family, part of it remaining in their possession until about 1850, when they removed to Ewing township, Mercer county, New Jersey.

Richard Hough took an active part in all the affairs of the county, political, social and religious. He was a member of Falls Meeting of Friends and his character and attainments gave him an important place in its proceedings. Prior to the erection of the Falls Meeting House, the Bucks Quarterly Meeting as well as meetings for worship were frequently held at his house. He was there, as elsewhere, intimately associated with Phineas Pemberton, Thomas Janney, William Yardley, William Biles, Nicholas Waln, Joseph Kirkbride and others, who, with him, were the leaders in the affairs of the county and province, though some of them, notably William Biles, with whom he was intimately associated in private affairs, differed from him in provincial politics, Biles being the Bucks county leader of the Popular party, with strong

Democratic tendencies, while Richard Hough was a strong adherent of the Proprietary party headed by James Logan. Richard Hough began early to engage in public affairs, and represened Bucks county in the Provincial Assembly in 1684, 1688, 1690, 1697, 1699, 1700, 1703, and 1704-5, and member of Provincial Council, 1693 and 1700. He was one of the commission to divide the county into township in 1692; was one of the justices of the county count, and appointed in 1700, with Phineas Pemberton and William Biles, by William Penn, a "Court of Inquiry" to investigate the affairs of the province. This bare record of the positions filled by Richard Hough can give but a very inadequate idea of the real position he filled in the affairs of the county and province, careful perusal of the records of both disclosing that he was one of the foremost men of his day. William Penn in a letter to Logan, 7 mo. 14, 1705, replying to one of Logan reporting the death of Hough, says: "I lament the loss of honest Richard Hough. Such men must needs be wanted where selfishness and forgetfulness of God's mercies so much abound." Richard Hough was drowned in the Delaware March 25, 1705, while on his way to Philadelphia from his home in Bucks county. By his will dated May 1, 1704, his home plantation of 400 acres was devised to his eldest son, Richard, one half to be held by his wife Margery, for life. His upper plantation, next the Manor of Highlands, went to his second son John; 350 acres and his Warwick plantation mentioned as 570 acres, but really nearly 900 acres, was devised to his youngest son Joseph; 271 acres, "next to John Palmer's," and 475 acres in Buckingham, purchased of his brother John, in 1694, were to be sold. The Warwick tract was one originally taken up by his father-in-law, John Clows, and purchased by Richard Hough of the heirs, and remained the property of his descendants for many generations, some of it for nearly two centuries. His daughters Mary and Sarah were given their portions in money. His wife Margery, son Richard, and "friend and brother," William Biles, were made executors.

Richard Hough married 8 mo. 17, 1683-4, Margery Clows, daughter of John and Margery Clows, theirs being the first marriage solemnized under the control of Falls Meeting. John Clows and Margery his wife and their children, Margery, Rebecca and William, came to Pennsylvania in the same ship with Richard Hough, from Gawsworth, Cheshire. Three other children, John, Joseph and Sarah, had preceded their parents, arriving in the "Friends' Adventure" 7 mo. 28, 1682. John Clows became a large landowner in Bucks county and represented the county in the Provincial Assembly in 1683 and 1684. He died 7 mo. 4, 1687. and his widow Margery 2 mo. 2, 1698. The eldest son John died in 1683; Joseph married Elizabeth Pownall;

William, Sarah Hanfield; Sarah, John Bainbridge, of New Jersey; Margery, Richard Hough; and Rebecca, John Lambert, of Nottingham, New Jersey.

The children of Richard and Margery (Clows) Hough were:

2. Mary Hough, born 6 mo. 1, 1685, died November 11, 1720; married April 6, 1690, William Atkinson, of Bristol, Bucks county, Pennsylvania.

3. Sarah Hough, born 4 mo. 7, 1690, married first, 4 mo. 23, 1708, Isaac Atkinson, brother of William; and (second) Leonard Shallcross, in 1724.

4. Richard Hough, married first, 1711-12, Hester Browne, and (second) 7 mo. 27, 1717, Deborah Gumley.

5. John Hough, born 7 mo. 18, 1693, married, 1718, Elizabeth Taylor.

6. Joseph Hough, born 8 mo. 17, 1695, died May 10. 1773; married 1725, Elizabeth West, daughter of Nathaniel and Elizabeth (Dungan) West.

Thomas Atkinson, father of William and Isaac Atkinson, was a minister of the Society of Friends, and was born at Newby, Parish of Ripon, West Riding of Yorkshire, England. He married Jane Bond at Knaresborough Meeting, 4 mo. 4, 1678, and in 1681, with his wife and son Isaac, born March 2, 1679, came to America and settled for a time in Burlington county, New Jersey, but soon after removed to Bristol township, Bucks county, Pennsylvania, where he bought a plantation. Thomas died 9 mo. 1, 1687, and the following year his widow Jane became the second wife of William Biles, before mentioned in this narrative. Another son, Samuel Atkinson, married Ruth Beakes, widow of William Beakes and daughter of Mahlon Stacy, of West Jersey. This family of Atkinson held high rank in colonial times. An account of Thomas Atkinson was published in a "Collection of Memorials of Deceased Ministers and others" (Phila. 1787) and also in "The Friend," vol. 27. In vol. 28 of "The Friend" is also a memorial of his wife, under the name of Jane Biles.

William Atkinson was a resident of Bristol borough and a member of town council there; was collector of excise eleven years, 1738-1749, coroner of Bucks county 1721, 1731-5, and 1737-1740; county commissioner 1722. He was for nearly thirty-three years an elder of Falls Monthly Meeting and a trustee for its real estate. He died in Bristol, October 29, 1749. The children of William and Mary (Hough) Atkinson were as follows:

(1). Sarah, born 1 mo. 10, 1704-5, died 10 mo. 1706.

(2). Hannah, born January 25, 1706-7, died December 9, 1760; married May, 1734, John Hall, of Bristol, his third wife. John Hall was a son of Robert Hall from the city of Westminster, England, who was the first coroner of Bucks county, and by his second wife, Elizabeth, daughter of George White, from Bucklebury, Berkshire, England, the ancestor of the White family of Bucks county. John Hall was a councilman of Bristol; member of Assembly 1717 and 1740 to 1750; several times sheriff of Bucks county; a justice of the county courts, and succeeded his father-in-law, William Atkinson, as collector of excise. He was born 6 mo. 12, 1686, and died 11 mo. 10, 1768; married first Rebecca Radcliffe, daughter of James Radcliffe, an eminent minister among Friends and an early settler in Bucks county, for whom Radcliffe street in Bristol is named. He married (second) January, 1715, Sarah Baldwin, daughter of John and Sarah (Allen) Baldwin, and granddaughter of Samuel Allen, who came from Chew Magna, Somerset, England, and founded a family of high standing in Bucks county and Philadelphia.

(3). William Atkinson, born 9 mo. 19, 1707, married 7 mo. 24, 1734, Sarah Pawley, daughter of George and Mary (Janney) Pawley, of Philadelphia (see Janney family). William Atkinson, Jr., was one of the early shipbuilders of Philadelphia, an industry for which that city is famous.

(4). Mary Atkinson, born 7 mo. 19, 1713, married July 9, 1745, at the First Presbyterian Church, Philadelphia, Daniel Bankson, of Bensalem, son of Daniel and grandson of Captain Andreas Bankson, one of the leading men among the early Swedish settlers at Philadelphia, whose descendants still hold a high place among the old families of that city.

(5). Joseph Atkinson, born 10 mo. 5, 1716, married first, 10 mo. 8, 1743, Janet Cowgill and (second) in 1762 Sarah Silver. He was a prominent man in Bristol borough, where his descendants are still people of high social standing. He succeeded his father as trustee of the real estate of Falls Meeting.

(6). Sarah Atkinson, born 9 mo. 4, 1719, died 2 mo. 7, 1726.

William Atkinson married (second) June 5, 1722, Margaret Baker, daughter of Henry Baker, well known in the early annals of Bucks county and had five children: Rachel, Rebecca, Samuel, Isaac, and Thomas. Rachel, the eldest, born 2 mo. 23, 1723, died 5 mo. 8, 1803, married, 10 mo. 18, 1750, Thomas Stapler, son of John and Esther. (See Stapler Family).

3. Sarah Hough married Isaac Atkinson, another son of Thomas and Jane, born in Yorkshire, March 2, 1679, died in Bristol township, Bucks county, January 3, 1720-1, where he was a landowner. They had issue: Jane, born 6 mo. 6, 1709, married 1728, John Wilson, of Middletown, son of Stephen and Sarah (Baker) Wilson, and grandson of Henry Baker above mentioned, and left numerous descendants in Bucks; (2) John; (3) Thomas. Sarah (Hough) Atkinson married second in 1724, Leonard Shallcross, by whom she had no children.

4. Richard Hough, eldest son of Richard and Margery, (Clows) Hough, inherited his father's home plantation of 416 acres

and lived thereon during his life. He sold 100 acres and his heirs about 100 acres more, the remainder going to his son Henry, and from him it descended to his grandson Phineas Hough, who sold it about 1850. Richard Hough, Esq. was one of the leading men of his time in Bucks county and took an active part in public affairs at a time when they were almost entirely in the hands of his class of gentlemen of landed estate. He was a justice of the peace and of the county courts for many years, and a member of Falls Meeting. He married February, 1711-12, Hester Brown, daughter of Henry and Margaret (Hardman) Baker, before mentioned, who had been the widow of Thomas Yardley, and of William Brown of Chichester, Chester county, Pennsylvania. Richard and Hester had one child, Richard, who died young. He married (second) 7 mo. 27, 1717, Deborah Gumley, (widow of John Gumley, of Philadelphia, formerly New Castle county) and had issue as follows:

8. William Hough, died without issue prior to 1755. 9. Deborah, married Thomas Davis, of Lower Makefield. 10. Margery, married Jonathan Saults, of Philadelphia. 11. Henry Hough, born 8 mo. 11, 1724 (O. S.) died 8 mo. 27, 1796, married 10 mo. 22, 1748, Rebecca Croasdale; see forward. 12. Mary, born 1726, died 1802; married 2 mo. 12, 1752 (O. S.) Anthony Burton, Jr., of Bristol. (See Burton Family).

11. Henry Hough, son of Richard and Deborah, inherited 215 acres of the Makefield homestead and lived thereon the life of a country gentleman, taking little part in public affairs. He was a member of Falls Meeting. He married 10 mo. 22, 1748, Rebecca Croasdale, born 1727-8, died 1800, daughter of William and Grace (Harding) Croasdale of Newton township and had eight children as follows: 13. Sarah, born 1751, married 1775, John Watson. 14. John, born 1753, married Hannah Watson and Mary Yardley. 15. Deborah, born 1755, died 1773, unmarried. 16. Mary, born 1759. 17. Jesse, born 1761, died 1794, married Mercy Merrick. 18. Rachel, born 1764, died 1793, married David Heston. 19. Rebecca, born 1766, married Isaiah Ross, grandson of Thomas Ross, an eminent minister among Friends and the ancestor of the eminent jurists, an account of whose family is given elsewhere in this work. 20. Henry, born 1768.

14. John Hough, born 9 mo. 16, 1753, eldest son of Henry and Rebecca (Croasdale) Hough, lived on his father's plantation in Lower Makefield. He was a member of Falls Meeting, but was married by the Rev. William Frazer, a Church of England minister, in 1782, to Hannah Watson, and they had one child, Beulah. He married (second) about 1790, Mary Yardley, daughter of Richard and Lucilla (Stackhouse) Yardley, and a great-granddaughter of Thomas Janney, Provincial Councillor. (See Yardley, Stackhouse and Janney family sketches in this volume.) The children of John and Mary (Yardley) Hough, were:

22. Phineas, born 12 mo. 20, 1700, died 5 mo. 6, 1876; 23. Lucilla, born 12 mo. 24, 1788, died 2 mo. 9, 1883, married Abraham Bond of Newtown, son of Levi and Hannah (Merrick) Bond, and a descendant of Phineas Pemberton, whom James Logan styles "The Father of Bucks County." (See Pemberton Family).

Phineas Hough (22) inherited a part his grandfather's plantation in Lower Makefield and lived thereon until sixty years old; selling it in 1850 he removed to Ewing township, Mercer county, and resided with his son William A. Hough until his death in 1875. He married Elizabeth Carlile, by whom he had no issue. On February 25, 1819, he married Deborah Aspy, daughter of William and Elizabeth Aspy, of Makefield, and had the following children: 24. William Aspy Hough, born December 4, 1819, died December 11, 1888, married Eleanor Stockton; see forward. 25. John Hough, born November 26, 1879, became a Methodist minister and removed to Delaware, where he married Rebecca E. Dukes. 26. Mary S., born July 7, 1824, married Jacob Hendrickson, of Mercer county, New Jersey. 27. Samuel Yardley Hough, born February 14, 1827, died August, 1862, married Wealtha Allen, from Massachusetts, and removed to Kansas, where he died. 28. Phineas, born January 24, 1830, died May 28, 1869, in Philadelphia; married Lizzie E. Lynn. 29. Benjamin Franklin, born March 16, 1833, lived in Philadelphia. unmarried 30. Edwin W., born April 27, 1837, died in Philadelphia, April 30, 1863, of disease contracted in the army, having served in the celebrated Anderson Cavalry, 160th Regiment, P. V.

William Aspy Hough (25) was born on the old homestead near Yardley, but in early life removed to property purchased in Ewing, New Jersey, and died there. He married Eleanor Stockton, of the distinguished family of that name in New Jersey and they were the parents of five children: 31. John Stockton, see forward. 32. William Henry, died while a student at Rutgers College. 33. Horace G., who inherited and is living on his father's plantation in Ewing. 34. Thomas J., and 35. Mary Emma, both died young.

John Stockton Hough, M. D. (31) eldest son of William A. and Eleanor (Stockton) Hough, was born on the old Hough plantation in Lower Makefield, Bucks county, December 5, 1845, and while a child removed with his parents to New Jersey. His education was obtained in the Ewing school, 1850-58; Trenton Academy, 1858-60; Model School, Trenton, 1860-61; Fort Edward Institute, New York, 1861-62; Eastman's Business College, Poughkeepsie, N. Y., 1862-63; Polytechnic College, Philadelphia, civil engineering course, 1864-67; University of Pennsylvania, Medical Department, 1865-68; received degree of M. D. at the University in 1868, and of Master of Chemistry at the Polytechnic in 1870. He lectured on botany, Philadelphia, 1866-67; was appointed adjunct professor of Chemistry, Central High School, Pheladelphia, 1868; resident physician, Philadelphia Hospital, 1868-9; lecturer on Physiology, Wagner Institute, Philadelphia, 1868-69 Philadelphia Dispensary, 1869; Lying-in Charity Hospital, 1869; medical adviser U. S. Life Insurance Company, 1869-73; Berkshire Life Insurance Company, 1875; and practiced medicine in Philadelphia 1869-74. While physician at Philadelphia Hopsital he made original discoveries in reference to trichinae. He invented a plan for fireproof building construction in 1870, and was the inventor of various surgical instruments in 1868-70. He was the author of about thirty papers and pamphlets on hygiene, biology, speculative physiology, social science, vital statistics, population and political economy, published in medical and scientific journals in this and foreign countries, from 1868 to 1886. These papers attracted much attention, and some were translated, and published in foreign languages, and through them membership in various learned societies was conferred on him, and a sketch of his life was published in Johnson's and Appleton's Encyclopædias, and in the Encyclopaedia Britanica. His magnus opus was a bibliography of medical literature of the fifteenth century, intended to be entitled "Incunabula Medica." He had lists printed of all the known medical books of that time, of which there were about 1,500, and sent copies of it to public libraries and private collectors all over the world, with the request to mark on the list such books as they had copies of, and to make certain remarks about them and return the lists. He also visited many important libraries and most of the famous Universities in France, Germany, and Italy, and mastered the languages of these countries, making eleven voyages to Europe in connection with this mammoth work, and traveled extensively in this country. Before his death nearly all the lists sent out had been returned, but he had not finished the compilation (which, besides the matter contained in the lists, was to include biographies of all the authors) when death overtook him. It is to be sincerely hoped that some day the work so well begun will be taken up and finished. During this period of his life he also gathered together a library on medical and related subjects estimated to contain 10,000 titles. It was his desire that this library should be kept intact, but leaving no will, it was sold by his administrators to the College of Physicians, who transferred about 1,900 volumes to the library of the University of Pennsylvania. He was much interested in local history and the history of old Bucks county families, and furnished considerable material for Davis's "History of Bucks County," first edition, 1876. In 1890 he purchased a property in Ewing township, where he had always retained his voting residence, and named it Millbank, and spent the remainder of his life there. He also owned, with his

brother Horace, a farm in Hopewell township, and a half interest in the Ewing flour mill near his home. He took a deep interest in that section where his boyhood was spent, and devoted great efforts for work of road improvements in that section, capably serving in the capacity of county supervisor of roads.

John Stockton Hough, M. D., as eldest son, back to Richard Hough, Provincial Councillor, was the head of the Hough family of Bucks county, Pennsylvania. He was one of the revivers of the Aryan Order of St. George, of the Holy Roman Empire in the Colonies of America, which was founded by Sir Thomas Forsythe, Viscount de Fronsac, a British-American officer, with the allies fighting the Revolution in France, who in 1798 was given authority by Emperor Joseph II to organize the American families who were descended from noble European blood, or from officers holding royal commissions in the colonies. A number of persons were admitted during the early years of its existence, but it was not thoroughly organized until 1879, when some of the members met in Boston for that purpose, and it was more formally organized in the rooms of the Maryland Historical Society, October 28, 1880.

Dr. Stockton-Hough, as he styled himself, was a member of the Protestant Episcopal Church, being confirmed by Bishop Stevens in Philadelphia in 1873. He married first, January 29, 1874, Sarah Macomb Wetherill, daughter of Dr. William Wetherill, of Fatland, Montgomery county, Pennsylvania, a descendant of Christopher Wethrul, of West Jersey, ancestor of the well known Philadelphia family of that name. She died in Florence, Italy, in 1875, leaving an only daughter, Frances Eleanor Agrippina Etrusca Hough, who was born in Florence, December 30, 1874, and died unmarried at Millbank, April 4, 1893. Dr. Hough married (second) June 30, 1887, in New York City, Edith Reilly, daughter of Edward and Anna Russun (Rogers) Reilly, of New York. Her father was a graduate of Yale, and a large mine owner in the west, and her mother's ancestors were prominent in Delaware and the eastern shore of Maryland. Dr. Stockton-Hough was a member of the Grolier Club and University Club of New York. He died at Millbank, May 6, 1900.

DESCENDANTS OF JOHN HOUGH, SECOND SON OF RICHARD AND MARGERY HOUGH. 5. John Hough, second son of Richard and Margery (Clows) Hough, born 7 mo. 18, 1693, inherited his father's upper tract adjoining the Manor of Highlands and included in Upper Makefield in 1737. It comprised 359 acres. It is not known how he disposed of it, and he left no will, and none of his children are known to have resided upon it in later years. It is probable that he conveyed a portion of it to the Taylors, his wife's brothers, as a descendant of Mahlon K. Taylor, who married Elizabeth

JOHN STOCKTON HOUGH

Hough, a great-granddaughter of John Hough, inherited it and founded Taylorsville. John Hough was a justice of the Bucks county courts for several years, and his death is said to have occurred while filling this position some time after 1733. He married 11 mo. 1718, at Falls Meeting, Elizabeth Taylor, daughter of Philip and Julianna Taylor, of Oxford township, Philadelphia county. Her brothers removed to Bucks county and founded a wealthy and influential family there. The children of John and Elizabeth (Taylor) Hough were:

40. John, born 11 mo. 3, 1720, died 1797, married Sarah Janney; see forward.

41. Joseph, born 5 mo. 20, 1722, died 1777; married 1746, Lydia Hurst, and their descendants removed to Loudoun County, Virginia, where one of his children married a Washington.

42. Benjamin Hough, born 4 mo. 14, 1724, died 2 mo. 10, 1803, removed to Philadelphia when a young man, accumulated a fortune, and spent the latter part of his life in traveling in the interests of religion. He lived for a time in Wilmington, Delaware, later at Nottingham, Cecil county, Maryland, and about 1771 located in Little Britain township, Lancaster county, where he died. He married first, 1748, Elizabeth West, daughter of Thomas, of Wilmington, by whom he had three children, of whom only Benjamin survived his father. He married (second) 1781, Sarah Janney, widow of Isaac Janney, of Cecil county, Maryland. Their only child, John, died at the age of seven years.

43. Isaac Hough, born 9 mo. 15, 1726, died 4 mo. 13, 1786, married Edith Hart; see forward.

44. William Hough, born 11 mo. 1, 1727-8, married 1749, Sarah Blaker, daughter of Samuel and Catharine of Warwick, Bucks county.

45. Thomas Hough, born 11 mo. 2, 1729-30, died 5 mo. 18, 1810; married 1857, Jane Adams; 1784, Mary (Bacon) Wistar. He removed to Philadelphia in early life and became one of the wealthy men of that time. He lived at No. 20 Pine street. By first wife had six children, all except two of whom died young; Elizabeth married James Olden, of the New Jersey family, and "Betsy Hough's wedding" is referred to in the "Journal of Elizabeth Drinker," one of Mrs. Drinker's daughters being a bridesmaid. Jane, the other daughter, married Halladay Jackson, of the Chester county family, well known in Friends' annals. One of her sons was John Jackson, the minister. One of her descendants is Mrs. Isaac H. Clothier. Mary (Bacon-Gilbert) Wistar, the second wife of Thomas Hough, was a daughter of John and Elizabeth (Test) Bacon, of Bacon's Neck, Cumberland county, New Jersey. She married first, Thomas Gilbert, of Northern Liberties, Philadelphia, and (second) Richard Wistar, whose family is prominent in the social life of Philadelphia to this day. There was no issue by the second marriage.

46. Septimus Hough, born 4 mo. 21, 1731, died in Philadelphia 9 mo. 3, 1749.

47. Elizabeth, born 12 mo. 15, 1732-3, married Nathan Tomlinson.

48. Bernard, born 11 mo. 15, 1734-5; said by an old record to have died "in France."

49. Martha, born 4 mo. 22, 1737, married David Bunting, son of Samuel and Priscilla (Burgess) Bunting, of the Bucks county branch of the descendants of Anthony Bunting, who came from Matlock, Derbyshire, and settled in Burlington county, New Jersey.

50. Samuel, born 2 mo. 15, 1739.

John Hough (40) eldest son of John and Elizabeth (Taylor) Hough, removed to Loudoun county, Virginia, where he became a very large landed proprietor, and built a fine mansion known as "Corby Hall." He was an elder of Farfax Monthly Meeting, and represented his Quarterly Meeting in Philadelphia Yearly Meeting; was well known in northern Virginia, and held in high esteem not only by the members of the Society of Friends but by the "cavalier" gentry of that section, with whom some of his children and grandchildren intermarried. When a number of prominent Philadelphia Quakers were exiled to Winchester, Virginia, during the Revolution, by order of the supreme executive council, John Hough visited them and was active in securing their release. A number of his letters on this subject are preserved in the Pemberton mss. collection in the library of the Historical Society of Pennsylvania. He is mentioned in the diary of George Washington, on the occasion of the latter spending a night at Corby Hall, and in other places. John Hough married, in 1742, in Bucks county, Sarah Janney, daughter of Joseph and Rebecca (Biles) Janney, a granddaughter of Thomas Janney and William Biles, both provincial councillors from Bucks county, and among the greatest of the founders of the county. Their nine children all married and reared families, most of them intermarrying with Virginia families, though some of the married into Bucks county families who had migrated to Virginia. They have left many distinguished descendants, among whom may be mentioned, Emerson Hough, of Chicago, novelist, historian and journalist, author of "Mississippi Bubble," and "The Way to the West," etc.

Isaac Hough (43) fourth son of John and Elizabeth (Taylor) Hough, removed early in life to Warminster township, Bucks county, where he purchased about 236 acres of land. He married, September 24, 1748, Edith Hart, born May 14, 1727, died March 27, 1805, daughter of John and Eleanor (Crispin) Hart, of Warminster, and sister of Colonel Joseph Hart, of the continental army, county lieutenant; member Bucks County Committee of Safety, etc., one of the most prominent figures in the Revolutionary struggle in Bucks county. (See Hart family). Her father, John Hart, was sheriff of Bucks county, justice of the county courts, coroner, etc. She was a granddaughter of Thomas Holme, surveyor-general of Pennsylvania and sometime president of Provincial Council of Pennsylvania, formerly of the Parliamentary army in the civil war in England. Also great-granddaughter of Captain William Crispin, acting rear admiral in the British navy, and one of Penn's commissioners for settling the Colony in Pennsylvania; and of Captain John Rush, also of the Parliamentary army, ancestor of the celebrated Dr. Benjamin Rush, signer of the Declaration of Independence, etc. She was granddaughter of John Hart, from Witney, Oxfordshire, an early minister among Friends who joined the Keithians, and finally became a Baptist preacher, one of the most learned men of the colony, and of Silas Crispin who, through his mother, Anne Jasper, was a first cousin to William Penn. Isaac Hough left the Society of Friends and joined the Baptists, to which sect his wife belonged. In 1775 he joined the Warminster Company of Associators, in the Second Battalion of Bucks County Militia, Colonel John Beatty. In July, 1776, he was appointed by the County Committee of Safety one of the committee to distribute allowances to families in need whose husbands were in the military service. On August 29, 1777, he was appointed one of the members of the committee from Warminster to attend to the driving off of cattle to prevent them from falling into the hands of the British. The children of Isaac and Edith (Hart) Hough were as follows:

60. Eleanor, born August 20, 1749, died March 1, 1802; married 1766, Thomas Craven, and had nineteen children. The family removed to Virginia during the Revolution.

61. Elizabeth, born August 21, 1751; married 1771, Silas Gilbert, her first cousin, son of William and Lucretia (Hart) Gilbert, and removed to Maryland. He was lieutenant in 1st Battalion, Bucks County Militia, 1777.

62. Susannah, born June 28, 1753; married 1773, Benjamin Jones, whose family furnished several members of Assembly and justices of Bucks county in colonial times.

63. John Hough, born March 12, 1755; married 1774, Charity Vandoren. He was a member of Warminster Associators 1775, and afterwards in Virginia militia. He moved to Philadelphia after the Revolution, and later to Moreland, Montgomery county.

64. Mary, born May 19, 1757, died unmarried.

65. Isaac Hough, born September 15, 1759, died March 17, 1801; member Warminster Associators; removed to Philadelphia after Revolution; many years chief clerk of United States Mint. One of his descendants is Judge Robert T. Hough, of Hillsborough, Ohio, sometime solicitor of Internal Revenue at Washington, D. C., recently candidate for the Democratic nomination for governor of Ohio. Isaac married first

Elizabeth Houghton; second, Mrs. Elizabeth Eberth.

66. Thomas Hough, born October 7, 1761; removed to Philadelphia; said to have been on officer in war of 1812; married 1790, Hannah Tompkins.

67. Oliver Hough, born August 27, 1763, died January 18, 1804; see forward.

68. Rev. Silas Hough, born February 8, 1766, died May 14, 1823. Baptist minister; also practiced medicine in Bucks and Montgomery counties. Married his cousin, Elizabeth Hart, daughter of County Treasurer John Hart.

69. Joseph Hough, born June 17, 1768, died July 3, 1799; married Elizabeth Marple.

70. William Hough, born September 12, 1770; died unmarried.

Oliver Hough (67) son of Isaac and Edith (Hart) Hough, became a large landowner in Upper Makefield, Bucks county. Hough's Creek, (formerly Milnor's Creek) took its name from him. In the latter part of his life he resided in Dolington. He married at Horsham Meeting, 4 mo. 16, 1790, Phebe Cadwallader, born 11 mo. 5, 1771, died 7 mo. 13, 1842, daughter of Jacob and Phebe (Radcliffe) Cadwallader, of Warminster. She was a descendant of Henry Baker before alluded to in this narrative, and from John Cadwallader, one of the prominent ministers among Friends, who died while on a religious visit to the Island of Tortola in 1742; also of Johannes Cassel and Thones Kunders, two of the principal founders of Germantown, and from Jan Lucken, the founder of the Lukens family in America. Her brother, Hon. Cyrus Cadwallader, before referred to in this volume, was in state senate 1816-25. The children of Oliver and Phebe (Cadwallader) Hough were; 71. Elizabeth, died young. 72. Rebecca, born 1792, married 1820, Joseph Johnson. 73. Mary, born 1794; married 1822, Samuel Yardley, a well known merchant of Doylestown, later of Philadelphia. 74. Elizabeth, born 1796, married 1817, Mahlon Kirkbride Taylor, founder of Taylorsville. 75, 76, 77, Isaac, Rachel and Phebe, all died young. 78. Oliver, born 2 mo. 14, 1804, died 7 mo. 20, 1855; born at Dolington, lived there until his marriage, when he removed to the Doron farm in Middletown township; soon after removed to a farm just outside Newtown borough on Yardley turnpike, where five of his children were born. In 1842 removed to Doylestown, and in 1846 to Philadelphia. Dealt largely in real estate, owning besides Bucks county property, coal and timber lands in Upper Lehigh Valley, also in Michigan, Tennessee and elsewhere. He died in Augusta, Georgia, July 20, 1855, while on a trip to Louisiana to view the property of the Louisiana Canal Company, of which he was a director. He was a member of Spruce Street Friends' Meeting, Philadelphia.

Oliver Hough married, 3 mo. 15, 1832, Martha Briggs, daughter of Joseph and

Martha (Dawes) Briggs, of Newtown, Bucks county, Pennsylvania, and had issue: Rebecca Jarrett Hough, died unmarried; Phebe Alice, unmarried, member Civic Club and Browning Society, Philadelphia, and of Bucks County Historical Society; managing committee of Friends' Central School, Philadelphia; Mary Yardley Hough, unmarried; from 1876 to 1897 proprietor and editor of "The Children's Friend," a juvenile magazine; author of numerous short stories for children; Elizabeth Taylor, died in childhood. Martha Dawes Hough, unmarried, elder of Spruce Street, Meeting, manager of Friends' Home for Children, Philadelphia, and Friends' Boarding House Association, Philadelphia. Oliver, died 1863 at Nashville, Tennessee, of camp fever, was a private in 160th Regiment Pennsylvania Volunteers, 15th (Anderson's) Cavalry. Isaac, see forward. The Misses Rebecca J., Phebe A., Mary Y. and Martha D. Hough lived for over forty years at 1340 Spruce street, Philadelphia. In April, 1904, they removed to the old William Linton Mansion, 24 South State street, Newtown, Bucks county, a picture of which appears in this volume. They inherited this house from their aunts Letitia and Francenia Briggs.

Isaac Hough, son of Oliver and Matha (Briggs) Hough, was born in Doylestown, Bucks county, Pennsylvania and moved to Philadelphia, with his parents when a child. He was a merchant, and engaged in the shipping trade with the West Indies. He was a charter member and director of the Maritime Exchange of Philadelphia, is a member of the Philadelphia Bourse; director of the Finance Company of Pennsylvania, and member of the Philadelphia Fencing Club, the Merion Cricket Club, of Haverford, Pennsylvania, and of the Union League. He married first, in 1867, Anna Alexander Duff, daughter of Edward Duff, common councilman, and member of the board of health of Philadelphia, by his wife, Mary Jane Diehl, a descendant of Captain Nicholas Diehl, a Revolutionary soldier and a member of the Committee of Safety of Chester county, of noble birth in Frankfort, Germany. Isaac and Anna A. (Duff) Hough were the parents of one child, Oliver Hough, 2d Lieutenant, Company 8,, 3d Regiment, Infantry, Penna. Vol. Spanish American war, 1898, to whom we are indebted for the foregoing history of the Hough family as well as data on numerous other families published in this volume. He is a member of the Bucks county Historical Society and has contributed a number of valuable papers to its Archives. He is the author of a number of papers on genealogy and local history and is now at work on an exhaustive history of the Hart and Atkinson families. Is a member of a number of patriotic Societies. Isaac Hough married (second) in 1877, Emilia Antionette, widow of Francis Thibault, of Phila-

delphia, and had one son, John Boyd, who died in 1895.

OLIVER HOUGH, son of Isaac and Anna A. (Duff) Hough, was born in Philadelphia, September 3, 1868, has lived in that city until the present time, and for about two years past has had a transient residence with his aunts, the Misses Hough, at the William Linton Mansion, at 24 South State street, Newtown. He received his early education at private schools, and entered the University of Pennsylvania in the class of '88, receiving the degrees of B. S. and P. C. on completion of course. He has been president, vice-president, secretary and treasurer Class of '88, and two terms secretary of the University of Pennsylvania Cricket Association. For thesis required for technical degree (P. C.) he made three original researches in chemistry, described under the titles: I. "An Attempt to Introduce Iodine into Parabroma-benzoic Acid"; II. Some Salts of Meta-nitro-para-bromo-benzoic Acid"; III. Some Compounds of Monochloro-dinitrophenol". Nos. I and II were published in the "Journal of the Franklin Institute," December, 1891. No. III resulted in the discovery of twelve previously unknown chemical compounds.

He has written a number of magazine and newspaper articles of historical or biographical character, the principal ones being: "Richard Hough, Provincial Councillor," (Penna. Mag. Hist. and Biog., XVIII, 20); "Captain Thomas Holme, Surveyor-General of Pennsylvania and Provincial Councillor," (Penna. Mag. Hist. and Biog., XIX, 413, XX 128, 248); "Captain William Crispin, Proprietary's Commissioner for Settling the Colony in Penna." (read before the Historical Society of Pennsylvania, January 10, 1898, and published in Penna. Mag. Hist. and Biog., XXII, 34); and "Thomas Janney, Provincial Councillor," (read before Bucks County Historical Society, July 20, 1897, and published in Bucks county newspapers).

In politics Oliver Hough has been secretary and chairman of the Seventh Ward Association, Municipal League of Philadelphia; a member of several committees in charge of independent candidates' campaigns (one of which resulted in the election of Alexander Crow, Jr., as sheriff of Philadelphia county); and from 1896 to date has represented the Fourteenth Division, Seventh Ward, in many conventions of the Republican party. Mr. Hough joined the National Guard of Pennsylvania as a private in Company D, First Regiment, Infantry, August 10, 1893; elected second lieutenant Company G, Third Regiment, Infantry, June 10, 1897. Served again with Company D, First Infantry, on riot duty at Hazelton, Pennsylvania, October, 1902. Is a member of the "Old Guard" of Company D. He was mustered into the United States service for the Spanish War as second lieutenant, Third Penna. Volunteer Infantry, July

OLIVER HOUGH

22, 1898; detailed as acting assistant quartermaster, A. A. commissary of subsistence, and A. A. ordinance officer; served in camps at Fernandina, Florida, and Huntsville, Alabama; mustered out October 22, 1898.

Mr. Hough is or has been a member of the following organizations: Society of Colonial Wars (by descent from Richard Hough, Thomas Janney and other early Bucks countians); Sons of the Revolution (by descent from Isaac Hough of the Bucks County Associators); Historical Society of Pennsylvania, and local historical societies of Bucks county, Montgomery county, Pennsylvania, and Harford county, Maryland; Genealogical Society of Pennsylvania (historian and member board of directors); American Catholic Historical Society of Philadelphia; Friends' Historical Society (England); Society of Chemical Industry (Great Britain); Franklin Institute of the State of Pennsylvania; Merion Cricket Club of Haverford, Pennsylvania; and Markham Club of Philadelphia.

ANCESTRY OF BENJAMIN HOUGH, OF WARRINGTON.

Joseph Hough, youngest son of Richard and Margery (Clowes)[1] Hough, a sketch of whose life and distinguished services is given in the preceding pages, was born in Lower Makefield, Bucks county, Pennsylvania, September 19, 1693, and died in Warwick township, now Doylestown, May 10, 1773. By the will of his father he inherited the Warwick plantation, originally taken up by his grandfather, John Clows, and purchased by his father in 1702. It comprised 841 acres as shown by a survey when divided between his two sons Joseph and John by deeds dated May 2, 1761, and lay on both sides of the Neshaminy, on the lower line of the present township of Doylestown, extending from the Bristol road to Houghville, or "The Turk." It was divided almost equally between the two sons in 1761, the Neshaminy being the dividing line for about one-third of the distance, John getting the end next Houghville, and Joseph the western end. Joseph Hough, Sr., married "out of meeting," his wife being Elizabeth West, daughter of Nathaniel and Elizabeth (Dungan) West, and granddaughter of the Rev. Thomas Dungan, who came from Rhode Island to Bucks county in 1683, and of Nathaniel West, of Rhode Island. Nathaniel West, Jr., was living at the time of the marriage of his daughter, on the Rodman tract, adjoining the Hough farm, which would imply that Joseph Hough had taken up his residence in Warwick prior to his marriage. A Joseph Hough was dealt with at Falls Meeting for marrying out of unity May 9, 1726, but whether Joseph of Warwick, or Joseph Hough, son of John and Hannah, who was about the same age, cannot be ascertained from the records. He evidently retained

a nominal membership, as his son Joseph was considered a member at Buckingham at the time of his marriage in 1756. The children of Joseph and Elizabeth (West) Hough, were as follows:

1. Sarah, married James Radcliffe, son of Edward and Phebe (Baker) Radcliffe, and grandson of James Radcliffe, the preacher, and of Henry Baker, whose distinguished services have been previously referred to.

2. Martha, born 1728, died 1785, married William Evans, son of Lewis Evans, a trooper in the battle of Boyne. For their children, see "Fox, Ellicott & Evans Families," Chas. W. Evans, Buffalo, N. Y., 1882. Four married Ellicots.

3. Mary, married Samuel Gourley, of Wrightstown, Bucks county.

4. Rebecca, married (first) a George, and (second) Samuel Williams, of Gwynedd.

5. Joseph, born 1730, died January 6, 1818.

6. John Hough, second son of Jeseph and Elizabeth (West) Hough, lived on the 414 acre tract conveyed to him by his father in 1761, as before recited, in Warwick township. Was probably not a member of the Society of Friends, though he adhered to their principles. His name appears on the roll of "Non-Associators" in 1775. He married, October 31, 1767, at St. Michael's and Zion Church, Philadelphia, Ruth Williams, and had issue five children, viz: Joseph, who married Eleanor Miller, who after his death married John Meredith; Thomas married (first) Ann Mathews, and (second), Lydia (Mathews) Drake, her sister; John, married Rebecca Thompson; Mary, married Robert Walker of Warrington; and Charlotte, died January 14, 1815, married John Meredith, who after her death married her brother's widow, Eleanor (Miller) Hough. John Thompson Hough, the wealthy inventor and manufacturer of safes, Pittsburg, Pennsylvania, is a descendant of John and Rebecca (Thompson) Hough.

7. Margery Hough, married Hugh Shaw.

8. Elizabeth Hough, married Robert Tompkins.

9. Hannah Hough, died April 18, 1819, married Simon Meredith, an uncle to John, who married Charlotte, daughter of John Hough. A grandson of Simon and Hannah married Rebecca, daughter of Joseph Hough; see below.

5. Joseph Hough, Jr., eldest son of Joseph and Elizabeth (West) Hough, born 1730, lived on the 420 acres conveyed to him by his father in Warwick. He was a member of the Society of Friends and was disowned for marrying out of meeting in 1756, but continued to adhere to their principles and was a "Non-Associator" in 1775. He married, in November, 1756, Mary Tompkins, daughter of Robert Tompkins, Esq., of Warrington. She died August 8, 1811, at the age of seventy-five years. They had issue: 1. Joseph, died 1796, married Rebecca Radcliffe, daughter of John and Rebecca (West) Radcliffe, niece of his aunt

Sarah's husband, and a descendant of Nathaniel West, as was her husband. 2. John who died young. 3. Richard, who married Pamela Walton. 4. Elizabeth, who married Henry Ditterline. 5. John, who married Mary Meredith. 6. Robert, who married (first) Francis Martin, of Maryland, and (second), Rachel Hopkins, of the Johns Hopkins family of Maryland, lived and died in Baltimore, and has left many distinguished descendants there. 7. Septimus Hough married Edith Wilson, daughter of Robert and Mary (Lundy) Wilson, of New Jersey. See Lundy Family. 8. Benjamin Hough. See forward. 9. Jacob, died young. 10. Lydia, who married Elias Anderson. 11. Charlotte, died unmarried. 12 and 13. Isaac and Jacob died young, and 14. Mary, married (1808) Dennis Conrad, a descendant of Thomas Kunders, one of the founders of Germantown.

John Hough, son of Joseph and Mary (Tompkins) Hough, was a prominent man in the community. He inherited a part of his father's plantation near Houghville, generally known as "The Turk," and when the county seat was about to be removed from Newtown was laid out streets there and made a plan of a town, and offered the site for the court house and public buildings. He was a large land owner and owned the Turk Mills at Houghville, and extensive warehouses in Philadelphia. He donated the land on which the Doylestown Academy was built, and was one of the commissioners of the lottery authorized by the legislature to raise $3,000 to complete the Academy. He married Mary Meredith, daughter of Thomas and Rachel (Mathew) Meredith, and niece of Simon Meredith, who married Hannah Hough, and had issue: John, who married Eliza Stuckert, and Harriet Ann Pierce, and Mary, who never married.

8. Benjamin Hough, son of Joseph and Mary (Tompkins) Hough, was born January 25, 1770, and died May 16, 1848. He purchased from his father in 1797 and 1806, and later his brother, Septimus Hough, portions of the old ancestral homestead, and at his death owned the greater part of the 400 acre tract, and lived thereon all his life. He was a prominent man in the community and filled many positions of public trust. He was a director of the poor in 1818, and served as a director of Doylestown Bank in 1832. He married, August 24, 1791, Hannah Simpson, born July 26, 1770, died April 3, 1848, daughter of John and Hannah (Roberts) Simpson, of Horsham, Montgomery county, Pennsylvania, and a sister to John Simpson, the grandfather of General Ulysses Simpson Grant.* John Simpson, her father, was born in 1738, and died August 16, 1804. His wife, Hannah,

was a daughter of Lewis Roberts, of Abington, and a sister to Colonel William Roberts, of New Britain, colonel of militia during the Revolution and a sheriff of Bucks county. Hannah (Roberts) Simpson died at the residence of her son-in-law, Benjamin Hough, in Doylestown township, January 22, 1821, aged seventy-nine. The children of Benjamin and Hannah (Simpson) Hough, were as follows: 1. John Simpson, born 1792, married, 1818, Elivia Lunn. 2. Joseph, born 1798, married Jane Cowell, and lived for many years in Tinicum; was brigadier general of Pennsylvania Militia. 3. Anne, born 1794, married George Stuckert. 4. Benjamin, see forward. 5. Silas, born 1804 married Sophia F. Moser, and their son, John S. Hough, was a candidate for governor of Colorado on its admission in 1876. 7. Hannah, born 1807, married, November 16, 1826, Daniel Y. Harman, member of Pennsylvania legislature in 1836, etc. 8. William Simpson, born 1809, married Elizabeth Neely. 9. Samuel Moore, born 1812, married Elizabeth N. Harman, sister of Daniel Y., and (second) his wife's niece, Araminta Beans, daughter of Isaac and Elizabeth (Harman) Beans. He was adjutant of 33d Pennsylvania Regiment, of which his brother, Joseph, was colonel. 10. Mary, born 1814, married John Barnsley, of Newtown. See Barnsley Family in this work.

Benjamin Hough, Jr., son of Benjamin and Hannah (Simpson) Hough, was born on the old homestead in Warwick, now Doylestown township, January 25, 1801. He was a merchant and farmer, and at one time owned and conducted the store at Buckingham. He later purchased the Barclay farm, later the Radcliffe farm at Warrington, which then included the site of the present store at Warrington, across the turnpike from the farm, a small triangular piece of land, whereon he erected a store building and conducted the mercantile business there for many years. He also purchased the farm now occupied by his grandson, Benjamin Hough, where he died in 1853. He was married by the Reverend John C. Murphy, February 5, 1824, to Maria Wentz, of New Britain, and they were the parents of ten children, viz: John, who removed to Valva, Illinois; Ellen, who married John S. Bryan; Silas, see forward; J. Finlay, who was a miller, lived first in Bedminster, later in Buckingham, died at Atlantic City, was the father of Dr. Hough of Ambler; Mary Jane, who married Edward Buckman, of Newtown, she died September 27, 1905; Anna, for many years a school teacher, died at Newtown in September, 1900; Simpson and Samuel H., twins, the former removed to Illinois and the latter for many years a miller in Warwick, Warminster and Hatboro, died in Hatboro in 1903; Benjamin, a soldier in the civil war, died at Leadville, Colorado, March 13, 1890; Henry, for many years a teacher in Doylestown and elsewhere, was appointed during President Grant's term to a position in the Pension office at Washington, D. C., and died there in 1901; and George, still living in Valva, Illinois.

Silas Hough was born and reared on the Warrington homestead, and on his marriage removed to the farm on which his son Benjamin now resides. He was a successful and prominent farmer, and filled many positions of public trust, frequently acting as guardian of minors and as executor and administrator in the settlement of estates. In politics he was a Republican, and took an active interest in the questions of the day, but never sought or held public office. He married, March 3, 1855, Hannah Horner, daughter of James and Ann (Long) Horner, of Warminster, Bucks county, both of Scotch-Irish ancestry. Silas and Hannah (Horner) Hough, were the parents of four children, of whom three died in childhood, leaving Benjamin Hough as only surviving heir. Hannah Hough died in 1890, and Silas in 1892.

Benjamin Hough, only son of Silas and Hannah (Horner) Hough, was born on the farm on which he still resides, in Warrington township, March 12, 1854, and it has been his place of residence almost continuously to the present, covering over half a century. He acquired a common school education, supplemented by a course at the Doylestown English and Classical Seminary. He was reared to the life of a farmer, and on his marriage he brought his bride to the old farm which he conducted until 1883, when he removed to Chester county and spent two years there on an experimental farm. After the death of his father he returned to the homestead, having in the meantime gained new knowledge of modern farming methods which he adapted to the use of the home place. He made substantial improvements and greatly improved the appearance of his beautiful home on the Doylestown and Willow Grove Turnpike and Trolley line, overlooking the beautiful valley of the Neshaminy. Mr. Hough is a Republican in politics and takes a keen interest in public affairs, but has never been an aspirant for office. He has filled the position of school director and other township offices. He married, September 28, 1876, Sarah Patterson, daughter of Jesse R. and Mary (Myers) Patterson, both natives of Bucks county, and granddaughter of William and Sarah (Rubinkam) Patterson, the former a native of Pittsburg, and the latter of Bucks county. William Patterson was of Scotch-Irish Presbyterian stock, and inherited the sterling as well as the genial qualities of his ancestors. He was a farmer in Bucks county, and reared a family of seven children, viz: Jesse, the father of Mrs. Hough; Mrs. Susan Bolinger, Margaret, William, of Doylestown;

Sheridan T., a farmer near Peoria, Illinois; Joseph, who died in the army during the civil war; and Thomas, who died in Illinois. Jesse Patterson, father of Mrs. Hough, was reared on his father's farm and early in life learned the miller's trade which he followed for many years. He was at one time the owner of the mills at Edisob, Bucks county, which he operated when the mill was destroyed by fire. He rebuilt and operated the mill during the civil war, and later turned his attention to farming. In 1880 he removed to Chester county, where he bought a farm and carried on agricultural pursuits until his death in 1885, at the age of fifty-eight years. His wife, Mary Myers, who was a daughter of Tobias Myers, of German descent, died in 1901. Her mother, a Miss Puff, was of English descent, and her brothers were Philip Puff, a merchant of Philadelphia, and Henry Puff, a carpenter. Jesse and Mary Myers Patterson were the parents of three children, of whom the youngest died in infancy, Sarah, Mrs. Hough, was the eldest. Her brother William is a prominent farmer in Chester county. Mrs. Hough is a member of the Baptist Church of Doylestown.

Benjamin and Sarah (Patterson) Hough are the parents of two children, Frederick F., born September 27, 1879, at present a school teacher in Bucks county, who was born on the old homestead in Warrington, and William P., who was born in Chester county, September 7, 1885.

WILLIAM H. HOUGH. More than a century has passed since the Hough family was established in Bucks county, for here occurred the birth of Charles Hough, the grandfather of William H. Hough, his natal year being 1801. He followed farming throughout his entire life and gave his political support to the Republican party. He held the office of supervisor for a number of years and was always faithful in matters of citizenship. The moral development of the community was also of deep interest to him, and his life was in harmony with his professions as a member of the Society of Friends. He married Miss Susan Neal, and they became the parents of ten children, six of whom have passed away. The living are: Rachel, the wife of James Lonsdale; Jasper, a carpenter of Langhorne, Pennsylvania; Henry; and Martha, the wife of James Subers.

Henry Hough, son of Charles Hough, was born in Edgewood, Pennsylvania, in 1838, and when a lad of twelve years went with his parents to the farm upon which his son William now resides. There he assisted in the development and cultivation of the fields and continued to engage in agricultural pursuits until 1861, when he established a hardware business in Yardley, continuing it for thirty-three years. In 1894 he sold this and removed to Solebury, where he has since given his attention to farming. Throughout his mercantile career he enjoyed an unassailable reputation, and his business life has ever been characterized by straightforward dealing and persistency of purpose. His efforts, too, have been directed along lines that have proved of value to his community, and at the same time have promoted individual success. He was one of the organizers of the Yardley Building and Loan Association, and for twenty-five years served as its treasurer. He was also one of the organizers of the Yardley National Bank. He held the office of school director for a number of years, the cause of education finding in him a warm friend; and his political allegiance has ever been given to the Republican party. He married Miss Elizabeth Parent, of New Jersey, and they became the parents of two children: Martha, deceased; and William H.

William H. Hough was born November 17, 1856, and acquired his education in the common schools of Yardley. When not occupied with his text books he assisted his father in the store, and was thus identified with mercantile interests for twenty-four years. In 1880 he opened a grocery store in Yardley, which he conducted with fair success for ten years. Since that time he has been engaged in the butchering business in connection with farming, and his keen discernment and enterprise have brought to him very creditable and gratifying success. Socially he is connected with the Improved Order of Red Men, No. 170, of Trenton, New Jersey, in which he has passed all of the chairs, a fact which indicates his popularity with his brethren of the fraternity. William H. Hough was married to Miss Anna Ford, a daughter of George and Anna Ford, of West Chester, Pennsylvania. They became the parents of seven children, of whom one died in infancy. The others are: Bertha J., wife of William J. Wilson; Edward T., Lillian I., Mabel C., Elsie and Bess, all at home.

EASTBURN FAMILY. The name of Eastburn is an old and honorable one. It originates in Yorkshire, England, where the Manor of Esteburne, (East stream) was created early in the Eleventh century. It comprised the parishes of Bingley and Thwaite-Keighly, from whence the Eastburns emigrated to America six centuries later. The name "de Eastburn" appears as a surname as early as 1200, and the more familiar names of Robert and John Eastburn in 1583. The first of the name to migrate to Penn's Province was John Eastburn, of the parish of Bingley, who brought a certificate from Brigham Monthly Meeting of Friends to Philadelphia, dated 5 mo. 31, 1682. He purchased 300 acres of land in Southampton township, Bucks county, in 1693, and married Margaret Jones, of Philadelphia 5 mo. 2, 1694. He died in Southampton about 1720. His children were: Elizabeth, born 8 mo. 16, 1695; John, born 6 mo., 22, 1697; Peter, born 1 mo. 5, 1699;

Thomas, born 9 mo. 22, 1700. Their mother died in 1740. There was also a daughter Mary, who married Thomas Studham. Elizabeth married Thomas Walton, of Southampton. Thomas died in 1748, leaving a widow Sarah and daughter Margaret. The eldest son John left several descendants.

ROBERT EASTBURN, probably a brother of John, at least son of another John, of the parish of Thwaite-Keighley, Yorkshire, married Sarah Preston, daughter of Jonas, of the parish of Rostick, near Leeds, England, 3 mo. 10, 1693. Their children were:

Esther, born 8 mo. 27, 1694, married 1717, Jonathan Livezey, ancestor of the Solebury family.

Benjamin, born 7 mo. 15, 1695, died 1741; surveyor general of Pennsylvania from 1733 to 1741, who married Ann Thomas in 1722, but left no issue.

John, born 1 mo. 12, 1697, married Grace Colston, and settled in Norriton, Montgomery county, Pennsylvania, where many of his descendants still reside.

Mary, born 11 mo. 17, 1698, died unmarried.

Samuel, born 2 mo. 20, 1702, died 1785 in Solebury, Bucks county, Pennsylvania; married Elizabeth Gillingham.

Joseph, born 1 mo. 21, 1704, died unmarried.

Sarah, born 12 mo. 10, 1706; married 1734, Hugh Thomas, of Philadelphia county, Pennsylvania.

Robert, born 2 mo. 7, 1710; married 1733, Agnes Jones; was captain in French and Indian war of 1756-8 under General Forbes, and was captured by the Indians in March, 1756, and carried to Canada and held until November, 1757. He, however, lived to render valuable service to Philadelphia Committee of Safety at the outbreak of the Revolution. He was the father of Rev. Joseph Eastburn, founder of the Mariners' Presbyterian Church, in 1818, and several other children.

Elizabeth, the youngest child of Robert and Sarah (Preston) Eastburn, was born after the arrival of her parents in Philadelphia.

The family as above given brought a certificate from Brigham Friends' Meeting in Yorkshire to Philadelphia, dated 12 mo. 6, 1713, and removed to Abington in 1714. Robert died 7 mo. 24, 1755, and Sarah 8 mo. 31, 1752.

Samuel Eastburn, third son of Robert and Sarah, born in Yorkshire, 2 mo. 20, 1702, came to Philadelphia with his parents in 1713. In 1728 he married Elizabeth, daughter of Yeamans Gillingham of Oxford, Philadelphia county, and removed to Solebury township, Bucks county, near Centre Hill, where he followed his trade, that of a blacksmith, as well as the conduct of a farm of 250 acres which he purchased in 1734. He brought a certificate from Abington Meeting, dated March 6, 1729, to Buckingham Meeting, of which he became one of the most active members, serving as overseer and clerk for several years. He was recommended as a minister in 1770, and travelled in that capacity through various parts of this state, as well as in New Jersey, New York and New England. He was also a prominent man in the community in which he lived. He donated the land upon which the first school house was built at Centre Hill, which was known for many years as "The Stone School House" before Centre Hill was known as a village. He died in 1785. His children were:

Benjamin, born 2 mo. 11, 1729, died 11 mo. 21, 1735.

Joseph, born 12 mo. 18, 1730, died 10 mo. 29, 1780; married 1753, Mary Wilson.

Ann E., born 12 mo. 18, 1732; married 1754, Joseph Pugh, son of Daniel, of New Britain.

Mary, born 2 mo. 16, 1734; married William Edwards.

Sarah, born 3 mo. 23, 1736; married 1756, Benjamin Smith.

Robert, born 6 mo. 23, 1739; married 1763, Elizabeth Duer; 1784, Rachel Paxson.

JOSEPH EASTBURN, born 1730, died 10 mo. 23, 1780, inherited from his father one-half of the homestead, 125 acres, and purchased considerable other land in Solebury, part of it being a tract of land purchased of Richard Pike in 1763, a portion of which is still in the tenure of his great-great-grandson, Eastburn Reeder. He married, 1 mo. 17, 1753, Mary, daughter of Samuel and Rebecca (Canby) Wilson, of Buckingham, and had by her eleven children, as follows:

Joseph, born 7 mo. 16, 1754; married 1777, Rebecca Kitchin, daughter of William and Sarah Ely Kitchin.

Benjamin, born 7 mo. 4, 1756; married 1778, Keziah Ross and removed to Maryland.

Samuel, born 6 mo. 20, 1759; married 1781, Macre Croasdale, and in 1786, Hannah Kierkbride.

John, born 4 mo. 28, 1760; married 1788, Elizabeth Wiggins, and in 1808, Hannah Hillborn.

Rebecca, born 4 mo. 4, 1762; married 1810, George Pierce.

Thomas, born 5 mo. 14, 1764; married 1795, Mercy Bailey.

Mary, born 6 mo. 22, 1766; married 1790, Joseph Phipps.

James, born 8 mo. 27, 1768, married 1791, Merab, daughter of John and Sarah (Simcock) Ely.

Amos, born 12 mo. 25, 1770; married 1705, Mary Stackhouse.

David, born 4 mo. 7, 1773; married 1801, Elizabeth Jeanes and removed to Delaware.

Elizabeth, born 1776, died 1777. Mary, the mother, died 11 mo. 19, 1805.

JOSEPH EASTBURN, born 1754, died 5 mo. 16, 1813, inherited from his father the Pike tract of land in Solebury, and lived and died thereon. He married Rebecca Kitchin, 9 mo. 19, 1777, and had seven children, of whom only five, all daughters, grew to maturity, and only the eldest, Elizabeth, born 9 mo. 13, 1778, married. She became the wife of Merrick Reeder, Esq., in 1802. An account of their descendants is given on another page of this work.

ROBERT EASTBURN, youngest son of Samuel and Elizabeth Gillingham Eastburn, born 6 mo. 23, 1739, died 1816, married (first) 11 mo. 22, 1763, Elizabeth Duer, and took up his residence on a part of the homestead farm where he was born, and spent the rest of his life there. His children by Elizabeth were: Sarah, born 1 mo. 12, 1766; married Thomas Phillips. Moses, born 4 mo. 1, 1768; married 1790, Rachel Knowles. Elizabeth, born 1770, died 1775. Aaron, born 1 mo. 10, 1773; married 1796, Mercy Bye. Ann, born 12 mo. 27, 1775, married 1798, John Comfort. Robert married (second) Rachel Paxson, a widow on 9 mo. 16, 1784, and had two children: Letitia, born 1793, married 1816, Samuel Metlar; Samuel, born 1800, married 1821, Mary Carver.

MOSES EASTBURN, born 4 mo. 1, 1768, died 9 mo. 28, 1846, married 10 mo. 21, 1790, Rachel, daughter of John and Mary Knowles. Mary Knowles, the elder, was a daughter of Robert and Mercy (Brown) Sotcher, and granddaughter of John and Mary (Lofty) Sotcher, Penn's faithful stewards at Pennsbury, and also granddaughter of George and Mercy Brown, and a cousin to General Jacob Brown. The children of Moses and Rachel Knowles Brown who grew to maturity were: John, born 1791, removed to the west; Elizabeth, born 1793, married 1813, Samuel Blackfan; Robert, born 1794, removed to the west; Jacob, born 9 mo. 14, 1798, married 1829, Elizabeth K. Taylor; Mary, born 9 mo. 15, 1800, married 1829, Thomas F. Parry; Sarah, born 1804, married John Palmer; and Moses, born 5 mo. 9, 1815, married 1845, Mary Anna Ely. Rachel Knowles Eastburn died 4 mo., 1843.

Moses Eastburn, son of Moses and Rachel, born 5 mo. 9, 1815, died 9 mo. 27, 1887, was a worthy representative of this old family. He was possessed in a marked degree of the best elements of good citizenship, quiet and unassuming in demeanor, but determined and unswerving in his devotion to principle and right. Though never holding any political office he held many positions of trust, and was always active in promoting and maintaining local enterprises for the benefit of the people of his native county. He was for many years a manager and afterwards president of the Bucks County Agricultural Society; one of the organizers and most active members of the Solebury Farmers' Club; a manager of the Farmers' and Mechanics' Mutual Insurance Association of Bucks County, probably the largest local insurance company in the county, and for many years its president, (1877 to 1886); a manager of the Lahaska and New Hope Turnpike Company, and its president for many years prior to his death; a manager of the Doylestown and Buckingham Turnpike Company from 1864 until his death; a manager of the Lambertville National Bank, and school director for many years. He was an active member of Solebury Monthly Meeting of Friends, being for thirty-five years clerk of the Meeting, and in every position he discharged its duties with ability and fidelity. Few men have been more honored and respected for sterling qualities than he. He was married 4 mo. 16, 1845, to Mary Anna, daughter of Hugh B. and Sarah M. Ely, of Buckingham, where she was born, 11 mo. 30, 1816. She died in Solebury, 7 mo. 2, 1879. Moses Eastburn inherited the farm upon which he was born and spent nearly his whole life there. It is now the property of his only son, Hugh B. Eastburn. The children of Moses and Mary Anna (Ely) Eastburn were: Hugh B., born 2 mo. 11, 1846; and Fannie, born 10 mo. 27, 1847, died 1851.

HUGH B. EASTBURN, of Doylestown, lawyer and banker, was born on the Solebury farm, 2 mo. 11, 1846. He attended the public schools of the neighborhood until 1859, and then entered the Excelsior Normal Institute at Carversville, graduating in 1865. For two years he taught in the Boys' Grammar School at Fifteenth and Race streets, Philadelphia, and subsequently in the Friends' Central High School. While there he began the study of law under the preceptorship of Hon. D. Newlin Fell, now justice of the supreme court, and was admitted to the Philadelphia bar in the spring of 1870. In June, 1870, he was appointed by State Superintendent Wickersham to fill a vacancy in the office of county superintendent of schools in Bucks county, and was elected to that position in 1872, and re-elected in 1875. Mr. Eastburn resigned the office of county superintendent in 1876 and entered the law department of the University of Pennsylvania, and was admitted to the Bucks County bar in August, 1877. In 1885 he was elected district attorney on the Republican ticket, receiving a handsome majority, though the county was at that time Democratic. Mr. Eastburn was one of the organizers of the Bucks County Trust Company in 1886, and has been one of the board of directors since organization and its president since 1895, and trust officer since

1892. He has always been deeply interested in educational matters, and his voice and pen have been potent in every movement for the advancement of education in his native county and state. He was for several years a member of the board of trustees of the West Chester Normal School, and has been a member of the Doylestown school board since 1890, and is now its president. In politics he is an ardent Republican, and has taken an active interest in the councils of his party. He has been its representative in many district, state and national conventions.

He was married 12 mo. 23, 1885, to Sophia, daughter of John B. and Elizabeth S. (Fox) Pugh, of Doylestown, and has two sons: Arthur Moses, born 9 mo. 27, 1886; and Hugh B., Jr., born 2 mo. 11, 1888.

ROBERT EASTBURN, of Yardley, Bucks county, Pennsylvania, was born in Solebury township, Bucks county, 3 mo. 2, 1833, is a son of Jacob and Elizabeth K. (Taylor) Eastburn. Jacob Eastburn was a son of Moses and Rachel (Knowles) Eastburn, mentioned in a foregoing sketch, and was born on the old Eastburn homestead in Solebury, September 14, 1793. He married in 1829 Elizabeth K. Taylor, who, like Rachel (Knowles) Eastburn, was a descendant of John and Mary (Lofty) Sotcher, through the marriage of their daughter Mary to Mahlon Kirkbride.

On the marriage of Jacob Eastburn his father purchased for him the farm now owned by John H. Ely, adjoining the homestead, and he spent the remainder of his life thereon. Jacob Eastburn was a prominent and successful business man and farmer. His elder brother Robert had heired a farm at Limeport, but, going west when young, had died without issue, whereby the farm descended to his brothers and sisters, subject to the life estate of their father, Moses Eastburn. During the lifetime of Moses the farm, which was a valuable one, as it included the then profitable lime kilns, quarries and wharfage on the canal, was occupied by Phineas Kelly. At the death of Moses Eastburn, in 1846, Jacob, as the eldest surviving son, was induced to take charge of this valuable plant and manage it for the heirs. He entered into a partnership with the late George A. Cook, who had been a clerk under Mr. Kelly, and the new firm built up a prosperous and profitable business. They eventually purchased the interest of the other heirs and continued the business until the death of Jacob Eastburn, which occurred August 26, 1860. Jacob Eastburn was an active and prominent man in the community, though never holding any elective office other than school director and was frequently called upon to act as guardian, trustee or executor

2-3

in the settlement of estates, and held many positions of trust. He was an active and consistent member of Solebury Friends' Meeting. Jacob and Elizabeth Eastburn were the parents of ten children, viz.: William T. and Anna, both of whom died in infancy; Robert, the subject of this sketch; Ellen Y., wife of Samuel Hart, of Doylestown township, born 10 mo. 27, 1834; Mary Anna, born 2 mo. 29, 1837, now widow of J. Simpson Betts; George, born 11 mo. 25, 1838, a prominent educator of Philadelphia; Elias and Timothy, twins, born 12 mo. 28, 1840—the former, now deceased, was a sheriff of Bucks county, and the latter is still living in Solebury; Rachel, died in infancy; Sarah, born 10 mo. 15, 1845, now deceased, was the wife of Mark Palmer, of Lower Makefield. Elizabeth K. Eastburn the mother, died 8 mo. 21, 1877.

Robert Eastburn was born and reared on the Solebury farm, and received a good education. Arriving at manhood, he was married, 2 mo. 12, 1857, to Elizabeth, daughter of Joseph E. and Letitia (Betts) Reeder, and in the following spring began farming on the Pownall farm at Limeport, purchased by his father-in-law. His wife Elizabeth died there 11 mo. 6, 1860, and the following spring he sold out and returned to the homestead. His father having died the preceding summer, he as eldest son and executor was occupied in the settlement of the estate and the conduct of the business for the next two years. These were trying times for the Quaker-bred youth of our section, the civil war having broken out, and excitement ran high. Though bred and trained as non-combatants, religious principles and parental injunction and restraint were insufficient to restrain many from responding to the numerous calls for men to go to the front in defense of our country. This family of four grown-up sons was no exception to the rule, and only the contention as to who should go and who remain at home to care for the widow and farm, probably prevented their early enlistment. Finally, when the rebels had entered our own state, the strain was too great, and three of the boys (Robert, George and Elias) enlisted in an emergency company formed at Doylestown, and started for the front, leaving Timothy to care for the home interests. Fortunately the tide of invasion was turned and the boys were gone but a few weeks, and came home to make peace with the grim elders of the meeting for their transgression of the discipline. In 1866, one year after the close of the war by the active work of our late friend, John E. Kenderdine, a prominent and active worker in Solebury Meeting, assuming the position that the boys going to the front were no more guilty than those at home contributing to the war, an acknowledgment of their deviation from one of the cardinal points of their faith (that of opposition to war) by in any way giving encouragement to the government in its armed support, was prepared and signed by forty-seven of the fifty male members of that meeting. Of that list but fourteen are living at this time.

In the summer of 1863 Robert Eastburn purchased the interest of his father in the lime business and removed to Yardley, where an office for the sale of the lime had been long established, and formed a partnership with George A. Cook, under the firm name of Eastburn & Cook, which lasted several years. Later he embarked in the coal and fertilizer business at Yardley, which he continued until 1897. In addition to this business, having been elected a justice of the peace in 1874, he started a real estate and general business agency, which he has continud to the present time in connection with the settlement of many estates and the transaction of official business, Mr. Eastburn having held the office of justice until the present time, a period of thirty years.

Robert Eastburn married (second) on October 20, 1863, Elizabeth, daughter of Charles White, of Solebury, and took up his permanent residence in Yardley. His wife died 11 mo. 5, 1866, and on 8 mo. 12, 1875, he married (third) Anna Palmer, who died 3 mo. 8, 1901. By his first marriage, with Elizabeth Reeder, Mr. Eastburn had two children: William T., born 8 mo. 31, 1859, married Alada Blackfan, and is now living at New Hope; and Jacob, born 11 mo. 6, 1860, now living in New York city. By his marriage with Anna Palmer he has one son, Walter N., born 2 mo. 6, 1881, married 11 mo. 11, 1902, Isabel Frances Stanbury, and now living in New York.

WILLIAM T. EASTBURN, of New Hope, son of Robert and Elizabeth (Reeder) Eastburn, was born in Solebury, 8 mo. 31, 1859. At the death of his mother, 11 mo. 6, 1860, he went to live with his grandparents, Joseph E. and Letitia Reeder, and was reared in their home in Solebury. He received a good education, and upon his marriage began farming at his present residence, where he has ever since resided. At the death of his grandfather in 1892 he was devised this property and the farm upon which he was born at Limeport. Mr. Eastburn is a progressive and intelligent farmer, and has gradually improved the property since it came under his tenure. He is a member of Solebury Friends' Meeting. He was married 10 mo. 5, 1887, to Alada E., daughter of the late William C. and Elizabeth (Ely) Blackfan, a lineal descendant of Edward Blackfan and Rebecca Crispin, the latter being a first

Charles T. Eastburn,

cousin to William Penn. William T. and Alada E. B. Eastburn have four children; viz.: Sybil Ethel, born 4 mo. 6, 1890; William B., born 4 mo. 30, 1894; Edward B., born 2 mo. 9, 1898; and Joseph Robert, born 10 mo. 20, 1901.

CHARLES TWINING EASTBURN, of Yardley, Bucks county, Pennsylvania, one of the most active and successful young business men of Bucks county, was born in Newtown township, Bucks county, Pennsylvania, October 9, 1873, and is a son of Franklin and Mary Elizabeth (Twining) Eastburn, both of whom are descendants of the earliest English settlers in Lower Bucks. Mr. Eastburn is a descendant in the seventh generation from Robert and Sarah (Preston) Eastburn, who migrated from Yorkshire, England, in 1713, through their son Samuel, who settled in Solebury township, Bucks county, in 1729. An account of the first three generations of this family is given above.

Amos Eastburn, son of Joseph and Mary (Wilson) Eastburn, and grandson of Samuel, above mentioned, was born in Solebury township, 12 mo. 25, 1770, being the ninth of eleven children. His father died when he was ten years of age. Early in life he learned the trade of a carpenter and joiner, and followed that vocation in connection with farming in Buckingham and Solebury townships, until 1811, when he removed to Middletown township and settled upon 135 acres of land that had been the property of the ancestors of his wife since 1699, nearly the whole of which is now included in the borough of Langhorne Manor, where he died 10 mo. 16, 1823. He married, 4 mo. 23, 1795, Mary Stackhouse, born in Middletown township, daughter of Jonathan and Grace (Comfort) Stackhouse, granddaughter of Isaac and Mary (Harding) Stackhouse, and great-granddaughter of Thomas and Ann (Mayos) Stockhouse, an account of whose arrival in Bucks county in 1682 is given in another part of this work. The land upon which Mrs. Eastburn spent nearly her whole life was part of a tract of 350 acres taken up by her great-grandfather (the last named Thomas Stackhouse) in 1699, and had been successively occupied by her direct ancestors down to the death of her father, Jonathan Stackhouse, in 1805, when fifty-five acres thereof was set apart to her as her share of her father's estate. Her husband later purchased of the other heirs an additional seventy-six acres adjoining, and it was her home from 1811 until her death, 11 mo. 31, 1831. Amos and Mary (Stackhouse) Eastburn were the parents of three children: Grace, born in Buckingham, 1 mo. 29, 1796, died in Fallsington in 1875,

unmarried; Jonathan, born in Buckingham, 12 mo. 25, 1797, died in Middletown, 4 mo. 9, 1840, married Sidney Wilson and had children: Mary Ann, Amos, Joseph Wilson and Isaac S.; and Aaron, born in Buckingham, 8 mo. 23, 1804, died in Newtown township, 2 mo. 6, 1889.

Aaron Eastburn, grandfather of the subject of this sketch, was reared from the age of seven years on the Langhorne Manor farm. His father died when he was nineteen years of age, and he remained with his mother until 1828, when he purchased the farm where the subject of this sketch was born, in Newtown township, and spent his remaining days thereon, dying 2 mo. 6, 1889, in his eighty-fifth year. He was an active member of the Society of Friends, and a trustee of Falls Meeting. He married 5 mo. 22, 1831, Sarah Cadwallader, daughter of Cyrus and Mary (Taylor) Cadwallader of Lower Makefield township, granddaughter of Jacob and Phebe (Radcliffe) Cadwallader, great-granddaughter of Jacob Cadwallader, and great-great-granddaughter of John Cadwallader, a native of Wales, who was an early settler in Warminster township and a noted minister among Friends. Through her mother, Mary Taylor, she was a great-granddaughter of John and Mary (Lofty) Sotcher, William Penn's trusted stewards at Pennsbury, the former of whom was for many years a member of colonial assembly.

Aaron and Sarah (Cadwallader) Eastburn were the parents of five children: Mary C., born 5 mo. 10, 1832, married Charles Moon; Cyrus, of Lower Makefield, born 12 mo, 2, 1833, married Asenath Haines; Charles, died in infancy; Mercy, born 7 mo. 11, 1838, married Charles Albertson; and Franklin.

Franklin Eastburn, father of the subject of this sketch, was the youngest child of Aaron and Sarah, and was born on the Newtown homestead, 11 mo. 2, 1842, and resided thereon until 1896 when he moved to 2107 Chestnut street, Philadelphia, where he now resides. He married, 10 mo. 28, 1869, Mary Elizabeth Twining, daughter of Charles and Elizabeth (West) Twining, of Yardley, Bucks county, Pennsylvania, and they are the parents of two children: Sarah C., born in 1871, now the wife of George William Balderston, of Trenton, New Jersey, and Charles.

Charles Twining Eastburn was born and reared on the old homestead in Newtown township, and acquired his education at the public schools and at Friends' Central School at Fifteenth and Race streets, Philadelphia, and Stewart's Business College at Trenton, New Jersey, leaving the latter February 28, 1892. The day following his leaving business college he entered the employ of Stephen B. Twining, in the stone quarry business, at Stockton, New Jersey. Upon the death of Mr. Twining, in July, 1894, he assumed charge of the entire operations. The following year he purchased the business, and has increased and expanded it from year to year until he is now the largest dealer in his line of trade in Eastern Pennsylvania, operating extensive quarries at Stockton, New Jersey, Lumberville, Yardley, Neshaminy Falls, and in Clearfield, Elk and Jefferson counties, Pennsylvania, and filling large contracts for furnishing stone to the Pennsylvania and other railroad companies, and for many large public and private building operations all over the country, employing from four hundred to seven hundred men in the conduct of his business. He also owns and conducts the homestead farm in Newtown township.

Mr. Eastburn married, January 8, 1903, Margaret B. Phillips, daughter of Theodore F. and Emma B. Phillips, of Langhorne, Bucks county, Pennsylvania, and they are the parents of one child, Sarah P., born June 17, 1904. Mr. and Mrs. Eastburn are members of the Newtown Presbyterian church. Mr. Eastburn is a Republican in politics, and has taken an active interest in the success of his party. He is a member of Newtown lodge, No. 426, F. and A. M.

SAMUEL COMFORT EASTBURN. Among the most enterprising business men of lower Bucks county is Samuel Comfort Eastburn, of Langhorne borough. He is a son of Joseph and Elizabeth (Comfort) Eastburn, and was born in Middletown township, Bucks county, August 2, 1848. An account of the first three generations of the paternal ancestors of the subject of this sketch is given in other pages, he being a descendant in the sixth generation of Robert and Sarah (Preston) Eastburn, who came from Yorkshire to Philadelphia in 1713, and settled near Abington, Montgomery county, Pennsylvania, a year later. Samuel Eastburn, the great-great-grandfather of Samuel C., removed to Solebury township, Bucks county, in 1729. His son, Robert Eastburn, and his first wife, Elizabeth Duer, were the great-grandparents of both the subject and his wife, Elizabeth (Maule) Eastburn.

Aaron Eastburn, youngest son of Robert and Elizabeth (Duer) Eastburn, born 1 mo. 10, 1773, married in 9 mo., 1796, Mercy Bye, of Buckingham, and lived in Solebury, dying at the age of seventy-three years, 3 mo. 24, 1846, and Mercy, his widow, dying 2 mo. 21, 1848, aged seventy-four years. They were the parents of ten children, seven daughters and three sons. Joseph Eastburn, the ninth child of Aaron and Mercy, and the only son who married, was born in Solebury township, 4 mo. 18, 1814. He

was reared in his native township of Solebury, but on his marriage, 11 mo. 19, 1846, to Elizabeth, daughter of Samuel and Elizabeth Comfort, of Middletown, settled on a portion of his father-in-law's farm in Middletown. At the death of Samuel Comfort in 1860 this farm descended to his daughter, Elizabeth C. Eastburn, and a part of it is the present home of the subject of this sketch. The children of Joseph and Elizabeth (Comfort) Eastburn were: Samuel C., born 8 mo. 2, 1848; Anna, born 6 mo. 24, 1852, married John G. Willetts; and Thomas, born 8 mo. 21, 1853. Joseph Eastburn, the father, died 10 mo, 31, 1891.

The maternal ancestors of the subject of this sketch were among the early Quaker settlers of this section. John Comfort was a resident of Amwell township, Hunterdon county, where he died in 1728. He brought a certificate from Flushing, Long Island, to Falls Meeting, 12 mo. 3, 1719. In 1720 he married Mary, daughter of Stephen and Sarah (Baker) Wilson, and had by her three children: Stephen, Sarah and Robert. Stephen Comfort married Mercy Croasdale, and settled in Middletown township, where he acquired several large tracts of land. He died in 1772, leaving sons Stephen, John, Ezra, Jeremiah, Moses, and Robert; and daughters Grace and Mercy. Stephen Comfort (2), married Sarah Stevenson, and settled on his father's farm on the Neshaminy, near Parkland, and later purchased considerable adjoining land, most of which became the property of his son Samuel at the death of his father in 1826. The other children of Stephen and Sarah Comfort were, Stephen, David and Jeremiah. Samuel Comfort lived upon the Neshaminy homestead until about 1850, when he removed to the village of Attleboro, where he died in 1860, leaving children: Mary Ann; Jesse; Elizabeth, wife of Joseph Eastburn, and Samuel. He was a prominent man in the community and filled many positions of trust.

Samuel Comfort Eastburn was reared on the Middletown farm, and received his education at the Langhorne Academy and at Westtown Boarding School. He later took a course at Crittenden's Commercial College, Philadelphia. He engaged in railroad surveying for a few years, and then in the dry goods business in Philadelphia, where he remained for ten years. In 1880 he took an agency for the Provident Life and Trust Company of Philadelphia, in the life insurance department, and has been connected with it ever since, now holding the position of general agent for Central Pennsylvania. Mr. Eastburn is an enterprising and successful business man, and has been closely identified with most of the vast improvements in and about his native town of Langhorne in the last twenty-five years. In 1886 he organized and developed the Langhorne Improvement Company, purchasing for it the 620 acres of land upon which the present borough of Langhorne Manor is built. In 1887 he built the Langhorne water works, which now supply water to the three boroughs of Langhorne, Langhorne Manor and Attleboro, and in the same year he built the Langhorne brick works. In 1888 he organized the Langhorne Electric Light Company. He was treasurer and superintendent of the Langhorne Manor Inn, now the Foulke and Long Institute. He has been largely instrumental in the sale and development of suburban real estate, and has been for many years a foremost advocate of the improvement of the public roads. He has always been an ardent advocate of progress and improvement, and has been a potent force along these lines in the community in which he lives. In religion he is a member of the orthodox branch of the Society of Friends. In politics he is a Republican, though never a seeker or holder of other than local office, being for some years a justice of the peace, and filling other local offices.

He married May 3, 1876, Elizabeth L., daughter of Joseph E. and Sarah (Comfort) Maule, of Philadelphia, who was born 2 mo. 10, 1851. She is a granddaughter of John and Ann (Eastburn) Maule, the latter being a daughter of Robert and Elizabeth (Duer) Eastburn, and a sister to Aaron Eastburn, the grandfather of the subject of this sketch. The children of Samuel C. and Elizabeth (Maule) Eastburn are: Herbert Maule, born 3 mo. 25, 1877; Samuel Arthur, born 10 mo. 3, 1878; Joseph Maule, born 4 mo. 25, 1880; and Howard Percy, born 2 mo. 15, 1887. Herbert is the general agent of the Penn Mutual Life Insurance Company at Trenton, New Jersey; Samuel A. is district agent for the Provident Life and Trust Company at Williamsport, Pennsylvania; Joseph M. is superintendent of the Redwood Lumber Manufactory, at Samoa, California, for Hammond & Co.; Howard P. is a civil engineer in the employ of the Good Roads Commission of Pennsylvania. All of the brothers are successful in their chosen careers, and all are single.

ROBERT KIRKBRIDE EASTBURN, Deceased, of Langhorne, Bucks county, Pennsylvania, was born in Morrisville, Bucks county, January 20, 1825, and was a son of Samuel and Huldah (Wooley) Eastburn and grandson of Samuel and Hannah (Kirkbride) Eastburn, the last named Samuel being a son of Joseph and Mary (Wilson) Eastburn, of Solebury, Bucks county, grandson of Samuel and Elizabeth (Gil-lingham) Eastburn, and great-grandson of Robert and Sarah (Preston) Eastburn, who were married in Yorkshire, England, 3 mo. 10, 1693. An account of the first three generations of the descendants of Robert and Sarah (Preston) Eastburn, and some account of their earlier antecedents in England, is given in the preceding sketches.

Samuel Eastburn, son of Joseph and Mary (Wilson) Eastburn, of Solebury, was born in that township, 6 mo. 20, 1759. He was reared on the old Solebury homestead, still in the tenure of the descendants of Joseph and Mary, and early in life learned the trade of a blacksmith, which he followed during the active years of his life, in connection with farming in various parts of the county. His father died when Samuel had just arrived at the age of twenty-one years, and prior to the death of the grandfather, who died in 1785. Under the will of the latter, Samuel acquired title to a part of the old homestead on the borders of the present borough of New Hope, and he followed his trade there until 1787, when he purchased a farm of 101 acres adjoining the homestead, which he conducted in connection with his trade until 1791. At about this time, having sold his farm, he removed to White Marsh, Montgomery county, where he operated a smith shop until 1803, when he removed to Morrisville, Bucks county, and purchased a portion of the Robert Morris tract and located thereon. He followed his trade in connection with farming at Morrisville for some years, and died at that place, 4 mo. 5, 1822, at the age of sixty-four years. He was twice married, having married 4 mo. 12, 1781, Macre Croasdale, who died 4 mo. 31, 1782; his son Joseph, by this marriage, born 1 mo. 13, 1782, died in infancy. He married again, 5 mo. 15, 1788, Hannah Kirkbride, daughter of Robert and Hannah (Bidgood) Kirkbride, of Doylestown, granddaughter of Mahlon and Mary (Sotcher) Kirkbride, and great-granddaughter of Joseph Kirkbride and John Sotcher, both of whom, as well as Mahlon Kirkbride, were provincial pustices and assemblymen for many years, and the most prominent men of their time in Bucks county. Samuel and Hannah (Kirkbride) Eastburn, were the parents of nine children, viz.: Robert, born 1 mo 31, 1789, died 7 mo. 28, 1796; Samuel, see forward; Jonathan, born 9 mo. 2, 1792, married first Beulah Gaskel, and second Sarah Crozier; David, born 2 mo. 23, 1795, married Louisa Willing; Mahlon, born 9 mo. 9, 1797, died unmarried, 12 mo. 7, 1870; Hannah, born 12 mo. 7, 1799, married Aaron Ivins, in 1839; Kirkbride, born 1 mo. 23, 1803, married Ann Reeves; Macre, born 2 mo. 14, 1806, died unmarried; and Ruth, born 1 mo. 20, 1810, also died unmarried.

Samuel Eastburn, son of Samuel and Hannah, was born in Solebury, Bucks county, 10 mo. 7, 1790. His early boyhood days were spent at White Marsh, where his parents resided until he was in his thirteenth year, the remainder of his life being spent in Falls township and Morrisville borough, Bucks county. He married, in 1813, Huldah Wooley, and they were the parents of seven children, viz.: Lewis, born 8 mo. 5, 1814; Elwood, born 11 mo, 22, 1816; Robert K., the subject of this sketch; Caroline, born 3 mo. 17, 1832; Maria Ann, who married and removed to the west; Hannah K., born 9 mo. 13, 1835; and Edward.

Robert Kirkbride Eastburn, third son of Samuel and Huldah, was born and reared at Morrisville. At the age of nineteen years he became a school teacher and taught in the nearby townships of Bucks county for several years. He later removed to Philadelphia, and was engaged in the manufacture of furniture, after some years becoming a member of the firm of Reeves & Eastburn, in which he continued for a member of years. His health failing, he was induced to accept a position as book-keeper for a mining company in New Mexico, and removed there with his family, and remained twelve years, entirely regaining his health in that delightful climate. While in New Mexico his duties required him to make his home in a rough mining camp among a turbulent element, not always controlled or animated by the refining influences of civilization, where every one except he weht armed, and human life was held exceedingly cheap. Mr. Eastburn always refused to carry arms, and, by his fearless though kindly defense of right and justice, won an influence among the rugged miners, and successfully enacted the role of peacemaker in many little disturbances in the camp, where he had the respect of all who knew him. He returned to Bucks county in 1894 and purchased a handsome home on Richardson Avenue, Langhorne, where he lived until his death on February 26, 1897, and where his widow still resides. He held to the faith of the Society of Friends, in which he and his ancestors had been reared, and his firm though kindly disposition won the respect and esteem of all who knew him.

Mr. Eastburn married, April 12, 1859, Miriam Ivins, daughter of George Middleton and Sarah (Buckman) Ivins, of Penns Manor, Bucks county, where her paternal ancestors had resided for several generations, she being a granddaughter of Aaron and Miriam (Middleton) Ivins, and great-granddaughter of Aaron and Ann (Cheshire) Ivins. On the maternal side she is a granddaughter of James and Sarah (Burroughs) Buckman, the former of whom was a son of

William and Jane Buckman, and a descendant of William Buckman, who came from England and settled at Newtown in 1684, and the latter a daughter of John and Lydia Burroughs, and granddaughter of Henry and Ann (Palmer) Burroughs, who came from New Jersey and settled in Lower Makefield, being a son of John Burroughs, who was born at Newtown, Long Island, in 1684, and died in Ewing, New Jersey, in 1772, and the last named John being a son of John and Margaret (Woodward) Burroughs, of Long Island and a grandson of John Burroughs, who came from England to Massachusetts prior to 1639, and died at Newtown, Long Island, in 1678, at the age of sixty-one years. To Mr. and Mrs. Eastburn were born two children, both born in Philadelphia, viz.: Henry Kirkbride, born November 19, 1861; and Edward Ivins, born March 17, 1866. Henry K. Eastburn is now engaged in the wool business in Philadelphia; he married, January 17, 1884, Carrie Gideon, of Philadelphia. Edwin I. is also a resident of Philadelphia.

Mrs. Eastburn, accompanied her husband to New Mexico, and spent twelve years in that territory. She now resides in Langhorne borough where she is highly esteemed by a large circle of friends.

———

EASTBURN REEDER, one of the most prominent farmers and dairymen in Bucks county, was born June 30, 1828, upon the farm on which he now resides, and which had been the property of his ancestors for five generations from 1763.

Charles Reeder, great-great-grandfather of the subject of this sketch, born in England, 6 mo. 24, 1713, came to America in 1734 and settled first near Philadelphia, removing later to Upper Makefield township, Bucks county, where he purchased 200 acres of land in 1765; he died there in 1800. He married in 1737, Eleanor Merrick, daughter of John and Eleanor (Smith) Merrick, of Lower Dublin township, Philadelphia county. John Merrick was a Friend, a native of Herefordshire, England, who came to Pennsylvania and settled in Lower Dublin township. In first month, 1702, he declared intentions of marriage, at Abington Friends' Meeting, with Eleanor Smith, and was married the following month. He died in 1732. His eldest son John subsequently removed to Wrightstown, having married Hananh Hulme, and was the ancestor of the Merricks of lower Bucks. Charles and Eleanor (Merrick) Reeder were the parents of eleven children, viz.: Joseph, born 9 mo. 3, 1738, removed to New Jersey, (his son John is supposed to be the ancestor of the Reeders of Easton,

Eastburn Reeder

HOMESTEAD OF EASTBURN REEDER

Pennsylvania); Charles, born 6 mo. 15, 1743; Benjamin, born 3 mo. 29, 1746, settled in Northumberland county, Pennsylvania; Jesse, born 8 mo. 25, 1748, was drowned in the Delaware river when a young man; David, born 5 mo. 3, 1750, married, in 1776, Elizabeth Montgomery; Abraham, born 7 mo. 8, 1752, married in 1780; Elizabeth Lee, of Wrightstown; Merrick, born 7 mo. 31, 1754, married in 1773, Elizabeth Collins; Hannah, born 8 mo. 15, 1756; Eleanor, born 2 mo. 3, 1758; John, born 11 mo. 29, 1761; and Mary, born 9 mo. 15, 1764.

Merrick Reeder, seventh son of Charles and Eleanor, was reared on the Makefield farm, and on arriving at manhood married Elizabeth Collins, and followed the vocation of a farmer. He was a tenant on the "Canaan Farm" in Upper Makefield for several years. In 1810 he and several of his children removed to Muncy, Lycoming county, Pennsylvania. He had thirteen children, viz.: Benajah, born 11 mo. 30, 1774, married Elizabeth Pownall, of Solebury, and removed to Muncy, in 1810; Merrick, born 2 mo. 8, 1776, was the grandfather of the subject of this sketch; Jonathan, born 6 mo. 10, 1777, married Sarah Palmer, and removed to Muncy; David, born 8 mo. 23, 1778, married Rachel Pownall, and removed to Muncy; Hannah, born 4 mo. 11, 1780, married Samuel Winder, and removed to Muncy; Mary, born 10 mo. 29, 1781, married John Robinson; Rebecca, born 5 mo. 20, 1783, died unmarried; Elizabeth, born 4 mo. 3, 1785, married Thomas Osborn and removed to Muncy; Charles, born 4 mo. 18, 1787, married Elizabeth Clark and removed to Baltimore, Maryland, where he has descendants; Andrew, born 6 mo. 12, 1789, married Anna Kemble, and removed to Muncy; John, born 5 mo. 18, 1791, married Rebecca Ellis, and removed to Muncy; Eleanor, born 11 mo. 4, 1793, married John Ross, and removed to Muncy, Lycoming county, with her parents; Jesse, born 8 mo. 19, 1796, married first Elizabeth Fell, and (second) Mary Fell, her sister; settled in Buckingham and is the grandfather of E. Wesley Keeler, Esq., of Doylestown, Pennsylvania.

Merrick Reeder, Jr., second son of Merrick and Elizabeth, born in Makefield, 2 mo. 8, 1776, was the grandfather of the subject of this sketch. He was reared on a farm in Upper Makefield, and received a good education. He came to Solebury as a school teacher in 1800, and in 1802 married Elizabeth, daughter of Joseph and Rebecca (Kitchin) Eastburn. He was a man of good business ability, and was for many years a justice of the peace in Solebury and New Hope borough. Soon after his marriage he settled on a portion of the Eastburn farm, (purchased by Joseph Eastburn, Sr., in 1763), and at the death of his father-in-law, Joseph Eastburn, Jr., in 1813, it was adjudged to him in right of his wife, and is now the property and home of Simpson B. Michener, of New Hope. Merrick Reeder was a surveyor and scrivener, and an active and useful man in the community. His wife, Elizabeth Eastburn, died 9 mo. 7, 1833, and he married (second) in 1836, Sarah Simpson. He died in 1 mo., 1851, aged seventy-five years. (For Eastburn ancestry of subject of this sketch, see Eastburn Family). Merrick and Elizabeth (Eastburn) Reeder were the parents of three children: Joseph E., born 3 mo. 28, 1803; David K., born 10 mo. 29, 1804, married Elizabeth M. Reeder, a daughter of Charles M. Reeder; and William P., born 4 mo. 26, 1815, married Mary Reeder, also a daughter of Charles M. Reeder. David K. Reeder heired his father's portion of the old plantation in Solebury and lived and died in that township in 1887. William P. removed to Philadelphia, and died in 1885.

Joseph E. Reeder, son of Merrick and Elizabeth, born in Solebury township, 3 mo. 28, 1803, was a farmer, and resided during his whole life on the parental acres. He married 4 mo. 11, 1827, Letitia, daughter of Stephen and Hannah (Blackfan) Betts, of Solebury, who bore him two children; Eastburn, the subject of this sketch; and Elizabeth, born 1 mo. 20, 1831, died November 7, 1860, married Robert Eastburn in 1857. Joseph E. Reeder died 7 mo. 28, 1892, aged eighty-nine years, and Letitia, his wife, died 12 mo. 2, 1892, aged ninety-one years.

Eastburn Reeder, born on the old homestead of his ancestors, June 30, 1828, has spent his whole life thereon. He received a good education, and on arriving at manhood turned his whole attention to the farm. He married, 12 mo. 15 1853, Ellen, daughter of John E. and Martha (Quinby) Kenderdine, and the following spring took charge of the home farm, which he conducted personally until 1898 a period of forty-four years, since which time he has retired from its active management. In 1872 he became interested in the breeding of Jersey cattle, and his handsome herds were the pride of the county for many years. He has always taken an active interest in the elevation of the calling of a farmer and the improvement of methods of tilling and utilizing the soil. He was one of the original thirty-three members of the Solebury Farmers' Club organized in 1871, and its first secretary, and is still one of its most active members. He was the representative of Bucks county in the State Board of Agriculture from 1877 to 1893, sixteen years; was appointed by Governor Robert E. Pattison, May, 1893, State Dairy and Food Commissioner, the first commissioner under the law creating the office, and served until July, 1895. He was active in the prosecution of the manufactures of oleomargarine and other imitations of pure food, and placed the office on a high plane of usefulness to the farmer. He is also the author of numerous papers on farming and dairying, and has done much to influence legislation for the protection and betterment of the farmer. He was a member of the Solebury school board for nine years, from 1865 to 1874, and its secretary for six years. In politics he is a Republican of the independent type. In religion is an active and earnest member of Solebury Meeting of Friends, as were his ancestors. Since his retirement from the active management of his farms he has devoted considerable time to literary pursuits, and has published a book entitled "Early Settlers of Solebury," and also a "History of the Eastburn Family."

Eastburn and Ellen K. Reeder are the parents of four children: Watson K., born October 3, 1854, the present station agent for the P. & R. R. R. at New Hope, who married 1879, Mary C. Beans, of Johnsville, Bucks county, Pennsylvania; Elizabeth, born 6 mo. 1, 1857, married in 1880, Newton E. Wood, of Moreland, Montgomery county, Pennsylvania; Letitia, wife of Dr. George W. Lawrence, of East Berlin, Connecticut, married in 1892; and Martha, wife of Charles Janney, of Solebury, married in • 1903.

THE VANSANT FAMILY. The Vansants of Bucks county are descendants of a common ancestor, Gerret Stoffelse Van Sandt or Van Zandt,* (otherwise Garret Van Sandt, son of Stoffel or Christopher), who emigrated from the Netherlands, probably from Zaandam in North Holland, or Zandberg in Drenthe, in or about the year 1651, and settled in New Utrecht, Long Island, on the records of which town he is frequently mentioned as Gerret Stoffellse. He was one of the fourteen patentees mentioned in the patent from Governor Thomas Dongan, May 13, 1686, for the Commons of New Utrecht, "on behalf of themselves and their associates, the present freeholders and inhabitants of the said towne." His land was located at Yellow Hook, "under the jurisdiction of the town of New Utrecht." He was a magistrate of New Utrecht in 1681.

By deed dated July 31, 1695, he conveyed his Yellow Hook plantation to Derick Janse Van Zutphen, and removed to Bucks county, where Joseph Growdon on 12 mo. 10, 1698-9, conveys to him 150 acres in Bensalem township, and on the same date conveys a like tract adjoining to his son Cornelius. It is probable that he was located for a time in New York, as he had two children baptized at the Dutch Reformed church there in 1674 and 1676, respectively. It is generally conceded that he was twice married, as the record of the baptisms above mentioned gives the name of his wife as Lysbeth Gerritz, while the later baptisms at New Utrecht and Flatbush churches give it as Lysbeth Cornelis. It is, however, possible that in one instance her father's surname is used and in the other his first name as was common on the Dutch records. Cornelius Gerrets was a member of the Dutch church at New Utrecht.

Garret Vansand died intestate in Bensalem township, Bucks county, Pennsylvania, prior to June 5, 1706, the date upon which his ten children make a conveyance of his land purchased as before stated in February, 1698-9. The record of baptism of seven of his ten children appears at the Dutch church of New Netherlands, and will be given in connection with a sketch of each child, taken in regular order of birth, later in this article. The names of the ten children were: I. Stoffell; 2. Cornelius; 3. Josias; 4. Harman; 5. Albert; 6. Johannes; 7. Jacobus; 8. George; 9. Jesina, and 10. Garret. (Harman was really the third child in order of birth, and Josias fourth).

I. STOFFEL VAN SANDT, eldest son of Garret, was born in the province of New York about the year 1670, and took the oath of allegiance at New Utrecht, Long Island, as a native of New Netherlands, in 1687. He probably removed to Bucks county at the same time as his father, in 1699. He was a member of the Bensalem Dutch Reformed church, with wife Rachel Courson; having joined by certificate in 1710. He seems, however, to have become a member of Abington Presbyterian church at its organization in 1714, and was made one of its elders. He purchased of Henry Paulin on May 23, 1706, 300 acres of land in Middletown, 200 acres of which he conveyed to his sons Garret and John, and died seized of the balance in 1749. He was a justice of Bucks county, 1715-18, 1723-27, and a member of colonial assembly, 1710, 1712, 1714, 1719. His children were: 1. Jannetje, baptized at Brooklyn, September 3, 1693, married November 3, 1711, William Renberg 2. Garret, baptized at Brooklyn, May 4, 1695, probably died young, as the son Garret, mentioned later, was certainly a younger man. (These children above were by Stoffel's first marriage with Annetje Stoffels, who probably died prior to the removal to Bucks county.) The children of Stoffel by his second marriage with Rachel Corson, daughter of Hendrick Courson, were eight in number and as follows:

3. Joshua, married February 20, 1728, Catharine Johnston, and settled in Kent county, Maryland, on land conveyed to him by his father, October 28, 1728.

4. John, who married Rebecca Cox, of Philadelphia, August 19, 1728, and settled in Middletown, on land conveyed to him by his father in 1738, and died there in 1750, leaving daughters Ann, Elizabeth, Catharine, Rebecca and Mary and one son, John.

5. James, who was baptised at Abington as an adult September 16, 1716, and had children. 1. Rebecca, 2. Flora, 3, John, 4. Jacobus, baptized there 1719-1733.

6. Garret, purchased land of his father in Middletown in 1742, died there in 1789, leaving large family of children; see forward.

7. Elizabeth, who married John Enoch in 1718, and left a large family.

8. Alice, or Alshe, married Samuel Rue and left a number of children.

9. Rachel, married Lewis Rue, March 24, 1736, and left children.

10. Jesina, who never married.

II. CORNELIUS VAN SANDT, son of Garret (1) was born in New York, probably about the year 1672. On 12 mo. 10, 1698-9, he purchased 150 acres of land adjoining his father in Bensalem township, Bucks county. On May 4, 1714, he conveyed this tract to Thomas Stevenson. It was probably in exchange for land in Cecil county, Maryland, as on the same date Stevenson conveyed to him 1,035 acres on the west side of Elk river, in New Munster township, Cecil county, Maryland. He was baptized at Pennypack Baptist church, September 14, 1712, and in 1714, with wife Dericka, was "dismissed to Welsh Tract" Baptist church in Pencader Hundred, New Castle county. This church was organized by a colony of Welsh Baptists at Milford Haven, when about to embark in America, in 1701. On arriving in America they located at Pennypack, where they remained until 1703, when they located in New Castle on land donated to them by James James, and were ever after known as the "Welsh Tract Baptist Church." Cornelius Vansant remained a member of this church, and was buried there May 1, 1734. His will, probated in Cecil county, mentions wife Mary and children Cornelius, Garret and Rebecca, apparently minors. He evidently married a second time after his removal.

III. Harman Van Sandt, son of Garret and Lysbeth Gerritz, was baptized at the Dutch Reformed church of New York, June 10, 1674, and died in Bensalem township, Bucks county, in 1759. He purchased August 1, 1704, 250 acres of land in Bensalem of Thomas Stevenson, and on April 26, 1712, 250 more. On May 26, 1713, he purchased 125 acres which had belonged to his brother Johannes, and devised it in his will to his daughter Catharine, wife of Daniel Severns. On May 20, 1741, he purchased 100 acres for his daughter Gazina, wife of Jacob Titus. He also purchased in 1711 50 acres in Southampton, which he conveyed to his brother Jacobus. Harman Vansant was three times married. His first wife, whom he married in New Utrecht, was Elizabeth Brouwers. He married (second) in 1733 Jane Joudon, and (third) on November 9, 1738, Judith Evans, who survived him. She had been twice married before becoming the wife of Harman Vansant, first to Cornelius McCarty, and second to John Evans, both of Basalem township. The children of Harman Vansant were as follows, all probably by Elizabeth, his first wife:

1. Garret, who died in 1755, leaving a widow Mary and four children—Harman, Peter, Elizabeth and Garret. Harman, who married Eleanor Vandegrift, was the administrator of his father in 1755, and executor of the will of his grandfather in 1759. He was devised by the latter 125 acres of the land whereon his father had lived, and subsequently purchased considerable other land in Bensalem where he died in 1815. His children were: Jacob, baptized at Southampton church, July 7, 1754; Joseph; Mary Van Horn; Eleanor, wife of Robert Wood; Sarah Cox; Ann Pleamess and Garret. Peter was devised 100 acres of land by his grandfather. Elizabeth and Garret were the ancestors of practically all the Vansants of Bensalem.

2. Gazina, who married Jacon Titus and lived on land devised to her by her father. She died prior to April 30, 1772, leaving children; Elizabeth, who married Ephraim Phillips, of Burlington, New Jersey; Olshe, who married Joseph Seaborne, of Warwick, Bucks county; Catharine, who married John Baker, of Mt. Holly, New Jersey; Charity, wife of Samuel Sutton, of Byberry. Jacob, Seruch and William, of Bensalem; and Sarah of Byberry.

3. Elizabeth, who married May 6, 1719, Volkert Vandegrift, and had nine children, and died before her father. See Vandegrift Family.

4. Katharine, who married Daniel Severns and lived on land in Bensalem devised to her by her father.

5. Harman, who married Alice Craven, daughter of James Craven, of Warminster, Bucks county, and died in 1735, leaving four children, mentioned in his father's will in 1755, three of whom were James, Harman and William. James

was born in 1731, and died in Northampton, January 31, 1798; he married August 23, 1756, Jane Bennett, daughter of William and Charity Bennett, and settled in Northampton in 1764; James and Jane were the parents of thirteen children: Harman, married Alice Hogeland and settled in Warminster; Charity, wife of John Corson, Esq.; William; Charles; Elizabeth; Eleanor, wife of John Brown; Richard; Isaac; John; Alice; James; Aaron, and Mary. Harman, son of Harman and Alice (Craven) Vansant, married Catharine Hogeland, and died in Warminster in 1823; was many years a justice; he left but one child, Elizabeth, wife of James Edams. William died in Warminster in 1805

IV. Josias Van Sandt, son of Garret and Lysbeth Gerritz, was baptized at the Dutch Reformed church of New York, October 29, 1676, but as we find no further record of him he probably died in childhood.

V. ALBERT VAN SANDT, son of Garret (1) was baptized at Flatbush, May 13, 1681. He married November 8, 1704, Rebecca Vandegrift, daughter of Leonard and Gertje (Ellsworth) Vandegrift. He probably removed with the rest of the family to Bensalem, Bucks county, as he joined in the deed conveying his father's real estate, but in 1708-9, in connection with his brother-in-law, Jacob Vandegrift, purchased 500 acres of land in St. George's Hundred, New Castle county. He seems also to have purchased land in Georgetown, Kent county, Maryland, which he conveyed to his brother George, May 14, 1737. In 1743 he and his wife Rebecca, of St. George's Hundred, New Castle county, Delaware, joined in the deed for his father-in-law's real estate in Bensalem. After this date and prior to December 16, 1751, the date of his will, he married a second wife, Sarah, who is named as executrix. His children were: Elizabeth, baptized October 3, 1705, married a Joudon; Leonard, baptized November 5, 1707, probably died young, not mentioned in will; Harmanus; James; John; Garret; Christina, married a Dushane; Rebecca, married a Martin; and Ann, who married a Brown.

VI. JOHANNES (or John) VAN SANDT, born on Long Island, son of Garret (1), married at the First Presbyterian church of Philadelphia, 12 mo. 17, 1702, Leah Groesbeck, probably daughter of Jacob Groesbeck, who accompanied the Vansants from Long Island to Bensalem and purchased land there. John Vansand, as he signed his name, purchased August 1, 1704, 125 acres of land in Bensalem of Thomas Stevenson, but reconveyed it to Stevenson, May 17. 1714, and the latter immediately conveyed it to Harmon VanSandt before mentioned. On the same date Stevenson conveyed to him 500

acrs of land on Elk River, Cecil county, Maryland. It is probable that his intention to move to Maryland was frustrated by his sickness and death. His will is dated October 30, 1714, and was proved the sixth of the following January. It devises to son John forty shillings, and to his wife Leah his personal estate and the use of his Maryland real estate, if not sold, during life for "the education and maintenance of. herself and children." Believing that it will be necessary to sell his Maryland real estate, he empowers Stoffel Vansand and Bartholomew Jacobs to sell it. If not sold, to be valued and divided between the two boys, they paying their sisters their equal shares. The only child mentioned was John. It is possible that the other of "the two boys" was Garret, who had a number of children baptized at St. Stephen's church, Cecil county, beginning with 1721. A daughter Rachel was baptized June 5, 1711.

JACOBUS (or James) VAN SANDT, son of Garret (1), was baptized at Flatbush, Long Island, February 15, 1685, and removed with his father to Bensalem, Bucks county, in 1699. He married at the First Presbyterian church of Philadelphia, on January 7, 1707-8, Rebecca Vandegrift, daughter of Nicholas and Barentje (Verkerk) Vandegrift, who had come to Bensalem from Long Island at the same date as the Vansants, (See Vandegrift Family). Jacobus and his wife joined the Bensalem church, Neshaminy branch, at its institution in 1710. On April 7, 1711, Benjamin Hopper conveyed to Jacobus Vansand, of Bensalem, yeoman, 100 acres of land in Southampton, and on January 1, 1712, his brother Harman Vansandt and Elizabeth his wife conveyed to Jacobus fifty acres adjoining the 150 which had been purchased by Harman of Ezra Bowen, June 13, 1711. He later purchased 144 acres of land of Cornelius Egmont, which he devised to his son Nicholas. The will of Jacobus Vansandt, of Southampton, is dated December 12, 1744, and was proven January 9, 1745. It devises to son Jacob the 150 acre farm on which he dwelt, reserving certain privileges to his wife Rebecca; the Egmont farm to son Nicholas; mentions daughters Elizabeth and Rebecca as having received their shares, the latter being deceased; sons Jacobus, Garret and Isaiah, and grandson Charles Inyard, to have equal shares. The will names "kinsman John Vansand" and friend Nathaniel Brittian as executors, but they renouncing, as also did the widow, letters were granted to the sons James and Nicholas. The will is signed "J. V." His widow Rebecca survived him two years, leaving will dated November 18, 1746, and proved January 13. 1746-7, and mentions the same children, and grandson Charles Inyard. The children of Ja-

cobus and Rebecca Vandegrift Vansandt
were: Jacobus (or James) baptized December 1, 1708; married 10 mo, 1, 1732,
Margaret Breece, daughter of Hendrick
and Hannah (Field) Breece of Bensalem;
see ancestry of Lewis R. Bond, in this
volume.

2. Elizabeth, baptized May 21, 1710;
married 4 mo. 1, 1732, Charles Inyard,
of Warminster, and left one son, Charles
Inyard.

3. Garret, married May 13, 1739, Ann
Groome of Southampton.

4. Nicholas, baptized January 1, 1711-12,
married May 18, 1744, Mary Brittian.

5. Rebecca baptized August 7, 1716,
married Isaac Larue.

6. Isaiah, married June 6, 1732, Charity (or Gertrude) VanHorn.

7. Jacob.

James, who married Margaret Breece,
was a mason, and in 1734 purchased of
Gidean de Camp 100 acres in Warminster, which he sold in 1748. At about
the same date he signed a release to his
brothers-in-law, Hendrick, and John
Breese for legacy left his wife by her
father, and probably accompanied his
brother-in-law Hendrick Breece to Harford county, Maryland. Garret, the second son, was a blacksmith in Southampton. His will dated 9 mo. 29, 1779, is on
file in the register of wills' office of
Bucks county, but does not appear to
have been proven. It mentions wife
Ann and the following children: William; Phebe, who married Miles Strickland, December 24, 1760; Mary and Rebecca Walton; Margaret Foster; daughter Elizabeth's three sons, Amos, Breece
and Mahlon Vansant; John; Ann Richardson; Esther Vansant and James.
Nicholas, the third son, married Mary
Brittian and had two children, Captain
Nathaniel Vansant, of the Revolution;
and Rebecca, who married January 9,
1768, Daniel Boileau. Nicholas died
about May 1, 1801, and his widow Mary
in March, 1808.

Isaiah, the fourth son, married Gertje
(or Charity) Van Horn, daughter of
Peter and Elizabeth Van Horn of Middletown. On March 18, 1736-7, he purchased at sheriff's sale 178¼ acres of
land in Makefield township. In 1754 he
purchased a small tract adjoining, and in
1768 purchased of John Scott 100 acres
in Upper Makefield. His children were:
Isaiah; Elizabeth, wife of Cornelius Vandegrift; Rachel, wife of George Merrick,
married 4 mo. 12, 1769; Charity; Sarah,
who married Christian VanHorn, June
14, 1764; Mary, who married Gabriel
VanHorn, January 18, 1772; Joshua;
Peter, who married Elizabeth Wollard
April 8, 1778, and (second) Alethia Curtis; Gabriel; and Cornelius, who married
Mary Larzelere. The will of Isaiah Vansant is dated April 15, 1786, and
was proved September 28, 1786. It

devises to son Joshua the land
bought of John Scott in Upper Makefield, and to Gabriel and Cornelius the
home plantation, "reserving one-fourth
of an acre for a graveyard, where I have
began to bury, for myself and my relations;" mentions Elijah, eldest son of
Isaiah, daughter Rachel's three children;
daughter Charity's four children, and
daughter Mary, and her daughter Charity; and daughter Elizabeth.

Jacob, the youngest son of Jacobus
and Rebecca Vansant, inherited from his
father the homestead in Southampton,
and died there in 1812, devising ninety
acres thereof to his daughter Elizabeth
Vansant, who married Samuel Dickson; and Margaret, who married Jacob Roads.

VIII. GEORGE VAN SANDT, son
of Garret (1) was baptized at Flatbush,
Long Island, April 24, 1687, and removed with the family to Bensalem,
Bucks county, in 1699. He married 12
mo. 17, 1706, Micah Vandegrift. He
joined his brother Jacobus in the purchase of his father's Bensalem farm in
1706, and purchased his brother's interest on April 2, 1711. On May 17, 1714,
he and wife Micah conveyed this 150
acres in Bensalem to Thomas Stevenson,
and removed to Cecil county, Maryland,
where he purchased of Gideon Pearce,
February 20, 1721, a tract of land called
"Forks and Revision," and in 1737 purchased of his brother Albert part of a
tract called "Tolchester." On October
17, 1733, he and wife "Mary" convey to
his son Nicholas, a tract called "Nicholas' Inheritance," and on same date,
they convey to son George other lands.
In 1745 they convey parts of "Tolchester" to sons Ephraim and Benjamin.
From the will of George Vansant, proven
March 22, 1755, we learn that his children were Nicholas, Cornelius, George,
Benjamin, Ephraim, John; Elizabeth,
wife of Peter Cole; Hester Newcombe,
Resultah Salisbury, and Ann Smith.

X. GARRET VAN SANDT, young-
est son of Garret (1) was a minor when
his father's real estate was conveyed in
1706. He settled in Wrightstown township, near Penn's Park, where he had a
large plantation. He died in 1746, leaving a widow Claunchy, sons Garret and
Cornelius, to whom he devised the plantation; and daughters Sarah Sackett,
Rachel Dungan and Rebeckah Vansant,
the latter a minor. Cornelius married
Mary Lee, December 6, 1748, and died in
March, 1789, without issue. His wife
Mary died in August, 1808. Garret, eldest son of Garret and Claunchy, inherited one-half of the Wrightstown homestead, and died there in June, 1806. He
married April 30, 1760, Rebecca Evans,
who survived him. She was possibly his
second wife. Their children were Elizabeth Addis, Rebecca McClellan, and
Mary, wife of Joseph Carver. Rebecca,

daughter of Garret, Sr., married a Brittian, whose son Joseph and grandson Cornelius are mentioned in the will of Cornelius Van Sant.

Garret Vansant of Middletown, son of Stophel, received by deed of gift from his father on October 21, 1742, 95½ acres of land, part of 300 acres purchased by Stophel of Henry Paulin in 1706, and on January 10, 1748, purchased 214 acres in Middletown of Charles and Ann Plumly. On June 25, 1789, he conveys the last mentioned tract in about equal parts to his sons, Garret, Jr., and John, and on July 31, 1789, he conveyed to his son George the 95½ acres conveyed to him by his father. No record appears of the name of his wife. A Garret. Vansant married Leah Nixon at Churchville, April 15, 1747, which was probably this Garret, although it may have been his cousin Garret, of Wrightstown. The will of Garret Vansant is dated July 7, 1789, and was proven August 7, 1789, only a week after the conveyance of his land. It mentions the children of his son Jacob, and their mother Mary Vastine; daughters Rachel Harrison, Keziah Sweetman, Vashti Vansant and Sarah Hise; sons John, Garret and George, and grandson James Vansant. Jacob, the eldest son, married Mary Richardson, daughter of Joseph Richardson, and settled in Falls township, Bucks county, where he died in April, 1785, leaving children: Elizabeth, James, Catharine and Garret. His widow married Benjamin Vastine prior to 1789. George Vansant married Sarah Johnston, December 24, 1783. He sold the old homestead to Joshua Woolston in 1794, and removed to Bristol township. John married Letitia Leaw and died in Middletown in 1812, leaving a son John, and daughters Ann Leah Lovett and Amelia Booz. Garret Vansant, Jr., remained on the homestead purchased of his father in 1789 until 1822, when he conveyed it to his sons James and John, and soon after removed to Newtown, where he died in 1842 at an advanced age. His wife Mary had died many years previously. The children of Garret and Mary Vansant were John, James, Martha; Jane, wife of Isaac Randall; Rachel, wife of Eber Randall; and Mary, wife of Jonathan Hunter. James died in Middletown in 1833, leaving a widow Amy and two children, Elizabeth, born March 11, 1821, and James born May 1, 1826.

JAMES TITUS VANSANT, of Middletown township, son of John and Mary (Hunter) Vansant, and grandson of Garret and Mary Vansant, last mentioned, was born in Middletown township May 23, 1837, where he was educated at the public schools, and has spent his whole life on the farm that has been the property of his direct ancestors since 1748, and part of it since 1704. On January 21, 1863, he married Lucy Ann Carman,

daughter of Samuel and Mary Ann (Brown) Carman, of Bensalem township, and granddaughter of Barzilla and Beulah Carman. Her maternal grandparents were Israel and Sarah (Hellings) Brown, the latter being a daughter of Nathan and Rachel Hellings, of an old Middletown, Bucks county, family whose progenitor was Nicholas Hellings, an early settler in Northampton. Mr. and Mrs. Vansant are the parents of eight children, viz.: Samuel Jennings, born August 15, 1865, died February 28, 1904; William Carman, born May 14, 1867; John Andrew, born August 11, 1869; Howard, born September 12, 1871; Clarence, born August 22, 1873; James Merton, born November 15, 1875. Joseph Winder, born January 10, 1879; Lucy Ann, born June 16, 1883. Samuel Jennings Vansant married August, 1891, Martha A. Tomlinson of Fox Chase, and they are the parents of three children—Roy, Arthur and Frederick. William Carman Vansant married January 1, 1894, Melvina Search, and they have four children—Charles Search, James Merton, Mary, and Edward. Mrs. Melvina Search died in December, 1904. John Andrew Vansant married April 13, 1900, Ella Sickle, and had one child Esther Helen. Clarence Vansant married, January 25, 1898, Clara Worthington, and their children are: Harriet, born October 21, 1898; and Samuel, born October 19, 1901. James M. Vansant married, March 6, 1900, Ada K. Hibbs, and their children are: Albert Hunter, born December 31, 1900; and Clifford Randall, born July 31, 1903. Joseph Winder Vansant married June 1, 1904, Matilda Prevost McArthur.

Mr. Vansant is one of the prominent and successful men of the county, and has held many positions of trust. He owns a large amount of real estate, in dwellings and farms and takes a lively interest in the affairs of the county. He and his family are members of the Methodist church. In politics he is a Republican. He is a member of Neshaminy Lodge, No. 422, I. O. O. F., of Hulmeville.

HOWARD VANSANT, fourth son of James T. and Lucy Ann (Carman) Vansant, was born in Middletown township, September 12, 1871, and received his elementary education at the public schools. He graduated from Pierce's Business College in 1891, and for one winter filled the position in that institution as teacher in the banking department. He then accepted the position of bookkeeper for Augustes Beitney, which he filled for six years, and then entered into the employ of Walton Bros., grain merchants of Philadelphia, as bookkeeper, and after a short time was promoted to the position of general superintendent, having general charge of their large warehouse. The firm has for many years done a large business, and is one of the largest dealers in that line in Philadelphia. In politics Mr. Vansant is a Republican, and takes an active interest in the affairs of the town in which he lives. He has been for many years a member of the borough council, and is now filling the position of clerk of that body. He is a member of the Masonic fraternity, being affiliated with Bristol Lodge No. 25, F. and A. M. He is also a member of Neshaminy Lodge, No. 422, I. O. O. F., of Hulmeville, of which he is a past grand. He married, November 12, 1895, Cora Wilson, daughter of Charles and Sarah (Snyder) Wilson, of Trenton, New Jersey, and a granddaughter of Christopher and Sarah (Snyder) Wilson. They are the parents of two children, Ella Praul, born February 23, 1900; and Elisha Praul, born March 9, 1904.

ANCESTRY OF MARTIN V. B. and NATHANIEL VANSANT, of Southampton.

Captain Nathaniel Vansant, only son of Nicholas and Mary (Brittian) Vansant, of Southampton, was born on the old homestead in that township, March 13, 1745. At the outbreak of the Revolution he was a resident of Bensalem township having purchased a farm there in 1777. He was commissioned first lieutenant of the Associated company of that township. From the very beginning of the arming for the conflict with the mother country, the Vansants were foremost in offering their services for home defense and militia service. Garret and Peter were members of the Bensalem company; Garret, of Southampton, brother of Nicholas, and uncle to Captain Nathaniel, was second lieutenant of the Southampton company in 1775, and was second lieutenant of the Fifth Company of the First Battalion in the reorganization of 1777. Nicholas, father of Captain Nathaniel, and Jacob, his brother were both members of the Southampton company in 1775. In Middletown, George and John, sons of Garret and grandsons of Stophel, were members of the Associated company of that township. James, son of Harman and grandson of Harman, Sr., the only member of the family in Northampton, joined the Associated company there in 1775. Peter, of Lower Makefield, son of Isaiah and grandson of Jacobus, was captain of the company of that township, and his brother Cornelius was second lieutenant.

The member of the family, however, who rendered pre-eminent service and suffered untold hardships in the defense of his country was Captain Nathaniel Vansant, of Bensalem. He was commissioned a captain January 5, 1776, in Colonel Robert Magaw's Fifth Pennsylvania Battalion of the Flying Camp, in which there was a large number of Bucks countians, who through the treachery of Ma-

gaw's adjutant, were badly routed at Fort Washington, New York, on November 16, 1776, and 2,700 American soldiers were taken prisoners, including Magaw and almost his entire command. Captain Vansant was captured with the rest, and for two years suffered the horrors of imprisonment in the floating hells in New York harbor and the loathsome warehouses in the city. Many of the letters written home to his wife while a prisoner are in the possession of the Bucks County Historical Society and of members of the family. The quaint chapeau worn by him in the service is also in possession of the Historical Society.

Captain Vansant married August 27, 1768, at the Dutch Reformed church of Southampton, Hannah Vansandt. There seems to be some dispute about the maiden name of Hannah Vansant; both the church records and that of the granting of the license by the civil authorities give it as Vanzandt, while his descendants claim that her name was Brittian, the same as that of the Captain's mother. It seems to be conceded that she was his cousin, and it is probable that she was the daughter of his uncle, James Vansandt, who married Margaret, daughter of Hendrick and Hannah (Field) Breece. Hannah was born January 16, 1746, and died August 19, 1818. The children of Captain Nathaniel and Hannah Vansant were as follows: Harman, who died of yellow fever in Philadelphia during the epidemic of that disease in the city, about the close of the century; and Nicholas, born February 25, 1771, died April 19, 1850.

Nicholas, as only surviving child of Nathaniel and Hannah Vansant, inherited the real estate of his father, who died August 8, 1825, intestate. He lived and died on the old homestead in Southampton, which remained in the family for six generations and until 1889, when it was sold, a period of at least one hundred and fifty years. Nicholas married Mary Larzelere, daughter of Nicholas and Hannah (Brittian) Larzelere of Bensalem township. She was born September 8, 1772, and died October 27, 1863. The children of Nicholas and Mary (Larzelere) Vansant were:

1. Mary, born September 6, 1795, married Jacob Vansant, and had two children, Franklin, who married a Hogeland, and Angelina.

2. Nathaniel, born April 14, 1797, married Alice Vanartsdalen; see forward.

3. Elizabeth, born February 24, 1799, married Silas Rhoads, and had one child, Mary Ann, who married William Goforth.

4. Benjamin, born February 14, 1803, died June, 1869; married (first) Sarah Campbell, born March 7, 1810, died March 10, 1853; and (second) Jane Lukens. The children of the first marriage

were: Lendrum L., born October 4, 1832; Elizabeth R., who married J. Paul Knight; Harriet P., who married George Shoemaker; and Charles R., who married Carrie Saurman. The only child of the second marriage was Dr. Benjamin Vansant.

5. Nicholas L., born September 7, 1807; married Margaret Vandegrift, and had two children, Mahlon and Mary Ann.

The children of Nathaniel and Alice (Vanartsdalen) Vansant, were:

1. Mary Amanda, born March 26, 1824, married Anderson Leedom, and had three children: Thomas, deceased; Alice, wife of John Tomlinson; and Nathaniel, who married Martha Comly.

2. Casper R., born April 3, 1826, died June 26, 1881, married Ellen Field, and had two children: Nathaniel, born October 12, 1859; see forward; and Levi, who married Ida Sickle.

3. Nicholas B., born January 28, 1828, went to California, where he probably died.

4. Hiram R., born January 12, 1831, died September 19, 1888.

5. Jacob W., born March 7, 1833; married Esther Buckman, and had five children: Alice, who married William Bradfield; Watson, who married a VanReif; Howard, who married Lydia Stout; Leonard, who married Sarah Yerkes; and Mary who married Horace Blaker.

6. Howard S., born February 13, 1835; married Elizabeth Fetter. He died July 9, 1866.

7. MARTIN VAN BUREN VANSANT, born on the old homestead in Southampton, February 4, 1839. He was reared on the old homestead and educated at the public schools. He learned the trade of a miller, and was engaged in the milling business at Churchville for a number of years. At his father's death in 1883 he purchased the old homestead in Southampton, and subsequently sold it to Dr. Benjamin Baer, of Philadelphia. Mr. Vansant was never married. In politics he is a Democrat. He never held other than local offices, having filled that of assessor, which office, by the way, was held by his great-great-grandfather under Colonial authority, the original commission being in possession of the Bucks County Historical Society.

NATHANIEL VANSANT, son of Casper (4) and Ellen (Field) Vansant, was born at Somerton, Philadelphia county, October 12, 1859, but was reared in Southampton township, Bucks county, and educated at the local schools. His father purchased a farm in Southampton in 1870, which he conveyed to Nathaniel in 1888, and he has always followed the life of a farmer. In politics he is a Democrat. He has filled the office of school director for several years. He was married in September, 1888, to Wilhelmina Depew, and they are the parents of two children: Blanche, born March 10, 1890; and Viola E., born October 8, 1892.

————

THE VANDEGRIFT FAMILY is of Holland descent, their progenitor being Jacob Lendertsen Van der Grift (that is, son of Lenerd) who with his brother Paulus Lenertsen Van der Grift, came from Amsterdam about 1644 and settled in New Amsterdam. Both of the Van der Grift brothers were in the employ of the West India Company. Paulus was skipper of the ship "Neptune" in 1645, and of the "Great Gerrit" in 1646. He was a large landholder in New Amsterdam as early as 1644. He was a member of council, 1647-1648; burgomaster 1657-1658, and 1661-1664; orphan master 1656-1660; member of convention, 1653 and 1663. On February 21, 1664, Paulus Leendersen and Allard Anthony were spoken of as "co-patroons of the new settlement of Noortwyck, on the North River." He had five children baptized at the Dutch Reformed church, and he and his wife were witnesses to the baptism of five of the eight children of his brother Jacob. Paulus Leendertsen Van der Grift sold his property in New Amsterdam in 1671, and returned with his family to Europe.

Jacob Lendertsen Van die Grifte, bottler, of New Amsterdam, in the service of the West India Company, on September 11, 1648, granted a power of Attorney to Marten Martense Schoenmaker, of Amsterdam, Holland, to collect from the West India Company such amounts of money as he (Van die Grift) had earned at Curocoa, on the ship "Swol", employed by that company to ply between the island of Curocoa and New Netherlands. The early records of New Amsterdam give a considerable account of this ship "Swol." It carried twenty-two guns and seventy-six men. In 1644 it was directed to proceed to New Amsterdam, and on arriving, "being old," it was directed to be sold. Another boat was, however, given the same name, being sometimes mentioned as the "New Swol."

On July 19, 1648, Jacob Lendertsen Van der Grist was married at New Amsterdam to Rebecca Fredericks, daughter of Frederick Lubbertsen. On March 7, 1652, he sold as attorney for his father-in-law, fifty morgens and fifty-two rods of land on East river. On February 19, 1657, Jacob Leendersen Van die Grift was commissioned by the burgomasters and schepens of New Amsterdam as a measurer of grain. To this appointment was affixed instructions "that from now nobody shall be allowed to measure for himself or have measured by anybody else than the sworn measurers, any grain, lime or other goods which are sold by the tun or schepel, or come here from elsewhere as cargoes and in wholesale, under a penalty of £3 for first transgression, £6, for second and arbitrary correction for the third." In 1656 Jacob Leendertsen Vandergrift was made a small burgher of New Amsterdam. In 1662 he was a resident of Bergen, New Jersey, where he subscribed toward the salary of a minister. On April 9, 1664, he and his wife, Rebecca Fredericks, were accepted as members of the church at "Breukelen," upon letters from Middlewout, (now Flatlands); his residence on the west side of the river must, therefore, have been of short duration. On May 29, 1664, then living under the jurisdiction of the village of Breukelen, Long Island, he applies to council for letters of cession with committimus to the court, to relieve him from his creditors on his turning over his property in their behalf, he being "burdened with a large family, and on account of misfortune befallen some years ago, not having been able to forge ahead, notwithstanding all efforts and means tried by him to that end, etc." There are records of a number of suits prior to this date, in which he appears either as plaintiff or defendant. In 1665 he was living on the strand of the North river, New Amsterdam, where he is assessed towards paying the expense of quartering one hundred English' soldiers on the Dutch burghers. On October 3, 1667, he received a patent from Governor Nicolls for land on the island of Manhattan, on the north side of the Great Creek, which he sold to Isaac Bedloe, in 1668. He probably removed at this date to Noordwyck, on the North river, where he purchased in 1671 the land of his brother Paulus, who had returned to Amsterdam. In 1686 he appears as an inhabitant of Newton, Long Island, where he probably died, though the date of his death has not been ascertained. His widow removed with her children to Bensalem, Bucks county, Pennsylvania, in 1697, and was living there in 1710. The children of Jacob Lendertsen and Rebecca Fredericks Van der Grift, baptised at the Dutch Reformed Church of New Amsterdam, were as follows:

1. Martje, baptised August 29, 1649, married Cornelius Corsen, March 11, 1666. He was baptised at New York, April 23, 1645, being the son of Cornelius Piterse Vroom, and Tryntje Hendricks. After the death of Vroom, Tryntje had married Frederick Lubbertsen, the grandfather of Marytje, father-in-law of Jacob Lendeertsen Van der Grift. Many descendants of Cornelius Corssen and Marytje Van de Grift still reside in Bucks county.

2. Christina Van de Grift, baptised February 26, 1651, married (first) Oc-

a widower, by whom she had two children, Abraham and Jacobus. She married (second) April 14, 1681, Daniel Veenvous, from Beuren, in Gelderland, by whom she had five children—Wilhelmina, Rebecca and Contantia; two others also named Rebecca died in infancy.

3. Anna Van de Grift, baptised March 16, 1653, married, September 29, 1674. *Jacob Claessen Groesbeck. They retober 9, 1678, Cornelius Jacobse Schipper, moved to Bucks county with the rest of the Vandegrift family in 1710, but little is known of them other than that he purchased land in Bensalem adjoining that of his brothers-in-law, and that two of his daughters married into well known families of Bucks. Their children were: Rebecca, baptised June 23, 1673; Elizabeth, baptised September 4, 1677; Leah, baptised February 11, 1680, married 12 mo. 17, 1702, Johannes Van Sandt; Rachel, baptised November 21, 1682, married November 8, 1704, James Biddle; and Johanna, baptised August 9, 1685.

4. Leendert (Leonard) Van de Grift, baptised December 19, 1655, died in Bensalem, Bucks county, 1725; married, November 20, 1678, Styntje Ellsworth. He, with his three brothers and two brothers-in-law, purchased land in Bensalem in 1697 of Joseph Growdon, Leonard's purchase being two tracts of 135 and 106 acres respectively. He subsequently purchased seventy-four acres of his brother Frederick. He and his wife were received at Bensalem church in 1710, and he was appointed junior elder. On December 30, 1715, he was commissioned a justice of the peace. Letters of administration were granted on his estate February 18, 1725, to his eldest son Abraham, known as "Abraham Vandegrift, by the River." The children of Leonard and Styntje (Ellsworth) Vandegrift were: 1. Jacob, baptised September 20, 1679; 2. Christoffel, baptised August, 1681, married July 7, 1704, Sarah Druith; 3. Rebecca, baptised December 15, 1683, married November 8, 1704. Albert Van Sandt; 4. Abraham, baptised July 4, 1686, married October 17, 1716, Maritje Van Sandt, died March, 1748, leaving six children—Leonard, of Bensalem; Garret and Abraham, of Philadelphia; Christine, wife of Yost Miller, of Salem county. New Jersey; Mary, wife of Mathew Corbet. and Jemima, wife of George Taylor, of Chesterfield. New Jersey. 5. Anneken, baptised April 7, 1689, married Andrew Duow. 6. Elizabeth, baptised at Brooklyn, October 8, 1691, married May 23, 1710, Francis Kroeson. 7. Annetje, baptised June 12, 1695, mar-

---

*Nicholas (or Claes) Groesbeck, father of Jacob, was a carpenter of Albany, New York, in 1662. On October 10, 1696. deposed that he was seventy-two years old. His will dated January 3, 1706-7, mentions wife Elizabeth, son Jacob and others.

ried December 22, 1715, Cornelius King. All of the above children of Leonard Vandegrift removed to New Castle county, Delaware, prior to the death of their father, except Abraham, to whom they conveyed the real estate in Bensalem in 1743. The above named heirs of Abraham conveyed the same to Leonard, eldest son of Abraham, in 1761.

5. Nicholas Vandegrift, baptised May 5, 1658, married at New Utrecht, Long Island, August 24, 1684, Barentje Verkirk, daughter of John Verkerk. They settled at New Utrecht, where he took the oath of allegiance to James II in 1687, and where he purchased land in 1691. He removed to Bucks county with his brothers and bothers-in-law in 1697, conveying his Long Island land after his removal. On July 1, 1697, Joseph Growdon conveyed to him 214 acres in Bensalem. He joined the Bensalem church in 1710, and became a junior deacon. The records of the Dutch Reformed church show the baptism of three children, viz.: Rebecca, baptised July 26, 1685, married 11 mo. 7, 1707, Jacobus Van Sandt; Jan, baptised January 1, 1691, married May 5, 1721, at Abington Presbyterian church, Anna (or Hannah) Backer; and Deborah, baptised April 1, 1695, married Laurent Jansen,* or Johnson. Nicholas Van de Grift removed to Sussex county, Delaware, conveying his land in 1713 to Jacob Kollock, whose widow Mary in 1722 conveyed it to Folert, son of John Vandegrift.

6. Frederick Vandegrift, baptised August 20, 1661, purchased of Joseph Growdon on July 1, 1697, 106 acres adjoining that of his brothers in Bensalem township, Bucks county, a part of which he conveyed a year later to Leonard Vandegrift. If ever a resident of Bucks county, he probably remained but a short time.

7. Rachel Vandegrift, youngest daughter of Jacob, was baptised at New York, August 20, 1664, and married, in 1689. Barent Verkerk, son of Jan, and brother to his brother Nicholas's wife. Barent Verkerk purchased in 1697 a tract of land in Bensalem adjoining his brothers-in-law, all the deeds being from Joseph Growdon, and bearing the same date, July 1, 1697. He died in 1739, leaving children: Jacob; John; Mary, married Niels Boon; Constantina, married James Fitchet; Dinah, married James Keirll; and another daughter, who married an Underwood.

8. Johannes Vandegrift, youngest son of Jacob Lendertsen and Rebecca Frederics Van der Grift, was baptised at New York, June 26, 1667, and died in Ben-

salem township, Bucks county, Pennsylvania, in 1745. He married, September 23, 1694, Nealkie Volkers, widow of Cornelius Cortelyou, who was living at date of his will in 1732, but died before 1740. He married (second) July 1, 1741, Elizabeth Snowden, a widow. He purchased 196 acres in Bensalem of Joseph Growdon, adjoining the tracts of his brothers and brothers-in-law, the deed bearing date July 1, 1697. He was an elder of the "Sammeny" church, having joined it at its organization in 1710. His will dated March 16, 1732, proved March 28, 1745, devises to son Abraham the farm he lives on, for life, and if he die without issue it is to go to his surviving brothers and sisters. Some years later the children of Johannes entered into an agreement by which the land was to vest in the heirs of those deceased, even though they did not survive Abraham, and inasmuch as Abraham died without issue in 1781, the subsequent conveyances of the land throw light on the family connections. In 1786 the representatives of Jacob, Rebecca, Christana, and Helena conveyed the land, 160 acres, to Jacob Jackson and later a partition thereof was had between Jackson and Abraham Harman and Cornelius, sons of Fulkert. The children of Johannes and Nealke (Volkers) Vandegrift were: 1. Fulkert, born 1695, died 1775; married May 6, 1719, Elizabeth Vansandt, and (second) August 10, 1742, Marytje Hufte. He was a considerable landholder in Bensalem. He had five sons: Folkhart, Harman, Abraham, Cornelius and John; and three daughters: Alice LaRue, Elizabeth Krusen and Elinor, most of whom have left descendants in Bucks county. 2. Jacob, baptised at New York, October 14, 1696, died in Bensalem in 1771, married Choyes Touley, October 23, 1716. 3. Abraham, born 1698, died 1781, married, but had no issue. 4. Rebecca, married John Van Horn, died 1786. 5. Christiana, married November 8, 1722, Joseph Foster. 6. Lenah, married a Fulton. 7. Esther, baptized in Bucks county, May 10, 1710.

Most of the Vandegrifts of Bucks county are descendants of Johannes and Nealke (Volkers) Vandegrift. Leonard, grandson of Leonard, remained in Bensalem, and the land originally settled by his grandfather descended to his son, Captain Josiah Vandegrift. John, son of Nicholas, became a large landholder in Bensalem; he died in 1765, leaving sons: Nicholas, Jacob, John, Joseph, for many years an innkeeper in Bensalem; and daughters: Catharine Sands; Esther, who married John Houten; and Rebecca Vansciver. Of the sons, John married Ann Walton, May 28, 1761, and had children: Joshua, Joseph, John, Jonathan, and Mary. The father died in 1777, and the widow Ann married Charles Fetters a year later.

---

*Laurent Jansen, or Lawrence Johnson, was doubtless son of Claus Jansen, who purchased several tracts of land in Bensalem some years earlier than the Vandegrifts. He died in 1723, devising his lands to his sons Lawrence, John and Richard. The families later intermarried.

C. S. Vandegrift

Jacob Vandegrift, son of Johannes and Nealke (Volkers) Vandegrift, baptized at New York, October 14, 1696, was but an infant less than a year old when his parents settled in Bensalem township, Bucks county. He married, October 23, 1716, Charity Touley. He became a large landholder and a prominent man in the community. He died in 1771. His children were, John, died 1805, in Bensalem, leaving five children, viz.: Jacob, who settled in Northampton township; John; Jane, who married a Johnson; Bernard, settled in New Jersey; and Abraham, who married Catharine Vandegrift a granddaughter of Fulerd. 2. Bernard, who was devised 200 acres in Upper Dublin township, and settled thereon; 3. Jacob, who was devised by his father 200 acres of land whereon he was living at his father's death. 4. Charity (or Catharine) who married John Praul, January 20, 1757. 5. Helen (or Elinor) who married Harman Vansant.

Jacob Vandegrift, third son of Jacob, married first Catrintje Hufte, May 19, 1753, and (second) Sarah Titus, February 5, 1775, as before stated he settled on 200 acres belonging to his father which descended to him at his father's death. He died in May, 1800, leaving five children; Jacob, married Elinor ——; David, married Sarah ——; William Bloomfield, the grandfather of Senator Vandegrift; Mary married —— Bennett; and Elizabeth, who married Daniel LaRue. William Bloomfield Vandegrift inherited from his father considerable real estate. He was the youngest son, and had just arrived at his majority when the will of his father was proved in 1800. He married Christiana Saunders. His death occurred in 1854. His children were seven in number, viz.; Sarah Ann, married Charles Tomlinson; Eliza L., married Jacob Johnson; Eleanor, married Enos Boutcher; Alfred; Charles Souders; William M., married Eliza Boutcher and Susan, married Peter Conover.

Alfred Vandegrift was born in Bensalem township in 1807, and died there in 1861. In 1849 his father conveyed to him and his brother jointly a store property at Eddington, where they conducted a mercantile business until the death of Alfred in 1861. In 1849 he also purchased of his father 31½ acres on the Buck road, which had been the property of his ancestors for several generations. He married Catharine Gibbs, daughter of John Gibbs, and granddaughter of Richard Gibbs, who was sheriff of Bucks county in 1771, and a prominent public man. His children were: John Gibbs, born September 2, 1834; William Bloomfield; Elinor, wife of William Lynesson Sayre; Charles Souders, Jr.; Augustus; Henry S.; Lewis H.; Susan; Mary; Christina; Alfred and Elizabeth LaRue.

HON. CHARLES SOUDERS VANDEGRIFT, son of Alfred and Catherine (Gibbs) Vandegrift, is a worthy representative of an old and eminent family. He was born in Bensalem township, August 20, 1839. He was reared on his father's farm, and attended the public schools until fifteen years of age, when he entered Captain Alden Partridge's Military School at China Hall, in Bristol township, where he remained for two years. At the age of seventeen he entered the employ of his uncle and namesake, Charles S. Vandegrift, Sr., in the country store at Eddington, where he remained as clerk and proprietor until 1873, when he sold out the store, and in connection with J. and E. Thomas opened a lumber yard on the Delaware at Eddington. This partnership continued until 1890, when he retired from the firm. Since that time he has been employed in the settlement of estates and the transaction of public business. In 1882 he was elected to the state senate and served four years. He was an active member of the upper house, and served on the ways and means, agriculture and other important committees. In politics he is a Democrat, and has served as representative to District, State and National conventions. He has always taken an active interest in local matters, and served his township officially at different periods. He is president of the Good Roads Association of Bensalem township, and one of its most active and efficient members. He is a director of the Farmers' National Bank; president of the Farmers' and Mechanics' Mutual Insurance Company of Bucks and Philadelphia counties; president of the Doylestown Publishing Company; and treasurer and trustee of the Vandegrift Burial Ground at Cornwells. He is a past master of Bristol Lodge, No. 25, A. Y. F. and A. M.; of Harmony Chapter, No. 52, R. A. M.; and St. Johns Commandery, No. 4, K.· T., of Philadelphia, and is the district deputy grand master for the eighth district. He is a member of The Netherlands Society of Philadelphia.

Mr. Vandegrift married, March 11, 1862, Mary Hannah Rowland, daughter of Charles Rowland, of Chester county, Pennsylvania. To this marriage have been born two children: Frederic Beasley, born December 22, 1862; and George Bloomfield, born May 22, 1864. The latter died in infancy. Mr. and Mrs. Vandegrift are members of the Presbyterian church.

———

FREDERIC BEASLEY VANDEGRIFT, son of Senator Charles S. Vandegrift, was educated at the public schools of Philadelphia, and at Smiths' Commercial College, after which he entered the office of John W. Hampton, Jr., custom house broker of Philadelphia, where he remained for eight years. He then entered into the business himself with offices in Philadelphia, New York and Chicago, and was also import freight agent. He continued to conduct the business of a custom house broker until his death. In 1893, feeling the necessity of a technical knowledge of the law in the transaction of his business, he entered himself as a student at law in the office of William S. Stanger, Esq., in Philadelphia, and was admitted to the Philadelphia bar in 1897, and was admitted to practice in the United States courts in January, 1899, but died on March 7, 1899.

Frederic B. Vandegrift made a close study of the tariff on imports and became an expert on that subject. Among the papers prepared and published by him on the subject was one on the McKinley Tariff, and another on the Dingley Tariff. He received an order for 1,500 copies of his work on the Dingley Tariff from the United States government, a copy of which was to be sent to every United States consul throughout the world. He received the prize offered by the United States government for the most perfect paper on the tariff. Mr. Vandegrift became a distinguished member of the Masonic fraternity. He was made a Mason on March 8, 1884, by his father, Past Master Charles S. Vandegrift, and became master of Bristol Lodge, No. 25, in 1888; joined Harmony Chapter, R. A. M., in 1889, and was elected king in 1899, which office he held at the time of his death. He joined St. Johns Commandery, K. T., in 1894, and held the office of captain general at the time of his death. He joined the Ancient and Accepted Scottish Rite, January 18, 1895, and on June 21st received his thirty second degree, S. P. R. S. He was also a member of Lulu Temple, A. A. O. N. M. S., and was representative of University Lodge in the Grand Lodge of Pennsylvania at the time of his death. On November 16, 1887, he married Harriet Elizabeth Harvey, of Philadelphia. This marriage was blessed with four daughters: Gertrude, Evelina, Loraine and Genevieve, all of whom are being educated at the Friends' Schools of Philadelphia.

JOHN GIBBS VANDEGRIFT, eldest son of Alfred and Catharine (Gibbs) Vandegrift, and brother to Hon. Charles S. Vandegrift, the subject of the preceding sketch, was born in Bensalem township, Bucks county, September 2, 1834. He was educated at the public schools, and later received an academic education. He was reared on the farm, and for several years followed the vo-

cation of a farmer. In 1873 he purchased the store at Eddington and followed the mercantile business there for the rest of his life. He was a justice of the peace for twenty years, and filled many positions of trust. He took a deep interest in educational matters, and was for many years a member of the school board, acting as its secretary. He was a vestryman of the Episcopal church. In politics was a Democrat, but never sought or held other than local office. He was a member of Bristol Lodge, No. 25, A. Y. F. and A. M.; of Harmony Chapter, R. A. M.; and St. Johns Commandery, K. T. Mr. Vandegrift married March 27, 1861, Mary Jane Creighton, daughter of Thomas and Rebecca Ashton Creighton. She was born May 10, 1832, at Holmesburg, Philadelphia, and died May 4, 1895. John G. Vandegrift died April 11, 1901. Two children were born to Mr. and Mrs. Vandegrift, Katherine and Lemuel.

Lemuel Vandegrift was born August 13, 1864. He was reared on a farm and attended public school. At the age of seventeen years he entered his father's store to assist him in the business, and at his death succeeded him in its conduct. He was also elected a justice of the peace to succeed his father. He is a vestryman of the Episcopal church. In politics he is a Democrat. He is a member of Bristol Lodge, No. 25, A. Y. F. and A. M., Philadelphia Chapter, R. A. M., and St. Johns Commandery, K. T. Mr. Vandegrift was married, April 6, 1893, to Mary Ella Carey, daughter of Seneca and Mary Ella (Moore) Carey. They are the parents of two children: Lemuel Creighton, born July 26, 1895, and Marian Katharine, born July 8, 1897. Their eldest child, John G., Jr., died in infancy. These children are being educated in the public school of Bensalem.

MOSES VANDEGRIFT. In the preceding sketch of the descendants of Jacob Lendertsen Van der Grifte, who came from Holland in 1644 to New Amsterdam, where he married in 1648, Rebecca Fredericks Lubbertsen, is given an account of the baptism and marriage of Johannes Van De Grift, youngest son of Jacob and Rebecca, and of the birth and marriage of his children. From two of the sons of Johannes and Nealke (Volkers) Vandegrift is descended the subject of this sketch, Folkhart, the eldest, and Jacob the second son.[1]

Folkhart (or Fulkerd) Van de Grift, eldest son of Johannes, was born in the province of New York in 1695, and was therefore but an infant when brought into Bucks county by his parents in 1697. He became a large landholder in Bensalem, a man of importance in the Dutch

G.G. Vandegrift

Moses Vandegrift

colony in Bucks, and a member of the Bensalem church. He was twice married, first on May 6, 1719 to Elizabeth Van Sandt, and second on August 10, 1742, to Marytje Hufte. Neither wife survived him. He died in November, 1775. Of his nine children, Fulkhart, Elizabeth, Harman, Alshe, Abraham, John, Cornelius and Elinor, the first eight are mentioned in his will.

Abraham Vandegrift, born about 1725 married Femmentje Hufte about 1752 and had six children. He died in Bensalem township about 1800. The children were: Elizabeth, baptized at Southampton church August 18, 1754, married John DeCoursey, and had eight children; Mary, married Benjamin Severns; Abraham; and Catharine, who married Abraham Vandegrift, her second cousin.

Jacob Van de Grift, second son of Johannes and Nealke, baptized at New Amsterdam, October 14, 1696, was the grandfather of Abraham above mentioned. John Vandegrift, eldest son of Jacob, known as "John Vandegrift, Esquire," to distinguish him from his cousins of the same name on the records, married November 14, 1750, Maria (or Mary) Praul, who died prior to 1786. He died in 1805; his will dated September 7, 1804, proved May 3, 1805, devised to his eldest son Jacob, (baptized at Southampton, April 18, 1753) a stone house "I am now erecting" and one acre of land, he having been "advanced 400 pounds towards purchasing a plantation." This plantation was in Northampton, where Jacob removed in 1783 and died leaving a large family. The will of John Vandegrift further devises to his son John, 162½ acres on the Dunk's ferry road where the testator lived; to his daughter Jane Johnson a lot on same road; to son Bernard a tract of land in New Jersey purchased of John Longstreth, and to his son Abraham seventy-two acres, "part of the land where he now lives, beginning at brother Jacob's lane end." etc.

Abraham, son of John and Maria (Praul) Vandegrift, was born in Bensalem in 1766. On his marriage his father set apart to him seventy-two acres of land and built a house for him thereon which has since been the home of his descendants. He was twice married; by his first wife he had a daughter Mary who married John Brodnax. His second wife was Catharine Vandegrift, daughter of Abraham and granddaughter of Folhart, as previously shown. By this marriage Abraham had two sons, John and Samuel, and two daughters: Elizabeth, who married Joseph Myers; and Phebe, who married Thomas Darrah. Abraham died in May, 1800, leaving a will made eleven years previously, which was contested by the widow and daughter Phebe, but proved in the court of common pleas in December of the same

year. The bulk of the landed property including the homestead descended to the son John.

John Vandegrift was born on the old homestead August 12, 1806, and died there in March, 1878. He was a successful farmer, a Democrat, and a member of the Presbyterian church. His wife was Susanna Sipler. She died July 3, 1898. John and Susanna (Sipler) Vandegrift were the parents of eight children: Jesse, who died young; Jesse (2); Moses; John; Philip, who served three years in the civil war and died January 12, 1900, in his fifty-eighth year; Samuel; Letitia; and George W.

Moses Vandegrift, the subject of this sketch, was born on the old homestead June 5, 1840. He was reared on the old farm and received his education at the Eddington school. On arriving at manhood he settled on the old homestead that had been the property of his ancestors for many generations, and has spent his whole life there. He is a member of the Presbyterian church and politically is a Democrat. He was elected supervisor of Bensalem township in 1888 for two years and was re-elected in 1900 for an additional term. He married January 26, 1879, Sarah Knight, daughter of Strickland and Caroline (Briggs) Knight, by whom he has six children: Eugene, born January 4, 1880; Walter, born January 5, 1882; Roland and Oscar, twins, born May 27, 1884, (Oscar died in infancy); Fannie, born November 4, 1885; and Russell, born November 8, 1887.

SAMUEL ALLEN VANDEGRIFT, eldest son of the late George V. and Mary Ann (Allen) Vandegrift, was born at Bridgewater, Bensalem township, Bucks county, Pennsylvania, March 21, 1830.

The educational advantages enjoyed by Samuel A. Vandegrift were obtained in the common schools of the neighborhood, and he remained a resident on the paternal homestead until he attained his majority. He then settled on the Jonathan Paxon farm in Bensalem township, and after a residence of twenty years there located on the farm owned by his brother William A., remaining nine years, and the following six years he resided on the Thomas Hamilton farm. He then took up his residence on the farm in Byberry, owned by Colonel Morrell, remaining three years, after which he located on the farm in Bensalem owned by his brother Frank, and in 1903 removed to the old Black farm in Bensalem township, owned by his son Charles, where he has since resided. Being practical and progressive in his methods of management, he met with a large degree of prosperity in the various localities where he resided, and his honorable and reliable transactions won for him an enviable reputation which he has always fully sustained. He is a firm advocate of the principles of Republicanism, and his support has always been given to the candidates and measures of that party.

On March 12, 1857, Mr. Vadegrift married Julia Ann Luck, born in Philadelphia but reared in Bucks county, a daughter of Joseph and Margaret (Leslie) Luck. Joseph Luck was a native of England, from whence he emigrated to the United States, entered the service of the United States government, and for many years had charge of the United States arsenal at Frankford, Pennsylvania. Four children were born to Mr. and Mrs. Vandegrift: George, born January 28, 1858, engaged in agricultural pursuits in Bensalem township, married Julia Miller, of Philadelphia, and they are the parents of one child, Frederick Vandegrift; Joseph, who died at the age of four years; Mary Ann, born February 19, 1863; Charles W., born December 16, 1865. The mother of these children, who was a most excellent woman in every respect, faithful and conscientious in the performance of her duties as wife and mother, died June 9, 1902.

LEWIS HERBERT VANDEGRIFT, of Bensalem, Pennsylvania, was born at that place, October 1, 1845, the son of Alfred and Catherine (Gibbs) Vandegrift. He was educated in the public schools of Bensalem, after which he engaged in farming, as an employe of his brother, John, with whom he remained until 1870, when he removed to the old homestead farm in Bensalem, which he purchased in 1892. After thirty years of farm life, he sold his farm and removed to Philadelphia, when he entered the employ of the Western Union Telegraph Company, with whom he is still engaged. Mr. Vandegrift has been twice married—first, January 7, 1874, to Margaret, daughter of James and Margaret (Ballantyne) Harvinson. By this union four children were born: 1. Alfred Eugene, born November 22, 1874, married, February 20, 1901, to Susannah Keifer, of Brooklyn, New York, daughter of John Colder and wife, Susannah (Jenninker) Keiffer, and they have one child, Margaret Susannah, born November 10, 1902; 2. Clara May, born January 29, 1877, married March 7, 1905, Eugene Gaskill, of Philadelphia; 3. Maud, born May 13, 1882; married, first Elwood E. Porter, by whom the issue was Milton Harvinson, born December 1, 1899; second, to Frank Peabody Hedges, of Trenton, New Jersey, May 1, 1904; 4. Bertha Irene, born May 20, 1883. Mrs.

Vandegrift died February 13, 1888, and for his second wife Mr. Vandegrift married, January 14, 1892, Margaret Brown, of Eddington, who was born May 4, 1854, daughter of Henry Jackson and Sarah (Staats) Brown, and the granddaughter of Alexander and Elizabeth (Darrah) Brown; also the granddaughter of Jacob and Maribel (Shaw) Staats. By his second marriage Mr. Vandegrift has one child—Lucy Eccleston, born October 13, 1893. Each of the above children, except Lucy, were educated in Bensalem. Alfred was graduated from Pierce's Business College of Philadelphia, and Lucy is attending Lincoln Grammar School in Philadelphia.

Mr. Vandegrift is a member of the Masonic fraternity, and affiliates with Newton Lodge, No. 427, A. F. and A. M. Both Mr. and Mrs. Vandegrift are members of the church of Christ (Episcopal) of Eddington, where they are efficient, earnest workers. Mr. Vandegrift has served on the school board very ably for three years, and has been its secretary. He has ever been much interested in educational matters, and is counted among the loyal citizens of his place.

GEORGE V. VANDEGRIFT. The death of George V. Vandegrift, April 24, 1853, removed from Bensalem township, Bucks county, Pennsylvania, where he resided all his life, one of its prominent, influential and public-spirited citizens. His birth occurred in 1804, a son of Joseph and Sarah (Byson) Vandegrift, and grandson of John Vandegrift. Joseph Vandegrift (father) was also a native of Bensalem township, Bucks county, the year of his birth being 1776. In early life he served an apprenticeship at the trade of weaver, and this he followed successfully throughout his active career. He was a member of the Episcopal church, the service of which he attended regularly. By his marriage to Sarah Bankson the following named children were born: Lydia, Rebecca, Mary, Amy, George V., Frances, Sarah Ann, Joseph, Julia Ann, and Jane. Mr. Vandegrift died in 1839, survived by his wife, who passed away in 1857.

George V. Vandegrift attended the common schools adjacent to his home, after which he learned the same trade as his father, that of weaver, but after following this for a number of years turned his attention to farming, which proved both a pleasant and profitable occupation. Upon attaining his majority he cast his vote with the Whig party, to whom he gave his allegiance up to the formation of the Republican party, and from that time up to his decease he advocated the principles of that great organization.

Mr. Vandegrift married, May 17, 1828, Mary Ann Allen, who was born in Bensalem township, October 26, 1808, and they were the parents of nine children, namely: Samuel Allen, born March 21, 1830, a sketch of whom appears in this work; Joseph T., born August 24, 1832, was twice married and had two children by each marriage, and died February 16, 1904; Jesse S., born August 24, 1836, resides in the western section of the United States; Georgianna, born September 23, 1839, resides on the old Allen farm with her brother; William Allen, born June 23, 1841, resides in Philadelphia; Israel Thomas, born August 24, 1843. and resides in Philadelphia; George W., born August 24, 1845; Jonathan, born March 25, 1848, died September 1, 1888; and Benjamin Franklin, born June 18, 1853, and resides in Philadelphia. Mr. Vandegrift and his wife held membership in the Neshaminy Methodist Episcopal church. Their deaths occurred respectively April 24, 1853, and March 19, 1864.

Mrs. Vandegrift was a daughter of Israel Allen, born May 29, 1766, and his wife Elizabeth Titus, born December 14, 1771. Isreal Allen was a son of Joseph and Sarah (Plumley) Allen. Joseph Allen was a son of William and Mary (Walsh) Allen. William Allen was born at what is now Bridgewater, Bensalem township, on the site of the Bridgewater Inn, a son of Samuel and Jane (Waln) Allen. Samuel Allen was a son of Samuel and Mary Allen, who came from England in 1681 and settled on the farm now owned by William Allen Vandegrift, in 1682, and one hundred acres of the original tract has never passed out of the possession of the family. The members of the Allen family have always adhered to the tenets of the Society of Friends.

J. WILSON VANDEGRIFT. Among the successful agriculturists of Buckingham is J. Wilson Vandegrift, who was born in that township January 1, 1863, being a son of Bernard and Mary Ann (Folker) Vandegrift, and a grandson of Lawrence Vandegrift of Northampton township, Bucks county, where his father Bernard was born June 30, 1829. The family is of Holland descent, being descendants of Jacob Lendert Van de Grift, who migrated from Holland in 1644, and settled on Long Island, from whence three of his sons (Leonard, Nicholas and John,) came to Bucks county in the latter part of the same century and settled in Bensalem, descendants of the last mentioned of whom settling in Northampton township a century later.

Bernard Vandegrift was a farmer all his life. In 1877 he purchased the farm now owned and occupied by the subject of this sketch, and resided thereon until his death, in September, 1900.. He married, December 27, 1851, Mary Ann Folker, daughter of James and Mary (Herlinger) Folker, of Buckingham, where she was born August 8, 1829. Her parents were both natives of Buckingham, her mother being a daughter of Captain Mathew Herlinger, who married the widow Else, whose husband died at sea on the voyage to America. Bernard and Mary Ann (Folker) Vandegrift were the parents of six children; Harry, of Elizabeth, Colorado; Susanna, wife of William Orem, of Buckingham; Wilmer, a wholesale commission merchant of Philadelphia; Mary, wife of William H. Atkinson, of Forest Grove, Buckingham township; J. Wilson; and Theodore, of Warwick township, Bucks county.

J. Wilson Vandegrift was reared on the farm and acquired a good common school education. In 1885 he purchased the home farm, which he has since successfully conducted. By industry and careful business methods he has acquired a competence. In 1899 he purchased an adjoining farm of 102 acres and in 1903, purchased a farm of 160 acres in Warwick township. He married, in November, 1894, Olive M. Fell, daughter of Wilson D. and Mary Jane (Trumbower) Fell, of Buckingham. She was born on the Fell homestead in Buckingham that had been in the tenure of her ancestors for over a century, January 19, 1863. She is still the owner of the farm, which is a portion of a tract purchased by her great-great-great-grandfather, Benjamin Fell, in 1753. This Benjamin Fell was born in 1703 in Cumberland, England, and came with his parents Joseph and Bridget (Wilson) Fell to America when an infant. His son John, born in 1730, married Elizabeth Hartley, and their son Seneca born 4 mo. 5, 1760, married Grace Holt of Horsham, among whose children was Stacy Fell, the grandfather of Mrs. Vandegrift. He was born in Buckingham in 1790, and died there in 1864; He married 10 mo. 14, 1812, Elizabeth Kinsey, of Buckingham, who was born in 1791 and died in 1863. They were the parents of seven children, the youngest of whom was Wilson D., father of Mrs. Vandegrift, who was born 12 mo. 2, 1832, and died April 28, 1895.

To Mr. and Mrs. Vandegrift have been born five children, Harry E. W., William Orem, Edwin Taylor, Wilson Fell and Gladys. Mrs. Vandegrift is a member of Doylestown Presbyterian church.

Wilson D. Fell married Mary Jane Trumbower December 1, 1854. She was the daughter of Philip and Catharine Trumbower of Bridge Point, now Edison, Bucks county, Pennsylvania. She was born April 11, 1833, and died April 15, 1904.

JENKS COAT-OF-ARMS.

THE JENKS FAMILY is of Welsh origin and can be clearly traced in the county of Montgomery, Wales, and the adjoining county of Salop, or Shropshire, England, from A. D. 900 down to the middle of the seventeenth century. On the records of the College of Arms, London, England, there is an Act in the year 1582, during the reign of Queen Elizabeth, by which "The Coat of Arms of the Anciente Family of Jenks, long in the possession of the same" at Wolverton Manor, Wales, was confirmed to them in the person of their representative, Sir George Jenks, of Salop, Gentleman, as certified by Robert Cooke, alias Clarencieux, one of the two first Provincial Kings-of-Arms, in England, whose jurisdiction of Clarenceux extended to all of England south of the Trent, Norroy holding a like jurisdiction north of the Trent.

The Jenks family of Bucks county, Pennsylvania, trace their descent from Thomas Jenks, of Shropshire, who, as shown by the will of John Penn, of the adjoining county of Montgomery, Wales, dated 1660, was a son of Thomas Jenks. Thomas Jenks the elder died 10 mo. 19, 1680, as shown by the records of the Monthly Meeting of Friends in Shropshire. He was one of the earliest converts to the principles of George Fox, and "Besse's Sufferings" gives a record of his arrest in 1656 as one of a party of Friends while attending a meeting of people of his faith. He was again arrested and fined in 1660. Thomas Jenks, son of the above, born in Shropshire, was married there and is supposed to have embarked for America with his wife Susan, and infant son Thomas, born January, 1699-1700. All that is definitely known, however, is that Susan Jenks, his widow, and her young son, Thomas, arrived in Bucks county soon after 1700, and located in Wrightstown. Susan Jenks married Benjamin Wiggins, of Buckingham, in 1708, and died soon after the birth of her son, Bezeleel Wiggins, in 1709.

Thomas Jenks was reared in the neighborhood of Wrightstown. We have little record of him until 1 mo. 1, 1725-6, when he applied for membership in Wrightstown Meeting. He was doubtless a birthright member of the Society, but the death of his father while on the voyage to America, or immediately preceding their sailing and the subsequent marriage of his mother to a non-member and her early death leaving him an orphan at ten years of age, his birthright privilege was no doubt neglected to be recorded. It was therefore necessary for him to be regularly admitted when he desired to become a member on reaching manhood.

Thomas Jenks married, 3 mo. 19, 1731, Mercy Wildman, daughter of John and Marah (Chapman) Wildman, of Middletown. The former, born in Yorkshire, England, in 1681, came to America with his parents, Martin and Ann Wildman, in 1690, and the latter, a daughter of John Chapman, the pioneer settler of Wrightstown, had married first John Croasdale, John Wildman being her second husband. Thomas Jenks, on his marriage, settled first in his home in Buckingham and three years afterward removed to a tract of land in Middletown township, two miles southeast of Newtown, along Core creek, containing 600 acres. Upon this tract he erected prior to 1740, a fulling mill one of the first in the county which was operated (by the family) until his death, doing a large business in dyeing, fulling and finishing the homespun goods of his neighbors, the early settlers of lower and middle Bucks. His ledger "C," exquisitely written and kept still in good preservation, is now in possession of his great-grandson, William H. Jenks, of Philadelphia. It covers the years 1743-56, and contains his accounts with nearly all the early families of Bucks east of the Neshaminy. He was an active and energetic business man, and retained his mental and physical faculties in a remarkable degree to extreme old age. He died at Jenks Hall (erected by him in 1734) from the effects of injuries received in being thrown from a wagon, 5 mo. 4, 1797, in the ninety-eighth year of his age. He had in the truest sense of the word "grown up with the country." Arriving in Bucks county when far the greatest part of it was a primeval wilderness, still inhabited by the Indians, he lived through its entire colonial period, and saw his country recover from the shock and trials of its war for independence, and become a thickly settled prosperous and enlightened community. He was six years older than Dr. Franklin, and thirty-two years older than George Washington, yet he survived the former seven years, and the latter survived him but little over two years, though both had lived to see the fruition of their long and noble struggle for their country's good. His wife Mercy died 7 mo. 26, 1787, aged seventy-seven years, after a married life of over fifty-six years. They were the parents of six children, as follows:

1. Mary, born 4 mo. 20, 1733, died 1803; married Samuel Twining.

2. John, born 5 mo. 1, 1736, died 1791, married in 1785, Sarah Weir. His son

John Wildman Jenks, born 6 mo. 21, 1790, studied medicine and removed to Jefferson county, Pennsylvania, where he died 4 mo. 4, 1850. He married in 1816, Mary Day Barclay, who bore him ten children, most of whom were distinguished in their professions, the youngest, George Augustus Jenks, being a member of the Forty-fourth United States Congress, and the Democratic nominee for governor of Pennsylvania in 1898.

3. Thomas, born 10 mo. 9, 1738, died 5 mo. 30, 1799, married, in 1762, Rebecca Richardson, daughter of Joseph and Mary (Paxson) Richardson, of Middletown.

4. Joseph, born 12 mo. 22, 1743, died 5 mo. 1820; married 6 mo. 22, 1763, Elizabeth Pearson, daughter of William and Elizabeth (Duer) Pearson; see forward.

5. Elizabeth, born 3 mo. 15, 1746, died 12 mo. 30, 1808; married 12 mo. 23, 1762, William Richardson, son of Joseph and Mary (Paxson) Richardson.

6. Ann, born 9 mo. 8, 1749, died about 1812; married 2 mo. 20, 1770, Isaac Watson.

Thomas Jenks, second son of Thomas and Mercy, was born and reared on the homestead in Middletown, and spent his whole life there. He was a prominent and influential man in the community. He served as a member of colonial assembly for the year 1775, and was a member of the constitutional convention of 1790, and was the first member of the state senate from Bucks under the constitution then adopted, and served continuously in that body until his death, May 4, 1799. For the first six years of his service the district which he represented was composed of the counties of Delaware, Chester and Bucks, while during his last two terms the district consisted of Chester, Montgomery and Bucks. He was an active member of the upper house and served on many important committees. He married, in 1762, Rebecca Richardson, and they were the parents of nine children, eight of whom lived to mature age. They were as follows:

1. Rachel, born 5 mo. 23, 1763, died 2 mo. 12, 1830; married 10 mo. 19, 1786, Thomas Story.

2. Mary, born 3 mo. 12, 1765, died in infancy.

3. Joseph R., born 9 mo. 16, 1767, died 6 mo. 26, 1858; married first 10 mo. 10, 1792, Sarah Watson; second, 6 mo. 6, 1809, Ann West; and third, 2 mo. 29, 1844, Ann Ely of Philadelphia, a widow. Joseph R. Jenks was a prosperous and prominent merchant in Philadelphia.

4. Mercy, born 10 mo. 20, 1769, died 10 mo. 19, 1836; married 10 mo. 18, 1792, Abraham Carlile.

5. Thomas, born 2 mo. 4, 1772, died 2 mo. 27, 1828; married first, in 1797, Thomazine Trimble, and second, in 1816, Rachel Wilson.

6. Rebecca, born 1 mo. 1, 1775, married 1 mo. 15, 1801, Jonathan Fell.

7. Mary, born 7 mo. 9, 1777, died in 1854, unmarried.

8. Phineas, born 5 mo. 3, 1781, died 8 mo. 6, 1851, married first, Eliza Murray, and second, Amelia Snyder, see forward.

9. Ruth, born 8 mo. 19, 1788, died 2 mo. 16, 1843, married 11 mo. 8, 1810, Joseph Dickson.

DR. PHINEAS JENKS, eighth child of Thomas and Rebecca (Richardson) Jenks, was reared on the old homestead in Middletown. He chose the medical profession, and was a student of the celebrated Dr. Benjamin Rush, and a graduate of the University of Pennsylvania. He began the practice of medicine in Newtown, and continued to practice there until his death in 1851, becoming one of the eminent physicians of his day. He was the first president of the Bucks County Medical Association, and continued at its head until his death. He took an active interest in the affairs of his county, state and neighborhood, and was one of the influential and prominent men, outside of his profession. He was a member of the state legislature for five years, 1815-19, and a member of the constitutional convention of 1837-38. He was one of the organizers of the St. Lukes Protestant Episcopal church of Newtown, of which he was rector's warden for many years. He was a good extemporaneous speaker, and was always counted on to lend his aid to any meritorious project in the neighborhood. He was twice married. His first wife was Eliza Murray, daughter of General Francis Murray of Newtown, whom he married 3 mo. 20, 1806. She died 3 mo. 16, 1807, leaving one daughter, who died in infancy. He married (second) on 3 mo. 28, 1820, Amelia Snyder, daughter of Governor Simon Snyder. She was born June 21, 1791, and died August 6, 1859. They were the parents of seven children, three of whom, (Simon Snyder, Frederick A. and Henry L.) died in childhood, the latter being a twin brother of General A. Jenks, Esq. Those who survived were: Elizabeth M., born July 29, 1822, died March 29, 1887; married Rev. Joseph I. Elsegood, rector of Trinity Protestant Episcopal church of East New York, Long Island, who died in 1884. William Wallace Jenks, born 11 mo. 2, 1825, a merchant in Philadelphia; he died 7 mo. 20, 1857. P. Frederick Jenks, born February 27, 1832, studied medicine and located at St. Louis, Missouri, soon after his graduation. At the outbreak of the civil war he enlisted in the First Missouri Light Artillery, and was in the battles of Fort Henry, Fort Donelson and Pittsburg Landing. He died at St. Louis, 1 mo. 9, 1863, from diarrhoea contracted in the service.

George A. Jenks, Esq., the only surviving child of Dr. Phineas and Amelia (Snyder) Jenks, was born at Newtown, October 9, 1829. He received his elementary education at the Newtown Academy, and then entered the University of Pennsylvania, from which he graduated. July 4, 1850. He entered himself as a student at law with James C. Van Dycke, Esq., of Philadelphia, then United States district attorney, and also entered the law department of the University, where he took a full course, and on July 3, 1853, the degrees of Master of Arts and Bachelor of Laws were conferred upon him.

On April 16, 1853, he was admitted to the bar of Philadelphia, and on October 8, 1855, was admitted to practice in the circuit and district courts of Pennsylvania, having been, admitted to practice in the supreme court on January 13, 1854. He practiced law in Philadelphia from 1853 to 1859, when he removed to Newtown, and was admitted to the bar of his native county, of which he is now the senior member. He is a careful student, and his thorough knowledge of the law and sound judgment have made him a safe counselor. In his long practice he has had many intricate cases to unravel, and in the vast number of disputed cases as to questions of law, referred to him by the courts as auditor, he has seldom been reversed in either the lower or upper courts. He has filled the office of justice of the peace for forty-four years, and has served his borough in the position of school director for nineteen years; and filled the office of chief burgess for seven years. He has always been actively interested in all that pertains to the interest of the locality in which he lived, and has been connected with nearly all the meritorious local enterprises of his town. He is president and one of the directors and active supporters of the Newtown Library, as was both his father and grandfather, George A. Jenks having served as a director for over forty years, and president for about thirty years. He is a member of the Bucks County Historical Society, and has always been actively interested in its work, and has furnished several historical papers for its archives. He is a member of Newtown Lodge, No. 427, F. and A. M., of which he was the first master, and Newtown Chapter, No. 229, R. A. M., of which he was the first high priest, and served as district deputy grand master for the district for five years. He is a member of St. Luke's Protestant Episcopal church of Newtown, of which his father was one of the founders. He was married, June 15, 1860, to Ella Davis, daughter of Jesse and Susan B. Davis, and they have been the parents of two children, Sylva P.

and Elizabeth M., both of whom died in early childhood. In politics he has been a lifelong Republican, but has never sought or held other than local office.

Joseph Jenks, third son of Thomas and Mercy (Wildman) Jenks, was born and reared on the old homestead in Middletown. He married, 6 mo. 22, 1763, Elizabeth Pearson, born in 1744, died 1768, daughter of William and Elizabeth (Duer) Pearson, and granddaughter of Enoch and Margaret (Smith) Pearson, of Buckingham, Enoch Pearson being a native of Cheshire, England, having come to Bucks county with his parents, Edward and Sarah (Burgie) Pearson, in 1687. Joseph and Elizabeth (Pearson) Jenks were the parents of three children: Margaret, born 6 mo. 6, 1764, died 1841; married 11 mo. 12, 1783, Samuel Gillingham. William, born 8 mo. 12, 1766, died 12 mo. 5, 1818; married 10 mo. 28, 1790, Mary Hutchinson. Elizabeth, born 10 mo. 21, 1768, died 1828, married, in 1787, Isaiah Shinn, of New Jersey, who was a general in the war of 1812. Joseph Jenks married a second time, 4 mo. 25, 1770, to Mary Ingham, who lived but a few years after the marriage, and he married a third time, on 5 mo. 30, 1776, Hannah Davids; neither of the last two wives left issue.

William, only son of Joseph and Elizabeth (Pearson) Jenks, was a lifelong resident of Bucks county, following the vocation of a farmer and miller on the homestead. He died at the early age of forty-two years, leaving a widow and ten children, six of whom were minors at the time of his death. His wife Mary was a daughter of Michael and Margery (Palmer) Hutchinson, of Lower Makefield township, a descendant of two old and prominent families of Makefield. The children of William and Mary (Hutchinson) Jenks, were:

1. Joseph, born 9 mo. 12, 1792, died 11 mo. 19, 1869, married 5 mo. 29, 1827, his second cousin, Eliza Jenks, daughter of Joseph R. and Sarah (Watson) Jenks.

2. Rebecca H., born 1 mo. 30, 1794, died 4 mo. 21, 1797.

3. Michael Hutchinson Jenks, born 5 mo. 21, 1795, died 10 mo. 16, 1867. He was a surveyor and conveyancer, as well as a justice of the peace, for very many years, and did an immense amount of local business, and was a very fine penman and draughtsman. He was county commissioner for the term of 1830-2, county treasurer in 1834, an associate judge of the county, and represented his district in the twenty-eighth congress, as well as filling a great number of other positions of trust. He was four times married; first, in 1821, to Mary Ridgway Earl, who was the mother of his nine children. His third daughter, Anna Earl, became the wife of Alexander Ramsey, first governor of Minnesota, and United States senator from that

Yours truly

Geo. A. Jenks

state. His other wives were Mary Canby, Ann Higgins and Sarah Leedom.

4. Eliza Pearson Jenks, born 2 mo. 14, 1797, died 12 mo. 13, 1884; married 10 mo. 13, 1825, George Yardley.

5. Charles, born 12 mo. 31, 1798, died 8 mo. 5, 1823; married 4 mo. 16, 1823, Mary Ann Newbold.

6. Margery, born 8 mo. 5, 1800, died 1 mo. 31, 1802.

Hannah, born 6 mo. 17, 1802, died 9 mo. 17, 1822, unmarried.

8. Mary Palmer Jenks, born 1 mo. 25, 1804, died 2 mo. 15, 1875; married 12 mo. 27, 1827, Edmund Morris.

9. Margaret, born 9 mo. 24, 1806, died 12 mo. 20. 1825, unmarried.

10. William Pearson, born 12 mo. 17, 1807, died 9 mo. 17, 1886, married 5 mo. 16, 1837, Elizabeth Story; see forward.

11. Ann, born 2 mo. 26, 1810, died 4 mo. 15, 1870, married 10 mo. 12, 1831, Charles M. Morris.

12. Susan W., born 6 mo. 3, 1812, died 7 mo. 25, 1857; married 7 mo. 4, 1838, Franklin Fell.

WILLIAM PEARSON JENKS, the tenth child of William and Mary (Hutchinson) Jenks, was born and reared in the old homestead at Bridgetown, in Middletown township. After finishing school he went to Paterson, New Jersey, where he learned the trade of a machinist. In 1828 he became interested in the manufacture of cotton yarns at New Hope, where he remained until 1832. In 1833 he went to Madison, Indiana, in the interest of the firm in Paterson with whom he had learned his trade, and remained there two years, establishing a factory for the manufacture of cotton goods. In 1835 he accepted the position of manager of .the Union Factories near Ellicott's Mills, Maryland, then the largest plant for the manufacture of cotton goods south of New England. He remained there until the autumn of 1846, when he was obliged to resign his position on account of failing health, and took a trip to Brazil to recruit. He returned in the summer of 1847 and joined his wife and three children in Philadelphia. Having regained his health, he was desirous of again engaging in business, and in the fall of that year joined Evan Randolph and formed the firm of Randolph & Jenks, cotton merchants, and did an extensive and prosperous business. He retired from active participation at the close of the year 1860. The firm continued, however, under the same name, the present members being his two sons, John Story Jenks and William H. Jenks, Evan Randolph, his partner, who married his only daughter, Rachel Story Jenks. in 1864, having died 12 mo. 3, 1887. William Pearson Jenks died 9 mo. 17. 1886, aged nearly seventy-nine years. He was a man of marked ability

as a merchant, and his life was full of active and intelligent energy. He prospered in his business and business enterprises, and took an interest in many of the financial institutions in Philadelphia. His wife, Elizabeth Story, born 3 mo. 6, 1807, was a daughter of David and Rachel (Richardson) Story, of Newtown, and a great-granddaughter of Thomas Story, a native of Northumberland, England, who came to Pennsylvania with William Penn on his second visit, in the ship "Centerbury," arriving at Chester 10 mo. 1, 1699. He settled in Bucks county, and in 1 mo., 1718, married Elizabeth (Wilson) Buckman, widow of William Buckman, of Newtown, who bore him one son, John Story. Thomas Story died 9 mo. 10, 1753, at the age of eighty-two years. His son, John Story, was born 11 mo. 26, 1718-19. He married 5 mo., 1747, Elizabeth Cutler, daughter of Thomas and Eleanor (Lane) Cutler, and lived all his life in the neighborhood of Newtown. He died .11 mo. 10, 1804, at the age of eighty-six, and is buried at Wrightstown. His son, David Story, was born 4 mo. 20, 1760, and died 2 mo. 23, 1833. He married 4 mo. 19, 1792, Rachel Richardson, daughter of William and Elizabeth (Jenks) Richardson. They had six children: 1. Rebecca; born 1 mo. 15, 1793, died 9 mo. 22, 1870; married 5 mo. 20, 1824, Dr. Ralph Lee, of Newtown. 2. Hannah, born 3 mo. 23, 1794, died 4 mo. 13, 1876; married 5 mo. 16, 1837, John C. Parry, of New Hope. 3. John, born 1 mo. 15, 1796, died 10 mo. 22, 1844; married 4 mo. 28, 1831, Esther A. Allibone. 4. William Story, born 9 mo. 10, 1797, died 9 mo. 16, 1822, unmarried. 5. Mary, born 3 mo. 23, 1800, died 5 mo. 22, 1846. unmarried. 6. Elizabeth, born 3 mo. 6. 1807, died 1 mo. 11, 1878, married 5 mo. 16, 1837. William Pearson Jenks.

John Story Jenks was born near Ellicott City, Maryland, 10 mo. 29, 1839, and came with his parents to Philadelphia in 1846. He married, 10 mo. 27, 1864, Sidney Howell Brown, and has three daughters, all of whom are married and reside in Philadelphia.

William H. Jenks was born in Maryland, 11 mo. 11, 1842, and married in Philadelphia, 9 mo. 9, 1869, Hannah Mifflin Hacker He has two sons, William Pearson Jenks and John Story Jenks, both of whom are business men of New York City, and two daughters who are married and reside in Philadelphia.

John Story Jenks and William H. Jenks, as before stated, succeeded their father, William Pearson Jenks, in the firm of Randolph & Jenks, and now comprise that firm. They have been prosperous merchants, and are interested in many of the financial; beneficial, social and political institutions of the city They are worthy descendants of their Bucks county ancestors, for whom they entertain the most profound love and respect. They are both members of the Bucks County Historical Society, and take a lively interest and pride in the county where their first ancestors on all branches were early settlers, and where all their later ancestors were born and reared.

B. FRANK HART, of 2010 Wallace street, Philadelphia, retired manufacturer and business man, was born in Warminster, Bucks county, Pennsylvania, March 22, 1825, and removed to Philadelphia when a young man and engaged in manufacturing interests there, where he has since resided. He has, however, always kept in touch with the county of his birth, and takes special pride in his distinguished Bucks county ancestry. On the paternal side all his direct ancestors from his father, John Hart, to his great-great-great-grandfather, John Hart, were prominent officials of the county and members of the law making body of the province and state, from Bucks county, making five successive generations to serve in that capacity.

John Hart, the ancestor of the Warminster (Bucks county) family of the name, was a son of Christopher and Mary Hart, of Witney, Oxfordshire, England, where he was born November 16, 1651. A brother, Robert, remained in England, a younger brother Joseph migrated to Jamaica, and the only sister Mary, born April 1, 1658, accompanied her brother to Pennsylvania in 1682. The family were members of the Society of Friends, and John brought a certificate from Friends at Witney. He had purchased of William Penn, July 16, 1681, 1,000 acres of land to be laid out in Pennsylvania. Of this 480 acres were located on the Poquessing, in Byberry, Philadelphia county, and the balance in Warminster township, Bucks county. The former was surveyed by virtue of warrant dated September 1, 1681, and on this John Hart located on arriving in Pennsylvania, and erected a house on the banks of the Poquessing. The Warminster tract was surveyey 7 mo. 25, 1684, and lay along the north side of the street road near Johnsville. It became the residence of John Hart in 1697 and remained the home of his descendants for several generations. John Hart was early identified with public affairs. He was a member of the first assembly of the province, from Philadelphia county, and his name is attached to the first charter of government, granted by Penn to his colonists, dated at Philadelphia, February 2, 1683. He was a minister among Friends, and the early meetings of the Society were held at his house from 1683 to 1686, when the meeting house was erected "near Takony." He was clerk of the meeting for many years. In 1691 he joined George Keith in his famous schism against Friends, and was one of his ablest advocates, and, when Keith's radical doctrines had carried him and his followers out of the Society, he united with the Baptists in

1697, and became their preacher at the meeting house originally erected by the Friends. He later became assistant preacher at Pennepack Baptist church, but was never ordained. He removed to Warminster in 1697, selling his land in Byberry, except one acre which was reserved as a burying ground. He died in Warminster, September, 1714, in his sixty-third year. He had married in the fall of 1683, Susannah Rush, daughter of William and Aurelia Rush, who had come to Pennsylvania in 1682 and settled in Byberry, and a granddaughter of John Rush, who commanded a troop of horse in Cromwell's army. Susannah, after the death of her husband, returned to Byberry and died there February 27, 1725. John and Susanna (Rush) Hart were the parents of five children; John, the ancestor of all of the name who remained in Bucks county; Joseph who married Sarah Stout, April 1, 1713, and died in 1714, without issue; Thomas, who inherited a portion of the land and conveyed it to his cousin, James Rush, in 1731, and left the county; Josiah, who removed to New Jersey, and Mary, who died unmarried.

John Hart, eldest son of John and Susannah (Rush) Hart, was born in Byberry, July 16, 1684. He does not appear to have occupied so important a place as his father in public affairs, though he held many posts of honor and responsibility. He was sheriff of Bucks county, 1737-8-9, and 1743-4-5, and 1749; coroner of Bucks county, 1741 and 1748; was commissioned justice June 9, 1752, and was succeeded by his son Joseph in 1761. When he was sworn in 1757, the record states he was "old, and impaired by apoplexy." He followed his father in matters of religion and united with the Baptists and was baptized at Pennepack November 15, 1706, by the Rev. Evan Morgan, and was thereafter closely associated with the sect. He was one of the organizers of Southampton Baptist church in 1746, and served as clerk, deacon and trustee, until his death March 22, 1763. He inherited from his father a large portion of the Warminster homestead and erected the family mansion there in 1750. He married November 25, 1708, Eleanor Crispin, daughter of Silas and Esther (Holme) Crispin, and grand-daughter of Thomas Holme, Penn's surveyor general, and of Captain William Crispin, one of Penn's commissioners for settling the colony of Pennsylvania. Though the latter never reached Pennsylvania, he was so closely identified with Penn and his family as to be of interest to Pennsylvanians. He was born in England in 1610, and was commander of the ship "Hope" in the service of the Commonwealth, under Cromwell, in 1652. In May, 1653, he was sent with the expedition against the Dutch, as captain of the "Assistance," under Rear Admiral William Penn, the father of the founder, and remained the remainder of that year cruising on the Dutch coast and preying upon their commerce. In 1654 he

HOMESTEAD of Col. John Hart. (APRIL 9.1787-JUNE 18. 1840)

WARMINSTER. BUCKS CO.PA. BUILT 1817

B. Frank Hart

was captain of the "Laurel," in the British squadron, sent against the Spanish possessions in America, arriving at Barbadoes, January 29, 1654-5. He participated in the capture of Jamica, May 17, 1655, was named as one of the commissioners for supplying Jamica, and remained there when Penn returned to England, but following him soon after, and with him retired to Kinsale, Ireland, where he lived for about twenty years. On Penn receiving the grant of Pennsylvania he named Captain Crispin as one of the three "Commissioners for the Settleing of the present Colony this year transported into ye Province," as stated in his letter of instructions, dated September 30, 1681. Captain Crispin, with his fellow commissioners John Bezar and Nathaniel Allen, sailed for Pennsylvania, but in different ships, Crispin sailing in the "Amity," which was blown off after nearly reaching the Delaware capes and put into Barbadoes for repairs. Crispin died there, and the "Amity" returned to England, and, returning to Pennsylvania in April, 1682, brought over Thomas Holme, Penn's surveyor general, who also succeeded Crispin as commissioner. Captain William Crispin married Anne Jasper, daughter of John Jasper, a merchant of Rotterdam, and a sister to Margaret, wife of Admiral Sir William Penn, and mother of the great founder. William and Anne Crispin were the parents of four children: Silas, above referred to, who came to Pennsylvania with Thomas Holme, and later married his daughter Esther; Rebecca, who married, August 24, 1688, Edward Blackfan, son of John Blackfan, of Stenning, county of Sussex, England; Ralph, who remained in Ireland and Rachel who married Thomas Armstrong and also remained in Europe. Edward Blackfan prepared to come to Pennsylvania, where William Penn had directed land to be laid out to him, but died before sailing, in 1690. His widow Rebecca and their only son William came to Pennsylvania and located in Bucks county at Pennsbury, where she lived for a number of years. She married, in 1725, Nehemiah Allen, son of Nathaniel, the commissioner. William, the son, married Eleanor Wood, of Philadelphia, and located in Solebury, Bucks county. They are the ancestors of the now numerous family of Blackfan. Captain Crispin married a second time, and had eleven children, most of whom located in the West Indies.

Silas Crispin, only son of the Captain by his first marriage, in 1684 located in Upper Dublin township, Philadelphia county, where he lived the rest of his life, dying May 31, 1711. He married a second time, Mary, daughter of Richard and Abigail Stockton, and widow of Thomas Shinn, who after his death married a third time, September 11, 1714. Richard Ridgway, Jr., son of Richard Ridgway, who was one of the earliest English settlers on the Delaware in Bucks county. Silas and Esther (Holme)

Crispin were the parents of eight children, six of whom lived to maturity: Sarah, married Lesson Loftus, of Philadelphia; Rebecca, married Joseph Finney; Marie, married John Collett; Eleanor, married John Hart; Esther, married Thomas Rush; Thomas, married Jane Ashton, and lived on his father's plantation in Lower Dublin; and William and Susanna who died young. By the second marriage Silas Crispin had six children; Joseph, who removed to Delaware; Benjamin, of Chester county; Abigail, married John Wright, of Chester county; Silas; Mary, married Thomas Earl, of New Jersey; and John.

John and Eleanor (Crispin) Hart were the parents of ten children, viz:-

1. John, born September 10, 1709, went to Virginia, where he was killed June 11, 1743 by the accidental discharge of a gun.

2. Susanna, born April 20, 1711, married March 31, 1731, John Price, and died two years later, leaving an only child, Joseph Price.

3. William, born March 7, 1713, died October 7, 1714.

4. Joseph, born September 1, 1715, died February 25, 1788; see forward.

5. Silas, born May 5, 1718, removed in early life to Augusta county, Virginia. At the organization of Rockingham county he became a resident of that county, filling the position of judge, sheriff, etc. He died without issue October 29, 1795.

6. Lucretia, born July 22, 1720, died December 15, 1760; was twice married, first, October 15, 1741, to William Gilbert, who died about 1750, and on March 5, 1752, to John Thomas; had three sons by first marriage, and a son and two daughters by the last.

7. Oliver Hart, born July 5, 1723, was for thirty years pastor of a Baptist church at Charleston, South Carolina, 1749-80, and fifteen years at Hopewell, New Jersey; died December 31, 1795.

8. Edith, born 1727, married Isaac Hough;—see Hough Family.

9. Seth, died at age of nine years.

10. Olive, died in infancy.

Colonel Joseph Hart, fourth child and eldest living son of John and Eleanor (Crispin) Hart at the death of his father, was born in the old family mansion in Warminster, September 1, 1715, and died there February 25, 1788. He was an active member of the Baptist church of Southampton, and a deacon from its organization in 1746, and succeeded his father as clerk and trustee in 1763. He entered into public life at an early age; was sheriff of Bucks county 1749-51; justice of the county courts 1764 to the time of his death. He was ensign of Captain Henry Kroesen's company of Bucks County Associators in 1747, and captain in 1756 of a Bucks county company. His most valuable services were however rendered during the Revolutionary contest, during which period to write of him is to write the history of the struggle in Bucks county, where he was in the forefront from the "protest" at Newtown, July 9, 1774, when he was appointed one of the committee from Bucks to meet the "Committee from the respective counties of Pennsylvania" at Philadelphia, July 15, 1774, until independence was established, almost always representing his county in the various conferences and conventions, serving as chairman of the committee of safety, county lieutenant, etc. He was commissioned colonel of the first battalion raised by the committee of safety, and took it through the Jersey campaign of 1776. He was vice-president of the convention that met in Carpenter's Hall, June 18, 1776, and was twice chairman of the committee of the whole in that famous convention. In 1777 he was elected to the supreme executive council, and served until October, 1779, when he became lieutenant of Bucks county. He was register of wills and recorder of deeds of Bucks county, 1777 to his death in 1788, being the first person commissioned for these offices by the supreme executive council. He was elected in 1782 to represent Bucks county on the "board of censors," and on June 7, 1784, was commissioned by council as judge of the courts of common pleas and quarter sessions. The records fully verify the truth of the lines inscribed on the tomb erected to the memory of him and his wife at Southampton; "His long and useful life was almost wholly devoted to the public service of his country; while the lives of both were eminent for piety and virtue."

He married October 8, 1740, his cousin Elizabeth Collett, daughter of John and Marie (Crispin) Collett, and granddaughter of Richard and Elizabeth (Rush) Collett. She was born in Byberry, May 14, 1714, and died February 19, 1788, six days before her husband's death. They were the parents of six children, all sons, William, John, Silas, Josiah, Joseph, and another Joseph, the first having died in infancy. William, the eldest died in 1760, at the age of nineteen, unmarried.

John the second son of Colonel Joseph and Elizabeth Hart, born November 29, 1743, was treasurer of Bucks county during the revolution, and was filling that position when the treasury at Newtown was robbed by the Doans and their gang of outlaws, October 22, 1784. He died at Newtown June 5, 1786. He married, September 13, 1767, Rebecca Rees, daughter of David and Margaret Rees, of Hatboro, and they were the parents of five sons and two daughters, of whom three died in youth. His son William was a physician in Philadelphia; John was a merchant at Jacksonville for many years, married Rachel Dungan and left numerous descendants; Elizabeth married Dr. Silas Hough, see Hough family; Joseph died unmarried.

Silas, the third son of Joseph and Elizabeth (Collett) Hart, born October 4, 1747, was a farmer and lived and died in Warminster; married Mary Daniel, and had ten children:

Joseph, the sixth son of Colonel Joseph Hart, born July 17, 1749, is treated of in the sketch of General W. W. H. Davis, whose grandfather he was.

Joseps, the sixth son of Colonel Joseph and Elizabeth Hart, and the ancestor of B. F. Hart, was born in Warminster, December 7, 1758. He was a man of liberal education and extensive information on public affairs, in which he took a deep interest, and always enjoyed the confidence of his fellow-citizens. During the famous Whiskey Insurrection he was paymaster of Colonel Hanna's brigade, and accompanied the army in its march to western Pennsylvania. He was a member of the state senate 1804-1809, and as such in 1805 was chairman of the committee which reported favorably the bill for building an alms-house in Bucks county, and in 1808 introduced the first resolution in the senate for the removal of the county seat from Newtown to a more central part of Bucks county, and which resulted in the location at the present site, Doylestown, two years later. He enjoyed a wide acquaintance with the distinguished men of his time in the state, as is evident by his correspondence. He married, December 25, 1783, Ann Folwell, of Warminster, whose family was one of the most respectable and influential in the county, and they were the parents of seven children, viz: Thomas, John, Charles, Lewis Folwell, Thomas, Eliza Ann, and Clarissa Maria. The first Thomas and Charles died in childhood. At the death of the father, on April 15, 1811, the homestead buildings and part of the home farm became the property of Thomas, the fifth son, who died in 1838, the balance being divided between John and Lewis F., who erected buildings thereon. The mother, Ann, died March 11, 1843. Eliza Ann, the eldest daughter, born December 8, 1797, married December 2, 1817, David Marple; and Clarissa Maria, the other daughter, married Joseph Carver.

Thomas Hart, the eldest son of Joseph and Ann (Folwell) Hart, born in Warminster, April 9, 1787, was a man of prominence in the county, and for many years had a considerable political influence. When the British threatened Philadelphia in 1814 he and his brothers, Thomas and Lewis, enlisted in Captain William Purdy's company in Colonel Humphrey's regiment, and served in the field until December, when the danger having passed, they were mustered out of service. After the return of peace he took an active interest in the military of the county, serving at one time as colonel of militia. He served one session in the state legislature, 1832, and filled a number of local offices. He was a warm patron of Hatboro Library, founded in 1755 by his grandfather and others. He married, March 10, 1810, Mary Horner, daughter of John and Mary Horner, of Warminster, who was born May 3, 1790, and they were the parents of eight children as follows

W. W. H. Davis

JOSEPH, the oldest son of John and Mary (Horner) Hart, born January 21, 1811, receiving a liberal education and graduated at Jefferson College, Cannonsburg, Pennsylvania. He followed the profession of teaching for many years, and was deeply interested in public affairs up to the time of his death in 1898. He married Jane, daughter of William and Ellen Vansant, and had four children,—George W., Charles H., Mary E., and Ella S. George W. followed the vocation of a farmer, married Jennie Valentine, had one child. Charles Vincent, who received a public school education, then graduated from West Chester Normal school, receiving a scholarship to Dartmouth, graduated from that institution and afterward from Jefferson University, Philadelphia, Pennsylvania, and is now practicing in Harrisburg, Pennsylvania. Charles H. was also a teacher, and at the time of his death, in 1881, was principal of a school in the Twenty-third Ward, Philadelphia. He was also connected with several newspapers, and enjoyed the reputation of being a deep thinker. Mary E. died in infancy. Ella S. taught school in Horsham, Montgomery county, for a few years, then returned home to attend her father in his declining years. She now lives in Hatboro, Pennsylvania.

WILLIAM H., second son of John and Mary (Horner) Hart, was born April 23, 1813. In 1845 he married Rachel Ayers, of Moreland, Montgomery county. They had three children, all of whom died in infancy.

JAMES, the third son of John and Mary (Horner) Hart, born December 15, 1820, married Rachel, daughter of Isaac and Emilie Hobensack. With his family he moved to Maryland and located near Baltimore, where as a farmer he continued to reside until the beginning of the civil war. Owing to the hostile feeling entertained toward northerners he was obliged to sacrifice his property and return with his family to Bucks county. He then enlisted in the First New Jersey Cavalry Regiment, in the company commanded by his cousin, Captain John H. Shelmire. In recognition of his bravery and courage he was promoted to major of the regiment, and at the same time held the commission as major in the United States army. He was repeatedly wounded, and finally killed, after the evacuation of Richmond, at the battle of Five Forks, Virginia, April 1, 1865. His remains were brought home and interred in the Southampton Baptist burial ground, along with his kindred. He left a widow and six children, all of whom are living.

GEORGE, the fourth son of John and Mary (Horner) Hart, born April 18, 1823, received a good thorough home education, and afterwards graduated at Yale. In 1849 he went to California, returned to Philadelphia, became a partner in the mercantile house of Shunway, Hart & Co., married

Louisa Webb, and had four children, one of whom is still living.

B. FRANK, the fifth son of John and Mary (Horner) Hart, and the subject of our sketch, born March 22, 1825, likewise received a liberal education and taught different schools in his native county and also in Philadelphia. He then located in Philadelphia, and was for many years associated with John P. Veree's rolling mill in Kensington, then became executive officer and general manager of one of the city passengers railways. After many years of close attention to business he retired from active life, and now resides with his family at 2010 Wallace street, Philadelphia. He is a member of the Bucks County Historical Society, and takes a lively interest in the affairs of the county with whose history his distinguished ancestors were so closely identified. April 9, 1867, he married Anna H., daughter of Thomas Barnett, Philadelphia, and had five children. John Davis, born March 25, 1868, died in infancy; Sarah, born May 23, 1869; Mabel, born November 10, 1870, died March 14, 1873; Walter, born October 5, 1874; and Lydia, born September 11, 1876. Sara, daughter of B. Frank and Anna (Barnett) Hart, married Rev. Madison C. Peters, the distinguished preacher, author and lecturer of Philadelphia, and has three children, Dorothy, Anna and Frank H. Walter Horner, son of B. Frank and Anna (Barnett) Hart, graduated from Colonel Hyatt's Military School and is now one of Philadelphia's rising business men. Lydia, daughter of B. Frank and Anna (Barnett) Hart, remains at home with her parents.

THOMPSON DARRAH, sixth son of John and Mary (Horner) Hart, born August 14, 1827, went to Philadelphia, where he engaged in business. He married Susan Snedecar, and had one child. At the beginning of the civil war he enlisted as first lieutenant in his cousin's (Colonel Alfred Marple's) company in Colonel W. W. H. Davis's 104th Regiment, Pennsylvania Volunteers, and was later commissioned as lieutenant-colonel and commanded a brigade at the siege of Charleston, South Carolina.

ANN ELIZA, daughter of John and Mary (Horner) Hart, born January 17, 1817, died June, 1900.

MARY DARRAH, daughter of John and Mary (Horner) Hart, born July 18, 1818, died.

GENERAL WILLIAM WATTS HART DAVIS, a veteran of two wars, author, journalist and historian, was born at Davisville, Southampton township, Bucks county, Pennsylvania, July 27, 1820, and comes of English, Welsh and Scotch-Irish ancestry, representing the commingling of the blood of these different nationalities to which we are indebted for many of the finest types of American citizenship.

On the paternal side, his great-grandfather, William Davis, was an early settler in Solebury or Upper Makefield township, Bucks county, and while tradition makes him of Welsh descent, his environment and associations indicate very strongly to the the writer of these lines that he was either a native of the north of Ireland, or a son of an Ulster Scot, who had made his way to Pennsylvania with the great army of Scotch Covenanters from the province of Ulster in the first quarter of the eighteenth century. He married, about 1756, Sarah Burleigh (or Burley) daughter of John Burley, of Upper Makefield, an Ulster Scot, who had settled in Upper Makefield about 1735 with the Torberts, McNairs and others with whom his family later intermarried. Little is known of the life of William Davis other than that he was a farmer in Solebury and Upper Makefield, and died in the latter part of the century. William and Sarah (Burley) Davis were the parents of seven children, viz: Jemima, born December 25, 1758, married John Pitner, and removed with him first to Maryland and later to New Castle, Delaware; John, the grandfather of General Davis, born September 6, 1760; Sarah, born October 1, 1763, married Lott Search, of Southampton, Bucks county; William, born September 9, 1766, became a sea captain and died at sea; Joshua, born July 6, 1769, removed to Maryland about 1800; Mary, born October 3, 1771, and Joseph, born March 1, 1774, of whom we have no further record.

John Davis, second son of William and Sarah (Burley) Davis, the grandfather of the subject of this sketch, was born and reared in Solebury, and at the age of sixteen years became a member of William Hart's company in the Bucks county battalion of the Flying Camp, under Colonel Joseph Hart, and participated with it in the New Jersey and Long Island campaign of 1776. Returning with the battalion to Bucks county he participated with General Washington in the Christmas night attack on Trenton. In 1777 he enlisted in Captain Thomas Butler's company in the Third Pennsylvania Regiment, later becoming a part of the Second Pennsylvania Regiment: then transferred to Captain Joseph McClelland's company, was at the storming of Stony Point, and wounded in the foot at Fort Lee on the Hudson, 1780. He was in the Ninth, under McClelland, at the time of revolt in New Jersey, proceeded from there to York in January, 1781, and from there the company was ordered south under Lafayette and participated in the battle of Yorktown, after which Davis was discharged on account of his disabled foot and returned to Bucks county. In 1782 he was commissioned ensign of Captain Neeley's company, Colonel John Keller's battalion, Bucks county militia, and was one of the members of that battalion to enter into active service for seven months. At the close of his military service John Davis married, June 26, 1783, Ann Simpson, daughter of William and Ann (Hines)

Simpson, of Buckingham, and rented the Ellicott farm in Solebury, where he lived until 1795, when he removed with his family to Ellicott's Mills, Maryland, where they resided until 1816, when he removed to Franklin county, Ohio, where he died January 25, 1832, at the age of seventy-two years. His wife, Ann, survived him, dying June 6, 1851, in her eighty-seventh year. Her father, William Simpson, was born in Ireland in 1732, and is said to have come to Pennsylvania about 1740 with his widowed mother and a brother John, who was the great-grandfather of General U. S. Grant. William Simpson married Ann Hines, daughter of Mathew Hines, of New Britain, and lived for a time in that township, removing later to Buckingham, where he died in 1816. The children of John and Ann (Simpson) Davis were: Sarah, born in Solebury, October 12, 1784; William born August 22, 1786; John, born August 7, 1788; Ann, born November 6, 1790; Samuel, born 1792, died in infancy; Joshua, born in Maryland, June 27, 1796; Samuel S., born September, 1798; Joseph, born January 27, 1803, and Elizabeth, born November 18, 1805. Most of these children removed with their parents to the banks of the Scioto, where they became useful and active members of the community and engaged in different branches of business and professions.

John Davis, the second son of John and Ann, born in Solebury, August 7, 1788, was the father of the subject of this sketch. He removed with his parents to Rock Creek, on the banks of the Potapsico, Maryland, at the age of seven years, and was reared to the life of a farmer. At the age of sixteen years he began to drive his father's Conestoga wagon with produce to Baltimore, and before he was seventeen was sent with his father's team to remove the goods of a neighbor to Pittsburg, crossing the Alleghenies and passing through what was then a wilderness with scattering settlers; the trip occupying about sixty days. In 1808, at the age of twenty, he bought his time of his father and began farming for himself. His opportunities for an education being limited, he supplemented what scholastic knowledge he had gained in his boyhood by the reading of books and periodicals of the day in the midst of a life of business activity. He had a thirst for knowledge, and, possessing a retentive memory, became exceptionally well informed on history and the issues of American politics of the day. On one of his visits to his uncle, Lott Search, in Southampton township, he made the acquaintance of his future wife, Amy Hart, daughter of Josiah and Ann (Watts) Hart, who was living with her widowed mother on the old Watts homestead in Southampton, and from that time until March 13, 1813, the date of his marriage, was a frequent visitor at his uncle's house.

Amy Hart was born June 30, 1784, and came of distinguished ancestry, her father,

Josiah Hart, being the fourth son of Colonel Joseph* and Elizabeth (Collet) Hart, born July 17, 1749, and died October 25, 1800. He was captain of one of the Bucks county companies of militia during the Revolutionary war, under his father, who was commissioned colonel of the first battalion organized in Bucks county, in 1776, for the Jersey campaign. Colonel Hart was one of the most prominent men of his day in Bucks county, serving as sheriff, 1747-1751; justice of the courts of Bucks county, 1764, to the time of his death in 1788, ensign of militia, 1747. In the Revolutionary struggle he was one of the leading spirits from the time he was appointed on the committee of Bucks county, July 9, 1774, to attend "a meeting of the several committees of the respective counties of Pennsylvania, to be held in Philadelphia the 15th of July, instant," until independence was achieved. He was born September 1, 1715, and died February 25, 1788, and was a son of John and Eleanor (Crispin) Hart, grandson of John Hart, who came from Witney, Oxfordshire, in 1682, and married Susanna Rush, of Byberry. On the maternal side Mrs. Davis was a granddaughter of Stephen, and great-granddaughter of Rev. John Watts, born at Leeds, England, 1661; came to Lower Dublin, Philadelphia county, 1686, and married Sarah Eaton. He become pastor of the Pennepack Baptist church, 1690, and died 1702. William Watts, brother of Mrs. Josiah Hart, was prothonotary, clerk of quarter sessions, and associate justice of Bucks county. Mrs. Hart, mother-in-law of John Davis, died in 1815, at Doylestown, of typhoid fever; also William W. Hart, a young member of the bar, her son, and Mrs. Miles, another daughter of Mrs. Hart, all dying in the George Brock house, Doylestown, within a few days, of the same fever.

Soon after his marriage John Davis settled on his mother-in-law's farm in Southampton, and, at her death, in 1815, it was adjudged to him in right of his wife, and he resided in that immediate neighborhood the remainder of his long and active life. He at once became active in the affairs of his native county, to which he returned while the second war with Great Britain was in progress. On news of the burning of Washington reaching Bucks county, a meeting was called at Hart's Cross Roads, now Hartsville, on Thursday, September 1, 1814, to raise volunteers to take the field. The list of the men enrolled is in the handwriting of William Watts Hart, brother of Mrs. John Davis, and John Davis's name heads the list. He became ensign of the company then formed, which, after two months' camp and drill at Bush Hill, Philadelphia, proceeded to Camp Dupont, in Delaware, where their three months' service was completed. Ensign Davis, soon after his discharge, entered

the volunteer militia of the county, became active therein, and was in constant commission for thirty-four years, holding in succession commissions as captain, brigade inspector, major, lieutenant-colonel, colonel, and was three times elected major-general of the division composed of Bucks and Montgomery counties. General Davis was a natural politician, a Democrat from conviction, and became a power in that party in Bucks county. Sturdy in the advocacy of what he conceived to be right and strong in the reasons and facts on which his conclusions were founded, he became a strong and eloquent advocate and was "on the stump" in many of the political campaigns of his day. He was appointed by Governor Wolf, 1833, a member of the board of appraisers of public works and held the office three years. In 1838 he was elected to congress from the Bucks county district, and made a splendid record as a congressman. His speech in favor of the passage of the Independent Treasury Bill, June 2/, 1840, was commented on throughout the country as a masterly and able one. He served on many important committees and took an active interest in all that pertained to the best interest of his district and the country at large. On March 4, 1845, he was appointed surveyor of the port of Philadelphia, and filled that position for four years. During the forty years from 1820 to 1860, General John Davis's position in the political arena was a prominent one and he was closely associated and in constant correspondence with the leading political lights of that time, A lifelong friend of James Buchanan, he used strenuous efforts to accomplish his election to the presidency. He, however, disapproved of Buchanan's Kansas and Nebraska policy, and refused to indorse it, and became estranged from many old-time comrades in the party.

During all these years General Davis remained a resident of Davisville, where he operated a farm and saw mill for many years. In 1829 he built a store building there, and conducted a general merchandise store for many years, and filled the position of postmaster. He was an excellent business man, frank and straightforward in his dealings, and of unswerving public and private integrity. He and his family were members of the Baptist church, and he took a deep interest in religious and educational matters. At the outbreak of the Civil war he was amongst the very first to raise his voice in favor of maintaining the Union and putting down the rebellion with a strong arm. Had his age permitted would have gone to the front, as did his only son, in defense of the government he loved and served.

Amy, the wife of General John Davis, died August 17, 1847, and he on April 8, 1876, and both are buried in the old graveyard at Southampton Baptist church. Their children were: Ann, who married, December 10, 1835, James Erwin, of Newtown,

*See preceding sketch.

whose only surviving child married Henry Mercur, of Towanda, Pennsylvania; Rebecca, who married, January 5, 1840, Alfred T. Duffield, who succeeded the General as storekeeper at Davisville, and died in September, 1871, and his wife in 1884, leaving three children: J. Davis Duffield, T. H. Benton Duffield, and Amy, wife of Judge Gustav A. Endlich of Reading; Sarah, who married Ulysses Mercur, of Towanda, later chief justice of the supreme court of Pennsylvania; Amy, who married Holmes Sells, a practicing physician at Dublin, Ohio, later a prominent physician and druggist at Atlanta, Georgia, where they resided during the Civil war; Elizabeth, who never married, and resides at the old homestead at Davisville; and an only son, William Watts Hart Davis, the subject of this sketch, who was named for his mother's brother, William Watts Hart, a member of the Bucks county bar, who was clerk of the orphans' court of Bucks county in 1814, and resigned to go in defense of his country when Washington was burned, and was adjutant of Colonel Humphrey's Bucks county regiment. At the close of the war he returned to Doylestown and died in 1815 of typhus fever.

William Watts Hart Davis was born at at Davisville, July 27, 1820. He was reared on the old homestead and his earliest educational advantages were obtained at a private school kept by Miss Anna Longstreth, at the Longstreth homestead nearby; later he attended the celebrated classical school at Southampton Baptist church, and the day school, a mile from Davisville, on the Bucks and Montgomery county line road. In 1832 he came to Doylestown and attended the Academy there, boarding at the public house of his father's old captain and friend, William Purdy; a few years later he attended the select school of Samuel Long, near Hartsville, and the Newtown Academy, finishing his elementary education at the boarding school of Samuel Aaron, Burlington, New Jersey. From the age of ten years the time not spent in school was spent behind the counter in his fathers' store, where he learned practical business methods and habits of industry from the best of teachers, by both example and precept. In 1841 he entered Captain Alden Partridge's University and Military School at Norwich, Vermont, and concluded a three years' course in sixteen months, graduating in 1842 with the degrees of A. M. and M. M. S. In the same year he was appointed an instructor of mathematics and commandant of cadets in the military academy at Portsmouth, Virginia, where he remained three years.

He then began the study of law in the office of Judge John Fox, at Doylestown, and in 1846, after his admission to the bar, entered the law department of Harvard University. On December 5, 1846, while a student of Harvard Law School, at Cambridge, Massachusetts, he enlisted in the First Massachusetts Infantry for the Mexican war; was commissioned first lieutenant, December 31, 1846, of Captain Crowningshield's company, Colonel Caleb Cushing's regiment; adjutant, January 16, 1847; aide-de-camp June 1, 1847; acting assistant adjutant general, July 18, 1847; acting commissary of subsistence, October 9, 1847; acting quartermaster and inspector, October 29, 1847; captain, Company I, First Massachusetts Infantry, March 16, 1848, spending the winter of 1847-1848 with Scott's conquering army in the Valley of Mexico. He was one of the officers who participated in the capture of General Valencia, in a night ride of seventy miles. He was mustered out July 24, 1848, at the close of the war.

He now returned to Doylestown, where he practiced law until 1853, when he was appointed by President Franklin Pierce (with whom he had served in the Mexican war) to the position of United States district attorney of the territory of New Mexico, and spent the next four years in that territory, during which time he filled the offices of attorney-general, secretary of the territory, acting governor, superintendent of Indian affairs and of public buildings. While there he also published a newspaper at Santa Fe in Spanish and English, and, with the assistance of an interpreter and his clerk he saved the valuable Spanish manuscript in the secretary's office which afterward furnished him the material from which he wrote "The Spanish Conquest of New Mexico," that was issued from the press of the "Doylestown Democrat" in 1869. While at Santa Fe he wrote his first work on New Mexico, entitled "El Gringo, or New Mexico and Her People," which Harper & Brothers published in 1857. While exercising the functions of government in our new territory, Mr. Davis met with some unique experiences. On one occasion, himself and party, while traveling on the plains, were captured by the Arapahoe Indians, but, by the exercise of a little diplomacy, escaped serious molestation.

Returning to Doylestown in the fall of 1857, he purchased the "Doylestown Democrat," then as now the organ of the Democratic party in the county, and owned and edited it until 1890, when he sold out to the Doylestown Publishing Company, but continued as its editor until 1900, since which time he has devoted his time to historical and literary work.

General Davis raised and took to the front the first armed force in the county for the defense of the country in the civil war, known as the "Doylestown Guards," of which he had been captain since 1858 as a volunteer militia organization. He served with this company through a campaign in the Shenandoah Valley under General Robert Patterson, an account of which campaign he later published, and which is considered an authority on that subject. The company was ordered to Washington in

1861, and was the first military force to pass through Baltimore after the riots of April 19, 1861. The company being mustered out at the end of their three months' service, Captain Davis, by order of the secretary of war, raised at Doylestown the One Hundred and Fourth Regiment, Pennsylvania Volunteers, and a battery known at its inception as the "Ringgold Battery," but later as "Durell's Battery," an excellent history of which has lately been written and published by Lieutenant Charles A. Cuffel, of Doylestown. Colonel Davis went to the front with his regiment November 6, 1861, and served throughout the war as its colonel, though frequently filling positions and exercising commands commensurate to a much higher rank. His military record during the civil war, as briefly summed up from the records of the War Department, is as follows: Captain Company I, Twenty-fifth Pennsylvania Regiment (Doylestown Guards), April 16, 1861, in the Shenandoah Valley campaign; mustered out July 26, 1861; colonel One Hundred and Fourth Regiment, Pennsylvania Volunteers, September 5, 1861; provisional brigade commander, November 11, 1861; commanding First Brigade, Casey's Division, Fourth Corps, November 30, 1861; wounded at Fair Oaks, May 31, 1862; commanded First Brigade, Second Division, Eighteenth Corps, January 11, 1863 (Second Division, First Corps, March 10, 1863; commanded United States forces at Port Royal Island, South Carolina, May 27, 1862, post of Beaufort, South Carolina, June 14, 1863; First Brigade, Terry's Division, July 8, 1863, at siege of Charleston, S. C.; commanded U. S. forces at Morris Island, South Carolina, January 19, 1864; District of Hilton Head, Port Pulaski, St. Helena and Tybee Islands, South Carolina, April 18, 1864; First Brigade, Hatch's Division, July 4, 1864; wounded at siege of Charleston, July 6, 1864, losing fingers of right hand; mustered out September 30, 1864; brevetted brigadier-general, United States Volunteers, March 13, 1865, "for meritorious services during the operations against Charleston, South Carolina." In connection with the distinguished services rendered by General Davis in the operations before Charleston we publish below a letter written by Major General Gilmore, then in command of the forces there, which shows in what light his services were held by his superior officers:

"Headquarters, Department of the South, "Folly Island, S. C., Nov. 26, 1863. "Col. W. W. H. Davis, 104th Pa. Vol. Inf., Commanding Brigade, Morris Island S. C.

"Dear Sir:—Although entirely unsolicited by you, directly or indirectly, I deem it my duty, as it is certainly a pleasure, on the eve of your departure for a short leave of absence in the North, to express to you, officially, my high appreciation of the zeal, intelligence, and efficiency which have marked your conduct and service during

the operations against the defences of Charleston, still pending. Much of our service here has been trying, indeed, upon both officers and men, but I have been most nobly sustained by all, and by none more zealously than yourself. I wish you a successful journey and a safe return to us. Very Respectfully, Your Obt. S'vt., (Signed)   Q. A. GILMORE, "Maj. Gen'l. Com'd'g."

The above letter, received on the eve of his departure for a short visit to his family and friends in Bucks county, was an entire and gratifying surprise to the general and is much prized by him.

The One Hundred and Fourth passed through the thick of the fight, and rendered valiant service in the defense of the Union, and left many of its numbers in their last sleep under Southern skies. General Davis was largely instrumental in securing the erection of a monument to the memory of his fallen comrades at Doylestown.

At the close of the war General Davis returned to the management and editorship of the "Democrat." He was honorary commissioner of the United States to the Paris Exposition in 1878; was Democratic candidate for congress from the seventh district in 1882, and for the state at large in 1884. In 1885 he was appointed by President Cleveland United States pension agent at Philadelphia, and filled that position for four years. In the midst of a life of business activity General Davis has devoted much time to literary and historical work. In addition to numerous lectures, addresses and papers on historical and other subjects, he is the author of the following publications, "El Gringo," 1857; "Spanish Conquest of New Mexico,"* 1869; "History of One Hundred and Fourth Regiment, Pennsylvania Volunteers," 1866; "History of the Hart Family of Bucks County," 1867; "Life of General John Lacey," 1868; "History of Bucks County," 1876; "Life of John Davis," 1886; "Doylestown Guards," 1887; "Campaign of 1861, in the Shenandoah Valley," 1893; "The Fries Rebellion," 1899; "Doylestown, Old and New," 1904, and a revised edition of the "History of Bucks County," 1905. All of these publications are considered the best authorities on the subjects treated and most of them now bring in the market double and treble their original subscription price. General Davis has been

*The eminent historian, George Bancroft, read the entire manuscript of the "Spanish Conquest of New Mexico" prior to its publication, and in a letter to General Davis, from Berlin, under date of February 17, 1869, said: "You are the only American I know who had the opportunity and the curiosity to investigate the subject, and our new acquisition is rising so rapidly in greatness and value that a new interest attaches to the romantic career of the adventurers who discovered it, and I trust that you will publish your valuable work." Thomas A. Janvier, author of the "Mexican Guide," and an extensive contributor to Spanish-American literature, in a letter to the General says: "Your history is one of the most scholarly and thoroughly satisfying works in the whole range of Spanish-American literature. It has the charm of style of the old chroniclers, and much of their charm of quaintness, with an exactness that is not, in all cases, an old chronicler's characteristic."

4-3

president of the Bucks County Historical Society almost from its organization, and its success as an organization is largely due to his untiring efforts in its behalf. Nearly his whole time since his retirement from the editorship of the "Democrat," in 1900, as well as a large part of his time prior to that has been spent in its rooms and in its service, and hundreds of books, pamphlets and curios on its shelves are of his contribution. At the age of eighty-five years his highest ambition is to live to see the Society successfully installed in its handsome new building, for which it is largely indebted to his untiring zeal in that behalf.

General Davis was married, June 24, 1856, to Anna Carpenter, daughter of Jacob Carpenter, of Brooklyn, New York, and of their seven children three survive: Jacob C., of Doylestown, now in the employ of the Philadelphia and Reading Railroad Company; Margaret Sprague, wife of Captain Samuel A. W. Patterson, of the U. S. Marine Corps, son of Rear Admiral Thomas H. Patterson, U. S. N., and grandson of Commodore Daniel T. Patterson, U. S. N., who commanded the Naval forces at the battle of New Orleans, 1865; and Eleanor Hart, residing with her father.

General Davis is a companion of the military order of the Loyal Legion, a member of the Aztec Club, Survivors of the Mexican War, of the Pennsylvania Society of the Sons of the Revolution, Post No. 1, G. A. R., Philadelphia, the American Historical Association and the Historical Society of Pennsylvania, and a member and one of the founders of Historical Society of New Mexico.

CAPTAIN SAMUEL AUCHMUTY WAINWRIGHT PATTERSON, U. S. Marine Corps, on board the United States battleship "Kentucky," of the North Atlantic squadron, U. S. N., was born at Washington, D. C., December 3, 1859, and is a son of Rear Admiral Thomas Harman Patterson, U. S. N., by his wife, Maria Montresor Wainwright, daughter of Colonel Richard D. Wainwright, first colonel of the United States Marine corps; and grandson of Commodore Daniel Todd Patterson, U. S. N.

Commodore Daniel Todd Patterson was born on Long Island, New York, in 1786. He entered the U. S. navy in 1800, and was a midshipman on board the frigate "Philadelphia" in the expedition commanded by Captain William Brainbridge, engaged in the blockade of Tripoli, October 31, 1803, when the frigate ran upon the rocks and the vessel and entire crew were captured and held prisoners in Tripoli for three years, until peace was declared. On January 24, 1807, he was promoted to the rank of lieutenant, and on July 24, 1813, to master-commander. As commander of the naval forces he co-operated with General Andrew Jackson in 1814-15 in the defense of New Orleans, lending such support as to assure the victory over the British, and received the expression of their appreciation from the U. S. congress. He commanded the expedition sent to capture the defenses of the corsair Lafitte, on the island of Grand Terre, in Batavia Bay, having been made captain February 28, 1815. He commanded the frigate "Constitution," 1826-29, and was appointed navy-commissioner in the latter year, holding the position for four years. In 1832-36 he was in command of the Mediterranean squadron, and on his return was made commandant of the navy yard at Washington, which he held at the time of his death in 1839.

Rear Admiral Thomas Harman Patterson was born at New Orleans, May 10, 1820, entered the navy from Louisiana as acting midshipman April 5, 1830, was promoted midshipman March 3, 1837, passed midshipman July 1, 1842. He spent the next five years on the frigate "Macedonia," the sloop-of-war "Falmouth," acting master and lieutenant on the brig "Lawrence," West India squadron, and on the brig "Washington," Coast Survey, from April 17, 1844, to October, 1848, when he was commissioned master. He was commissioned lieutenant June 23, 1849, and served on the sloop-of-war "Vandalia," Pacific Squadron, until October 12, 1852.

At the breaking out of the civil war he was serving on the steam sloop "Mohickan," on the coast of Africa; returning home he was put on active duty; was commissioned commander of sham gunboat "Chocura," July 16, 1862, in Hampton Roads, Virginia; and was present at the siege of Yorktown, and opened up the Pamunkey river for McClellan's army, co-operating with the Army of the Potomac. In November, 1862, he was ordered to the South Atlantic Blockading Squadron in the steamer "James Adger," which he commanded until June, 1865, participating in the capture of a flying battery near Fort Fisher, in August, 1863; captured the "Cornubia" and "Robert E. Lee," and the schooner "Ella" off the North Carolina coast. He was senior officer in the outside blockade off Charleston, South Carolina, September 15, 1864; commanded the steam-sloop "Brooklyn," flagship of the South Atlantic Squadron, from September 19, 1865, to September 18, 1867, being commissioned captain July 25, 1866; promoted to commodore November 2, 1871, and commanded Washington Navy Yard 1873-6; was commissioned rear admiral March 28, 1877, and commanded the Asiatic Squadron until 1880, which completed his twenty-five years of active sea duty. He retired May 10, 1882. He was elected January 2, 1868, a member of the Military Order of the Loyal Legion of the United States. He died at Washington, D. C., after a long and painful illness, April 9, 1889. He married Maria Montresor Wainwright, daughter of Colonel Richard Wainwright, of the United States Marine Corps, who died in

1881. They were the parents of three sons and one daughter.

Captain Samuel A. W. Patterson entered the Naval Academy at Annapolis in 1876, and graduated in 1882, after making several cruises as a student. After graduation he was attached to the flagship "Hartford," of the Pacific Squadron, where he served two years. He left the navy in 1884, and in 1885 was appointed as a clerk in the United States Pension Office at Philadelphia under General W. W. H. Davis, pension agent, and filled that position for four years and six months. From 1886 to 1896 he resided in Doylestown, Bucks county, Pennsylvania. In May, 1896, he entered the U. S. Revenue Cutter service, where he served until January 17, 1900. He was in the blockading squadron at Cuba during the Spanish-American War. He re-entered the U. S. navy in January 1900, and was stationed at the Boston Navy Yard until ordered to China, June, 1900, as second lieutenant of the U. S. Marine Corps, and was promoted to first lieutenant, July, 1900, during the Boxer troubles in China, where he participated in the famous march to Pekin to relieve the imprisoned legations. At the close of the Chinese imbroglio he was ordered to the Philippines, and served on the U. S. S. "New Orleans," at China and Japan, and at Cavite and Olongapo, Philippine Islands. After two years and eight months' service abroad he was stationed for a time at the New York Navy Yard, from whence he was ordered to the Isthmus of Panama, where he served for six months. Returning to the New York Navy Yard he was promoted captain in November, 1903, and is now (1905) cruising on board the U. S. battleship "Kentucky," of the North Atlantic Fleet.

Captain Patterson, February 18, 1886, married Margaret Sprague Davis, daughter of General W. W. H. Davis, of Doylestown, Bucks county, Pennsylvania, a sketch of whose distinguished career and ancestry is given in this volume. Captain and Margaret (Sprague) Davis Patterson have been the parents of three children, Anna Davis, born December 27, 1886, died December 1, 1894; Thomas Harman, born April 15, 1889, died August 12, 1889; and Daniel Walter, born April 14, 1891, who survives.

CORNELL FAMILY. Gulliame Corneille, (variously spelled, Cornele, Cornale, Cornelise, in the Dutch records of New Netherlands) was of undoubted French origin, probably a Hueguenot, and possibly of the same family as Pierre and Thomas Corneille, the noted dramatists and poets of Rouen, a supposition strengthened by the fact that he named his eldest son Peter, the French of which would have been "Pierre." He settled on Long Island early in the seventeenth century, and died at Flatbush prior to July 17, 1666, at which date his son Pieter Guilliamse paid for the burial of both his father and mother, as shown by the town records. On August 9, 1658, he procured from Director Stuyvesant, a patent for a large plantation at Flatbush, and in 1661 he and his son Pieter purchased a "bouwery" and several building lots in Flatbush. He left five children Pieter, Guilliam or Gelyam, Cornelis, Jacob and Maria, who have left numerous descendants in Kings county, Long Island, New York, New Jersey, and in Bucks county and other parts of Pennsylvania. The name for nearly a century was spelled Cornele, with the accent on the e.

Pieter Wuellemsen, as he wrote his name, the eldest son of Guilliam Cornele, was a prominent man in the early history of Flatbush and Kings county. As above stated he was joint purchaser with his father of a large plantation in Flatbush, and later was alloted other building lots in the town. He was commissioned as "Pierre Guilleaum" on October 8, 1686, a lieutenant of the Flatbush company of Kings county militia. His will is dated May 23, 1689. He married in 1675 Margueritie Vercheur, or Vernelle, as the marriage record gives it, and they were the parents of at least five children: Gulliame, born 1679; Cornelis, 1681; Jacob, 1683; Maria, 1686, and Pieter. Cornelis, the second son, married Jannetje—and had children: Johannes, baptised September 21, 1718; Adrien, baptised November 19, 1721; Cornelis, married Anne Williams in Philadelphia in 1746, and probably several others, some of whom are said to have settled in Bucks county. Pieter, the youngest son of Pieter and Margaret, married Catharine Lanning and settled in New Jersey. Adrien, son of Cornelis, is erroneously confounded with Adrien, son of Guilliam, who settled in Bucks county; the former probably never lived in Pennsylvania.

Gilliam Cornell, eldest son of Peter and Margaret, was born at Flatbush, Long Island, in 1679, married November 4, 1714, Cornelia Van Nortwyck, daughter of Simon and Folkertje Van Nortwyck, of Blanckenburg, in the Netherlands, and remained until 1723 at Flatbush, removing from there to New Utrecht, and is said to have accompanied some of his children to Bucks county prior to 1750, of which latter fact we have no proof, unless a tombstone, beside those of his sons Gilliam and Wilhelmus, in the old Dutch Reformed burying ground near Feasterville, marked "G x C," may be considered as proof. He purchased a house and lot in Flatbush as early as 1708. His children as shown by the records of the Dutch Reformed churches of Flatbush and New Utrecht and from the Bucks county records, were: Adrien: Jacobus, baptised October 2, 1720; Wilhelmus, baptised July 29,

1722; Gilliam, baptised October 23, 1724; Johannes, baptised June 16, 1727, married May 23, 1750, Maria Lott, and remained in Flatbush; Simon, baptised July 13, 1729; and Abraham, baptised October 10, 1731. Margaretta Cornell, who married Rem Vanderbelt, of Southampton, and had a son Gilliam baptised at Southampton in 1742, is also supposed to have been a daughter of Gilliam. Of the above named sons of Gilliam and Cornelia Cornell, four (Adrien, Wilhelmus, Gilliam and Simon) came to Bucks county, and settled in Northampton and Southampton, and where the first three left numerous descendants. Adrien was the ancestor of most of the Cornells who now reside in Bucks, and a more detailed account of him will be given below.

WILHELMUS CORNELL, born at Flatbush, Long Island, July 13, 1722, probably came to Bucks county with his elder brother Adrien and their parents prior to 1740. He was married at the Southampton church, April 14, 1744, to Elshe (or Alice) Kroesen. His first purchase of land was in connection with his younger brother Gilliam in 1755, and consisted of three tracts of land near Churchville, eighty-two acres on the Northampton side of the Bristol road, and 115 acres opposite in Southampton, including the present site of the church. In 1762 he conveyed his interest in these tracts to Gilliam, and purchased of Jacob Duffield 233½ acres in Southampton, and subsequently acquired considerable other land there. He died October 14, 1783, and his wife Elshe died October 8, 1802, at the age of seventy-seven years; they are buried side by side in the old grave yard at Feasterville. They were the parents of seven children: Gilliam, born January 2, 1745, died August 17, 1755; John, born January, 1750, died January 24, 1811, leaving sons Gilliam, Wilhelmus, Jacob, John and Isaac and daughters Elizabeth, wife of Henry Feaster, and Cornelia, wife of Gilliam Cornell; Cornelia, baptised February 11, 1753, married William Craven; Margaret, baptised December 14, 1755, married Henry Courson; Elizabeth, baptised June 7, 1761; and Gilliam, baptised September 17, 1758, married Jane Craven. The latter was known locally as "Yompey Cornell." He was buried on his farm at Southampton Station.

Gilliam Cornel, born on Long Island in 1724, married there May 23, 1750, Margaret Schench, and removed to Bucks county. He purchased land as above recited in 1755 in connection with his brother Wilhelmus, and purchased the latter's interest therein six years later. He died in Northampton, July 17, 1785, and his wife Margaret died September 5, 1805. They had seven children: 1. Phebe, who married her cousin Cornelius Cornell, the son of Simon. 2.

Cornelia, baptised April 11, 1757, married William Bennett. 3. John, baptised December 31, 1758, married Catharine Sleght. 4. Abraham, baptised January 28, 1760, died August 31, 1801, married Agnes Bennett. 5. Gilliam, baptised August 27, 1764, married Rachel —— and left Bucks county. 6. Margaret, baptised 1767. 7. John, baptised June 12, 1774, died young. 8. Maria, baptised August 24, 1778.

Simon Cornell, born on Long Island in 1729, married Adrienne Kroesen and settled in the neighborhood of Southampton, though probably in Philadelphia county; his sons Cornelius and John were baptised at Southampton church in 1761 and 1772 respectively. The former married Phebe, daughter of his uncle Gilliam, and had children Gilliam, John, Cornelius, Isaac, Jane, who married Peter Bailey, and Margaret.

ADRIEN CORNELL, eldest son of Gelyam and grandson of Peter Guilliamse Cornel, was born in Flatbush, Long Island, August 22, 1713, as shown by his family Bible now in possession of Thompson Cornell of Philadelphia, a great-great-grandson, and died July 28, 1777. He was eldest son of Gelyam Cornell by the first marriage of Gelyam, who was a landholder in Flatbush as early as 1708. Historians have erroneously stated that he was a son of Cornelis, the brother of Gelyam. Bergen, in his "Early Settlers of Kings County," makes that statement and gives the date of his baptism as November 19, 1721, but this is effectually disproven by the Bible record, as well as by the will of Gilliam of Bucks county, who is shown to be a son of Gelyam and Conelia, and makes "my nephew Gilliam Cornell, son of my brother Adrien," one of the executors of his will. Adrien Cornell married Mattie Hegeman, born at Brooklyn, Long Island, November 1, 1718, daughter of Rem and Peternella (Van Wycklen) Hegeman, grand-daughter of Elbert and Marytje (Rappalye) Hegeman, great-granddaughter of Joseph and Femmeltje (Remse) Hegeman, and great-great-granddaughter of Adrien and Catharine Hegeman, who emigrated from Amsterdam in 1650, settling first at New Albany, but later removing to Flatbush, Long Island, where Adrien was a magistrate in 1654 and died in April, 1672. Adrien Cornell removed to Bucks county prior to June 7, 1739, at which date he purchased 250 acres in Northampton township, where he was already a resident. In 1751 he purchased sixty-one acres adjoining his first purchase and 205 acres additional in 1772. This land was located in the heart of the Dutch settlement known as Holland, and much of it still remains the property of his descendants. He died on his plantation purchased in 1739, July 27, 1777, and his wife Mattie died July 4, 1790;

Adrian Cornell

both are buried at Richboro. Their children were: Gilliam, born April 26, 1741, died March 2, 1809, married Jannetje Suydam, daughter of Lambert Suydam; and Rem, born June 9, 1744, died July 18, 1825, married Peternelletje Hegeman, born 1751, died December 19, 1816.

Gilliam and Jane (Suydam) Cornell were the parents of nine children: Adrien, born May 18, 1765, died February 28, 1841, married Rachel Feaster; Abigail, born December 17, 1769, married Henry DuBois; Lambert, born July 14, 1772; James, born October 20, 1774, died April 1, 1850, married first Cynthia, daughter of Rem Cornell, and second Margaret Vandegrift; Rem, born April 4, 1777, died young; Mattie, born April 23, 1779, married Aaron Feaster; Jane, born May 15, 1781, married Christopher Vanarsdalen; John, born March 29, 1783, married Elizabeth Vandegrift; and Gilliam, born May 13, 1785, married Elizabeth Krewsen, November 16, 1809. In the division of the real estate of Adrien Cornell between his two sons Gilliam and Rem, the latter retained 203 acres of the homestead tract of 250 acres, and forty-one acres of the Vanduren purchase adjoining, and conveyed to his brother Gilliam the balance of the homestead, fifty-six acres, and 205 acres purchased by their father of Van Horn in 1772. These lands were devised by the brothers to their respective sons, and a portion of both tracts still remain in the tenure of their descendants of the name. Gilliam divided the homestead between his sons Lambert, James and Gilliam, settling his son Adrian on eighty-five acres purchased in 1785 of William Thomson, and John on 100 acres purchased of Henry Dyer.

Rem Cornell, second son of Adrien and Mattie (Hegeman) Cornell, born in Northampton in 1744, married Peterneelitie Hegeman, and lived all his life on the old homestead in Northampton, acquiring later considerable other land in the vicinity. He was an active and prominent man in the community, and a member of the Dutch Reformed church of North and Southampton. He died July 18, 1825, in his eighty-second year. His wife died December 19, 1816, in her sixty-fifth years, and both are buried in the old graveyard at Richboro. They were the parents of three children: Mattie, born 1770, married John Kroeson; Cynthia, born 1776, died June 7, 1808, married her cousin James Cornell; and Adrien.

Adrien Cornell, only son of Rem, born on the old homestead in Northampton in May, 1779, and, inheriting it from his father in 1825, spent his whole life there. He was a prosperous farmer and a good business man and acquired a large estate, owning at his death in 1857 over 700 acres of farm land and a fine mill property in Northampton, and over 400 acres in Upper Makefield township. His wife was Leanah Craven, daughter of James and Adrianna (Kroesoh) Craven, and was baptised at Churchville, February 21, 1779. The children of Adrien and Leanah (Craven) Cornell were as follows: 1. James Craven, baptised November 4, 1804, died February 1, 1865, married Judith S. Everett. 2. Eleanor, baptised January 10, 1807, married James Krusen. 3. John Lefferts, baptised January 10, 1807, died January 14, 1836. 4. Ann Eliza, baptised August 28, 1810, married James S. McNair. 5. Charles, baptised March 21, 1812. 6. Lydia, January 18, 1815, married Henry Wynkoop. 7. Cynthia, baptised August 11, 1816, married William R. Beans. Adrian, see forward, and Mary Jane, wife of Frances Vanartsdalen.

Adrien Cornell, youngest son of Adrien and Leanah (Craven) Cornell, was born on the old homestead in Northampton, December 21, 1818. He was reared on the farm that had been the home of his ancestors since 1739, and in the house erected by his great-great-grandfather in 1747. This house he tore down in 1861, and erected the present mansion house. He was an active and successful business man. He was connected for many years with the Bucks County Agricultural Society, of which he was for several years president, succeeding his brother James C. Cornell in that position. He married January 8, 1840, Mary Ann Van Horn, daughter of Abraham Van Horn, who survived him many years. He died on the old homestead, September 17, 1870.

GEORGE W. CORNELL, only child of Adrien and Mary Ann, was born on the old homestead, October 17, 1841, and resided there until the spring of 1904, when he removed to Newtown borough, where he now resides. He was educated at the public schools of Northampton, supplemented by a three years course at the Tennent School at Hartsville, Pennsylvania. He married October 10, 1871, Sarah C. Luken, who died May 23, 1873. On June 6, 1877, he married Elizabeth B. Camm, his present wife, who is a daughter of Joseph C. and Martha (Feaster) Camm, and a granddaughter of Aaron and Matilda (Cornell) Feaster, Matilda being a daughter of Gilliam and Jannetje (Suydam) Cornell. Her paternal great-grandfather, John Camm, was a native of England and located in Philadelphia, where his son William and grandson Joseph C., were born and reared. Her father, Joseph C. Camm, located in Northampton township, Bucks county, after his marriage, and Mrs. Cornell was born and reared in that township. On the Feaster side she is of Holland descent. Her great-great-grandfather, John Feaster, was born on Long Island in 1798, and died in Northampton township, Bucks county, December 19,

1775. His wife Mary, born in 1706, died May 28, 1774. Their son David, born April 8, 1740, married Mary Hegeman, born March 8, 1743; he died September 28, 1808, and his wife May 28, 1783. Their son Aaron, the grandfather of Mrs. Cornell, was born in October, 1772, and died July 18, 1860. Mr. and Mrs. Cornell have no children. Mr. Cornell still owns the old homestead in Northampton, but lives retired in Newtown. In politics he is a Republican. He and his wife are members of the Dutch Reformed church.

Gilliam Cornell, youngest son of Gilliam and Jannetje (Suydam) Cornell, of Northampton, was born on the old homestead May 30, 1785. He married November 16, 1809. Elizabeth Krewsen, and settled on a portion of the old homestead purchased by the grandfather of the Van Horns in 1772, 103 acres of which Gilliam inherited at his father's death in 1809. His two children were: Jacob Krewsen, born September 28, 1810, and Martin H., born May 29, 1820.

Jacob Krewsen Cornell was reared on the old Northampton homestead, but on his marriage purchased of Samuel McNair a farm in Southampton, at Churchville, part of the land purchased in 1755 by Wilhelmus and Gilliam Cornell, and settled thereon. He married January 7, 1834, Elizabeth Finney, who bore him eleven children, seven of whom lived to maturity and raised families, viz.:

1. Mary, born June 26, 1835, married Charles Van Artsdalen, January 10, 1856, and had one daughter, Alice, born December 1, 1856, who married James L. Cornell.

2. Alice, born December 18, 1837, died May 28, 1838.

3. Jane M., born August 21, 1840, married December 26, 1861, Thomas Beans, and has three children—George, William and Howard.

4. Alice L., born June 5, 1842, married (first) Henry McKinney and (second) Joseph J. Yerkes, and has a son Jacob.

5. John Corson, born August 2, 1844, a prominent merchant of Oakford, Pennsylvania, married April,· 1870, Margaret J. Stevens.

6. Jacob Krewsen, Jr., born June 10, 1846, now deputy recorder of deeds of Bucks county; married January 8, 1884, Alice E. Woodruff; has no children.

7. Charles F., born June 10, 1848, died August 8, 1848.

8. Gilliam, Jr., born June 22, 1849; married January 24, 1878, Jane, daughter of Joseph Hogeland; one son, Joseph Remsen, born January 8, 1885.

9. Martin Harris, born February 19, 1851, married October 7, 1874, Mary H. Agin; now reside in Doylestown; one daughter, Carrie Ruth, born July 7, 1884.

10. Charles Finney, born 1853, died 1861.

11. Henrietta, born 1857, died 1863,

Jacob Krewsen Cornell married (second) Ruth Anna Morrison, daughter of Judge Joseph J. and Ellen (Addis) Morrison, by whom he had the following children: Joseph M., born December 18, 1862, see forward; Ella M., born October 4, 1864, married January 14, 1897, J. Warner Cornell, and has two children—Ruth and Charles; Edith, born May 10, 1870; and Albert, born October, 1871, died July, 1872.

JOSEPH MORRISON CORNELL was born on the old homestead at Churchville, Southampton township,, Bucks county, December 18, 1862, and is the eldest son of Jacob Krewson Cornell by his second marriage with Ruth Ann Morrison. He was reared on the farm and acquired his education at the local schools. On arriving at manhood he followed farming five years in that vicinity, and then purchased his father's farm, where he has since residéd. He has always taken an active interest in the affairs of his native township, and has filled several local offices. He was for three years supervisor, and has also filled the office of township assessor. Mr. Cornell was married November 27, 1884, to Emma E. Fetter, daughter of John Carrel and Mercy C. (Lefferts) Fetter, and they have been the parents of two children: John Fetter, born December 1, 1887, died July 17, 1890; and Joseph M. Jr., born January 16, 1894.

Mrs. Cornell was born March 20, 1864, and is one of the three children of John C. and Mary (Leffets) Fetter. Her great-grandfather, George Fetter, was one of twelve children, and was born January 13, 1768. His wife, Rebecca Wynkoop, was born August 28, 1868, and they were the parents of nine children, of whom William, the eldest, born October 7, 1797, was the grandfather of Mrs. Cornell. He married Sarah Carrell, December 26, 1821, and had six children, of whom the eldest, John C., born August 18, 1824, was the father of Mrs. Cornell. On the maternal side Mrs. Cornell is of Holland descent, being descended from Leffet Pieterse, who came to Long Island with his parents in 1669 from Haughwout, North Holland, and settled at Flatbush, Long Island. His son, Pieter Lefferts, born May 18, 1680, married Ida, daughter of Hendrick Suydam, and their son, Leffertse Leffertse, was the first of the family to settle in Bucks county, where he has left numerous descendants.

THE JANNEY FAMILY of Bucks county are descendants of the Cheshire family of that name who, according to various authorities, "are supposed to be" or "considered to be" descended from the house of De-Gisne, or Gyney, of Heverland, Norfolk, who were of French extraction, and the name to be derived from Guisnes, near Calais, France.

The earliest lineal ancestor of the American family of Janney of whom there is any authentic record was Randull Janney, of Stiall, parish of Wilmeslome, Cheshire, England, who died about the year 1596, being mentioned in the will of his son Thomas Janney, made in 1602, as having left legacies to daughters of Thomas, the youngest of whom was baptised in 1595. Thomas Janney, before mentioned, was married at least twice, if not three times. Investigations recently conducted in Cheshire by Miles White, of Baltimore, indicate that he married first Ellen ———, who was buried February 7, 1578, and by whom he had a daughter Alyce, who was baptised November 7, 1570, but as no further record of this Alice is found, and she is not mentioned in Thomas's will, there is no proof that the record above refers to Thomas of Stiall. He married, December 7, 1578, Jane Worthington, who was buried August 10, 1589, and (second) on November 4, 1590, Katharine Cash, of Stiall. By the first marriage he had two sons, Randle and Henry, and daughters Margerie and Maud. By the second marriage he had six children, two at least of whom died in infancy. He was possessed of a considerable freehold of lands in Cheshire, which he devised to his sons Randle and Harry, and personal estate to Thomas and daughters Maud, Margaret and Anne.

Randle Janney, the eldest son of Thomas and Jane (Worthington) Janney, was baptised February 23, 1579-80, and was buried October 30, 1613. He married, July 14, 1602, Ellen Abrodd, and lived and died at Stiall, Cheshire. They were the parents of four children: Thomas, baptised June 27, 1605, died 12 mo. 17, 1677, married September 3, 1625, Elizabeth Worthington, who died 12 mo. 19, 1681-2; Randle, baptised May 26, 1608, married July 16, 1636, Anne Knevet; Heine, baptised March 24, 1610, buried March 3, 1611; and Richard, baptised February 20, 1613, settled in Ardwick, Lancashire, where he died in 1691, wife Mary. Of these four children of Randle Janney, of Stiall, only the two eldest has special interest to the Janneys of America, as through the two sons of the former, Thomas and Henry, and William, son of the latter, are descended all the Janneys who today are scattered over the United States.

Thomas Janney, eldest son of Randle and Ellen (Alrodd) Janney, baptised June 27, 1605, was married September 3, 1625, to Elizabeth Worthington, and both joined the Society of Friends soon after it came into existence, and are frequently mentioned in the early annals of the Society, meetings being frequently held at their house at Stiall, and later at Mobberly, Cheshire. He suffered distress of goods, was imprisoned, and otherwise persecuted on account of his faith as related in Besse's sufferings. He and others purchased and presented to the Meeting the land for the burial ground and meeting house at Mobberly. He was evidently possessed of considerable property, and in his will made in 1677 left a legacy to the poor of the town. He died 12 mo. 17, 1677, and his widow Elizabeth on 12 mo. 19, 1681-2, and both are buried in the Friends' burying ground at Mobberly. His will is still preserved at Chester, and his name thereto is spelled Janney, though mentioned in the records as Janey. His will names the children mentioned below, his brother Richard, and William Janney of Handworth. The children of Thomas and Elizabeth (Worthington) Janney were:

1. Mary, baptised March 19, 1625-6, died 7 mo. 3, 1698, married 12 mo. 3, 1663-4, Robert Peirson, of Pownall Fee, Cheshire, and had a son Enoch, born 11 mo. 30, 1665, died 8 mo. 2, 1680-1. Thomas and Robert Pearson, who came to Pennsylvania in 1683 and 1682 respectively, were probably related to Robert.

2. Margaret, baptised March 16, 1627, died 11 mo. 11, 1673, is buried at Mobberly.

3. Martha, baptised June 6, 1630, died 2 mo. 4, 1702, married 12 mo. 12, 1672, Hugh Burges, of Pownall Fee, who died 3 mo. 23, 1713, aged seventy-four years. Both are buried at Mobberly. It was at their house, that her brother Thomas Janney, of Bucks county, Pennsylvania, died in 1696, while on a religious visit to England.

4. Randle, baptised December 16, 1632, died 3 mo. 17, 1674, buried at Mobberly.

5. Thomas, the ancestor of the Janneys of Bucks county, baptised January 11, 1634, died 12 mo. (Feb.) 2, 1696, and is buried at Mobberly; see forward.

6. Henry, baptised January 1, 1637, died at Eaton Norris, Lancashire, 6 mo. 3, 1690, and is buried at Mobberly. He married at the house of Thomas Potts, Pownal Fee, 1 mo. 3, 1674, Barbara Baguley, of Stockport, was a tailor and chapman or cloth dealer. His daughter Elizabeth, born 9 mo. 7, 1677, came to Philadelphia in 1698, and married in 1710 Pentecost Teague, a distinguished Friend of Philadelphia. Mary, born 11 mo. 1, 1680, and Tabitha, born 7 mo. 29, 1687, also came to Philadelphia, the former marrying in 1708 Joseph Drinker, and the latter in 1709 William Fisher. A son Thomas and daughter Martha died in infancy.

Before proceeding to give an account of Thomas Janney, the distinguished ancestor of the Janneys of Bucks county, it might be well to say a word or two in reference to William Janney, (son of Randle and Mary, and grandson of Randle and Ellen Alrodd Janney), whose two sons, Randle and Thomas, also came to Pennsylvania.

William Janney was baptised December 8, 1641, died 8 mo. 4, 1724, and is buried among his kinsman in the old burying ground at Mobberly. He married 7 mo. 30, 1671, Deborah Webb, and was then living at Handforth; after his wife's death he removed to Morley. He was a prominent member of the Society of Friends, and suffered persecution for his faith. Meetings were frequently held at his house. His son Randle, born 2 mo. 10, 1677, in 1699 obtained a certificate from the Meeting at Morley and emigrated to Philadelphia, where he became a prominent merchant, was a friend of Penn, and a large landowner in Pennsylvania and Cecil county, Maryland. He married at Philadelphia, in 9 mo., 1701, Frances Righton, daughter of William and Sarah Righton, of Philadelphia. Their only child died in infancy. In 1702 and 1706 he visited England, and in 1715 obtained a certificate to visit the Bermudas, but died before starting, 10 mo. 7, 1715. His will mentions his brother Thomas and his sister Mary, wife of George Pawley, who had also come to Philadelphia, and their children, Debora, Mary, Sarah and Thomas.

Thomas Janney, brother of Randle, was born in Cheshire, England, 3 mo. 18, 1679, and died in Cecil county, Maryland, about 1750. In 1702 his brother Randle obtained a certificate for him to Philadelphia, which, with the one brought from the Morley Meeting by Randle in 1699, is preserved among the records of Philadelphia Monthly Meeting. In 1706 he went to England with his brother, and after his return settled in West Nottingham township, Chester county, on land formerly owned by Randle, and later found to be in Cecil county, Maryland. His will was proven in Cecil county, March 22, 1751, and in it he mentions his wife Magdalen, son-in-law Robert Lashly, and children Jemima Janney, Debora Lashly, William, Thomas and Isaac Janney, who are the progenitors of the Janneys of Cecil county. Robert Lashly was Robert Leslie, who married Debora Janney, in 1740, and is the ancestor of Charles Robert Leslie, R. A., the noted author and artist, and his talented sisters. Deborah Pawlee, daughter of George and Mary (Janney) Pauley, married 9 mo. 21, 1727, Samuel Siddons, son of Thomas and Lowrey (Evans) Siddons, who have descendants in Bucks county. Sarah Pawley, another daughter of George and Mary, married 7 mo. 24, 1734, William Atkinson, Jr., of a Bucks county family.

THOMAS JANNEY, second son of Thomas and Elizabeth (Worthington) Janney, baptised at Stiall, Cheshire, England, January 11, 1634, "was convinced of the truth as held by Friends" at the first preaching thereof in Cheshire in 1654, and the next year took up the ministry in that sect and traveled extensively in England and Ireland. He married, 9 mo. 24, 1660, Margery Heath, of Horton, Staffordshire. The marriage took place at the house of James Harrison, in the township of Pownal Fee, in which Stiall the home of the Janneys was situated. Ann, the wife of James Harrison, was a sister of Margery, as was also Jane, the wife of William Yardley, both of whom came with their husbands to Pennsylvania and settled in Bucks county in 1682, as shown by an account of each family given in this volume. They lived at Stiall, where their four sons were born, until 1683, when they followed their brothers-in-law to Pennsylvania and settled on a tract of land in Makefield, Bucks county. Thomas Janney had purchased of William Penn, 6 mo. 12, 1682, 250 acres of land to be laid out in Pennsylvania, and it was laid out in Lower Makefield, fronting on the Delaware. He and his wife Margery, their four sons and two servants, John Nield and Hannah Falkner, arrived in the Delaware river in the Endeavor, 7 mo. (September) 29, 1683. He eventually purchased other lands in the vicinity; the tract fronting on the Delaware below the present borough of Yardley containing 550 acres was confirmed by patent in 1691, and another tract of 1000 acres lay back of the "River Lots" and extended into Newtown and Middletown townships, where the line between these townships joins the line of Lower Makefield. The latter tract was of irregular form and was well watered, Core creek running through it. A saw mill was erected on it soon after its occupation in 1683, and Jacob Janney erected a grist mill near the old family mansion in 1816, which was in use until a few years since, that portion of the plantation still being owned and occupied by descendants of the name. Thomas Janney was related by blood or marriage to many of the most prominent settlers of the county. William Yardley, for many years a justice of the county courts and a member of provincial assembly, and James Harrison, Penn's confidential agent in Pennsylvania, were, as before stated, his brothers-in-law, and Phineas Pemberton, called by Logan "the father of Bucks County," was therefore his nephew, and John Brock, another prominent official of the county, was his cousin. Thomas Janney was also an intimate friend of Penn, who entertained a high opinion of him and mentioned him lovingly in many of his letters. Thomas Janney continued his labors as a minister of the Society of Friends, but that did not preclude his engaging actively in civil affairs, and upon his arrival in America he at once took a prominent place in the affairs of the colony. He was elected to provincial council for a term of three years, and was qualified as a member 1 mo. 20, 1684, and was again elected and commissioned in 1691. He was also commissioned April 6, 1685, one of the justices of the courts of Bucks county, which commission was renewed January 2, 1689-90. He was one of the commission of twelve men appointed to divide the county into townships in 1690, and filled many other important official positions. In the ministry he visited Friends' meetings in New England, Rhode Island, Long Island, New Jersey, Pennsylvania and Maryland, and was an esteemed counsellor in all matters pertaining to the Society, as well as of the county and province. In the early part of 1695 he began to make preparations for a visit to Friends in England, executing a power of attorney to his eldest son, Jacob Janney, to transact business for him in his absence, and making his will, which is dated 3 mo. 21, 1695. This will was doubtless proved and recorded in the county of Bucks, but the records of the county (with the exception of deeds) from 1693 to 1713 are entirely lost, and it is only through a copy found among the papers of Samuel M. Janney, the Quaker historian, that we learn what its provisions were. He was accompanied on his visit to England by Griffith Owen, and they started by way of Maryland 3 mo. 31, 1695. Landing in London, they traveled through England and Wales, visiting many meetings. Janney was taken sick in the spring of 1696, while in Derbyshire, but, partially recovering, attended the Quarterly Meeting in London, and then started to pay a visit to his relatives in Cheshire, and, though detained in Hertfordshire by a severe attack, eventually reached Cheshire, and so far recovered as to visit meetings there and in Lancashire, and made preparations to return to Pennsylvania in 11 mo., 1696, but, being taken seriously ill, returned to the home of his sister, Mary Burgess, where he was born, and died there the 12th of the 12th mo., (February) 1696-7, at the age of sixty-three years, having been a minister for forty-two years. His wife Margery survived him and died somewhere between 1697 and 1700. Their children were six in number—four sons: Jacob, Thomas, Abel, and Joseph, who accompanied their parents to America; and two daughters, Martha and Elizabeth, who died in England.

1. Jacob Janney, born at Pownall Fee, Cheshire, 3 mo. 18, 1662, buried in Bucks county, 8 mo. 6, 1708, married at Falls Meeting, Bucks county, 10 mo. 26, 1705, Mary Hough, born in Bucks county, 7 mo, 6, 1684, daughter of John and Hannah Hough, of Newtown. After her husband's death she married, 3 mo. 2, 1710, John Fisher, by whom she had one child, Mary, who married in 1740 John Butler. The only child of Jacob and Mary (Hough) Janney was Thomas, born 12 mo. 27, 1707-8, died 4 mo. 8, 1788.

2. Martha Janney, born at Cheadle, Cheshire, 5 mo. 17, 1665, died there 12 mo. 4, 1665-6.

3. Elizabeth, born at Pownall Fee, 11 mo. 15, 1666-7, died 11 mo. 17, 1666-7.

4. Thomas Janney, born at Pownall Fee, Cheshire, 12 mo. 5, 1667-8, died in Bucks county. He married 9 mo. 3, 1697, Falls Meeting records, Rachel Pownall, born in Cheshire, England, daughter of George and Eleanor Pownall, of Bucks county. They had four children; Henry, born 4 mo. 20, 1699; Sarah, born 8 mo. 26, 1700, married 1722, Thomas Pugh; Mary, married 1725, Thomas Routledge; Abel, born in Bucks county, died there 1748, married June 5, 1740, Elizabeth Biles.

5. Abel Janney, born at Mobberly, Cheshire, 10 mo. 29, 1671, married in New Jersey, 1700, Elizabeth Stacy, born at Dorehouse, Yorkshire, 8 mo. 17, 1673, daughter of Mahlon and Rebecca (Ely) Stacy, of Trenton, New Jersey. They had seven children; Amos, born 11 mo. 15, 1701-2, died in Fairfax county, Virginia, 1747, married, 1727-8, at Falls, Mary Yardley, daughter of Thomas and Ann (Biles) Yardley; Rebeckah, born 9 mo. 9, 1702, died at Wilmington, Delaware, married Joseph Poole, of Bucks county, born in Cumberland, England, 1704, died in Bucks county, Pennsylvania, 1767; Mahlon, born in Bucks county, 2 mo. 18, 1706; Thomas, married 1735, Hannah Biles, daughter of William and Sarah (Langhorne) Biles; Jacob, born 4 mo. 10, 1710, died in Delaware 11 mo. 14, 1782, married Elizabeth Levis, at Kennett, Chester county, was a prominent minister; Abel, removed to Virginia, 1742; Elizabeth, married 10 mo. 22, 1737, John Stackhouse, and (second) David Wilson, both of Bucks county. Abel Janney, the father of the above named children, was a justice of the peace 1708-10, and a member of assembly 1710-21.

6. Joseph Janney, born at Pownall Fee, Cheshire, 1 mo. 26, 1675-6, died in Bucks county, about 1729, married at Falls Meeting, 6 mo. 18, 1703, Rebeckah Biles, born in Bucks county, 10 mo. 27, 1680, daughter of William and Joanna Biles, and had six children: Martha, married Nicholas Parker and settled in New Jersey; Ann, died young; Abel, married at Falls, 8 mo. 2, 1733, Sarah Baker, and removed to Virginia; William, married at Falls, Elizabeth Moon, born 10 mo. 16, 1719, daughter of Roger and Ann (Nutt) Moon, and removed to Virginia; Jacob, married at Falls, 1725, Hannah Ingledew, and removed to Virginia; Mary, married at Falls, 1720, John Hough, of Bucks county and removed to Virginia; they are the ancestors of Emerson Hough, of Chicago, the novelist and historical writer, editor of "Forest and Stream."

Thomas Janney, born 12 mo. 27, 1797-8,

only son of Jacob and Mary (Hough) Janney, is the ancestor of the Janneys at present resident within the county of Bucks. He married at Wrightstown Meeting, Bucks county, 10 mo. 28, 1732, Martha Mitchell, daughter of Henry and Sarah (Gove) Mitchell; the former a son of Henry· and Elizabeth (Foulds) Mitchell, was born at Marsden Lane, Lancashire, and the latter was a daughter of Richard Gove of Philadelphia. By the will of Thomas Janney, the pioneer and provincial councillor, he devised to his son "Jacob the house and plantation which we do live in and upon, with all the lands and appurtenances thereunto belonging," and, Jacob dying in 1708, it descended to his infant son and only child Thomas Janney, and has continued to be the home of his descendants to the present day. On a visit to the old homestead in May, 1905, the writer of these lines was shown the old family Bible nearly a century old, in which was inscribed, in the quaint handwriting of long ago, the dates of the birth of the children of Thomas and Martha (Mitchell) Janney. Martha, the mother, died 9 mo. 19, 1785, and Thomas, the father, 4 mo. 8, 1788. Their children were: Jacob, born 8 mo. 15, 1733, died 3· mo. 26, 1761, without issue; Thomas, born 2 mo. 17, 1736, died 11 mo. 16, 1754; Richard, born 8 mo. 22, 1738, died 9 mo. 5, 1766, see forward; Mary, born 1 mo. 18, 1741, died 2 mo. 24, 1795, married 3 mo. 19, 1788, William Linton, no issue; Sarah, born 10 mo. 19, 1743, married 11 mo. 11, 1762, Daniel Richardson, and had one son, Daniel; Alice, born 10 mo. 4, 1747, married John Dawes, and settled in New Jersey; Martha, born 9 mo. 11, 1750, married Isaac Warner. None of these sons survived their father, and the homestead was devised by his will to his grandson Jacob Janney, the only grandson of the name.

Richard Janney, third son of Thomas and Martha (Mitchell) Janney, born 8 mo. 22, 1738, married, in 1764, Sarah Worth, daughter of Joseph Worth, of Stony Brook, Burlington county, New Jersey. She was born in 1741, and died in Wrightstown township, Bucks county, August 20, 1833, at the age of ninety-two years, having been a widow for forty years, though three times married. Richard Janney died 9 mo. 5, 1766, leaving an only child, Jacob· Janney, born 4 mo. 10, 1765. His widow married Stephen Twining in 1773, and had two children; Mary born September 16, 1774, died March 8. 1815, married Joseph Burson; and Stephen Twining, born 1776, died 1849. Her second husband dying in 1777, Sarah married (third) 2 mo. 6, 1782, James Burson.

Of the youth of Jacob Janney, only child of Richard and Sarah (Worth) Janney, little is known. Tradition relates

that he lived for a time in New Jersey. If this were true, it was probably with his maternal grandparents. As his mother's last two husbands both resided in Wrightstown, it is probable that he was reared there or on the old homestead in Newtown, with his grandparents, Thomas and Martha Janney. Certain it is that that was his residence at the time of his grandfather's death in 1788, when he is devised the plantation and made executor of the will of his grandfather. He married, 11 mo. 16, 1792, Frances Briggs, born 10 mo. 19, 1773, died 8 mo. 21, 1851, daughter of John and Letitia Briggs, and continued to reside on the old homestead until his death, 2 mo. 19, 1820. The children of Jacob and Frances (Briggs) Janney, all born on the old homestead at Newtown, are as follows:

1. Thomas, born 8 mo. 9, 1794, died in Newtown borough, 3 mo., 1879, married 10 mo. 11, 1838, Mary ·Kimber, daughter of Emmor and Susanna, born 2 mo. 10, 1807, and had two children: Anna, married a Bergner, and is still living in Newtown; and Emmor Janney, of Philadelphia. Thomas lived on the old homestead until 1842, when he rented it to his youngest brother, Stephen T. Janney, and removed to Newtown. He was a large landowner in Newtown and Makefield.

2. Richard, born 3 mo. 13, 1796, died in Lower Makefield, 8 mo., 1877, married (first) Ann Taylor, and (second) Achsah Yardley, and lived and died in Lower Makefield. He had seven children: Mercy Ann, married Heston Lovett, of Lower Makefield, and is deceased; Taylor, died unmarried; Susan, married (first) Lovett Brown, of Falls, and (second) Oliver Paxson, of New Hope, where she still resides; Franklin, lives in Philadelphia; Jacob, married Matilda Ely, of Lambertville, and is living in Philadelphia; Frances, married Jonathan Schofield, of Lower Makefield, and is deceased; and Mary, married William Linton, of Newtown, and is deceased.

3. Jacob, born 4 mo. 24, 1798, married Esther Betts, daughter of Stephena and Hannah (Blackfan) Betts of Solebury, and removed to Cecil county, Maryland, and after several years residence there returned to Bucks county, and later removed with his family to Michigan, where he died 12 mo., 1869. They had seven children: Hannah, married Amasa Atkinson; James Worth, married Loisa· Beitzel; Edward B., died single in Michigan; Frances, married John Sumner, and is recently deceased; Elwood, married Almeda Allen; Robert Simpson, married Urania Baldwin; Dr. Joshua Janney, of Moorestown, New Jersey, who married Amanda Eastburn, of Solesbury.

4. John L., born 5 mo, 31, 1800, died on his portion of the homestead. 4 mo.

12, 1872. He married Mary Jenks, daughter of Thomas and Thomazine (Trimble) Jenks, of Middletown. (See Jenks Family). By the will of Jacob Janney the homestead was devised to his sons Thomas and John L., and they in 1829 made partition of it and a tract purchased by them adjoining, the new purchase and a small part of the homestead on the east going to John L., where he lived and died, and where his son Thomas and daughters Elizabeth and Thomazine still reside. The children of John L. and Mary (Jenks) Janney were: Charles, married first Anna Yardley, and second her sister, Julia Yardley, was a merchant at Dolington for many years, and died on a farm in Solebury in 1902; Thomas J., who was prothonotary of Bucks county, 1895-7, and is now cashier and accountant in the office of the Newtown, Bristol and Doylestown Electric Railway Company at Newtown; John L., Jr., married Matilda Wynkoop, and resides in Newtown borough, though still conducting the old homestead farm; and Elizabeth and Thomazine, before mentioned.

5. Martha, born 10 mo. 14, 1801, died 12 mo. 6, 1876, married Robert Simpson, of Upper Makefield, and had five children: Jacob, of Buckingham, deceased, married Elizabeth Johnson; William, of Upper Makefield, deceased, married Julia Johnson; Elizabeth, wife of Benjamin Smith, many years principal of Doylestown English and Classical Seminary, now of Plymouth Friends' School; Martha, wife of Albert Hibbs, of Kansas; and James, who married an Eisinbrey, of Solebury, and died in Kansas.

6. Benjamin, born 1 mo. 17, 1804, died 1 mo. 8, 1806.

7. Mary, born 6 mo. 8, 1805, died 7 mo. 31, 1807.

8. Sarah, born 10 mo. 21, 1806, died 10 mo. 10, 1851; married Joshua Dungan, no issue.

9. Letitia, born 9 mo. 25, 1808, died 1 mo, 22, 1813.

10. William, born 3 mo. 31, 1810, died 3 mo. 7, 1891, married 12 mo. 15, 1830, Rebecca Smith, daughter of William and Sarah (Moore) Smith, of Solebury, where she was born in 1810. He was a farmer in Lower Makefield for several years, and later lived retired in Newtown borough, where his widow and two daughters still reside. They were the parents of nine children: Richard H., residing on the old Smith homestead in Solebury, married Mary Hibbs, of Pineville, and had three children: Dr. William Smith Janney, of Philadelphia, see forward; Sarah Smith, living with her mother in Newtown; Stephen Moore, of Newtown, married Elizabeth Nickelson, of Yardley; Oliver, of Wrightstown, married Hannah Willard, of Newtown; George, of Solebury, married Elizabeth

Ellis, of Langhorne; Martha, wife of Harrison C. Worstall, a hardware merchant of Newtown; Rebecca Frances, died in infancy; and Mary Ella, living with her mother in Newtown.

11. Joseph, born 9 mo. 19, 1812, died 10 mo. 19, 1887, married 11 mo. 21, 1833, Mary Ann Taylor, daughter of David B. and Elizabeth, of Lower Makefield, lived and died in Philadelphia. They had children: Barton Taylor, of Emilie; Benjamin, Samuel and Joseph, of Philadelphia; Frances, wife of Joseph Lovett, of Emilie; Elizabeth, died in Philadelphia; and Emma, wife of Charles Walton, of Langhorne.

12. Mahlon, born 12 mo. 15, 1815, married Charlotte Brown, and removed to the west where he died.

13. STEPHEN T. JANNEY, youngest child of Jacob and Frances (Briggs) Janney, was born 11 mo. 15, 1817, and died 11 mo. 12, 1898, on the homestead where he was born and always resided. He was but three years of age at the death of his father, and remained with his mother on the homestead, and was educated at an academy in Wilmington, Delaware. On his marriage in 1842, he rented the homestead of his brother Thomas, and purchased it in 1855, and continued to conduct it until his death. He married Harriet P. Johnson, born in Buckingham, 10 mo. 20, 1820, died 1891, daughter of William H. and Mary (Paxson) Johnson, and granddaughter of Samuel and Martha (Hutchinson) Johnson, all of Buckingham. (See ancestry of Hon. E. M. Paxson, where an account of the distinguished ancestry of Mrs. Janney, maternal and paternal is given). The children of Stephen T. and Harriet P. (Johnson) Janney, were: Calvin D., born January 12, 1843, residing on the homestead, married March 8, 1892, Frederica, daughter of Frederick and Anna M. Linton, of Newtown, who died at the birth of their only child. Frederick, December, 1892; Horace, born September 1, 1846, farmer and nurseryman at Newtown; William H., born October 1, 1849, a farmer in Lower Makefield, married February 3, 1873, Anna M. Torbert, daughter of James L. and Maria (Van Artsdalen) Torbert, of Lower Makefield, and had two children: Elizabeth, wife of Erwin J. Doan, of Philadelphia, who has three children—Frances J., Anna Jean and Harriet J.; and Harriet, wife of LeRoy Suber, of Newtown. Mrs. Anna M. Janney died 3 mo. 11, 1893, and William H. married (second) June 8, 1905, Ella J. Burroughs, daughter of Robert and Phebe (Beans) Burroughs of Newtown. Marietta Janney, third child of Stephen and Harriet, is still single, and resides with her brother Calvin on the homestead. Frances J. Janney, the youngest daughter, married, September

26, 1877, Wilmer A. Briggs, son of Theodore S. and Sarah B. (Leedom) Briggs, of Upper Makefield, and they reside at Glen Ridge, New Jersey.

DR. WILLIAM SMITH JANNEY, of 1535 North Broad street, Philadelphia, Pennsylvania(second son of William and Rebecca (Smith) Janney, was born in Lower Makefield township, Bucks county, Pennsylvania, August 12, 1833. He acquired his elementary education at the public schools, Newtown Academy, Bellevue Academy at Langhorne, and finished as a private pupil of Joseph Fell, of Buckingham. At the age of seventeen years he taught school at Brownsburg, Upper Makefield township, and later at Lumberville, in Solebury, at the same time taking up the study of medicine. He attended lectures at the Pennsylvania Medical College at Philadelphia in the winters of 1852 and 1853, and graduated in March, 1854. He practiced medicine at Tullytown, Bucks county, for two years, and in April, 1856, removed to Leavenworth, Kansas, just in time to become involved in the noted "Border War." Returning to Bucks county in the fall of the same year, he located at Woodsville, Mercer county, New Jersey, where he remained until 1870. In the meantime, however, (in 1862 he enlisted in the army as assistant surgeon of the Twenty-first New Jersey Volunteers, and was promoted to surgeon of the Twenty-second Regiment. His regiment during its ten months service took part in the battles of Chancellorsville and Fredericksburg, and the doctor had ample opportunity for the use of his skill as a surgeon. Returning to Woodsville, New Jersey he resumed his practice, which continued until 1870, when he removed to a plantation in Caroline county, Virginia, where he remained until 1874. when he resumed the practice of his profession at Eighth and Oxford streets, Philadelphia, removing in 1877 to his present location, where he has since practiced. In 1880 he was elected coroner of Philadelphia by 20,000 majority. He was for sixteen years surgeon of the Philadelphia Hospital, and for the last fourteen years has had charge of the hospital of Girard College, and stands deservedly high in his profession. He is a member of Post No. 2, G. A. R., and of the Loyal Legion, and in politics is a Republican. He married, in November, 1855, Sarah Ellen Beans, born April, 1835, daughter of Benjamin and Mary Beans, of Lower Makefield, Bucks county, Pennsylvania. They have been, the parents of four children, two of whom, a son and daughter, died in infancy; those who survive are: Marianna, born November 2, 1873; and William, born February 18, 1876, a graduate of the University of Pennsylvania, both residing with their father.

THE JAMES FAMILY. The James family of Bucks county is of Welsh origin, being descended from John James and Elizabeth, his wife, who with sons Thomas, William, Josiah, and Isaac, and daughters Sarah, Rebecca and Mary, migrated in the year 1711 from the parish of Riddillyn, Pembrokeshire, South Wales, and settled in Montgomery township, Philadelphia, (now Montgomery) county. They were Welsh Baptists, and the vanguard of the little colony of that denomination who eight years later organized themselves into a church known as the Montgomery Baptist church, of which the James family were members for many years. New Britain and Hilltown Baptist churches were offshoots of this ancient church. The James family contributed largely to the moral and financial support of the New Britain church for many generations.

Whether the family settled originally in Montgomery or in New Britain is problematical. According to Rev. Morgan Edwards, the great Baptist historian, the Rev. Abel Morgan, pastor of Pennypack church, preached to the little colony at Montgomery prior to the organization of the church, at the house of John Evans, who arrived from Pembrokeshire a year prior to the arrival of the James family, and the James family formed part of the assembly. At that period all the land on the Bucks county side of the line belonged to other than actual settlers, in large tracts, and it is more than probable that the James family were tenants on some of this land. In 1720 John James and his eldest son Thomas purchased one thousand acres in New Britain township, Bucks county, including a portion of the present borough of Chalfont, and extending eastward at least two miles, and north westerly at its western end nearly as far, being in the shape of the letter L. Between that date and 1726, when they made a division of the land between them, they conveyed nearly one half of this tract to the other three brothers, William, Josiah and Isaac, and William and Thomas had purchased other tracts adjoining on the northeast until the family owned nearly if not quite 2,000 acres, extending from Chalfont far into what is now Doylestown township, and up across Pine Run and North Branch to the old highway leading through New Galena. Two of the brothers, Josiah and Isaac, do not seem to have left descendants in Bucks county, though both owned portions of the original 1,000 acre purchase. Josiah married, May 21, 1724, Elizabeth, daughter of Thomas Perry of Great Valley Baptist church, Chester county, and a year later she was received as a member of Montgomery church, but June 16, 1727, they received a dismissal to Great Valley and probably settled in Chester county. Isaac James was a blacksmith, and resided in Montgomery township. He married, November 26, 1729, Ann Jones. We have no further record of him other than his conveyance of his New Britain land about 1742. Josiah had received 235 acres of the 1,000 acre purchase in 1722, and conveyed it to his brother in 1725. Of the daughters of John and Elizabeth James, Sarah, the eldest, as shown by the records of Montgomery church, married Benjamin Phillips, March 2, 1727, but in the will of her father twenty years later she is mentioned as Sarah Lewis. Rebecca, we learn from the same source, was married to a miner. Mary was single at her father's death in 1749, and was requested to live with her brother Thomas. Elizabeth James died prior to her husband.

Thomas James, eldest son of John and Elizabeth, was born in Wales about 1690, and died in New Britain in April, 1772. As previously stated, he was one of the original purchasers of the 1,000 acres of which he retained possibly 300 acres, and in 1731, purchased over 200 acres of the society lands of Joseph Kirkbride, most of which, however, he conveyed to his sons several years prior to his death. He married, May 15, 1722, Jane Davis, and she was baptized as a member of Montgomery church, November 19, 1725. They had four sons and two daughters, Thomas, the eldest, lived and died on a portion of the old plantation in New Britain, but is said to have left no issue to survive him. Elizabeth, the eldest daughter, married Benjamin Butler about 1746, and had one daughter, Ann, who married (first) Thomas Morris, and (second) Moses Aaron. Benjamin Butler died about 1750. James James, second son of Thomas and Jane, married Elizabeth Eaton in 1762. His father had conveyed to him in 1755, 167 acres, part of which is now the property of the estate of Eugene James, deceased, one-half mile west of New Britain, and here he lived until the close of the Revolution, when he exchanged with Peter Eaton for land in Rowan county, North Carolina, and removed thither taking with him three of the children of his brother John.

John James, third son of Thomas and Jane, received by deed from his father in 1761 a farm of two hundred acres, and lived thereon his entire life. He was a member of the New Britian Company of Associators in 1775, and a private in Captain Henry Darrah's company, when in service under Lieutenant Colonel (later General) John Lacey, November 1, 1777. He died in March, 1779. John James was twice married, first on August 13, 1762, to Magdalena Keshlen, (or Keshler) a German woman, by whom he had two children; Margaret, born 1763,

died March 3, 1821, married Morgan James, son of John, and grandson of William James; and Benjamin James, born 1765, removed to Bryant's Settlement, Rowan county, North Carolina, with his uncle James James about 1785. John James married (second) June 14, 1766, Edith Eaton, a sister to his brother James' wife, and had by her two children Catharine and James. In his will dated February 10, 1779, proved March 10, 1779, he directs that Catharine's share of his estate be left in the hands of her "Aunt Elizabeth James;" this was the wife of James James, with whom all three of the younger children removed to North Carolina. James, the youngest son, was devised 200 acres of land in Chestnut Hill township, Northampton county.

Samuel James, youngest son of Thomas and Jane, received from his father a farm of about 150 acres just northeast of Chalfont, and died there in 1804. He married, April 8, 1765, Anna Keshlen, a sister to his brother John's first wife, and had five children; 1. Samuel, who married Elizabeth Shewell, and removed to Maryland, where he died in 1847; 2. Levi, who married Rebecca Polk and was the father of Samuel P. and grandfather of Levi L. James, late a member of the bar, and father of Robert James, deceased, whose son Louis H. was also a lawyer, and Lydia, who married John G. Mann; 3. Elizabeth, married Isaac Oakford; 4. Margaret, married John Wolfe; and 5. Ann James. Levi married late in life Mary Polk, nee Good, who survived him many years.

William James, son of the emigrant John James and Elizabeth his wife, from whom most of the family now residing in Bucks county are descended, was born in Pembrokeshire about 1692, and died in New Britain township, Bucks county, in 1778. He seems to have been the favorite son, and was the largest land-owner of the family. In the year 1725 his father and brother Thomas conveyed to him 206 acres of the 1,000 acre purchase, and in the same year he purchased of his brother Josiah his allotment of 235 acres of the same. In 1738 he purchased of John Kirkbride 207 acres of the society lands, part of which is still the property of his descendants. He also owned other tracts of land near Chalfont, which became the property of his sons-in-law. He conveyed practically all of his land to his children in his life time—in 1749 to John the 206 acres, and to Isaac the 207 acres; and in 1758 to Abel the 235 acres. William James married in 1718. The name of his wife was Mary, but nothing more is known of her. She was baptized at Montgomery church in 1719 as "Mary, wife of William James." She died about 1765 William and Mary James had five children;

John; Isaac; Margaret, who married Henry Lewis; Abel; and Rebecca, who married Simon Butler, Jr.

John James, eldest son of William and Mary, born 1719, died 1785, was a carpenter and joiner by trade, but, since he retained possession of his farm and resided thereon his whole life, it is to be supposed his principal occupation was the tilling of the soil. He married, May 20, 1740, Elizabeth, daughter of Lewis Evans, and was the father of ten children, nine of whom grew to maturity, viz: 1. Josiah, born 1741, died December 11, 1816, married Elizabeth Evans. 2. William, born 1742, died May 10, 1828, married January 25, 1769, Rebecca Williams. 3. Isaac, born 1744, married Jemima Mason, and removed to the state of Ohio. 4. Ebenezar, born 1746, died 1815, had no children. 5. Simon, born 1748, died 1814, married Elizabeth Hines. 6. Morgan, born April 27, 1752, died April 18, 1816, married Margaret James, daughter of John, as before stated. 7. Elizabeth, married John Callender. 8. Mary, married Nathan Evans. 9. Alice married Thomas Mathias. Of the above Josiah and Elizabeth were the great-grandparents of Robert E. James, Esq., of Easton, Pennsylvania, and the children of William and Rebecca all removed to the west. The only one who left descendants in Bucks of the name was Morgan, and Margaret.

Morgan James, sixth son of John and Elizabeth James, was born on the old plantation in New Britain, April 27, 1752. At the breaking out of the Revolution he, with his brothers Josiah, William, Isaac, became members of the Associated Company of New Britain militia. Morgan was later a private in Captain Henry Darrah's company, and was in active service under General John Lacey. His brothers, Isaac, Ebenezer, Simon and William, were also in this company. Morgan James married, as before stated, Margaret James, daughter of John and Magdalene. Their children were: 1. Lydia, who married Mathew Thomas. 2. Benjamin, born November 28, 1786, died May 24, 1865, married Elizabeth, daughter of Moses Aaron, and widow of James Poole, left no issue. 3. Naomi, born February 26, 1793, died November 4, 1871, married Jacob Conrad. 4. Isaiah, born August 27, 1798, died September 23, 1886, married Caroline James, daughter of Abel James.

Isaac James, second son of William and Mary James, born in New Britain about 1726, received from his father in 1749 a deed for over 200 acres of land upon which he lived his entire life. He was constable of New Britain township for many years. He died very suddenly in 1766, aged about fifty years. His wife, whom he married in 1751, was Sarah Thomas, daughter of John Thomas, who came to New Britain from Wales in

1726 and died there in 1750. The children of Isaac and Sarah (Thomas) James were: 1. Abiah, born 1745, died December 1, 1834, married September 22, 1773, Rachel Williams. 2. John, born 1747, a soldier in the Revolution, married Dorothy Jones. 3. Abel, born 1749, died 1798, married Elizabeth Hines. 4. Nathan, born 1754, died 1845, married Sarah Dungan. 5. Samuel, born 1760, died 1848, married Elizabeth Cornell and removed to North Carolina in 1785. 6. Uslega, born 1762, died 1844, married Joseph Morris. 7. William, born 1764, died 1854, removed to Reading, Berks county, Pennsylvania. 8. Benjamin, born 1766, died 1854, married Ann Williams. Tracy, died young. Of these, Abiah, Abel, Nathan, and Benjamin have descendants residing in Doylestown, and will be noticed later in this sketch.

Abel, the youngest son of William and, Mary James, born about 1729, died September, 1770, at Dover, Delaware, was in some respects the most prominent of the family in his generation. He received a liberal education and was possessed of ample means and early evinced a taste for mercantile pursuits. He married Mary, daughter of Thomas Howell, of Warwick, in 1756, and entered into business in Philadelphia and Dover, Delaware, and was for several years very successful. An unfortunate speculation ruined him. and the worry and strain of his financial difficulties brought on a fever from which he died while at Dover. His plantation of 235 acres in New Britain had been heavily mortgaged to tide him over a financial speculation and was sold. He left five sons and four daughters, viz: 1. Daniel, the eldest son, was a clerk for his father at Dover at the time of the failure; after his father's death he secured a position as clerk at Durham Iron Works, then operated by Joseph Galloway. At the closing of the furnace in 1776 he returned to Delaware and joined Proctor's Delaware regiment as a lieutenant, was promoted to captain, and served throughout the war. 2. William, the second son, was also a soldier in the Revolution, first enlisting in Captain Edward Jones' company recruited in Hilltown, and later serving in Captain John Spear's company in the Eleventh Pennsylvania Regiment. 3. Margaret, married William Kerr, of Warwick. 4. John James was a noted millwright, and lived and died in Lower Dublin township, Philadelphia county. 5. Mary, married Abel Thomas of Hilltown; they removed first to Harford county, Maryland, and later to Rockbridge county, Virginia. 6. Martha, married Asa Thomas, brother of Abel.*

Abel H., youngest child of Abel and Mary (Howell) James, was born Jan-

---

*Catharine, another daughter, married Mr. Hilt, an iron master, having iron works in the extreme western end of Virginia.

uary 1, 1771, a few months after his father's death. When quite a youth he went with his brother-in-law, Abel Thomas, to Maryland, and a few years later to Virginia, near the Natural Bridge, where he engaged in the transportation of produce down the James river. The boats were built at Lexington, and on reaching tidewater were sold as well as the cargo, and a new one built for the next trip. He returned to Bucks county in 1803 to marry Catharine Owen, daughter of Griffith Owen, Esq., of Hilltown, intending to return with her to Virginia. He was, however, persuaded to remain in Bucks county, and in 1804 he opened a' store at what is now Hagersville, on the Bethlehem road, above Dublin, which he conducted a few years when he opened a store at Lewis' Tavern, in Hilltown. A few years later he purchased the store property at Leidytown and remained there one year, when he purchased the tavern and store known as Lewis', at what is now Hilltown postoffice and remained there until his death, June 11, 1838. His wife died August 12, 1810, and he married (second) Gainor Mathias, a widow. His children were: Caroline, born September 2, 1804, died September 5, 1888, married Colonel Isaiah James, before mentioned; Mary, born March 6, 1806, died young. Owen, born 1807, died young. John Owen James, the great Philadelphia merchant, born March 8, 1809, died June 26. 1883. Catharine Owen, who married Abel H. James, was born in Hilltown township, Bucks county, June 17, 1781. She was the eldest daughter of Griffith Owen, Esq., and his wife Jane Hughes.

Griffith Owen, the grandfather of the Griffith mentioned above, was a native of Wales and came to America in 1721, settling in Hilltown. He was received into Montgomery Baptist church, and on June 30, 1731, married Margaret, daughter of Thomas Morgan, who it is said accompanied him from Wales to Bucks county. Griffith Owen, Sr., was one of the most prominent men of Hilltown. He was captain of the Hilltown company of Associators in 1747-8, raised for the defence of the frontiers and was a member of colonial assembly from 1749 to 1760. He died October 18, 1764. He had three sons, Owen, Ebenezer and Levi; and one daughter, Rachel Erwin. His eldest son, Owen Owen, married Catharine Jones about 1756, and had eight children; Abel, Elizabeth, Griffith, Edward, Owen, Margaret, Sarah and Mary. Griffith, the second son, was born February 9, 1758. He was one of the trustees of Hilltown Baptist church, and a very prominent man in the community. He was commissioned a justice of the peace in 1801, and served in that office until prevented by the infirmities of age from discharging its duties. He died Feb-

ruary 5, 1840. His wife, Jane, was the daughter of Christopher Hughes, of Bedminster and was born September 1, 1759, died January 9, 1841.

Isaiah James was a very prominent man in local and county affairs, a member of New Britain Church, he always took an active part in all its affairs and was a consistent member thereof. After his marriage he lived for a number of years in Hilltown township. In 1849 he purchased the New Britain farm, now owned by the estate of his son, Eugene, and made his home thereon for several years, conveying it to Eugene in 1870. Like all the family he was an ardent Democrat in politics and always took an active part in his party's councils. He was a member of the Assembly, 1834-1838, and Prothonotary of Bucks county 1848-1851. The children of Isaiah and Caroline James were Abel H., born April 16, 1825, died September 20, 1850. He was a man of more than ordinary culture and fine ability. He served as Deputy Prothonotary during his father's incumbency of that office up to the time of his death. Isabella, born August 9, 1828, married Dr. Thomas P. Kephard; she is now residing in Doylestown with her daughter Florence. Eugene, born March 31, 1831, died August 22, 1896, married Martha J., daughter of Abiah J. and Miranda (James) Riale. Isaiah James, the father, was for many years a Colonel of militia, and was almost universally known as Col. James.

Abiah James, eldest son of Isaac and Sarah (Thomas) James, born in 1745, died December 1, 1834. He accepted the 222 acre farm of his father, under proceedings in partition in 1789, but soon after conveyed a portion thereof to his brothers. He married September 22, 1773, Rachel Williams, and had six children, viz: 1. Margaret, married Joshua Riale and had, Abiah J., who married Miranda, daughter of Joseph and Martha (Mann) James; Rachel who married Joseph Evana; Elizabeth, who married Josiah Lunn, Ann, and Sarah who married David Stephens. 2. Col. Nathan James, a soldier in the U. S. army who served through the war of 1812. 3. Elizabeth who married William Hines, and had children, Nathan, Dr. A. J., deceased, late of Doylestown, Elizabeth and Emily. 4. Abiah, married Pamela Jones. 5. Martha, died unmarried, and Benjamin W., who married Elizabeth Black, daughter of Elias and Cynthia (James) Black.

Abel James, second son of Isaac and Sarah (Thomas) James, born 1749, died 1798, married Elizabeth Barton, and had four children, Barton, who removed to Baltimore, Maryland. James, who removed to Ohio. John, who died unmarried and Cynthia, who married Elias Black, the latter being the parents of Elizabeth, who married Benjamin W. James. Benjamin W. and Elizabeth had one son, Abiah R., who married Josephine Leavitt and is now living in Doylestown township. A sketch of their only son Wynne James, Esq., will follow. Nathan James, third son of Isaac and Sarah (Thomas) James, born 1754, died 1845, married Sarah Dungan, and had four children, 1. John D., for many years Court Crier, married Sarah Cline, and had Elizabeth who married Asher Cox, Nathan C., a life long member of the Bucks County bar, Sarah, who married Jacob Shade, and Henrietta. 2. Ann, or Nancy, married Jesse Callender. 3. Joseph, married, Martha Mann, and had Miranda, who married Abiah J. Riale, Wilhelmina, Charles, Joseph, Louisa, and Susan. 4. Simon, married Mary Meredith.

Benjamin youngest son of Isaac and Sarah (Thomas) James, born 1766, died 1854, was a farmer and resided in New Britain township. He married Ann or Nancy Williams, daughter of Benjamin Williams. She died in 1838. Their children were: 1. Uslega, married Edward Roberts; 2. Isaac W., married Ann Meredith; 3. Abiah, married Charlotte Aaron; 4. Thomas C. never married; 5. Elizabeth M., died unmarried; 6. Sarah Maria, married (first) Hervey Mathias, (second) John G. Mann; 7. Abel, died unmarried; 8. Silas H. died unmarried; 9. Oliver P., M. D., and two daughters who died young.

HOWARD I. JAMES, Esq., of Bristol, Bucks county, Pennsylvania, senior member of the firm of Gilkeson & James, is the second son of Eugene and Martha A. (Riale) James, of Doylestown township, whose ancestry is given on other pages of this work, and was born on his father's farm in Doylestown township. He was educated at the public schools and Doylestown Seminary, and read law with his brother, Henry A. James, Esq., and was admitted to the Bucks county bar May 9, 1892. He opened an office at Bristol, Bucks county, and began the practice of his profession, forming a partnership with his brother Henry A., who had an office at Doylestown. In 1898 he formed a co-partnership with Hon. B. F. Gilkeson, of Bristol, under the firm name of Gilkeson & James. This firm was for many years the leading one at the local bar, and did an immense amount of legal business, the routine work of which devolved largely upon Mr. James. At the death of Mr. Gilkeson, in 1904, Mr. James continued the business for the family, and on the admission of B. F. Gilkeson, Jr., to the bar about a year later, he became a member of the firm, the old firm name of Gilkeson & James being continued. Mr. James has been a successful practitioner, and is one of the leaders among the younger members of the bar, and highly respected by his fellow attorneys.

WYNNE JAMES, lawyer and real estate agent, Doylestown, was born November 2, 1865, in Doylestown township, on a part of the plantation that had been in the tenure of his direct ancestors for over a century, and where his father, grandfather and great-grandfather were born. He comes of the good old James stock. His great-great-grandfather Abel James, through his maternal grandmother, was second lieutenant of Captain William Pugh's company, Fourth Battalion of Pennsylvania militia, and saw active service in 1777 under Lieutenant Colonel William Roberts. Several other members of the family were also in the service, among them John James and Isaac James, who served under Captain Henry Darrah, in the battalion of Lieutenant Colonel (afterward General) John Lacey, the former being a brother to Abiah James, the great-grandfather of the subject of this sketch. Abiah James was also a member of the militia.

Abiah R. James, the father of the subject of this sketch, as before stated, was born on the old homestead in Doylestown township, formerly New Britain, being the son of Benjamin W. James and Elizabeth Black, the former being a son of Abiah James and Rachel Williams, and the latter a granddaughter of Abel James and Elizabeth Barton. Abiah R. was educated in a school established on the home farm by his father, and where many prominent men were educated under the tuition of Professor Clark, a graduate of Yale College, and an eminent educator. Arriving at manhood he married Josephine Levitt, of Memphis, Tennessee, whose family had sought refuge in the north during the trying scenes of the civil war in their native state. At the death of his father he inherited the farm that had descended from father to son for six generations, and still owns it. Failing health induced him to leave the farm and he and his wife live retired in Doylestown township. He is a trustee of New Britain Baptist church, of which his ancestors have been members since its organization. In politics he is a Democrat, but has never sought nor held office. The subject of this sketch is the only child.

Wynne James was educated at the public schools of his native township and at Doylestown English and Classical Seminary, where he graduated in 1885. He taught school in Doylestown township for one year, in Southampton for three years, and again in Doylestown township for one year. In 1891 he entered as a student at law in the office of Nathan C. James, Esq., at Doylestown, and was admitted to the bar in March, 1893, since which time he has practiced law and conducted an extensive real estate business, his practice being mainly in the orphans' court and in connection

Wynne James

with real estate titles and conveyancing. He is a member of Doylestown Lodge, No. 245, F. & A. M.; Doylestown Chapter, R. A. M.; and Philadelphia Consistory; Doylestown Lodge, No. 94, I. O. O. F.; the Royal Arcanum and the Knights of the Golden Eagle. He was married in 1895 to Madeline Mai Gentry, of Memphis, Tennessee, and has two children, Madeline A., and Wynne, Junior.

HENRY A. JAMES, attorney and counselor at law, Doylestown, son of Eugene and Martha A. (Riale) James, was born in Doylestown borough, October 22, 1865. Through the various intermarriages of his ancestors, as shown by the preceding sketch of the James family, Mr. James is a descendant of two of the sons of the emigrant John James, viz: William and Thomas, and a lineal descendant of three of the sons of the former.

Eugene James, the father of Henry A. James, was the son of Col. Isaiah and Caroline James, and was born at Warrington, Bucks county, where his father was at the time conducting a store, March 31, 1831. Most of his boyhood days were spent in Hilltown, where his father was engaged in the mercantile business. In 1849 his father purchased the old James plantation in New Britain, and Eugene, at the age of eighteen years, became its principal farmer, his father at the time being prothonotary of the county. He remained on the farm until his marriage in 1864 to Maria A. Riale, daughter of Abiah James and Miranda (James) Riale, when he settled in Doylestown. His father-in-law, Abiah J. Riale, dying at about this time, Eugene purchased his interest in the mercantile firm of Bell & Riale, who conducted a store where George W. Metlar, is now located, and became a member of the firm. He continued in the store business until the spring of 1870, when he purchased his father's New Britain farm and lived there until his death, August 22, 1896. He was an active and prominent man in the community, and won the esteem of all who knew him. He held many positions of trust; was one of the directors of the Doylestown National Bank, from January, 1884, until his death; president for many years of the Whitehall Fire Insurance Company; a director of the Whitehall Turnpike Company, and one of the managers of the Doylestown Agricultural and Mechanics Institute. Eugene and Martha A. (Riale) James were the parents of three children—Henry A.; Howard I., a prominent member of the Bucks county bar; and Gertrude Miranda, wife of Rev. Purdy Moyer.

Henry A. James was reared from the age of five years on the New Brit-

ain farm, and received his early education at the public schools. He later attended the Doylestown English and Classical Seminary, from which he graduated in 1884. In the following year he registered as a student at law in the office of J. M. Shellenberger, Esq., at Doylestown, and was admitted to the bar of Bucks county, January 30, 1888. For two years he remained in the office of his preceptor, and then opened an office for himself, and has since practiced his chosen profession in all its branches, and has met with success. In politics he is a Democrat, and has taken an active interest in the councils of his party, frequently representing his home district in state, congressional and district conventions. He has been a member of the Doylestown school board for several years. He is a member of the Historical Society of Pennsylvania, and of the Bucks County Historical Society. He is one of the directors and counsel for the Whitehall Fire Insurance Company, vice-president of the Fellowship Horse Company, president of the Doylestown Fire Company, and one of the board of censors and examiners of the Bucks County Bar Association. He is a member of Doylestown Lodge, No. 245, F. & A. M., and Aquetong Lodge, No. 193, I. O. O. F.

He married, April 30, 1902, Miriam Watson, daughter of ex-Judge Richard and Isabella T. (McCoy) Watson, of Doylestown. They have no children. Mr. and Mrs. James are members of St. Paul's Protestant Episcopal church, of Doylestown, of which Mr. James has been a vestryman and accounting warden for a number of years.

IRVIN MEGARGEE JAMES, of Doylestown, was born in that town, November 25, 1860, and is a son of the late Nathan C. and Maria (Megargee) James, the former of whom was for many years a prominent member of the Bucks County bar, and died August 10, 1900.

Nathan James, the great-grandfather of Irvin M., as shown by a preceding sketch, was a son of Isaac and Sarah (Thomas) James, and a great-grandson of John James, the emigrant ancestor of the family. He was an officer of militia during the revolutionary war, having been commissioned first lieutenant on May 6, 1777, of the Eighth Company, Captain John Thomas, Second Battalion, Colonel Arthur Erwin, Bucks County Militia, and was promoted May May 10, 1780, to captain of the Seventh Company, Fourth Battalion, Colonel McElroy. Captain Thomas' company was in active service in August, 1777. Captain James married Sarah Dungan, daughter of John Dungan, of New Brit-

5-3

ain, and had four children, viz: John D.; Nancy, wife of Jesse Callender; Joseph, and Simon. John Dungan James, son of Captain Nathan and Sarah (Dungan) James was the grandfather of Irvin James. He was an officer in the war of 1812-14, in the company of his cousin, Captain Nathan James, as was also his brother Simon. John D. was crier of the courts of Bucks county for forty years. He married Sarah Cline, and had seven children; Elizabeth; Nathan C., above mentioned; Sarah, Silas, Henrietta, Mary Ann, and Elizabeth.

Irvin Megargee James was born and reared in Doylestown, and was educated at the Doylestown Seminary and the Cheltenham Academy at Ogontz, Pennsylvania. In 1879 he accepted a position as clerk in the wholesale dry goods establishment of William B. Kempton & Co., of Philadelphia, where he remained for two years. The next three years he held a similar position with Riegel, Scott & Co., in Philadelphia. On July 5, 1885, he was appointed a clerk in the United States pension office at Philadelphia, which position he filled acceptably for five years, four under General W. W. H. Davis, and one year under his Republican successor, Pension Agent Shelmire. In 1890 he entered the employ of the Philadelphia & Reading Railroad Company, where he remained for one year. when he accepted a responsible position in the offices of the Pennsylvania Railroad Company, where he remained until April, 1903. He now follows a general insurance and real estate business at Doylestown.

Mr. James has been a member of the Doylestown school board for the past four years, and is now the secretary of the board: he is also clerk of the town council. He married, November 27, 1889, Elizabeth C. Firman, daughter of the late Samuel A. and Hannah (Doan) Firman. Their only surviving child is Marie Megargee, born July 5, 1893. Mr. and Mrs. James are members of St. Paul's Protestant Episcopal church of Doylestown, of which Mr. James has been a vestryman for a number of years.

DR. OLIVER P. JAMES, late of Doylestown, deceased, was the youngest son of Benjamin and Nancy (Williams) James, and was born in New Britain township, Bucks county, Pennsylvania. in 1815. He was a descendant in the fifth generation from John and Elizabeth James, who emigrated from Pembrokeshire. Wales, in 1711, as shown by the preceding sketch. On the maternal side he is said to be a descendant of the Roger Williams family of Rhode Island.

Dr. James was reared upon the New Britain farm, on Pine Run, and received his education at the schools of the neighborhood. At the age of nineteen, believing that a mechanical trade was his sphere in life, he took up that of a carpenter. He did not bind himself as an apprentice, as was the custom in those days, but, after assisting in building a house erected for his father in 1834, he went to Philadelphia and worked at the trade for two years. Becoming convinced by that time that he had mistaken his calling, he abandoned the saw and plane, and in 1837 entered himself as a student of medicine in the office of his cousin, Dr. Robert E. James, of Upper Mount Bethel, Northampton county, Pennsylvania, father of Robert E. James, Esq., of Easton, and read the allotted time with the Doctor, and during the winter season attended lectures at the Jefferson Medical College, Philadelphia, where he graduated in March, 1840. During his studies it developed that he possessed a peculiar aptitude for his chosen profession. During the year succeeding his graduation his cousin and preceptor, Dr. Robert E. James, was serving a term in the state legislature and the young doctor took charge of his practice in his absence. He opened an office in New Britain, where he soon built up a large practice. In the first or second year of his practice he was appointed physician at the Bucks County Almshouse, a position he retained for seventeen years. This position attracted attention to the rising young physician, and assisted in securing him a large practice that soon extended into the far surrounding sections. He continued his residence in New Britain until 1859, when he removed to Doylestown, purchasing the present Ginsley property, on Main street, the former residence of General Samuel A. Smith. Soon after the war he purchased the handsome residence on North Main street, where he spent the remainder of his life, and where his widow and daughter still reside.

Dr. James became very prominent in the practice of his profession. Prior to his retirement from active practice, a few years before his death, he was one of the most prominent physicians of the county, and enjoyed an extensive and lucrative practice. He was always closely identified with the interests of his town and county, and in his prime his high ability, courtly manners and kindly nature commanded the highest respect and gave him a wide influence among men.

In politics he was a Democrat. and from early manhood he took an active interest in politics. In 1864 he was elected to the state senate over his old neighbor, William Godshalk, by a majority of 989 votes. In 1878 he was the candidate of his party for congress from the Seventh District, and, though he ran far ahead of his ticket in many of the precincts, was defeated by his old opponent, William Godshalk. In local societies and institutions Dr. James took a deep interest. He was a member of Doylestown Lodge, No. 245, F. & A. M., and its treasurer for many years, holding that position at the time of his death. He was president of the Doylestown borough council for several terms. He was treasurer of the Doylestown Agricultural and Mechanics' Institute from its organization in 1866 to its dissolution in 1892. He was for twenty years a director of the Doylestown National Bank, and was a member of the board of directors of the Doylestown and Willow Grove Turnpike Company, and treasurer of the company for many years.

Dr. James died at his residence in Doylestown on the evening of November 19, 1894. He had been in failing health for some time, being confined to the house for upwards of a month. The cause of his death was valvular disease of the heart.

Dr. James was married in 1859, to Sarah A. Gordon, of Montgomery county, who survives him. Their only son, Oliver B., died when a young man, several years ago. Two daughters survive: Martha A., wife of Rev. George H. Lorah, D. D., of Philadelphia; and Sarah M., residing in Doylestown.

THOMAS A. JAMES, of Doylestown, son of Louis H. James, is descended from Thomas James, eldest son of John and Elizabeth, who accompanied his father from Wales in 1710 and joined him in the purchase of the one thousand acres of land in New Britain in 1720. He married Jane Davis, May 15, 1722, and lived all his life on the old farm plantation, and died there in 1772, leaving Thomas; Elizabeth, who married Benjamin Butler, and second, Moses Aaron; James, John and Samuel.

Samuel James, born 1730, succeeded to one hundred and fifty acres of the homestead, and married Anna Kachline, died in 1804, leaving three children: Samuel, Levi and Elizabeth, who married Isaac Oakford.

Levi married Rebecca Polk, of an old Scotch-Irish family of Warwick, whose pioneer ancestor, Samuel Polk, came from Ireland, in 1725, and after her death married Mary Good. His children by the first wife were: Robert, Samuel, Elizabeth, Lydia Ann, and Isabella. He was a prominent man in the community. He died in 1857.

Robert, the son, married Ann Bayard, a relative of the distinguished Delaware family of that name. He was almost a giant in stature, modest, unassuming, intelligent, a man of unquestioned integrity. He participated actively in the affairs of the county, both politically and socially. He was elected to the legislature at the same election in which Francis R. Shunk was made governor, and while at Harrisburg a warm friendship was cemented between the two men. He died in his eighty-eighth year, and was survived by his wife and five children: Louis H., Nancy C., Frank, Emma C. and Louise.

Louis H. married Mary E. Laughlin, of Philadelphia, studied law in the office of George Lear, and as a lawyer had a large clientage throughout the county. Like his father, he took a very active part in politics, and was one of the leaders of his party. He died in the latter part of 1900, and was survived by his wife and six children: Robert C., Helen, Thomas A., Carrie Y., Margaret C., and Mary E.

THE PARRY FAMILY OF NEW HOPE, PENNSYLVANIA. ("CORYELL'S FERRY" OF THE REVOLUTION.)

The Parrys herein mentioned are descended from an ancient and honorable family, long resident in Caernarvonshire, Wales. THOMAS PARRY, the founder of the family in Pennsylvania, was born in Caernarvonshire, North Wales, A. D., 1680, and came to America towards the close of the seventeenth century, settling in that part of Philadelphia county—long afterwards set aside as Montgomery county, and still so called. In 1715 he married Jane Morris, by whom he had issue ten children, all born between the years 1716 and 1739 inclusive. Eight of these were sons, and two daughters, named Mary and Martha. The eldest son Thomas having been born July 26, 1716, the third child, John, (ancestor of this branch) July 25, 1721, and Martha, the youngest, March 3, 1739.

THOMAS PARRY, THE ELDER, born 1680, was a considerable landholder and is recorded as having been owner of over one thousand acres of land in Montgomery county, Pennsylvania, to a part of which his son John Parry, of Moorland Manor, subsequently succeeded. Of the above thousand acres, Thomas Parry conveyed 200 acres to John Van Buskirk, September 2, 1725, and 300 acres he conveyed to David Maltby, December 29, 1726. Thomas Parry was a man of most excellent good sense, and judgment, and he and his neighbor and acquaintance, Sir William Keith, of Graeme Park. Governor of Pennsylvania under the Penns, consulted together about their internal local affairs, such as roads, etc., and certainly the roads were bad enough in their day, as Indian trails and bridle paths were frequently the best that they had before. It is only since comparatively late years that there were turnpikes from Willow Grove, in Montgomery county to either Doylestown or New Hope, in Bucks county. The descendants of Thomas and Jane Morris Parry are to be found at the present day not only in Pennsylvania, but in parts of Ohio, Indiana, Tennessee, New Jersey, and Virginia. By intermarriage the Parrys have become allied with some of the oldest colonial families in the United States, such as Tyson, Randolph, Paxson, Morris, Waldron, Gerrish, Winslow, and others of note. A paper, stained yellow with age, found recently among some old family papers recites quaintly that "Thomas Parry dyed ye 30th day of ye seventh month, in the year of our Lord, one thousand seven hundred and Forty Eight." (7 mo. 30, 1748). His widow, Jane Parry, survived him many years, dying September 6, 1777, aged eighty-two years. Both Davis "History of Bucks County, Pennsylvania" 1876, and "Munsell's American Ancestry" Vol. 7, page 21, note the coming to America of this Thomas Parry.

JOHN PARRY, of "Moorland Manor," so styled to distinguish him from another John of the same name, the third child of Thomas Parry, born 1680, and Jane Parry, his wife, was born July 25, 1721, married September 21, 1751, Margaret Tyson, daughter of Derick and Ann Tyson, and granddaughter of Renier (sometimes spelled Reynear) Tyson, who, with Daniel Pastorius, the three brothers Updegraff, Jan Lukens, and others, came to America in 1683, from Crefeld in Germany, and were the original settlers of Germantown, Pennsylvania. Renier Tyson was twice chief burgess of Germantown; he in early days, removed to Montgomery county, then a part of Philadelphia county, acquired a large estate, and became ancestor of the Pennsylvania and Maryland Tysons. John Parry and Margaret Tyson Parry, his wife, had seven children: Thomas, John, Benjamin, Phebe, Stephen, David and Daniel, the eldest born August 20, 1752, and the youngest April 21, 1774. John Parry lived on the back road, near the present "Heaton station" of the North-East Pennsylvania Railroad, the road running into the old York Road at about this point. This estate was derived from his father, Thomas Parry and his house, a large double stone mansion, still stands, but has since that time been altered by carrying the attic up square, making it now (1905) a double three-story structure, but losing in its colonial style, which was originally not unlike the "Old Parry Mansion" at New Hope, Pennsylvania, built in 1784. John Parry was an elder in the Society of Friends, had many city acquaintances and, being a man of means

and much given to hospitality, entertained largely in this ancient home in his day; it passed out of the ownership of the family, however a number of years ago. Several of John Parry's books containing his autograph and dated and an oaken and iron-bound wine chest once owned by him containing a number of very thin bottles bearing curious cut devices and most of them unbroken, with the wine glasses and two small glass funnels, each dotted with cut stars gilt are still in existence and much valued by their owner, a great-grandson, residing at New Hope, Pennsylvania. A stout gold-headed walking stick or cane of this John Parry's and engraved with his name and date, A. D., 1751, was also in the possession of his great-grandson, Judge William Parry, now deceased, and doubtless is still preserved in that branch of the family. John Parry, of Moorland Manor died November 10, 1789, his wife, Margaret Tyson Parry, surviving him for eighteen years and dying November 24, 1807.

BENJAMIN PARRY, a prominent and influential citizen of Bucks county. Pennsylvania, during the latter part of the eighteenth and early part of the nineteenth centuries, was the third child of John Parry, of "Moorland Manor" and Margaret Tyson, his wife, and was born March 1, 1757, and married November 4, 1787, Jane Paxson, daughter of Oliver Paxson the elder, of "Maple Grove," Coryell's Ferry (now New Hope) Pennsylvania, by whom he had issue, four children as follows:

1. Oliver, born December 20, 1794 (and noted later on) died February 20, 1874, in eightieth year.

2. Ruth, born January 4, 1797 and died October 28, 1885 in ninetieth year, unmarried.

3. Jane, born August 27, 1799, and died September 28, 1879, in eighty-first year, unmarried.

4. Margaret, born December 7, 1804, and married C. B. Knowles, and had no issue. Died July 26, 1880, aged seventy-six years.

Benjamin Parry is mentioned at considerable length in General Davis' "History of Bucks County, Pennsylvania," 1876, in Hotchkin's "York Road, Old and New," Philadelphia, 1892, and in divers other published works. Under the chapter upon New Hope, General Davis in the historical pages of this work gives some account of Benjamin Parry and the old Parry Mansion, which is unnecessary to repeat here.

Benjamin Parry was the original promoter of the New Hope Delaware Bridge Company and in 1810, first agitated the subject, with his friend, the Hon. Samuel D. Ingham of Solebury, secretary of the United States Treasury, under President Jackson. At that early day, real-

Eng. by E. C. Williams & Bro. N.Y.

Benjamin Parry

Born March 1 1757

izing the great importance of bridging the Delaware River at New Hope, these two men never rested until it was accomplishd, in 1813-1814. Benjamin Parry headed the subscription list and Mr. Ingham signed, as second subscriber. The first public meeting towards organization was held September 25, 1811, at the Tavern of Garret Meldrum in New Hope at which vigorous action was taken towards securing the building of the bridge. Benjamin Parry and Mr. Ingham were the commissioners, to superintend its construction as noted in the very interesting paper of the Reverend D. K. Turner, upon "Our Bucks County Congressmen" read before the Bucks County Historical Society, January 22, 1895. It was necessary to obtain charters from both the states of Pennsylvania and New Jersey, and charters were granted in both states in 1812—about fifteen months after the first eventful meeting at "Meldrum's Tavern." The charters gave the bridge company banking privileges and acting under the same, and the written opinion of their counsel, the Hon. George M. Dallas, once vice-president of the United States, a banking business was conducted and bank bills were issued, for many years and became largely the currency of the country, both in Pennsylvania and New Jersey. The first president of the New Hope Delaware Bridge Company was the Hon. Samuel D. Ingham and Benjamin Parry was a member of the First Board of Managers in 1811. It may perhaps be of some interest to note that in 1905, ninety-four years later, the family are still closely connected with this ancient corporation and one of its members (a grandson of Benjamin Parry) has been for a number of years president of the company. Daniel Parry, born April 21, 1774, a younger brother of Benjamin, was its treasurer in 1814. The present treasurer is John S. Williams. From 1784 to about 1815 "Coryell's Ferry," (now New Hope) was admittedly the most active and thriving town in Bucks county and the means, hand and influence of Benjamin Parry, were those which mainly guided the helm; so much so was this that in early times he was known and styled "the Father of Coryell's Ferry." Besides his linseed oil mills, flour and saw mills in Pennsylvania, Benjamin Parry was owner of flour mills in Amwell township, New Jersey, on the opposite side of the river from New Hope and was interested with his relatives, Timothy Paxson (one of the executors of the rich Stephen Girard) in the flour commission business in Philadelphia. A letter from the late Martin Coryell of Lambertville, New Jersey, states as follows, "Benjamin Parry had a very large and profitable trade, for the product of his flour mills with the West Indies and other tropical

countries, having in A. D., 1810, invented a process by which malt, flour, corn meal, etc., would resist the heat and moisture of voyages through tropical climates and remain sweet and wholesome" and "that the amount of production was the only limit for the demand in foreign ports." This patent from the United States to Benjamin Parry is dated July 10, 1810; and is recorded in both Washington and Philadelphia; the record in Philadelphia being in Book 25 "L. W." of Miscellaneous Records, page 67, etc., Recorder of Deeds Office. It was long known as the "Kiln Drying Process" and was not superceded by any different method for a period of nearly seventy-five years. Some of the business affairs of Benjamin Parry were conducted under the firm name of Benjamin Parry & Co., and others as Parry & Cresson. Some time between 1791 and 1794, the name of "Coryell's Ferry" was changed and it became known as New Hope and a private map of the settlement, made for Benjamin Parry, bears the name of New Hope and is dated, in printed letters A. D., 1798. Mr. Parry died as before stated, November 22, 1839, in his eighty-third year at "The Old Parry Mansion,"* New Hope, and he is buried with so many others of his name and race, in the family lot at Solebury Friends' burying ground, Bucks county.

OLIVER PARRY, GENTLEMAN, of Philadelphia and Bucks county, Pennsylvania, only son of Benjamin Parry, born 1757, was born at "The Old Parry Mansion," Coryell's Ferry, now New Hope, Bucks county, Pennsylvania, December 20, 1794, and married May 1, 1827, Rachel Randolph, daughter of Captain Edward F. Randolph, a patriot of 1776, who had served in many of the principal battles of the Revolutionary war and who became an eminent citizen of Philadelphia. His portrait in oil, painted by Robert Street, hangs upon the walls of the "Historical Society of Pennsylvania," at Philadelphia. Oliver and Rachel Randolph Parry had twelve children, four sons and eight daughters, all born between March 24, 1828, and August 17, 1848. Of the sons, Oliver Paxson Parry, born June 20, 1846, died in 1852, aged 6 years, and the others will be noted later. Oliver Parry, the elder, born 1794, was a large landholder and his name appears upon the records of Philadelphia county oftener perhaps, than that of any other person of his day. A part of his property was a large tract of the once famous "Bush Hill Estate" long the residence of Governor Andrew Hamilton, in colonial days. This property Mr. Parry owned jointly with his

_____

*An account and description of "The Old Parry Mansion" follows this narrative.

nephew Nathaniel Randolph. In Watson's "Annals of Philadelphia," much mention is made of "The Bush Hill Estate." Rachel Randolph Parry, the wife of Oliver Parry, died at "The Old Parry Mansion," New Hope, September 9, 1866, his own death occurring February 20, 1874, at his city residence, 1721 Arch street, Philadelphia, and both are buried in the family lot at Solebury Friends' burying ground, Bucks county, Pennsylvania. The close of an obituary notice of Oliver Parry in a Philadelphia newspaper of the day, thus pays tribute to his high character, and standing: "Born a member of the Society of Friends, he lived and died in that faith, walking through life with a singleness and direct honesty of purpose which made the name of Oliver Parry synonymous with truth and honor." (Edward, Richard, George and Oliver, the four sons of Oliver, are noted below.)

MAJOR EDWARD RANDOLPH PARRY, U. S. army, born July 27, 1832, eldest son of Oliver Parry (born 1794) was a brave and gallant officer, who served from the beginning to the end of the Civil war of 1861. The following notice of him, appeared in many of the newspapers, after his death, which event occurred at "The Old Parry Mansion" April 13, 1874:

Major Edward Randolph Parry, late of the United States army, died at his residence, New Hope, in this county, on the 13th of April, 1874, and was buried on the 16th, at Friends' Solebury burying ground. He was a son of the late Oliver Parry of Philadelphia, and was born at New Hope, July 27, 1832. In May, 1861, he entered the army as first lieutenant in the 11th United States Infantry, and served throughout the war, with great credit. In 1864 he was made captain in the 11th; afterwards transferred to the 20th, and on reorganization of the army was promoted to a majority for gallant service. He was in the terrible fighting along the line of the Weldon railroad, and before Petersburg, Virginia, commanding his regiment in several actions. In 1865 he was assistant general of the regular brigade, Army of Potomac, and served upon the staff of General Winthrop when he was killed. At Lee's surrender he was attached to army headquarters. In 1868 Major Parry commanded Forts Philip and Jackson, at mouth of Mississippi river, and Fort Ripley in Minnesota in 1869. He resigned on account of ill health in 1871. Major Parry was the grandson of Major Edward Randolph, who served from the beginning to the end of the Revolutionary war.

A portrait of Major Parry hangs upon the walls of the "Bucks County Historical Society" at Doylestown, Pennsylvania. Major E. R. Parry married December 17, 1863, at Boston, Massachusetts, Frances, daughter of General Justin Dimick, U. S. A., and had three children. She, with one child, an unmarried daughter (named Katharine) survives him. The other two children, daughters, died in childhood

RICHARD RANDOLPH PARRY, GENTLEMAN, of New Hope, Pennsylvania, second son of Oliver and Rachel (Randolph) Parry, was born in Philadelphia, December 5, 1835, and married October 11, 1866, in Saint Luke's Protestant Episcopal church, Portland, Maine, Miss Ellen L. Read, of Portland, and they have issue, three children, as follows:

1. Gertrude R. Parry, unmarried.
2. Adelaide R. Parry, unmarried.
3. Oliver Randolph Parry, born March 29, 1873, married on October 15, 1898, in New York city, Miss Lida M. Kreamer and has one child, Margaret (born May 3, 1901,) at "The Old Parry Mansion."

R. R. Parry was educated at private schools in Philadelphia and at Haverford College, Pennsylvania. From 1856 to 1862, he resided at Mankato, Minnesota, where he was engaged in the banking business. In "Neill's History of the Minnesota Valley" page 549, published in Minneapolis, 1882, and in "Mankato, Its First 50 Years" published at Mankato 1903, Mr. Parry is described as one of the early pioneers of the valley. In 1862 he returned to Pennsylvania to live. He is a member of the "Bucks County Historical Society" and a life member of "The Historical Society of Pennsylvania" since 1855. He is also a member of the "Pennsylvania Society of the Sons of the Revolution;" and a companion of the Military Order of the Loyal Legion of the United States, commandery of Pennsylvania. He is senior warden of "St. Andrew's Protestant Episcopal Church", Lambertville, New Jersey, and for many years past has been president of "The New Hope Delaware Bridge Company." Mr. Parry is a man of literary tastes, and historical interests and has frequently contributed articles to the press and published works. He resides at the "Old Parry Mansion," in New Hope borough, erected for his ancestor, Benjamin Parry in 1784. Two different portions of this estate were occupied by the Continental troops, in December, 1776, just prior to the "Battle of Trenton" as more fully mentioned elsewhere in this volume.

DR. GEORGE RANDOLPH PARRY, of New Hope, Pennsylvania ("Coryell's Ferry"), third son of Oliver and Rachel (Randolph) Parry, was born September 3, 1839 in Philadelphia, and was educated in private schools of that city. He began the study of medicine in the Philadelphia College of Pharmacy from which he graduated, in the class of 1862.

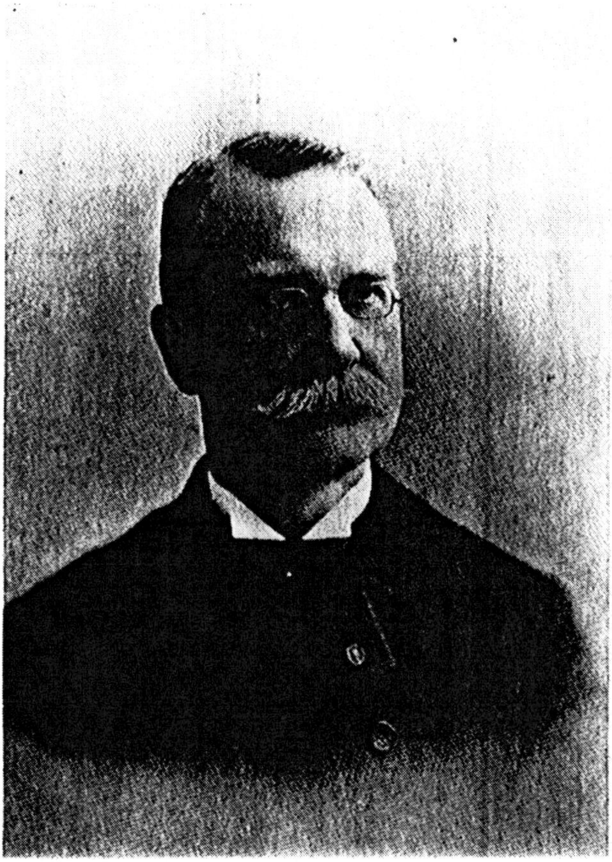

Richd. Randolph Parry

OLD PARRY MANSION—INTERIOR VIEW

OLD PARRY MANSION

In 1864 he entered the Medical Department of the University of Pennsylvania and was graduated in 1867. For some years he practiced his profession in Cayuga county, New York. On returning to Pennsylvania in 1880 he located at the old homestead at New Hope, living at the "Old Parry Mansion" until his death June 12, 1893. He enjoyed a large practice, and died much esteemed and lamented. Dr. Parry married March 2, 1869, Miss Elizabeth Van Etten, of Vanettenville, New York, whom he survived twelve years. They had two children, Elizabeth R. and Jane Paxson, the latter deceased. Dr. Parry was a member of the Medical Societies of Bucks county, Pennsylvania and Hunterdon county, New Jersey; and was also a member of the "Bucks County Historical Society" and a life member of the "Historical Society of Pennsylvania, Philadelphia." He also was much interested in Free Masonry and belonged to a commandery of Knights Templar in New York state.

OLIVER PAXSON PARRY, fourth son of Oliver and Rachel (Randolph) Parry was born 1846, and died December 13, 1852, in his seventh year.

DANIEL PARRY, ESQ., of New Hope, Pennsylvania, son of John Parry, of "Moorland Manor" and Margaret Tyson, his wife, was born April 21, 1774, and married Martha Dilworth of Dilworthtown, Pennsylvania, having but one child, named for his grandfather, John. Parryville, Carbon county, Pennsylvania, an important point for shipment of coal on the Lehigh river, was named for this Daniel Parry, who was a gentleman of fortune and owned large tracts of land, in Carbon, Wayne, Luzerne and other counties of Pennsylvania; a part of which were obtained through the Marquis de Noailles of France. Daniel Parry died July 16, 1856, aged eighty-two years. Martha Dilworth Parry, his wife, died April 3, 1831, aged fifty-three years. Their son John died in childhood and all three lie buried in their family lot, at Friends burying ground in Solebury township, Bucks county. The Doylestown papers, in noticing the death of Daniel Parry, spoke of him as "a man of large benevolence, and a generous friend to the destitute," and many poor persons indeed mourned the loss of a friend ever ready to help them.

"THE OLD PARRY MANSION," New Hope Borough, Bucks County, Pennsylvania ("Coryell's Ferry," of the Revolution).

The ancient colonial double stone mansion still standing at the corner of the old York road and the Trenton or River road in New Hope borough, erected in 1784 for Benjamin Parry, which has bravely stood in three centuries has long been known as "The Old Parry Mansion" and has been the home of the Parrys of New Hope (Coryell's Ferry) for five generations. Two different portions of this property were occupied by troops of the Continental army, in the Revolutionary war. In 1776, just prior to the Battle of Trenton, a considerable body of American soldiers under General William Alexander (Lord Stirling) were quartered here and the village placed in a state of armed defence by Stirling, who threw up a strong redoubt on top of the hill across the pond, in a southwesterly direction from "The Old Parry Mansion," and a part of this estate. These earth works extended from where the yellow public school house now stands, in an easterly direction, a considerable distance towards the Delaware river, at the termination of the old York road at the river's brink above and below the Ferry landing. Upon another part of the Parry property, (purchased of the Todd's) entrenchments were erected and batteries placed. Lord Stirling also had another redoubt thrown upon the old York road facing the river at the corner of Ferry street, and the present Bridge street, opposite where "the old Washington Tree," cut down November 28, 1893, then stood and near the site of the present Presbyterian church. From this elevated position he likewise commanded the approach from the Delaware river. Such were the defenses of Coryell's Ferry at this period of the Revolution, when it (then an important strategic point, and crossing of the Delaware) was saved to the American cause from British plans and designs. At page 175, Volume I of *Washington and his Generals" in speaking of General Alexander (Lord Stirling) it is stated "That in his new capacity of Major General, he joined the army in its memorable retreat through New Jersey and took part in the operations on the Delaware river, where he again signalized himself by his successful defense of Coryell's Ferry."

Lord Stirling's headquarters at New Hope, are said to have been in the old hip roof house known as "The old Fort" which then stood on the site of the present hipped roof home of Mr. P. R. Slack on the Old York road, just opposite the avenue and entrance to "Maple Grove" then and now owned and occupied by the Paxson family and where Benjamin Parry's wife Jane Paxson was born January 24, 1767.

Looking backward through the long vista of more than a century and a quarter, it seems difficult to realize that New Hope ("Coryell's Ferry") and the now

---

*Published by E. Meeks, Philadelphia, 1885.

peaceful highways about it once resounded with the bustle of war, and the frequent tramp of armed men, as our patriot sires hurried forward to do battle for their country or fell back in the sadder marches of retreat. The years have come and gone since the days of the Revolution, bringing with them many changes, but the old settlement at "Coryell's" still remains, nestling close beside the noble river, at the "Ferry" which our forefathers defended in the old heroic days. Many of the boats used by General Washington on Christmas night, 1776, to make that memorable crossing of the Delaware, now known the world over in history, as "Washington's Crossing" and made additionally famous by the artists' brush, were collected at New Hope ("Coryell's Ferry") and kept secreted behind Malta Island, then densely wooded over and were floated by night, down the river to "Knowles Cove," just above Taylorsville, Pennsylvania, the point where Washington crossed to fight and win the Battle of Trenton. "Malta Island" has since filled up and become mainland, the present "Union Mills" paper manufacturing company's plant at New Hope is just at the north end of Malta Island. Former mills here were owned many years ago by Daniel Parry Esq., (born April 21, 1774) a younger brother of Benjamin Parry. Many letters of General Washington and other of his prominent Generals, are at different times, during the Revolutionary War, dated at "Coryell's Ferry."

In both Benjamin Parry's day and that of his son Oliver Parry, the "Old Parry Mansion" was the scene of much hospitality and its doors were thrown open wide upon many an occasion to bid hearty welcome to both city and country guests and during the life time of the latter and his hospitable and popular wife, Rachel Randolph, this ancient homestead was often called by their friends "Hotel de Parry" and sometimes "Liberty Hall." Many distinguished persons have been entertained beneath its broad roof in the long period in which it has stood and had it lips, much it could speak of events in three centuries. Interesting mementos of bye-gone days have been sacredly treasured up and much old family furniture is yet preserved in this home; some of it nearly (or quite) 200 years old, and brought from over the sea; the ancient high clock standing half way up the stairs, on the broad landing, has ticked in and out the lives of many generations of the family and still shows upon its familiar face the moon, in all its phases. In this connection it may be perhaps of some interest to note the occurrence of an event so unusual in its character as to become historic, and worthy of passing notice in the birth in this home, on May 3, 1901,

of a daughter to Mr. and Mrs. Oliver Randolph Parry (named Margaret Kreamer Parry) in the same room in which her great-grandfather Oliver Parry was born in 1794, one hundred and eleven years ago, and in the same old mansion, in which her great-great-grandfather Benjamin Parry lived and died. Seldom do we find homes in the United States passed on beyond the second or third generations. Many sketches of "The Old Parry Mansion" have appeared from time to time, in various published works, and newspaper articles, a comparatively recent one on July 15, 1901, issue of *The Philadelphia Inquirer* by its historical editor, being illustrated. In the "York Road, Old and New" by Rev. S. F. Hotchkin, published 1892 in Philadelphia, this old colonial home of the Parrys of "Coryell's Ferry" is thus described: "As viewed from the outside—this ancient mansion, presents a quiet and dignified appearance, in keeping with the family for whom it was built; the quaint and handsome carved ornamentations, over the windows, small window panes, pointed corners, and hoods, betoken its age, and are charmingly attractive. Over the front door remains the ancient bonnet or hood of our forefathers' day, beneath which is the massive old-fashioned door, with its transverse panels, brass knocker, cumbrous lock and huge iron hinges, which stretch across the whole width. This door opens into a wide wainscoted and paneled hall, running through the middle of the house and dividing the long parlor upon one side from the dining room and the parlor or sitting room, on the other; in these rooms and in daily use, are yet preserved the corner cupboards of a hundred years ago" now (1905) 121 years old. "The upper floors are approached, by low broad steps and half way up the stairs on the broad landing, stands in one corner, relic of a past age—the old eight-day clock which has ticked in and out, the lives of so many of the family and still showing upon its familiar face, the moon in all its phases. Five bed chambers, most of them communicating upon the second floor, open out upon an upper hall, the full width of that beneath; the inside shutters over the house—both in the main building and wing—are secured for the most part by long wooden bars, stretching across, and fitting into the deep window frames. In most of these rooms may be seen great open mouthed chimneys and fire places, the brick floors of which are painted in bright tile colors; immense closets, with brass door knobs in one of these chambers fill up entirely one end of the room, taking several feet off its length but compensating by the additional convenience afforded the family. The rooms and halls of this old mansion contain much valued, handsome and ancient furniture, belonging to the family for several generations, much of it being carved in solid mahogany and walnut woods. In one of the rooms on the first floor is a trap door in the floor leading into a cellar, partitioned off and shelved as a wine cellar, but which may have been intended in earlier times, as a means of escape from sudden danger. In the great attic overhead the children, grandchildren and great-great-grandchildren of the original owner, have often played and wondered at the contents of numerous chests, high cases of drawers and boxes, since found to have contained much linen-stuffs, and other articles of family value, and far up amid the rafters on the fourth floor, a dark secret room only reached by a long ladder (always removed after each visit) afforded a safe hiding place for papers, and such valued matter as seemed to require extra security and care in the time of the original owner, which was to his grandchildren, of course, a place of especial wonder, tinctured somewhat perhaps, with a species of fear. In the wing of the mansion, in a capacious fire place, still swings an ancient iron crane, with its outstretched arm at rest after a long term of service, much prized by the family and shown visitors as a curious relic. A huge bake oven of an early period and no longer used in the kitchen adjoining was torn out a few years ago for the lost space which was needed. An elaborately cut stone circle in the north gable end of the house, under the roof, bears a tablet inscribed Benjamin Parry, A. D., 1784, and to this home in 1787 he brought his wife Jane Paxson, as a bride" and here on December 20, 1794, was born their only son, the late Oliver Parry, Esq. whose son Major Edward Randolph Parry of the United States army, died at "The old Parry Mansion" in 1874 of disease brought on by hardships and exposure endured during the late terrible Civil war. Major Parry received a brevet from Congress "for gallant services during the war." This old mansion has never been out of the Parry family and name; it is now (1905) owned and occupied by Richard Randolph Parry. Of the male descendants of Benjamin Parry (of the name) in the next generation, Oliver Randolph Parry, born March 29, 1873, son of above Richard, is the only one living, at the present time.

HON. DAVID NEWLIN FELL, justice of the Supreme Court of Pennsylvania, was born in Buckingham, November 4, 1840, and is a son of Joseph and Harriet (Williams) Fell.

Joseph Fell, the pioneer ancestor of the family, was born at Longlands, the seat of the family for several generations in the parish of Rockdale, Cumberland, England, October 19, 1668. In 1698 he married Bridget Wilson, and two sons, Joseph and Benjamin, were born to them at Longlands. In 1704 with his wife and two sons, he emigrated to America, and located for a short time in lower Bucks county, removing to Buckingham in 1706, when he became a large landholder and a prominent man in the community. Two daughters, Tamar and Mary, were born to him in Bucks county. His wife dying when the latter was eleven days old, he married three years later Elizabeth Doyle, daughter of Edward and Rebecca (Dungan) Doyle, who had come to Bucks county from Rhode Island in 1683. Their seven children were John, Isaac, Titus, Thomas, George, Sarah, and Rachel. He died in 1748, his widow surviving him several years.

Joseph Fell, eldest son of Joseph and Bridget (Wilson) Fell, was born at Longlands, Cumberland, England, June 29, 1701. He married, March 4, 1735, Mary Kinsey, daughter of Edmund and Sarah (Ogborn) Kinsey of Buckingham, the former a native of New Castle, Delaware, for many years a noted minister among Friends at Buckingham. Joseph Fell, Jr., settled on a farm on the Durham road above Mechanicsville, conveyed to him by his father, which remained the property of his descendants until 1890, a period of one hundred and seventy-five years of continuous occupancy. He died there February 22, 1777. His children who lived to maturity were: Joseph; Sarah, who never married; Rachel, who married William Lownes; David; and Martha, who married Edward Rice, Jr. Mary (Kinsey) Fell, the mother, was born in Buckingham, April 29, 1715, and died December 29, 1769.

Joseph Fell (3) son of Joseph and Mary (Kinsey) Fell, born October 31, 1738, on the Buckingham homestead, married October 21, 1767, Rachel Wilson, who was born in Buckingham June 5, 1741, and died March 8, 1810. She was the daughter of Samuel and Rebecca (Canby) Wilson, the granddaughter of Thomas Canby and Stephen Wilson, both early pioneer Friends in Bucks county and a great-granddaughter of Henry Baker, a provincial councillor and one of the most prominent public men in the infant colony on the Delaware. Soon after his marriage Joseph Fell removed to Upper Makefield township, Bucks county, where he purchased a farm and resided until his death, March 26, 1789. He was the father of eight children, six of whom grew to maturity: Joseph, born 1768, married Esther Burroughs; John, born 1770, married Edith Smith; Martha, married Benjamin Schofield; David, married Phebe Schofield; Jonathan, born 1776, married Sarah Balderston and returned to the Buckingham homestead in 1831; and Rachel, born 1783, married John Speakman.

David Fell, M. D., second son of Joseph and Rachel (Wilson) Fell, born in Upper Makefield, Bucks county, July 1, 1774, was the grandfather of Judge Fell. He received a liberal education, and, having chosen the medical profession, entered the University of Pennsylvania, from which he graduated with the degree of M. D. in 1801. He began the practice of medicine in Upper Makefield, but soon after removed to Buckingham, where he built up an extensive practice and became one of the prominent physicians of his day. He died February 22, 1856, in his eighty-second year. He married, March 16, 1803, Phebe Schofield, who was born September 26, 1774 and died January 10, 1858. She was the daughter of Samuel and Edith (Marshall) Schofield, of Solebury, Bucks county, Pennsylvania. They were the parents of five children: Joseph, born March 12, 1804; Edith Newlin, died unmarried in 1857; Sarah Ann, died unmarried in 1872; Bushrod, died in infancy; and Elizabeth, married Ezra B. Leeds, of Germantown, and later removed to Columbiana county, Ohio.

Joseph Fell, son of David and Phebe (Schofield) Fell, was born at Lurgan, Upper Makefield, Bucks county, Pennsylvania, March 12, 1804, and died in Buckingham, March 11, 1887. He was one of the best known and highly respected men of Bucks county. He began teaching at Union School, Buckingham, and was later an instructor in the school of John Gummere at Burlington, New Jersey. In 1830 he began to teach at the Friends School at Buckingham Meeting House, where he remained several years, making it one of the famous local schools. He later made a journey to Ohio and on his return purchased the Buckingham homestead, still owned by his grandchildren, and spent his remaining days there. During the winter for several years he continued his teaching at Tyro Hall and the Hughesian School.

He was elected to the state legislature in 1837, and was prominently identified with the adoption of the common school law of Pennsylvania, and rendered efficient services in placing it in effect in his native county. He was a member of the first school board of Buckingham, and its secretary for many years. When the office of county superintendent was created in 1854 he was elected as the first superintendent of Bucks county, and did much to place the office on the high plane of usefulness it has since attained. After filling the position for three years he declined a reelection. In 1855 he held the first teachers' institute. Retiring to his farm in 1857 he devoted himself to the affairs of his farm and neighborhood, filling many important positions of public trust. He was for many years a trustee and director of the Hughesian Free School, and continued an active interest in educational matters during his whole life. He was a lifelong member of the Society of Friends, and an active, fearless and outspoken Abolitionist, his home being one of the stations of the "Underground Railroad." He was a man of high intellectual ability, and kept in touch with the important public movements, and was fearless and outspoken in all his convictions on public questions.

He married, March 28, 1835, Harriet Williams, born September 25, 1807, died March 28, 1890, a daughter of Samuel and Sarah (Watson) Williams, of Buckingham, and a descendant of Jeremiah Williams, who came to Tinicum township, Bucks county, from Westbury, Long Island, about 1743, and they were the parents of five children: William W., born May 25, 1836, died unmarried, January 4, 1874, was a lawyer of Philadelphia; Emily C., born June 15, 1838, married William T. Seal; David Newlin; Edward Watson, born September 27, 1843, married Elizabeth M. Kenderdine, and resided on the old homestead, died April 30, 1900; and Lucy W., who never married.

Hon. David Newlin Fell, born and reared on the Buckingham farm, was educated under the direction of his father, and graduated from the First Pennsylvania State Normal School at Millersville, in the class of 1862. In August of 1862, he entered the army as lieutenant of Company E, 122d Regiment, Pennsylvania volunteers, the company being mainly recruited from the students of the school.

He studied law in the office of his brother, William W. Fell, and was admitted to the bar March 17, 1866, and at once began the practice of his chosen profession at Philadelphia. After eleven years of successful practice he was appointed May 3, 1877, by Governor Hartranft, as judge of the court of common pleas of Philadelphia county, and in the November following was elected to the same position for a term of ten years, and reelected in 1887, receiving on both occasions the nomination of both the Republican and Democratic parties. He has always manifested an active interest in the public affairs of the city of his adoption, and at the time of his appointment to the bench was a member of the city council for the twentieth Ward, and was a member of the municipal commission created by the act of legislature to devise a plan for the better government of the cities of the commonwealth. He is a member of Post No. 2, G. A. R., of Philadelphia, and has served as senior vice commander and judge advocate general of the Grand Army of the Republic of Pennsylvania. He was elected to the Supreme Bench in 1893.

He married, September 1, 1870, Martha P. Trego, born July 31, 1846, daughter of Smith and Anna (Phillips) Trego, and

Engraved by James H. Rice, Phila.

Harman Yerkes

they are the parents of seven children:
Joseph Williams, born June 24, 1871, died
December 8, 1901; Anna Trego, born
February 16, 1873, married John H.
Ruckman, April 26, 1900; David Newlin,
born June 3, 1875; Edith Newlin, born
August 1, 1879; Emma Trego, born December 17, 1881; Edward Watson, born
August 22, 1888; and Alfred Moore, born
January 30, 1891. Judge Fell and his
family have made Buckingham their
summer residence for many years, he
having erected a handsome residence on
a part of the old homestead overlooking
the beautiful valley of Buckingham.

HON. HARMAN YERKES, of Doylestown, was born in Warminster township,
Bucks county, October 8, 1843. He is of
French and Holland descent, being son of
Stephen and Amy Hart (Montayne) Yerkes,
and sixth in descent from Anthony Yerkes,
who emigrated from Holland about 1700
and settled in Germantown. This pioneer
ancestor of the Yerkes family in America
was accompanied to our shores by his wife
Margaret and two sons Herman and Adolphus. The first record we have of him is
in the year 1702, when he was burgess of
Germantown, a position which he filled
for three years. In 1709 he purchased the
plantation in the "Manor of Moorland,"
now Moreland township, Montgomery
county, Pennsylvania. He married (second) Sarah (Eaton) Watts, widow of
Rev. John Watts, pastor of Pennypack
Baptist church.

HERMAN YERKES, son of Anthony and
Margaret, born in Holland in 1689, died in
Moreland in March, 1751. He was a farmer and miller. He married February 8,
1711, Elizabeth, daughter of Rev. John
and Sarah (Eaton) Watts, born April 15,
1689. (Rev. John Watts was a native of
Leeds, England, and his wife of Wales).
Herman Yerkes probably settled on his
father's plantation in Moreland at its purchase in 1709. His father conveyed to
him two hundred acres on Pennypack
creek in 1723. In 1744, in conjunction with
Walter Moore he erected a mill on Pennypack and set apart nineteen acres of land
therewith. This mill he devised to his
sons, and it later became the property of
Jacob and John Shelmire, and is to this
day known as "Shelmire's Mill." The
children of Herman and Elizabeth (Watts)
Yerkes:

1. Anthony, born November 28, 1712,
died March 9, 1791.
2. John, born February 21, 1714, died
1790; married Alice McVeagh.
3. Sarah, born July 15, 1716, married
Jacob Hufty.
4. Josiah, born November 28, 1718, died
1793; married Mary ——
5. Herman, born January 18, 1720, died
November 29, 1804; married (first) Mary
Stroud, and (second) Mrs. Mary Clayton,
and (third) Mrs. Eliza Tompkins.

6. Silas, born February 15, 1723, died
1795; married Hannah Dungan.
7. Elizabeth, born January 29, 1725, died
1793; married John Howell.
8. Stephen, born August 3, 1727, died
1811; married Rebecca Whitesides.
9. Elias, born February 7, 1729, died
January 17, 1799; married Rebecca Foster.
10. Titus, born 1731, died 1762; married
Margaret Paul.

HARMAN YERKES, fourth son of Herman
and Elizabeth (Watts) Yerkes, was born
in Moreland, January 18, 1720, and died
there November 29, 1804. Like his father
he was a farmer and miller. He also followed the mercantile business at Plymouth
Montgomery county, in the years 1752-5,
where he had purchased a tract of land
from his brother John in 1747. In 1762 he
removed to Warminster township, Bucks
county, being the first of the family to
make a home in this county. He purchased
181 acres of land near Johnsville, which
still remains the property of his descendants. He returned to Moreland in 1788
and died there November 29, 1804. He was
an active supporter of the war for independence. His name appears on the list
of Associators in Warminster in 1775, and
he served on various committees under the
committee of safety. His Warminster
home witnessed some of the bloody carnage and rout following the battle of
Crooked Billet in 1778. An incident is
related of an American soldier being saved
from slaughter by four British soldiers
who were pursuing him, by the strategy
of Mrs. Mary Yerkes, the second wife of
Harman, who, when the soldier had sought
refuge in the house, conducted him to a
rear exit and found him a place of concealment in a pile of buckwheat straw in
a neighboring field. His pursuers entered
the house and made a diligent search for
the fugitive, thrusting their bayonets
through beds and up the chimney, to the
terror of the women and children of the
household.

After locating at Plymouth, Mr. Yerkes
became enamored of a Quaker lass, Mary,
the daughter of Edward Stroud, of White
Marsh, and uniting himself with the Society, was married to her by the simple
ceremony of the Society March 22, 1750-1.
She died in 1771, and he married (second)
Mary (Houghton) Clayton, widow of
Richard Clayton. His second wife died in
1785, and he married in 1787 Elizabeth
(Ball) Tompkins, widow of John Tompkins, of Moreland. She was the proprietress of an inn on the Old York road, and
his remaining years were spent as "mine
host" at this old hostelry. His widow died
in 1819. The children of Harman and
Mary (Stroud) Yerkes, were:

1. William, born 1752, died in infancy.
2. Elizabeth, born September 5, 1753;
married 1779 John Hufty.
3. Catharine, born June 19, 1755, died
1821; married Major Reading Powell.

4. Edward, born April 19, 1757, a Revolutionary soldier and sea captain, died at sea.

5. Sarah, born 1759, died in infancy.

6. Stephen, born October 20, 1762, died 1823; married Alice Watson.

7. Mary, born January 5, 1765, died unmarried.

8. Harman, born July 25, 1767, died February 12, 1827; married Margaret Long.

9. William, born July 25, 1769, died 1823, married Letitia Esther Long.

Harman, son of Harman and Mary (Stroud) Yerkes, was born in Warminster, July 25, 1767. He spent his whole life on the Warminster homestead, one hundred acres of which he purchased in 1793, upon which he erected the large stone mansion still standing. In 1800 he purchased the remainder of the 180 acres that had been his father's and later bought the Noble tract on the county line, making three farms which he devised to his sons. He married in 1790 Margaret, daughter of Captain Andrew Long, of Warrington, born January 8, 1771, died March 4, 1849. He died February 12, 1837.

The children of Harman and Margaret Long Yerkes were 10, viz:

1. Mary, born 1791, died 1816; unmarried.

2. William, born July 8, 1792, died 1826; married Penelope McDowell.

3. Andrew L., born August 25, 1794, died 1862; married Eliza Everhart.

4. Edward, born July 11, 1797, died 1799.

5. Elizabeth, born May 26, 1800, died 1875; married John C. Beans.

6. Clarissa, born October 2, 1802, died December, 1873; married Samuel Montayne.

7. Edwin, born November 28, 1804, died 1864; married Catharine R. Williamson.

8. Harman, born March 9, 1807, died 1889; married Rebecca Valentine.

9. Stephen, born May 19, 1809, died July 25, 1865; married Amy Hart Montayne.

10. Margaret, born October 8, 1815, died December 29, 1815.

Stephen, son of Harman and Margaret Long Yerkes, was born on the old homestead in Warminster, May 19, 1809, and died there July 25, 1865. He commenced life as a farmer on the west side of the York road, but at the death of his father in 1837 he removed to the original homestead devised to him by his father. He later added to this two other farms now occupied by his sons. He married January 13, 1831, Amy Hart Montayne, daughter of Rev. Thomas B. Montayne, and great-granddaughter of Jean de la Montaigne, who came to New York in 1624, and was director-general of New York under the Dutch government. Mrs. Yerkes was born October 23, 1811, and died March 22, 1856. The children of this marriage were:

1. Thomas, born November 14, 1831.

2. Harman, born February 8, 1833, died May 24, 1840.

3. Stephen, born April 11, 1835; married Elizabeth Jamison, and is now living on the Warminster homestead.

4. Adolphus, born January 31, and died February 31, 1837.

5. Anna Margaret, born January 17, 1841, died at Germantown, March 13, 1903; married Captain George H. Bucher.

6. Harman, the subject of this sketch, born October 8, 1843; married Emma Buckman.

7. Alfred Earle, born June 7, 1846; married Mary A. Hazlett, living in Warminster.

8. Edwin Augustus, born October 24, 1849, died May 21, 1900.

Judge Yerkes' boyhood days were spent on the Warminster farm. He attended the public school of the neighborhood and later the Tennent school at Hartsville, and then entered Williston College at Easthampton, Massachusetts, from which he graduated in the class of 1862. He read law with Thomas and Henry P. Ross, at Doylestown, and was admitted to the bar November 3, 1865, and at once began the active practice of his chosen profession. He was elected district attorney in 1868, and discharged the duties of the office with special ability. In 1873 he was elected to the state senate and was re-elected in 1876. He was a prominent figure in the upper house of the state, and served on many important committees. He drew the laws regulating the separate orphans courts and the civil and criminal courts of the state under the new constitution of 1874. He was a member of the state board of managers of the Centennial Exposition at Philadelphia in 1876, and took a prominent part in the management. He introduced the bill creating the Hospital for the Insane at Norristown and was one of the original trustees to which position he has been a second time appointed. He has been a life long Democrat and has always been prominent in the councils of the party. He was chairman of the judicial committee of conference in 1869, and was a delegate to the judicial conventions of 1871 and 1872. He was a delegate to the Democratic national convention at Baltimore in 1872, but was one of the twenty-one members of that memorable convention that refused to vote for the nomination of Horace Greeley, giving the vote to Hon. Jeremiah S. Black, of this state. He was a national delegate again in 1880, and delegate to the state conventions of 1873, 1874, 1877, 1878 and 1882. In 1883 he was elected president judge of the district and was re-elected in 1893, receiving at that time the unanimous endorsement of the bar of the county. As a judge Mr. Yerkes displayed remarkable ability, his promptness in the despatch of business, his eminent fairness of his decisions, the deep study and wide research shown by the opinions rendered and his intense earnestness in the prosecution of the suits brought before him, made him very popular. He has frequently been called upon to hold court outside the county, and was universally considered a learned and able judge. He was one of 'six Democratic nominees for the superior court at the Williamsport convention in 1895, and received on the first ballot 349 out of a total of 454 votes in the convention. In the election that followed, while he ran far ahead of most of the ticket, receiving a handsome plurality in his home county, he was defeated by his colleague, Justice Smith, of Wilkesbarre. In 1901 he was the Democratic nominee for justice of the supreme court, and ran far ahead of his ticket. On the expiration of his second term as president judge he was unanimously re-nominated for the position, but was defeated at the polls by Hon. Mahlon H. Stout. On retiring from office he at once resumed the practice of law, associating himself with the grandsons of his old preceptor, Thomas and George Ross, and enjoys a large practice.

Judge Yerkes and his family are members of St. Paul's Protestant Episcopal Church of Doylestown, of which he is a member of the vestry. He is a member of Doylestown Lodge No. 245, F. and A. M.; of the Historical Society of Pennsylvania; the Bucks County Historical Society; the Colonial Society; the Society of the Sons of the Revolution, and the Pennsylvania Germans' Society. He was extremely active in bringing about the erection of the Bucks County Historical Society building, and was largely instrumental in securing funds for the purpose, and as chairman of the building committee had principal charge of the erection of the building. He was married June 24, 1869, to Emeline, daughter of Monroe Buckman, of Doylestown, but has no children.

THE ADAMS FAMILY. Among the earliest members of the Adams family who emigrated to America were Henry Adams, of Braintree, Massachusetts, and Robert Adams, of Oxford township, Philadelphia county, and Walter Adams, his brother, all of whom it is said were descended from Lord John Ap Adams, son of Ap Adams, who "came out of the Marches" of Wales. Thomas ·Adams, brother of Henry Adams, of Braintree, Massachusetts, was one of the grantees named in the charter of Charles I. in 1629. He was high sheriff and lord mayor of London.

Henry Adams with his eight sons settled at Mount Wollaston, in Braintree, and Walter and Robert Adams were his brothers. It is thought, however, that they came to this country at a later date. They settled in Pennsylvania and, like the majority of the early colonists of that state, Walter was a Quaker.

The earliest record of the English branch of the Adams family is that of John Ap Adams, of Charlton Adams, in Somersetshire, who married Elizabeth, daughter and heiress to Lord Gowrney, of Beviston and Tidenham county, Gloucester, who was summoned to parliament as baron of the realm, 1226 to 1307. In the upper part of a Gothic window on the southeast side of Tidenham church, near Chopston, the name of John Ap Adams is still to be found, together with "arms argent in a cross gules, five mullets or," of Lord Ap Adams. The design is probably executed on stained glass of great thickness and is in perfect preservation. This church originally stood within the boundary of Wales, but at a later period the boundary line was changed so that it is now upon English soil. The arms and crest borne by the family are described as argent in a cross gules; five mullets or, out of a ducal coronet a demi-lion. The legend is "Loyal au mort;" a motto commonly used by this branch of the family is "Aspire, persevere and indulgence," all other "sub cruce veritas."

,The following is the line of direct descent to the Adams family of the Lehigh Valley. (1). Ap Adams came out of the Marches of Wales. Lords of the Marches were noblemen who in the early ages secured and inhabited the Marches of Wales and Scotland, living there as if they were petty kings, having their own private laws. These laws, however, were subsequently abolished. (2) Sir Ap Adams, knight, lord of Ap Adams, married Elizabeth, daughter of Lord Gowrney. (3) Sir Thomas Ap Adam; (4) William Ap Adam; (5) Sir John Ap Adam; (6) Thomas Ap Adams; (7) Sir John Ap Adam, Knight; (8) Sir John Ap Adam, who was the first to attach the letter "s" to his name; (9) Roger Adams; (10) Thomas Adams; (11) John Adams; (12) John Adams; (13) Nicholas Adams; (14) Richard Adams; (15) William Adams; and (16) Henry Adams, who is said to have emigrated about 1634. In February, 1641, he was granted forty acres of land near Boston, of which Braintree is a part. His brothers were Robert, Thomas and Walter. The last named came to America by way of the Barbadoes, West Indies, and after living there for a time took up his abode in Pennsylvania.

(1) Walter Adams married Elizabeth ———. Their children were: Richard, Anne, William, and Robert. Walter Adams was the brother of Robert Adams, of Oxford township, Philadelphia, who died in 1719, leaving no children; he devised the estate to his nephews and nieces, the children of his brother Walter and Elizabeth, his wife.

(2) Richard Adams, of New Providence township, now Montgomery county, Pennsylvania, died in 1748. His first wife's name is not known. His second wife was Alice or Aishe Withers, and they were married in 1726. His children were as follows: Abraham, married Alse ———; William, of Braken township, Lancaster county; Isaac, of Coventry township, Chester county; Susanna, married Conrad Custard,

or Kistard; Catharine, married John Morris; Mary, married Israel Morris; Margaret, married Paul Casselberry; Elizabeth, married Thomas Bull; Ann, married Jacob Umstadt; Hannah, married Owen Evans.

(3) Abraham Adams died in 1738, and letters were granted to Rachel, his daughter, a spinster. There is mention of two children, Ann and Abigail.

Walter Adams and his brother were brothers of Henry Adams, who came to New England and was a founder of the Adams family there, at Braintree, Massachusetts. Walter, his son Richard, and his son Abraham were Quakers.

Conrad Custard, husband of Susanna Adams, (daughter of Richard), owned a large tract of land immediately adoining the tract surveyed to Ensign John Adams, of Nockamixon township, in 1763.

John Adams and James Adams, possibly and probably brothers, lived in Nockamixon township, Bucks county. There are a few records at Doylestown, Pennsylvania, which bear James Adams's signature. He was also an ensign in the provincial service, Associated Companies of Bucks county, in 1747. (See Colonial Records, vol. v., p. 209; also Pennsylvania Archieves, second series, vol. ii., p. 505). This was nine years before John Adams held a like commission in the provincial service in the Associated Companies of Bucks county. There is nothing to establish that James Adams and John Adams were related, neither can be found any data of their former residence or whose children they were. The only solution is that they were both possibly sons of Abraham Adams; the latter having died intestate no list of his children is obtainable. The fact that John Adams held land adjoining that of Conrad Custer is a possible solution, he having been raised by his aunt Susanna.

Richard Adams, of Providence township, Philadelphia, whose will is dated February 1, 1847-8, and probated March 24, 1747-48, mentions son Abraham's children, Ann and Abagail, then letters were granted to Abraham's daughter Rachel. There at once seems to be some discrepancy which is most difficult to explain.

James' commission in the provincial service, as above stated, was dated in 1747, which tends to show that he might have been disinherited by his grandfather. Then, again, there is a possibility that James and John Adams are one and the same man, but this is very doubtful, as their names are mentioned distinctly and separately in the old records.

(1) John Adams, ensign, Provincial Service, of Nockamixon township, Bucks county, Pennsylvania, died in Nockamixon township, May 22, 1807. He married Mary ——. He was buried in the old Nockamixon church graveyard. His will dated March 21, 1807, proved June 8, same year, is recorded in Will Book No. 7, p. 278, in the registrer of wills office, Doylestown, Pennsylvania.

John Adams, of Nockamixon, served in the provincial service in 1756. He held a commission as ensign in one of the companies of the Associated Companies of Bucks county. (See Pennsylvania Archieves, vol. iii., p. 19; also Pennsylvania Archives, second series, vol. ii., p. 531). Captain William Ramsey was captain of the company in which John Adams served and held his commission as ensign in 1756, and was also from Nockamixon township, Bucks county. John Johnson was the lieutenant of the company. John Adams of Nockamixon, and Mary his wife, had the following children: Mary, Elizabeth, Margaret, George, Henry, John Jacob.

George and Henry, sons of John Adams of Nockamixon, served in the Nockamixon Company of Associators in 1775. George was sergeant of the company, and the son, John was a soldier in the Continental army during the Revolutionary war.

The first record that we have of John Adams of Nockamixon owning any land is a warrant that was granted March 26, 1754, to John Adams, for land in Nockamixon township, Bucks county, upon which a survey was returned for fifty-four acres and 113 perches. A patent for this same land was granted April 26, 1726, to Abraham Fryling. John Adams had some trouble with this land, for on May 19, 1763, he entered a caveat against the acceptance of a survey made for Archibald Merrin, which took in the above mentioned land and improvements. (See Pennsylvania Archieves, third series, vol. ii., p. 275). The above land was surveyed by J. Hart, for which he gave a receipt, June 26, 1763, which is recorded in Doylestown, Pennsylvania, in Deed Book No. 32, p. 169. This receipt also mentions the date of the warrant, March 26, 1754.

(II) John Adams, private in Captain Samuel Watson's company, of Durham township, Bucks county, Pennsylvania, was a son of John Adams of Nockamixon township, Bucks county, Pennsylvania, born in Nockamixon township, November 3. 1759, died in Durham township, November 12, 1826. He married Christina Klinker, December 15, 1789, at the Tohickon German Reformed church. Some time after the Revolutionary war he moved into Durham township, where he lived until his death. He is buried in the old Durham church graveyard. Christina Klinker, the wife of John Adams, of Durham, was born in Nockamixon township August 15, 1770, died in Durham township October 2, 1847, and is buried in the old Durham church graveyard. She was the daughter of John and Mary Klinker of Nockamixon township, Bucks county, Pennsylvania.

John Adams, of Durham township, Bucks county, Pennsylvania, was a soldier in the Continental army during the Revolutionary war. He served as a private in Captain Samuel Watson's company of the Second Pennsylvania Battalion under Colonel

.rthur St. Clair. He enlisted February 12, 776. (See Pennsylvania Archieves, second :ries, vol. x, p. 98). Several of the memers of his company were from upper lvcks county. Captain Watson died at 'hree Rivers and was succeeded by 'homas L. Moore, who was promoted to 1ajor of the Ninth Regiment, May 12, 1779, nd was succeeded as captain by John Henerson. The company was transferred or ecame a part of the Third Battalion, :welfth Regiment, July 1, 1778, and thus ıecame associated with other companies ıf Bucks county. For his services he reeived from the state of Pennsylvania two ıundred acres of "donation land" in Robnson township, Westmoreland county, ²ennsylvania, which was returned for patnt October 9, 1786. (See Pennsylvania ١rchives, third seriês, vol. vii, p. 723). This ınd he sold to Hugh Hamill, November ١, 1786, for £37 10s. The witnesses to this Ieed were Thomas Delap (Dunlap), John ⊃onnell and Jacob Glassmyer, all residents ⊅f Nockamixon township at that date. (Reːorder's office, Philadelphia, Pennsylvania, Ieed book D-17, p. 322.) John K., son of Iohn Adams of Durham, was a soldier for ⅰome time during the ⸗war of 1812-1814, ⸗rivate in Captain John Dornblaser's com⸗ⱥany (Pennsylvania Archives, second ser⸗es, vol. xii, p. 105).

John Adams of Durham, and Christina, ⱥis wife, had the following children: ≡lizabeth, Mary, Margaret, John K., Hen⸗y, Jacob, Samuel, Susan, married Joseph ℝetschlin, and Daniel.

John Adams of Durham was quite a ⱥarge land owner. In 1706 he owned one ⱥundred acres of land and a grist and a ⱥaw mill in Nockamixon township, Bucks ːounty, Pennsylvania. April 20, 1799, he ⊃ought of Solomon Lightcap 263 acres of ⱡand. (Bucks county deed book 30, p. 310). April 11, 1808, he bought two tracts, one of 155 acres and the other óf twelve acres. (Bucks county deed book 39, p. 135). John Adams of Durham died without making a will. It is impossible to give the date when John Adams was mustered out of the service, for the muster rolls of the Twelfth Regiment have practically never been found.

Tax lists of · Nockamixon township show the holdings of John Adams, the father of the above John Adams, and his sons George and Henry, elder brothers of John. John Adams appears as a "single man" first in the year of 1785, notwithstanding that he was of age in 1780. He therefore served, in all probability, up to about that date (1784-1785) in the Twelfth Pennsylvania Regiment. Captain Samuel Watson's company records date to November 25, 1776, only.

(III) Henry Adams, of Durham township, Bucks county, Pennsylvania, son of John Adams, was born in Durham township June 17, 1806, and died there December 15, 1838. He married Elizabeth Bitz, August 25, 1828, at her home in Spring-

field township, Bucks county, Pennsylvania. He is buried in the old Durham church graveyard. Elizabeth Bitz, the wife of Henry Adams, of Durham, was born September 18, 1811, in Springfield township, Bucks county, Pennsylvania, and died March 28, 1878, in Bethlehem, Pennsylvania. She was the daughter of John Bitz and Susan Riegel, his wife, of Springfield, Bucks county, Pennsylvania. Henry Adams's will is recorded in Doylestown, Pennsylvania. It is dated April 28, 1838, and is proved December 22, 1838. Henry Adams of Durham and Elizabeth, his wife, had the following children: John, Hannah, Catharine and Samuel. After the death of Henry Adams in 1840, Elizabeth Bitz was married a second time to Christian Nicholas. She had no children by this union. Christian K. Nicholas was born in Nockamixon township, Bucks county, Pennsylvania, January 23, 1817, and died in upper Saucon township, Lehigh county, Pennsylvania, November 3, 1893, and was buried in Friedensville November 7, 1893, and body removed to Nisky Hill Cemetery, Bethlehem, December 16, 1899.

(IV.) Samuel Adams of south Bethlehem, Northampton county, Pennsylvania, son of Henry Adams, of Durham township, Bucks county, Pennsylvania, was born in Durham township July 25, 1837, and died in South Bethlehem, Pennsylvania, February 22, 1902. He married Susie Weaver, September 14, 1865, at her home in Allentown, Pennsylvania. He is buried at Nisky Hill Cemetery, Bethlehem, Pennsylvania. Susie Weaver, wife of Samuel Adams, was born in Allentown, Pennsylvania, May 5, 1847. She was a daughter of Joseph Weaver and Salome, his wife, of Allentown, Pennsylvania. Samuel Adams ,and Susie Weaver, his wife, had the following children: John, Joseph H., Henry and Susie. Samuel Adams when quite a young man started out in farming, and then in iron ore mining. He entered the employ ƀf the Thomas Iron Company of Catasaqua, Pennsylvania, and was given charge of their mining interests. Mr. John Fritz induced him to come to Bethlehem and accept the position as his assistant in the Bethlehem Iron Company. Here he remained for nearly thirty years, and then had to resign on account of his health. He then organized the Ponupo Mining and Transportation Company, Limited, and went to Santiago de Cuba as general manager of the company. Here he bought a railroad for the company, the Ferro-Carril de Santiago de· Cuba, and became its president, and also built an extension to the railroad to connect ,with the company's manganese mines. He remained in Cuba with his family for over two years, when he resigned and returned north. He was in Cuba part of the year 1892, all of 1893, and part of 1894. After returning from Cuba he assisted in forming the Sheffield Coal, Iron and Steel Company of Sheffield, Alabama.

He stayed in Sheffield with his family one year, then sold out his interest and came north. While with the Sheffield Coal, Iron and Steel Company he held the positions of general superintendent and assistant treasurer, and also director of the company. He then retired from active business and devoted himself to farming, having a tract of one hundred acres near Friedensville, Pennsylvania, about 130 acres above Bingen, Pennsylvania, and a tract of woodland along the P. & R. of forty acres, above Bingen, Pennsylvania. He was also interested in and a director of the following companies at the time of his death: Ponupo Mining and Transportation Company, Cuban Mining Company, Jones and Bixler Manufacturing Company, South Bethlehem National Bank.

Henry, son of Samuel Adams, was a soldier during the Spanish-American war of 1898. He organized the first volunteer company in the state. He and his company were taken into the Ninth Pennsylvania Regiment to help make up the Third Battalion of that regiment. He was commissioned as captain of Company K, Ninth Pennsylvania Regiment, United States Volunteer Infantry. The regiment was in the Third Brigade, Third Division, First Army Corps.

(V.) Joseph W. Adams, of South Bethlehem, Northampton county, Pennsylvania, son of Samuel Adams, was born in Bethlehem, Pennsylvania, January 19, 1872. He married Reba Thomas, of Pittsburg, Pennsylvania, daughter of David J. Thomas and Susannah Edwards, of Pittsburg, June 14, 1899, at her home. Reba Thomas, the wife of Joseph W. Adams, was born in Pittsburg, November 11, 1877.

Joseph W. Adams was educated at the Moravian parochial school of Bethlehem, Pennsylvania, the Hill school of Pottstown, Pennsylvania, and the Lehigh University of South Pennsylvania, where he joined the Delta Upsilon fraternity. He started to work in the drawing rooms of the Bethlehem Iron Company. He went to Cuba with his father and was treasurer of the Ferro-Carril de Santiago de Cuba, 1892-93. He went to Alabama as assistant to the general superintendent of the Sheffield Coal, Iron and Steel Company in 1895, and part of 1896. He returned home and took up his studies again at Lehigh University in metallurgy and mineralogy, and then read law for over a year. In 1899 he and his brother Henry formed the Cuban Mining Company, and he was elected secretary and treasurer of the company and also a director. He is connected with the following companies: Director and vice-president of the South Bethlehem National Bank; director and president of La Paz Mining Company; director, secretary and treasurer of the Cuban Mining Company; director and executive committee of Delaware Forge and Steel Company; director and committee of Guerber Engineering Company; director of Lehigh Valley Cold Storage Company; director, secretary and treasurer of the Roepper Mining Company; director of Valentine Fibre Ware Company; acting trustee of the estate of Samuel Adams. He is a member of the following clubs and societies: Society of Colonial Wars in the State of New York; Empire State Society; Sons of the American Revolution; Pennsylvania Society of Sons of the Revolution; Pennsylvania German Society, and the local town and country clubs; and of Masonic bodies—Bethlehem Lodge, Zinzendorf Chapter, Bethlehem Council, Allen Commandery, Caldwell Consistory, and Rajah Temple. He is captain of commissary, Fourth Regiment Infantry, N. G. P. His children were: John, born January 23, 1901; David Samuel, born March 15, 1903.

Henry Adams, captain of Company K, Ninth Pennsylvania Regiment, U. S. V. I., son of Samuel Adams, of South Bethlehem, Northampton county, Pennsylvania, was born in Bethlehem, Pennsylvania, November 2, 1873. He married Annette Talbot Belcher, of New London, Connecticut, July 9, 1902.

Henry Adams, mining engineer, was educated at the Moravian parochial day school of Bethlehem, Pennsylvania, the Hill school of Pottstown, Pennsylvania, and the Lehigh University of South Bethlehem, Pennsylvania, where he joined the Delta Upsilon fraternity. He started to work with Thomas Edison at Edison, N. J. He went to Cuba and was assistant superintendent and then superintendent of the Ferro-Carril de Santiago de Cuba. He went south to Alabama and was in charge of the coal and coke department of the Sheffield Coal, Iron and Steel Company at Jasper, Alabama. He went to Mexico and erected an electric light plant for the Mexican National Railroad, and then was supervisor of a division of that road. He resigned and was made constructing engineer for Tumer Nunn & Company of Mexico, Mexico, with headquarters in Pueblo. In December of 1897 and January of 1898 he was in Cuba in the city of Santiago and the surrounding country, and visited the insurgents several times.

When war broke out with Spain in 1898 he raised the first company of volunteers in the state, with the assistance of Colonel Wilson and Captain Juett of Bethlehem. He and his company were mustered into the United States service, and he received his commission as captain of volunteers on July 6, 1898. His company was attached to the Ninth Pennsylvania Regiment, United States Volunteer Infantry, as Company K, to help complete the Third Battalion. The regiment was in the Third Division, Third Brigade, First Army Corps. Company K, of the Ninth Pennsylvania Regiment of United States Volunteer Infantry, is thus mentioned in the "Record of Events which may be Necessary or Useful for Future Reference at the War Department."

"This company was organized in July at South Bethlehem, and mustered in at South Bethlehem, July 6, 1898, which company left by rail for Chickamauga Park, July 7, 1898, arriving in camp July 19, 1898. Remained in camp until August 26, 1898, when company left by rail for Camp Hamilton, Lexington, Kentucky, arriving in camp August 28, 1898. Left Camp Hamilton for regimental headquarters at Wilkesbarre, September 17, 1898, arriving there September 19, 1898. Company left by rail for home station, September 20, 1898, arriving same day, when company was verbally furloughed for thirty days."

The above is taken from the muster-out roll of the company. The company was mustered into service on the 6th day of July, 1898, and was mustered out of the service on the 29th day of October, 1898. It was the first volunteer company formed in the state of Pennsylvania, and was taken to help fill out the Third Battalion of the Ninth Pennsylvania Regiment. The other companies were Captain Green's, of Reading; Captain Mercer's, of Summit Hill, above Mauch Chunk; and Captain Moor's, of Towanda.

On Friday evening, April 22, 1898, there was a meeting held in the Fountain Hill Opera House, and a call for volunteers made. These met in Doxon's Hall afterward and elected Henry Adams, captain; Leighton N. D. Mixsell, first lieutenant; and Dick Enright, second lieutenant. Mr. Enright failed to pass his physical examination and was re-elected. A. Alison Mitchell, of Wilkesbarre, was appointed in his place. The South Bethlehem Market Hall was used as an Armory by the company.

Henry Adams is a member of the Pennsylvania German Society, 1899; a member of the Society of Foreign Wars, Pennsylvania Commandery, 1899; general manager of the Cuban Mining Company at Neuvitas, Cuba, 1899-1902, and the mines of this company were discovered by him; a member of the Empire State Society of the Sons of the American Revolution, and was presented a medal of honor by the society for service in the Spanish-American war; and of Masonic bodies—Fernwood Lodge, No. 543, Philadelphia, and Caldwell Consistory, 32d degree. He was vice president and general manager of the San Domingo Exploration Company and San Domingo Southern Railway Company, San Domingo, R. D., West Indies, 1902.

HON. GEORGE ROSS, an eminent jurist and statesman, was born in Doylestown, August 24, 1841. He came of a distinguished and honored ancestry. His earlier ancestors were of the clan Ross, of the Highlands of Scotland. His great-great-grandfather Thomas Ross was born in the year 1708, in county Tyrone, Ireland, where his parents had sought a refuge from the horrors of civil

and internecine war in their native Scotia. Emigrating to America at the age of twenty-one he settled in Solebury, Bucks county. He joined the Society of Friends and became a distinguished preacher. He was a man of superior education and intellectual ability, and traveled extensively in later life both in the American colonies and in England and Ireland. He died at the home of Lindley Murray, the great grammarian, in York, England, while on one of his religious visits in 1786. He married Keziah Wilkinson in 1731, and had by her three children: John, Thomas, and Mary, who married Thomas Smith. John Ross married Mary Duer in 1754, and had seven children; Sarah, who died in childhood; Thomas; Keziah, who married Benjamin Eastburn; John; Joseph; Isaiah; and Mary, who died in infancy.

Thomas, the great-grandfather of the subject of this sketch, as one of the executors of his father's will, joined in the conveyance of the Solebury homestead, patented to his father in 1737, to Jacob Van Horn in 1787, and the latter conveyed it back to Thomas by deed dated two days later. In 1796 he conveyed it to his son Thomas, who by will in 1814 devised it to his brother, Judge John Ross, of Easton, who devised it to his son Thomas, the father of the subject of this sketch, who conveyed it to Edward Vansant in 1853. Thus the original homestead of the Ross family in Bucks county remained in the family for one hundred and sixteen years, notwithstanding the fact that for three generations the owners had been much more eminent as jurists than as farmers. John Ross, eldest son of Thomas and Keziah, removed to Philadelphia. His son Joseph removed to the West. John became an eminent physician. Thomas married Rachel Longstreth and settled in West Chester. He was a lawyer, and had a large and lucrative practice.

THOMAS ROSS, younger son of Thomas and Keziah (Wilkinson) Ross, born on the old homestead in Solebury, was the great-grandfather of the subject of this sketch. He married (first) a Miss Clark, and (second) Jane Chapman, who was the mother of his six children: Thomas, John, William, Cephas, Hugh and Samuel. He lived on the Solebury plantation until 1796, when he removed with his family to Newtown, where he died about 1814. His eldest son Thomas was appointed prothonotary and clerk of the courts of Bucks county in 1801, and held those offices for eight years. He was born in 1767 and was admitted to the bar of Northampton county in 1793, practiced but a year or two, when he removed to New York city. He returned to Newtown in 1800 and practiced law until appointed prothonotary and clerk. His wife was Mary Lyons, of Long Island. He died in 1815, while visiting his brother John at Easton and left no children. Hugh Ross studied law with his brother John at Easton and on being admitted to the bar returned to Newtown, later went to Trenton, New Jersey and finally settled in Milford, Pike county, Pennsylvania. Samuel, the youngest child of Thomas Ross (2) born 1779, married in 1815 Mary Helena Wirtz, and settled in Philadelphia. He had six children. Cephas Ross, another son of Thomas (2) remained in Bucks county, where he still has numerous descendants. He died in Plumstead in 1840.

Hon. John Ross, the grandfather of the subject of this sketch, son of Thomas and Jane (Chapman) Ross, was born on the Solebury homestead, February 24, 1770. He received a liberal education, but it appears that his family were averse to his following a professional career. From a number of letters written by him in 1790 to his benefactor, Richard Backhouse, it would seem that by reason of the difference with his parents' as to his future career he was cast upon his own resources. These letters are now in the possession of the Pennsylvania Historical Society. He commenced life as a school teacher at Durham, where he attracted the attention of Richard Backhouse, then proprietor of the furnace. To Mr. Backhouse the youth confided his intention of going South to seek his fortune. Mr. Backhouse urged him to take up the study of law, and generously offered to give him sufficient financial aid to complete his studies and start him in the practice of law. Taking up with this generous offer, the embryo judge began the study of law with his cousin, Thomas Ross, of West Chester, then in the same judicial district as Bucks county, and he was admitted to the bar of the district in 1792. He settled at Easton, Northampton county and began the practice of law, and at once sprang into prominence. Hon. Henry P. Ross, his grandson, once said: "No member of the family approached him in ability," and his brilliant professional career warrants the assertion, superlative though it be. A born politician, he early launched into the arena of politics. He was elected to the state legislature in 1800. In 1804 he was a candidate for congress, but the jealousies aroused by the rival claims of the three counties of Northampton, Bucks and Montgomery, then composing the district, caused his defeat. He renewed the fight in 1808 and was then elected. At the expiration of his term he was appointed prothonotary of Northampton county. Was elected to congress again in 1814, and re-elected in 1816 and resigned to accept the appointment of judge of the seventh judicial district, comprising the counties of Bucks, Montgomery, Chester and Delaware, January 25, 1818. He had married November 19, 1795, Mary Jenkins, whose family resided at Jenkintown, and on taking up the duties of his office he located there. The act of March, 1821, placed Montgomery and Bucks in one judicial district and Judge Ross removed to Doylestown, then the county seat of Bucks.

He purchased the old tavern stand where the National Bank now stands, and converted it into a residence, and it remained the home of his descendants until 1896. Judge Ross was appointed justice of the supreme court April 16, 1830, after which much of his time was spent in Jenkintown. He died of apoplexy in Philadelphia January 31, 1834, in his sixty-fourth year. While in Northampton county he had purchased a tract of 348 acres near the Wind Gap in what is now Monroe county, and named it Ross Common. He set apart upon this tract a family burying ground. Here his favorite brother Thomas was buried, and here the famous jurist and statesman himself lies buried.

The children of Judge John Ross were: George, a graduate of Princeton, who studied law with his father and was admitted to the bar in 1818; (he became involved in a quarrel which resulted in a duel on the Delaware river, and he was never afterwards heard from) Charles J.; Lord; Camilla, who married General Peter Ihrie, of Easton; Serena; John, an invalid, though he lived until 1886; Thomas; Jesse Jenkins, who was at one time consul to Sicily; Adelaide, who married Dr. Samuel R. Dubbs, and Mary. Of these, George, Thomas, William and Jenkins all were college graduates and all lawyers, though Thomas was the only one who continued to practice. William became a teacher. Mary Jenkins Ross died in December, 1845.

Thomas Ross, the father of the subject of this sketch, was born in Easton, December 1, 1806. He graduated at Princeton in 1825, studied law, and was admitted to the bar February 9, 1829. Inheriting the abilities of his distinguished ancestors, he was a fine pleader and a logical thinker and became one of the eminent lawyers of his day. He was elected to congress from the tenth district comprising Bucks and Lehigh in 1848, and re-elected in 1851, and the district was never more ably represented. As an orator he obtained a national reputation. He died July 7, 1865. His wife was Elizabeth, daughter of Levi Pawling of Montgomery county, a member of the fiftieth congress, and granddaughter of Governor Heister. The children of this marriage were Henry P., George and Mary.

Henry P. Ross, born December 16, 1836, who became president judge of the seventh judicial district, graduated at Princeton in 1857, studied law with his father and was admitted to the bar in December, 1859. He practiced law with his father until the death of the latter in 1865, when he took his brother George into the firm. He was elected district attorney in 1862. He was a brilliant lawyer and an accomplished speaker. He was a leader of his party, and twice its candidate for congress. He was elected additional law judge in 1869, and succeeded Judge Chapman as president judge two years later. When the district was divided in 1874 he chose Montgomery county and, finishing his term there, was re-elected in 1881, but died at Norristown, April 13, 1882.

George Ross, son of Thomas and Elizabeth (Pawling) Ross, was born August 24, 1841. He obtained his preparatory education at the Tenent school at Hartsville, conducted by the Rev. Mahlon and Charles Long, and at the Lawrenceville, New Jersey Academy, under the tutorship of Dr. Hamill. He entered Princeton in January, 1858, and graduated in the class of 1861. He at once began the study of law with his father and brother at Doylestown and was admitted to the bar of the county June 13, 1864. At the death of his father the following year he formed a partnership with his elder brother, Hon. Henry P. Ross, which lasted until the elevation of the latter to the bench in 1869, when he became associated with Levi L. James, under the firm name of George Ross & L. L. James. At the death of Mr. James in 1889, J. Ferdinand Long became the junior partner.

Mr. Ross, like his father and grandfather, was a trained and erudite lawyer, by years of study and patient industry he had mastered the great principles of common and statute law, and soon earned the proud distinction of being the recognized leader of the bar in his native county. He was a forceful speaker, quiet and undemonstrative in his manner, not given to self-assertion in oratory. One of his contemporaries has said of him, "if the absence of art is the highest quality of oratory, he was an orator indeed. His remarkable knowledge of the law, his subtle power of logic, and his indomitable perseverance in the advocacy of the cause of a client, have made his memory dear to the people he served, and made his name remembered and honored in the community in which he lived." In 1872 he was a member of the constitutional convention that framed our present state constitution, representing the counties of Bucks and Northampton in that body. He was elected to the state senate in 1886, and succeeded himself four years later, a distinction exceedingly rare in the history of his county. He was a life-long Democrat, and therefore represented the minority in the law-making body of the state. Notwithstanding this fact he soon became known as the recognized leader in all that pertained to the best interests of his state. At the organization of the senate on January 2, 1895, Senator Brewer, of Indiana county, who was not of his political faith, in calling the attention of the body to the death of Senator Ross, said in part: "Seldom has any legislative body been called upon to mourn the loss of a more distinguished member. This is not the proper time to pay a tribute to the distinguished services he rendered his state. There is such a thing as leadership, known and recognized among men, and the members of this body, irrespective of party, accorded to George Ross leadership. Although we

have scarcely passed the threshold of this session, his absence is noticed and his counsel is missed. " Mr. Ross stood deservedly high in the counsels of his party. He was a delegate to the national conventions of 1876, 1884, and 1892. He was the Democratic nominee for congress in the seventh district in 1884, but was defeated at the polls by Hon. Robert M. Yardley. He was also the caucus nominee of his party for the United States senate in 1893. He was deeply interested in the local institutions of his county and district was one of the original directors of the Bucks County Trust Company, and its president at the time of his death. He was also a trustee of the Norristown Insane Asylum until his death. He died at his home in Doylestown, November 19, 1894. The disease which caused his death had given his family and friends much concern for probably a year. The state senate, of which he was a member at the time of his death, appointed a committee of five to draft resolutions expressive of the sense of that body upon his death, and fixed a special session on January 23, 1895, to receive and consider the report of such committee. At this special session the resolutions adopted and the speeches of his colleagues show the merited appreciation of his public services and private virtues. We quote from one of these speeches the following: "Our friends was not of humble origin, nor could he boast of being wholly a self-made man. He had great advantages, coming from a long line of distinguished ancestors, a race of lawyers, some of whom had worn the judicial ermine; he had the benefits of a most liberal education, and claimed the famous college of Princeton for his alma mater. This scion of one of the most illustrious families of Pennsylvania, in whose veins flowed some of the best blood in this grand old Keystone state, worthy of his origin, was a prince among men."

George Ross married, December 4, 1870, Ellen Lyman Phipps, a daughter of George W. Phipps, of Boston, Massachusetts. The children of this marriage are: Thomas, born September 16, 1873; Elizabeth P., George; Ellen P., Mary, Gertrude.

Thomas, the eldest son, was educated at Lawrenceville and Princeton, and graduated at Princeton in the class of 1895. He studied law under the preceptorship of Hon. Harman Yerkes, and was admitted to the bar December, 1897. He formed a partnership with his father's old partner, J. Ferdinand Long, which terminated with the death of the latter in January, 1902.

George Ross was born May 28, 1879. He graduated at Lawrenceville in 1896 and at Princeton in 1900. He studied law with his brother Thomas at Doylestown and at the University of Pennsylvania Law School and was admitted to the bar December 22, 1902, and entered into partnership with his brother. In 1904 Hon. Harman Yerkes became a member of the firm.

HON. MAHLON H. STOUT, president judge of the courts of Bucks county, was born in Richland township, Bucks county, Pennsylvania, March 10, 1852, being the son of Jacob and Amanda (Headman) Stout, both of German descent.

Jacob Stout, the great-great-grandfather of the subject of this sketch, was born in Germany in the year 1711, and came to this country at the age of twenty-six years. He arrived in Philadelphia in the ship "Samuel," August 30, 1737, accompanied by an elder brother John, aged thirty years. In the year 1739 Jacob Stout married Anna Leisse, widow of John Leisse, of Rockhill township, Bucks county, Pennsylvania. John Leisse, LaCene, Lacey, or Licey, as the name has been variously spelled, arrived in the ship "Adventurer," from Rotterdam, with wife Anna, aged twenty-four years, a brother, Paul La Cene, with his wife Luisa and three children, and a brother-in-law, Michel Miller, September 23, 1732. John Leisse purchased in 1735 two hundred acres in Rockhill under the name of "John Lacey." He died in 1738, and the following year his widow married Jacob Stout. The two hundred acre farm purchased by Leisse included a large part of the present borough of Perkasie. In 1759 Johannes and Hendrick Licey, the sons of John Leisse, deceased, conveyed this tract to their stepfather, Jacob Stout, and he and wife in turn conveyed to them tracts in Hilltown, portions of 266 acres purchased by Jacob Stout in 1757. The first purchase of land by Jacob Stout was a tract of land adjoining the Durham tract, now in Williams township, Northampton county, 243 acres, purchased September 9, 1750; his residence at that date was given as "Durham township, Bucks county." In 1753 he purchased a mill property at Church Hill, in Rockhill township. In 1767 he purchased the Pine Run mill property and one hundred and nineteen acres, and in 1774 a tract of one hundred and fifty acres in New Britain township. These later purchases were doubtless to provide homes for his daughter, Salome, who had married Abraham Freed, a miller, and to whom he conveyed the mill and forty-one acres three years later; and Catharine, who had married Jacob Schlieffer, who occupied and later heired the New Britain property. Jacob Stout was a potter by trade and was a successful and prominent man in the community. The last twenty years of his life were doubtless spent on his Perkasie farm, where he lies buried in a neat little burial lot close to the P. & R. R. R. station. He died April 30, 1779, aged sixty-eight and a half years. The children of Jacob and Anna (Miller-Leisse) Stout were: Abraham, Isaac; Salome, married (first) Abraham Freed and (second) Gabriel Swartzlander; and Catharine, wife of Jacob Schlieffer.

Abraham Stout, eldest son of Jacob and Anna Stout, was born August 17, 1740. He was probably one of the best educated Pennsylvania Germans of his time in Bucks county. Most of his education was acquired in the old Germantown Academy, under the tuition of Hilarius Becker, professor of German, and David J. Dove as instructor in English. He thus acquired a thorough knowledge of the English language, a rare accomplishment at that date or for many years later among the German colonists of upper Bucks. He was an excellent accountant and penman as well as a good business man, and his services were much in demand as a surveyor, scrivener and accountant among his German neighbors for over a quarter of a century. From an examination of the old papers on file in the county offices it would appear that he drew a great majority of the deeds, wills and other legal papers for the middle section of upper Bucks during that period. In addition to this he was constantly in demand by the court to serve as one of the auditors appointed to prepare and state the accounts of administrators and executors under the rule then in vogue, and many of these papers now on file in the orphans' court are models of penmanship, conciseness and neatness. At the death of his father in 1779 his brothers and sisters conveyed to him the homestead farm at Perkasie, whereupon he was born, and he spent his whole life there, the Durham farm going to his brother Isaac, while the sisters were provided for as before stated. He died June 8, 1812, and is buried beside his father, mother and wife in the family burial lot at Perkasie. His life presents a fine example of German-American citizenship. Though he was in the height of his local usefulness during the period of the Revolutionary war, he seems to have held aloof from active participation therein. He was elected to represent Rockhill township in the committee of safety in 1775, but after several meetings had been held he asked to be relieved and another was appointed in his place. It is probable that the traditions of the sufferings of his ancestors from the civil wars in the Palatinate had their effect in deterring him from taking an active part in the struggle. He was a delegate from Bucks county to the constitutional convention of 1790, and took an active part in the framing of the constitution of our commonwealth. He married October 21, 1772, Mary Magdalen Hartzell, daughter of Henry Hartzell of Rockhill. She died November 8, 1811, in her sixty-first year. Their children were: Hannah, who married a Worman, and was left a widow young and for many years resided with her parents; Abraham; Henry H.; Jacob H.; Anna, who married Jacob Hartman; Margaretta, who married Tobias Rule; (later spelled Ruhl) and Magdalene, who married John Gearhart.

Jacob Stout, second son of Abraham and Magdalen, was the grandfather of Judge Stout. He was born on the Perkasie homestead January 9, 1775, and died there August 15, 1820. His wife was Elizabeth Barndt, born November 27, 1778, and died

Mahlon H. Stout.

November 7, 1821. They resided on a portion of the old homestead and raised a family of eight children, viz: Isaac; Abraham; Jacob B.; Samuel; Sarah, who married Charles Leidy; Anna, who married Isaac Drumbore; Mary Magdalen, who married Jacob Groff; and Elizabeth, who married Enos Kile.

Jacob B. Stout, the father of Judge Stout, was born at Perkasie, November 8, 1814, and died near there in April, 1896. He married Amanda, daughter of Michael Headman. They resided for a time at the old Headman Pottery in Rockhill, but returned later and purchased a farm adjoining the old Perkasie homestead, where the remainder of their lives were spent. The children of Jacob and Amanda Stout were: Maria, who married Tobias Weil; Emma, who married George W. Kratz; and Mahlon H., the subject of this sketch.

Judge Stout spent his boyhood days on the Rockhill farm and attended the public schools of the neighborhood and the First State Normal School at Millersville, and taught school for four years. He afterwards entered Franklin and Marshall College, at Lancaster, Pennsylvania, from which he graduated in 1878. He at once took up the study of law in the office of Adam J. Eberly, Esq., at Lancaster, and was admitted to the Lancaster county bar April 4, 1880, and to that of his native county in May of the same year. After two years of practice at Doylestown he located in 1882 at Hulmeville, opening a law office there and having a branch office at Bristol. He was also a justice of the peace at Hulmeville. In 1886 he came to Doylestown and formed a law partnership with ex-Judge Richard Watson, under the firm name of Watson & Stout, which continued until the death of Judge Watson in 1894. Mr. Stout was elected district attorney of Bucks county in 1888, and was unanimously nominated by his party to succeed himself three years later, but was defeated at the polls by the late Paul H. Applebach, the candidate of the then dominant party.

Mr. Stout was married November 13, 1894, to Miss Harriet Miller, of Downingtown, Pennsylvania. In 1898, his wife's health failing, he sacrificed his business and removed with her to Pasadena, California, with the hope of saving her life. While there he was admitted to the bar of that state and practiced law at Pasadena. His wife died December 24, 1899, and their infant son Max on December 25, 1898.

Mr. Stout returned to Doylestown in the spring of 1900, and again took up the practice of law. In 1901 he formed a partnership with Harvey S. Kiser, Esq., under the firm name of Stout & Kiser, which continued until the elevation of Mr. Stout to the bench. He was elected president judge in November, 1903, and entered upon the duties of his office in January, 1904. Judge Stout has always been a close student, and as a lawyer had the reputation of being one of the best counsellors at the bar, and his administration of the high office to which he has been elevated merits the trust reposed in him by the large majority of voters who elected him. His calm and even temperament, his uniform courtesy, his sterling common sense, his devotion to principle and right, and his unquestioned knowledge of the law, have made his administration popular with all classes.

JOHN C. SWARTLEY was born in Franconia township, Montgomery county, Pennsylvania, September 14, 1865, and is a son of Jacob S. and Elizabeth (Cassel) Swartley, both of whom are descendants of early German settlers in that locality of the Mennonite faith.

John Schwardley, the pioneer ancestor of the subject of this sketch, was born in Eppingen, in Necker, grand duchy of Baden, Germany, in the year 1754. At the age of eighteen years, accompanied by his younger brothers, Jacob and Philip, he emigrated to Pennsylvania, arriving in Philadelphia September 30, 1772, in the ship, "Minerva," Captain James Johnston, from Rotterdam. He soon after found a home among his compatriots in Franconia township, where he married Magdalena Rosenberger, born December 18, 1759, daughter of the Rev. Henry Rosenberger, Mennonite minister at Franconia, and grand daughter of Henry Rosenberger, the pioneer ancestor of the Rosenberger family, who had taken up a large tract of land in Franconia in 1728. Rev. Henry Rosenberger was born December 2, 1725, and died in 1809. He married in 1745 Barbara Oberholtzer, born in 1726, died February 3, 1765, daughter of Jacob and Barbara Oberholtzer, (or Overholt), who were early settlers in Bedminster township, Bucks county, where Jacob purchased land in 1749. Rev. Henry and Barbara (Oberholtzer) Rosenberger were the parents of eight children, five of whom survived and left descendants, viz: Anna, who married (first) Michael Leatherman and (second) John Loux, both of Bedminster; Elizabeth, married Mark Fretz; Barbara, married Daniel Rickert; all of Bucks county; Magdalena, above named; and Sarah, who married Philip Schwardley, the youngest brother of John Schwardley, above named. John and Magdalena Schwardley lived and died on a portion of the Rosenberger homestead in Franconia, still in the tenure of their descendants, and were the parents of nine children, viz: John, Jacob, Samuel, Abraham, Joseph, Henry, Philip R., Elizabeth and Mary.

Philip R. Swartley, son of John and Magdalena, was born on the old homestead in Franconia, January 2, 1795, and died there July 30, 1880. He married Annie C. Shoemaker, and their son Jacob S. Swartley, born in 1821, died 1867, was the father of the subject of this sketch. He was born and reared on the old homestead in Franconia, and followed farming and milling during the brief period of his manhood. His wife, Elizabeth Cassel, was a descendant of early German settlers on the Skippack, who have left numerous descendants of the name in Bucks and Montgomery counties and elsewhere. She is still living in Lansdale, Pennsylvania.

John C. Swartley, the subject of this sketch, left an orphan at the age of two years, was reared in the family of his maternal uncle, Abraham F. Delp, in the township of New Britain, Bucks county, and acquired his elementary education in the public schools of that township. He entered the First state normal school at Millersville in 1885, and graduated in 1888. For the next two years he was principal of the North Wales high schools, in Montgomery county. In 1890 he entered the law department of the University of Pennsylvania, from which he graduated in 1893, in the meantime reading law in the office of Henry Lear, Esq., at Doylestown. He was admitted to the Philadelphia bar in June, 1893, and in August of the same year to the bar of Bucks county, and at once began the practice of his profession at the county seat. Soon after admission to the bar he became active and influential in political circles, and served for three years as chairman of the Republican county committee. In the fall of 1897 he was elected to the office of district attorney for the term of three years, and filled that position with ability. He has always been active in the councils of his party, and has served as delegate to state and congressional conventions. He was appointed January 1, 1903, assistant United States attorney for the Eastern District of Pennsylvania, a position which he still fills. In 1903 he formed a co-partnership at law with Wesley Bunting, Esq., and the firm have a good practice in the several courts of Bucks county.

Mr. Swartley was married on October 24, 1900, to Agnes Darlington, daughter of the late Henry T. and Susan Darlington, of Doylestown, and this union has been blessed with two children—John C. Jr., and Margaret Darlington.

(A sketch of the career and ancestry of Mrs. Swartley's distinguished father, Henry T. Darlington, will be found in this volume.)

LEE S. CLYMER, of Riegelsville, Bucks county, Pennsylvania, one of the prominent manufacturers and business men of upper Bucks, was born at Mt. Laurel Furnace, Berks county, Pennsylvania, (Temple post-office) April 2, 1863, and is a son of William Hiester and Valeria (Smith) Clymer. His father was for many years proprietor of the Mt. Laurel furnace. Mr. Clymer comes of a distinguished ancestry both in this country and in Europe, only brief mention of which can be given in the scope of this brief sketch. Richard Clymer, the paternal ancestor, was a native of Bristol, England, from whence he migrated to

Philadelphia, Pennsylvania, in 1705, accompanied by his mother, Catharine Clymer, and a brother William, who died in 1740 without issue. Richard Clymer was a shipping merchant and shipbuilder; he died August 18, 1734, leaving several children, of whom only his sons, Christopher and William have left descendants. George Clymer, the signer of the Declaration of Independence, was a son of the former.

William Clymer, son of Richard, was a captain in the English navy, commanding the frigate "Penzance" during the reign of George II, and was lost at sea, leaving a will dated October 16, 1760. He married at Christ Church, Philadelphia, January 19, 1742, Ann Judith Roberdeau, daughter of Isaac and Mary (Conyngham) Roberdeau, and sister to General Daniel Roberdeau, the friend of Franklin, and one of the most distinguished patriots in Pennsylvania during the Revolution. Ann Judith (Roberdeau) Clymer was born on the Island of St. Christopher, West Indies, in the year 1725, and died at Morgantown, Berks county, Pennsylvania, April, 1782. Isaac Roberdeau, father of Mrs. Clymer, was a native of Rochelle, France, and fled to the island of St. Christopher, one of the British West Indies, on the revocation of the Edict of Nantes in 1685. Here he met and married Mary Conyngham, born at Cayou, on that island, April 4, 1699, daughter of Robert Conyngham, born in Scotland, March 24, 1669, and his wife Judith Elizabeth de Bonneson, a native of Morlais, France, the former of whom traced his descent back through a long line of kings and princes royal to William the Conqueror, and in his own direct line to Malcolm, son of Friskine, who assisted Malcolm Canmore, afterwards King of Scotland, to escape from MacBeth's tyranny and treason, and was in return made Thane of Conyngham, from which his posterity afterwards took their surname. Robert Conyngham, of St. Christopher, left an immense estate in St. Christopher and in Scotland, a portion of which he entailed in the male line, and which was the subject of litigation a century later on the male line bearing his surname becoming extinct. Isaac and Mary (Conyngham) Roberdeau were the parents of three children, all born at St. Christopher, viz: Elizabeth, born 1724, who died unmarried; Ann Judith, who married William Clymer; and Daniel, the eminent merchant, statesman and patriot before referred to. Isaac Roberdeau died at St. Christopher, and his widow and children removed to Philadelphia while the children were still in their minority, where the widow married a man by name of Keighly, but was again a widow many years prior to her death, which occurred March 13, 1771.

Daniel Conyngham Clymer, only son of William and Ann Judith (Roberdeau) Clymer, was born in Philadelphia, April 6, 1748. His father dying when he was a child, he was educated under the care of his distinguished uncle, General Daniel Roberdeau. He graduated at Princeton in 1766, studied law and became eminent in his profession. At the beginning of the Revolution he at once joined the Associators of that city and was commissioned a lieutenant. April 8, 1776, he was commissioned lieutenant-colonel and placed in command of a rifle battalion. He was appointed in 1775 and again in 1776 by Congress as a signer of Bills of Credit, and held the offices of deputy commissary-general of prisoners and commissioner of claims of the treasury. During the closing years of the Revolution he removed to Reading, Berks county, and represented that county in the legislature in 1782 and several succeeding terms. He died at Reading, January 25, 1810. He had married in 1782 Mary Weidner, daughter of Peter and Susan Weidner, of Berks county, who died December 5, 1802, in her forty-sixth year. Their children were Ann, born 1782, who died unmarried in 1852; William, born 1788, died October 10, 1845, an eminent lawyer of Reading; and Edward Tilgham, born August 14, 1790, died March 6, 1831. Edward Tilghman Clymer was born at Reading, Berks county, and was educated at Princeton. He married June 11, 1818, Maria Catharine Hiester, daughter of William and Anna Maria (Meyer) Hiester. She was born March 4, 1793, and died March 24, 1845. Edward Tilghman was a man of scholarly attainments, and follows

1. Daniel Roberdeau, a merchant and lawyer of Reading, born March 31, 1819, died May 5, 1889, aged seventy years.

2. William Hiester, the father of the subject of this sketch; see forward.

3. Edward Myers, born July 16, 1822, died May 25, 1883, in New York City, projector and first president of the East Pennsylvania railroad, later president of a coal company connected with the N. Y., L. E. & W. Railroad Company, with offices in New York.

4. Wiedner, born May 12, 1824, died July 16, 1824.

5. Mary Hiester, born July 19, 1825, drowned in the English Channel November 26, 1878, with two of her children; married August 10, 1852, her cousin, William Bingham Clymer, son of Henry, and grandson of George Clymer, the Signer, who was born April 18, 1801, at Morrisville, Bucks county, Pennsylvania, died May 28, 1873, at Florence, Italy.

6. Hon. Hiester Clymer, born November 3, 1827, died June 12, 1884; lawyer, state senator, congressman, Democratic candidate for governor, president of Union Trust Company, etc.

7. George Edward Clymer, born January 8, 1830, died July 7, 1895, major of Sixth Pennsylvania Cavalry in the civil war and prominent in the iron and steel industries.

William Hiester Clymer, the father of the subject of this sketch, was born at the Clymer homestead in the Conestoga Valley, near Morgantown, Berks county, October 9, 1820. His father dying when he was eleven years of age, he was placed with his uncle, William Hiester, at New Holland, Lancaster county, and was educated at Lititz, and assisted his uncle in his store. He later removed to Reading, where he and his brother, Daniel R., conducted a dry goods store until 1846, when he sold out to Daniel, and with his brother Edward M., purchased the Mt. Laurel iron furnace. They built the Temple iron furnace in 1867, and, having seven years previously purchased the old Oley furnace, became extensive manufacturers of iron, organizing the Temple Iron Company in 1870, and later the Clymer Iron Company, both of which William H. Clymer was president, until September, 1882, when he resigned and removed with his family to Reading, where he died July 26, 1883. He was president of the First National Bank of Reading from 1876 to his death. He married, June 12, 1855, Valeria Smith, eldest daughter of Levi B. Smith, who was born March 14, 1828, and died August 17, 1901. They were the parents of six children: Emily Smith; Edward Tilghman; William Hiester; Lee Smith; Valeria Elizabeth; and Frederick Hiester.

The ancestors of Maria Catharine Hiester, the grandmother of the subject of this sketch, were of Silesian origin, her first American ancestor being Daniel Hiester, the youngest of three brothers, John, Joseph and Daniel, who emigrated from Witgenstein, in Westphalia, to Pennsylvania, early in the eighteenth century, and took up their residence in Goshenhoppen, now Montgomery county. Daniel had several sons, of whom John, born April 9, 1745, was a member of congress from Chester county 1807-8 and was succeeded by his son Daniel; Daniel, a representative in congress from Montgomery county, 1789-97, and from Maryland 1801-5; Gabriel, for thirty years a member of the state legislature from Berks county; and William. All four of these sons of Daniel Hiester were in the continental service during the revolution, the two elder as colonels, the third as a major, while William, the youngest, born June 10, 1757, being required to look after his aged parents, did not serve but one campaign. Joseph Hiester, governor of Pennsylvania, was the only son of John, and a cousin of the four brothers above named.

Daniel Hiester, the elder, was born in the town of Elsoff, county of Witgenstein, province of Westphalia, in Silesia, Germany, January 1, 1713, and died in Bern township, Berks county, Pennsylvania, June 7, 1795. His wife was Catharine Schuler, whom he married September 29, 1742. She was born September 10, 1717, and died August 17, 1789, aged seventy-two years, eleven months and seven days.

William Hiester, the great-grandfather of the subject of this sketch, born at Goshenhoppen, Upper Salford township, Montgomery county, June 10, 1757, was the youngest son of Daniel and Catharine

(Schuler) Hiester. He was seventeen years of age when his parents removed to Reading, and remained with his parents in Reading for ten years. He then removed to Bern township, where he died July 13, 1822. He was a private in Captain George Will's company, in 1777, in the battalion commanded by his brother, Major Gabriel Hiester. He married, March 18, 1784, Anna Maria Meyer, daughter of Isaac Meyer, the founder of Meyerstown, Pennsylvania. She was born December 28, 1758, and died October 4, 1822. They were the parents of eight children, the fifth of whom, Maria Catharine, born March 4, 1793, was the wife of Edward Tilghman Clymer.

LEE S. CLYMER, born at the Mt. Laurel Furnace, April 2, 1863, was educated at Lafayette College, Easton, Pennsylvania, taking a special course in chemistry. On leaving college he accepted a position as chemist for the Minnesota Iron Company, which he filled for one year. In 1885 he opened a general laboratory at Reading, Pennsylvania. In December, 1886, he left Reading and took a position as chemist for the Carnegie Company at the Edgar Thomas Furnace, Braddock, Pennsylvania, where he remained for one year. In October, 1887, he came to Bucks county as chemist for the Durham Iron Company, and filled that position for two years, when he was made superintendent of the Pequest Iron Furnace, near Oxford, New Jersey, where he remained until the furnace was about to be closed in the autumn of 1890. He then accepted a position as superintendent of the Lehigh Iron Company's works near Allentown, Pennsylvania, where he remained for about eight months. During a part of the next two years he was superintendent for the Thomas Iron Company's furnaces at Hellertown, Pennsylvania. In 1895 he erected and equipped the Durham Knitting Mills, at Riegelsville, Bucks county, which he has since sucessfully operated. He also operates several fine farms in Durham· township, and is interested in the breeding of standard bred horses and thoroughbred cattle. He recently became half owner of what was the Lehigh Power Company, located at Raubsville, Pennsylvania. It is proposed to operate this plant under the name of the Clymer Power Company.

He married, June 11, 1891, Clara Matilda Riegel, daughter of the late John L. and Lydia (Stover). Riegel, by whom he has two children, John Riegel, born April 14, 1892, and Valeria Smith, born January 12, 1896.

JACOB F. CLYMER. The Clymer family, of which Jacob F. Clymer, a prosperous farmer of New Britain township is a worthy representative, is one of the oldest in the township, and have always been highly esteemed for the many excellent characteristics displayed by them both in public and private life. Jonas Clymer, grandfather of Jacob F. Clymer, resided on the farm now owned by Jacob F. Clymer. He was a shoemaker by trade, and this occupation he followed in connection with agricultural pursuits during the early years of his life, but as he advanced in years he abandoned the former line of work entirely, devoting his entire attention to the latter. He served as supervisor of his township for seven years, his long term of office attesting to his capability. He adhered to the tenets of the Mennonite church, in which he served as trustee; he was formerly a Whig in politics, and later a Republican. He married Hannah Clymer, daughter of Henry Clymer, and their children were: John, William C., Henry, Levi, Elizabeth, Sarah, Amanda and Hannah.

William C. Clymer, father of Jacob F. Clymer, was reared on his father's farm in New Britain township, educated in the common schools of the neighborhood, and upon the death of his father succeeded to the homestead. In connection with his extensive farming operations he engaged in the produce commission business for thirty years, deriving a goodly income from both enterprises, and thus was enabled to provide a comfortable home for his family. The esteem in which he was held by his fellow-townsmen was evidenced by the fact that he was the incumbent of the office of school director twelve years and supervisor one year. He was a trustee of the Mennonite church, the doctrines of which he firmly believed in, and his political views were in accord with those of the Republican party. By his marriage to Elizabeth Fretz, only child of Joseph and Mary (Markley) Fretz, four children were born: Jacob F., Charles who died at the age of twenty years; Jonas, who is engaged in business in Philadelphia; and Harvey, also engaged in business in Philadelphia. Mary (Fretz) Clymer, mother of these children, died in 1884, and Mr. Clymer married for his second wife Lydia A. Swartley, widow of Philip Swartley.

Jacob F. Clymer was born in New Britain township, Bucks county, Pennsylvania, March 16, 1862. He was reared on the old homestead, and his educational advantages were obtained by attendance at the common schools. His whole life has been spent on the farm where he was born, his occupation being that of farming, for which he is eminently qualified, as is clearly shown by the appearance of his broad acres and commodious outbuildings. Mr. Clymer has served as supervisor of the township nine years, his duties during that time being performed in a highly creditable and efficient manner. In religious and political faith he follows in the footsteps of his forefathers, being a member and trustee of the Mennonite church and a Republican. In 1887 Mr. Clymer married Anna Mary Swartley, daughter of Philip and Lydia Swartley, and they are the parents of one son, Vincent, born June 30, 1892.

THE FOULKE FAMILY that has been prominent in the official, professional and business life of Bucks, Montgomery and Philadelphia counties for many generations as well as in that of far distant states and cities, is descended from Edward Foulke, who emigrated from Wales in 1698 and settled in Gwynedd, now Montgomery county, Pennsylvania. An acount of his ancestry, tracing in unbroken line to "John King of England, born December 24, 1166, crowned May 27, 1216," and an account of his coming to America, etc., the latter written by himself under date of 11-mo. 14, 1702, contains among other things the following:

"When arrived at mature age, I married Eleanor, the daughter of Hugh, ap (son of) Cadwallader, ap Rhys of the parish of Spytu in Denbighshire. Her mother's name was Gwen the daughter of Ellis ap William, ap Hugh, ap Thomas, ap David, ap Madoc, ap Evan, ap Cott, ap Evan, ap Griffith, ap Madoc, ap Einion, ap Meredith of Cai-Fadog; she was born in the same parish and shire with her husband. I had by my said wife nine children, whose names are as follows: Thomas, Hugh, Cadwallader, and Evan; Grace, Gwen, Jane, Catharine, and Margaret. We lived at a place called Coedy-foel, a beautiful farm belonging to Roger Price, Esq., of Rhiwlas, of Merionethshire, aforesaid. But in progress of time I had an inclination to remove with my family to the Province of Pennsylvania; and in order thereto we set out on the 3d day of the 2d-month, A. D. 1698, and came in two days to Liverpool, where with divers others, who intended to go the voyage, we took shipping, the 17th of the same month, on board the "Robert and Elizabeth," and the next day set sail for Ireland, where we arrived, and stayed until the 1st of the 3d month, May, and then sailed again for Pennsylvania, and were about eleven weeks at sea. And the sore distemper of the bloody flux broke out in the vessel, of which died five and forty persons in our passage. The distemper was so mortal that two or three corpses were cast overboard every day while it lasted. But through the favor and mercy of Divine Providence, I, with my wife and nine children, escaped that sore mortality and arrived safe at Philadelphia, the 17th day of the 5th-month, July, where we were kindly received and hospitably entertained by our friends and old acquaintances. I soon purchased a fine tract of land of about seven hundred acres, sixteen miles from Philadelphia, on a part of which I settled, and divers others of our company, who came over sea with us, settled near me at the same time. This was the beginning of November, 1698, aforesaid, and the township was called Gwynedd or North Wales."

According to his own narrative Edward Foulke was born 5th mo. 14th, 1651, and taking the age given by the Meeting Records at time of his death would place the date of his death in 1739. All of his nine children lived to mature age, married and reared families. The only two in whom Bucks countians have any especial interest were his eldest son Thomas, and second son Hugh. Gwen, the eldest daughter, married Alexander Edwards, Jr., who was a land owner in Bucks county and has descendants here. Grace married John Griffith, of Merion, Chester county. Jane married Ellis Hugh, and settled at Exeter, Berks county, and left numerous descendants of the name of Hughes. Catharine married Theophilus Williams, of Montgomery. Margaret married Nicholas Roberts. Thomas Foulke, eldest son of Edward and Eleanor, born in Merionethshire, Wales, immigrant to Gwynedd, 1698, with his parents, married at Gwynedd, 4 mo. 27, 1706, Gwen Evans, daughter of David, of Radnor, and settled at Gwynedd on part of the Edward Foulke tract. He died in 1762, and his wife in 1760. They were the parents of eight children, of whom the two oldest Edward (1707-1770) and William (1708-1775) had descendants in Bucks. Dr. Joseph Foulke, for many years a practicing physician of Buckingham, was a great grandson of Edward, through his son Hugh (1752-1831), a noted minister among Friends, who married Ann Roberts, their son Joseph (1786-1863), who married Elizabeth Shoemaker, being the father of the Buckingham physician. Dr. Charles Foulke, born December 14, 1815, died December 30, 1871, for many years a practicing physician at New Hope, Bucks county, and the father of Dr. Richard C. Foulke, still practicing there, was also a great-great-grandson of Thomas Foulke and Gwen Evans. His father, Edward Foulke, of Gwynedd (1784-1851), married Tacy Jones, and his grandfather, Amos Foulke, (1740-1791) one of the firm of Caleb and Amos Foulke, merchants of Philadelphia, was the son of William, second son of Thomas and Gwen, who married Hannah Jones, of Montgomery.

Hugh Foulke, second son of Edward and Eleanor, born in Merionethshire, in 1685, married, in 1713, Ann Williams, born 11 mo. 8, 1693, died 9mo. 10, 1773, daughter of John Williams, of Montgomery, and settled in Richland, Bucks county, soon after his marriage, and died there 5mo. 21, 1760. He was a minister of the Society of Friends for forty years. He is the ancestor of many present residents of Bucks county, through comparatively few of the name now reside in the county. The children of Hugh and Ann (Williams) Foulke were;—Mary, born 1714, died 2mo. 29, 1756, married James Boone, of Exeter, Berks county, son of George the elder, and brother of Squire Boone, the father of Daniel, the pioneer of Kentucky. Their eldest daughter, Ann, married Abraham Lincoln, of the family of the martyred president. Martha, born 5mo. 22, 1716, died 4mo. 17, 1781, married (first), October 4, 1738, William Edwards, of Milford, Bucks county, and (second) John Roberts. Samuel, born 1718, died 1797, married Ann

Greasley. He was one of the most prominent men in upper Bucks county, serving in the Provincial Assembly 1761 to 1768. He was a surveyor and conveyancer, and transacted a large amount of public business for his neighbors. He was clerk of Richland Meeting from its organization in 1742 for thirty years, and an elder until his death, notwithstanding the fact that he and his brothers, John Thomas, and Theophilus and nephew, Everard, were disowned in 1781 for having taken the oath of allegiance, the action of the Meeting not being sanctioned by the Yearly Meeting. He translated the "narrative" of his grandfather, Edward Foulke, from Welsh into English. John Foulke, born 12mo. 21, 1722, died 5mo. 25, 1787, married Mary Roberts, daughter of Edward Roberts, a noted minister among Friends of Richland. John was also a member of Provincial Assembly from Bucks county from 1769 to 1775. Thomas Foulke, born in Richland 8mo. 14, 1724, died 3mo. 31, 1786, married Jane Roberts, another daughter of Edward Roberts, of Richland. See forward. Theophilus Foulke, born in Richland, 12mo. 21, 1726, died 11mo. 4, 1785, married Margaret Thomas, daughter of Samuel and Margaret. Of their twelve children Benjamin, born 11mo. 19, 1766, died 2mo. 28, 1821, was a member of assembly from Bucks county, 1816 to his death in 1821, at Harrisburg in attendance upon the session of the legislature. He was given an official funeral, which was attended by both houses, the governor, and heads of departments, and resolutions were adopted that crape should be worn during the remainder of the session. William Foulke, born 12mo. 10, 1728, died 4mo. 11, 1796, married Priscilla Lester, daughter of John of Richland. Edward Foulke, born 10mo. 19, 1729, died March 1, 1747, unmarried. Ann Foulke, born 1mo. 1, 1732, married William Thomas. Jane Foulke, born 1mo. 3, 1734, died 8mo., 1771, married John Greasley.

Thomas Foulke, of Richland, son of Hugh and Ann (Williams) Foulke, born 1mo. 14, 1724, died 3mo. 31, 1786, was a life long resident of Richland township, and a prominent man in the community. He was a member of Richland Monthly Meeting, and like his brothers was dealt with for taking the oath to the United Colonies in 1781. His wife, Jane Roberts, born 11mo. 3, 1732, died 7 mo. 25, 1822, was a daughter of Edward and Mary (Bolton). Roberts, of Richland, the former a native of Merionethshire, born 3mo., 1687, came to Pennsylvania in 1699, and settled in Byberry, Philadelphia county. He married, in 1714, Mary Bolton, born in Cheltenham, Philadelphia county, Pennsylvania, November 4, 1687, daughter of Everard and Elizabeth Bolton, who came from Ross, Hertfordshire, England, in 1682, and settled in Cheltenham. Everard Bolton was a justice of Philadelphia county, and a very prominent man in Colonial times. The

children of Thomas and Jane (Roberts) Foulke were:—Everard, born 9mo. 8, 1755, died 9mo. 5, 1827; Abigail, born 10mo. 4, 1763; Susan, born 11mo. 5, 1766; Samuel, born 11mo. 19, 1767; Edward and Samuel, died in infancy.

Everard Foulke, son of Thomas and Jane, was one of the justices of the peace of Richland for many years. He was one of the assessors of the United States taxes, when John Fries raised his rebellion in 1798, in upper Bucks and Northampton counties, against the collection of the tax, and was one of the assessors attacked in Lower Milford and at Quakertown by the insurrectionists and forced to desist from performing their duty. He married, in 1778, Ann DeHaven, of Holland ancestry and they were the parents of nine children, as follows:—Abigail, born 5 mo. 18, 1779, married Abel Penrose, see Penrose family in this work; Eleanor, born 7mo. 18, 1781, died 4 mo. 28, 1815, unmarried; Caleb, see forward; Samuel, born 3 mo. 28, 1786, married Elizabeth Johnson; Thomas, born 4 mo. 13, 1789, died in Kentucky; Susanna, born 9 mo. 18, 1791, died 1883, married David Johnson; Anna, born 5 mo. 3, 1794, died 9 mo. 16, 1820; Margaret, born 12 mo. 24, 1796, married Peter Lester in 1820; Everard, born 7 mo. 21, 1800, married Frances Watson, daughter of John Watson, of Buckingham, and removed to Illinois.

Caleb Foulke, son of Everard and Ann (DeHaven) Foulke, was born in Richland, 8 mo. 28, 1783, died 2 mo. 22, 1852, was also a lifelong resident of Richland. He married, 11 mo. 26, 1807, Jane Green, born 2 mo. 8, 1785, died 3 mo. 3, 1835, daughter of Benjamin and Jane (Roberts) Green. Benjamin Green was a son of Joseph and Catharine (Thomas) Green, of Springfield, Bucks county, and was born in Springfield, 4 mo. 27, 1750, died in Quakertown. He was a hatter in Springfield and later in Quakertown. The children of Caleb and Jane (Green) Foulke were:—Caroline, died in infancy; Caroline, born 2 mo. 25, 1810, died 12 mo. 17, 1838; Maryetta, born 7 mo. 30, 1811, died 4 mo. 26, 1851, married Aaron Penrose; Benjamin G. (see forward); and Eleanor, born 3 mo. 12, 1816, died 8 mo. 13, 1842, married Samuel J. Levick.

Benjamin G. Foulke, son of Caleb and Jane (Green) Foulke, was born at Quakertown, and died there 8 mo. 14, 1888. He was clerk of the men's branch of the Philadelphia Yearly Meeting from 1873 to 1886. He was a prominent business man of Quakertown for a half century and was highly respected by all who knew him. He was a surveyor and conveyancer and did a large amount of public business. He married, in 1838, Jane Mather, born 3 mo. 24, 1817, daughter of Charles and Jane Mather, of Whitpain, Montgomery county, Pennsylvania. Their children were, Caleb, born 12 mo. 3, 1839, died 10 mo. 20, 1865; Charles M., born 7 mo. 25, 1841, educated at Foulke's school at Gwynedd, and Friends' Central School, Philadelphia; entered mercantile business in Philadelphia, 1861, retired 1872, married at Paris, France, December 10, 1872, Sarah A. Cushing, of New York city; Job Roberts, born 2 mo. 23, 1843; Anna S., born 1846; and Eleanor, 1850.

Job Roberts Foulke, son of Benjamin G. and Jane (Mather) Foulke, born at Quakertown, 2 mo. 23, 1843, has been trust officer of the Provident Life and Trust Company of Philadelphia for many years. He married, 5 mo. 25, 1869, Emma Bullock, daughter of Samuel and Jemima R. Bullock, of Mt. Holly, New Jersey, and has two children; Roland Roberts, and Rebecca Mulford. Roland Roberts, a member of the Philadelphia bar, married, June 6, 1900, Ellen R. Griffith, daughter of Manuel E. and Mary E. Griffith, of Philadelphia.

Eleanor Foulke, daughter of Benjamin G. and Jane (Mather) Foulke, is the only one of the family to retain her residence in Bucks county. She resides at the old family mansion at Quakertown, and is unmarried.

WILLIAM HENRY FOULKE, one of the enterprising, practical farmers of Bucks county, Pennsylvania, was there born in Richland Centre, July 4, 1841, on the farm he now occupies and cultivates, it being one of the original Foulks homesteads. William is the son of Hugh and Sarah (Roberts) Foulke, and grandson of Hugh Foulke, who was a farmer by occupation and the founder and a trustee of the subscription schools of his district. He is a descendant of Hugh Foulke, the first of the name born in America. An old Bible now in the possession of Mrs. Susan Hannah Biehn, sister of William Henry Foulke, gives the record of his birth, July, 1685, and death, May 21, 1760. He married Ann ――――, who was born November 3, 1693, and died September 10, 1773. They were the parents of the following named children: 1. Mary, born September 24, 1714; 2. Martha, June 2, 1716; 3. Samuel, December 4, 1718; 4. Ellen, January 19, 1720; 5. John, December 21, 1722; 6. Thomas, January 14, 1724; 7. William, December 10, 1728; 8. Edward, October 19, 1729; 9. Ann, January 1, 1732; 10. Jane, January 3, 1734.

Hugh Foulke, father of William Henry Foulke, was born in Richland township, Bucks county, Pennsylvania. His education was obtained in the subscription schools of his district, and the followed the quiet but useful calling of a farmer. He married Miss Sarah Roberts, daughter of John and Sarah Rob-

erts, and the following children were the issue of this union: 1. Catherine, born September 6, 1835, married Isaac Tomlinson, of New Britain township; 2. Julia Ann, born December 4, 1839, married Henry Dotts of Montgomery county, Pennsylvania; 3. William Henry, mentioned at length herein after; 4. Sarah Martha, born August 19, 1843, married (first) David Hillegas, of Quakertown, and (second) Henry Sonders, farmer, of lower Richland township; 5. Charles Edward, born in 1845, married, 1870, Anna, the daughter of Warner and Alice (Singley) Haycock, farmers, Whitemarsh township, Montgomery county, Pennsylvania; 6. Elizabeth, born March 6, 1847, married Charles Miller, and resides at Hockerstown, Montgomery county; 7. Hester Ellen, born November 16, 1850, married Nicholas Martin, of Stowe, Montgomery county; 8. Susan Hannah, born October 25, 1852, married Andrew Biehn, lives at Paletown, Richland township; 9. Anna, born April 15, 1860, married Francis Fellman.

William Henry Foulke, third child and eldest son of Hugh and Sarah (Roberts) Foulke, obtained his educational training in the Rocky Ridge public school at Paletown, remaining there until his nineteenth year. After leaving the school William assisted with the farm work, and later he and his brother, Charles Edward, purchased the place. They were engaged in the cultivation of the farm until 1891, when the partnership was dissolved. William sold his interest in the property to Charles and purchased the Hugh Foulke farm, the old family homestead, comprising seventy-two acres of improved land and forest. Mr. Foulke is an industrious, useful member of the community, and an excellent farmer. In matters of politics he affiliates with the Republican party, and, although he takes a deep and lasting interest in the welfare of that organization has never aspired to public office. He is actively interested in educational affairs, and served twelve years as school director.

January 25, 1883, William Henry Foulke was united in marriage to Mary Elizabeth, daughter of Charles Pilgrim, V. S., of New York city, and widow of George S. Plant, Esq., of Norfolk, England. Mrs. Foulke was born at Hudson, on the Hudson river, near Albany, New York, May 31, 1847. During her first husband's life she lived for a time in England, and later near Quakertown. Mrs. Foulke is a woman of bright and active disposition and assists in the management of the home farm. Mr. and Mrs. Foulke are the parents of one child, Mary Elizabeth, born June 5, 1888; she was educated in the public schools of Paletown, and now resides at home with her parents.

CHARLES EDWARD FOULKE, an old resident and worthy representative of Bucks county, Pennsylvania, was there born in Richland Center in 1845, the son of Hugh and Sarah (Roberts) Foulke. Mention of the ancestral history of Mr. Foulke is made in the preceding sketch of his brother, William Henry Foulke. Charles obtained his education in the Rockridge public school, continuing there until he was eighteen years of age. He then engaged in assisting with the home farm work, and later spent six months in Quakertown with Mr. Richard Moore. He subsequently purchased the home farm in partnership with his brother William, and in the spring of 1891 purchased his brother's interest, and has since continued alone in the conduct of the farm. Mr. Foulke is one of the progressive farmers of the county, his farm comprising one hundred and seven acres of mostly improved land. In politics. Mr. Foulke is a strong advocate of the principles of the Republican party, has always taken a lively interest in local affairs, and has served as committeeman of his township. He and his wife are members of the Society of Friends of Quakertown Meeting.

In 1870 he was united in marriage to Miss Anna Hoycock, daughter of Warner and Alice (Singley) Hoycock, farmers of White Marsh township, Montgomery county, Pennsylvania. The following named children were born to Mr. and Mrs. Foulke: 1. Linford, born December 21, 1872, married, June 6, 1900, Miss Mary C. Gerhart, daughter of Edward and Caroline (Lewis) Gerhart; Linford Foulke, lives at Quakertown, is carrier of U. S. mails, rural free delivery, and a dealer in agricultural implements, wagons and farmers' supplies; 2. Joseph, born August 27, 1874, married Miss Katharine, daughter of William and Elizabeth Neanan, of Richland; he lives in Quakertown, Pennsylvania, and is a carpenter for J. W. Stoneback; 3. Herbert Theophalus, born September 17, 1875, lives at home and assists his father on the farm; unmarried; 4. Oschar Clifford, born January 20, 1878, married January 1, 1904, Martha, daughter of Peter and Sarah (Weaver) Smith; lives at Quakertown, Pennsylvania, stove moulder for Roberts, Winner & Company. 5. Chester A. Foulke, born August 25, 1881, lives at home, unmarried, and is a weaver in the Quakertown silk mill.

THE VAN HORN FAMILY. The family of Van Horn has been a prominent one in Bucks county for two centuries, filling important positions in the official, professional and business life of the county in every generation and constantly sending out its representatives to fill like important positions in other localities and states, its representatives now being found in nearly every state in the Union.

The pioneer ancestor of the family was Christian Barendtse, that is Christian, son of Barendt, who it is said came from Hooren, a city of the Zuyder Zee, about twenty-five miles from Amsterdam. The exact date of his arrival in America is not known. He was a carpenter by trade, and the records of New Amsterdam show that he and a fellow craftsman, Auke Jansen, were appointed, March 10, 1653, by the burgomasters and schepens of New Amsterdam to view a house, about the building of which there was some litigation. These records further show that he was frequently appointed a referee during the next four or five years. And he is shown to have contributed towards the strengthening of the city wall on October 15, 1655. He is also said to have been with the force sent out from New Amsterdam, September 5, 1655, against the Swedes and Finns on the south (now Delaware) river, at Fort Christina. On his return to New Amsterdam he was appointed January 18, 1656, a fire warden, in place of Johan Paul Jacquet, who had resigned and "removed to the South River in New Netherlands." On April 17, 1657, he was admitted a "Small Burgher" of New Amsterdam, an honor which carried with it the freedom of trade and a right to membership in the respective guilds of the town, and conferred upon natives of the city, residents there one year and six weeks before the date of the charter, burgher's sons-in-law, city storekeepers, salaried servants of the company and all paying the sum of twenty-five guilders. On August 1, 1657, Christian Barentze, carpenter, was granted by Peter Stuyvesant, director general of New Netherland, a lot in New Amsterdam, by the Land Gate, (now at Broadway and Wall streets) for a house and garden. He also owned several other properties in the neighborhood, some of which are said to have covered a part of the present Trinity churchyard. Probably as a result of his trip to the South river, Christian Barentse and Joost Rugger and possibly others obtained a grant of land on the south side of None Such creek, a tributary of the Chrisiana, near the present site of Wilmington, Delaware, and began the erection thereon of a tide water mill. According to Amos C. Brinton, who has given much attention to the ancient mill sites of Delaware Barentse and Rugger, he began the erection of this mill in 1656. From the dates previously given, however, as well as from other records, it would appear, that the date of Christain Barentse, removal to the Delaware was sometime in the year

1657. Contemporary records also refer to the mill as a "horse mill," the truth of the matter being most probably that the horse mill was set up to serve until the tide water mill was completed. The low marshy nature of the land and the turning up of the mud to the sun caused an epidemic from which Barentse died July 26, 1658. A letter written by Vice-Director Jacob Alricks, from New Amstel, (New Castle) to Stuyvesant, under date of September 5, 1658, and published in documents relating to the Colonial History of New York, vol. xii, p. 224, relates entirely to the affairs of the widow and children of Christian Barentse. It states that the widow had requested within three days of his burial that she desired to return to New Amsterdam, and that the property which he left be sold and that though he consents thereto he "advised and proposed to her that it woulld be for her best to remain in possession, she should be assisted in completing the mill, with income whereof, which through the grists she would be able to diminish the expenses and live decently and abundantly with her children on the surplus, besides that she had yet three or four cows with sheep and hogs, which also could help her to maintain her family, she and her children should have remained on and in her and the father's estate, which was in good condition here, wherein the widow with the children could have continued reputably and in position to much advantage; but she would not listen to advice, * * * that she was to be restricted in her inclinations and well being, which I shall never think of, much less do." The wife of Christian Barentse was Jannetje Jans, and it is probable that they were married before coming to America, as the baptism of their eldest child is not recorded in the New York church. On December 12, 1658, Jannetje Jans, widow and executrix of Christian Barents, presented an inventory of his goods and chattels to the court at New Amsterdam, and requested that Vice-Director Alricks, "Director of the City's Colony on the South River, where her husband died, be written to in order that the chattels which are there may be sent from the South river to this place." The widow married on September 12, 1658, Laurens Andriessen Van Boskerk, who was born in Holstein, Denmark. He was a member of Bergen court in 1667, its president in 1682, a member of the governor's council for many years. He died in 1693 and Jannetje on July 13, 1694. They were the parents of four children, Andries, Lourens, Peter, and Thomas, the two latter, according to the Dutch custom, being known as Lourensons, appear later to have become known by the name of Lawrence. Peter joined his half-brother, Barant Christian Van

Horn, in his purchase of land in Bucks county in 1703. His youngest son John married Alce Van Horn, granddaughter of Christian Barents, and his daughter Jannetje, married Cornelius Corson, of Staten Island, and became the ancestress of the Bucks county Corsons. The children of Christian Barents and Jannetje Jans were as follows: Barendt Christian Van Horn, born in Holland, married Geertje Dircks; died in Bergen county, New Jersey, in 1726. 3. Cornelius Van Horn, baptized August 3, 1653, married Margaret Van de Berg, died in Bergen county in 1729. 4. Jan Van Horn, baptized March 18, 1657, married Lena Boone, died in Bergen county.

2. Barent Christian Van Horn, eldest son of Christian Barents and Jannetje Jans, as before stated was probably born in Holland, a theory which is borne out by the early date at which he acquired title to land. On March 26, 1667, Governor Philip Carteret granted to Barent Christian, of Menkaque, planter, fifty acres of land at Pembrepach and eighty-five acres on the bay called Kill Van Kull, both in Bergen county. On September 29, 1697, he obtained a grant from the proprietors of East Jersey, 160 acres on "Hackingsack River," joining that of his half brother Thomas Lawrenson (Van Boskerk). On May 15, 1703, Barnard Christian and his half-brother, Peter Lawrence, purchased 1,000 acres of Robert Heaton, on Neshaminy creek, in Bucks county, which on September 18, 1707, they partitioned between them. Two days later, September 20, 1707, Barnard Christian conveyed his portion to his two sons, Peter and Christian Barnson, Peter receiving 257 acres and Christian 294 acres. On September 29, 1707, Barnard Christian purchased 550 acres in Bucks county, of Thomas Groom, 274 acres of which he conveyed to his son Barnard Barnson, June 17, 1714. He also acquired other land in Bucks county, and on June 2, 1722, conveyed to his son, Isaac Van Horn, 276 acres, and on May 6, 1722, 290 acres to his son, Abraham Van Horn. He thus owned in all 1381 acres of land in Bucks county, though he continued to live in Bergen county, New Jersey, and died there in 1726. He married, in 1679, at the Bergen Dutch Reformed church, Geertje Dircks, daughter of Dirck Classen, who was baptized in New York, March 5, 1662. The children of Barent Christian Van Horn and Geertje Dirckse were:

5. Richard Barentsen Van Horn, born at Bergen, New Jersey, died at Hackensack, New Jersey, in 1763; married, April 11, 1704, Elizabeth Garretsen.

6. Christian Van Horn, born October 24, 1681, died in Northampton township, Bucks county, November 23, 1751; see forward.

7. Nicholas Van Horn, born in Bergen county, New Jersey, died in Delaware; he was for a time a resident of Bucks county, and the baptism of two of his children Barnet on July 24, 1715, and Rachel on April 29, 1720, are recorded at Abington Presbyterian church.

8. Peter Barentsen Van Horn, born at Bergen, 1686, died in Middletown township, Bucks county, February 20, 1750. He married (first) Tryntje (Catharine) Van Dyck, and (second) Elizabeth Gabriels, on May 9, 1706. She was baptized at Albany, New York, May 12, 1689, and died November 3, 1759. She was a daughter of Gabriel Tomase Struddles. Peter settled on land conveyed to him by his father in Northampton in 1707 and 1715, and later purchased 425 acres in Middletown. According to the Rev. Samuel Streng, Peter Van Horn joined the Episcopal church, and was a vestryman of St. James Protestant Episcopal church at Bristol, 1734-7. His children, all with the possible exception of Barnard, his eldest son, being by the second wife Elizabeth, were as follows: Catharine, baptized June 4, 1710, died 1755, married Thomas Craven, of Warminster, Bucks county; Barnard, who married Patience Hellings; Charity, who married. June 6, 1732, Isaiah Vansant (see Vansant family) Jane baptized October 16, 1715, married, August 10, 1732, Edmund Roberts; Gabriel, baptized March 3, 1716, died 1789, married Martha Brelsford; Elizabeth, who married April 21, 1737, Peter Praul; Peter, baptized August 25, 1719, married in 1746, Margaret Marshall; Mary, who married William Gosline, of Bristol, Bucks county; Benjamin, who married, June 5, 1749, Hannah Davis; Richard, born 1726, died unmarried, February 1, 1756; John, twice married, second wife being Mary Collett, a widow; and Garret, who married Mary Neal, and died in 1801.

9. Barent Barentsen Van Horn, born in Bergen, New Jersey, April 3, 1691, died in Bucks county, in 1776. He married (first) February 23, 1712, Jannetje Pieters, and (second) January 25, 1726, at Bergen, Elizabeth Klinkenberg. He received by Deed in 1714 276 acres in Northampton township, Bucks county, from his father. He had fourteen children, most of whom married and reared families.

10. John Van Horn, born in Bergen, New Jersey, 1692, died in Lower Dublin, Philadelphia county, 1758, and is buried in the Vandegrift burying ground. He married Rebecca Vandegrift, daughter of Johannes and Nealke (Volkers) Vandegrift, of Bucks county, and had one son John and six daughters.

11. Abraham Van Horn, born in Bergen, New Jersey, died in Northampton, Bucks county, in 1773, on farm of 290 acres received by deed from his father

in 1722. He married first Mary Dungan, and second Mary Vansciver, and had six sons, Barnard, Isaac, Abraham, David, Jacob, and Jeremiah, and three daughters, Mary, wife of Derrick Krewson, Charity, and Martha, who married a Van Sciver.

12. Jane Van Horn, born at Bergen, New Jersey, April 18, 1697, married Adrien La Rue, and resided at Six-Mile Run, New Jersey.

13. Isaac Van Horn, born at Bergen, New Jersey, died in Solebury township, Bucks county, Pennsylvania, in 1760. He married Alice Sleght (or Slack) and had eight children: Bernard, who married first Sarah Van Pelt and second Jane Slack; John, who married Catharine Neafie; Catharine, who married a Van Pelt; Charity, Geertje, Elsie, Isaac, baptized 1749,[*] married Alice Neafies; and Jane.

14. Jacob Van Horn, born at Bergen, New Jersey, died there April 14, 1775.

15. Benjamin Van Horn, born at Bergen, January 10, 1705.

(6) Christian Van Horn, second son of Barendt and Geertje (Dirckse) Van Horn, born at Bergen, New Jersey, October 24, 1681. He married Williamtje Van Dyck, daughter of Hendrick Janse and Jennetje (Heermans) Van Dyck, and granddaughter of Jan Tomasse Van Dyck, who emigrated from Amsterdam in 1652 and settled in New Utrecht, Long Island. His sixth child, Hendrick Janse, baptized July 2, 1653, married, February 7, 1680, Jannetje Hermans, daughter of Herman Janse Van Barkeloo, and settled on Staten Island, where he was a constable in 1689 and assessor in 1703. In 1704 he purchased land in Bucks county and removed there. At the organization of Bensalem church, in 1710, he produced a certificate from the Staten Island church. He purchased four tracts of land in Middletown, two of which he retained until his death in 1721, and devised to his daughter Williamtje, wife of Christian Van Horn, and his granddaughter, Susanna Van Vleck, who later married her cousin, Henry Van Horn. He had but two children, Williamtje, and Jannetje, who became the wife of the Reverend Paulus Van Vleck, the first pastor at Neshaminy.

Christian Van Horn located in North-

---

[*] Isaac Van Horn, of Solebury township, Bucks county, Pennsylvania, was commissioned January 1, 1776, ensign of Captain John Beatty's company, Bucks county's contingent of the Flying Camp. Fifth Pennsylvania Battalion, Colonel Robert Magaw, and was taken prisoner at Fort Washington, November 16, 1776. Exchanged in 1778, and promoted to lieutenant, Sixth Pennsylvania Battalion, captain lieutenant, July 1, 1779; captain, Second Pennsylvania, June 19, 1781. Retired from service January 1, 1783. Settled in Westmoreland county, Pennsylvania. 1781. Member of seventh and eighth congress. (1801-1803) from Pennsylvania. Receiver of public monies at Zanesville, Ohio in 1815. Died in Muskingum county, Ohio, February 2, 1834. Pennsylvania Archives. Second Series.

ampton township, Bucks county, on, 294 acres conveyed to him by his father in 1707. In 1737 two hundred acres of the land belonging to the estate of his father-in-law, Hendrick Van Dyck, in Middeltown township was conveyed to him by Jeremiah Langhorne, as "straw man" in effecting the transfer from the devises of Van Dyck to Christian Van Horn. He represented Bucks county in the Pennsylvania assembly for the years 1723-1732 and 1734-1737, thirteen years in all. He died November 23, 1751, and his wife May 6, 1760. She was born on Staten Island, July 4, 1681. The will of Christian Van Horn devised to his eldest son Bernard the home plantation of 205 acres in Northampton, to his son Henry 200 acres on which Henry was living in Newtown, purchased of George and Joseph Randal in 1726; to his son John thirty-two acres in Northampton, to his daughter Charity Van Duren another tract adjoining containing forty-one acres, and to his son Christian 187 acres in Northampton, when he should come of age; the other children receiving their shares of his estate in money. To his son ·Barnard he bequeathed his large Bible. This Bible is now in the possession of Dr. Wilmer Krusen, of 127 North Twenty-ninth street, Philadelphia, having descended to him from his ancestors, the Hegemans, John Hegeman having married Jane Van Horn, daughter of Christian. who inherited it from her brother, Barnard Van Horn, who died in 1760, without issue. It was printed at Dordrecht in 1690, and was purchased by Hendrick Van Dyck in December, 1701, and presented to his daughter Williamtje, who married Christian Van Horn. On the fly leaf it contains the record of the birth of the children of Hendrick Van Dyck, those of Christian and Williamtje Van Horn, and those of John and Jannetje (Van Horn) Hegeman.

The children of Christian and Williamtje (Van Dyck) Van Horn were:

16. Barnard Van Horn, born February 19, 1701-2, died April 22, 1760. married December 31, 1741, Jannetje Van Boskerk, had no children.

17. Henry Van Horn, born September 15, 1707, died in Newtown township, Bucks county in 1761. He married his first cousin, Susanna Van Vleck. daughter of Rev. Paulus and Jannetje (Van Horn) Van Vleck. She inherited from her grandfather, Hendrick Van Dyck, one half of his real estate, and 173 acres thereof was conveyed to Henry by the same proceedings as in the case of his father, and the latter at his death devised to Henry 200 acres, in Newtown, and it was devised by the will of Henry in 1761 to his sons, Christian and Henry. Susanna. the widow of Henry, died in June, 1776. They were the parents of four children, Christian, who married,

June 14, 1764, Sarah Vansant,—see forward; Henry Van Horn, died 1777, married Elizabeth Vansant; Jane, who married John Johnson; and Susannah, who married Euclides Longshore.

18. Geertje or Charity, baptized May 21, 1710, married Godfrey Van Duren, who was the first innkeeper at Ruckman's, in Solebury township, Bucks county.

19. Antje of Ann, baptized March 22, 1712, died in infancy.

20. John Van Horn, born December 8, 1713, married, May 30, 1739, Lena Van Pelt, (See Van Pelt Family) and died in 1760. John and Lena (Van Pelt) Van Horn were the parents of five children, all of whom were baptized at Southampton church, viz: Catharine, baptized August 11, 1741, married January 12, 1764, John Subers, see forward; Christian, baptized October 4, 1743, died young; Willimentje, baptized May 11, 1746, died in infancy; Willimentje, born March 1, 1748; and Joseph, born May 30, 1750, married, January 7, 1773, Ann Searle.

21. Ann Van Horn, born July 19, 1716, died 1753, married Cornelius Corson, and had seven children, viz: Blandia; baptized March 26, 1738, Willemeynje, baptized February 24, 1740; Marytje, baptized May 23, 1742; Jannetje, baptized July 19, 1744; Antje, baptized December 26, 1746; Benjamin, baptized April 13, 1749; and Cornelius, baptized November 16, 1751.

22. Catharine Van Horn, born April 13, 1719, married Hendrick Hegeman, and had four children, viz: Adrien, baptized March 26, 1738; Maria, baptized April 7, 1740; Jannetje, baptized June 6; 1742; Catrintje, baptized March 24, 1745.

23. Jane Van Horn, born May 20, 1721, died September 7, 1783, married, October 20, 1741, John Hegeman, born January 10, 1718, and had nine children; Mary, born March 8, 1743; Christian, born August 8, 1745; Henry, born January 5, 1748; John, born July 26, 1750; Henry, born January 11, 1753; Benjamin, born November 19, 1755; Adrian, born September 16, 1758; Barnet, born February 23, 1761; and Jane, born May 15, 1765.

24. Christian Van Horn, born August 29, 1728, died December 17, 1753.

Christian Van Horn, eldest son of Henry (17) and Susanna (Van Vlecq) Van Horn, born in Newtown township, Bucks county, married, June 14, 1764, Sarah Vansant. daughter of Isaiah and Charity (Van Horn) Vansant, of Lower Makefield. Her mother, Charity (Van Horn) Vansant. being a daughter of Peter (8) and Elizabeth (Gabriels) Van Horn. Christian Van Horn inherited from his father 126 acres of land in Newtown township, on the Neshaminy creek, part of the land purchased by his grandfather, Christian Van Horn, in 1726, whereon he lived until his death in 1777, when it was divided between his sons Henry and Isaiah. Sarah (Vansant) Van Horn died in 1785. They were the parents of but two children, viz: Henry and Isaiah. Henry, married, April 26, 1787, Elizabeth McCorkle, and had three children; Amos, born March 4, 1792, died at Newtown, September 5, 1823, married, January 8, 1817, Mercy Starkey; Susan, born October 25, 1794, died in Michigan, September 5, 1872, married Joseph Roberts; and Elizabeth, born January 27, 1797, married Joseph Winship, and died at Newtown, May 12, 1868.

Isaiah Van Horn, second son of Christian and Sarah (Vansant) Van Horn, was born in Newtown township, Bucks county, married, December 31, 1794, Catharine Suber, daughter of John and Catharine (Van Horn) Suber, and his first cousin. He was adjudged fifty acres of the homestead farm by the orphans' court in 1787, but on March 15, 1791, sold it to his brother Henry, and on his marriage in 1794 took up his residence on a farm belonging to the estate of his father-in-law, Isaiah Vansart, in Upper Makefield, where he died in 1802. His widow, Catharine, married John Wynkoop, January 31, 1805. The only child of Isaiah and Catharine(Vansant) Van Horn, was Sarah, born February 29, 1796; died January 27, 1838. She married (first) on January 16, 1812, Aaron Winder, and (second) August 24, 1825, Abner Morris. (See Winder Family in this volume). Catharine Wynkoop, the mother, died in December, 1820.

R. Winder Johnson, of Philadelphia, to whom we are indebted for the above account of the Van Horn family, is a grandson of Aaron and Sarah (Van Horn) Winder, great-grandson of Isaiah and Catharine (Suber) Van Horn, great-great-grandson of both Christian and Sarah (Vansant) Van Horn, and John and Catharine (Van Horn) Suber, and great-great-great-grandson of Henry and Susanna (Van Vlecq) Van Horn, John and Lena (Van Pelt) Van Horn, and Isaiah and Charity (Van Horn) Vansant, and great-great-great-great-grandson of Christian and Williamtje (Vandyck) Van Horn, and Peter and Elizabeth (Gabriells) Vanhorn, the last mentioned Christian and Peter Van Horn, being sons of Barendt Christianzen Van Hoorn and his wife Geertje Dircks Classen, and grandsons of Christian Baretzen Van Hoorn and Jannetje Jans, the pioneer ancestors of the family in America. An account of the Van Pelt, Vansant, Vandegrift, Winder and Johnson families also largely the result of investigations also made by Mr. Johnson, will be found elsewhere in this work.

Henry Van Horn, son of Henry and Susanna (Van Vlecq) Van Horn, was reared on the old homestead purchased by his grandfather, Christian Van Horn, in 1726, and at the death of his father, in 1761, inherited a one-half interest therein with his brother Christian. They made a division of the 252 acres, each conveying to the other 126 acres in 1773. After the reverses on Long Island in November, 1776, and at Fort Washington when the Continental forces were so badly routed and so many of the Bucks county contingent were taken prisoners, Henry Van Horn raised an independent company of militia and was commissioned their captain, December 6, 1776, (See Penna. Arch. vol. xiv p. 175) and took them into the service. He died of camp fever late in 1777. He married Elizabeth Vansant, daughter of Isaiah and Charity (Van Horn) Van Sant, and they were the parents of eight children: Joshua, born February 21, 1759; Isaiah, born October 24, 1760, was drummer in his father's company, 1776-7; Mary, born May 5, 1764, married Isaac Gillam, died April 18, 1823; Christian, born July 13, 1766; Susanna, born October 9, 1768, married Jesse Willett, who had previously married her sister Sarah; Elizabeth, married an Anderson, and died January 26, 1813; Sarah, born February 7, 1773, married Jesse Willett, died prior to 1809; Henry, born April 5, 1777. Elizabeth the mother, died November 25, 1807, aged about eighty years.

Henry Van Horn, youngest child of Captain Henry and Elizabeth (Vansant) Van Horn, born in Newtown township, April 5, 1777, learned the trade of a carpenter and cabinet maker and located at Yardley, Bucks county, where he followed the trade of a cabinet maker for several years. His sign uniquely painted is now in possession of his grandson, Richard H. Van Horn, of Lambertville, New Jersey. He also purchased a farm of 93 acres in Lower Makefield in 1805, which, in 1811, he conveyed to his brother-in-law, Isaac Gillam. He purchased a farm of 200 acres in Upper Makefield, near Eagle Tavern, where he resided the balance of his life. He died in February, 1849. He married, in 1798, Hannah Reeder, of Canaan, Upper Makefield, and their six children who grew to maturity were as follows:

1. Abraham, born 1802, married, in 1829, Eliza Hampton, by whom he had one child, Margery. He married (second) Christiana Neald, and a son Henry K. was born in 1834. He married (third) Elizabeth Sampsel. He sold his farm in Upper Makefield and removed to Sandy Spring, Maryland, where he reared a family of thirteen children.

2. Elizabeth, born 1804, married William Ryan, of Upper Makefield, born 1810. They settled near Rocksville, Northampton township, Bucks county, and engaged in the milling business. Three of their children

survive: Edward H., born 1832; Mary, born 1835; and Hannah, born 1839.

3. Eleanor H., born 1810, married Cornelius Slack, and settled in Lower Makefield. He was lately a merchant at Dolington. Their children are: Watson, born 1832; John H., born 1833; Henry V., born 1836; Jane E., born 1839; Sarah E., born 1841; William H., born 1843; Anna M., born 1847; and Hannah, born 1850.

4. Moses H., born January 15, 1812, at Yardleyville, removed with his parents to Upper Makefield, where he spent his entire life, inheriting at his father's death, in 1849, 100 acres of the old homestead. He was a successful farmer, and a prominent man in the community, holding many positions of trust and honor. He and his wife and family were lifelong members of the Society of Friends. He married, April 13, 1843, Rebecca Scattergood, born February 7, 1820, daughter of John* and Catharine (Hepburn) Scattergood, of Makefield, who died September 15, 1895. Moses died February 13, 1885. They were the parents of nine children: Richard H., born 1844; Mary Anna, born 1846; Samuel S., born 1848; William T., born 1851; George F., and Catharine S., twins, born 1854; Hannah E., born 1857; Benjamin F., born 1860; and Emma L., born 1863.**

5. Mary A., born 1816, married Christian Van Horn, born 1814, and settled on a farm near Dolington. Their surviving issue are: Cyrus B., Jane E., Cornelius S., Hannah E., and Callender C.

6. John R., born 1820, married Rebecca Feaster, and settled on a portion of the old homestead in Upper Makefield. Their surviving children are: James P., David F., Emeline, Watson, Martha F., and Joseph F.

RICHARD H. VAN HORN, eldest son of Moses and Rebecca (Scattergood) Van Horn, born at the old homestead of his grandfather, in 1844, was reared on the Upper Makefield farm, acquired a limited education at the public school and later took a course at Union Business College in Philadelphia. After a few years experience in the mercantile business in Philadelphia, he started into that business for himself at Lambertville, New Jersey, in 1868. By strict application to business and a close study of the wants and needs of the community, he soon built up a large trade and his remodeled store in 1884 named "Grand Depot" enjoyed much more than a local reputation and soon outgrew its early modest quarters. In 1877 an adjoining building was added and the volume of business doubled. Seven years later the entire property was remodeled and both stores thrown into one, making a large and commodious department store, and his brother, Samuel S., who had been for some years a clerk in the establishment was given an interest in the business, and the firm name became R. H. Van Horn & Brother. The partnership of the growing establishment extended far beyond the limits of Jersey into their native county, and the country districts and towns of New Jersey. In 1889, the brothers dissolved partnership and Richard H. continued the business alone until 1892, when his son Henry came of age and was admitted as a partner. Ten years later the younger son, Edmori E., becoming of age, also became a partner, and the firm of R. H. Van Horn & Sons, continue to conduct the popular and successful establishment that has grown from its modest beginning of 1868. To an additional L a new building, the floor space of which combined with the original "Grand Depot" covers now (1904) about three-quarters of an acre.

Richard H. Van Horn married, in 1869, Lydiana Beatty Warner, born in 1845, daughter of Edwards Edmunds Warner, of Philadelphia, and of New England ancestry, and they are the proud parents of two sons, both of whom, as before stated, are members of the firm. Henry E., the eldest, born April 21, 1870, married Era Runkle, of Hunterdon county, New Jersey; and Edmori E., born in October, 1879, married Jessie Hoffman of the same place. Mr. R. H. Van Horn is an active member of the Society of Friends, having many years since transferred his certificate of membership from Wrightstown Monthly Meeting to Solebury Friends' Meeting where he and his wife Lydianna were subsequently appointed elders. R. H. Van Horn has always shown an active spirit in his town affairs but little interest in "Political Pulls"; he has, however, served in the school board, acted as a member of the board of trade, and at present is next to the oldest director in the Amwell National Bank of Lambertville.

SAMUEL SCATTERGOOD VAN HORN, second son of Moses and Rebecca (Scattergood) Van Horn, whose ancestry has been given in the preceding pages, was born in Makefield township, Bucks county, Pennsylvania, October 28, 1848, and was reared on the Upper Makefield farm; acquiring his education at the public schools of that township. In 1870 he went to Lambertville, New Jersey. In 1889 Samuel S. Van Horn embarked in the general merchandise business in Lambertville, where he carried on a successful business for three years. He then purchased

---

*John Scattergood (a descendant of Thomas Scattergood, of Burlington county, New Jersey, a noted minister among Friends) was born 6 mo. 14, 1774. He married 5 mo. 4. 1794, Sarah Forman, and second Catharine Hepburn, who was the mother of Mrs. Rebecca (Scattergood) Van Horn. John Scattergood died 12, 12, 1842.

**George F. and Benjamin F. Van Horn, sons of Moses H., left the Upper Makefield homestead on arriving at age. George learned the printing business, and subsequently both brothers, after a few years engagement with their brother, Richard H, learning the mercantile business at Lambertville, New Jersey, went in 1890 into business on their own account near Pittsburg, Pennsylvania, where by much energy and hustle they met with great success, but owing to poor health both have retired from business, 1905.

his present location, where he has since conducted a successful business.

Mr. Van Horn married, in 1888, Ella M. Dilley, daughter of Louis and Caroline (Larison) Dilley, of Kingwood, Hunterdon county, New Jersey. To this marriage has been born two sons, Lloyd and Earl. Mr. Van Horn is an extensive real estate owner in Lambertville, owning fifteen resident properties. He is a member of the Society of Friends.

LAWRENCE JOHNSON AND HIS DESCENDANTS. The family of Johnson, from which Lawrence Johnson descended, belonged to the yeomanry and lived in Lincolnshire, England, having settled in Barrow-on-Humber in 1684, after the marriage of Robert Johnson and Mary Hall, nee Ledgard. Here five generations of the family lived and owned property. Edward Johnson removed to Hull after his marriage in 1796. Previous to 1680 the family had lived and owned property at Grasby, in Lincolnshire.

Edward Johnson had a large family of children, and, believing that their prospects for advancement would be greater in America, he was induced by his sons to sell his property in Hull, and emigrate with his family to America. On July 4, 1818, with his wife and ten children, he sailed from Grimsby on the brig General Ripley" for New York, where the vessel arrived August 28, 1818. The people of New York looked so pale that Edward Johnson thought it could not be a healthful place, and accordingly sailed immediately up the Hudson to Albany, where he bought a farm of one hundred and twenty-fice acres near Cato, Cayuga county, New York.

Lawrence Johnson, son of Edward and Ann (Clayton) Johnson, was born in Hull, England, January 23, 1801, and was baptized in Holy Trinity church, March 2, 1801. Immediately after coming to America with his parents in 1818, he found employment in the office of the "Troy Budget," a newspaper published at Troy, New York, but the following spring went to New York city, where he was employed in several printing establishments. About 1820 he settled in Philadelphia and established a stereotype foundry, to which he later added the industry of making type, under the firm name of L. Johnson & Company, and built up an immense business. He became interested in many prominent enterprises in Philadelphia and elsewhere in Pennsylvania, the development of coal lands, building of street horse-car lines, and many other enterprises, and acquired a fortune. He was also president of the Commonwealth Bank. He died in Philadelphia, April 26, 1860.

In the spring of 1851 Lawrence Johnson purchased a farm and country seat in Bristol township, Bucks county, known as "Lansdowne," where he spent much of his time, and which has ever since been occupied by members of his family.

Mr. Johnson had married May 3, 1825, Sarah B. Murray, of Philadelphia, who died August 21, 1834, leaving one child, a daughter. He married a second time, on May 29, 1837, Mary Winder, daughter of Aaron and Sarah (Van Horn) Winder, of Lower Makefield township, Bucks county, Pennsylvania, who was born June 18, 1814, and died February 16, 1877. (See Winder Family). Lawrence and Mary (Winder) Johnson were the parents of ten children, viz: 1. Edward Winder; 2. Anna Rebecca; 3. Mary Ella; 4. Caroline Fletcher; 5. Howard Lawrence; 6. Russel Hampden; 7. Lawrence; 8. Walter Richards; 9. Robert Winder; 10. Alfred Clayton.

1. EDWARD WINDER JOHNSON, eldest son of Lawrence and Mary (Winder) Johnson, was born in Philadelphia, April 12, 1838. In the summer of 1847 he accompanied his father on a trip to Europe. He was educated at Mr. Fay's boarding school at Elizabeth, New Jersey, and at Dr. Faires' and other private schools in Philadelphia. In 1856 he traveled under the care of an agent of his father to Havana, Mexico, Texas, and up the Mississippi river, and to Cincinnati, Ohio. In the latter place he remained for some months, working in a branch type foundry established there by his father. On October 23, 1857, he was commissioned as a midshipman on the flagship "Powhattan," and on December 9, following that frigate left Norfolk, Virginia, on a long cruise, with ex-President Franklin Pierce and wife on board. She sailed first to Maderia, St. Helena, and Cape Town, preceeding thence to Hong Kong, stopping on the way at Mauritius and Singapore, and arrived at Hong Kong in May, 1858, and proceeded to Japan in the following July. Becoming ill in Japan, Midshipman Johnson obtained a dismissal from service on the U. S. frigate "Powhattan," and embarked as a passenger on board the "Minnesota," October 2, 1858, to return home, arriving in Boston, Massachusetts, May 29, 1859. On September 26, 1860, he sailed from New York on the clipper "Messenger" for Hong Kong, intending to enter into business with A. W. Habersham, in Japan. He arrived in Yokohama, April 20, 1861, where he remained for some time, engaged in business. On learning of the outbreak of the civil war in America he left Japan on the steamship "Carrington," and arrived in San Francisco, California, October 20, 1861, from which place he proceeded at once to New York. He enlisted in August, 1862, in Company G of the Anderson Cavalry, and fought in the battles of Antietam and Murfreesboro. Afterwards his regiment was reorganized, and he became a member of Company A of the Anderson Cavalry. He was also in the battle of Chickamauga, under General Rosencrans. On December 30, 1863, he returned home on a furlough,

and did not again enter the army. He died, at Lansdowne, Bristol township, Bucks county, January 12, 1874, unmarried.

2. Anna Rebecca Johnson, second child of Lawrence and Mary (Winder) Johnson, was born in Philadelphia, December 15, 1839. She was educated at the school of Professor Charles D. Cleveland, in Philadelphia. In 1858 and 1859 she traveled extensively in Europe, Egypt, and Palestine, under the care of Mr. and Mrs. Gardel. She was married in Philadelphia, December 3, 1863, to Theodore Hoe Mead, of New York. Theodore Hoe and Anna Rebecca (Johnson) Mead have been the parents of six children, three of whom survive, viz: Lawrence Johnson Mead, who married, June 29, 1901, Anna Frances Ely, of Doylestown, Bucks county, Pennsylvania, daughter of Samuel L. and Mary (Knight) Ely; Anna Johnson Mead, who married, October 7, 1902, Herbert Gordon Thomson, of New York; and Gilbert Mead, who married, July 25, 1903, Mary Comly Ely, daughter of Samuel L. and Mary Comly (Knight) Ely, of Doylestown, Bucks county. (See Winder Family.)

3. Mary Ella Johnson, third child of Lawrence and Mary (Winder) Johnson, was born in Philadelphia, September 22, 1841. After spending five years in Professor Cleveland's school in Philadelphia, she traveled in Great Britain, Europe, Egypt, the Sinaitic Peninsula, Palestine and Syria, as well as the rock-hewn city of Petra, to which, it is said, no ladies had previously ventured with the exception of two English ladies, somewhat earlier in the same year. Miss Johnson married, December 4, 1862, William D. Stuart of Philadelphia, who died April 7, 1863, leaving no children. Mrs. Stuart married a second time, January 11, 1870, Dr. James Cheston Morris, of Philadelphia, by whom she has eight children, all residing in Philadelphia.

4. Caroline Fletcher Johnson, fourth child of Lawrence and Mary (Winder) Johnson, was born in Philadelphia, July 10, 1843, and was educated at Dr. Cleveland's school. She married, February 21, 1871, Anthony Taylor, son of Robert Taylor, and a nephew of Hon. Caleb Newbold Taylór, of Bristol, Bucks county, Pennsylvania. Anthony Taylor enlisted in the Pennsylvania cavalry August 8, 1862, was promoted sergeant, October 30, 1862; first sergeant, March 1, 1863; first lieutenant of 15th Pennsylvania Cavalry, May 8, 1863; and captain, June 1, 1865. He was awarded a medal of honor for signal acts of bravery, and was honorably mustered out June 21, 1865. He died in Philadelphia, May 21, 1894. Anthony and Caroline F. (Johnson) Taylor were the parents of two children Mary Lawrence Taylor, who married, February 25, 1893, Bromley Wharton, now private secretary to Governor Samuel W. Pennypacker; and Elizabeth Elmslie Taylor, who married, December 31, 1904, Houston Dunn.

5. Howard Lawrence Johnson, born October 31, 1845, died June 25, 1891; married, May 7, 1876, Mary Evangeline Bradley. They had no children.

6. Russell Hampden Johnson, son of Lawrence and Mary (Winder) Johnson, was born in Philadelphia, September 15, 1847, and received his preliminary education in private schools in Philadelphia. He entered Princeton University at the age of seventeen years, and graduated in the class of 1868, after a four years' course, with the degree of Bachelor of Arts. He then made an extensive tour of Europe, and on returning entered the medical department of the University of Pennsylvania, where he received the degree of Doctor of Medicine in 1871. After serving as resident physician in the Episcopal Hospital of Philadelphia, he once more visited Europe, spending two years in travel, chiefly for the further prosecution of his medical studies in the University of Vienna. Returning to Philadelphia he began the practice of medicine there, where, excepting occasional visits abroad, he has since lived and practiced his profession. He married, December 13, 1877, Grace H. Price, of New York. Five children blessed this union, all, like their father, devotedly attached to the old home on the Neshaminy, in Bucks county, where the youngest daughter was born. The children are: Russel Hampden, Jr., born September 16, 1878; Lawrence, born September 17, 1880; Anna Price, born September 20, 1881; Louisa, born May 20, 1883; and Paul Sears, born October 24, 1896.

7. Lawrence Johnson, seventh child of Lawrence and Mary (Winder) Johnson, was born in Philadelphia, September 28, 1849, and was educated at private schools there and at Princeton University. In 1868 he began his business career as a clerk in the shipping house of Isaac Hough & Morris, where he remained for about two years. On coming of age in 1870 he began business for himself, under the firm name of Lawrence Johnson & Company, shipping and commission merchants and foreign bankers, which business he has since followed. On November 21, 1891, he was elected a director of the Philadelphia National Bank, and he is also a director of the Pennsylvania Company for Insurances on Lives and Granting Annuities, the Insurance Company of North America, and the Philadelphia Warehouse Company. He married, December 6, 1877, Louisa Philler Gaw, daughter of Henry L. Gaw, of Philadelphia. They have one child, Millicent Gaw Johnson, born November 22, 1884.

8. Walter Richards Johnson, eighth child of Lawrence and Mary (Winder) Johnson, was born at Lansdowne, Bucks county, August 24, 1851. He was educated at Dr. Faires' and other private schools of Philadelphia. He married, October 31, 1876, his cousin, Mary Rebecca Winder, daughter of Moses and Margaretta Winder. He purchased a farm on the right bank of the Neshaminy, in Bensalem township,

Bucks county, between Hulmeville and Newportville, where he lived the remainder of his life, and was actively engaged in agricultural pursuits. He was also actively interested in political affairs and held several political offices. He died March 25, 1897, leaving one child, Winder Lawrence Johnson, since deceased, who married, October 11, 1899, Susan D. Fine.

9. Robert Winder Johnson, ninth child of Lawrence and Mary (Winder) Johnson, was born Sunday, May 7, 1854, at No. 727 Pine street, Philadelphia. He prepared for college at Mr. Gregory's private school on Market street, near Eleventh, and entered the freshman class of the University of Pennsylvania, September, 1870 (class of 1874,) but left the University in the spring of 1871 and accompanied his mother to Europe, where he studied and traveled until October, 1874. He again traveled abroad in 1875 and 1876. In January, 1877, he entered the office of Lawrence Johnson & Company, doing a large business as importers and exporters and bankers, and in July, 1879, was admitted as a member of the firm and has since been actively associated with its business. He was elected a member of the Historical Society of Pennsylvania in 1874 and a life member in 1877; was elected a member of the Rittenhouse Club in 1883; a member of the vestry of St. Peter's church in 1891; member of the board of managers of Christ Church Hospital in 1892; member of the Genealogical Society of Pennsylvania in 1892; member of the Colonial Society of Pennsylvania in 1897; member of the Society of the Protestant Episcopal Church for the Advancement of Christianity in Pennsylvania in 1897; member of the Board of managers of the Children's Hospital in 1897; member of the Netherlands Society of Philadelphia in 1899; and a life member of the Bucks County Historical Society in 1903. He takes a deep interest in the local history of Bucks county, where his maternal ancestors, the Van Horns, Van Dycks, Van Sandts, Van Pelts, Vandegrifts, Winders, and others were among the earliest and most prominent settlers, and has devoted much time and expense during the last twenty-five years in tracing out the history of these early families of Bucks. Mr. Johnson was married on November 10, 1887, to Rosalie Morris, daughter of George Calvert and Elizabeth (Kuhn) Morris, at St. Peter's Church, Third and Pine streets, Philadelphia. Their children are as follows: Morris Winder, born July 5, 1889, at Chestnut Hill, Philadelphia; Lawrence Edward, born July 9, 1892, at Lansdowne, Bucks county; Robert Winder, Jr., born August 19, 1894, at Lansdowne, Bucks county; and Rosalie Eugenia, born October 12, 1900, at Chestnut Hill.

10. Alfred Clayton Johnson, youngest child of Lawrence and Mary (Winder) Johnson, was born in Philadelphia, Sep-

tember 17, 1856. He was educated at private schools in Philadelphia and at Dresden, Saxony. He read law under P. Pemberton Morris, Esq., of Philadelphia, and also attended lectures on law at the University of Pennsylvania, and was admitted to the Philadelphia bar April 3, 1880. He was appointed consul to Stuttgart, Germany, in 1893 and vice consul general at Dresden in 1898. He married in Dresden, July 21, 1888, Countess Toni von Baudissin, and they have one child, Mary Winder Johnson, born in Bristol township, Bucks county, Pennsylvania, June 11, 1889.

THE WINDER FAMILY.* The progenitor of the Winders of Pennsylvania and New Jersey was Thomas Winder of England, who settled in Hunterdon county, New Jersey, in 1705. He was in New Jersey in 1703, and was one of the purchasers of Maidenhead and Hopewell, and participated in the agreement with Daniel Coxe, one of the proprietors of West Jersey, in relation to that purchase. Soon after the consummation of the purchase he returned to London, and was married at St. Margaret's, Westminster, June 5, 1704, to Sara Bull, and returned to West Jersey, settling in Hunterdon county, where he became a large landowner. In 1721 he purchased six hundred acres at Newtown, Bucks county, of John Walley, and in 1727 purchased three hundred and forty-one acres in Makefield, Bucks county, which descended to his son John, and remained in the tenure of his descendants for several generations until it was sold in 1837. He was a prominent man in Hunterdon county, and was commissioner of highways in Amwell township in 1723. He married (second) in 1731, Rebecca Gregory, who survived him, and married Edward Collins in 1736. Thomas Winder died, and letters of administration were granted on his estate May 23, 1734. The children of Thomas and Sara (Bull) Winder were as follows:

1. John Winder, born 1707, died August 9, 1770, married Rebecca Richards.

2. Thomas, settled in Amwell, where he was living in 1736.

3. James, removed to Prince George county, Maryland, where he died in 1789.

4. Jane, who married John Slack and settled in Lower Makefield, Bucks county, where many of her descendants still reside.

5. Elizabeth, married Peter Phillips of Amwell, where they lived and died.

Elinor, daughter of Thomas and Rebecca (Gregory) Winder, married July 31, 1751, Thomas Guinnup, of Philadelphia.

John and Rebecca (Richards) Winder settled on the land purchased by his father in Lower Makefield, Bucks county, the other heirs making conveyances to him for their interest therein at various periods af-

*Condensed from "Winders of America," by R. Winder Johnson.

J. M. Winder

ter the death of Thomas. His wife, Rebec-,
ca Richards, was born September 19, *1714,
and died January , 19, 1788. The family
were not members of the Society of Friends
until 1747, when he and his wife applied
for membership at Falls Meeting, and were
admitted as members. John died in Makefield, August 9, 1770. The children of
John and Rebecca (Richards) Winder,
were as follows:

1. Thomas, married, May 11, 1758, Elizabeth Linton, daughter of Joseph and Mary
(Blackshaw) Linton, of Northampton
township.

2. James, married (first) December 28,
1763, Sarah Bailey, and (second) Mary
Booz.

3. John, married, January 23, 1760, Margaret Briggs. He removed first to Delaware and later.to Fayette county, Pennsylvania, and still later to the state of Ohio.

5. Elizabeth, married (first) in April,
1759, Joseph Linton, son of Joseph and
Mary, before mentioned, and on April 2,
1795, married David Feaster.

6. Sarah, married, April, 1761, Robert
Whitacre, and removed to Catawissa, Pennsylvania.

7. Hannah, married in 1770, Timothy
Brooks. Moses, Aaron and Rachel died unmarried.

11. Rebecca, married March 26, 1772,
John Nutt, and removed to Fairfax, Virginia.

12. Mercy, died unmarried.

13. Ann married May 13, 1779, Absalom
Knight.

14. Aaron Winder, born September 14,
1759, died July 2, 1824, married January 16, 1812, Sarah Van Horn,
born February 29, 1796, died January 27, 1838, daughter of Isaiah and Catherine (Subers) Van Horn, of Makefield.
He purchased in 1788 two hundred acres
of the Makefield homestead, and built a
house thereon in 1790. It is related that
Catherine Subers, whose daughter he
eventually married, was the first love of
Aaron Winder, and on her marriage to his
successful rival in her affections, Isaiah
Van Horn, he abjured matrimony and lived.
single until the age of fifty-three years,
when he married her daughter though Mrs.
Van Horn, the mother, had been a widow
almost from the birth of the daughter.
The children of Aaron and Sarah Van
Horn Winder were as follows:

1. Joel, born March 8, 1813, died in
infancy.

2. Mary, born June 18, 1814, died February 16, 1877, married Lawrence Johnson. (See Johnson Family).

3. Rebecca, born February 22, 1817, died
September 26, 1854, married General John
Ely and had four children, but two of
whom lived to mature age; Mary Winder
Ely, born November 19, 1840, died July
12, 1860, married October 19, 1859, Joseph
Parry Brosius; and Samuel Lawrence Ely,
born May 24, 1847, died March 19, 1886,
married December 29, 1865, Mary Comly

Knight. He was sheriff of Bucks county
for the term of 1881-83.

4. Dr. Aaron Winder, born October 17,
1821, died December 28, 1883, married
August 21, 1846, Mary S. Gillam, and had
three children; William G. Winder, M.
D., of Andalusia, Bucks county and Phila-
delphia; Mary Ely Winder, wife of Henry
B. Knight of Bucks county; and Lawrence
Johnson Winder, M. D.

5. Moses Winder, born December 20,
1823, died April, 1864, married December
25, 1844, Margaretta Thornton, and had six
children, five of whom grew to maturity,
viz: Sarah, born 1849, married Blackstone
P. Doddridge; Mary Rebecca, born 1851,
died 1893, married Walter Richards Johnson, of Bensalem, Bucks county, Pennsylvania; Anna Louisa, born February 4,
1854, married April 6, 1885, Isaac Holbor-
row Robertson; John Ely Winder, born
1857, died 1866; and Aaron Augustus Winder, born February 8, 1859, married October 12, 1880, Jane Phillips Slugg, died
September 5, 1903.

Sarah (Van Horn) Winder married
(second)August 24, 1825, Abner Morris,
and had four children.

JACOB M. WINDER, of Bristol,
was born in that borough August 28,
1858, and is a son of Isaac and Mary
Jane (Hetherington) Winder. He is of
English descent, his paternal ancestors
having been early English settlers in
New Jersey. Samuel Winder, the great-
grandfather of the subject of this sketch,
was a farmer in Falls township, and
died there in April, 1816, devising his
small estate to his wife Sarah who survived him several years.

Giles Satterthwaite Winder, son of
Samuel and Sarah, was born in Falls
township about 1795, being just arrived
at legal age at the death of his father,
and was named as executor of the will.
He received a good education and taught
school in Middletown township for
thirty years. He died in Bristol in
1857. He married Sarah Yonker,
daughter of George Yonker, of Middletown, and granddaughter of Daniel
Yonker, of Solebury. George Yonker
was the father of twelve children, one
son George, and eleven daughters, all
of whom lived to mature age, and all except two of whom married and reared
families. The father resided on his farm
in Middletown, near Langhorne, until
1859, and then sold it on account of in-
ability to care for it, being very old
and infirm, and lived with a married
daughter in Burlington for one year,
and then removed to Bristol, Bucks
county, where he died in 1861 at a very
advanced age. Sarah Satterthwaite was
his eldest daughter. She also lived to
an advanced age, dying in Bristol, June
21, 1880. The children of Giles S. and

Sarah (Yonker) Winder were: George Y., Daniel Y., Samuel, Isaac, Eliza and Mary.

Isaac Winder, father of the subject of this sketch, was born in Middletown township, Bucks county, in 1832, and died in Bristol in 1860. He married Mary Jane Hetherington and they were the parents of one child, Jacob McBrien Winder, the subject of this sketch.

Jacob M. Winder was born and reared in Bristol, Bucks county, and acquired his education at public and private schools in Bristol and Philadelphia. He graduated from Bryant and Stratton's Business College in 1877. For the greater part of his business life he has been engaged in the wholesale liquor business in Bristol, where he has always resided. In politics he is a Democrat, and has always taken a prominent part in the councils of his party. He was postmaster of Bristol for the term of 1895-1899, discharging the duties of that responsible position efficiently and to the satisfaction of its patrons. Mr. Winder married in August, 1878, Margaret Scott Irwin, daughter of Robert and Dorothy (McCartney) Irwin, of Philadelphia. Mr. and Mrs. Winder are members of the Protestant Episcopal Church of Bristol.

ISAAC S. JOHNSON, of Buckingham, was born in New Britain township, on February 20, 1850, being a son of Jacob B. and Lydia (Swartz) Johnson. Jacob B. Johnson was a son of Jacob Johnson, a native of England, and was born in Montgomery county, Pennsylvania, and while still a young man removed to New Britain township, Bucks county, and later located in Plumstead township, where he still resides. He was a prominent farmer for many years, but is now living a retired life with his son Harry. When the turnpike was built from Doylestown to Dublin, Mr. Johnson was the builder under contract with the newly organized company. Jacob B. and Lydia Swartz Johnson were the parents of nine children, of whom seven survive, viz.: Henry S., of Plumstead; John S., of New Britain; Isaac S.; Abraham S., of Montgomery county, Pennsylvania; Sallie S., wife of John Funk, of Fountainville; Mary Ann, wife of Reuben Detweiler, of Hilltown; Susan, wife of Harry High, of Plumstead.

Isaac S. Johnson, the subject of this sketch, was reared on the farm and acquired his education at the public schools of the neighborhood. In 1873 he married Mary A. Myers, of Pipersville, Bedminster township, and settled on and conducted his father's farm in Plumstead for ten years. He then rented the Lead Mine farm in New

Britain, which he conducted for four years. In 1887 he purchased his present farm in Buckingham, eighty-six acres, where he has since resided. He is a successful farmer and a man of high standing in the community. Mr. and Mrs. Johnson are the parents of four children, viz.: Laura, for several years a school teacher in Buckingham, now the wife of Clarence Buckman; Monroe M., a graduate of the Hughesian Free School, West Chester Normal School and Pierce's Business College, now filling a clerical position in Philadelphia; Franklin M., living at home; Rosa, residing at home and teaching school in Buckingham, who acquired her education at the Hughesian School, Doylestown High School and at West Chester Normal School. Mr. Johnson is a member of the Mennonite meeting, as was his father. In politics he is a Republican, but has never sought or held office.

THE VAN PELT FAMILY. The emigrant ancestor of the Van Pelt family was Teunis Jansen Lanen Van Pelt, who emigrated in 1663 from Liege, Belgium, with wife, Grietje Jans, and six children and settled in New Utrecht, Long Island. He was known as "Tunis the Fisher." The children of Teunis Jansen L. Van Pelt were, John Van Pelt, died after 1720, married Maria Peters; Anthony Van Pelt, died February 2, 1720-1, married Magdalen Joosten; Hendrick Van Pelt, married Annetje Meinards; Wouter Van Pelt, married Maria Jansen Schaers; Jacomytje, married Jochem Gulick; and Aerte, married Nieltje Jansen Van Tuyl. Bergen in his "Early Settlers of King's County" mentions three other children of Teunis Jansen L. Van Pelt, viz.: H. Teuntje, married Hermanus Gelder, Rebecca, married Abraham De La Montaigne, and Elizabeth.

Anthony Van Pelt, son of Teunis Janse, came to this country with his parents in 1663. He was a landholder in New Utrecht in 1683, and ten years later was constable of New Utrecht. In 1700 he joined with his brothers and sister, the six above mentioned, in a conveyance of land taken up by his father in New Utrecht, on July 27, 1713; he conveyed his land to his sons John and Tunis with a provision that he and his wife were to remain thereon during their natural lives. He died on February 2, 1720-1. His wife was Magdalena or Helena Joosten. Their children were: Joost. (Joseph) baptized at Flatbush, September 28, 1679; Maria, baptized October 14, 1681, married Adrien Schoute; Adriantje, baptized February 3, 1684, died young; Grietje, baptized June 3, 1685, married Barendt Bond; Tunis, who removed to Staten Island, 1719, married

Maria Degreau; Adriantje, baptized May 25, 1690, married Charles Taylor; John, of Staten Island, married Susanna La Tourette; Helena, baptized May 29, 1695, married Teunis Stoutenburgh, and Sarah, who married Cornelius Dorlandt. Of the above, at least two, Joseph Van Pelt and Adrien Schoute, (Scout) and Maria Van Pelt his wife settled in Pennsylvania, Joseph in Byberry, Philadelphia county, and Scout in Warminster township, Bucks county.

Joseph Van Pelt married Catharine ———, and the baptism of three of their children appears of record in Staten Island, Catharine, baptized May 4, 1714. Joost, baptized March 20, 1716, and Johannes, baptized September 8, 1717. He removed to Pennsylvania prior to December 6, 1719, as his daughter Sarah was baptized at Abington Presbyterian church on that date. Another son Derrick was baptized at the same church May 7, 1721. His other children were: Joris (George), who married Catharine Sleght, June 2, 1743, and had children, Joseph John, Catharine and Sarah, baptized at the Dutch Reformed church of North and Southampton, (1744 to 1756); Lena, who married John Van Horn; Anthony, who died in Buckingham in 1754, and Elizabeth, who married John Bennett. On November 7, 1730, Joseph Van Pelt purchased 180¾ acres of land in Byberry of Jacob Hibbs. He died intestate and letters of administration were granted to his widow Catharine March 17, 1739. His widow married John McVeagh, May 17, 1745. His son Joseph must have died young as he does not appear in connection with the conveyance of his father's real estate. John Van Pelt, the second son, married May 12, 1739, Cornelia Sleght, and settled in Northampton township, Bucks county. Their children were: Joseph, baptized December 11, 1742; Catharine, baptized April 2, 1745; John, baptized August 31, 1749; Daniel, baptized October 15, 1751; Isaac, baptized August 11, 1754, married December 30, 1788, Jane Henderson, and removed to Wrightstown township, Bucks county. Helena, baptized January 2, 1757; Jacob, baptized August 12, 1759, married Sarah Ryan. He died in New Milford, Ohio, August 31, 1831. He was the father of eleven children. Sarah, baptized September 23, 1761. Catharine Van Pelt, eldest daughter of Joseph and Catharine Van Pelt, married Abraham Carroll, January 29, 1737. Sarah, daughter of Joseph and Catharine Van Pelt, married Barnard Van Horn, January 17, 1753, and their son Isaac Van Horn was baptized at Southampton, March 17, 1754. Derrick Van Pelt married February 14, 1742, Mary Britton. He was an innkeeper in Whitpain township, Philadelphia county, at his death in 1767. His sons Joseph and John were residents of Upper Dublin township in 1770, but both removed to New Britain township, Bucks county, prior to 1776. The other children of Derrick and Mary were: Abraham, Mary, Anne, Samuel, Catharine, married Isaac Newhouse, and Mercy, married Jacob DeHaven.

Isaac Van Pelt, who married Jane Henderson in 1788, removed to Wrightstown township, Bucks county, in 1795, later removed to Buckingham where he died in 1811. His children were: Mary, married Robert Jones; John; Isaac; Thomas; Jane, married Thomas D. Wolf; and Eleanor, married William Vansant. Jane (Henderson) Van Pelt died in Buckingham in 1835.

Three of the sons of Joseph Van Pelt, viz.: John, Isaac and Daniel—were privates in Captain Folwells Associated Company in Southampton in 1775, John was commissioned a lieutenant in Lower Solebury, May 10, 1779. Isaac also saw actual service in the revolution. John became a captain.

Isaac, son of Isaac and Jane Henderson Van Pelt, was born in Wrightstown in 1797. He was a shoemaker by trade and lived in Wrightstown until 1836, when he purchased a farm in Buckingham, where he died May 27, 1865. He was twice married. His first wife was Sarah, daughter of Peter D. and Rebecca (Lewis) Cattell, (originally De-Cattel). The children of this marriage who survived were: Seth C., born August 24, 1829; Jane Ellen, married Joseph S. Ely, Esq., of Newtown; William, of Upper Makefield; Wilhelmina, married Charles H. Warner. Isaac Van Pelt married (second) Mary Ann Richardson and had three children: Joseph, born October. 8, 1844, Elizabeth, married Joseph Starkey, and Matilda Caroline, who never married, living with her sister Elizabeth at Forest Grove.

SETH C. VAN PELT, deceased, was born near Penns Park, Wrightstown township, Bucks county, Pennsylvania, August 24, 1829, a son of Isaac and Sarah (Cattell) Van Pelt. He was reared on a farm until twenty years of age, acquiring a good education in the common schools adjacent to his home. He then entered the store of Jesse P. Carver, at Pineville, as clerk, where he remained until December 1, 1872, when, having been elected to the office of prothonotary of Bucks county, he removed to Doylestown and there resided until the spring of 1877, when he returned to Pineville and rented a store for two years. At the expiration of this period of time he purchased the same and continued the management of it until his death, May 31, 1889. He was a man of sterling integrity, and in all his career as clerk, accountant, postmaster, merchant and public official enjoyed the unbounded respect and esteem of all with whom he came in contact.

Mr. Van Pelt married, May 30, 1877, Carrie A. Bodine, daughter of John R. Bodine, and sister of General Robert L. Bodine, who participated in the civil war. One child was the issue of this union, Arthur C., who now resides in Pittsburg. Mr. Van Pelt was survived by his wife, who now makes her home in Doylestown. Their son, Arthur C. Van Pelt, born in 1879, is now residing in Bellevue, a suburb of Allegheny City, Pennsylvania. He married Claudia Geer, and has two daughters: Marian and Margaret.

WILLIAM VAN PELT, of Upper Makefield, son of Isaac and Sarah (Cattell) Van Pelt, was born in Wrightstown township, Bucks county, May 27, 1833. He was reared on the Wrightstown farm, and acquired his education at the local schools. In 1857 he married Hannah D. Tomlinson, daughter of Samuel Tomlinson, of Pineville, Bucks county, and took charge of the .home farm, which he conducted for four years, when he removed to Taylorsville, where he conducted a temperance hostelry for one year. He then removed to Searchville, and conducted a small farm for one year, and then removed to Titusville, New Jersey, and engaged in the butcher business. In the fall of 1861 he enlisted in Company F, Twenty-second Regiment New Jersey Volunteers, for a term of nine months, and went to the front in defense of his country. At the expiration of his term of enlistment he returned to Titusville, and was employed in a store there for a short time. His father being taken sick, he returned home and took care of him until his death, May 27, 1865. After his father's death he removed to Pineville, and worked at carpentering for a short time, and then purchased a lot of land and erected buildings and began buying and slaughtering calves and poultry for the New York market, and conducted a local butchering business. In 1878 he sold out his business to his half-brother, Joseph Van Pelt, and Hiel Quinn, and purchasing his present farm in Upper Makefield, has since devoted his attention to farming and stock raising. He has bred and owns a number of high bred horses. In politics Mr. Van Pelt is a Democrat. He is a member of Captain Angel Post, G. A. R., of Lambertville, New Jersey.

Mrs. Van Pelt died October 17, 1900. They have been the parents of seven children, four of whom survive: Josephine, wife of Augustus Poore, a conductor on the P. & R. R. R., residing at Doylestown; Isaac, residing in New

Hope, Bucks county; Seth, who now has charge of the home farm; and Clara, wife of Harry S. Woolsey, of Doylestown.

JOSEPH VAN PELT, deceased, of Pineville, Pennsylvania, was born in Buckingham township, Bucks county, Pennsylvania, October 8, 1844, a son of Isaac and Mary Ann (Richardson) Van Pelt. He was reared on his father's farm, and obtained such education as could be acquired at the common schools in the vicinity of his home. At his father's death, in 1865, he went to live with his brother-in-law, Joseph Starkey, on the Buckingham farm. In 1869 he came to Pineville and entered the employ of his half-brother, William, in the butcher business. Ten years later he began the business of butchering in partnership with Hiel G. Quin, under the firm name of Van Pelt & Co. Making a specialty of pork butchering, they built up a large and lucrative trade, turning out a finished product of two hundred and twenty-five thousand pounds in a year. The success attained by the firm was entirely due to the energy, perseverance and pluck displayed in their management of affairs, and also by honorable and straightforward business principles which characterized their career from the beginning. In politics Mr. Van Pelt was a Democrat.

Mr. Van Pelt married, December 31, 1874, Rachel R. Tomlinson, daughter of William H. and Sarah (Phillips) Tomlinson. Five children were born to them, of whom Jennie died at the age of two years and eleven months, and Harry in his sixteenth year. The surviving members of the family are: Eugene K., a bookkeeper in Philadelphia; Mary A., a graduate of Doylestown high school, resides at home; and Lewis W., who also resides at home. William H. Tomlinson, father of Mrs. Van Pelt, was a son of Samuel and Hannah (Doan) Tomlinson, and grandson of Joseph Tomlinson, whose mother was a descendant of William Buckman, who came from Sussex county, England, arriving here in the "Welcome," 8 mo., 1682. Joseph Van Pelt died January 5, 1905.

CHARLES LANGHORNE TAYLOR, of Trevose, son of the late Charles Williams Taylor, and Sarah (Paxson) Taylor, his second wife, was born on the Trevose estate in Upper Bensalem township, Bucks county, Pennsylvania, the home of the Taylor family for several generations, and the residence in Colonial times of the Growdons, ancestors of the Taylor family.

The founder of the Taylor family in America was Thomas Taylor of Virginia, who was a son of Thomas Taylor, of London, England. The latter was a son of John, who was a son of one Nathaniel Taylor, who lived in Colchester, Essex, at the time of the commonwealth under Cromwell. Thomas Taylor, the American progenitor of the family, went to Virginia when young and became a planter. He was prosperous and became possessed of a large landed estate which he devised to his son Caleb at his death. Thomas Taylor, third son of Caleb and grandson of Thomas Taylor of Virginia, was born in 1753, joined the Society of Friends, and settled in York, Pennsylvania, where he died in 1837, aged eighty-four years. His son, Caleb, Jr., was born in 1789, and went into the wholesale drug business at 24 North Front street, Philadelphia, in 1810, at the age of twenty-one. In the space of ten years he built up a large and profitable business. In 1820 he died, leaving a widow, Lydia, and four children: Caleb, third; George W., Charles W., father of the subject of this sketch; and Sarah, wife of the late Thomas Paul, of Germantown, whose niece, Mary Paul, married William Waldorf Astor, of New York city. Caleb Taylor, Jr., married in 1814 Lydia Williams, a woman of superior mental attainments and of distinguished ancestry. She was a lineal descendant of Thomas Langhorne and of Lawrence Growdon, the elder, and Joseph Growdon, prominent men in and early settlers of the province of Pennsylvania; also from the English Mauleverers of Arncliffe. She was the daughter of Charles Williams and Sarah Dickinson, his wife. The original parchment marriage certificate reciting their marriage in 1788 by Frends' ceremony, is still in the possession of the family, and is an interesting document. Charles Williams was the son of Hezekiah Williams, Jr. and Grace Langhorne Biles, his wife. The latter was a daughter of Charles Biles and Anne Mary, his wife. Charles Biles was the son of William Biles and Sarah Langhorne, his wife.

William Biles was one of the early settlers of the county. He took up nearly three hundred acres just east of the present borough of Langhorne. He was a man of eminent talents and of great influence. He was a member of the assembly, overseer of the highways, and a constable under Governor Andros and the Duke of York. Sarah Langhorne, his wife, was the daughter of Thomas Langhorne, and sister of Jeremiah Langhorne, a noted minister of the religious Society of Friends, and later judge of the provincial courts. Hezekiah Williams, Jr., was the son of Hezekiah Williams, Sr., and Sarah Abbott, his wife. The latter was the daughter of John Abbott, and Anne Mauleverer, his wife. Anne Mary, wife of Charles Biles, was the daughter of Thomas Hooper and Ganfeier (Growdon) Hooper, who was the daughter of Joseph Growdon, the father of Lawrence Growdon the younger. Joseph Growdon was a son of Lawrence Growdon the elder, of Trevose,

Cornwall, England. He with his son Joseph in 1681 together obtained a grant of ten thousand acres of land from the proprietor of the province of Pennsylvania. At the death of Joseph his share of the estate went to his wife Anne, and at her death it went to Lawrence Growdon the younger. The Growdon tract comprised nearly the whole of what is now the present township of Bensalem. The present Trevose estate is all that is now left of it, and it is one of the historic estates of Pennsylvania. The boundaries of the tract as it then existed began on or near the farm of one Charles Vandegrift, on the Poquessing creek, and extended in an irregular line to the Neshaminy creek, a short distance above the present village of Newportville; thence following the Neshaminy until it reached the range of the Southampton township line; thence along this line to the Poquessing, and down that stream until it reached the farm of Charles Vandegrift, at the place of beginning. The Growdons also took up under their patent from Penn three hundred acres of land in the southern point of Bensalem, between the Poquessing creek and the Delaware river.

After a short residence in Philadelphia, after he came over from England, Lawrence Growdon erected a mansion house at Trevose, set up a manorial establishment, and maintained much pomp and circumstance. The mansion house was at that time a large stone building with pointed finish, two stories high, with open stairway and hall. When it was completed in 1687 it was one of the finest residences in the province. Two wings, one adjoining the east end of the house, and the other adjoining the west end, with an open court-yard between them, were used for kitchen, scullery, store house and slave quarters respectively. At the east end of the dwelling house Growdon erected a small stone fireproof building, with brick arched roof, and an iron door. Here the county records were stored while the county seat was at Bristol and while Growdon was prothonotary, and here at a later date were kept many of the valuable papers of Benjamin Franklin, who was an intimate friend of Joseph Galloway, son-in-law of Lawrence Growdon. In the iron door at present on this building there still may be seen bullet holes from shots fired by soldiers in the Continental army during the Revolutionary war. In front of the mansion house the main door opened into the spacious hall, and from this door a splendid view could be had of distant Jersey and the Delaware river, as well as the lower lands of Bensalem, Byberry and Bristol. A fine lawn of original forest trees surrounded the house, while back were stables and garden. Back of the house and towards the "Neshaminy river" was Growdon's famous orchard of one thousand apple trees of English importation. This was the home, or Manor farm. The farms retained and rented were South Trevose, East Belmont, West Belmont, South Richlieu, West Richlieu, and

Richlieu Forest. Part of the southern lands were subsequently sold to the Rodmans. Gabriel Thomas, in his book entitled "An Historical Description of the Province of Pennsylvania," published in London in 1698, describes the Growdon mansion as situated on the "Neshaminy river" and further says that "Judge Growdon hath a very noble and fine house, very pleasantly situated; and likewise a famous orchard adjoining to it, wherein are contained above a thousand apple trees of various sorts." Growdon's mansion house, which this quaint historian refers to, is still standing, and is as solid as it was when built over two hundred years ago. There have been but slight changes to alter its appearance with the exception of a half story which was added in 1847. The old house in its day had seen many a distinguished guest. Here Penn held council, and here laws were formulated for the better government of the province. Here, in the next generation, Benjamin Franklin rehearsed his theories regarding the then undiscovered science of electricity with his friend the eminent and erratic Galloway.

Lawrence Growdon, the younger, was a member of the general assembly from Philadelphia in 1685. In 1693 he was elected to represent Bucks county in the same body, and served as speaker of the house for a number of consecutive terms. He was appointed a provincial judge in 1706, and was one of the judges of the supreme court in 1715. Proud speaks of him as being attorney general in 1725. For further information on this subject the reader is referred to an interesting paper entitled "The Growdon Mansion," read before the Bucks County Historical Society, January 19, 1897, by Henry W. Watson, Esq., of Langhorne.

Lawrence Growdon died in 1769, and left surviving him two daughters, Elizabeth and Grace. The latter married Joseph Galloway, one of the eminent men of his day. He was an able lawyer, and at the beginning of the Revolution had built up a large practice in the courts of Pennsylvania, New Jersey and Delaware. He was a man of great activity and indefatigable industry. He was a member of the provincial assembly eighteen years, and speaker of the house twelve years. He was sent by the assembly as a delegate to the Continental congress. After the death of Lawrence Growdon, his father-in-law, Joseph Galloway, resided at Trevose. He believed that the difficulties between Great Britain and the Colonies which eventually led to the Revolution could be settled amicably and without bloodshed. These views he boldly upheld in the Continental congress. His influence was so great that his opponents saw that he must be silenced. In the autumn of 1776, while Galloway was supposed to be living at Trevose, a squad of soldiers appeared there in search of him. They did not find him, however, as he had been warned and had left. They sacked the mansion, and plundered the wine cellar. As they left they fired a parting shot at the iron door of the old record office. The bullet holes may be seen to this day. After hostilities commenced Galloway upheld the British cause. His wife and daughter went to Philadelphia, where he rejoined them shortly after, entering the city with the British army under Sir William Howe. Joseph Galloway had one daughter, known to history as "Betty." In her day she was a great belle. Among her admirers was a British army officer, William Roberts, whom she afterwards married. Galloway took a determined stand against the young man and forbade his daughter to have any association with him, and threatened to shoot him if he ever came on his property. The colored servants sympathized with the young lovers and carried letters between them. An elopement from Trevose and a marriage followed. When Galloway discovered this he was enraged. He immediately resolved to sell all his slaves, and accordingly advertised and sold them in the open court yard at the rear of the mansion house and between its wings. This occurred about ten years before the Revolutionary war.

Some time after this, Galloway turned his mind to religion and wrote and published a work entitled "Galloway's Comments on Divine Revelation," an old work yet in many libraries. Meeting the far-famed Christian philanthropist, Anthony Benezet, one of the best men of any age or country, Galloway asked him very pompously if he had read his great work on "Divine Revelation." "No," replied Benezet, "neither shall I, for I think that a man who sells his fellow beings at public sale had better leave Divine Revelation alone, and everything else that is Divine."

To prevent her property from being confiscated, Galloway's wife Grace, by her will dated December 30, 1781, and recorded at Doylestown, devised all her real estate, including Trevose, to nine persons therein named, their heirs and assigns, without any restrictions or limitations whatever. The devisees took possession and held her estate until in 1801, when the survivors of them recorded in Doylestown "A Declaration of Trust," in which they declared that they held the estate in trust for Elizabeth Galloway, her heirs and assigns, covenanting to convey at her request. The tracts Trevose, South Trevose, East Belmont, West Belmont, Richlieu, and Richlieu Forest were so conveyed to Elizabeth Galloway Roberts, and were sold by her grandchildren to George Williams, great-uncle of the subject of this sketch.

The Galloways lived at Trevose in accordance with their social position and wealth and were looked up to as great folk, by the people of the community. On every fair day "Betty" Galloway could be seen cantering on horseback over the roads of the neighborhood, followed by a colored groom. Her riding habit has been minutely described by a local historian :

"The habit consisted of a black hat and plume, with coat and bodice and flowing skirt of green velvet, faced with gold." Her father wore the short trousers of the day with silk stockings and a powdered wig on all important occasions.

An interesting discovery was made at Trevose in 1888. It was part of the neighborhood tradition that before Mrs. Grace (Growdon) Galloway was forced to leave her home at the time of the Revolution, she buried a good deal of her treasure, which was too bulky to take with her. In August, 1888, this tradition was confirmed. A laborer while working on the farm unearthed the remains of what had been a box of rare and costly eggshell or India china. It was unfortunately nearly all broken when found, but enough remained to show that it had been hand-painted with pictures of Chinese life, with the funny and impossible perspective so much in use by the artists of the Flowery Kingdom for the last thousand years. Just enough remained to show what once had been. They had evidently been carefully packed. Saucers and tea plates were found standing on their edges in rows, and there was a strong partition in the box separating them from the larger and heavier pieces of china. There were also a number of pieces found belonging to a children's toy tea set of common blue ware. There was but one other article deserving of mention, and this was a bowl of the commonest ware ornamented with a likeness of King George III., taken when he was a young man, with the words "George III., King," on a scroll at the base of the portrait. There seems to have been no reason why so worthless an article should have been hidden away, excepting that, as it indicated the loyalty of the family, it was dangerous to allow it to be exposed to view. A similar box of china was dug up in 1847 by the late William Ridge, who was then lessee of the property.

In 1847 the Burtons, grandchildren of Betty Galloway, sold Trevose to their second cousin, George Williams, a lineal descendant of the Growdons. At his death he devised it to his niece Lydia (Williams) Taylor, wife of Caleb Taylor; Lydia at her death devised it to her son, the late Charles W. Taylor, father of the subject of this sketch. It is somewhat singular that, from the time of the Growdons down to the time of the Burtons, there is no mention in any deed or will conveying the property to any male heir being born to the estate. There has always been a female heir in each generation for whom the property was held in trust. From 1681 to the present time the property has been sold but twice. Through the Williams family the present owner is a lineal descendant from the Growdons, the first purchaser from William Penn, and while the property has not always descended in a direct line, yet it is interesting to note that it has never passed out of the hands of the descendants of Lawrence Growdon the elder, since the time he

received it by grant from Penn, the proprietor of the province of Pennsylvania.

Lydia (Williams) Taylor, wife of Caleb Taylor, was also a lineal descendant of Thomas Langhorne, father of Jeremiah Langhorne, of Langhorne Park. The latter was an interesting contemporary of Lawrence Growdon. He was a branch of the Langhorne family of Wales, "a family of much wealth, and great note." They were the owners of all the country from St. Davids' to Carmarthan, over sixty miles. St. Brides' was the family seat of the Langhornes, settled by one Thomas Langhorne during the reign of Richard II. Langhorne Castle was dismantled by Cromwell. Thomas Langhorne, of Kendall meeting, Westmoreland, England, came to Bucks county in 1684. He took up some eight hundred acres of land covering the ground between the present borough of Langhorne and Glen Lake, and was one of the first settlers. His mansion house was situated about one half-mile south of the present borough of Langhorne Manor, and on the property now owned by J. Hibbs Buckman, Esq. He had four children: Jeremiah; Elizabeth, who married Lawrence Growdon; Sarah, who married William Biles; and Grace, who died at the age of thirty-four, unmarried.

Jeremiah Langhorne was farfamed as one of the ablest ministers of the religious Society of Friends. He was chief justice of the province, and held court in many places in it. He lived a single life with his sister Grace until her death, and after that alone with his servants. Besides Langhorne Park, his residence, he owned several thousand acres in Lehigh county. As to the date of his death there is no known record. His remains are said to lie in the Middletown meeting graveyard in the borough of Langhorne. His will was proved in 1774. By marriages and deaths without issue Jeremiah Langhorne's estates went largely to the Growdons and the Galloways of Trevose. For an interesting essay on "Jeremiah Langhorne and his Times" the reader is referred to a paper read before the Bucks County Historical Society on August 9, 1898, by Samuel C. Eastburn, Esq., of Langhorne, from which much of the information herein contained is taken.

The Williams family are also descended from the Mauleverers of Arncliffe, England. Hezekiah Williams, Jr. (ante) great-grandfather of the late Charles W. Taylor, was the son of Hezekiah Williams, Sr., and Sarah Abbott, his wife. The latter was a daughter of Anne Mauleverer and John Abbott, of Burlington county, New Jersey, who were married April 16, 1696. John Abbott was born in Nottinghamshire in 1663, and arrived in Philadelphia in 1684. Anne Mauleverer was the daughter of Edmund Mauleverer, of West Auyton, Yorkshire, and Anne Pearson, his wife. He died 27 November, 1679. Edmund's father was James, who married Beatrice, daughter of Sir Timothy Hutton, Bart. Records in St.

Mary's church, York, show that he was buried there 25 April, 1664. James's father was William, who married Eleanor, daughter of Richard Aldborough. William Mauleverer was buried at Arncliffe, the family seat of the Mauleverers, 11 April, 1618. William's father was Sir Edmund, who married Mary, daughter of Sir Christopher Danby, Bart. He was buried at Arncliffe, 27 April 1571. Sir Edmund's father was Robert, who married Alice, daughter of Sir, Nimian de Markenfield. Robert's father was Sir William Mauleverer (knighted at Flodden in 1513) who married Anne, daughter of William, first Lord Conyers, and Anne de Neville his wife. The latter was a daughter of Ralph de Neville, third earl of Westmoreland. Lord Conyers was the son of Sir John Conyers, Bart, and Alice de Neville, his wife. Through the Nevilles, and John of Gaunt, the line may be readily traced to Edward III., and so on back, by any one familiar with English history. For further research on this matter the reader is referred to "Descent of Anne Mauleverer Abbott," by Charles Marshall and John B. Clement, 1903, Times Printing House, Philadelphia. See also "Inglesby Arncliffe, and its Owners," by William Brown, F. S. A., 1901, John Whitehead & Son, Alfred street, Boar Lane, Leeds. The descent in all its details is beautifully traced in the Marshall-Clement chart, to which the reader is referred.

Sarah (Paxson) Taylor, second wife of the late Charles W. Taylor, and mother of the subject of this sketch, was born April 13, 1841, at "Brushy Park," near Eddington, Pennsylvania, and died at Trevose, February 22, 1889. She was the daughter of Joseph Paxson and Elizabeth (Gallaher) Paxson, his wife, and a member of the Rodman family. Joseph Paxson was born February 12, 1803, and died September 24, 1867. He was the eldest son of John Paxson, of Brookfield, and Sarah (Pickering) Paxson, his wife. John Paxson's father was Joseph, who married Sarah Rodman. He was born 25 December, 1744, and resided at Brookfield until his death in 1795. Sarah Rodman's father was John Rodman (fourth) of Brookfield, who married (second) Mary Harrison Rodman. He was born in 1714 at Flushing, Long Island. He removed to Burlington, New Jersey, with his father, in 1726; thence September 1, 1748, to Bensalem township, Bucks county, Pennsylvania, residing until his death in 1795 on the farm called Brookfield, which he purchased from the Growdons. His father was John Rodman (third) who married Margaret Grosse. John Rodman (third) was born in the Island of Barbadoes, May 14, 1679, and accompanied his father to Newport, Rhode Island, in 1682. He resided at Newport after he became of age, and was admitted as a freeman of that city May 1, 1706. He removed to Flushing, Long Island, in 1712, where he continued to reside until 1726. He was a member of the Society of Friends,

and a practicing physician. He was a member of the ninth assembly of the province of New Jersey in 1727, from the city of Burlington. From 1738 until his death, a period of eighteen years, he acted as King's Councillor for New Jersey. King George II. appointed him 8 January, 1741, a member of a commission to settle the controversy between the Mohegan Indians and the colony of Connecticut. He was the son of John Rodman (second) and Mary (Scammon) Rodman, his wife. John Rodman (second) was born in 1653. His name appears among the inhabitants of Christ church parish, Barbadoes, December 22, 1679, as the owner of forty-seven acres of land and thirteen negroes. He was a member of the Religious Society of Friends, and while he lived in Barbadoes was fined 1,350 pounds of sugar "for default of appearing in the troop." He purchased land in Newport, Rhode Island, in 1682, and in Burlington, New Jersey, in 1686. He died July 10, 1731, at the age of seventy-eight. He was the son of John Rodman (first) of the Island of Barbadoes, the progenitor of the Rodman family in America, and Elizabeth Rodman, his wife. Of John Rodman little is known. He died in the Island of Barbadoes some time between the 16th September and 4th December, 1686. His will bears the former date, and it was proved on the latter date. From whence he came is not now known. No memorials now exist in the family showing this fact, and the researches necessary to discover it from other sources have not been made. The only fact which tends to throw any light at all upon the subect is found on page 366 of Rutty's "History of the Quakers in Ireland," published in 1751: "In the year 1655 for wearing his hat on in the Assizes in New Ross, was John Rodman committed to goal by Judge Louder, kept a prisoner three months and then banished the country." The inference from this passage is that John Rodman originally came from Ireland, and upon his banishment went to the Island of Barbadoes. See "A Genealogy of the Rodman Family from 1620 to 1886," by Charles Henry Jones, Philadelphia, 1886, Allen Lane & Scott, publishers.

The Brookfield Farm above mentioned as the home of the Rodmans for so many generations is still owned by their descendants, and the subject of this sketch inherited an interest in it through his mother. It is worthy of remark that from the early part of the seventeenth century until the present time, a period of two hundred years, this property has never been out of their hands, but has been owned and occupied by seven or eight successive generations of the family.

Charles W. Taylor, father of the subject of this sketch, was born in Philadelphia in 1817. He was educated at the Westtown Friends' School, and at the Friends' Academy, then on Fourth street, below Chestnut street, Philadelphia. Soon after coming of age he became associated with his great

Benjamin J. Taylor

uncle, George Williams, in the China and East India trade. In 1847 he gave up active business owing to ill health, and took up his residence at Trevose, where he resided until his death, May 30, 1893. He was a man of great force of character, of earnest piety, and much respected by those among whom he lived. In early life he was a member of the Society of Friends, as were all his family before him. In later years he became an Episcopalian. He was an attendant at Christ church, Eddington, and Grace Protestant Episcopal church, Hulmeville. For a number of years he was vestryman and rector's warden of the latter church, and represented it at the Episcopal convocation of Germantown. While he was possessed of more than ordinary ability and took a great interest in the public affairs of his time, yet he was of a retiring disposition, and, although he was often strongly urged, he never held public office. While living a retired life at Trevose he was active in every work for the advancement of the community. He was a fluent and graceful writer, and a frequent contributor to current newspapers and magazines on floricultural and historical subjects. He was especially interested in the latter subject, and was one of the charter members of the Bucks County Historical Society.

Charles Langhorne Taylor, the subject of this sketch, was prepared for college by a private tutor, and at the Abington Friends' School, Jenkintown, Pennsylvania. He entered the University of Pennsylvania in 1893 and was graduated B. S. in 1897; attended Harvard College, but did not graduate; was graduated LL. B. from Harvard Law School, 1900; also graduated LL. B. from the Law School of the University of Pennsylvania, 1901; was admitted to practice law at the Philadelphia bar on motion of George Wharton Pepper, Esq., in 1901; was admitted to the bar of the supreme court of Pennsylvania in 1904, and has practiced his profession in Philadelphia since 1901. In the latter year he was one of the organizers of the Bucks County Country Club at Langhorne, near Trevose; later became one of its charter members, and a member of the board of governors; was elected secretary of the club in 1904. He is a Republican in politics, and a member of several clubs and societies, among which may be mentioned the Harvard Club of Philadelphia, the Bucks County Historical Society, and Historical Society of Pennsylvania.

BENJAMIN J. TAYLOR, of Bristol, Bucks county, Pennsylvania, president of the Farmers' National Bank of Bucks county and prominently associated with the business interests of lower Bucks, was born in Burlington county, New Jersey, and is a representative of a distinguished family that has been prominently identified with the business, official and social life of Bucks and Philadelphia counties, and of the

neighboring state of New Jersey for over two centuries.

Samuel Taylor, the emigrant ancestor of the family, was a native of the parish of Dore, Derbyshire, England, and sailed from Bristol, England, in the fly-boat, "Martha," in the year 1677, and landed at the point where Burlington, New Jersey, now stands. He was one of the proprietors of West Jersey, owning one thirty-second share in the lands of West Jersey, the papers for which were executed by his brother, William Taylor, of Dore, county of Derby, England, who had purchased the land of George Hutchinson, when in England and sold it to Samuel, but being lost before reaching America, the land was conveyed to Samuel by Hutchinson in 1681. He located in Chesterfield township, Burlington county, owning large tracts of land there and elsewhere. He died in December, 1723, leaving a family of eight children, four sons, John, George, William and Robert, and four daughters who married into prominent families of New Jersey.

Robert Taylor, youngest son of Samuel, was the executor of his father's will and inherited a large portion of the homestead tract, which descended to his son Anthony, the great-grandfather of the subject of this sketch, and remained in the tenure of his descendants until quite recently. The five hundred acre tract known as Brookdale farm was Robert's portion. His son, Anthony, who inherited Brookdale and lived thereon until his death in 1785, was an ardent patriot during the revolution and rendered material service to the cause of national liberty.

Anthony Taylor, Jr., third son of Anthony, and great-grandson of Samuel, the founder, was born at Brookdale farm in 1772, and when quite young was placed with John Thompson, a prominent merchant of Philadelphia, to be trained for a mercantile and business career. On attaining his majority he formed a partnership with Thomas Newbold, whose sister Mary he later married, and engaged extensively in the East India trade, the firm name being Taylor & Newbold. In 1810 Mr. Taylor retired from active business pursuits and settled at Sunbury," his fine country seat in Bristol township, Bucks county, which had been his summer home for some years previously. He later purchased several other large tracts of land in lower Bucks county, and at his death in 1837 was the largest landowner in the county. Anthony Taylor married, in 1802, Mary Newbold, tenth child of Caleb Newbold, of Springfield township, Burlington county, New Jersey, and a descendant of Michael Newbold, of Sheffield Park, Yorkshire, England, who in 1678 purchased one eighth of three nintieth parts of the province of West Jersey, and settled in Springfield township, Burlington county, where he died in 1693, leaving a large number of children and grandchildren, some of whom were still in

England. Many of his descendants eventually became residents of Bucks county. Anthony and Mary (Newbold) Taylor were the parents of eleven children, Robert, Anthony, Sarah, William, Edward, Lawrence, Michael, Caleb Newbold, Mary Ann, Thomas, Emma L. and Franklin. The seventh of these children, Hon. Caleb Newbold Taylor, born at "Sunbury," July 27, 1814, was for over fifty years one of the most prominent men in Bucks county, being an acknowledged leader first of the Whig and later of the Republican party in Bucks county, representing his county in state and national conventions almost continuously after attaining his majority, and four times was the candidate of his district for congress, being twice elected, in 1866 and 1868, respectively. He was also one of the most prominent business men in the county and amassed a large estate, owning at one time about 3,000 acres of land in Bucks county. He was president of the Farmers' National Bank of Bucks county, of which his father, Anthony Taylor, had been president for many years at his death in 1837. He died unmarried.

Dr. Robert Taylor, eldest son of Anthony and Mary (Newbold) Taylor, was the father of the subject of this sketch. He was born in Philadelphia in 1803, and was reared in Bucks county. On attaining manhood settled in Philadelphia, removing later to Burlington county, New Jersey, and late in life to Bristol, Bucks county, residing at Sunbury Farm, where he died in August, 1872, at the age of sixty-nine years and was buried in the graveyard of the Protestant Episcopal church of St. James, the less, at the Falls of Schuylkill. He married Elizabeth Jones, daughter of Benjamin Jones, of Philadelphia, and a great-granddaughter of John Jones, a large landowner in Bucks and Philadelphia counties in colonial times. Dr. Robert and Elizabeth Ash (Jones) Taylor were the parents of five children: Benjamin J., Captain Anthony, Robert, Frances, and Alice J. Elizabeth Taylor, the mother of these children, died at Bristol, January 29, 1893, aged eighty years.

Captain Anthony Taylor, the second son of Dr. Robert Taylor, born in Burlington county, New Jersey, October 11, 1837, rendered distinguished services to his country during the civil war. He enlisted August 8, 1862, in the Fifteenth Pennsylvania Cavalry as a private, was made sergeant, October 30, 1862; first sergeant, March 1, 1863; first lieutenant of Company A, May 8, 1863; and Captain, June 1, 1865; having had command of the company as lieutenant, commanding almost from the date of his commission as first lieutenant. Prior to 1865 he was under Brigadier General Rosencrans, in the Army of the Cumberland, and participated in the battles of Antietam, Stone River, Chickamauga and many other engagements. From June 1, 1865 until the close of the war he served on the staff of General William J. Palmer, as aide-de-camp, and was honorably mustered out June 21, 1865. In 1893 he was awarded a medal of honor by the United States congress for signal acts of bravery and meritorious service. He married, February 21, 1871, Caroline Fletcher Johnson, daughter of Lawrence and Mary (Winder) Johnson, and died in Philadelphia, May 21, 1894, leaving two daughters, Mary Lawrence, now wife of Bromley Wharton, private secretary to Governor Pennypacker; and Elizabeth Elmslie, wife of Houston Dunn.

Benjamin J. Taylor, was born in Burlington county, New Jersey, and received his education at the Friends' Select School and at the Protestant Episcopal Academy of Philadelphia. He received a thorough business training, and followed mercantile pursuits in Philadelphia for eight years. In 1863 he served for three months in the Grey Reserves, and was at the shelling of Carlisle by General Fitz Hugh Lee. He also saw military service in Tennessee and Mississippi as volunteer aide on the staff of different commanders. After retiring from active mercantile pursuits he made his residence at the old family homestead at Sunbury Farm, in Bristol township, and devoted much of his time to the transaction of business, acting as agent for others and assisting in the care and management of the large estate belonging to the family. He has been a director of the Farmers' National Bank of Bristol for many years, and on the death of Pierson Mitchell, in 1894, was elected its president, representing the third generation of his family in succession to serve in that capacity. Mr. Taylor has inherited many of the sterling business qualities of his ancestors, and is interested in most of the local business enterprises. He and his sister Alice are the owners of Sunbury Farm, comprising 400 acres, which has been the home of his ancestors and their families for four generations, covering a period of over a century. He is a member of H. Clay Beatty Post, G. A. R., and other social, fraternal, and patriotic associations.

THE HICKS FAMILY of Bucks county descend from Pilgrim stock, their first American progenitor being Robert Hicks, who landed at Plymouth, Massachusetts, November 11, 1621, having sailed from London in the ship "Fortune," which followed the "Mayflower," and brought over those left behind the previous year by that famous vessel. The family of Robert Hicks were natives of Gloucestershire, England, and traced their ancestry in an unbroken line back to Sir Ellis Hicks, who was knighted by Edward, the Black

Prince, on the battle field of Poitiers, September 9, 1356, for conspicuous bravery in capturing a stand of colors from the French.

Robert Hicks settled at Duxbury, Massachusetts, and died there at an advanced age. His sons John and Stephen in 1642 joined an English company which acquired by patent an extensive tract of land about Hempstead and Flushing, Long Island. Stephen Hicks purchased several thousand acres at Little Neck, Long Island, and erected a large mansion where he lived to an advanced age and died without leaving male descendants.

John Hicks settled at Hempstead, and from him are descended the extensive family of the name on Long Island, in New York, Philadelphia and Bucks county, as well as in many other parts of the Union. He was educated at Oxford, and was a man of intelligence and natural force of character, and therefore soon became a leader in the youthful colony, and took an active part in public affairs, his name appearing in nearly all the important transactions of the time.

Thomas Hicks, only son of John, inherited his father's intellectual ability and force of character, and occupied a prominent position in public and social life, filling many positions of trust and honor. He was the first judge of Queens county, New York, and filled that office for many years. In 1666 he obtained from Governor Nicolls a patent for four thousand acres of land including Great Neck, Long Island, and lands adjacent, and lived there in English manorial style. He was a remarkable man in many respects, and retained his mental and physical powers unimpaired to an extreme old age. He was twice married, his first wife being Mary Washburne, by whom he had two sons, Thomas and Jacob, the latter being the father of the famous Quaker preacher, Elias Hicks, the founder of that branch of the Society of Friends known to this day as Hicksites. Judge Hicks married (second) Mary Doughty, by whom he had ten children—six sons; Isaac, William, Stephen, John, Charles, Benjamin; anl four daughters; Phebe, Charity, Mary and Elizabeth. A paragraph in the "New York Post Boy" of January 26, 1749, in referring to the death of Judge Hicks, says: "he left behind him of his own offspring above three hundred children, grandchildren, great-grandchildren and great-great-grandchildren." He died in his one hundredth year.

Isaac Hicks, eldest son of the Judge by his second marriage with Mary Doughty, was, like his father, a prominent man in public affairs. He was judge of Queens county, Long Island, for the years 1730-1738, and a member of the colonial assembly of New York from that county, 1716 to 1739. He married Elizabeth Moore, and they were the parents of evelen children—nine sons: Charles, Benjamin, Isaac, Gilbert, James, Thomas, Henry, John, Edward; and two daughters, Margaret and Mary.

Gilbert Hicks, fourth son of Isaac and Elizabeth (Moore) Hicks, was born in Queens county, New York, September 19, 1720, and married April 24, 1746, Mary Rodman, born February 17, 1717, a daughter of Joseph Rodman. They were the ancestors of all the Hickses of Bucks county. Both were born at Flushing, Long Island. As a wedding present to the youthful couple, Joseph Rodman conveyed to them six hundred acres of land in Bensalem township, on the Neshaminy creek, twenty miles northeast of Philadelphia, which he had recently purchased. Hither they came in 1747 and made their home in a comfortable log house until they erected a more commodious dwelling, to defray the expense of which he sold off two hundred acres of the land to Lawrence Growdon. They subsequently sold the remaining four hundred acres and purchased one hundred acres, coming to a point at Four-Lanes-End, (now Langhorne) on which he erected in 1763 a commodious brick house which is still standing.

On June 9, 1752, Gilbert Hicks was commissioned by the governor and council one of the justices of the peace for Bucks county, and on May 11, 1761, he was commissioned chief justice of the court of common pleas. On March 29, he and Hugh Hartshorne were commissioned by John Penn, then governor, to hold court for the trial of negroes, whether slave or free. Gilbert Hicks was a man of superior mental abilities, and stood very high in the community, commanding the respect of all. On July 9, 1774, he was chairman of a public meeting held at Newtown, then the county seat of Bucks, in pursuance of previous notice, and in a short address explained the objects of the meeting as being to consider the injury and distress occasioned by the numerous acts of oppression inflicted on the colonies by the English parliament, in which the colonies were not represented, and entirely concurred in the resolutions then adopted, looking toward a congress composed of delegates from the different colonies, "to use every lawful endeavor to obtain relief and to form and promote a plan of union between the parent country and colonies." See Penna. Archives, Second Series, Vol. XV, page 343.

When, however, General Howe issued his proclamation calling on the loyal subjects of George III to lay down their arms and seek peaceful means of redress, Judge Hicks, being greatly impressed with the power of England and the futility of armed resistance, while he condemned the injustices of the mother country toward the colonies, and being conscientious in regard to the oath he had taken as a justice, read the proclamation from the court house steps at Newtown, and counselled his friends and neighbors to pause before it was too late, and to postpone any over action or resistance until the colonies grew stronger. Excitement ran high at the time, and he was branded as a traitor and forced to flee the country and spend the remainder of his days in Nova Scotia, where he was supported by a pension from the British government, and where he was waylaid and murdered by highwaymen on March 8, 1786, for the quarterly pension he had just drawn. From the nature of the advice he gave to his eldest son Isaac, who visited him while in New York immediately after his flight, there is every reason to believe that if reasoned with calmly he would have realized that matters had progressed too far for peaceful measures to prevail, and would have lived to render to the patriot cause the same eminent service that he gave to his county under royal authority. His extensive property was confiscated, and his family reduced to almost penury. His son Isaac, who at the time was clerk of the several courts of Bucks county, was cast under suspicion and removed from office. Mary Rodman Hicks, the wife of Gilbert, died August 17, 1769, years before his flight and disgrace. They were the parents of five children: 1. Isaac, born April 21, 1748, married his first cousin, Catharine Hicks, daughter of Colonel Edward Hicks and Violetta Ricketts, of New Jersey. 2. Sarah, born November 3, 1749, died unmarried. 3. Elizabeth, born April 7, 1751, married June 4, 1768, General Augustine Willet, of Bensalem township. 4. Mary, born January 15, 1753, married May 8, 1772, Samuel Kirkbride. 5. Joseph Rodman, born November 12, 1756, married July 29, 1777, his cousin, Margaret Thomas.

Joseph Rodman Hicks purchased in 1780 a farm of one hundred acres near Dolington, in Upper Makefield township, and spent the remainder of his life there. He died May 28, 1816. His wife was an approved minister among Friends at Makefield Meeting, adjoining the farm, the land upon which the meeting house was built being originally part of the farm. She continued in the ministry from 1790 to the date of her death, May 2, 1842. In 1822 Mrs. Hicks and her children sold the farm, and she took up her residence with her son Charles in Philadelphia.

Joseph Rodman and Margaret (Thomas) Hicks were the parents of eight children, viz: Charles, married Elizabeth Cooper; Joseph, married Jane Bond; Elizabeth, married Jacob Wollery; Margaret, married Amos Carlile; Gilbert, married Phoebe Mathews; Mary, married Elias Slack; William, died unmarried; and Isaiah married Mary Flannagan.

Joseph Hicks, second son of Joseph Rodman and Margaret (Thomas) Hicks, born June 12, 1780, died October 4, 1827, married January 2, 1804, Jane Bond, of Newtown, Bucks county, and had nine children, the seventh of whom was Thomas Hicks, the eminent artist.

Charles Hicks, eldest son of Joseph Rodman and Margaret (Thomas) Hicks, was born June 12, 1778. At the age of sixteen years he removed to Philadelphia, and learned the carpenter trade, which he followed in that city during the ative years of his life. He died April 20, 1855. He was married August 10, 1804, to Elizabeth Cooper, born June 19, 1780, died April 17, 1858, and they were the parents of nine children, viz,: William C., Isaac, Ann C., Joseph, Willet, Charles C., Cooper, Rodman, and Elizabeth.

Willet Hicks, fifth son of Charles and Elizabeth (Cooper) Hicks, born February 21, 1814, died December 12, 1853, married April 16, 1836, Margaret Mintzer, born June 26, 1816, died January 5, 1899, and had six children, viz.: George A.; Edwin M.; S. Elizabeth; Albert M.; William U.; and Harry H.

George A. Hicks, to whom we are indebted for a history of the earlier generations of the Hicks family, is the eldest son of Willet and Margaret Mintzer Hicks, and was born in Philadelphia. Early in life he learned the trade of a plumber, and has followed that business to the present time in his native city. He takes deep interest in Bucks county, the home of his ancestors. He is one of the active members of the Bucks County Historical Society, and is a regular attendant at its meetings, and contributing largely to its success. Previous to manhood he united himself with the United States Hose Company, No. 14, (late Volunteer Fire Department of Philadelphia) and served as its secretary for many years. He is a member of the Veteran Firemen's Association, the Firemen's Association, State of Pennsylvania, and a life member of the Association for the Relief of Disabled Firemen. He is an honorary life member of Columbia Lodge No. 91, F. and A. M., and an honorary life member of Harmony Chapter, No. 52, R. A. M.; a member of the Master Plumbers' Association, and a stockholder in the Mercantile Library, all of Philadelphia. Mr. Hicks was never married.

EDWARD P. HICKS. Isaac Hicks, the eldest son of Gilbert and Mary (Rodman) Hicks, an account of whose ancestry from the Pilgrim ancestor Robert Hicks down to his father Gilbert Hicks, is given in, the preceding sketch, was born in Bensalem township, April 21, 1748, and died in Newtown, Bucks county, October 5, 1836. He received a good education, and was a man of fine intellectual ability and excellent business capacity. On June 6, 1772, he was commissioned prothonotary and clerk of the several courts of Bucks county, and filled those positions with eminent ability until 1777, when he was directed to turn in all papers and books relating to these offices to be deposited in the fire-proof at Newtown, the political views of his father (Gilbert Hicks) having cast a suspicion upon him. He was also commissioned a justice of the peace an April 9, 1774, and held that office for three years. The continued good and loyal deportment of the son had its proper effect to convince the public that the suspicion was groundless. After the close of the Revolution he was again commissioned a justice of the peace, and held the office many years while residing at Newtown. His office for many years was in the western end of what is now the White Hall Hotel. Here by close attention to his duties and an honorable course of life he built up a large business. It is said that in dress he adhered to the old style of breeches and knee-buckles.

He was married at Newtown, on November 17, 1771, to his cousin, Catharine Hicks, daughter of Col. Edward and Violetta (Ricketts) Hicks, who was born in New York, November 4, 1745, and died at Burlington, New Jersey, October 19, 1781. Her brother William was prothonotary of Bucks county, 1770-1772. The children of Isaac and Catharine Hicks, were:

1. Gilbert Edward, born March 11, 1773, who became a prominent physician at Catawissa, Pennsylvania, where he married Catharine Hibbs, daughter of James Hibbs. His grandchildren now living are: Dr. J. J. John, historian and prominent business man of Shamokin, who spent some little time in Bucks county in early life; Emma Walters, of Catawissa; and Anna M. Ormsby, widow of Henry George Ormsby, of Philadelphia.

2. William Richard, born November 17, 1774, died February 5, 1777.

3. Edward Henry, born June 29, 1776, died August 20, 1776.

4. Eliza Violetta, born March 17, 1778, married October 4, 1807, Thomas G. Kennedy, sheriff of Bucks county for the term 1815-1817. She was drowned in Newtown creek, near her home in Newtown, July 28, 1817, in an effort to save her child, who had fallen in the creek.

5. Edward, born April 2, 1780, died August 23, 1849.

8-3

Isaac Hicks married (second) October 20, 1792, Mary (Gilbert) Young, widow of Edward Young, of Philadelphia, who was born August 3, 1757, and died at Newtown February 22, 1812.

Edward Hicks, youngest son of Isaac and Catharine, was born at Attleboro (now Langhorne, then known as Four-Lanes-End) April 2, 1780. His mother dying when he was but eighteen months old, he was left to the care of her faithful servant Jane, a colored woman. His father's home was entirely broken up by the confiscation of all the property belonging to his father, Gilbert Hicks, and this, with sickness and deaths in his family, reduced him for a season to a great strait. He later secured a home for his infant son in the family of David Twining, where he remained until thirteen years of age. Edward Hicks in his "Memoirs" gives abundant testimony of his appreciation of the kindness received at the hands of his adopted mother, Elizabeth Twining. In April, 1793, he was apprenticed to the coach-making trade with William and Henry Tomlinson, at Four-Lanes-End, where he remained until 1800, when he set up business for himself. In the autumn of 1801 he entered the employ of Joshua C. Canby, then a coach-maker at Milford (now Hulmeville) and remained a resident of that village until April, 1811, when he removed to Newtown, Pennsylvania. He became a member of Middletown Monthly Meeting of Friends in the spring of 1803, and later became a prominent minister in the Society, traveling extensively in the ministry. Like his distinguished cousin, Thomas Hicks, he possessed considerable artistic talent, and a number of his paintings of high merit are still preserved. He was an ardent temperance advocate, and claimed to have built the first house in Bucks county erected without the use of intoxicating liquors, in 1804. He married 11 mo. 17, 1803, Sarah Worstall, daughter of Joseph and Susanna (Hibbs) Worstall. He died in Newtown 8 mo. 23, 1849, and his widow died 12 mo. 30, 1855. Their children were: Mary, born 10 mo. 12, 1804, died 2 mo. 7, 1880, unmarried; Susan, born 11 mo. 9, 1806, married 5 mo. 17, 1832, John Carle, Jr., of New York, and died in New York, 1 mo. 24, 1872; Elizabeth T., born 8 mo. 24, 1811, married Richard Plummer, of Baltimore, Maryland, 11 mo. 11, 1852, and died in Newtown, 3 mo. 22, 1892; Sarah B., born 12 mo. 24, 1816, married Isaac C. Parry, of Warminister, 5 mo. 23, 1844, and died in Warminister 2 mo. 23, 1895; Isaac W., born 1 mo. 20, 1809, and died 3 mo. 28, 1898.

Isaac W. Hicks, only son of Edward and Sarah (Worstall) Hicks, was born at Hulmeville, and reared in Newtown, Bucks county, where he lived from the age of two years until his death. He assisted his father in the coach painting business and farming, but after his fathers death he devoted himself mostly to farming. He was greatly interested in the incorporation of Newtown as a borough in 1838, and the laying of the brick walk on Penn street which led from a ladies seminary at the corner of Penn and Congress street to the heart of the town, and was the first improved walk in the new borough. Throughout his life he was interested in everything that would add to the best good of the town. His entire life after he was twelve years of age was spent in the house on Penn street, Newtown borough, built by his father about 1821 and remodeled by himself in 1870, and still occupied by his daughter Sarah. He married 6 mo. 4, 1857, Hannah L. Penrose, daughter of William and Hannah (Jarrett) Penrose, of Horsham. She was born at the historic Graeme Park, the former residence of Sir William Keith, colonial governor of Pennsylvania, 2 mo. 20, 1820, and died at Newtown 9 mo. 23, 1894. The children of Isaac W. and Hannah Penrose Hicks are:

Sarah W., born 4 mo. 9, 1858, still residing at the old homestead in Newtown.

Edward P., born 8 mo. 27, 1859, married 2 mo. 24, 1903, Lydia Harper Barnesley, daughter of William and Mary Ellen (Paff) Barnesley, of Newtown, and resides in Newtown borough, in the house on Penn street, opposite the old homestead built by his father about 1833, and remodeled by himself in 1904. Their daughter, Mary Barnesley Hicks, was born 7 mo. 24, 1904. Mr. Hicks took a prominent part in 1898 in establishing the standard telephone system at Newtown which was a matter of much importance to Newtown. He was for seven years a member of the Newtown town council and during this time many very important improvements were inaugurated which have proved beneficial to the town. He is somewhat retiring in disposition but one of the useful and highly respected citizens of the town and county.

William Penrose Hicks, born 9 mo. 6, 1864, married 5 mo. 23, 1890, Nellie Brown, daughter of William B. and Hannah (Hough) Brown, of Brownsburg, and resides on "Fountain Farm," adjoining Newtown borough. Their children are: Hannah Brown Hicks, born 12 mo. 1, 1891; and Cornelia Carle Hicks, born 3 mo. 1, 1898.

PENROSE HICKS. Bucks county is rich in memories of her honored citizens of the past, among whom must be numbered Penrose Hicks, for many years a respected resident of Richland township. Mr. Hicks belonged to a family whose name is a memorable one in the annals of the Society of Friends. William Hicks was a native of Bucks county, and was the father of five sons and two daughters. One of the sons, George, was a farmer and married Ann, daughter of John and Ann Penrose. To Mr. and Mrs. Hicks were born eleven children, of whom one was Penrose, mentioned at length hereinafter. In religious belief all the family were Friends.

Penrose Hicks, son of George and Ann (Penrose) Hicks, was born May 9, 1802, in Milford township. In his youth he learned the trade of a wheelwright and ploughmaker, but at the age of twenty-one became a farmer, devoting himself to agricultural pursuits until he was forty-two years of age. Some years later he retired from active labor. He was one of the directors of the Turnpike Company. He was chosen by his neighbors a member of the council, in which he served with honor to himself and satisfaction to his constituents. He was a Republican in politics, and always took an active interest in the affairs of the organization. He was a birthright member of Richland Monthly Meeting.

Mr. Hicks married Mary, daughter of William and Martha (Cadwallader) Ball, and they were the parents of a number of children. After the death of his wife Mr. Hicks married, November 13, 1862, Elizabeth, daughter of Hugh and Elizabeth (Roberts) Foulke.

The death of Mr. Hicks occurred July 11, 1886, when he had reached the advanced age of eighty-four. He left behind him the memory of a good husband and father, a kind neighbor, and a useful, public-spirited citizen.

J. WILMER LUNDY, of Newtown, Bucks county, was born at Rancocas, Burlington county, New Jersey, May 3, 1869, and is a son of Joseph and Mary (Evans) Lundy. Though a native of New Jersey, as have been his ancestors for four generations, his paternal ancestors were among the earliest settlers of the county in which he now resides.

Richard Lundy, the first American ancestor of the subject of this sketch, was a son of Sylvester Lundy, of Axminster, in the county of Devon, England, and came to Boston, Massachusetts in 6 mo., 1676, "and from thence came to the Delaware River the 19th of the 3d mo., 1682." So says the ancient record in the quaint little tattered "Book of Arrivals" in the handwriting of Phineas Pemberton (the first clerk of the Bucks county courts), now in possession of the Bucks County Historical Society. The same volume records the arrival in the Delaware river in "8th mo. 1683, in the ship Concord of London, the Master William Jeffry, of Elizabeth Bennett, daughter of William Bennett of Hammondsworth, in the county of

Middlesex (now deceased) and now the wife of the aforesaid Richard Lundy." William Bennett was accompanied to America by his wife Rebecca and daughters Elizabeth, before mentioned, Ann and Sarah. This book also gives the record of the marriage of Richard Lundy and Elizabeth Bennett, 6 mo. 24, 1684. Elizabeth survived her marriage but three years, and was buried 6 mo. 14, 1687. Still another entry in the old "Book of Arrivals" is interesting to the descendants of Richard Lundy, that which records the arrival of James Harrison and the Pembertons in the ship "Submission," on 5 mo. 7, 1682, at Choptank, Maryland, and their subsequent trip overland to Bucks county, detailed in this volume in a brief sketch of "The Pemerton Family," in which is given a list of the passengers on the ship "Submission." With the family of James Harrison came Jane Lyon, who was to serve in his family for four years to 9 mo. 2, 1686, and was then to receive fifty acres of land. On 4 mo. 24, 1691, this Jane Lyon became the second wife of Richard Lundy, at Middletown Meeting of Friends. Jane was born in the year 1666, and was therefore sixteen years of age when she arrived in Pennsylvania, and twenty-five years old when she became the wife of Richard Lundy. On 10 mo. 6th, 1682-3 there was laid out to Richard Lundy two hundred acres in what is now Bristol township, just west of the Manor of Pennsbury, which was patented to him 5 mo. 6th, 1684. 8 mo. 7th, 1685, he exchanged this tract with Jacob Telner for 1000 acres in what is now Buckingham, "back in the woods", as it is described in the deed recorded at Doylestown under date of 2 mo. 12th, 1688. It comprised all the land below the York road, eastward from the west line of Judge Paxson's "Nonesuch" farm to the village of Holicong, and extending to the top of Buckingham mountain.

Richard Lundy did not at once take up his residence "back in the woods" of Buckingham, but purchased of Samuel Burgess a tract of 103 acres on the upper side of Pennsbury Manor, part of the same tract on which Falls Meeting House was erected, and probably resided there until close to 1700. He finally conveyed this land to Thomas Duer, and took up his residence on his Buckingham purchase, either where Charles J. Smith now resides, or across the creek at the old Ely homestead now owned by the estate of Anna J. Williams. On 7 mo. 12, 1692, he conveyed to Francis Rossel, 500 acres off the western end of his tract, lying in about equal quantities on both sides of the present Durham Road. Rossel dying in 1695, devised it to William Smith. Ralph Boon and the "sons of Samuel Burgess." By various conveyances prior to 1705 that

west of the Durham road came to Mathew Hughes, whose family owned and occupied it for over a century, or until the death of Amos Austin Hughes in 1811. The east side of the road was first occupied by Lawrence and Enoch Pearson in 1702-3, and came to be the home of Thomas Canby in 1729. On 4 mo. 7, 1709, Richard Lundy, then re-residing in Buckingham, conveyed 100 acres to Joseph Large (now the Broadhurst farm) and some time prior to 1719 sold to his son Richard Lundy, Jr., 300 acres of the remaining 400 acres of his tract "back in the woods." The date was probably that of the marriage of Richard, Jr., in 1714: He, however, failed to convey the land to his son, and he having agreed to sell it to Isaac Norris, Richard Lundy, Sr., and Jane his wife and Richard, Jr., and Elizabeth his wife in 1710 conveyed it to Norris, and a year later it became the property of Hugh Ely, and remained in the family several generations. In 1724 Richard Lundy, Sr., conveyed the remaining 100 acres to Hugh Ely. This was probably the approximate date of the death of his wife Jane, and he took up his residence with his son Richard, Jr., who at this date had removed to Plumstead township and located on land belonging to his brother-in-law, Ebenezer Large, which he subsequently purchased.

Richard Lundy was a prominent member of Falls Meeting, and is frequently mentioned on their records. On his removal to Buckingham he became affiliated with the Meeting there, then a branch of Falls Meeting, and on it becoming a separate monthly meeting with Wrightstown in 1720, became one of the overseers and elders. On 8 mo. 5, 1737, he requested a certificate to remove himself to Maiden Creek, Berks county, where his son and family had removed two years previously, and though the Friends remonstrated against his removing himself so far back on the frontiers at his advanced age, he persisted, and was granted a certificate to Exeter Meeting, which he deposited there the month following. He probably died at Maiden Creek soon after his removal there, as we find no further record of him, and at the marriage of his grandson there in 1789 his name does not appear among the witnesses.

Richard Lundy (2), son of Richard and Jane (Lyon) Lundy, was born 3 mo. (May) 20, 1692, in Bucks county, probably in Falls township, and died 2 mo. (February) 28, 1772, at Allamuchy, Warren county. New Jersey. At least part of his boyhood days were probably spent on the Buckingham plantation, 300 acres of which was conveyed to him on his marriage in 1714. His wife was Elizabeth Large, daughter of Joseph Large, then deceased, and they were married at Buckingham under the auspices of Falls Meeting, 4 mo. 3, 1714. He was for ten years caretaker of Buckingham Meeting House and "grave digger." The records of the Meeting on 10 mo. 2, 1724, recites the fact that he had "moved too for off" to further officiate in this capacity, and fixes the date of his removal to Plumstead, where he was later made one of the trustees of the land on which Plumstead Meeting House was erected though the deed for the land (200 acres) on which he lived was not made to him until November 2, 1734, less than six months before the date on which he conveyed it preparatory to his removal to Berks county, viz.: 3 mo. 24, 1735. On 3 mo. 5, 1735, he was granted a certificate by Buckingham Meeting to remove with his family to Maiden Creek, Berks county, the certificate being directed to Gwynedd Meeting, from which Exeter was organized two years later, and of which latter meeting he was appointed an elder in 1737. Richard Lundy and his family remained in Berks county twelve years, removing in 5th mo., 1747 to the valley of Pequest river, in what is now Allmuchy township, Warren county, he and his family bringing certificates to Bethlehem (later Kingwood, and now Quakertown Meeting) in Hunterdon county, New Jersey., but becoming later attendants at Hardwick Meeting,. a branch of Kingwood. Several of his children had married prior to the removal to New Jersey, but all removed there with their families, though a few years later several of his children and grandchildren removed elsewhere. On March 28, 1749, Richard Lundy was commissioned a justice of the peace for the county of Morris, in which his residence was then included. In the same year he was made an elder of the Friends Meeting at Great Meadows, and frequent mention is made of meetings being held at his house. He died in Allemuchy, 2 mo. 28, 1772, and was buried at Hardwick Friends' burying ground. On the records of Kingwood Monthly meeting is recorded a testimony of his worth, which says among other things, "he was a man much esteemed among Friends and others, being of a meek and quiet spirit, exemplary in life and conversation, and a pattern of plainness and simplicity * * * He was an affectionate husband, a tender father, a kind friend, punctual and just in his dealings among men, evidencing to the world that he was concerned to do to others as he would have them do to him." His eighty years of life had not been lived in vain.

The children of Richard and Elizabeth (Large) Lundy were nine in number, all of whom were born in Buckingham and Plumstead townships. Bucks county, Pennsylvania, and all of whom removed with their parents to Berks county, and all of whom either preceded or accompanied them back to New Jersey; they were as follows:

1. Richard, born 4 mo. 23, 1715, in Buckingham, died at Allemuchy, New Jersey, 11 mo. 7, 1757; married at Maiden Creek, Berks county, in 1739, Ann Wilson, and removed to the Pequest Valley, New Jersey, in 1746. He had eleven children, ten of whom grew to maturity: Samuel, William, Amos, Sarah, Richard, Ann, Ebenezer, John Eleazer and Azariah. Samuel and William removed to Canada, Samuel to Newmarket, and William to Lundy's Lane, it being upon his property that the famous battle of Lundy's Lane was fought in 1814. Ebenezer and Azariah returned to Bucks county. Amos, Sarah (Kester) Richard, John, and the family of Azariah removed to Virginia.

2. Mary Lundy, born in Buckingham, Bucks county, 11 mo. 6, 1716, married in Plumstead in 1734, Robert Wilson, removed with him to Berks county, Pennsylvania in 1735, and to Sussex county, New Jersey, in 1748, where she died 3 mo. 4, 1807, at the age of ninety years. She left numerous descendants, some of whom still retain the Sussex homestead.

3. Joseph Lundy, born in Buckingham 4 mo. 24, 1719, removed with the family to Berks county in 1735, married there in 1743 Susanna Hutton, and removed to Warren county, New Jersey, in 1745; died there about 1759; left children: Sarah, who married Joseph Carpenter, and returned to Berks county, as did his son Enos, who in 1805 removed to York county, Ontario. His daughter Hannah married Samuel Shotwell, and settled in Sussex county, New Jersey.

4. Jacob Lundy, born in Buckingham 6 mo. 15, 1721, married at Maiden Creek, 1748, Mary Wilson, removed to New Jersey same year, and died there in 1800, leaving children, Jacob, Mary (Schmuck), Jonathan, and Deborah (Dennis).

5. Martha Lundy, born in Buckingham, 6 mo. 1, 1723, married in New Jersey in 1755, Benjamin Schooley; died there 9 mo. 11, 1803; left four children.

6. Thomas Lundy, born in Plumstead, Bucks county, and died in Warren county, New Jersey, about 1775; he married there in 1750, Joanna Doan, and had six children. See forward.

7. Samuel Lundy, born in Plumstead, Bucks county, 12 mo. 13, 1727, died in Sussex county, New Jersey, 2 mo. 14, 1801. He was a judge of Sussex county court, and was twice married, first in 1731 to Ann Schooley, and second in 1765 to Sarah Willets, and had twelve children. His son Levi removed to Ohio, Samuel to Seneca county, New York, and Jesse to Ontario, Canada. The others of his children remained in New Jersey.

8. Elizabeth Lundy, born at Plumstead, Bucks county, married at Hard-

wick, New Jersey, in 1748, Gabriel Wilson, and settled at Great Meadows, in Warren county, New Jersey, where she died 5 mo. 25, 1811; their eight children removed to North Carolina, Indiana, Canada and Kentucky.

9. Margaret Lundy, born at Plumstead, Bucks county, 12 mo. 14, 1732, died at Hardwick, New Jersey, in 4 mo., 1776. She had married in 1750 John Wilson, who removed with her family from Maiden Creek, Berks county, Pennsylvania, in 1745. No record of children.

Thomas Lundy, sixth child of Richard and Elizabeth Large Lundy, was a mason by trade, and was the first of the family to remove from Berks county to the Pequest Valley in New Jersey. He helped to erect the first jail of Warren county in 1754. His wife Joanna Doan was probably a granddaughter of Daniel and Mehetabel Doan, of Bucks county. Thomas and Joanna had six children: Susanna, who married Thomas Parker, son of Humphrey Parker, of Wrightstown, Bucks county. Reuben, born 3 mo. 13, 1752, married in 1776 Esther Bunting, daughter of Joseph and Sarah (Bidgood) Bunting, of Bristol, Bucks county, and later settled in Columbia county, Pennsylvania. Ephraim, son of Thomas and Joanna, married in 1776, Elizabeth Patterson, and after living for twenty years in New Jersey removed with their five children to Catawissa, Lycoming county, Pennsylvania. Thomas, son of Thomas and Joanna, married in 1779 Elizabeth Stockton, and in 1787 removed to North Carolina. Elizabeth, youngest daughter of Thomas and Joanna (Doane) Lundy, born 8 mo. 30, 1763, married in 1782, Israel Bunting, son of Joseph and Sarah, of Bucks county, and settled in Warren county, New Jersey, where their seven children were born.

Joseph Lundy, son of Thomas and Joanna (Doane) Lundy and the great-grandfather of the subject of this sketch, was born in Warren county, New Jersey, 3 mo. 19, 1762, and died at Rancocas, Burlington county, New Jersey, 8 mo. 13, 1846. He married 4 mo. 26, 1787, Elizabeth Shotwell, born 1762, daughter of Benjamin and Amy (Hallet) Shotwell, of Rahway, New Jersey, who bore him one son, Benjamin Lundy, the eminent abolitionist and editor of "The Genius of Universal Emancipation." He was born in Sussex county, New Jersey, 1 mo. 4, 1789, and on 10 mo. 5, 1809 was granted a certificate of removal to Westland Meeting Washington county, Pennsylvania, and settled in Wheeling, West Virginia, where he learned the trade of a harness maker, and in 1812 located in Mt. Pleasant Ohio, where he carried on his business of harness making. Becoming strongly impressed with the horrors of human

slavery, he about this time began to speak against it and organize anti-slavery societies, also contributing articles to the "Philanthropist," a paper published in Mt. Pleasant. In 1821 he started the publication of "The Genius of Universal Emancipation," the first paper published, devoted exclusively to that cause. He later traveled extensively in the interest of emancipation, and became one of the noted exponents of the emancipation of slaves. He died in Lowell, La Salle county, Illinois, 8 mo. 22, 1839.

Joseph Lundy, the father, having lost his first wife, married a second time, 1 mo. 15, 1795, Mary Titus, of Westbury, Long Island. He continued to reside in Hardwick, Sussex county, New Jersey, until 1810, when he removed with his family to Willingboro township, Burlington county, New Jersey, where he purchased a farm of 160 acres on Rancocas Creek. The children of Joseph and Mary (Titus) Lundy were eight in number: Abigail, born 9 mo. 30, 1795, died 5 mo. 14, 1875, married Daniel Woolston, of Eyrestown; Richard, born 1 mo. 30, 1797, died 7 mo. 30, 1875, at Rancocas, married Mary Ward; Elizabeth, born 6 mo. 2, 1709, died 9 mo. 22, 1840, unmarried; Phebe, born 2 mo. 6, 1802, died May, 1849, married William Hilton; Lydia Shotwell, born 7 mo. 25, 1804, died 5 mo. 27, 1864, married Joel Wierman; Deborah, born 4 mo. 29, 1806, died 5 mo. 7, 1896, married Ezra Walton; Asenath, born 1808, died 1809; Mary, born 3 mo., 26, 1811, died 10 mo. 2, 1887, married William Barnard, a minister of the Society of Friends and prominent in the anti-slavery cause.

Richard Lundy, second child of Joseph and Mary (Titus) Lundy, was the grandfather of the subject of this sketch. He was born at Hardwick, Sussex county, New Jersey, and removed to Rancocas with his parents at the age of thirteen years, and spent the remainder of his life there. His wife, Mary Ward, born 9 mo. 27, 1805, died 6 mo. 14, 1888, was a daughter of George and Edith (Wood) Ward, from near Salem, New Jersey. Richard and Mary were the parents of four children, viz.: George Ward, born 6 mo. 25, 1835, married Maria Haines, and resides at Mt. Holly, New Jersey; Edith M., born 6 mo., 21, 1838, died August 28, 1871, married Isaac S. Wright, of Falls, Bucks county, and left three children, all born in Bucks county—Walter S., Mary Ellen, wife of George H. Betts, and Ruth Anna; Joseph, born 11 mo. 11, 1840; Charles, born 11 mo., 11, 1847, died 2 mo. 6, 1904, was twice married, and left one child, Mary.

Joseph Lundy, the father of the subject of this sketch, was born at Rancocas, 11 mo. 11, 1840. He was educated at the Friends' schools, and has been a farmer in Burlington county all his life. He married June 15, 1864, Mary Evans, daughter of Darling anl Rachel (Matlack) Evans, and they are the parents of two children: Maurice E., born 8 mo. 19, 1865, married Laura S. Thompson and has one child, Florence T., born 11 mo. 8, 1891; and J. Wilmer, the subject of this sketch.

The first maternal ancestor of Mr. Lundy to land in America was William Evans, of South Newenton, Oxfordshire, carpenter, who came to New Jersey prior to 1682 and purchased one-half of a one-fifteenth share of the lands of West Jersey in that year, and several hundred acres were laid out to him on the Rancocas creek in Burlington county. He died in 1688, leaving a wife Jane; a daughter Sarah, wife of Thomas Eves, or Evans; and a son William. William (2) died in 1728, leaving children Thomas, Jane and John. Of these Thomas, born 12 mo., 12, 1693, died February, 1793, married 10 mo. 1, 1715, Esther Haines, and had children: William, Elizabeth Isaac, Esther, Jacob, Nathan; of whom William, born 1716, died 1761, married Sarah Roberts, and had children, John, Hannah, Enoch, Esther, Mary, Rebecca and William, of whom William, born 10 mo. 5, 1760, died 5 mo. 22, 1845, married 11 mo. 17, 1785, Rebecca Ballinger, and had children, Enoch, Joshua, Sarah, Mary, Darling and Hannah; of whom Darling, born 3 mo. 14, 1799, died 12 mo. 19, 1891, married 1 mo. 19, 1826, Rachel Matlack, and had children, William, Sarah, Enoch, Rebecca, wife of Thomas Lawrence, Mary, wife of Joseph Lundy, and Ezra, of Trenton, New Jersey.

J. Wilmer Lundy was born and reared on the farm near Rancocas, and was educated at the Friends' school there and at Moorestown Friends' high school. After teaching school one year he entered Trenton Business College, from which he graduated in 1889. From that date until 1893 he filled the position of bookkeeper for his uncle, Ezra Evans, a Trenton grocer. In the latter year he went to Mt. Holly as bookkeeper in the plumbing establishment of George D. Worrel, where he remained until 1900, when he formed a partnership with Elmer J. Shinn, and bought out the plumbing, heating, tin and stove business of Franklin Smith, at Newtown, Bucks county, which business he has since conducted, his partner having charge of a branch establishment at Princeton, New Jersey. Mr. Lundy is a member of the Society of Friends, and politically is a Democrat. He is a member of Mt. Holly Lodge No. 14, F. and A. M., the Junior Order U. A. M., and the Knights of Pythias. He married April 30, 1895, Lizzie Morris Roberts, daughter of Stacy and Harriet Roberts, and they have one child, Elizabeth, born January 5, 1900.

CAPTAIN WILLIAM WYNKOOP, of Newtown, is a representative of a family that has been prominent in the history of our country for over two centuries, many of them at different periods filling high and honorable positions in church and state, in local, state and national affairs.

The American progenitors of the family were Peter and Cornelius Wynkoop, who migrated from Holland to New York in 1639 and 1642, respectively. Peter was born in 1616 and came to New Amsterdam in 1639, and settled in New York state near the present site of Albany five years later, where he became prominent in the Dutch colony. His descendants were prominent in the affairs of that section for many generations. A grandson Evert, son of Cornelius, was a captain in the French and Indian war and died of camp fever in 1750. Adrian Wynkoop, another descendant, was commissioned major of the First Regiment of Ulster county, New York, May 1, 1776, and in the same year was placed in command of two hundred men to guard the passes of the Hudson. His brother Jacobus was a captain of the Fourth New York Regiment in 1775, and was later transferred to the naval service on recommendation of General Schuyler, to take command of all the vessels on Lakes George and Champlain. Another Cornelius was a colonel in the Continental service in New York. Cornelius, a son of Peter, married Maria Janse Langedyck, and their third son Gerrit (or Gerardus, as the name came to be spelled later) married Hillitje Folkert, and in the year 1717 came to Pennsylvania with his sons Nicholas and Gerritt. He lived for a time in the manor of Moreland, but later removed to Northampton township, Bucks county, where he died in 1747, leaving sons Cornelius, Nicholas, Gerrit and Philip, and daughters Jannetje Van Buskirk and Jacomyntje Van Meter. He purchased in 1727 five hundred and twenty acres in Northampton, which he conveyed in equal parts to his two sons Nicholas and Gerrit in 1738, and part of the latter is still the property of the subject of this sketch, having descended from father to son for five generations. Nicholas, the third son, married Ann Kuypers, and their only son was Judge Henry Wynkoop, who was in the opinion of many the most prominent man in the history of Bucks county. He was for many years the leading justice of the courts of Bucks county, and its first president judge. From the time the relations between the colonies and the crown became strained, he was the leader of the patriot cause in Bucks county, was one of the delegates to the meeting of the provincial deputies at Carpenter's Hall in July, 1774, was appointed to attend

the provincial conference in May, 1775, and was again a delegate to the conference that drafted the first constitution in 1776. He was the leading member of the committee of safety in Bucks, and the county's first representative in the congress of the United States, which assembled in New York on March 4, 1789. He died in 1816, after a long career of unexampled usefulness in public life..

Gerrit Wynkoop, second son of Gerrit and Lilletje (Folkert) Wynkoop, was born in New York, about 1700, and came to Bucks county with his father in 1717, and died in Northampton township, May 12, 1769, on the 260-acre farm conveyed to him by his father in 1738. He and his wife, Susanna Vliet, were members of the Dutch Reformed church of Northampton and Southampton. They were the parents of several children, only two of whom survived him, Gerardus and Adrian. The latter was baptized at Southampton, October 4, 1743.

Gerardus, eldest son of Gerrit and Susannah, was born in Northampton, and was joint heir with his brother Adrian of the paternal homestead, which he purchased entire in 1770, and spent his entire life thereon. He was first lieutenant of the Northampton County Associators in 1775. He was elected a member of assembly in 1774, and served continuously in that body until 1794, and was for several years speaker. He died in June, 1812. His wife, whom he married December 7, 1758, was Elizabeth, daughter of Isaac Bennett. They were the parents of eight children—six sons: Isaac, John, Garret, Mathew, David, and William; and two daughters, Susannah, wife of David Wylie, and Elizabeth, wife of Stephen Rose.

William, youngest son of Gerardus and Elizabeth, inherited one hundred and twenty-eight acres of the old homestead in Northampton, and spent his life thereon. He married April 13, 1801, Mary Longstreth, and died in 1833. His widow Mary survived him several years. Their children were: Thomas L., Gerardus, Christopher; Elizabeth, wife of Charles McNair; Catharine, wife of Dr. James McNair; Susannah, Margaret, Anna Maria, Susan, Mary Frances and Caroline.

Thomas L. Wynkoop married Elizabeth Torbert, daughter of James and Margaret (McNair) Torbert, of Scotch-Irish ancestry, a descendant of Samuel Torbert, who came to Newtown, Bucks county, from Carrickfergus, Ireland, in 1726. Thomas and Elizabeth (Torbert) Wynkoop were the parents of five children, viz. James, Catharine, William, Samuel, and Thomas Henry. The latter was a member of General W. W. H. Davis' 104th Pennsylvania Regiment, and was killed in action in June,

1862. Thomas L. Wynkoop, the father of the above named children, died in 1879, and devised the old homestead where he had lived all his life to his son William, the subject of this sketch, who still owns it.

The subject of this sketch has lived an eventful life. He served three years during the war of the rebellion in the First New Jersey Cavalry, enlisting as a private and was promoted successively to sergeant, second lieutenant, first lieutenant and captain. He served on the staff of Brigadier General Davis, in Gregg's Cavalry Division, as provost-marshal, ordnance office and assistant adjutant general; was three times wound and received an honorable testimonial for meritorious services.

Soon after the war Captain Wynkoop removed to Newtown, where he has since resided. He was engaged in the real estate business for nearly twenty years, and transacted a large amount of public business as assignee, executor, administrator, and agent. He served in the office of justice of the peace for fifteen years; was three years chief burgess of Newtown borough, and borough treasurer for several years. He has been president of the school board for the past ten years, and is an active member of the school directors' association of Bucks county, which he has served as president. He was one of the assignees of the Newtown Banking Company on its failure in May, 1878, and was an important factor in winding up its complicated affairs.

Captain Wynkoop comes of good old Presbyterian stock, his ancestors for eight generations having been officers of the Presbyterian or Reformed churches in the localities where they resided. He has served as ruling elder of the Newtown Presbyterian church since 1872, during which period he has acted as clerk of the session. In the same year he was chosen superintendent of the Sabbath school connected with the church, and was re-elected to that position for twenty-eight consecutive years, then declining a re-election. In 1879 he was elected president of the Bucks County Sabbath School Association and served in that position for eight years. He has been identified with the Bucks County Historical Society for many years, and has prepared a number of valuable historical papers for its sessions. He is now one of the board of trustees of the Society. He is an active member of the G. A. R., and commander of T. H. Wynkoop Post, No. 427, at Newtown. This Post was named in honor of his brother, who died in the service of his country, having enlisted in Colonel Davis' 104th Regiment, when twenty years of age, and was killed in action nine months later. Captain Wynkoop served as aide-de-camp, to General John L. Black, commander-in-chief of the G. A. R. of the United States in 1904.

He married Rachel Ann Blaker, who died in January, 1895, leaving four children, their eldest child having died in her eighteenth year; those who survive are: Elizabeth, wife of George R. Luff, who resides with her father at Newtown, with her five children, William, Ruth, Mabel, Katharine and Rachel. Katharine, who married (first) Henry C. Wylie, who died six years later, leaving a daughter, Margaret; she afterwards married G. F. Reynolds of Scranton, Pennsylvania, and has two sons, William and Arthur. Evelyn, married H. L. Harding, of Scranton. The only son, James Wynkoop, entered Princeton University in 1900, intending on his graduation to study for the ministry but failing health compelled him to relinquish his studies during his first year at college; he is at present employed in a bank at Scranton, Pennsylvania, with greatly improved health. He is the only male descendant of the Wynkoops in Bucks county, of the younger generation, that bears their name. He was married in 1904 to Cora B. Gernon, of Scranton.

Captain Wynkoop is still in active life and health. He is president of the Excelsior Bobbin and Spool Company of Newtown, president of the Mutual Beneficial Insurance Association of Bucks county, and a director in six other Bucks county corporations, and has served as secretary of the Newtown Cemetery Company for the last thirty years. He is widely and favorably known in business and social circles, and has traveled extensively both in this country and Europe.

HON. OLIVER HENRY FRETZ, A. M., M. D., of Quakertown, Bucks county, Pennsylvania, one of the leading physicians of upper Bucks, was born on his father's farm in Richland township, Bucks county, Pennsylvania, April 9, 1858, and is descended from the earliest German settlers in upper Bucks county, whose descendants have been identified with the affairs of that section since it was inhabited by the aborigines, a period of nearly two centuries. John Fretz, the paternal ancestor of Dr. Fretz, came to Pennsylvania about the end of the first quarter of the eighteenth century, accompanied by two brothers Christian and Mark, the latter of whom is said to have died at sea. John Fretz located for a time in what is now Montgomery county, where he married Barbara Meyer, daughter of Hans Meyer, an early German emigrant, who had settled in Salford township, now Montgomery county. About 1737 John Fretz purchased a tract of 230 acres in Bedminster township, Bucks county, and set-

tled thereon. His wife Barbara died about 1740, and he married a second time. He reared a family of eight children, five of whom were by his first wife, all except one of which were born in Salford. John Fretz died early in the year 1772. According to the historian of the family, Rev. A. J. Fretz, of Milton, New Jersey, he has to-day 5,000 living descendants.

Jacob Fretz, second son of John and Barbara (Meyer) Fretz, was born in Montgomery county, in 1732, came with his parents to Bucks county when a child and was reared in Bedminster township. About 1755 he married Magdalena Nash, daughter of William Nash, of Bedminster, and settled in Tinicum township, near Erwinna, but later returned to Bedminster township, where he purchased a farm and lived and died there. He and his wife as well as all the earlier generations of the family were Mennonites and worshiped at the historic old Deep Run Meeting House erected about 1746, and where many of the family are buried. Jacob and Magdalena (Nash) Fretz were the parents of six sons and three daughters, only the eldest of the latter having married, viz: Elizabeth, who became the wife of the Rev. John Kephardt, for many years pastor of the Doylestown Mennonite congregation. Abraham the eldest son, located in Hilltown; he was a teamster in the Revolutionary army and endured many hardships. He married and has numerous descendants in Bucks. John, Jacob, William and Joseph Fretz were farmers in Bedminster, where they reared families.

Isaac Fretz, youngest son of Jacob and Magdalena (Nash) Fretz, was the grandfather of Dr. O. H. Fretz. He was born on the homestead in Bedminster township, June 11, 1781, and on arriving at manhood married Mary Moyer, and followed farming in Bedminster until 1822, when they removed to Richland township, where he also followed agricultural pursuits until his death on December 27, 1855. His wife, Mary Moyer, was born August 24, 1786, and died March 27, 1855. They were the parents of two children, William and Magdalena, the latter of whom died July 1, 1854, unmarried.

William Fretz, only son of Isaac and Mary (Moyer) Fretz, was born in Bedminster township, April 9, 1811, and removed with his parents to Richland at the age of eleven years. Early in life he learned the trade of a carpenter, which he followed until the death of his parents in 1855, when he returned to the homestead and resided thereon until 1866, when he removed to Quakertown, where he lived retired until his death on December 22, 1869. He took an active interest in local affairs and served as supervisor of Richland township for several years. He was a member of the German Reformed church. He married, in 1854, Catharine Hofford, daughter of Daniel and Snsanna (Maugle) Hofford, and they were the parents of two children, Edwin Penrose, and the subject of this sketch. Edwin Penrose Fretz, born March 3, 1856, on the homestead in Richland township, attended the public schools there until his fifteenth year, when he learned the shoemaker trade with A. B. Walp & Co. Later he entered Washington Hall Collegiate Institute at Trappe, Montgomery county, Pennsylvania, and later Allentown Business College, from which he graduated in 1878. He was employed for some time in the shoe factory of A. B. Walp & Co. He is now proprietor of a shoe store at Lansdale, Pennsylvania.

Hon. Oliver Henry Fretz, A. M., M. D., second and youngest son of William and Catharine (Hofford) Fretz, was born in Richland township, Bucks county, April 9, 1858. There he lived till he was ten years old, when he removed with his parents to Quakertown, Pennsylvania, where he received the best school advantages the borough afforded. He later attended Oak Grove Academy, a school conducted under the auspices of the Society of Friends. During 1878 and 1879, he was a student of Muhlenberg College, at Allentown, Pennsylvania. He began the study of medicine in 1879, first under that able practitioner, and scientist, Dr. I. S. Moyer, and afterward in the same year he entered the Jefferson Medical College, Philadelphia, Pennsylvania, and, after pursuing a three years' graded course of study, graduated March 30, 1882, receiving the degree of Doctor of Medicine. He began the practice of medicine at Salfordville, Montgomery county, Pennsylvania, but, owing to ill health, at the end of three years he sold his practice and removed to Quakertown, where he is now successfully engaged in the drug business, combined with a large and lucrative office and consulting practice. In 1886-87 he took a post-graduate course of instruction at the Philadelphia Polyclinic and College for Graduates in Medicine. He also pursued a course of instruction at the eye, ear, nose and throat department of the Philadelphia Dispensary, fitting himself as a specialist in diseases of the eye, ear, nose and throat. In 1889 he completed a course in pharmacy at the National Institute of Pharmacy, Chicago, Illinois. Since 1886, when he was elected a school director of Quakertown borough, he has been closely identified with the educational interests of his town and the county. He was re-elected school director in 1889, and served three years as president and one year as treasurer of the board.

In 1890 Dr. Fretz was nominated on the first ballot for assembly by the Bucks county Democratic convention, and was elected by nearly three hundred majority. He represented his county in the legislature of 1891 with marked ability, and to the utmost satisfaction of his constituents. In the fall of 1892 he was renominated by acclamation and re-elected by a largely increased majority. In the session of 1893 he served on the following important committees: educational, municipal corporations, public health and sanitation, and congressional apportionment. He introduced a number of bills in the legislature, the most important of which was, an act to authorize the state superintendent of public instruction to grant permanent state teachers' certificates to graduate of recognized literary and scientific colleges. He was also elected by the house of representatives a member of the Pennsylvania election commission for 1893-94, whose duty it was to open, compute and publish the vote for state treasurer. On June 21, 1893, Ursinus College recognized his ability by conferring the honorary degree of Master of Arts (A. M.) upon him. In January, 1894, Dr. Fretz was appointed a clinical assistant in the eye department of the Jefferson Medical College Hospital, Philadelphia, Pennsylvania. He received the appointment of borough physician of Quakertown in 1888, and has since been reappointed annually. In July 1893, he was appointed by the borough council a member of the borough board of health, a position he still holds, he being president of the board. November 2, 1898, he was elected president of the Bucks county Medical Society. He is also a member of the State Medical Society of Pennsylvania, the Lehigh Valley Medical Association, the American Medical Association, the American Academy of Political and Social Science of Philadelphia, the Pennsylvania Forestry Association and the Bucks County School Directors' Association, of which he served as vice president. He is also surgeon for the Philadelphia and Lehigh Valley Traction Co., and medical examiner for numerous life insurance companies. On November 21, 1898, Dr. Fretz was elected by the board of trustees a censor of the Medico-Chirurgical College of Philadelphia. He pursued a course of study at the Chicago School of Psychology, graduating therefrom March 15, 1900, receiving the degree of Doctor of Psychology (Psy. D.). On March 7, 1905, he completed a course of study at the South Bend College of Optics, South Bend, Indiana, graduating therefrom with the degree of Doctor of Optics, (Opt. D.). He is a member of the following organizations: Quakertown Lodge, No. 512, F. and A. M.; Zinzendorf Chapter, No. 216, Royal Arch Masons, Bethlehem, Pennsylvania;

Pennsylvania Commandery, No. 70, Knights Templar of Philadelphia; Quakertown Lodge, No. 714, I. O. O. F.; Secona Tribe, No. 263, I. O. of R. M., and Marion Circle, No. 16, B. U. (H. F.) of Pennsylvania.

On October 26, 1882, Dr. Fretz married Elmira A. Roeder, daughter of Nathan C. and Lucinda (Antrim) Roeder, of Spinnerstown, Pennsylvania. Both are members of the Reformed church. Their union was blessed with two children: Roberts Bartholow, born January 19, 1884, and died October 1, 1884, and Raymond Lamar, born April 24, 1885. The latter received his primary education in the public schools of Quakertown, Pennsylvania; later he attended Perkiomen Seminary for two years, and the Bethlehem Preparatory School, an adjunct to Lehigh University for one year. He then entered his father's drug store as a student of medicine and pharmacy, and in May, 1905, he graduated in the Era Course of Pharmacy of New York. He is also a member of Marion Circle, No. 16, B. U. (H. F.) of Pennsylvania, also of the Quakertown Mandolin Club.

YARDLEY FAMILY. John Yardley, treasurer of the Doylestown Trust Company, is a son of Mahlon and Elizabeth (Brock) Yardley, and was born in Doylestown, 6 mo. 15, 1852, and belongs to the fourteenth generation of the descendants of John Yardley, of county Stafford, England, who married a daughter of Marbury of Dadesbury, in 1402. The family of Yardley (formerly spelled Yeardley) is an ancient one with residence in Staffordshire, where the heads of the family were known as the "Lords of Yeardley." Their coat-of-arms is: "Argent on a chevron azure, three garbs or, on a canton gules, a fret or;" Crest: "A buck courant, gu. attired or."

The pioneer emigrant of the family was William Yeardley, who with wife Jane and three sons, Enoch, William and Thomas and a servant Andrew Heath, emigrated from Ransclough, near Leake, in the county of Stafford, and arrived in the river Delaware in the good ship "Friends' Adventure," 7 mo. 29, 1682. They located on five hundred acres of land purchased of William Penn 3 mo. 30, 1681, (just sixteen days after Penn received the grant of Pennsylvania from Charles II). This tract was located on the Delaware river, near the present site of the borough of Yardley, and was called "Prospect Farm." William Yardley was fifty years of age on his arrival in Bucks county. He was a member of the Society of Friends, and had been called to the ministry among them in his twenty-third year. He had traveled through different parts of England preaching the Gospel, and had suffered imprisonment and fines for his faith. He became at once and continued to his death one of the most prominent men of the province. He was a member of the first Colonial Assembly in 1682, and again in 1683; member of Provincial Council in 1688-9; justice of the peace and of the courts of Bucks county, April 6, 1685, to January 2, 1689; sheriff, February 11, 1690, to April 29, 1693. 'He died 5 mo. 6, 1693, aged sixty-one years.

Enoch Yardley, eldest son of William and Jane, was a member of Colonial Assembly in 1699. He married 10 mo. 1697, Mary, daughter of Robert Fletcher, of Abington, Philadelphia county, Pennsylvania, and had by her three daughters, Jane, Mary and Sarah, all of whom died in infancy. He died 11 mo. 23, 1702-3. His brother William died unmarried 12 mo. 12, 1792-3. Thomas, the other brother, married 9 mo. 6, 1700, Hester Blaker, and had two children, William and Hester, both of whom died in infancy. He died on the same day as his brother, 11 mo. 23, 1702-3. Mary, the widow of Enoch Yardley, married (second) Joseph Kirkbridge, one of the most prominent men of the Province, who had emigrated from the parish of Kirkbride, in Cumberland, England. She was his third wife, and bore him seven children—John, Robert, Mary, Sarah (married Israel Pemberton), Thomas, and Jane, who married Samuel Smith, the historian of New Jersey. Hester, the widow of Thomas Yardley, married 8 mo. 1704, William Browne, of Chichester, Chester county, Pennsylvania.

William Yardley, his wife, children and grandchildren all being dead, his real estate in Bucks county descended to his brother Thomas, of "The Beeches," in the parish of Rushton, Staffordshire. In the year 1704 Thomas Yardley, Jr., son of Thomas of Rushton, came to Bucks county with a power of attorney from his father and his brother Samuel to claim the real estate. "Prospect Farm" was sold under this power of attorney, 5 mo. 25, 1710, to Joseph Janney, who as "straw man" conveyed it back to Thomas Yeardley, Jr., 6 mo. 14, 1710. This Thomas Yeardley (as he always wrote his name) was the ancestor of all the Yardleys of Bucks county. He married 12 mo., 1706-7, Ann, the youngest daughter of William and Joanna Biles, who had emigrated from Dorchester, in the county of Dorset, England, and arrived in the river Delaware 4 mo. 4, 1679. The children of Thomas and Ann (Biles) Yardley were ten in number:

1. Mary, born 8 mo. 4, 1707, married, 12 mo. 30, 1728-9, Amos Janney of Loudoun county, Virginia.

2. Jane, born 11 mo. 20, 1708-9, married Francis Hague, of Loudoun county, Virginia.

3. Rebecca, born 7 mo. 27, 1710, never, married.

4. Sarah, born 7 mo. 30, 1712, married (first) Benjamin Canby, (second) David Kinsey.

5. Joyce, born 10 mo. 3, 1714, never married.

6. William, born 3 mo. 25, 1716, died 8 mo. 3, 1774.

7. Hannah, born 11 mo. 13, 1718-19, never married.

8. Thomas, born 11 mo. 1, 1720-1, died 3 mo. 12, 1803, married Mary Field. Entered military service of the Province and was disowned by Friends therefore in 1756.

9. Samuel, born 4 mo. 16, 1723, died 8 mo. 12, 1726.

10. Samuel, born 7 mo. 13, 1729, died 1759, married Jane.

Thomas Yeardley was returned as a member of the Provincial Assembly in 1715 and again in 1722. He was commissioned a justice of the several courts of Bucks county, May 12, 1725, and continued to serve as such until 1741. He was one of the most prominent and active of the judges, being present at nearly every sitting of the court. He became a very large land holder, acquiring in 1726 five hundred acres adjoining Prospect Farm, and in 1733 a tract of six hundred acres in Newtown township. He also acquired title to the Solebury Mills, erected by Robert Heath in 1707. He died in 1756. He devised his Makefield lands to his sons William and Thomas, and his Solebury property, to his son Samuel.

William Yardley, born 3 mo. 25, 1716, married 4 mo. 20, 1748, Ann Budd, of New Jersey, and had: Ann, born 4 mo. 10, 1749, married Abraham Warner. Sarah, born 2 mo. 17, 1751, married Timothy Taylor. Margaretta, born 12 mo. 6, 1752, married Stacy Potts, of Trenton, New Jersey. Anna (Budd) Yardley died 1753, and William married, 3 mo. 31, 1756, Sarah, daughter of Mahlon and Mary (Sotcher) Kirkbride. Mahlon Kirkbride was the son of Joseph, before mentioned, by his second wife, Sarah, daughter of Mahlon and Rebecca (Ely) Stacy, who were married at Cinder Hill, near Mansfield, Yorkshire, England, in 1668, and emigrated to New Jersey in 1676. Mahlon Stacy was the first settler at the present site of Trenton, New Jersey, where he built a mill which was the sole resources for the farmers on the Pennsylvania side of the Delaware for many years. Mahlon Stacy was a prominent official of the Province of West Jersey, while Joseph Kirkbride, his son Mahlon, John Sotcher, father of Mary Kirkbride, and Penn's steward at Pennsbury, and William Biles. all ancestors of the subject of this sketch, were all members of Colonial Assembly and justices of the court at different times. The children of Will-

iam Yardley and his second wife Sarah Kirkbride were:

Mary, born 1 mo. 27, 1757, married Jonathan Woolston.

Hannham, born 3 mo. 19, 1758, married 1779, John Stapler.

Achsah, born 2 mo. 17, 1760, married 1794, Thomas Stapler.

Letitia, born 7 mo. 12, 1762, married 1782, Jonathan Willis, of Philadelphia.

Thomas, born 10 mo. 2, 1763, married 1785, Susanna Brown.

Mahlon, born 7 mo. 17, 1765, married 1787, Elizabeth Brown.

Samuel, born 2 mo. 28, 1767, died in infancy.

William, born 6 mo. 8, 1769, married 1793, Elizabeth Field.

Joseph, born 3 mo. 19, 1771, married 1798, Sarah Field.

Sarah (Kirkbride) Yardley, died 1 mo. 21, 1783.

William Yardley, served as sheriff of Bucks county from October 4, 1752, to October 4, 1755; and as justice of the courts of Bucks county December 7, 1764, to 1770. He died 8 mo. 3, 1774.

Mahlon, son of William and Sarah (Kirkbride) Yardley, born 7 mo. 17, 1765, married 4 mo. 26, 1787; Elizabeth, daughter of John and Ann (Field) Brown, of Falls township. (Benjamin Field, father of Ann Brown, was a member of Provincial Assembly 1738-45.) The children of Mahlon and Elizabeth (Brown) Yardley, were:

Sarah, born 4 mo. 16, 1788, married 1813, Joseph Paul.

Ann, born 2 mo. 6, 1790, married 1812, Jesse Lloyd.

Achsah, born 9 mo. 1, 1792, married 1834, Richard Janney.

John, born 12 mo. 1, 1794, married 1823, Frances Hapenny, 1841, Anna Van Horn.

Hannah, born 4 mo. 25, 1797, married 1819, Samuel Buckman.

Robert, born 1 mo. 18, 1799, married 1829, Ellen Field.

Charles, born 8 mo. 4, 1802, married Anna Warner.

Elizabeth, born 7 mo. 21, 1807, married 1831, Mahlon B. Linton.

Elizabeth (Brown) Yardley, died 1 mo. 22, 1824.

Mahlon Yardley died in Makefield, 11 mo. 17, 1829.

John, son of Mahlon and Sarah (Kirkbride) Yardley, born 12 mo. 1, 1794, married, 1 mo. 23, 1823, Frances Happenny. Their children were: Mahlon, born 2 mo. 4, 1824, married 12 mo. 11, 1850, Elizabeth, daughter of Stephen Brock. Strickland, born 10 mo. 18, 1826, married Martha Johnson. Franklin, born 6 mo. 26, 1830, died in infancy. John Yardley, married (second) Anna Van Horn, 6 mo. 16, 1841; their children were: Fannie, born 12 mo. 10, 1844. Hon. Robert M., born 10 mo. 9, 1850, member of congress, Seventh District. Mary

Eliza, born 1 mo. 14, 1854. John Yardley during the later years of life was a member of the firm of Yardley & Justice, coal and lumber merchants, at Yardley, Pennsylvania. He died at Yardley, 5 mo. 24, 1874.

Mahlon Yardley was born in Makefield township, 2 mo. 24, 1824, where his early boyhood was spent. He graduated at Lafayette College, Easton, Pennsylvania, in the class of 1843, and at once began the study of law at Easton. He was admitted to the Bucks County bar February 2, 1846, and began the practice of law at Doylestown. At the organization of the Republican party he became an ardent advocate of its principles. In the fall of 1851 he was its nominee for state senator from the Sixth district, and, although the district was then overwhelmingly Democratic, was elected, defeating the late General Paul Applebach, of Haycock. The term at that period was three years, and he was therefore in the state senate at the breaking out of the war.

When in April, 1861, the Doylestown Guards were on their way to the front, they were met at the station at Harrisburg by Senator Yardley and two colleagues and a bountiful supper served to them. When General W. H. H. Davis recruited and organized the 104th Pennsylvania Regiment at Doylestown, September, 1861, Mr. Yardley enlisted and was commissioned first lieutenant of Company K. He was with the regiment at the siege of Yorktown, and in the beginning of the hostilities along the Chickahominy. In the skirmishes at Savage's Station and Seven Pines, preliminary to the battle of Fair Oaks on May 24, 1862, he narrowly escaped being killed. General Davis, in his "History of the 104th Regiment," says, in speaking of this engagement: "There were many narrow escapes. Lieutenant Yardley moved his head to one side just in time to prevent a shell that passed along, from taking it off. A soldier named Brown, immediately back of him, was struck in the head and instantly killed. After the battle the regiment was encamped on the edge of a dense swamp, and many of the men were taken sick with fevers. Among these was Lieutenant Yardley. In the latter part of the month he was carried home by some friends who were on a visit to the regiment, and never rejoined the command. When sufficiently recovered he was placed in the recruiting service and was subsequently appointed provost marshal for the Fifth District, with headquarters at Frankford."

Mr. Yardley never fully recovered from the severe attack of typhoid contracted in the Chickahominy swamps, and was ever thereafter afflicted with a severe cough, which no doubt hastened his death. After being in bed for about

four months, he opened a recruiting office at Doylestown. On April 10, 1863, he was appointed provost marshal for this district, then comprising three wards of the city of Philadelphia, and promoted to the rank of captain. At the close of the war he was appointed internal revenue collector for the same district, a position he filled until his death. He died June 23, 1873. His wife, whom he married 12 mo. 11, 1850, was Elizabeth, daughter of Stephen and Mary (Jones) Brock. The Brocks are one of the oldest families in Bucks county. The emigrant ancestor of the family was sheriff of the county in 1685, and his son, Thomas Brock, held the same office for the term 1693-5. Stephen Brock, father of Mrs. Yardley, was twice elected sheriff of Bucks county, in 1821 and again in 1827.

John Yardley, the only child of Mahlon and Elizabeth, was born in Doylestown, June 15, 1852. He was educated at private schools in Doylestown, and entered Lehigh University in 1868, remaining two years, after which he entered the silk house of Watson & Janney, of Philadelphia, as clerk. He returned to Doylestown in the autumn of 1872 to assist his father in the revenue office. On February 1, 1873, he was appointed a clerk in the Doylestown National Bank, and remained in the employ of the bank until 1896, when he resigned to accept the position of treasurer of the Doylestown Trust Company, which position he still fills. Mr. Yardley has always been active in everything that pertains to the best interests of the town he lives in. He was for many years a member of the school board and has held other borough offices. He was one of the organizers of the Doylestown Electric Company and of the Doylestown Gas Company, and has been a director of both companies from their organization. He has also been interested in several other local enterprises. He is a member of Doylestown Lodge, F. and A. M., No. 245; Aquetong Lodge, No. 193, I. O. O. F.; Doylestown Encampment, No. 25, I. O. O. F.; and Lenape Council, No. 1117, Royal Arcanum. He married, October 19, 1876, Emma, daughter of David and Lucy (Lear) Krewson. Their only child is Mahlon, born May 19, 1878, who resides with his parents.

SAMUEL YARDLEY, of Edgewood, Lower Makefield township, was born in Upper Makefield township, Bucks county, October 19, 1834, and is a son of Joseph H. and Esther B. (Knowles) Yardley, and is without doubt of the same lineage as Thomas Yardley, son of Thomas Yardley, of Rushton Spencer, Staffordshire, England, the former of whom came to Bucks county in 1704, as

Robert M. Yardley

the heir of his uncle, William Yardley, of Ransclough, near Leake, county Stafford, who had come to Bucks county in 1682, an account of whom is given in this work.

Richard Yardley appears in Bucks county soon after the arrival of Thomas, with whom he was closely associated. He was probably a grandson of John Yardley, of Rushton Spencer, uncle of William and Thomas, above mentioned, who married Alice, daughter of Richard Sutton, of Rushton Spencer, and had sons, Edward, William, Ralph, John, Richard, and Thomas. As before stated Richard Yardley appears in Bucks county soon after the emigration of Thomas Yardley to this county, and the latter sold him in 1753 six hundred acres of land near Newtown, purchased in 1742. Richard never lived on this land, and at his death in 1761 was operating the mill belonging to Thomas Yardley, in Solebury township. His will, dated January 5, 1761, and proved March 4, 1761, mentions wife Mary, daughter Mary, wife of Joseph Harvey; and sons, Thomas, Samuel, Richard, Enoch, William, and Benjamin.

Richard Yardley, son of the above Richard, married November 1, 1759, Lucilla Stackhouse. He purchased in 1773 of Thomas and Mary (Field) Yardley 107 acres of land in Lower Makefield, on which he lived and died. He was a wheelwright by trade and followed that vocation in connection with farming. He died in 1786 leaving two sons, Samuel and William; and three daughters: Anna, wife of John Leedom; Hannah, wife of James White; and Mary, wife of John Hough. William, the youngest of the children, was born in 1777. Lucilla Stackhouse, wife of Richard Yardley, was born 4 mo. 9, 1738, and was a daughter of John and Elizabeth (Janney) Stackhouse, her maternal grandfather being Abel Janney, whose daughter Elizabeth, John Stackhouse married at Middletown 10 mo. 22, 1737, their only other child being Abel Stackhouse, born 4 mo. 4, 1740. John Stackhouse was born 3 mo. 11, 1708, and died 7 mo. 23, 1743, and was a son of John and Elizabeth Stackhouse, of Middletown, the former of whom came to Middletown from England with his uncle, Thomas Stackhouse, in 1682.

Samuel Yardley, eldest son of Richard and Lucilla (Stackhouse) Yardley, was a man of considerable prominence in the community, and at one time a considerable landholder in the Makefields. He married Ann Vansant, daughter of Cornelius and Ann (Larzelere) Vansant, and had two sons, Richard and Joseph Harvey Yardley.

Joseph H. Yardley was born near Yardley in the year 1797. He was a natural mechanic, and in early life followed the trade of a carpenter, in connection with the conduct of a farm near Taylorsville. In April, 1841, he purchased at sheriff's sale the Jacob Janney farm of 115 acres, which included the farm now owned and occupied by his son, the subject of this sketch, and spent the remainder of his life thereon, dying in 1880 at the age of eighty-three years. In politics he was a staunch Republican, and was an active and prominent man in the community, holding the office of justice of the peace for many years. He was also one of the directors of the Yardley Delaware Bridge Company, and held several other positions of trust. His wife was Esther B. Knowles, of an old and prominent family in Upper Makefield, and they were the parents of six children: Elizabeth; Julia, widow of Charles Janney, of Solebury; Anna, first wife of the above named Charles Janney; Rebecca, who died young; Samuel, the subject of this sketch; and Gulielma, wife of Robert Yardley Linton, of Makefield.

Samuel Yardley was born near Taylorsville, Upper Makefield township, October 19, 1834, but from the age of seven years was reared on the farm upon which he still resides. He was educated at the local schools and at the Norristown Academy. He was reared to the life of a farmer, and has always given his attention to the tilling of the soil. In politics he is a Republican, but has never sought or held other than local office. He is one of the highly respected citizens of Lower Makefield, where he has always resided. Mr. Yardley has been twice married, his first wife being Sarah Swartzlander, who died December 21, 1865; and his second wife was Jane* P. Swartzlander, who died November 28, 1902, both being daughters of Abraham and Rebecca Swartzlander.

William R., only son of Samuel and Sarah (Swartzlander) Yardley, married Mary Vanhorn, and they are the parents of eleven children, as follows: Florence K., born February 6, 1884; Joseph H., born July 21, 1885; Bernard V., born October 4, 1887; Mary S., born November 16, 1889; Sarah S., born January 22, 1892; Oscar V., deceased; Jane P., born March 12, 1897; Maud L., born August 1, 1898; Samuel Y., born February 5, 1900; Virginia, born May 30, 1901; Esther K., born January 8, 1903.

HON. ROBERT M. YARDLEY, deceased. On the ninth day of December, 1902, passed away in Doylestown, Bucks county, Pennsylvania, one of the most popular and distinguished citizens of the county, one who by reason of eminent ability and distinguished services had achieved a fame far beyond the borders of his native county, and who by his generous, kindly and affable traits had intrenched himself in the hearts of the people.

Robert M. Yardley was born in Yardley, Bucks county, Pennsylvania, October 9, 1850, a son of John and Ann (Van Horn) Yardley. Of a distinguished ancestry who had rendered to their county, state and nation distinguished and eminent services in nearly every generation, he rendered fully his meed of service. He was reared in the village, (now borough) of Yardley, and received a good academic education. As a young man he was engaged for a few years in assisting his father in the conduct of a large lumber and coal business at Yardley. At the age of eighteen he began the study of law in the office of his half-brother, Mahlon Yardley, Esq., and was admitted to the bar of Bucks county in 1872. He located in Doylestown, and immediately began the practice of his chosen profession. He was a careful and conscientious student, a logical and forceful reasoner and an eloquent speaker, and soon proved himself an able and strong lawyer, and merited and held the confidence of a large clientage.

In 1879 he was elected district attorney of the county against an adverse majority, and filled the office for three years with eminent ability. In politics he was an ardent Republican, and represented his party and county in the national convention of 1884. He was elected to the Fiftieth Congress in 1886, from the Seventh District, over Hon. George Ross, and made an enviable record. Returning to Doylestown and declining a re-election, he resumed the practice of his profession and soon reached the first rank as a lawyer. His reputation as an orator placed him upon the platform at many political and other assemblies, and his eloquent addresses, touched with a vein of humor, were always incisive, instructive and to the point. He was appointed receiver of the Keystone National Bank, Philadelphia, in 1891, and his excellent administration of its affairs led to his appointment as receiver of the Spring Garden Bank, in 1894. He was interested in all that pertained to the best interests of his town and county, and generously contributed to every good cause, public or private. He was a director of the Bucks County Trust Company of the Doylestown Electrical Company, the Doylestown Gas Company, and an officer in several other local institutions. He was president of the Doylestown school board for several years prior to his death, and an active member of the local board of health. He was a member of the Masonic fraternity and of the I. O. O. F.

Mr. Yardley was twice married, first in 1874, to Clara Bell, who died in 1883, and second, on April 21, 1892, to Rebecca P., widow of Levi L. James, Esq., and daughter of John M. and Sarah (Roberts) Purdy, who survives him. An account of the ancestry of Mrs.

Yardley, is given on another page of this work. The news of the death of Mr. Yardley on December 9, 1902, was heard with profound regret and sorrow in all parts of Bucks county. The end came without warning; he had gone to his office as usual in the morning, and a few minutes after entering his private office died in his chair from heart failure.

HENRY W. COMFORT. It is definitely known that it was at a very early epoch in the settlement of the new world when the Comfort family was established in America, for John Comfort came from Flushing, Long Island, to the Friends Monthly Meeting held in Falls township, Bucks county, December 3, 1719, bringing with him a certificate from the former place. He settled in Amwell, Hunterdon county, New Jersey, and his life was devoted to reclaiming the wild land for purposes of civilization and to more advanced agricultural interests. He married Miss Mary Wilson, August 6, 1720, and they had three children: Stephen, Sarah and Robert.

(II) Stephen Comfort, of the second generation, was married to Mercy Croasdale August 25, 1744. They had nine children; John; Ezra; Jeremiah; Stephen; Grace, the wife of Jonathan Stackhouse; Mercy, the wife of Aaron Phillipps; Moses; Robert; and Hannah.

(III) Ezra Comfort, son of Stephen Comfort, was born August 11, 1747, and married Alice Fell, January 9, 1772. He was a recorded minister of the Society of Friends and exerted strong influence in behalf of the moral as well as material development of his community. In his family were six children: Elizabeth, who became the wife of Peter Roberts, and after his death married Benjamin White; Mercy, wife of Joshua Paxton; Grace, twin sister of Mercy, and the wife of Benjamin Gillingham; John; Ezra; and Alice.

(IV) Ezra Comfort, who was born April 18, 1777, was also a recorded minister of the Society of Friends. He married Margaret Shoemaker, October 16, 1800, and they had nine children; Sarah, wife of Hughes Bell; Grace, wife of Charles Williams; Jane, who became the wife of Jones Yerkes, and after his death married Charles Lippencott; Ann, who married Isaac Jones; John S.; Alice, the wife of George M. Haverstick; Jeremiah; David; and Margaret, wife of Henry Warrington.

(V) John S. Comfort, son of Ezra Comfort, was born May 25, 1810, in Plymouth, Montgomery county, Pennsylvania. In early life he engaged in a lime business, building and owning kilns about ten miles from Easton on the Delaware division of the canal. He shipped the first boatload of lime that was ever sent over the canal, and for a number of years supplied most of the farmers in the lower part of Bucks county. Later he turned his attention to the lumber business, which he conducted quite extensively in the Lehigh valley. About 1835 he purchased the farm where his son, George M. Comfort, now resides, situated in Falls township, about a mile and a half from the village of Fallsington, whereon he spent his remaining days, passing away in 1891. He married Jane C. Comfort, a daughter of Jeremiah and Sarah (Cooper) Comfort. Their only child was

(VI) George M., who was born April 10, 1837, in the house which is yet his home. He early engaged in agricultural pursuits, in which he was much interested, finding it both congenial to his tastes and satisfactorily remunerative. He was a member of the first board of directors of The Peoples' National Bank of Langhorne, and is yet a member of the board of directors of the First National Bank of Trenton, New Jersey, and is president of the Bucks County Contributionship for Fire Insurance. Like his ancestors for several generations, he is a member of the religious Society of Friends, and from early life has been actively engaged in its work. He married Ann Elizabeth, daughter of Moses and Mercy Comfort, of Penns Manor, on October 14, 1858. Their children are: Edward C., who died in childhood; Henry W., born February 27, 1863; and William S., who died in childhood.

(VII) Henry W. Comfort, the only surviving son of George M. and Ann Elizabeth Comfort, resides on and is operating the farm in Falls township which has been the family home for three generations. It includes an area of 225 acres, on which he keeps a large herd of high grade dairy cows, the milk from which is delivered daily to customers in the city of Trenton, New Jersey. This business was started by his grandfather in 1847, and the milk route has been constantly served from this farm ever since. Mr. Comfort is president of the John L. Murphy Publishing Company, president and treasurer of the International Pottery Company, of Trenton; a director of the Yardley National Bank, and is interested in, and vice-president of The William H. Moon Nursery Company. He has been actively associated with affairs touching the general interests of the neighborhood, is a director of the Morrisville Building and Loan Association, and of the Fallsington Library Company, and is one of the managers of The Friends' Asylum for the Insane at Frankford, Philadelphia.

Mr. Comfort has been twice married. His first wife was Edith, daughter of Samuel Ellis and Sarah B. DeCou, and his present wife was Lydia P., daughter of Ellwood and Mercy A. Parsons.

THE ELY FAMILY. The earliest mention of Ely as a family surname in England occurred during the reign of the Plantaganets after the Norman Conquest. The English "Book of Dignities" records William De Ely as lord treasurer for King John and Richard I; Richard De Ely, lord treasurer for Richard I and Henry II; Ralph De Ely, baron of the exchequer for Henry III, (1240); Philip De Ely lord treasurer for Henry III (1271); Nicholas De Ely, lord chancellor, in 1260, Lord treasurer in 1263, and Bishop of Worcester 1266 to 1289. One branch of the family is known to have lived at Utterby, Lincolnshire, from this early period down to the present day, L. C. R. Norris-Elye being the present Lord of the Manor of Utterby and patron of the old thirteenth century church of St. Andrew at that place. Wharton Dickinson, the New York genealogist, traces this line back to a connection with Ralph De Ely, Baron of the Exchequer. The Manor House has the Ely arms, (a fesse engrailed between six fleurs-de-lis) cut in stone over the entrance, dated 1639. The same arms are also found in the church. Another branch is said to have settled in Yorkshire, and Burke gives the arms the same as above, but red instead of black. Papworth's "British Armorials" states that these arms were borne also by Nicholas De Ely and Sir Richard De Illey. In Bailey's "History of Nottinghamshire," John De Ely is stated to have been appointed the first vicar of St. Mary's Collegiate church at Nottingham in 1290, and its author adds that the name has "Come down to the present day." Another John De Ely was Lord of the Manor of Thornhaugh and Wiggesley in Nottinghamshire in 1316 (within a mile of Dunham, where Joshua Ely resided before embarking for America in 1683.)

The ancestors of the Elys of Bucks county, Pennsylvania, came from that part of Old England known as the Peak District, famous both for its natural beauty and historic interest. It comprises Upper Derbyshire, Southwestern Yorkshire, and Western Nottinghamshire. The family were related to the Revells of Derbyshire, an ancient and powerful family, descendants of the Norman nobility. Hugh De Revell was grandmaster of the Knight Hospitalers, and this family in England throughout the Crusades were trustees of the Knight Templar property in England. The Stacyes of Yorkshire, who held the estate known as Ballifield from the time of the Norman Conquest, were also closely connected with the Elys. The Stacye and Ely families were among the earliest of the English churchmen to follow the teachings of George Fox, the founder of the Society of Friends. Great religious meetings were held at Ballifield Hall, the home of the Stacyes, by Fox in his journeys to Yorkshire, and there is still to be found at Ballifield Hall, an antique black oak table inlaid with a silver plate inscribed as follows: "This called by Fox the Quaker's Table, made before 1593, was for many years at Synder Hill and afterwards for sixty years in the Tool House there, then restored and placed in Ballifield Hall by Thomas Watson Cadman, Esq., in December, 1868."

The connection between this branch of the Ely family and those of the same name mentioned in the earlier history of this section of England is not known. In the Feudal history of Derbyshire by Yeatman in the days of Henry VII and Henry VIII, Hugh*, Thomas*, Roland*, and John Ely are memtioned and still earlier, Nicholas le Hele, Sir William "Delly," Knt. and John "Eallee" are also mentioned, but no positive. lineage is known back of the grandparents of those who came to America. Joshua Ely and Rebecca Ely Stacye, who landed in West Jersey in 1683 and 1678 respectively, were the children of George Ely, of Mansfield, Nottinghamshire. Other children were: Hugh of Mansfield, who married Marie Roos; Ruth, who married Lionell Revell; and Elizabeth, whose tomb is in a good state of preservation in the private cemetery of the Stacyes at Ballifield Hall. Another Hugh Ely is known to have married Rosamond Bullock at Chesterfield, Derbyshire, between 1600 and 1640, and Alicia, a daughter of Hugh Ely, was baptized at Chesterfield in 1614.

A history of the Ely, Stacye and Revell families is in preparation under the supervision of Warren S. Ely of Doylestown, Pennsylvania, Dr. William S. Long, of Haddonfield, New Jersey, and Daniel B. Ely of Montclair, New Jersey.

The wife of George Ely, of Mansfield, was doubtless Sarah Heath, as at the time Joshua Ely, their son, proposed intentions of marriage at Mansfield Quarterly Meeting, England, 7th month, 1673, with Mary Seniar, the following entry was made on the minutes of that meeting:

"Joshua Ely and Mary Senierd, both of Mansfield, declare intentions of marriage with each other. Present, his grandmother, Elizabeth Heath, his relations and guardians Mahlon and Rebecca Stacy, his brother-in-law, Lionel Revely who married his sister Ruth Ely, and Alse Senierd, mother of said Mary Senierd."

Mahlon Stacy had married Rebecca Ely in 1668, at Cinder Hill, a part of the Ballifield estate. From another source we have the following records: "Joshua Ely of Mansfield and Mary Seniar of same place, daughter of Alice Seniar married 8th month, 29, 1673, at G. Cockerman's House at Skegby in Nottinghamshire." "John Ely, son of Joshua and Mary, buried 9th month, 25, 1676. George Ely, son of Joshua and Mary, died 3rd month, 3, 1676."

Mahlon Stacy, of the ancient family of Ballifield, with his wife Rebecca Ely, their children and servants, in the year 1678 embarked in the "Shield," and on November 10, 1678, landed on the east bank of the Delaware, in New Jersey, where they and their descendants were destined to take an important part in the founding and preservation of an English colony and nation in America. In the same ship came their cousin, Thomas Revell, of Chesterfield, Derbyshire, who, unlike them, was not a convert to the gentle teachings of George Fox, but represented the High Church Tory party, and later took an active part in the affairs of the West Jersey colony, filling the positions of surveyor general, recorder, surrogate, member and almost a dictator in the governor's council, and finally a justice on the supreme bench. He was, however, an aristocrat of the aristocrats and was unpopular with the colonists, and after the downfall of Lord Cornbury was finally removed from office at the instigation of the colonists and on the advice of William Penn.

Mahlon Stacy became a very prominent man, filling many important government positions. His daughters intermarried with the Kirkbrides, Pownalls and Janneys of Bucks county, who were prominent in the affairs of Bucks county and the province of Pennsylvania. He took up a tract of land on the site of the present city of Trenton and erected a mill there, the first to furnish meal to the early colonists of Bucks county. It was through him that his brother-in-law, Joshua Ely, who, after his marriage, had settled at Dunham, Nottinghamshire, came to America in 1684 with his wife and children, and located on 400 acres, conveyed to Joshua by Mahlon Stacy, on both sides of the Assinnipink, by deed dated April 20, 1685. This tract fronted on the river, about five eighths of a mile from a point thirty-two and one-half chains north of the mouth of the creek upward, and extended inland one mile.

Joshua Ely became a prominent man in the colony, and was commissioned a justice in 1700 and recommissioned the following year. He became a large landholder, owning at different periods two other tracts of 400 acres each, be-

---

*These Christian names are also common in the Revell pedigree. It is also known that the Elys of Utterby Manor are descended from the Elys of Derbyshire.

sides his original purchase on the site of Trenton, of which he died seized. His wife, Mary died in 1698, and he married (second) November 9, 1699, Rachel Lee, who bore him two children, Benjamin and Ruth, twins. He died 4th month, 1702, at Trenton. The children of Joshua and Mary (Seniar) Ely were John and George, before mentioned, who died in infancy in England; Joshua, born in England 1680; George, born 1682 in England; John, said to have been born on the voyage to America; Hugh, born at Trenton about 1686; Elizabeth, and Sarah, the latter born in the same year that her mother died. Of Rachel, the widow and her two children, nothing is known.

Joshua Ely, the eldest son, bought a portion of the homestead in 1705. Letters of administration were granted on his estate to George Ely in 1760, but whether his son or not we are unable to determine; nothing is known of his descendants.

George Ely, the second son, it would seem, was about to marry Christian, the daughter of Nathaniel Pettit, who lived on an adjoining tract, at the death of his father, and the latter, in his will, expresses decided objections to the marriage and practically disinherits George in case of its consummation. What became of Christian Pettit remains a mystery, but in 1703 George Ely married Jane Pettit, daughter of Nathaniel, but whether the same person or another daughter is a matter of conjecture. George Ely purchased 100 acres of the old homestead of his father's executors at Trent Town (as it came to be known after the purchase by William Trent of the Stacy mill and lands) and lived thereon until his death in 1750. He was active in the affairs of the embryo city, and a member of its first town council, at the incorporation in 1746. The children of George and Jane (Pettit) Ely were: Joshua, born March 16, 1704; George, born 1706; Rebecca, who married Eliakim Anderson, and has descendants in Bucks county; Joseph; Mary, who married Richard Green, and is the ancestress of Mrs. Ethan Allen Weaver of Philadelphia; Sarah, who married John Dagworthy;* and Elizabeth, who married James Price of Hopewell.

John Ely, the third son of Joshua and Mary (Seniar) Ely, married Frances Venables, daughter of William and Elizabeth Venables, of Bucks county, Pennsylvania, in 1706, and died at Trenton, in 1732. Their four children, John, who married Phebe Allison; William; Mary, wife of William Hill; and Elizabeth, wife of Joseph Higbee, have left numerous descendants in New Jersey. The

descendants of John and Phebe are especially numerous in southern New Jersey.

Hugh Ely, the youngest son of Joshua and Mary (Seniar) Ely, born at Trenton about 1686, married December 12, 1712, Mary Hewson, and in 1720 settled in Buckingham township on 400 acres of land purchased in the "Lundy Tract," extending from Broadhurst's lane to Holicong and from the York road to Buckingham Mountain, and lived there the remander of his life, dying in 1771. He became a member of Buckingham Friends' Meeting, and, his wife Mary having died, he married May 16, 1753, Phoebe Smith, widow of Robert Smith, of Buckingham, and daughter of Thomas Canby, an eminent minister among Friends. Phoebe was also an accepted minister. The children of Hugh Ely, all by his first wife, were:

1. Thomas, who married January 22, 1734, Sarah Lowther, daughter of William and Ruth Lowther, of Buckingham and about 1775, removed with most of his grown up children to Maryland. Gen. Hugh Ely of Baltimore county, veteran of the second war with Great Britain, congressman, United States senator, etc., was a son of Mahlon and grandson of Thomas and Sarah (Lowther) Ely. Many of the male descendants of Thomas migrated to Ohio, where the family is now quite numerous.

2. Hugh Ely, Jr., married Elizabeth Blackfan, and remained on the homestead in Buckingham, part of which is still owned and occupied by his descendants. He reared a family and has very numerous descendants in Bucks county and elsewhere.

3. Ann Ely married Peter Matson.

4. Anna Ely, married John Wilkinson.

Of Elizabeth and Sarah Ely, daughters of Joshua and Mary, little is known. The descendants of the three sons, George, John and Hugh, are now widely scattered over the United States, and many of them have filled honored positions in the official, professional and business life of the sections in which their lot was cast.

George Ely, second son of George and Jane (Pettit) Ely, married Mary Prout, and settled in Amwell township, near Lambertville, New Jersey, in 1748-1750. He was proprietor of Wells Ferry, now New Hope, and resided there, and also was the owner of considerable land in the Ferry Tract, Solebury. He had sons Joseph, John and George, the last named of whom was colonel of a New Jersey regiment during the revolutionary war, and at its close removed to Shamokin, Pa., where he died in 1820. He married Susanna Farley, of Amwell and had nine children, many of whose descendants now reside in western Pennsylvania and Ohio.

U-8

Joshua Ely, eldest son of George and Jane (Pettit) Ely, born at Trenton, New Jersey March 16, 1704, married in 1729, Elizabeth Bell, daughter of Henry and Elizabeth Bell, of Burlington county, New Jersey. He removed to Pennsylvania permanently in 1737, but it would appear that he had established a residence there some years earlier, as he was admitted a member of Buckingham Meeting in 1734. Though the minutes of that meeting fail to show any record of his removal, he and his wife Elizabeth received a certificate of removal from Chesterfield Meeting to Buckingham in 1738. In 1737 he leased of William Blakey 400 acres in Solebury township, Bucks county, the greater part of which is still owned and occupied by his descendants of the name. The lease was for ten years, and under its provisions, he was to clear sixty acres of upland and ten acres of meadow, and build an addition to the house, Blakey to furnish "nails and shingles," and to build a frame barn. The lease was renewed in 1747, but in 1749 he contracted for its purchase, which failed of consummation until two years later by reason of the death of Blakey before the deed was delivered. Here Joshua Ely lived until his death in 1783, building a stone house soon after his purchase, which is still occupied by his great-great-grandson, William L. Ely. He became a prominent man in Solebury but, being a consistent member of the Society of Friends, took no part in the revolutionary struggle, his name and those of his sons appearing on the list of "non-associators" in 1775. He was made an elder of Buckingham Meeting in 1752 and was recommended as a minister in 1758. He was a successful farmer, and in addition to the 400 acres acquired another large tract of land, part of the Pike tract adjoining. The children of Joshua and Elizabeth (Bell) Ely were as follows:

1. Joshua, born at Trenton in 1730, died on a part of the Solebury homestead in 1804. He married Elizabeth Hughes, daughter of Mathew and Elizabeth (Stevenson) Hughes, of Plumstead, and has left numerous descendants. The farm of 150 acres received by him of his father was occupied successively by his son and grandson, both named Jonathan, the latter dying in 1867, when the farm went to 'another branch of the family, and is now conducted by a great-great-grandson of his brother George, George H. Ely.

2. George Ely, born at Trenton, New Jersey, November 9, 1733, died in Newtown township in 1815. He married September 24, 1760, Sarah Magill; see forward.

3. John, born May 28, 1738, married Sarah Simcock, and inherited the homestead tract of his father. For his de-

scendants see sketch of William L. Ely, who still resides there.

4. Sarah Ely, born June 14, 1736, married William Kitchin, to whom her father conveyed a portion of the homestead lying next to the Delaware river, upon which he erected a mill for his half-brother Aaron Phillips, whose descendants of the name operated it until about 1890.

5. Hugh Ely, born August 8, 1741, married Elizabeth Wilson. He inherited from his father a farm in the "Pike Tract," but sold it and resided in New Hope, where he was a noted clock maker a century ago.

6. Hannah, married James Dubree, and left two children Absalom and Hannah.

7. Jane, married Jonathan Balderston, and lived and died in Solebury.

George Ely, second son of Joshua and Elizabeth (Bell) Ely, born at Trenton, November 8, 1733, married November 24, 1760, Sarah Magill, daughter of William and Sarah (Simcock) Magill, of Solebury, the former a native of Ulster, Ireland, located in Solebury about 1730 Sarah Simcock was a daughter of Jacob Simcock, Jr., and Sarah Waln, of Ridley, Chester county; Sarah Waln being a daughter of Nicholas Waln, for many years a member of colonial assembly, at whose house in Middletown, Bucks county, the early Friends Meetings were held. John Simcock, of Ridley, the grandfather of Jacob, Jr., born in Cheshire, England, in 1630, came to Chester county with his wife Elizabeth about 1682; he was one of Penn's five commissioners, and a member of provincial council, 1683-1700; judge of Chester county, 1683-86; puisine judge of province, 1686-90; provincial judge, 1690-93; and speaker of assembly, 1696; died 1703. His son Jacob, who was coroner of Chester county in 1691, married Alice Maris, daughter of George Maris and Alice his wife, who came from Worcestershire, England, to Chester county in 1682, a member of the governor's council, 1684 to 1695, member of assembly, justice, etc., died 1705. In 1760 George Ely received from his father 112 acres of the homestead, on which he erected a house still standing, and which is still owned by his descendants, being the home of his great-granddaughter Laura Ely Walton. He later purchased considerable other land in Solebury and elsewhere, much of which is also occupied by his descendants. He was a prominent man in the community, and a member of colonial assembly in 1760. He was a resident on the old homestead until 1802, when he transferred it to his son George Ely, Jr., and removed to Newtown township to a farm purchased of Hampton Wilson, where he died in 1814. The children of

George and Sarah (Magill) Ely were as follows:

1. Joseph, born August 13, 1761, married Mary Whitson, daughter of Thomas Whitson, Jr., and granddaughter of Thomas Whitson, who came from Bethpage, Long Island, and a descendant of the Powells, Hallecks and Estes of Long Island. Joseph Ely received from his father the Rabbit Run farm, now occupied by his great-grandson Thomas Magill, and lived and died there.

2. Jane Ely, born January 5, 1764, married Benjamin Paxson.

3. Joshua, born July 4, 1766, died young.

4. Amos, born February 6, 1769.

5. George, born July 25, 1772, married Sarah Smith, and lived and died on the homestead, where his sons, Robert, Smith, George and Gervas, late of Lambertville, New Jersey, were born and reared.

6. William, born November 26, 1774, inherited his father's Newtown farm.

7. Aaron married Alada Britton, was the father of Hiram and Britton Ely, of New Hope, and the grandfather of Daniel Britton Ely, of Montclair, New Jersey.

8. Joshua, born October 24, 1779, died young.

9. Mark, born September 18, 1781; see forward.

10. Mathias, born September 5, 1783, was twice married, and was the grandfather of Esward W. Ely, of Doylestown.

11. Amasa, born November 12, 1787.

Mark Ely, ninth child of George and Sarah (Magill) Ely, born on the old homestead, September 18, 1781, was a shoemaker by trade, and followed that vocation in connection with farming all his life. He inherited from his father a small farm adjoining the homestead, and lived thereon until his death in 1835. He was twice married, first on June 2, 1802, to Hannah Johnson, who bore him three daughters, and second, December 12, 1815, to Rachel Hambleton, born May 23, 1787, died August 21, 1878, daughter of James and Elizabeth (Paxson) Hambleton, of Solebury, later of Drumore, Lancaster county, granddaughter of Stephen and Hannah (Paxson) Hambleton, and great-granddaughter of James and Mary (Beakes) Hambleton, of Solebury. James Hambleton came to Solebury in the early part of the eighteenth century from Maryland, where his ancestors had resided for two or three generations. Hannah Paxson, wife of Stephen Hambleton, born December 28, 1732, died November 1, 1812, was the daughter of James and Margaret (Hodges) Paxson, and granddaughter of William and Abigail (Pownal) Paxson; and Elizabeth, the wife of James Hambleton, was a daughter of Henry and Elizabeth (Lupton) Paxson,

and granddaughter of Henry and Ann Plumly Paxson, the latter being a brother to William before mentioned, and both sons of James and Jane Paxson, who came from Bucks county, England, in 1682. Mary Beakes, wife of James Hambleton, was a daughter of Stephen and Elizabeth (Biles) Beakes, both of whom were natives of England, the former born April 28, 1665, in Blackwell, Somerset, England, son of William and Mary (Wall) Beakes, came to Pennsylvania with his parents in 1682 and died in 1699. Both he and his father were members of colonial assembly. His wife Elizabeth, born in Dorchester, England, June 3, 1670, was a daughter of William and Joanna Biles, who came to Bucks county in 1679, William was a member of the first provincial council, and represented his county for many years.

Of the three daughters of Mark and Hannah (Johnson) Ely, one married a Hall, and had a large family of children; Rachel married Amos C. Paxson, of Solebury, and had a large family, most of whom are now deceased; and Rachel Ann, married first Joseph Lownes, and second Samuel Cooper, having several children by the first marriage, and one (Mrs. Rachel Pidcock, of New Hope) by the second.

The children of Mark and Rachel (Hambleton) Ely, were.

1. James H. died September 29, 1905, in Solebury, married Emeline Magill, and had four daughters and one son, Mark, of Ewing township, Hunterdon county, New Jersey. Of the daughters, Henrietta married Ellis Walton, and is living in Solebury; Josephine is the wife of George Quinby, of Warrington; Elizabeth married Joseph Lear, and is deceased; and Amy, unmarried, resides with her father.

2. Amy, married Isaac Heston Worstall, and is deceased, leaving two children, Mrs. George Wiley of Solebury and Mrs. Emma Wilson of California.

3. Mercy, married William H. McDowell, and resided for many years in Cecil county, Maryland, both are deceased leaving four sons and a daughter.

4. Mary, married Howard Paxson of Solebury and has been a widow for many years, residing with her daughter Mrs. Harvey Warner in Solebury.

5. Isaac Ely, second son of Mark and Rachel, born in Solebury, May 23, 1819, was reared in that township and lived there and in the borough of New Hope all his life. He was a farmer, and, after renting a farm for about five years, purchased a farm in the Pownall tract adjoining the homestead of his ancestors, where he lived until 1865, when he purchased the farm on which his grandparents, George and Sarah (Magill) Ely, had settled in 1760, and where his father was born, and lived there until 1884, when he retired from active business and

resided in New Hope until his death, on March 3, 1898. In 1867 he purchased the farm given by his great-grandfather, Joshua Ely, to his son, Joshua, Jr., on which his eldest son, William M. Ely, settled and still resides. Isaac Ely was a prominent and successful farmer and business man. He took an active interest in local affairs, and held a number of positions of public trust. He was for many years a member of the local school board, and took an active interest in the cause of education. During the civil war, though a member of the Society of Friends and constant in the attendance of Solebury Meeting, he was active in raising the quota of soldiers required to carry on the war, from his section, and in rasining funds and materials for the care of the sick and wounded in the hospitals. He was for many years a director of the Bucks County Agricultural and Mechanics' Institute, and one of the active members of the Solebury Farmers' Club. He married December 25, 1841, Mary Magill, born October 23, 1820, died March 2, 1897, daughter of John and Anne (Ely) Magill. The former, born July 12, 1779, died February 10, 1866, was a son of John and Amy (Whitson) Magill, and a grandson of William and Sarah (Simcock) Magill, before mentioned; and the latter a daughter of Joseph and Mary (Whitson) Ely before mentioned. Amy Whitson, the wife of John Magill, Sr., was born July 18, 1739, and was a daughter of David and Clemence (Powell) Whitson, who came from Long Island to Solebury in the first half of the eighteenth century. The children of Isaac and Mary (Magill) Ely were:

Sarah Ellen, born 1842, died August 3, 1876; married John S. Abbott.

William M. Ely, born January 29, 1844; has been for many years a justice of the peace of Solebury, residing on 150 acres of the land taken up by his ancestor, Joshua Ely, in 1737. He married December 19, 1876, Agnes S. Michener, daughter of Hugh and Sarah (Betts) Michener, and they are the parents of two children: George H., born June 30, 1880, is married to Marion Rice, daughter of Hon. Hampton and Emma (Kenderdine) Rice, and resides with his two children, Wilton and Helen, on the same farm; and Mary D., born December 12, 1880.

Anna M. Ely, born June 7, 1845, married March 29, 1873, Frederick L. Smith, for many years engaged in the mercantile business at Penns Park and New Hope, now living retired in Doylestown. Their only child, Ely J. Smith, born December 16, 1877, is a member of the Bucks county bar.

Edgar C. Ely, born October 14, 1846, and Rachel Anna, born June 4, 1850, both died August 25, 1851.

John H. Ely, born November 17, 1851,

married in 1882, Martha S. Gilbert, daughter of John W. and Letitia (Smith) Gilbert, of Buckingham; he was a farmer in Solebury for several years, and is now residing in New Hope borough. They have no children.

Laura Ely, born August 18, 1853, married Seth T. Walton, of one of the oldest families of Montgomery county, and has three children, Edna M., Mark Hubert, and Marguerite.

Warren S. Ely, born October 6, 1855; see forward.

Alice K., born January 17, 1860, married Clarence T. Doty, a prominent business man of Jacksonville, Florida, where they reside.

Martha C., born December 10, 1861, married Thomas B. Claxton, a farmer in Buckingham.

WARREN SMEDLEY ELY, tenth child and fourth son of Isaac and Mary (Magill) Ely, was born in Solebury township, October 6, 1855. He was educated in the common schools and Lambertville Seminary. On April 1, 1878, he took charge of the paternal farm, upon which he had been reared, and conducted it for two years. March 1, 1880, he purchased a farm in Buckingham, to which he removed and cultivated it for five years, during the same period acting as one of the managers and the treasurer of the Buckingham Valley Creamery Association. On October 26, 1881, he experienced a distressing accident by the loss of his right arm in farming machinery. This necessitated his seeking other employment than that to which he had been accustomed, and in the winter of 1881-82 he engaged in business as a real estate and general business agent, and during the ensuing four years was busily engaged in that capacity, at the same time continuing his residence upon the farm and directing its management. In the spring of 1885 he sold the farm and purchased a mill in Buckingham, which he remodeled and refitted throughout, equipping it with the latest improved roller process machinery for the manufacture of flour and granulated cornmeal. He was the pioneer in eastern Pennsylvania in the manufacture of the latter product, and his "Gold Grits" enjoyed a more than local reputation, and commanded a ready sale, as did his roller process flour, and he conducted a prosperous business for several years.

In the autumn of 1893 he was elected on the Republican ticket to the office of clerk of orphans court of Bucks county, and in the spring following removed to Doylestown, where he has since resided. After his retirement from office on the expiration of his official term, he was appointed a deputy clerk of the same court, acting more especially as advisor

Warren P. Ely

The Lewis Publishing Co

and assistant to his chief, and during a large portion of this same period also serving as deputy register of wills, and for some time as deputy recorder of deeds and deputy sheriff. In March, 1900, he went to Jacksonville, Florida, to fill a position in the mercantile house of Doty-Stowe Company, but returned to Doylestown May 1st of the same year to accept the position of business manager of the "Republican," a daily and weekly newspaper. He was so engaged until August, 1901, when he resigned to take charge of the work of arranging, recopying and filing the papers and records of the orphans' court office under the direction of the court, a task which employed him constantly for nearly two years. Since the completion of this labor his entire time has been devoted to historical and genealogical work, and much of the contents of the genealogical department of these volumes (History of Bucks County) is from his pen.

Proud of the achievements of the sons of Bucks county, abroad as well as at home, Mr. Ely has made a close study of the part the county has taken in the rise and development of the province, state and nation, and is recognized as an authority in matters relating to its local history, and particularly the genealogy of its early families. He was directed into this channel of thought and investigation during his incumbency of the office of clerk of the orphans, court, and while rendering efficient service in that capacity, found congenial occupation in his contact with the ancient records of the county not alone in his official investigations, but in the fund of information opened up to him with reference to the old families of the county. He became an active member of the Bucks County Historical Society, was its first regularly constituted librarian, and has occupied that position to the present time. He has contributed a number of papers to the archives of the Society, these including one of particular merit, on "The Scotch-Irish Families of Bucks County."

Mr. Ely is deeply interested in general educational affairs, and gave capable service as one of the trustees and directors of the Hughesian Free School, in Buckingham, until his removal from the township rendered him ineligible for the office. He is a member of the fraternity of Odd Fellows, affiliated with Aquetong Lodge, No. 193, in which he is a past grand, and Doylestown Encampment, No. 35, in which he is a past chief patriarch; he has represented both in the grand bodies of the state for a number of years, and for some time filled the position of district deputy. He is also a past select commander of the Ancient Order, Knights of the Mystic Chain, of Pennsylvania, affiliated with Buckingham Castle, No. 208, which he represented in the select castle for several years, also serving for three years as trustee of the state body.

Through his marriage, Mr. Ely is related to a family as old in America as his own. March 29, 1882, he married Hannah S. Michener, a daughter of Hugh and Sarah (Betts) Michener. She is descended on the paternal side from John and Sarah Michener, who came from England about 1690 and settled in Philadelphia, later removing to Moreland township, Montgomery county, whence William Michener removed in 1722 to Plumstead, Bucks county, where Mrs. Ely's ancestors were prominent farmers for several generations. On the maternal side she is descended from Colonel Richard Betts, who came from England to Ipswich, Massachusetts, about 1648, and soon afterward to Long Island, where he filled many high and honorable positions under the colonial government—member of the provincial assembly, commissioner of highways, sheriff, officer of volunteers, etc., and died November 18, 1673, at the remarkable age of one hundred years. Among the maternal ancestors of Mrs. Ely were also the Stevenson, Whitehead, Powell, Whitson, De la Plaine, Cresson, Cock, Halleck, Este, Field and other prominent families of Long Island and New Jersey and the Blackfan, Simpson, Warner, Wiggins, Croasdale, Chapman and Hayhurst families of Bucks county. Many of her lineal ancestors have held high official positions in the early days of the colonies, as have those of her husband.

The children of Warren S. and Hannah S. (Michener) Ely are as follows: M. Florence, born July 19, 1884; Laura W., born February 21, 1887, died February 25, 1903; and Frederic Warren, born February 16, 1889, now a student at Swarthmore College.

HON. IRVING PRICE WANGER, the present representative in congress from the Eighth Congressional District, comprising the counties of Bucks and Montgomery, while not a native or a resident of Bucks, nevertheless holds a conspicuous place in the interest and regard of the people of the county he has so ably and conscientiously represented in the law making body of the nation for the past twelve years, and some account of his career and antecedents will be of interest to the readers of this historical work.

He was born in North Coventry township, Chester county, Pennsylvania, March 5, 1852, and is the eldest son of George and Rebecca (Price) Wanger, and a descendant of early settlers in Montgomery county, of the religious sects known as the Brethren (Dunkards) and Mennonites. His paternal ancestor, Henry Wanger (or Wenger, as the name was then spelled) came from Switzerland with other Mennonites in 1717, and located on one hundred acres now included in the borough of Pottstown, Montgomery county, purchased September 15, 1718, with his wife Elizabeth and several children. He was a farmer by occupation, and later purchased additional land in that locality. He died in 1753, and is supposed to be interred in the Mennonite burying ground at East Coventry, Chester county. John Wanger, son of Henry and Elizabeth, was born on his father's farm at what is now Pottstown, December 10, 1726, and in 1754 purchased part of the plantation, on which he resided until 1762, when he removed to Union township, Berks county, where he had purchased 293 acres of land on which he lived until his death, January 5, 1803. He was court martial officer of Captain Thomas Parry's company, Fifth Battalion Berks County Militia, commissioned May 17, 1777, under Colonel Jacob Weaver.

Abraham Wanger, son of John, was born at Pottstown, December 15, 1761, and died in Berks county, March 18, 1793. His wife was Susanna, daughter of Jacob and Magdalena Shantz, and their son, Abraham, born December 11, 1787, was the grandfather of Congressman Wanger. He was born on the old Berks county homestead, which was acquired by his father in 1788, and remained in that county until late in life, when he removed to Chester county, where he died April 23, 1861. He married Mary Berge, daughter of Abraham and Susanna (Shantz) Berge, and they were the parents of ten children, five of whom grew to manhood and womanhood.

George Wanger was born in Berks county in 1820, and was reared to manhood in that county, and then removed with his parents to Chester county, where he followed the occupation of a farmer during life. He was a soldier in the civil war, enlisting first in the Keystone Guards, organized for state defense, in Company E, Nineteenth Regiment, and was in service a short time. Later he served for two months in Company D, Forty-second Regiment Pennsylvania Volunteer Militia, which went to Chambersburg. George Wanger, though a Mennonite by birth, became a member of the official board of St. James' Methodist Episcopal Church at Cedarville, Chester county, the site of which church he presented to the congregation. He died in North Coventry township, December 30, 1876. He was known as a man of great force of character and high standing in the community; a strong advocate of the public school system, he served for a number of years on the local school board. Originally a Whig, he cast his first presidential vote for Henry Clay. He was a strong advocate of the restriction and abolition of slavery, and his home was one of the stations of the "Underground Railroad" through which many runaway slaves were assisted to freedom. He was active in the formation of the Republican party, and foremost in the temperance movement in his locality. He married Rebecca, daughter of Rev. John and Mary (Reinhart) Price, whose direct ancestors for five generations had been preachers in the denomination known as German Baptist Brethren; the first, Rev. Jacob Price (or Priesz), was a native of Witzenstein, Prussia, and united with the sect soon after its establishment at Schwarzenau in 1708, and early became a preacher and missionary. Driven by religious persecution to Serverstin, Friesland, he came to Pennsylvania with the first party of German Baptists in 1719, and settled on Indian Creek, Montgomery county. His son, Rev. John Price, was born in Prussia and accompanied his father to America in his seventeenth year. He was a poet and preacher, and a personal friend of Christopher Saur, the noted German printer who in 1753 published a collection of Mr. Price's poetry. He was one of the founders of the mother church at Germantown in 1723. He had two sons, John and Daniel, both of whom became preachers, the former settling in Indiana county, Pennsylvania, where he has left many descendants. Rev. Daniel Price was born in Montgomery county, December 11, 1723, and died there February 11, 1804. He married in 1746 Hannah Weickard, and left a large family. He owned two hundred acres of the land taken up by his grandfather, and was active in local matters, serving as township auditor and supervisor. Rev. George Price, son of Daniel, was also a preacher among the German Baptists. He was born in Montgomery county, November 1, 1753, but removed to East Nantmeal, Chester county, in 1774, and to Coventry in 1794. His wife was Sarah Harley, and they were the parents of several children.

Rev. John Price, son of George and Sarah, was the father of Mrs. George Wanger, and the grandfather of the subject of this sketch; he was a farmer and preacher, and was born in Chester county, August 6, 1782, and died April 12, 1850. His wife was Mary, daughter of John and Hannah (Price) Rinehart, born May 17, 1783, died April 23, 1863, and they were the parents of twelve children, three of whom and the husband of a fourth became preachers.

George and Rebecca (Price) Wanger were the parents of six children, five sons and one daughter, of whom four survive—Irving P., Newton, George F. P., assistant postmaster of Pottstown, and Joseph P. Wanger.

Hon. Irving P. Wanger was born and reared on the old homestead in Chester county, and was educated in the public schools and the Pottstown Hill and high schools. He taught school for one year and in 1870 became a clerk in the prothonotary's office at West Chester, and in the following year was appointed deputy prothonotary, which position he resigned at the end of a year, and in January, 1872, began the study of law in the office of Franklin March, Esq., at Norristown, Montgomery county. In December, 1872, he was appointed deputy prothonotary of Montgomery under William F. Reed, the first Republican ever elected to that office in Montgomery. He continued the study of law and was admitted to the bar of Montgomery county in December, 1875. Being an earnest student and an eloquent forcible advocate, he soon acquired a practice from all parts of Montgomery county. His talent for public speaking caused his services to be in demand in behalf of the candidates of his party, and he soon became a prominent figure in Montgomery county politics, being an earnest and logical advocate of the principles of the Republican party. In 1878 he was elected burgess of Norristown, and in 1880 to the office of district attorney of Montgomery county. In the latter position he instituted several reforms, among them, the dividing the list of criminal cases to be tried among the several days of the term, thus obviating the necessity of all the witnesses and parties interested to attend during the whole term, and thereby making a great saving to the taxpayers. This custom has been uniformly followed since. In 1880 Mr. Wanger was a delegate to the Republican national convention, and voted continuously for the unit rule and for the nomination of James G. Blaine for the presidency, until the final ballot, when, as requested by the friends of the latter, he voted for James A. Garfield, the nominee. In 1886 he was again elected to the office of district attorney by a majority of 1187 votes, running several hundred votes ahead of his ticket, notwithstanding the fact that his opponent was one of the most capable candidates ever nominated by the Democracy. In 1889 he was chairman of the Republican county committee. In 1890 he was unanimously nominated for congress in the Bucks-Montgomery district, but, owing to the unpopular candidacy of George W. Delameter for governor, was defeated by 187 votes, the Republican ticket being defeated in both counties by a much larger vote. Two years later he was again nominated, and elected, though the district gave a majority for Cleveland. In 1894 he was elected by a majority of 4826, and has been re-elected in 1896, 1898, 1900, 1902 and 1904, by increased majorities, his majority in

the latter year being 10,252, showing that his course at Washington had been such as to commend him strongly to the people of the district. His support has not been confined to members of his own party, voters of other party affiliations testifying their appreciation of his worth by their votes at each election. As a congressman Mr. Wanger has taken an active part in the debates in the house on the tariff, the currency, the Philippine legislation, and other questions of national interest, but his strong point has been his conscientious attention to all matters affecting his constituents, doing everything possible to promote the prosperity and welfare of the people of his district, as well as of the country at large. He has always voted with his party upon questions involving its principles, ably and earnestly upholding the policy of McKinley and Roosevelt, whenever it has been a matter for action in congress or elsewhere. It was upon his motion that the special committee was appointed which investigated the hazing of cadets in the United States Military Academy at West Point, and suggested important legislation on the subject, which was adopted. His principal committee service has been as a member of the committee on foreign and interstate commerce, and as chairman of the committee on expenditures in the postoffice department. He has always been a faithful exponent of the wishes and interests of his constituents, as his repeated re-elections testify.

As a public speaker, Mr. Wanger stands deservedly high; he is argumentative, logical, clear and deliberative, appealing always to the reason and judgment of his hearers, rather than to their prejudices and personal or partisan feelings. He is a ready debater and parliamentarian, quick to take advantage of the weak point in the argument of his opponent. He has always kept in close touch with the measures and policies of the two dominant parties in congress, and is quick to perceive and defend the interests of his constituents in any proposed legislation. During his service he has made many friends among the representatives of other districts and states, frequently securing their services and support, when occasion required in his home district.

Mr. Wanger was married on June 25, 1884, to Emma C. Titlow, daughter of John Titlow of North Coventry, Chester county, a playmate and schoolmate of his youth. They are the parents of three children—George, Ruth and Marion. Two others, Lincoln and Rebecca, died in infancy. He resides with his family in the old Chain homestead, 827 West Main street, Norristown. His mother, from whom he inherits many of his characteristics, resides with him. She is a member of the Methodist church, Marshall street, Norristown. Mr. Wanger is himself a member of St. John's Episcopal church. He is a member of the Independent Order of Odd Fellows and the Improved Order of Red Men, and of the various branches of the Masonic fraternity, having been grand commander of the Knights Templar of Pennsylvania in 1894-5.

WILLIAM WATSON, one of the most enterprising and progressive farmers of Buckingham, was born on the old Watson homestead upon which he still resides, February 17, 1862, being only son of Henry and Emeline P. (Rich) Watson.

The first American ancestors of the subject of this sketch were early settlers in Chesterfield township, Burlington county, New Jersey. Mathew Watson and Anne Mauleverer, his wife, migrated form Scarborough, in Yorkshire, England, about 1682, and settled in Chesterfield. They were members of Chesterfield Monthly Meeting of Friends. Mathew's occupation is given as "chemits." He purchased in 1683 of Thomas Hutchinson, late of Beverly, in Yorkshire, a one-twelfth share in the province of West Jersey, and appears to have been a man of wealth and education. He died in Chesterfield, 7 mo. 13, 1703, and his wife Anne died there 11 mo. 16, 1721. Their children were: Mathew, Jr., born at Burlington, 10 mo. 2, 1682; and Marmaduke, born 8 mo. 13, 1685. Mathew seems to have been engaged in a shipping business, as on 3 mo. 27, 1724, he takes a certificate from Chesterfield Meeting to "transport himself to other parts on account of trading."

Marmaduke Watson, second son of Mathew and Anne, was married at Burlington Meeting, 1 mo. 27, 1718, to Elizabeth Pancoast, daughter of William and Hannah (Scattergood) Pancoast. He inherited from his father large tracts of land in different parts of West Jersey, allotted as part of the one-twelfth share of the province, among them a tract in Bethlehem township, Hunterdon county, on the Musconetcong creek, which he devised in his will to his son Aaron. This will is dated in Chesterfield township, Burlington county, 3 mo. 14, 1746, and was proven July 24, 1749, and mentions, beside the son Aaron, wife Elizabeth, son Marmaduke, and daughter Anne, wife of Joseph Curtis.

Aaron Watson, son of Marmaduke and Elizabeth (Pancoast) Watson, was born in Chesterfield about 1720. It is possible that on arriving at manhood he became associated with his uncle Mathew in the "trading" business, as he seems to have followed a migratory life for some years. In 1744 he brings a certificate from Chester, Pennsylvania,

Meeting to Philadelphia, where he remained until after his father's death. In 1750 he takes a certificate to his old home at Chesterfield, but probably located at once on his inheritance at Bethlehem, now Kingwood, though he does not take a certificate to Kingwood Meeting until 1754, when about to marry Sarah Emley, a member of that Meeting. The children of Aaron and Sarah (Emley) Watson were: John, Lucy, Anne and Sarah, all born at Kingwood, New Jersey.

John Watson, eldest child of Aaron and Sarah, born at Kingwood, about 1755, was reared on the Jersey farm. During the Revolution he removed to Shrewsbury, and engaged in the manufacture of salt on the Jersey coast, where Point Pleasant is now located. He sold the product to the continental army, and thus incurred the special enmity of the British, who destroyed his residence and plant, thereby ruining him financially. He married about 1778 or 1779, at Shrewsbury, Mary Jackson, a descendant of Daniel Jackson, who migrated from Stangerthwaite, in Yorkshire, about 1693, and located in Bristol township, Bucks county, whose descendants had removed to Shrewsbury prior to the revolution. John Watson returned to Kingwood in 1781, with wife and daughter Sarah. His eldest son John was born there 10 mo. 25, 1781. In the autumn of 1782 he removed to Middletown, Bucks county, where his son Aaron was born, and his eldest child, Sarah, died. He removed to Buckingham in 1785, where the rest of his ten children were born, viz.: Hannah, married William Gillingham; Sarah, married George Hughes; Elizabeth, married James Shaw; Joseph; Charles; Ann; Marmaduke and John. In 1794 he purchased 140 acres of land lying on both sides of the Mechanicsville road, and including the present Watson farm, the original buildings being on the northwest side of the road, where John Riniker now lives. He died on this farm in 1818, and the farm was partitioned through the orphans' court, the farm now occupied by the subject of this sketch being adjudged to his oldest son, William Watson.

William Watson, son of John and Mary (Jackson) Watson, was born in Kingwood, 10 mo. 25, 1781, and was but a child when his parents removed to Buckingham. He married, May 10, 1809, Elizabeth, daughter of Samuel and Margaret (Jenks) Gillingham, who was born 11 mo, 21, 1784, and died June 28, 1868. Upon his marriage William Watson settled on the farm still occupied by his grandson the subject of this sketch, the building then being first erected for him by his father. William Watson was a prominent and useful man in the community, and filled many positions of trust. He was one of the original trus-

Henry Watson

tees of the Hughesian Free School, and filled other responsible positions; was one of the solid substantial men of his day, a prosperous farmer and conservative business man. He and his family were members of Buckingham Meeting of Friends. The children of William and Elizabeth (Gillingham) Watson were: Samuel G., born 4 mo. 10, 1810, married Sarah H. Thomas; Jenks, died an infant; Margaret Jenks, born 1814, died 1835; Mary, born 4 mo., 17, 1817, married Joshua Fell; Henry, the father of the subject of this sketch; Elizabeth, born 1822, died 1861; and Sarah, born 1825, died 1904. Neither of the last two were married, and lived and died at the residence of their brother Henry, on the old homestead.

Henry Watson, the father of the subject of this sketch, was born on the farm upon which he still resides, on 12 mo. 17, 1819. He is one of the most highly esteemed men of his neighborhood. Like his father, he is a member of Buckingham Friends' Meeting, and has fully maintained the standing of this old and respected family. He succeeded his father as a trustee and director of the Hughesian Free School, and has served as director of the public schools for many years, and held many other positions of trust. He married Emaline P., daughter of Moses Rich, of Buckingham, who was born in 1822 and died January 3, 1903. They were the parents of five children: John Rich, who died in infancy; Caroline M., born 10 mo. 19, 1852, died 11 mo. 8, 1898, married Lewis D. Rich; Martha Rich, born 7 mo. 25, 1855, died 3 mo. 12, 1903, married James McNair; Fannie, born 4 mo. 8, 1858, married William E. Wilson; and William, born 2 mo. 27, 1862.

The subject of this sketch was reared on the farm, and obtained his education at the public schools and at Doylestown English and Classical Seminary. Being the only son, the care of the farm devolved upon him at an early age, his father being occupied with public affairs and the oversight of several other farms owned by the family. Like his father and grandfather, he is an excellent farmer, and takes great pride in the old farm, which is one of the best tilled and productive in the township. In politics Mr. Watson is a Republican, and, though never an office seeker, takes a keen interest in all that pertains to the best interests of his party, and has served as a delegate to several state and district conventions. He is a member of Buckingham Friends' Meeting. Socially he is a member of Doylestown Lodge, No. 245, F. and A. M.; a past high priest of Doylestown Chapter, No. 270, R. A. M.; a member of Pennsylvania Commandery No. 70, K. T.; Philadelphia Consistory, A. and A. S. S.; and of Aquetong Lodge,

No. 193, I. O. O. F., and Doylestown Council, No. 1117, Royal Arcanum.

He was married on 12 mo. 5, 1893, to Caroline M., daughter of the late Captain John S. Bailey, of Buckingham, and has one child, Edward Blackfan Watson, born in 1894.

PROFESSOR A. J. MORRISON, one of the best known educators in Philadelphia, was born in Northampton township, Bucks county, Pennsylvania February 14, 1844, and is a son of Judge Joseph and Eleanor (Addis) Morrison.

John Morrison, the great-grandfather of Professor Morrison, was a native of the north of Ireland, and was one of the great army of Ulster Scots who, having fled from religious persecution and internecine strife in their native Scotia, took temporary refuge in the province of Ulster, Ireland, from whence many emigrated to Pennsylvania in the first half of the eighteenth century. John Morrison settled on the banks of the Brandywine, where his son, John Morrison, was born in 1767. On attaining manhood he located in Northampton township, Bucks county, where he died March 17, 1858, at the age of ninety-one years. He married Hannah Yerkes, daughter of Elias Yerkes, of Southampton, who was born June 30, 1772, and died February 12, 1844. Her paternal grandfather, Silas Yerkes, was born in Moreland township, Montgomery county, February 15, 1723, and died there September 25, 1795. He was a son of Herman Yerkes, born 1687, and grandson of Anthony Yerkes, one of the first burgesses of Germantown. Silas married June 14, 1750, Hannah Dungan, daughter of Thomas and Esther Dungan, and granddaughter of the Rev. Thomas Dungan, who founded the first Baptist church in Bucks county, in 1684. Their son Elias was born in Warminster (where his parents resided for many years) December 7, 1751, and died in Moreland, January 15, 1828. Elizabeth (Watts) Yerkes, the mother of Silas, born April 15, 1689, died October 11, 1756, was the daughter of Rev. John and Sarah (Eaton) Watts of Southampton.

The children of John and Hannah (Yerkes) Morrison, were: Joseph, born October 18, 1794; Hannah, born February 10, 1796, married Joseph Erwin; Benjamin, born 1798, died in infancy; Mary, born February 5, 1799, married Benjamin Longstreth; Martha, twin to Mary, died single in 1882; Eliza, born March 19, 1802, married Charles Blaker; Ann, born May 11, 1803; David and Benjamin, born April 18, 1805; John, born October 28, 1807; Esther, born February 10, 1809, died unmarried; Matilda, born November 5, 1810, married Joseph Erwin; Rebecca Ann, born March 19, 1813, married John Campbell; Jonathan J., born May 4,

1815, married Jane Rapp; and Sarah, born May 30, 1818, married Jonas Yerkes.

JOSEPH MORRISON, eldest son of John and Hannah (Yerkes) Morrison, born October 18, 1794, died July 30, 1880, became one of the most distinguished citizens of Bucks county. He was born in Delaware county, and learned the trade of a miller with Amos Addis, in Moreland, and on his marriage to the daughter of his preceptor he removed to Northampton township, Bucks county, where he owned and operated the Rocksville Mills for fifty years. Early in life he took an active interest in the organization of the local militia, and eventually filled every commissioned position in the organization from captain to brigadier-general, and was esteemed the best informed man in the county on military tactics. He was elected to the office of commissioner of Bucks county in 1836, and served three years. In 1840 he served a term as county treasurer. He filled the responsible position of recorder of deeds for the term 1852-4. He served as associate justice of Bucks county courts for fifteen years, 1863 to 1878. He married in 1822 Eleanor Addis, born December 11, 1802, died January 8, 1870, daughter of Colonel Amos Addis, who for many years operated a mill in Moreland township, Montgomery county, Pennsylvania. He was born in Moreland or Oxford township, and was a son of Nehemiah and Grace Addis, and a grandson of John Addis, an early settler in Oxford township, Philadelphia county, where he died in 1724. Richard and John Addis, the pioneers of the family in Northampton township, Bucks county, from whose family, Addisville (now Richboro) took its name, were older brothers of Nehemiah Addis. The children of Joseph and Eleanor (Addis) Morrison were: Amos Addis, born May 27, 1823, married Mary Coxhead; John, born March 13, 1827, died in Tennessee in 1864, while a soldier in the Union army; Johnson, born November 16, 1827, married Mary Hobensack; Ruth Ann, born July 30, 1830, married J. Krewson Cornell; Charles B., born March 31, 1832, married Mary A. Feaster; Eliza Ann, born September 9, 1835; Mary Ellen, born October 12, 1839, married Joseph F. Whitall of Southampton; Hannah Rebecca, born May 7, 1841; and Andrew Jackson. Judge Joseph Morrison, married (second) Mary Ann Lashley, widow of Lambert Lashley, of Wrightstown, and died at the Anchor, in Wrightstown, July 30, 1880.

Professor Andrew Jackson Morrison was born and reared in Northampton township and acquired his education at the Central High School of Philadelphia, the Tennent Academy at Hartsville, Bucks county, and the University of Pennsylvania. He has devoted his whole life to the cause of education. He was successively principal of the Tillyer, Wheat Sheaf, Landreth, Irving, and Northern Liberties Grammar Schools, and of the Kaighn Grammar School of Camden, New Jersey. From 1881 to 1883 he was professor of mathematics in the Central High School, Philadelphia; from 1883 to 1898, senior assistant superintendent of public schools in Philadelphia; and acting superintendent during the year 1891. Since 1898 he has filled the position of principal of the Northeast Manual Training School of Philadelphia. In 1901 the honorary degree of Doctor of Philosophy was conferred upon him by Cedarville College.

Professor Morrison has always kept to the fore front in the cause of education. He has served two terms as president of the Teachers' Institute of Philadelphia, and two terms as president of the Educational Club of Philadelphia. He is an active member of the National Educational Association and of the State Teachers' Association, as well as of all the teachers' organizations of Philadelphia. He and his family are members of the Second Reformed Church of Philadelphia. He is a member of Phoenix Lodge, No. 130, F. & A. M., and of Kensington Chapter, No. 233, R. A. M. He is also a member of the Penn Club, and of the Schoolmen's Club.

Professor Morrison was married at Feasterville, Bucks county, March 9, 1865, to Julia H. Jones, daughter of Asa Knight Jones, and they are the parents of five children, viz.: Anna Jones Morrison, born January 18, 1866, graduate of the Girls' Normal School; Jennie Singer Morrison, born December 5, 1867, now the wife of Rev. H. W. Haring, D. D., of Lancaster, Pennsylvania; Egbert Heisler Morrison, born March 14, 1870, a graduate of the Central High School, now agent for the Garlock Packing Company; Clara Maria Morrison, born October 16, 1877, a graduate of the Girls' Normal School, residing at home; and Horace Stanton Morrison, born March 20, 1879, a graduate of the Northeast Manual Training School and of the University of Pennsylvania, now associate editor of the Publications of Commercial Museums of Philadelphia.

———

H. S. PRENTISS NICHOLS, Esq., of Philadelphia, was born in Columbia, Lancaster county, Pennsylvania, November 2, 1858. and is a son of Dr. Joseph D. and Emily (Darrah) Nichols. His grandfather was also a physician and a native of New Hampshire. Dr. Joseph D. Nichols, was the proprietor of an academy at Columbia, Lancaster county, and died in 1874. His wife Emily Darrah was a daughter of Robert Darrah, of Warminster Bucks county, and a great-granddaughter of Captain, Henry Darrah of the Revolution.

The pioneer ancestor of the Darrah family was Thomas Darroch, native of Londonderry, Ireland, who with his wife Mary, emigrated to Pennsylvania about 1730, with the colony of Scotch Irish who settled on the banks of the Neshaminy, about the famous "Log College." He settled for a time in Horsham township, but in 1740, purchased of Mathew Hughes, a tract of land in Bedminster, Bucks county, on the Swamp Road, below the present village of Dublin, purporting to be 500 acres of land, but really containing nearly 800 acres. He died there in March, 1750. The children of Thomas and Mary Darroch were Robert, Thomas, Agnes, wife of John Davis, Esther, wife of George Scott, William, Henry, James, and Susanna. Robert died in Bedminster in 1793, leaving a son Robert and several daughters. He represented his township in the Bucks County Committee of Safety in 1776, and was active in the struggle. Thomas also died in Bedminster leaving two sons Thomas and Mark and several daughters. William was lieutenant of Captain, later Col. Robinson's company of Bucks county militia in 1775, and is also said to have served in the Colonial war of 1756-7. He left two sons Archibald and William and several daughters. one of whom Hannah, married David Kelly of Buckingham and became the mother of Hon. William D. Kelly, for many years a member of Congress from Philadelphia and known as the "Father of the House." Another daughter Susannah, married John Shaw and was the mother of Commodore Thompson Darrah Shaw. Still another Agnes married James Smith of Buckingham, son of Hugh, and was the mother of Gen. Samuel A. Smith of Doylestown.

Henry Darroch, fourth son of Thomas and Mary, was a miner at the death of his father in 1750. By the will of the latter about 190 acres of the homestead was devised to each of the elder sons, Robert and Thomas and the residue to the three younger sons William, Henry and James, subject to a life interest of their mother. On part of this residue. containing 185 acres Henry probably took up his residence on his marriage in 1760 though it was not conveyed to him by his brothers until 1763, when he was about to convey it to Henry Rickert. In 1767, he purchased a farm of 207 acres on the west bank of the Neshaminy, on the Bristol Road, between Tradeville and New Britain villages, now in Doylestown township, on Sheriff's sale as the property of his brother-in-law John Davis. Here he lived until 1773, when he purchased 237 acres further west in New Britain township, on the line of Warrington township, and now included in the latter township, later purchasing about 50 acres adjoining. This remained his home until his death in 1782. Henry Darroch was one of the most illustrious of our Bucks county patriots in the trying days of the war for independence. He was a member of the New Britain company of Associators in 1775, and was commissioned in May, 1776, first lieutenant of Captain William Roberts Company of the Flying Camp, under Col. Joseph Hart, and served with distinction in the Jersey campaign of 1776. Returning to Bucks county in December, 1776, his company was one of the few that responded to the second call in the winter of 1776-7. On the reorganization of the Militia in the Spring of 1777, his old captain and lifelong friend William Roberts was made a Lieut. Colonel and Lieut. Darroch was commissioned Captain May 6, 1777, and his company was soon after in active service under Colonel, later Gen. John Lacey. In 1778, it was again incorporated in Col. Roberts' Battalion, which in 1781, came under the command of Col. Robinson. Captain Darroch's company of Militia was one that was almost constantly in service and he died in the Spring of 1782 from a cold contracted in the service of his country. His will is dated March 17. 1782, and his friends, Col. William Roberts. Col. William Dean and his brother-in-law William Scott are named as executors. It is related that George Washington was a great admirer of Captain Darroch and visited him at his house.

Captain Henry Darroch married August 13, 1760. Ann Jamison, daughter of Henry and Mary (Stewart) Jamison of Warwick township, Bucks county. Tradition relates that Henry Jamison did not approve of the attentions of young Darroch to his daughter, because he was too much of a dashing young man and too fond of fast horses to settle down to the life of a farmer; and that the young people settled the matter for themselves by his taking her up behind him on one of his fast horses and outdistancing the irate father in a race to the parson's. Henry Jamison was a native of the north of Ireland. and came to Bucks county with his father, Henry Jamison and brothers Robert and Alexander about 1720. Henry the elder is said to have been born in Midlothian, Scotland, and removed to the Province of Ulster, Ireland in 1685, with his parents, from whence he migrated to Pennsylvania. He purchased in 1724, 1.000 acres partly in Northampton township and partly in Warwick, and was one of the founders of Neshaminy Church in 1727. In 1734 he conveyed the greater part of his real estate to his sons and returned to Ireland. where he died. His son Henry, Jr., the father of Ann Darroch, was one of the original trustees of the "new lights" of the Neshaminy Church in 1743, a large landowner and prominent man in the Scotch-Irish settlement on the Neshaminy. He sailed for Florida in 1765, and was never heard of afterwards. His wife Mary Stewart was one of a large and influential family of the names that were early settlers in Warwick, New Britain, Warrington, Plumstead and Tinicum. The children of Henry and Mary (Stewart) Jamison were, Isabel, who married - Tristram Davis, brother of John who married Agnes Darroch; Jean, wife of Captain Thomas 'Craig; Ann, wife of Captain Darroch; Alexander; William, Robert and John.

In the possession of the descendants is a beautifully written letter yellow with age written by Ann Darroch to her husband while he was in the army. The children of Captain Henry and Ann (Jamison) Darroch, were, James, see forward Ann, who married Hugh Shaw; Margaret who married William Hewitt; William, born 1767, died July 11, 1838; John and George, the last two of whom died young.

James Darrah, eldest son of Captain Henry and Ann (Jamison) Darroch, was born in 1764, and reared in New Britain township. In 1789, the executors of his father's will conveyed to him 170 acres of the homestead tract in New Britain and the balance 114 acres to his brother William. James married Rachel Henderson, born in Warminster July 27, 1762, daughter of Robert and Margaret (Archibald) Henderson, of Warminster. In 1794, James Darrah purchased of his wife's sisters and their husbands the 250 acres farm in Warminster belonging to the estate of Robert Henderson, formerly the property of Rev. Charles Beatty, pastor of Neshaminy Church, and they sold the New Britain farm and made their home on the Warminster farm, all of which is still owned by their grandsons, John M. and R. Henderson Darrah. Rachel (Henderson) Darrah died November 18, 1802, and James married second Rebecca McCrea. James Darrah died February 17, 1842, aged 78 years. His children, both by the first wife, were Robert Henderson and Henry. The latter married his cousin Martha Stinson, daughter of Elijah and Mary (Henderson) Stinson and lived for a time in Warminster, but removed later to Richboro, Northampton township where he died August 10, 1849, aged 58 years.

Robert Darrah, eldest son of James and Rachel (Henderson) Darrah, was born on his grandfather's homestead in New Britain, February 8, 1789, and removed with his parents to the Warminster homestead at the age of nine years, and spent the remainder of his days there. He was an ensign in the war of 1812. Among the cherished mementoes now owned by the family are three swords, that of Captain Henry Darroch, of the Revolution; the sword of Ensign Robert Darrah of the war of 1812 and that of Lieutenant Robert Henderson Darrah of the Civil war. Robert Darrah was an industrious and enterprising farmer and accumulated a considerable estate. He had a sawmill on the farm which he operated in connection with his farming. He also had a lime kiln and burned the lime used on his plantation. He early realized the value of a dairy and gave much attention to this branch of husbandry, marketing the product in Philadelphia. He married September 4, 1819, Catharine Galt of Lancaster county, born January 26, 1799, a woman of fine intellectual ability and both she and her husband took a deep interest in and devoted their energies and means to the cause of morality, temperance, education and religion. In 1835, at the urgent request of his wife, he erected a school house on his farm which was afterwards enlarged and in connection with Josepn Hart and others secured college graduates as teachers for their own and their neighbors children for many years. In 1849, he built a fine stone mansion house on the Bristol Road and retired from active farming, introducing water, bath, any many modern improvements, and this was the happy home of his family for forty years. His wife entered into all his plans and was his wise and prudent adviser. She lived to the good old age of ninety-one years, surviving her husband thirty years, he having died August 5, 1860. The Darrahs were of strong Scotch-Irish Presbyterian stock. For more than a century the family have occupied the same pew in the historic Neshaminy Church, and the first two generations were intimately associated with the equally historic church at Deep Run, near their first Bucks county home, then presided over by Rev. Francis McHenry. Robert Darrah left a family of three sons and six daughters. His eldest son, Rev. James A. Darrah, born in 1821, was one of the pioneer home missionaries and teachers in the West. He graduated at Princeton in 1840 and studied law under Judge John Fox at Doylestown and was admitted to the bar in 1843. But feeling called to the ministry he took a three years' course in the Theological Seminary of Yale College and was licensed to preach by the Presbytery of Philadelphia September 23, 1846. For some months he labored as a missionary at Winchester, Va., and then removed to St. Louis, Mo., where he was pastor of a church and principal of the preparatory department of Webster college for nine years and then was called to the pastorate of a church at West Ely, Mo. He died at Zanesville,

Ohio, Feb. 24, 1882. The other children of Robert and Catharine (Galt) Darrah were, Rachel H., first wife of Rev. D. K. Turner, the eminent Presbyterian divine of Hartsville, lately deceased; Eliza M., who married Dr. Freeland of Chester county; Emily, the mother of the subject of this sketch; Rebecca, the second wife of Rev. D. K. Turner; Mary A., who died unmarried; John M., of Hartsville; Kate, who married Theodore R. Graham of Philadelphia; and ·R. Henderson, still residing on the homestead.

Prior to the death of her husband Dr. Joseph D. Nichols, Mrs. Nichols returned to Bucks county and resided with her mother at the old stone mansion, on the Bristol road now owned by the subject of this sketch, her son M. S. Prentiss Nichols, where she died in 1898.

H. S. Prentiss Nichols came to Philadelphia in 1872, and since that time has had a home in the old homestead on the Bristol Road at Hartsville, Bucks county, though most of his time has been spent in Philadelphia. He graduated from the college department of the University of Pennsylvania in 1879; studied law and was admitted to the bar of Philadelphia county, where he has since practiced with success, and has since been admitted to practice at the Bucks county bar. He is a member of the Bucks county Historical Society and takes a lively interest in Bucks county, the home of his distinguished maternal ancestors. He is a member of the Pennsylvania Society of the Sons of the Revolution.

He married, June 4, 1895, Isabel McIlhenny, of Germantown, daughter of John and Berenice (Bell) McIlhenny, both natives of the north of Ireland, now living in Germantown, but formerly of North Carolina, where Mrs. Nichols was born. Mr. and Mrs. Nichols reside at 346 Pelham Road, Germantown, but the summer months are generally spent at their country home at Hartsville, Bucks county.

HENRY SYLVESTER JACOBY, Professor of Bridge Engineering, in Cornell University, Ithaca, New York, was born April 8, 1857, in Springfield township, Bucks county, Pennsylvania, between Bursonville and Springtown, and is a son of Peter L. and Barbara (Shelly) Jacoby, both of German descent.

The paternal ancestor of Professor Jacoby came to Pennsylvania, as is supposed, prior to 1750, but little is known of him. His widow Elizabeth survived him many years, dying at an advanced age at the home of her son-in-law, Andreas Schneider, in Richland, about 1790, letters of administration being granted on her estate January 9, 1790.

Her children as shown by the distribution account filed were: Conrad, "eldest son," Henry, who settled in Lower Mount Bethel township, Northampton county; George, who settled in Lehigh county; John, who settled in York county; and Margaret, who married Andreas Schneider, of Richland, a native of Zweibrucken, who came to this country in 1759. Margaret, probably the youngest of the Jacoby family, was born January 6, 1749, and died March 22, 1828.

Conrad Jacoby was born June 7, 1730, and was certainly in Bucks county May 18, 1751, when a warrant for survey for a tract of land in Bedminster township, Bucks county, was issued to him. His later Bucks county residence was in Milford township, the threshold of German immigration into the county of Bucks. On April 1, 1768, he purchased of Jacob Geil 220 1-2 acres of land in Springfield township, on the line of Durham township. In this deed he is styled "Conrad Jacobi, of Lower Milford township, Blacksmith." This farm is on the road from Bursonville to Durham, and adjoins the farm still owned by Professor Henry S. Jacoby, on the northeast. On March 6, 1787, he purchased a farm of 152 acres in Bedminster township, the present residence of Gideon S. Rosenberger, and lived thereon until his death March 26, 1795. On April 11, 1791, he purchased 259 acres in Durham township, being Nos. 5 and 6 of the Durham tract, and adjoining his Springfield purchase. This tract he conveyed to his sons, Peter and John and John Reigle, respectively, in 1792 and 1793. His wife Hannah died November 27, 1828, at the age of ninety-nine years six months, and is buried at St. Peter's German Reformed church, in Leidytown, her later days having been spent with her youngest son, Leonard, in Hilltown township. Conrad Jacoby is buried in the graveyard of the old Tohickon church at Church Hill. He and his wife Hannah were the parents of nine children: John, Philip, Peter, Benjamin, Margaret, Catharine, Elizabeth, Henry and Leonard. John lived on the Durham land conveyed to him by his father in 1793, until his death as did his brother Peter. Philip lived for a time in Nockamixon, and from 1783 to 1787 he lived on a farm of 196-½ acres at Stony Point, in Springfield township. He then removed to Hilltown township, where he died in 1827. Benjamin settled in Haycock township on a tract of 165 acres, patented to him as No. 15 of the Lottery Lands in 1789, near Haycock Run postoffice, where he lived until his death. One of the daughters, either Margaret or Catharine, married a Woolsleyer. Elizabeth married (first) John Fluck, and after his death married Robert Darroch, Jr., and they resided in Bensalem township, Bucks county, during the latter part of their lives. Henry lived for a time in Bedminster, removed thence to Gwynedd, and a year later to Andalusia, Bensalem township, Bucks county. Leonard lived for fifty years near the Mennonite meeting house in Hilltown, and then removed to Allentown.

Peter Jacoby, third son of Conrad and Hannah, was born in Bucks county on New Years day, 1759. He learned the trade of a blacksmith with his father, and probably followed it for a number of years. On June 9, 1792, he purchased of his father seventy-one acres of the Durham tract No. 6. He built in 1801 the stone house and later the barn, both of which are still standing, and later, purchasing other land adjoining, lived there all his life. While attending the February term of court, 1815, as a juror, he was taken ill and died March 11, 1815. He was a member of Durham Reformed church, a trustee of the church from its organization and was later an elder. He married Catharine Trauger, born September 29, 1763, died September 4, 1844; daughter of Christian and Ann Drager (Trauger) of Nockamixon. The former, born March 30, 1726, in Bechenbach, grand duchy of Hesse Darmstadt, came to Pennsylvania in the ship "Restoration," arriving in Philadelphia, October 9, 1747, and died in Nockamixon, January 8, 1811. His wife, Anna Barbara, was born March 5, 1729, and died November 5, 1821. The children of Peter and Catharine (Trauger) Jacoby were: John, who settled in Doylestown township; Elizabeth, who married George Hartman, of Rockhill, who after living for twenty-seven years in that township, removed to near Bloomsburg, Pennsylvania; Mary, who married Jacob Hartman, of Rockhill; Benjamin, who finally settled in Springfield township; Barbara, who died in youth; Catharine, who married Frederick Laubach, of Lower Saucon, later of Durham township; Hannah, who married George Overpeck, of Springfield, and later removed to near Milton, Pennsylvania; Sarah, who died in youth; Peter, who lived and died on the old homestead in Durham; Samuel, who finally settled in Northumberland county, Pennsylvania; and Susannah, who married Jacob Schlieffer, of Springfield township.

Benjamin Jacoby, son of Peter and Catharine (Trauger) Jacoby, was born September 9, 1786. He was a mason by trade. In the fall of 1809 he married Margaret Landes, daughter of Samuel and Susannah Landes, and on September 10, 1810, purchased a small farm in Nockamixon, where he lived for six years, following his trade in summer and teaching school during the winter months. He then bought a farm of ninety acres two miles from Frenchtown,

New Jersey, where he lived until 1826, when he purchased the farm in Springfield, adjoining the farm purchased by his grandfather in 1768, and removed thereon. This farm has remained in the family ever since, and is now the property of the subject of this sketch. Here Benjamin Jacoby lived until the spring of 1839, when he rented the farm to his son, Peter L. Jacoby, and removed to the village of Springtown, where he lived until his death, October 29, 1850. He served for three months in the army during the war of 1812-14, his company being stationed at Marcus Hook, to guard the approach to Philadelphia after the burning of Washington in 1814. His wife Margaret died in 1827, and he married in 1829 Margaret, daughter of Peter Werst, who died September 26, 1844, without issue. The children of Benjamin and Margaret (Landes) Jacoby were: Samuel, who finally settled at Bethlehem, Pennsylvania; Peter L., who lived nearly all his life on the Springfield homestead; Catharine, who married Aaron Heckman and settled near Milton, Pennsylvania; Caroline, who married John Schlieffer, of Springfield; Susannah, who married Samuel Fulmer, of Springtown; Anna, who died in infancy; Benjamin L., who during his later years resided in Philadelphia; John L., who lived for some years in Springfield and later removed to Allentown, Pennsylvania; and Levi L., who was a minister of the German Evangelical association and stationed at various points in New York state, being located at Newark, New York, at the time of his death.

Peter L. Jacoby, second son of Benjamin and Margaret (Landes) Jacoby, was born in Nockamixon township, Bucks county, February 9, 1813, and, aside from teaching school for a brief period was a farmer all his life. He married, August 20, 1837, Barbara Shelly, daughter of John and Mary Shelly, of Milford township, Bucks county, and lived in Milford township until the spring of 1839, when he took charge of his father's farm in Springfield, renting it until his father's death, when he purchased it, later purchasing other land adjoining, and lived on the homestead until his death, July 3, 1876. With the exception of ten years residence in New Jersey and one year at a select private school, his whole life was spent in Bucks county. He was better educated than most men of his day in that vicinity, and appreciated the advantage of a higher education. He was a prosperous farmer, and actively interested in the important public interests of his neighborhood. His wife died at Bethlehem, June 12, 1904. Their eldest child, Mary Ann, died at the age of twenty-two years. Those who survive are: Titus S., now residing in Bethlehem; Amanda, who married Henry Unangst, of Williams township, Northampton county, Pennsylvania, and later settled near Pleasant Valley, Bucks county; Lewis Shelly, and John S., both now residing in Allentown, Pennsylvania; and Henry Sylvester, who now resides in Ithaca, New York.

Henry Sylvester Jacoby, born on the old homestead near Bursonville, April 8, 1857, was reared on the farm and attended the public school during the winter sessions, and during the summer months attended the private school of David W. Hess for eight years. He attended the Excelsior Normal Institute at Carversville, Bucks county, during the terms of 1870-72, and the preparatory department of Lehigh University, 1872-3. He then took the regular four-years course at Lehigh University, receiving the degree of Civil Engineer in 1877. During the season of 1878 he was stadia rodman on the Lehigh Topographical Corps, of the Second Geological Survey of Pennsylvania. From November, 1878, to November, 1879, he was engaged on surveys of the Red River, Louisiana, with the U. S. A. Corps of Engineers, under Major W. H. H. Benyaurd. From November, 1879, to March, 1885, he served as chief draughtsman in the United States Engineer's Office at Memphis, Tennessee. From May, 1885, to August, 1886, he was bookkeeper and cashier for G. W. Jones & Co., wholesale druggists in Memphis. From September, 1886, to June, 1890, he was instructor in civil engineering at his alma mater, Lehigh University. In September, 1890, he was elected assistant professor of Bridge Engineering and Graphics at Cornell University, was promoted to an associate professorship in the same department in 1894, and in 1900 was made full professor of Bridge Engineering in the University, and has since filled that position.

In August, 1887, he was admitted a member of the American Association for the Advancement of Science; was made a fellow of the Association in 1894; secretary of "Section D" in 1895, and vice president and chairman of Section D. (Mechanical science and Engineering) in 1901. On November 5, 1890, he became an associate of the American Society of Civil Engineers; in August, 1894, a member of the Society for the Promotion of Engineering Education, of which he was secretary 1900-1902. On February 22, 1888, he became a member of the Honorary Scientific Society of Tau Beta Pi, and of the Honorary Scientific Society of Sigma Xi on May 1, 1893.

Professor Jacoby, in addition to contributing numerous articles on Engineering and kindred subjects, for periodicals devoted to that science, is the author of the following publications: "Notes and Problems in Descriptive Geom-

erty," (1892); "Outlines of Descriptive Geometry" Part I, 1895, Part II, 1896, Part III, 1897; "A Text Book on Plain Lettering," (1897). He is joint author with Professor Mansfield Merriman of a "Text Book on Roofs and Bridges," in four volumes (1890-1898) embracing the following branches: Part I, "Stresses in Simple Trusses," 1888, entirely rewritten in 1904; Part II, "Graphic Statics," 1890, enlarged in 1897; Part III, "Bridge Design," 1894, re-written 1902; Part IV, "Higher Structures," 1898. Professor Jacoby served as editor of the Journal of the Engineering Society of Lehigh University for the years 1887-1890.

Professor Henry S. Jacoby married May 18, 1880, Laura Louise Saylor, daughter of Thomas S. and Emma A. Saylor, of Bethlehem, Pennsylvania, and they are the parents of three children, John Vincent, Hurlbut Smith, and Freeman Steel, all of whom reside with their parents at Ithaca, New York.

Professor Jacoby retains a lively interest in the affairs of his native county, and makes many extended visits to the old homestead in Springfield (the ownership of which he still retains), as well as to other points of Bucks county, taking a proper and commendable pride in his Bucks county ancestry.

PHILIP H. FRETZ. Among the representatives of the old and honored families of Bucks county who, with their respective ancestors, have witnessed the settlement and development of our beloved county from a primitive wilderness, inhabited by a primitive race, to a thickly settled, prosperous, wealthy and enlightened community, is Philip H. Fretz, of Doylestown township. He was born in the township in which he still resides, November 22, 1846, and is a son of Philip K. and Anna (Stover) Fretz, the ancestors of both of whom had been prominent factors in the development of the natural resources of Bucks county, those of the latter being the pioneer millers of Tinicum and Bedminster and her emigrant ancestor being Henry Stauffer, who emigrated from Alsace in 1749 and settled in Bedminster soon after that date. His son Jacob, born May 13, 1757, was the grandfather of Mrs. Fretz, and Henry, son of the last named, born October 17, 1786, was her father. Her mother was Barbara Stout, daughter of Isaac Stout, of Williams township, Northampton county, and a granddaughter of Jacob Stout, the emigrant ancestor of the Stout family of Bucks, an account of whom is given in this work. Barbara was educated at the Moravian school at Bethlehem, and her husband, Henry S. Stover, at the Doylestown Academy, under the Rev. Uriah Dubois, both receiving unusual advantages in this respect for their day and generation.

The paternal ancestor of Mr. Fretz was John Frets, who with a brother, Christian emigrated from Manheim, in Baden, Rhenish Prussia, about 1720, and settled for a time in Upper Salford, now Montgomery county, where he married Barbara Meyer, daughter of Hans Meyer, who bore him five children—John, Jacob, Christian, Abraham and Elizabeth. In 1737 John Fretz settled in Bedminster township, Bucks county, where he purchased 300 acres of land and lived until his death in February, 1772.

Christian Fretz, son of John and Barbara, born in Upper Salford, May, 1734, was reared in Bedminster township, Bucks county, and married in 1757 Barbara Oberhotzer, born November 10, 1737, died May 8, 1823, daughter of Martin Oberholtzer, who was born near Frankfort-on-the-Main in 1709, and settled in Bedminster soon after attaining manhood. Christian Fretz, on attaining manhood, settled in Tinicum township, where he lived until his father's death, when, having inherited the old homestead, he returned to Bedminster, where he died May 1, 1803. During the boyhood and early manhood of Christian Fretz the Indians were still quite numerous in that vicinity, and tradition relates many incidents of the association of the family with the "noble red man." At the time of the death of Barbara Fretz, widow of Christian, in 1823, she was the mother of twelve children, one hundred and nine grandchildren, and one hundred and three great-grandchildren. The children were: John; Agnes, wife of Abraham Bebighouse; Joseph; Henry; Martin; Jacob; Abraham; Isaac; Barbara, wife of Henry Fretz; Christian; Mary, wife of Henry Tyson; and Elizabeth, wife of Abraham Meyer.

John Fretz, eldest son of Christian and Barbara, was born in Bedminster, May 24, 1758, and was reared in the Mennonite faith, his parents being members of the old Deep Run Meeting, the oldest Mennonite congregation in Bucks county. He purchased land adjoining the homestead in Bedminster, and lived there until 1792, when he purchased 300 acres of the Rodman tract in Warwick, now Doylestown township, and settled thereon, building in 1795 the stone house which was standing until about 1898. He later purchased considerable adjoining land, owning at one time 800 acres along both sides of the Neshaminy, marked on the old maps of the region as "Fretz Valley." He died December 20, 1804. His wife was Anna Kratz, born in Plumstead township, November 4, 1764. She died August 4, 1813. John and Anna Kratz Fretz were the parents of nine children, viz: Christian; Susan, wife of William Garges; Elizabeth, wife of

Thomas Z. Smith; Mary, wife of Henry Gill; John; Rachel, wife of Abraham F. Stover; Barbara, wife of John Smith; Anna, wife of Samuel Dungan, and Philip, died young.

Christian, eldest son of John and Anna (Kratz) Fretz, was born in Bedminster township, November 17, 1782, and was reared from the age of ten on the Fretz Valley farm in Doylestown township, where he spent the remainder of his life. He was a successful business man and acquired considerable real estate. He was a farmer and hotelkeeper, establishing the "Fretz Valley Inn," near the homestead on the Easton road, opposite the almshouse, which he conducted for a number of years. He died January 28, 1840. He married April 14, 1808, Mary Stover, daughter of Ralph and Catharine (Funk) Stover, and granddaughter of Henry Stauffer above referred to, and a great-granddaughter on the maternal side of the pioneer, Bishop Henry Funck.

Ralph Stover, father of Mary (Stover) Fretz, was born in Bedminster, Bucks county, January 10, 1760, and died there November 7, 1811. He was one of the prominent business and public men of his time. For many years a justice of the peace, he did a large amount of legal business pertaining to the transfer of real estate and the settlement of estates. He was a member of state assembly from 1783 to 1799, and was one of the first board of directors of the poor, created under act of assembly of April 10, 1807, and superintended the erection of the almshouse opposite the Fretz homestead. His daughter Mary was born December 15, 1787, and died in New York, where she had gone to undergo a surgical operation, November 17, 1855. The children of Christian and Mary (Stover) Fretz were six in number, as follows:

1. Ralph Stover Fretz, born in Warwick, November 13, 1809, died in California, June 6, 1867. He had an eventful career. Early in life he engaged in business in Philadelphia and later in New York city. At the latter place he met Commodore Garrison and became interested with him in several important enterprises. For some years he ran a line of steamboats on the Mississippi river, and later engaged in a trading and shipping enterprise with Commodore Garrison at the Isthmus of Panama, in which he was later joined by his brothers John and Christian Augustus. In 1849 he sailed from the Isthmus to San Francisco, where in connection with the commodore he established a bank and amassed a fortune of a half million of dollars. The eighth clause of his will reads as follows:

"Eighth: Considering that I have been greatly blessed and that I have an undying attachment to the Government of the United States, the country of my birth, and remembering that by reason of my age and infirmities during the recent unnatural rebellion to destroy it, I was unable to render service in the field to put down and punish that great crime, and being not unmindful that a huge public burden of indebtedness has been necessarily incurred in accomplishing that object, I -desire not only to leave behind me when I am gone an humble testimonial of the gratitude I feel towards those whose virtues, valor and sacrifice and services preserved what I regard as the best government man was ever permitted to have, but beyond that and in addition to paying the ordinary taxes on my estate, I think it my duty out of the means Providence in His bounty has enabled me to acquire, and the Laws of the Country has aided me to preserve, to do something towards extinguishing the National Debt; Therefore moved thereto by the foregoing causes only, I hereby give and bequeath unto the Secretary of the Treasury of the United States of America, in trust and to be applied only towards cancelling the National Dollars, the sum of Twenty Thousand Dollars." Dated at San Francisco, May 1, 1867.

2. John Fretz, born October 2, 1811, in Warwick, died at White Sulphur Springs, California, where he was operating a gold quartz mill, June 26, 1863. He had also been associated with his brothers in enterprises at Panama. Neither of the above were married.

3. Philip Kratz Fretz, see forward.

4. Elizabeth Fretz, born February 23, 1818, in Doylestown township, died there February 9, 1897, married John Farren, of Lancaster county, Pennsylvania, January 1, 1844. He was born March 1, 1809, and died in Doylestown township December 16, 1878. He was a contractor, and was associated with his brother-in-law, Philip K. Fretz, in railroad building, etc. He and his family were members of the Roman Catholic church. Their children were: Mary Jannetta and Frances Annetta, who died in infancy; John Augustus, born April 21, 1855, died December 17, 1884, married January 25, 1882, Alleta Bleiler; he left no issue. Mary Cecilla Farren, born February 21, 1858, died; married June 16, 1881, Samuel J. Penrose, and has left children, Cyril F., Ralph and Norman.

5. Christian Augustus Fretz, born February 23, 1824, died December 1, 1859. He was a provision merchant at Panama for seven years prior to his death. He was never married.

6. Mary Catharine Fretz, born January 13, 1827, died March 4, 1842, unmarried.

Philip K. Fretz, third son of Christian and Mary (Stover) Fretz, was born on the old homestead at Fretz valley, now Doylestown township, September

14, 1813, and died on board the steamship "Henry Chauncey" off the coast of the Carolinas, March 13, 1867, while on his way to California. Mr. Fretz was one of the prominent men of his community, not in the sense of seeking or holding public office, but in the doing day by day, as occasion offered, those things that tend to uplift humanity and stimulate in others that love of country and home which is the sheet-anchor of American liberties and citizenship. He inherited from his forefathers a stern sense of duty, a loving and jovial disposition, and an unswerving directness in following the course which his conscience dictated as right and proper. One who knew him well has said of him, "To write of him as he was known is to write of the day by day life of the earnest loving Christian who had at heart first, his township, then his county, next his state and finally the best country that God Almighty ever made." At the time of the civil war he was one of the foremost in calling meetings to raise funds to clear his district and neighbors of the draft, and, when the money could not be raised in time, advanced it himself and went to Philadelphia and cleared his district of the draft. He was president of the Democratic club of Pennsylvania before and during the civil war. About 1850 the cholera, which was prevalent in many parts of the country, broke out with great virulence at the almshouse, and many of the inmates died of the dread disease, several in a single day, and it was impossible to obtain assistance to bury the dead or care for the living; the steward was dying of the disease, and his son was already dead and unburied, when Mr. Fretz, after removing his wife and family to her father's residence at Erwinna, with Davis E. Brower, went to the almshouse and worked till the scourge was abated. Being unable to find an undertaker who would bury the steward's young son, he secured a hearse and buried the lad himself.

Mr. Fretz succeeded his father as proprietor of the Fretz Valley Inn, which he conducted until January 9, 1846, the first anniversary of the birth of his daughter, Mary Catharine, when he cut down the sign pole and closed the inn as a public house. He was extensively engaged in contract work in connection with his brother-in-law, John Farren, and was one of the contractors to build the horse-shoe curve of the Pennsylvania railroad over the Allegheny mountains. He was buried in the Atlantic ocean. His wife, Anna Stover, whom he married February 18, 1841, was born in Tinicum township, at Point Pleasant, where her father, Henry S. Stover, was an extensive miller, September 11, 1812. She was a fitting helpmate for an earnest loving husband. Their children were: Charles Augustus, born May 31, 1843, married Susan Derby, and resided on the homestead until his death, August 12, 1900, without issue; Mary Catharine, born January 9, 1845, married September 8, 1868, Theodore P. Austin, of Hancock county, Maine; Philip H. and John S. Anna (Stover) Fretz died at the residence of her son, Philip Henry, Fretz, October 8, 1889.

Philip Henry Fretz, second son of Philip K. and Anna (Stover) Fretz, was born on the old homestead, in Doylestown township, November 22, 1846. He was educated at the public schools of Doylestown and at the famous Tennent School, at Hartsville. On arriving at manhood he went to New York city, where he engaged for a short time in the manufacture of silver plate. He sailed from New York for San Francisco, where he engaged in the banking business for a short time, and then returned to the old home in Doylestown township. His partner in the banking business was Judge Pratt, of California. The return trip was made overland across the plains by stage coach, having for traveling companion on the trip his uncles' old partner, Commodore Garrison. In 1871 he erected the buildings and handsome residence now occupied by his brother, John S. Fretz, and married and lived there until 1879, when, having erected his present handsome residence one mile south of Doylestown, he moved there and has since made it his home, operating his farm and looking after his other properties. He is the owner of the old Turk mills, one of the oldest mill properties in this section, it having been operated by Hugh Miller as early as 1745. Mr. Fretz is a broad-minded and public-spirited man and is interested in whatever inures to the benefit of the community in which he lives. He has been an elder of Doylestown Presbyterian church for nearly thirty years. He was largely instrumental in the building of the chapel at Edison, which was placed under the control of the sessions of the Doylestown Presbyterian church, and is used for Sunday school purposes. Mr. Fretz being the superintendent of the Sunday school held there, and which by the way is said to be the oldest Sunday school ever held in Eastern Pennsylvania outside of Philadelphia. It was originally held in the old school house at Edison, which was originally built by and for the use of the neighborhood, long before the days of the public school system, and was rented by the directors after the organization of the public schools for some years, the upper story being used for religious and other local meetings. After the school directors erected another school house, the old one was sold and the proceeds with liberal contributions from the neighbors

was used to erect the present chapel on land donated by Aaron Fries. In 1881 Philip H. Fretz was elected to the office of justice of the peace and filled the same for one term of five years. He was one of the original directors and managers of the Bucks County Trust Company at its organization in 1888, and still fills that position.

Philip H. Fretz married, September 19, 1871, Margaret Wilhelmina Johnston, born in Doylestown township, June 1, 1848, daughter of Robert and Wilhelmina (McHenry) Johnston. Her father, Robert Johnston, was born in Doylestown township, December 5, 1817. He died January 25, 1905. He was a son of David and Susanna (Riale) Johnston. His father, David Johnston, was a son of Robert Johnston, an early settler in Huntingdon county, and died in Doylestown township, October 28, 1867. He was a soldier in the war of 1812 under Captain William Magill. His wife Susanna Riale, was a daughter of John Riale, Esq., of Scotch-Irish descent. She died August 26, 1866, in her ninety-sixth year. Wilhelmina McHenry, mother of Mrs. Fretz, was born in the old Ross Mansion at Doylestown, April 6, 1818, and was a daughter of Captain William McHenry, who was born 9 mo. 22, 1794, and died 10 mo. 22, 1880. He was a son of William and Mary (Stewart) McHenry, both of whom were of Scotch-Irish descent, the former, born May 6, 1744, died November 25, 1808, was a son of the Rev. Francis McHenry, the first settled pastor of Deep Run and Red Hill Presbyterian churches, and one of the ablest divines of his time. He was born on the island of Rathlen, Ireland, October 18, 1710, and came to this country when a lad of fourteen and was educated at the famous Tennent Log College at Neshaminy. He was licensed to preach in 1738, and preached for a time at Neshaminy Presbyterian church, and Deep Run. In 1748 he took charge of Deep Run and Red Hill churches and settled in Bedminster, where he died January 22, 1757. His son Charles was a lieutenant in the continental army. Mr. and Mrs. Philip H. Fretz have been the parents of six children: Dr. John Edgar Fretz, of Easton, Pennsylvania; Anna Leola Fretz, residing with her parents, Ralph Johnston, deceased; Philip H., deceased; Marguerite Wilhelmina, now a student, preparing for Bryn Mawr; and Edna McHenry, died February 21, 1897.

Dr. John Edgar Fretz was born in Doylestown township, November 29, 1872, and was educated at Lafayette College, graduating in the class of 1893. He graduated at medical deparment of Pennsylvania University in 1897. He began the practice of medicine at Easton. He was recently honored by the offer of the position of physician and professor of hygiene, anatomy and physiology, in Williams' College, at Williams-town, Massachusetts, to fill the vacancy caused by the death of Professor Luther Dana Woodbridge, M. D. He however, chose to follow his profession at Easton, where he has a lucrative practice. He was married, December 7, 1904, to Frances Josephine Rodenbough, daughter of Joseph S. Rodenbough, of Easton.

Ralph Johnston Fretz, second son of Philip H. Fretz, was born February 25, 1878, and died December 24, 1899. He prepared for college under Dr. John Gosman, of Doylestown, and entered Lafayette College in the class of 1901, and had returned home to spend the Christmas holidays, when he was taken suddenly ill with acute myelitis, and lived but three days. He was a bright manly boy and much beloved by his family and class mates, and his sudden and untimely demise was a sad blow.

John S. Fretz, youngest son of Philip K. and Anna (Stover) Fretz, was born on the old Fretz Valley homestead in Doylestown township, September 22, 1850. He was but seventeen years of age at the death of his father, and resided for some years with his brother, Philip Henry Fretz, the subject of the preceding sketch. In 1879 he purchased of his brother his present residence, and has since made it his home. He soon after erected and equipped a large steam saw mill near his residence, which he has operated for many years. He is a member of the Doylestown Presbyterian church, and takes an active interest in all charitable objects. He is the owner of the old Fretz homestead that has been the home of his ancestors for over a century. He married, in November, 1879, Mary W. Long, daughter of Henry Long, of Doylestown, and they are the parents of one son, Augustus Henry Fretz, who graduated at Lafayette College in the class of 1903, and is now taking a post graduate course there in mechanical engineering.

THE HALL FAMILY. The pioneer ancestor of this family was Mathew Hall, who came from Birmingham, England, about 1725, and settled in Buckingham township, Bucks county, Pennsylvania, where he married in 1731 Sarah (Scarborough) Haworth, widow of George Haworth, daughter of John and Mary Scarborough, and granddaughter of John Scarborough, a coachsmith of St. Sepulchre, London, England, who came to America in 1682 accompanied by his son John. Sarah was born in Solebury township, Bucks county, Pennsylvania, 2 mo. 4, 1694, and married George Haworth at Falls Meeting, 9 mo. 20, 1710. Mr. Haworth, who died in 1725, purchased 500 acres on the north cor-

ner of Buckingham and settled thereon, and at his demise was seized of 339 acres thereof which descended to his six children; George, Stephanus, Absalom, James, Mary, who became the wife of John Michener; and John. Of these George and John remained in Bucks county, the former dying in 1749, and James and Absalom removed to the Shenandoah valley in Virginia. Mathew Hall settled on the land belonging to the estate of his wife's first husband, nearly the whole of which he subsequently purchased of his step-children. His wife died 3 mo. 4, 1748, and on 7 mo. 13, 1750, he married Rebecca (Rhoads) Massey, widow of Mordecai Massey, of Marple, Delaware county, Pennsylvania, and daughter of Joseph and Abigail Rhoads. On 8 mo. 3, 1752, with a certificate to Haverford Meeting, he removed with his family to Blockley, Philadelphia, where he purchased a large tract of land, and in 1756 removed to Marple, Delaware county, and purchased 194 acres of land there, whereon he died 9 mo. 1766. His second wife, by whom he had no children, died prior to his death. He was not a member of the Society of Friends on his arrival in Bucks county, but became a member after his first marriage. He was an overseer of Springfield (Chester county,) Meeting from 3 mo. 28, 1757, to 3 mo. 23, 1759. The children of Mathew and Sarah (Scarborough) (Haworth) Hall were as follows: 1. David, born in Buckingham, 7 mo. 7, 1732, died in Marple, Delaware county, 1802. He married, 12 mo. 21, 1758, Deborah Fell, daughter of Edward Fell, of Springfield, and had children: Beulah, who married William Broomall; David, who married Hannah Parnell; Sarah, who married Joseph Levis; Edward and Joseph. 2. Mahlon, born in Buckingham 11 mo. 12, 1733-34; see forward. 3. Margery, born 1 mo. 23, 1734-35, married, 11 mo. 10, 1753, at Merion Meeting, Arnold Warner, of Blockley, son of Isaac and Veronica Warner, of Blockley, and had four daughters, of whom Gulielma, wife of William Widdifield, was for many years an accepted minister of Friends in Philadelphia. 4. Sarah, born 11 mo. 24, 1736-37, married at Buckingham Meeting, 5 mo. 12, 1756, John Pearson, and had children, Enoch, Margaret, Mahlon and William. The family removed to Bush River, South Carolina, in 1772, with the exception of Enoch, who removed to Gunpowder, Maryland, in 1780.

Mahlon Hall, second son of Mathew and Sarah Hall, born in Buckingham, 11 mo. (January) 12, 1733-34, took a certificate from Buckingham Meeting to Falls in 1752, and from there to Chester Meeting in 1756. He married at Bristol, Bucks county, 4 mo. 21, 1757, Jane Higgs, daughter of James and Elizabeth (Andrews) Higgs, of Bristol. Jane was born 8 mo. 17, 1728, and died 5 mo. 10, 1812. On their marriage they settled on a tract of land in Blockley township, Philadelphia, devised to him by his father later, much of which is now within the limits of the park. It adjoined Belmont, the residence of Judge Peters, and Lansdowne, the residence of Governor John Penn, the last of the colonial governors. Mahlon Hall related to his granddaughter, Matilda Heston, that during the revolutionary war a party of British soldiers visited his home, and the officer in command after some conversation with Mahlon Hall told him that he was a native of Birmingham, England, and on learning that the father of Mahlon Hall was also a native of that place gave strict orders that nothing about the place should be disturbed by the soldiers. Mahlon Hall died 7 mo. 26, 1818, and he and his wife are buried at Merion Meeting. Their children were as follows: 1. John, born at Blockley, 6 mo. 16, 1758, died there 1 mo 17, 1842, married, 11 mo. 21, 1783, Anna Morris, daughter of Edward Morris, of Montgomery township, now Montgomery county, Pennsylvania; she died 6 mo. 17, 1845, aged ninety-one years; they had children: Martha, who married Nathan Dickinson, and was the mother of Mahlon Hall Dickinson, late president of the State Board of Charities, and an eminent Philadelphian; James, George, John, Morris, Hannah, Sarah and Charles. 2. Mahlon, born 11 mo. 29, 1759, died 4 mo. 7, 1805; see forward. 3. Sarah, born 4 mo. 16, 1763, died 8 mo. 18, 1856, married 11 mo. 18, 1784, Edward Warner Heston, the founder of Hestonville, now part of the city of Philadelphia. She was his second wife, he having previously married Mary Griffith, by whom he had children; Abraham, Isaac, Bathsheba, Mary, who married Mahlon Hall; Jacob F. and Thomas W. The children of the second wife, Sarah Hall, were; Jane, who married Joseph Worstall, of Newtown, Bucks county, in 1808; Rachel, Anna, Matilda, Isaac, Sarah, William Penn and Louisa.

Mahlon Hall, second son of Mahlon and Jane (Higgs) Hall, was born in Blockley township, Philadelphia county, 11 mo. 29, 1759. He married, 5 mo. 15, 1791, Mary Heston, born 3 mo. 26, 1775, died 12 mo. 12, 1858, daughter of Edward Warner and Mary (Griffith) Heston, of Blockley, before mentioned. Edward Warner Heston was born in Bucks county, and was a son of Jacob and Mary (Warner) Heston, of Makefield, and a grandson of Zebulon and Dorothy Heston, early settlers in Wrightstown, Bucks county. He inherited from his father the lands at what was named Hestonville, in Blockley township, and was the founder of the village. He was an officer of the Seventh Battalion,

Pennsylvania Militia, during the revolution and saw active service and was subsequently one of the judges of the court of common pleas of Philadelphia county. His second wife was a sister of Mahlon Hall, who married his daughter. On his marriage Mahlon Hall erected a house on what is now Elm avenue, West Philadelphia, close to Fairmount Park, where he died 4 mo. 7, 1805. He was an active business man of Philadelphia. His widow married William Sanders, born 5 mo. 22, 1810. Mahlon and Mary (Heston) Hall were the parents of nine children: 1. Edward H., born at Hestonville, 4 mo. 30, 1792, died in Columbiana county, Ohio, 4 mo. 10, 1831, married at West Chester, Pennsylvania, 2 mo. 5, 1816, Jane Paxson, daughter of Benjamin and Jane (Ely) Paxson, of Solebury, and removed to Ohio in 1820. 2. Mahlon, born 3 mo. 11, 1793, died in Doylestown township, Bucks county, 11 mo. 3, 1872; see forward. 3. Thomas W., born 3 mo. 4, 1795, died in Caln township, Chester county, 4 mo. 7, 1896, aged over one hundred and one years; he married Mary Heston, daughter of Abraham Heston, and had nine children. 4. Isaac, born 4 mo. 29, 1796, died 4 mo. 21, 1810. 5. John, born 8 mo. 17, 1797, died 2 mo. 3, 1897, at West Chester. He married, 10 mo. 23, 1862, Sarah (Thatcher) Yarnall, a widow, who survives him. He was a farmer at Hestonville for many years and removed to West Chester in 1872. 6. Jane, born 11 mo. 24, 1798, died at West Chester, 10 mo. 4, 1876, unmarried. 7. William H., born 1 mo. 21, 1801, died in West Chester, 5 mo. 20, 1886, married Ann Paxson, but had no children. 8. Sarah, born 12 mo. 28, 1802, died at West Chester, 2 mo. 3, 1900, married Edward Dickinson, leaving no issue. 9. Ann, born 3 mo. 29, 1804, died 12 mo. 23, 1813. This family was very remarkable for longevity, one of them having exceeded the century mark, another came short of it but six months, while four others passed four score years.

Mahlon Hall, second son of Mahlon and Mary (Heston) Hall, born at Hestonville, Philadelphia, March 11, 1793, was the father of Mathias H. Hall and the grandfather of William W. Hall, sketches of whom follow. He was a blacksmith by trade, and came to Buckingham, near Pineville, Bucks county, when a young man and followed his trade there for some years, returning later to Philadelphia where he was a partner with his brother John in the milk business. Subsequently he removed again to Bucks county, and in 1836 purchased a farm of fifty acres in Doylestown township, where his son, Isaac H. Hall, still lives, and thereon died November 3, 1872. He married (first) Hannah P. Hampton, of Buckingham, by whom he had five children: Thomas, a prominent business man of Philadelphia; John; William; Moses P., for many years a merchant in Buckingham; and Benjamin, the father of Squire Hall. Mr. Hall married (second) Isabella Robinson, daughter of John Robinson, who was a soldier in the war of 1812 and stationed at Marcus Hook, by whom he had twelve children, of whom eleven survived him: Mary, who never married; Hannah, who married her cousin, Albert P. Hall, son of Edward H. and Jane (Paxson) Hall, who is a dry goods merchant at West Chester, Pennsylvania; Jane H., who married William Seal; Martha R., who married George Geil; Edward D.; Isaac H., who lives on the homestead in Doylestown township; Sarah D., who married J. Gilpin Seal; Matthias H., a prominent farmer of Upper Makefield township; Charles Henry; George W., and Emma P. Hall. Isabella (Robinson) Hall, widow of Mahlon Hall, died in Doylestown township, June 29, 1879.

Benjamin Hall, third son of Mahlon and Hannah P. (Hampton) Hall, was born in Bnuckingham, Bucks county, Pennsylvania, September 30, 1823, and resides with his son, William W. Hall, at Danboro. He went to Philadelphia when a boy, and for some time drove a milk wagon for his uncle. Returning to Bucks county he clerked in the store of his brother Thomas at Mechanics Valley until 1850, when in partnership with his brother, Moses P. Hall, he purchased the store at Buckingham, which they conducted for four years. On April 1, 1854, he purchased and removed to the present homestead farm at Danboro, where he resided for the following thirteen years. In April, 1867, he purchased a property at Smith's Corner in Plumstead township and opened a store, which he conducted for two years. He then removed to Mechanics Valley, where he conducted the store for six years, and in 1875 returned to the old homestead, where he has since resided. Mr. Hall was the pioneer milk shipper to Philadelphia market from Doylestown. He married Sarah Carlile, daughter of Benjamin and Elizabeth Carlile, of Plumstead, who was born on the present Hall homestead, where her father died January 9, 1833. Benjamin and Sarah (Carlile) Hall were the parents of two sons and a daughter, of whom William W., mentioned hereinafter, alone survives.

MATTHIAS H. HALL, third son of Mahlon and Isabella (Robinson) Hall, was born in Doylestown township, Bucks county, Pennsylvania, April 29, 1844. He was reared to the life of a farmer and acquired his education at the public schools of that vicinity. His whole life has been devoted to agricultural pursuits in the county of his birth. The following spring after his marriage he began farming for himself in Wrightstown township, and after five years' residence there he removed to Upper Makefield, and in 1883 purchased his present farm in that township, on the line of Wrightstown, near the site of the historic Indian village of Playwicky, where he has since resided. While conforming to the tenets of the Society of Friends. in which faith his paternal ancestors were reared, he is not a member of the society. Though deeply interested in the affairs of his county, state and nation, he has taken little part in partisan politics. He is an active member of the Bucks County Historical Society, and a regular attendant of its meetings. He recently contributed a valuable paper to its archives on the local history and folk-lore of his locality, so rich in historic interest as the border line between the original settlement of the pioneers of Penn's colony in America and the land taken up by their descendants and the later arrivals. He married, November 18, 1874, Sarah Wiggins, daughter of Jesse and Margaret (Hampton) Wiggins, of Wrightstown. She is a descendant of Benjamin Wiggins, one of the earliest settlers in the locality in which she lives, and who is said to have come thence from New England. He married in 1708, Susan Jenks, widow of Thomas Jenks, of Shropshire, England, on the borders of Wales, who came into Bucks county with her infant son Thomas, about 1700, and is the ancestress of the prominent family of that name in Bucks county. By her second marriage with Benjamin Wiggins she had one son, Benzaleel Wiggins, born in 1709, from whom the prominent family of that name as well as numerous others of Wrightstown, Buckingham. Solebury and Makefield are descended. The pioneer maternal ancestor of Mrs. Hall was John Hampton, of Ephingstoun, East Lothian, Scotland, who purchased land at Amboy Point, East Jersey, November 23, 1682, and later settled at Freehold, New Jersey, where he died in February, 1702-3, leaving sons: John, Joseph, Andrew, David, Jonathan and Noah. Joseph Hampton, his son by a second marriage with Jane Ogburn, widow of John Ogburn, and mother of Sarah Ogburn, wife of Edmund Kinsey, was one of the first ministers among Friends of Buckingham. Jane was four times married and came to Buckingham about 1720, then the widow Sharp, and died there in 1731. Joseph Hampton either accompanied or preceded his mother to Bucks county and located in Wrightstown. He married Mary, daughter of Thomas Canby and has left numerous descendants. He died in 1767, leaving two sons, John and Benjamin, and three daughters. The children of Matthias H. and Sarah (Wiggins) Hall are: Frances, Margaret, Hanna, Jesse, and Emma, all of whom reside with their parents.

WILLIAM W. HALL, only surviving son of Benjamin and Sarah (Carlile) Hall, was born in the village of Buckingham where his father and uncle Moses were at the time engaged in mercantile business, November 2, 1851. His parents removing to the present homestead in 1854, he was reared on the farm upon which he still resides and was educated in the schools of Plumstead township At the age of thirteen years, during the civil war, he and four companions went to Philadelphia and offered their services in the Union army. It is needless to say that their services were declined on account of their age. He returned home and entered the store at Buckingham as a clerk, remaining as such for eight years, and then returned to the farm. In politics Mr. Hall is a Republican and has taken an active interest in the councils of his party. He has held a number of local positions, and has been a justice of the peace since 1888. He has served as delegate to state and congressional conventions and as a member of the county committee. He is an active member of the Independent Order of Red Men, and has served as representative grand chief for five terms to the grand council of the order. He is also a past chief of the Knights of the Golden Eagle. Mr. Hall married, October 26, 1880, Anna Fry, daughter of Michael Fry, of Plumstead, and they are the parents of ten children: Chester Arthur; Roscoe C.; Nellie B., deceased; Warren Russell; Florence Ethel; Norman D.; Althea Fry; Eleanor E., deceased; and Sarah Esther, and Emma Pauline Hall.

HOWARD PURSELL, M. D. of Bristol, was born in Bridgeton (formerly Nockamixon) township, Bucks county, March 23, 1847, and is a son of Brice M. and Martha Merrick (Poore) Pursell.

The Purcell-Pursell family of Pennsylvania and New Jersey are descendants of the noble family of Purcell in Ireland, whose founder, Sir Hugh Purcell, was a grandson of Sir Hugh Purcell who went from Normandy to England with William the Conqueror, and traced his descent through many generations from Charlemagne of France. Sir Hugh Purcell is said to have been the first of the conquering Normans to land on British soil at Pevensey Bay, and the first to effect a deed of arms by storming the ruins of a Roman castle where a party of King Harold's soldiers lay entrenched. The Irish Purcells were adherents of the House of Stuart, and were swept away by the rebellion of 1641, though several distinct branches

of them later recovered their lands and titles at the restoration and were again badly broken on the accession of William of Orange.

John Purslone Pursley or Purssell, as his name is variously spelled, came to America from Dublin, Ireland, in the ship "Phoenix," arriving in the river Delaware in August, 1677, and settled in Bucks county. He was appointed constable for the "further side of Neshaminah" 7 mo. 9, 1685, and on the 8th of 7 mo. 1689, was again appointed constable for the "upper parts of the settlement, between Neshaminah and Poquessing." In the same year he appears as a witness in the Bucks county courts, and on being attested gives his age as "about sixty years." He was again appointed constable in 1690, for "upper parts of Neshaminah." He married in 1684, Elizabeth, widow of Thomas Walmsley, who with her husband and six children migrated from Yorkshire in 1682 and settled in Byberry, Philadelphia county, bringing a certificate from Settle Monthly Meeting of Friends in Yorkshire. At about the same date of the arrival of John Purslone in Bucks county, Thomas Purcil appears at Flatlands, Long Island. He acts as an appraiser in that town in 1679, and was one of the patentees of Newton, Long Island, in 1686. He or a son of his with the same name removed to the Raritan, in Somerset county, New Jersey, prior to 1703, and had children baptized at the Raritan Dutch Reformed church. The descendants of Thomas Pursell became numerous in Somerset, Middlesex and Essex counties, New Jersey, prior to 1760. In 1710 he purchased a large tract of land in Somerset county, though then living in Middlesex, and in 1719 conveyed one-half of it to his son Daniel, who in 1728 conveyed a part of it to Gysbert Krom, of Amwell township, Hunterdon county. A Daniel Purcell settled later in Alexandria township, Hunterdon county and in 1783 bought a tract of land in Tinicum, Bucks county, Pennsylvania, and erected a grist mill which he operated for two years. He then returned to Kingwood, New Jersey, where he died in 1804, leaving sons, Peter, Benjamin and Thomas, and daughters, Ruth Middleswarts, Sarah Tinsman and Hannah Jones.

On September 28, 1728, "Denes Purcell of Pennsylvania" married Ruth Cooper, daughter of Henry and Mary (Buckman) Cooper, of Newtown, Bucks county, and settled in Bethlehem township, Hunterdon county, New Jersey. Whether he was a son of John and Elizabeth (Walmsley) Purssell, of Bucks county, or of Thomas, of New Jersey, is problematical, but certain it is that Dennis and Ruth Cooper were the parents of John Pursell, "of Pennsylvania," who married in 1761 Ann Coone (Coomb), of

HOWARD PURSELL

Tinicum township, Bucks county, and settled in Nockamixon township, Bucks county, Pennsylvania, where he purchased land in 1773. Another John Pursell, also of Pennsylvania, married in 1765 Mary Logan, and settled in Falls township, Bucks county, where he died in 1778.

John Pursell, of Nockamixon, died in that township in December, 1804, and his will was probated February 5, 1805. It is probable that his father, Dennis Pursell, settled in Nockamixon while John was a young man, as a Denes Pursle was sergeant of the Nockamixon company of Associators in 1775, and, though John had a son Dennis, it is hardly probable that he could have been of sufficient age to have held a commission at that date. The children of John and Ann (Coomb) Pursell were: 1. John, Jr., who married Mercy Iliff, and died in 1816, leaving eleven children. 2. Thomas, who married Catherine Crause, and died in 1841, leaving six sons, Dennis, William, John, Thomas, Jacob and Frederick, and one daughter, Mary, who married Jacob Fulmer. 3. Brice, mentioned hereinafter. 4. Dennis, who went west and left no descendants in Bucks county. 5. Ruth, who became the wife of Daniel Strawn, born 1752, son of Jacob and Christiana (Pursell) Strawn, of Haycock, the former of whom was a half-brother of Ruth (Cooper) Pursell, by the second marriage of Mary (Buckman) Cooper with Launcelot Strawn. 6. Elizabeth, who became the wife of Benjamin Holden. 7. Mary. 8. Ann. 9. Hannah, who became the wife of John Williams, a son of Benjamin and Mercy Stevenson Williams. 10. Margaret. 11. Jane, who became the wife of Jacob Hauseworth. Mary, Ann and Hannah, aforementioned, were triplets; all grew to womanhood, married and all died at the birth of their first child. Either Mary or Ann married a Henry, and left a daughter Ann.

Brice Pursell, third son of John and Ann (Coomb) Pursell, was born in Nockamixon, August 15, 1776, and died there August 12, 1830. He lived on a portion of the homestead which had been devised to the three eldest sons, John, Thomas and Brice, and was partitioned between them in 1806. He later purchased considerable other land adjoining, becoming a large landholder and a man of prominence in that community. He was a justice of the peace for twenty-one years and performed a large amount of public business. He married Catharine Moore, who was born May 25, 1784, and died August 12, 1848, and they were the parents of nine children: 1. Ann, who became the wife of John Fisher. 2. Thomas, who married Eliza Marshall. 3. John, who married Sarah Williams. 4. Evaline, who became the wife of Abram Arndt. 5.

Brice Moore, mentioned hereinafter. 6. Hugh, who married Jane B. Eltonhead. 7. Daniel, who married three times; his first wife was Susanna Unangst; his second wife was Margaret Rebecca Eilenberger; and his thrid wife was Rachel Quinn. 8. Hannah, who became the wife of Cyrenius Slack, of Hunterdon county, New Jersey. 9. Mary, who died at the age of six years.

Brice Moore Pursell, father of Dr. Howard Pursell, was born in Nockamixon, August 31, 1811, and died there June 18, 1885. He was a farmer and lived on the old family homestead. He married, July 19, 1837, Martha Merrick Poore, born February 18, 1817, in Upper Makefield township, Bucks county, died in Bristol, Pennsylvania, May 2, 1902. She was a daughter of Daniel and Maria (Merrick) Poore; the former a son of John Poore, was born October 12, 1793, and died April 12, 1888, and the latter was born April 23, 1798 and died October 1, 1879. They were married May 2, 1815. The Merricks are descendants of John Merrick, a native of Herefordshire, England, who settled in Lower Dublin, Philadelphia county, prior to 1700. His son John Merrick was an early settler in Makefield, where he has left numerous descendants. Brice Moore and Martha M. (Poore) Pursell were the parents of four sons: 1. Augustus, born May 3, 1839, married November 12, 1868, Evalina Eilenberger, daughter of David and Susan (Arndt) Eilenberger, who bore him one child, Jessie Martha Pursell; Evalina's death occurred at his home in Muncy, Pennsylvania, July 27, 1904. 2. Horatio N., born December 4, 1841, died August 31, 1863, after his return from the civil war; he was unmarried. 3. Howard, born March 23, 1847, mentioned hereinafter. 4. Stacy, born November 20, 1849, married, April 22, 1885, Josephine K. Williams, daughter of Barzilla and Sarah (King) Williams, no issue.

Howard Pursell, third son of Brice and Martha M. (Poore) Pursell, was was born and reared in Nockamixon (now Bridgeton) township. He graduated from the medical department of the New York University, March 1, 1867, and practiced medicine at Ceres, New York, until 1869. In the latter year he removed to Bristol, Bucks county, Pennsylvania, where he has conducted a drug store and practiced medicine ever since. He is a member of the Bucks County Medical Society, the Medical Society of Pennsylvania, and the American Medical Association. He is president of the board of health of Bristol, which position he has held since 1893. He is a member of the board of United States examining surgeons for Bucks county. In politics he is a Republican. He is a past master of Bristol Lodge, No. 25, Free and Accepted Masons.

Dr. Pursell has been twice married, first on February 22, 1869, to Vestilla Smith, daughter of James and Achsah (Lear) Smith. His second marriage occurred at Milford, New Jersey, June 4, 1879, to Nellie Carpenter Bartolette, daughter of Dr. Charles R. and Ann M. (Carpenter) Bartolette. His children are as follows: James Everett, born June 12, 1870; Ethel Bartolette, born May 12, 1882; Charles Howard, born September 30, 1885, died February 18, 1886; and Carrie Nesbit, born February 2, 1888.

WILLIAM EDGAR GEIL, the distinguished author, traveller and orator, was born near Doylestown, Bucks county, Pennsylvania, and is the son of Samuel Geil, still residing in Doylestown, by his late wife Elizabeth Seese, deceased. On the paternal side Mr. Geil is of French and German descent. His great-grandfather, Jacob Geil, was born in the province of Alsace, in the year, 1742, and accompanied his parents to America in the ship "Duke of Bedford," arriving in Philadelphia, September 14, 1751. The family lived for a time in Philadelphia and then located on the Skippack, in what is now Montgomery county, Pennsylvania, where Jacob Geil married Anna, daughter of John Clymer (or Klemmer) and granddaughter of Bishop Valentine Klemmer, who came from Switzerland in 1717. By deed dated April 18, 1763, William Crook conveyed to him by name of "Jacob Choel, of Philadelphia county," 194 acres in Springfield township, Bucks county. He was a weaver by trade. On April 1, 1768, Jacob Geil and Anna his wife conveyed the Springfield farm to Conrad Jacoby, and on April 18, 1768, Samuel Barnhill and wife conveyed to him 153 acres near New Galena in New Britain township, Bucks county. Here his wife Anna died, and he married a second time and in 1786 sold his farm and removed with the younger members of his family to Chester county, and from thence to Rockingham county, Virginia, where he died about 1802. The children of Jacob Geil were: Mary, who married Samuel Godshalk, of New Britain; Abraham, John, Philip, and Margaret. The first two were by the first wife, and the last three by the second. Philip and Margaret were minors on their return to Bucks county in 1802, and guardians were appointed for them by the Bucks county court.

John Geil, son of Jacob, was born in New Britain, Bucks county, April 1, 1778, and removed with his father to Virginia, where he was apprenticed to the tanning trade, but, liking neither the trade or his master, he returned to Bucks county about 1796, and probably resided for a time with his elder brother, Abraham Geil. Abraham was a farmer, and later

located near Doylestown, where Samuel Hart now lives, and reared a family of eight children, of whom but two married, and none so far as known left male descendants. John Geil married April 22, 1802, Elizabeth Fretz, daughter of Mark Fretz, who owned and operated the grist and saw mills later known as Curley's Mills, in New Britain. John Geil settled in New Britain, where he owned a farm, and resided there until near the close of his life. He was ordained as minister of the Mennonite congregation at Line Lexington in 1809, and preached there for forty-two years. Late in life he removed to Plumstead, where he died January 16, 1866, at the age of eighty-eight years. His wife was born January 27, 1781, and died November 6, 1849. She was the daughter of Mark and Elizabeth (Rosenberger) Fretz, the former a son of John and Maria Fretz of Bedminster, and the latter the daughter of Rev. Henry Rosenberger, for many years pastor of the Mennonite congregation in Franconia, Montgomery county. Rev. John and Elizabeth (Fretz) Geil were the parents of nine children: Jacob, the eldest son, married Anna Funk, and had three sons: John F., Enos F. and Samuel; the first and last removed west; Samuel became a distinguished lawyer in Ohio, and removed later to California, where he recently died. The remaining children of Rev. John Geil were: Barbara, who married Abraham Landis; Elizabeth, who married Martin D. Rosenberger, of Hilltown, (see Rosenberger family); Mark, who died young; Catharine, who married John Krabehl; Mary, who married Joseph Landis; John, born August 20, 1819, killed by a fall in his barn in New Britain, August 26, 1890; Anna, who married Mathew Hare and removed to Illinois; and Samuel.

Samuel Geil, of Doylestown, youngest son of Rev. John and Elizabeth (Fretz) Geil, was born in New Britain, Bucks county, March 11, 1825. He was a youth of more than ordinary intellectual ability and of a studious temperament. Early in life he studied civil engineering and surveying. After teaching school for some years he followed topographical engineering and surveying, and for many years made and published township, county and state maps. He made a survey of Morris county, New Jersey, in 1850, and his last map published, which was a triumph in map-making, was that of the state of Michigan, made in 1863-65. He then settled on his large farm in New Britain, where he resided until 1878, when he removed to Doylestown, and for several years was engaged in the hard wood lumber business. In 1856 he injured his spine by a fall from which he never fully recovered. Samuel Geil married Elizabeth Seese, of Plumstead, whose ancestors came over in the Mayflower and they were the parents of two children: Ella, residing with her father in Doylestown; and William Edgar, the subject of this sketch.

William Edgar Geil, the great traveler, author and orator, was born in New Britain township, Bucks county, near Doylestown, October 1, 1865. He acquired his education at the public schools, the Doylestown English and Classical Seminary, and Lafayette College, Easton, Pennsylvania, graduating from the latter institution in the class of 1890. At an early age he manifested a deep interest in religious matters and became an earnest and active member of the church. An indefatigable student, he early became thoroughly versed in the Scriptures as well as in most of the important sacred literature, ancient and modern.

On leaving college where he was famous as an orator he engaged in evangelistic work, with credentials from the Doylestown church, and soon after made several trips to Europe. Later he visited Asia, Egypt, the Holy Land, and many of the ancient cities of the Mediterranean. Returning to America he again engaged in evangelistic work. He then began his life work in earnest, and his success was phenomenal. He held revival meetings in various parts of New Jersey, New York and New England, and later made a tour of the south and west, addressing meetings of thousands of hearers and making thousands of converts. The "Cincinnati Inquirer" says of him: "His success has been more pronounced than that of any evangelist since Moody;" and the "Lowell (Mass.) Citizen" says that the meetings conducted by him were "the most remarkable series of meetings ever held in this city." In 1896 he made another extended trip abroad, revisiting the Holy Land and its ancient environs, and many of the ancient towns of Asia Minor, and the Mediterranean. Among other points he visited the Isle of Patmos, and on his return wrote and published his book, "The Isle that is called Patmos," which reached a sale of many thousands, and was rewritten, enlarged and republished in 1904, after his second visit to the island, in that year. The alarming illness of his mother, to whose early training he says he owes most of his success, called him home in the early part of 1897, and soon after closing the eyes of his beloved parent in her last sleep, on May 2, 1897, he returned to Europe for a brief sojourn and then again took up his work in his native country with increased success.

The crowning feat, however, of his younger days, was his remarkable trip around the world, visiting missions in obscure and distant parts of heathendom, and occupying a period of nearly four years. The purposes of this trip are best described by his Doylestown pastor, who says: "The purpose of the tour is that of independent observation of the whole missionary field, in its actual condition, operations, modes of organization, instruction and efforts, its different peculiarities, its needs, its difficulties, its relations to existing heathen religion, to international and denominational policies of political events; and what encouragement or discouragement may exist in the great work of extending the gospel to the world, and especially to the neglected parts of heathendom. A special object is to visit schools, colleges and institutions of sacred learning in connection with missionary operations and report the results to the whole Christian church." This purpose Mr. Geil fulfilled to the letter. Leaving Philadelphia on April 29, 1901, he crossed the continent to California, and, sailing from the Golden Gate for the Sandwich and South Sea Islands, visiting the Hawaiian, Samoan, Fiji, and many other archipelagoes, inspecting the missions, and intelligently noting their condition and work, as well as the condition and characteristics of the inhabitants, and the relation of governmental and commercial matters to the propagation of the Gospel of Christ. He proceeded thence to New Zealand, and Australia, reaching Sydney in November, 1901, where, and in Melbourne the following April and May, he organized and participated in the greatest religious revivals the continent has even known, speaking daily to audiences of 3,000 at noon and 10,000 at night. From Australia he proceeded to New Guinea, the Philippines and Japan. The results of this part of the trip are beautifully told in his book, "Ocean and Isle," published in 1904. He also made an extensive trip through China, going up the Yangtse river in a native gunboat, and was carried over the mountains of western China in a bamboo mountain chair. His popular work, "A Yankee on the Yangtse" tells the story in brilliant language. He visited Manchuria, Korea and Siberia, and later traveled extensively in Burmah and journeyed across Africa from Mombassa on the eastern coast to the Pigmy Forest, and thence down the Congo to the western coast. William Edgar Geil is the greatest living traveler. He is the only living white man who has crossed both China and tropical Africa. His great book "A Yankee in Pigmy Land," is just published. After spending sometime lecturing to vast audiences in England and Scotland, where he was welcomed by immense crowds, he returned to Bucks county and in June, 1905, delivered an address before the alumni of his alma mater, Lafayette College, and received from that institution the degree of A. M. One feature of his return to his native town was the large and enthusiastic reception tendered him by his fellow townsmen in the courthouse at Doylestown, when addresses were delivered by many prominent Bucks countians, and at least one thousand people packed the "Temple of Justice" while others climbed up to the windows on ladders to welcome the distinguished traveler on his return to his native heath. In August, 1905, he again sailed for foreign lands, and, after spending some months in England, Scotland and Wales, intends making an extended trip to Persia and other Asiatic points to finish up the work of his renowned trip around the world.

Mr. Geil, in addition to numerous and noted magazine articles, is the author of a number of books that have had enormous sales. One of his earliest publications was "The Pocket Sword," a vestpocket book of scriptural phrases and texts and the lessons drawn from them, that has been immensely popular and has reached a sale of over 100,000 copies. Among his other books are, "Judas Iscariot and other Lectures;" "The Isle That is Called Patmos;" "A Boy in the Sun;" "Laodicea, Or the Marble Heart;" "Smyrna, or the Flight of the Angel;" "Trip Stories;" "Ocean and Isle;" "A Yankee on the Yangtse;" "The Man of Galilee;" "A Yankee in Pigmy Land." Mr. Geil's new books "The Men on the Mount;" "The Automatic Calf," and "The Worker's Testament," have just passed throught the press. He has delivered six thousand lectures to large audiences in many states and countries. He is a Fellow of the Royal Geographical Society of London, and a member of a number of other noted societies. In all his wanderings the heart of the great traveler still clings to Doylestown as his "home," in all the truest sense of that much abused term.

HON. EDWARD M. PAXSON, of Bycot House, Buckingham township, Bucks county, Pennsylvania, ex-chief Justice of the Supreme Court of Pennsylvania, was born in Buckingham, September 3, 1824, and is a son of Thomas and Ann (Johnson) Paxson, and comes of an old and distinguished family that have been residents of Bucks county from its earliest settlement.

James, Henry and William Paxson, brothers, came to Pennsylvania in the ship "Samuel," arriving in the river Delaware the middle of the eleventh month, 1682. Another brother, Thomas, died at sea on the same ship as did the wife and son (Henry) of Henry. Henry Paxton came from Bycott House, in the parish of Stowe, Oxfordshire, and James and William from the parish of Marsh Gibbon, county of Bucks, near Stowe. Bycot House is said to have been the ancestral home of the family for many generations. The subject of this sketch, in a visit there several years ago, found a Henry Paxton then occupying the premises. The family were Friends

prior to their coming to Pennsylvania, and brought certificates from Bucks Monthly Meeting in Buckinghamshire, England. The family settled in Middletown, where Henry took as a second wife, Margery, the widow of Charles Plumly, August 13, 1684, his nephew, Henry Paxson, son of James, marrying her daughter, Ann Plumly. Elizabeth, the only child of Henry Paxson, Sr., who reached Pennsylvania with him, married Richard Burgess, who in 1696 purchased two hundred acres on the river Delaware in Solebury, and what was long known as "Paxson's Island," in the river adjoining, then known as "Turkey Point." This tract and island later became the property of William Paxson, son of James, and remained in the family many generations. Henry Paxson was also a very extensive land holder in Solebury, owning about one thousand acres there, and numerous large tracts elsewhere. He died about 1725, and, having no living descendants, devised his immense holdings of real estate to his nephews, the Solebury land going to William and Henry, the sons of his brother James.

James Paxson and Jane his wife, who came from Marsh Gibbon, in the county of Bucks, England, as before recited, were the parents of four children: Sarah, born in England, 8mo. 28, 1671, married 1692, John Burling; William, born 10mo 25, 1675, married Abigail Pownall; Henry, born in Bucks county, 7mo. 20, 1683, married Ann Plumly; and James, born 4mo. 10, 1687, died 7mo. 16, 1687. Jane, the mother, died 2mo. 7, 1710, and James, the father, 2mo. 29, 1722.

William Paxson, the second son of James and Jane, born in Bucks county, England, on Christmas day, 1675, was the direct ancestor of Judge Paxson. He married, February 20, 1695, Abigail Pownall, youngest daughter of George and Elinor Pownall, of Laycock, Cheshire, England, who, with their son, Reuben and daughters Elizabeth, Sarah, Rachel, and Abigail, came to Pennsylvania in the ship "Friends' Adventure," arriving in the Delaware river 8mo. (October) 11, 1682, and located in Falls township, where George was killed by a falling tree thirty days after his arrival. Another son George was born eleven days after his father's death. The widow Elinor later married Joshua Boare. Abigail was born in England in 1678. She became a recommended minister among Friends, and died in Solebury, Bucks county, 4mo. 17, 1749. Her husband, William Paxson, died in 1719. Their children were: Mary, born 11mo. 2, 1696; Abigail, born 6mo. 20, 1700; James, born 9mo. 5, 1702, married (first) Mary Horsman in 1723, and (second) Margaret Hodges in 1730; Thomas, born 9mo. 20, 1712, married Jane Canby; Reuben, who married Alice Simcock; Esther, who married a Clayton; and Amy, who never married.

Thomas Paxson, son of William and Abigail (Pownall) Paxson, in the division of the real estate in Solebury fell heir to the farm lately occupied by the Johnson family near Centre Bridge, and the island lying opposite. He later purchased other large tracts of land in Solebury, some of which still remain in the tenure of his descendants. Thomas died in 1782. He married in 1732 Jane Canby, daughter of Thomas Canby, an eminent preacher among Friends, (son of Benjamin Canby of Thorn, Yorkshire) who had come to Pennsylvania with his uncle Henry Baker. He was three times married, and had nineteen children who intermarried with the most prominent families of Bucks county and have left numerous descendants. The children of Thomas and Jane Canby Paxson, were: Joseph, born 9mo. 10, 1733, married 6mo. 28, 1758, Mary Heston; Benjamin, born 8mo. 1, 1739, married 6mo. 16, 1763, Deborah Taylor, (second) in 1797 Rachel Newbold; and (third) in 1807 Mary Pickering; Oliver, born 7mo. 9, 1741, married, 1766, Ruth Watson; Rachel, born 3mo. 6, 1744, married, 1764, John Watson; Jacob, born 11mo. 6, 1745, married in 1769 Lydia Blakey; Jonathan, born 11mo. 14, 1748, married, 1771, Rachel Biles; Isaiah, born 9mo. 20, 1751, married, 1775, Mary Knowles; and Martha, who died young. Of the above named sons of Thomas and Jane (Canby) Paxson, Joseph was devised a farm at Limeport, Solebury township; Benjamin, a farm at Aquetong, still owned by the children of his grandson, Elias Ely Paxson, one of whom is the wife of Colonel Henry D. Paxson; Oliver, who married (second) Ruth Johnson, was left a farm in the Pike tract, near New Hope; Isaiah, the island known as Paxson's Island, where he died without issue; Jacob, the homestead farm at Centre Bridge; Jonathan, the farm at Rabbit Run, now owned by Thomas Magill.

Jacob Paxson, born 11mo. 6, 1745, in Solebury township, fourth son and fifth child of Thomas and Jane (Canby) Paxson, was the grandfather of Judge Paxson. He married 6 mo. 19, 1769, Lydia Blakey, and at about that date purchased a farm and mill property on Tacony creek, in Montgomery county, Pennsylvania, and settled thereon. Here his wife died, leaving him two children, and he married a second time, in 1777, Mary Shaw, born in Plumstead township, Bucks county, 5mo. 28, 1759, daughter of Johnathan and Sarah (Good) Shaw, the former born in Plumstead, June 15, 1730, died there May 24, 1790, was a son of James and Mary (Brown) Shaw, the pioneers of the Shaw family in Plumstead. James being the son of John and Susanna Shaw, early English settlers in Northampton, and born January 9, 1694, and married at Abington Friends' Meeting, September 24, 1718, Mary Brown, daughter of Thomas and Mary Brown, who came from Barking Essex county, England, and after residing for some time in Philadelphia settled near Abington, Montgomery

county, Pennsylvania. Thomas Brown was one of the earliest landowners in Plumstead township, and he and his sons were pioneer Friends in that section and the founders of Plumstead Meeting. In 1724 Thomas conveyed to his son-in-law, James Shaw, two hundred acres of land on the upper line of Buckingham township, that remained the Shaw homestead for over a century and a half. The ancestors of Sarah (Good) Shaw, were also early Quaker settlers in Plumstead and adjoining parts of New Britain. Jacob and Mary (Shaw) Paxson were the parents of twelve children, all born in Abington township, Montgomery county, where Jacob Paxson continued to reside until his death in Buckingham, in 1832, while on a visit to his son-in-law, William H. Johnson. The children of Jacob and Mary (Shaw) Paxson were: John, Sarah, Isaiah, Jonathan, Jane, Thomas, Jacob, Oliver, and Ruth, most of whom married and reared families, whose descendants are now widely scattered over Bucks, Philadelphia, Montgomery and Chester counties and elsewhere.

Thomas Paxson, sixth child of Jacob and Mary (Shaw) Paxson, was born in Montgomery county in 1793, and reared in that county. He married, in 1817, Ann Johnson, daughter of Samuel and Martha (Hutchinson) Johnson, of Buckingham, and granddaughter of William Johnson, who was a native of Ireland, and came to America about the year 1754, in his nineteenth year. He was a man of high scholastic attainments, and a great student on scientific subjects, and delivered numerous lectures on electricity and kindred subjects of the highest merit. He married Ruth Potts, of an eminent New Jersey family, and resided for a time in Philadelphia, where his son Samuel was born in 1763. He soon after removed with his family to Charleston, South Carolina, where he died in 1767 at the age of thirty-two years. His widow and four children returned to Philadelphia and later removed to Trenton, New Jersey, where they resided at the time of the memorable battle of Trenton, on Christmas night, 1776. His eldest daughter Mary married Thomas Mathews of Virginia, and Hon. Stanley Mathews of the United States supreme bench was a descendant. The second child was Hon. Thomas Potts Johnson, an eminent lawyer of New Jersey.

Samuel Johnson, third child of William and Ruth (Potts) Johnson, born in Philadelphia, in 1763, removed with his parents to South Carolina, and returned with his mother to Philadelphia in his fourth year. He was reared at Trenton, New Jersey, and came to Bucks county in 1786, purchasing "Elm Grove," on the York road, east of Holocong, now the residence of his great-grandson, Colonel Henry D. Paxson. He later purchased a farm including the site of the present "Bycot House," and removed thereon. He was a man of high intellectual ability and literary attainments, a poet of more than ordinary merit. Two volumes of his poems have been published, the last one in 1845. In 1801 he retired from active business and, making his home with his son-in-law, Thomas Paxson, devoted his time to literary pursuits and social intercourse with congenial spirits. He died at the age of eighty-one years, his wife having died a few years previously. She was a daughter of Mathias Hutchinson, Esq., a prominent public official of Buckingham and Solebury, for many years a justice of the peace and an associate justice of the Bucks county courts. He was a grandson of John and Phebe (Kirkbride) Hutchinson, of Falls township, the latter being a daughter of Joseph and Phebe (Blackshaw) Kirkbride. Mathias Hutchinson married, in 1765, Elizabeth Bye, whose ancestors were the first settlers on the land now occupied by "Bycot House." Ann Johnson, who married Thomas Paxson, was born at "Elm Grove" in 1792. She was a woman universally loved and respected in her neighborhood for her many acts of Christian charity and kindness. Whenever by sacrifice and self devotion a fellow being in want or sickness could be made more comfortable by help in counsel or material assistance, she acted the part of the Good Samaritan with a cheerfulness that was highly appreciated. She was a writer of much merit, both in poetry and prose. She died in 1883, in her ninety-second year. William H. Johnson, a brother of Mrs. Paxson, married her husband's sister Mary Paxson. He was a classical scholar and mathematician, and an extensive writer on temperance and anti-slavery, contributing numerous essays to the *"Intelligencer"* and other journals.

Thomas Paxson, at his marriage to Ann Johnson in 1817, settled on the homestead at Abington, but moved to Buckingham two years later and purchased a portion of the Johnson homestead near the mountain, now occupied by his son, Hon. Edward M. Paxson, where he spent his remaining days, dying in April, 1881, at the age of eighty-eight years. He was a member of the Society of Friends and a constant attendant at Buckingham Meeting. He took an active part in the affairs of his neighborhood, and had strong convictions of right and wrong. He was conservative in his views, and the old landmarks of Friends that had distinguished them as a people were held in reverence by him; while an earnest advocate of all true reforms for the improvement of mankind, he believed the religious society of which he was an earnest member had a mission to fulfill with the Christian religion as a enduring basis. In him the Society of Frends lost an earnest supporter and a living example of sacrifice and devotion to principle rarely met with. The children of Thomas and Ann (Johnson) Paxson, were:

1. Samuel Johnson Paxson, born in Montgomery county in 1818, died in Buckingham, May 28, 1864. He was editor and proprietor of the *"Doylestown Democrat"* from 1845 to 1858, when he sold it to General W. W. H. Davis; he was a writer of recognized ability. He married Mary Anna Broadhurst in 1840, and had two daughters: Helen, widow of J. Hart Bye, now living at Germantown; and Carrie, who married Watson B. Malone, and is now deceased, leaving two daughters, and a son Arthur, a business man of Philadelphia.

2. Albert S. Paxson, born in Buckingham in 1820, died there. At the age of nineteen he became a teacher at a school in Montgomery county where his father had taught many years before. A year later, 1840, he returned to Buckingham and taught for some years at "Tyro Hall" and at the Friends School at Buckingham. From 1851 to 1856 he was local editor and general manager of the *"Doylestown Democrat,"* owned and edited by his brother, Samuel Johnson Paxson. In 1856 he removed to the old Ely homestead, near Holicong, that had been in the continuous occupancy of his wife's ancestors since 1720. He was elected to the office of justice of the peace in 1873, and served for ten years. He devoted considerable time to literary pursuits and was a writer of known merit. He married first, in 1844, Mercy Beans, daughter of Dr. Jesse Beans, who died in 1849, leaving a daughter Mary, who married Robert Howell Brown, of Mount Holly, New Jersey. She died at Bycot House, July 20, 1887, leaving a son, T. Howell Brown, now residing in Solebury. Mr. Paxson married (second) in 1854, Lavinia Ely, daughter of Aaron Ely, of Buckingham, and a descendant of Joshua and Mary (Seniar) Ely, who came to Trenton, New Jersey, from Nottinghamshire, England, in 1684. Their children are: Edward E., born May 7, 1860, engaged in the banking business in Philadelphia, with summer residence at the old homestead; and Colonel Henry D. Paxson, born October 1, 1862, a member of the Bucks county and Philadelphia bar, for many years an officer of the National Guard of Pennsylvania, and a prominent lawyer of Philadelphia. He married Hannameel Canby Paxson, a daughter of Elias Ely Paxson, of Aquetong, and they reside at Elm Grove, in Buckingham.

3. Hon. Edward M. Paxson, the third son of Thomas and Ann (Johnson) Paxson, was born in the old homestead in Buckingham, September 3, 1824. He was educated at the Friends' School at Buckingham, then a famous educational institution, where many young men, who later distinguished themselves in legal and other professional life were educated. Judge Paxson did not have a collegiate education, but fitted himself in the classics and higher branches of learning, chiefly by his own exertions. At an early age he had ambitions for a journalist career, and, having mastered the practical art of printing, in

1842, at the age of eighteen years, started the *"Newtown Journal,"* at Newtown, Bucks county, and successfully conducted it until 1847, when he sold out and established the *"Daily News"* in Philadelphia, but sold it out also the following year and removed to Doylestown, where he studied law in the office of Hon. Henry Chapman, later the judge of the Bucks county courts. He was admitted to the bar of Bucks county April 24, 1850, and after two years practice at Doylestown removed to Philadelphia, where he practiced his chosen profession for seventeen years, building up a large practice and establishing a reputation as a counselor at law that marked him for a career as a jurist. He was appointed as a judge of the common pleas court of Philadelphia on the resignation of F. Carroll Brewster in 1869, and, showing marked ability as a judge, was unanimously nominated to succeed himself, and elected the following October. After seven years' service on the common pleas bench, he was elected to the supreme bench in 1874, and at once took a commanding position among his fellow justices. His career on the supreme bench on which for eighteen years he served as chief justice, was marked by promptness in the discharge of business, and always by careful considerations of the questions of law. His opinions were models of terseness, clearness and appropriate diction, and showed an accurate knowledge of the law, expressed in clear and concise language and terms that could be clearly understood. Many notable cases were committed to his hands, and his reputation as a supreme justice was an enviable one. He resigned from the bench in 1893 and besylvania; fourth, receiver of the Philadelphia & Reading Railroad Company, a position he filled for four years. The only four public positions ever held by Chief Justice Paxson were the following: First, a member of the board of guardians of the poor, of Philadelphia; second, judge of the court of common pleas, of Philadelphia; third, chief justice of the supreme court, of Pennsylvania; fourth, receiver of the Philadelphia & Reading Railroad, all of which positions he resigned. He has for many years had charge of several large estates, to the management of which and that of his own large interests he has devoted much of his time in recent years, his summers being spent at "Bycot House" and his winters in Philadelphia. He is one of the largest real estate owners in Bucks county, owning many farms in Buckingham and Solebury, aggregating nearly 2,000 acres.

Judge Paxson married, April 30, 1846, Mary Caroline Newlin, of Philadelphia, daughter of Nathaniel and Rachel H. Newlin, of Delaware county, Pennsylvania. She died at Bycot House, June 7, 1885. He married (second) December 1, 1886, Mary Martha S. Bridges, widow of Hon. Samuel A. Bridges, of Allentown. He has no children.

WILLIAM CLAYTON NEWELL, of Doylestown, Pennsylvania, was born in Philadelphia, October 23, 1856, and is a son of William C. and Susan (Bispham) Newell.

William (first) and Martha (McGee) Newell, the great-grandparents of William C. Newell, came from Belfast, Ireland, to Philadelphia in 1780. He was a wholesale merchant and importer and conducted a large mercantile establishment at Water street, below Market street, Philadelphia, for many years. He died January 7, 1883, and Martha, his wife, died in 1843 at the age of eighty-four years. They were the parents of nine children, all of whom were born in Philadelphia: John in 1789; Elizabeth in 1790; William, February 25, 1792; James in 1797; Ann in 1800; Stewart in 1802; Samuel in 1804; Robert in 1808, and Martha, in 1806.

William Newell (second) son of William and Martha (McGee) Newell, born in Philadelphia, February 25, 1792, succeeded his father in the wholesale business in Philadelphia, and was a large importer of teas and coffees, owning two docks on the river front and doing a large business. He was a member of the First Troop Philadelphia City Cavalry, 1820 to 1831, and was the bearer of government despatches to France in 1842. He married, April 10, 1823, Eliza ——, born in Philadelphia, October 19, 1795, and died August 2, 1863, and they were the parents of two children, William and Rebecca.

William C. Newell (third) son of William and Eliza, was born in Philadelphia, September 5, 1825, and died there June 27, 1865. He was reared and educated in Philadelphia, and on arriving at manhood engaged in the wholesale tea business in Philadelphia, and was a large importer of tea from China, to which country he was the bearer of government despatches in 1846. He married, June 16, 1852, Susan Bispham Dunlap, of a prominent family of that city, where she was born in May, 1824. They were the parents of three children: Susan, wife of Dr. James Hendrie Lloyd, of Philadelphia; William Clayton, the subject of this sketch; and Rebecca W., wife of Grellett Collins, of Philadelphia.

William Clayton Newell, son of William C. and Susan (Dunlap) Newell, born in Philadelphia, October 23, 1856, was reared in that city and acquired his education at the Central High School. At the close of his school days he engaged in the wholesale provision business, in 1877, with which he was connected for several years. In 1892 he accepted a position with the Provident Life and Trust Co. of Philadelphia, and has since filled a responsible position with that company, having charge of the real estate department. He is a member of the Pennsylvania Society of the Sons of the Revolution, and of the Society of the War of 1812. He has been a resident of Doylestown since 1880, and is a vestryman of St. Paul's Protestant Episcopal church of Doylestown. Mr. Newell married, 27 April 1880, Sarah Rex Harvey, daughter of Dr. George T. and Mary L. Rex Harvey, of Doylestown, who is a descendant of one of the oldest families in Bucks county. Mathias Harvye, the great-great-great-grandfather of Mrs. Newell, came from England and settled in Flushing, Long Island, where he was a justice of Kings county, New York, commissioned October 1, 1690. On January 1, 1697, he purchased 1050 acres in Upper Makefield, Bucks county, Pennsylvania, and settled thereon. By his will dated April 5, 1699, his land was devised to his three sons Mathias, Thomas and Benjamin, Mathias, the eldest, getting the dwelling house and four hundred acres, and Thomas and Benjamin each three hundred acres. All three of the sons reared large families and left numerous descendants in Bucks county. Mathias married Elizabeth Margerum and died in 1742. Benjamin died in 1730. Mathias, the father, was twice married, the three sons above named being by the second marriage, June 2, 1689, to Sarah Harrington.

Thomas Harvye, the second son of Mathias and Sarah (Harrington) Harvye, born at Flushing, Long Island, October 22, 1692, came with his parents to Makefield when a child. As above stated he inherited from his father three hundred acres of land in Upper Makefield, on which he lived and died, his death occurring in January, 1759. He married Tamar ———, and had eleven children, five sons: Thomas, who died in 1749; Benjamin, who also died before his father; Joseph, Mathias and William; and six daughters: Hannah, who married John Milnor in 1741; Ann, who married Edward Bailey; Elizabeth, married a Coryell; Mary, married Richard Holcomb; Letitia, married Nathaniel Ellicott; and Sarah.

Joseph Harvey, son of Thomas and Tamar, was born in Upper Makefield, Bucks county, February 8, 1734, and died there February, 1779. He inherited from his father one-half of the homestead in Makefield, and lived there all his life. He was twice married, his second wife Margaret, surviving him. By his first wife, Mary, he had six children: Thomas, Joseph, Letitia, William, Enoch and Joshua.

Enoch Harvey, son of Joseph and Mary, was born in Upper Makefield in 1767, and came to Doylestown about 1790, where he followed the trade of a saddler for a few years and was later the proprietor of the inn now known as the Fountain House for a few years. He was a large landowner and an influential citizen, and took an active part in the improvement of Doylestown as it grew from a cross-road village into a town and borough. He died July 15, 1831, in his sixty-fifth year. He married, March 20, 1792, Sarah Stewart, daughter of Charles Stewart, of Doylestown, of Scotch-Irish ancestry, a granddaughter of Captain Charles Stewart, a soldier in both the pro-

vincial and revolutionary wars. Sarah died February 16, 1847, aged seventy-three. The children of Enoch and Sarah (Stewart) Harvey, were: Joseph, Charles, Mary, Pleasant, Letitia, Sarah and George T. Harvey.

George T. Harvey, youngest child of Enoch and Sarah (Stewart) Harvey, was born at Doylestown, February 27, 1813. He was educated at a school kept at Bridge Point by Samuel Aaron, and at the Doylestown Academy. At the age of twenty years he began the study of medicine with Dr. Abraham Stout, of Bethlehem, and, entering the medical department of the University of Pennsylvania, graduated in 1835. He then removed to Missouri, where he practiced medicine until 1840, when he returned to Doylestown and erected a drug store on the site of the present Hart building at Court and Main streets, where he kept a drug store for nearly half a century. He was a prominent and influential citizen, was three times postmaster of the town and several years a member of town council, being a member of that body when water was first introduced into the borough in 1869. He was second lieutenant of the Doylestown Guards, the first company organized in Bucks county for the civil war, and later served three years and three months as captain of Company E, 104th Regiment Pennsylvania Volunteers. Dr. Harvey married (first) June 27, 1842, Mary K. LaRue, of Philadelphia, by whom he had two children, Emma and Edward, the latter judge of the Northampton county courts. Dr. Harvey married (second) in 1856, Mary L. Rex, of Montgomery county, by whom he had three daughters: Mary, Sarah, (Mrs. Newell) and Emily.

The children of William Clayton and Sarah (Harvey) Newell are: George Harvey, born June 25, 1881, died July 28, 1881; William Clayton, born September 16, 1883; Edward Harvey, born September 4, 1885; Louis H. F., born November 16, 1887; Mary Louise, born April 4, 1890; and Margaret, born September 10, 1891, died October 5, 1891.

———

"ANDALUSIA." This place has been handed down in uninterrupted succession to the members of the same family since its acquisition in the year 1795. It was purchased at that time by Mr. John Craig, a well known and distinguished merchant of Philadelphia, and, through his eldest daughter's marriage in 1811 to Mr. Nicholas Biddle, has descended to their issue, and is occupied by them and their descendants at the present time.

The Biddle family has been prominent in Pennsylvania since a very early day. William Biddle (3d) married in 1730 the daughter of Nicholas Scull, surveyor-general of the province of Pennsylvania, and, dying in 1756, left a numerous family. His son Charles was an active patriot during the revolution, and vice president of the State of Pennsylvania between 1785 and 1788, when Benjamin Franklin was the president. Another son was Captain Nicholas Biddle, a comrade in early life of Horatio Nelson, when both were midshipmen in the English navy. His later career in the navy of our own country is well known. It was of him Paul Jones, writing of the "five Captains" appointed in the revolution, said: "Four of them were respectable skippers; and they all outlived the war! One of them was the kind of naval captain that the God of Battles makes. That one was Nick Biddle—poor, brave Nick! and he died in hopeless battle with a foe double his own strength—half of his flagship going down, and the other half going up by explosion of his magazine."

Vice-president Charles Biddle married, in 1778, Hannah Shepard, and had ten children. Two of these, Edward and James, went into the United States navy. Edward died during his first voyage, but James became one of the most famous naval officers. He served under Commodore Bainbridge on the coast of Tripoli, and shared with the crew of the ill-fated "Philadelphia" the long period of imprisonment to which they were condemned by the Tripolitans. He was first lieutenant of the sloop-of-war "Wasp," in the sea fight with the British sloop-of-war "Frolic," and led the boarders when the decks of the Englishman were carried. He was captain of the "Hornet," in the action with the British ship "Penguin," when the latter was captured after a furious conflict, her captain being among the list of killed. He was afterwards commander of the navy yard and governor at the naval asylum at Philadelphia, from 1838 to 1842. Among special services rendered by him was the taking possession of Oregon territory in 1817; the signing of a commercial treaty with Turkey in 1826; he exchanged ratifications of the first treaty with China, and acted as United States commissioner to that country; he also touched at Japan and made an earnest effort to conciliate by kindness and forbearance its singular and exclusive people.

Nicholas Biddle, whose name is first associated with "Andalusia," (son or Vice-president Charles) was during many years the most noted member of the family. He was secretary to General Armstrong, United States Minister to France, in 1804, and was present at the coronation of Emperor Napoleon in Paris. At this time the purchase of Louisiana and the indemnification for injuries to American commerce were in progress, and, although but eighteen years of age, young Biddle managed the details with the veterans of the French bureau, in whom his juvenile appearance and precocious ability excited much surprise. Leaving the legation, he traveled in the continent of Europe, adding to his classical attainments a thorough mastery of the modern languages which he retained through life. On reaching England, he became secretary to Mr. Monroe, then our Minister to London. On his return to America in 1807, he engaged in the practice of the law and devoted a portion of his time to literary pursuits. He became associated with Joseph Dennie in the editorship of the "Portfolio" in 1811. His papers on the fine arts, biographical sketches and critical essays exhibit a discriminating taste. When Lewis and Clark had returned from their explorations their journals and memoradums were placed in the hands of Mr. Biddle, who prepared from them and the oral relation of Clark the narrative of the expedition. Published in 1814, it has gone through various editions, and is recognized to-day as an authoritative and admirably compiled account of this noted journey.

He was in the state legislature in 1810, advocating a system of popular education. It was not until 1836 that the ideas broached by him were fully carried out by legislative enactment. When the renewal of the charter of the old United States Bank was under discussion in 1811, he advocated the measure in a speech which was widely circulated at the time, and gained the distinguished approval of Chief Justice Marshall. During the war with England he was elected to the state senate and gave a zealous and powerful support to the measures of the national administration for carrying on the contest. He and all of his brothers were now engaged in the service of the country—in public councils, the navy, the army, and the militia; of whom Commodore James Biddle, Major Thomas Biddle, and Major John Biddle gained particular military reputation. The youngest of the brothers, Richard Biddle, during the war a volunteer at Camp Dupont, afterwards settled at Pittsburg and was for many years an acknowledged leader of the bar of that city.

After the capture of Washington; when an invasion of Pennsylvania was expected, Nicholas Biddle in the senate initiated the most vigorous measures for the defense of the state. Towards the close of the war he replied to the address of the Hartford convention by an elaborate report which was adopted in the Pennsylvania legislature, a state paper which attracted universal attention and added greatly to the reputation of its author. In 1819 he became a government director of the Bank of the United States on the nomination of President Monroe, and under a resolution of Congress prepared a work on the laws and regulations of foreign countries relative to commerce, moneys, weights and measures. This was known in its day as "The Commercial Digest." In 1823, on the retirement of Mr. Langdon Cheves, Mr. Biddle was elected to the presidency of the bank and to the conduct of its affairs he thenceforth devoted all his energies. The history of the bank is public knowledge, it has been recounted and touched upon in writings and biographies dealing with the events and characters of the time. Only recently (1903) a work entitled "The Second Bank of the United States," by Ralph C. H. Catterall, published under the auspices of the University of Chicago, has appeared giving a full account of what in its day was long a "burning question." After the smoke of battle had cleared and when passions had cooled, it was found that political antagonists were ready to bear testimony to the high character of Nicholas Biddle. Mr. C. J. Ingersoll, a political opponent on the bank question, writing of the war, says: "Nicholas Biddle was as iron-nerved as his great antagonist, Andrew Jackson; loved his country not less, and money as little." The last years of Mr. Biddle's life were spent at Andalusia and there he died on the 27th of February, 1844.

"Andalusia" is noted for the fine timber growing upon it, splendid specimens of the American tulip, catalpa, chestnut, Spanish chestnut, and varieties of oak, adorning the lawns, while towering evergreens surround the mansion house. Many of these trees were planted in the time of Mr. Craig. Nicholas Biddle did much to adorn and beautify the place, adding a very striking portico in the Grecian style with. Doric columns to the river-front of the house. He was an enthusiastic agriculturist, devoting time and thought to the cultivation of the grape and importing the first Alderney cattle to this country.

He was a member and served as president of the Agricultural Society, resigning only the month before his death. His son, Judge Craig Biddle, inherited his tastes in this direction, serving the society before its dissolution in the capacity of president, also, and he continues to direct the farming operations at "Andalusia."

CHARLES HENRY MATHEWS, of Philadelphia, is a descendant of the early settlers in Bucks county, and was born in Doylestown, Bucks county, Pennsylvania, April 21, 1844, being a son of Dr. Charles H. and Margaret (Rodman) Mathews, the former an eminent physician of Bucks county, and the latter belonging to a family that had been prominent in the affairs of the county since the time of Penn. Simon Mathew, the paternal ancestor of Dr. Mathews, was a native of Langenych, South Wales, from whence he emigrated with a colony of Welsh Baptists in 1710, and settled in the Welsh Tract, New Castle county, now Delaware. He was accompanied from Caermarthenshire by Anthony Mathew, either his father or brother, and among others by Simon Butler, who was in some way connected with him by ties of blood or marriage, and with whom he was closely associated during his whole life, both in New Castle and Bucks counties. The Welsh Tract comprised a large tract of land granted to a colony of Welsh Baptists who, having formed themselves into a church at Milford Haven just prior to sailing for America, migrated to Pennsylvania in September, 1701, in the "James and Mary," and settled at Pennypack, where they remained for a year and a half, and, being joined by later arrivals from Pembroke and Caermarthenshire, removed in 1703 to Pencader Hundred, New Castle county, where they built a church and founded a colony, both known by the name of "Welsh Tract" for a century. In course of time, the spelling of the name has been changed in two particulars. One "t" has been dropped, and the oldest legal documents do not show that it has been used since the emigration to America. The final "s" at first was not used; but old deeds of a date previous to the Revolution show that the name had come to be spelt "Mathews."

In 1720 Simon Mathews and Jane his wife, Anthony Mathews, Simon Butler and Ann his wife, and Daniel Rees and Jane his wife, removed from Pencader Hundred to New Britain township, Bucks county, bringing certificates from Welsh Tract church to Montgomery Baptist church, the parent of New Britain Baptist church, founded in 1741. Simon Mathew and Simon Butler purchased large tracts of land comprising the greater part of the present borough of Chalfont, where they jointly erected what was known for many years as "Butler's Mill," Butler being the miller, and Mathew a millwright. This mill was the nucleus of the present town, and was the objective point of many of the early roads laid out from the ferries on the Delaware and points in Upper Bucks during the first half of the eighteenth century. Anthony Mathew died in New Britain, March 3, 1726. Simon Mathew died about July 1, 1755, and his wife Jane prior to December 28, 1751, the date of Simon's will. By this will the testator's half interest in the mill, mill lots and dwelling house was devised to his son Edward, as well as a tract of land adjoining, the remainder of the real estate, about 150 acres, the homestead, was devised to the youngest son Thomas.

The children of Simon and Jane Mathew, were: John, married Diana Thomas, and is the ancestor of Edward Mathews, of Lansdale, the historian of the family; Simon, who removed to Virginia; Benjamin, who also removed to Virginia; Edward, who lived in New Britain, on Pine Run; Margaret, who married a Thomas; Ann, who married Simon Morgan; and Thomas. John, the eldest son, died in New Britain in 1783, and his widow Diana in 1799. Their children were: Benjamin; Margaret, married John Young; Mary, married Thomas Barton; Joseph; Rachel, married James Meredith; Ann, married Jonathan Doyle, and removed to Huntingdon county, Pennsylvania, and Susanna, married —— Thomas.

Thomas Mathew, youngest son of Simon and Jane, was born in New Britain in 1728. He inherited the homestead farm near Chalfont, and was a prominent and successful farmer, acquiring considerable other land in the vicinity. He married Mary Stephens, daughter of David Stephens and granddaughter of Evan Stephens, an early Welsh settler in New Britain. He died in 1795.

Edward Mathew, son of Thomas and Mary (Stephens) Mathew, was born on the old homestead in New Britain (purchased by his grandfather in 1720), in 1755. In 1779 he purchased a farm of one hundred acres in New Britain, on which he resided until 1791, when his father conveyed to him the homestead farm of 127 acres, whereon he resided until his death in the winter of 1813-14. He married Eleanor Thomas, daughter of Ephraim and Eleanor (Bates) Thomas, of Hilltown, and granddaughter of "Elder" William Thomas, who was born in Llanerwarth, Wales, in 1678, and came to Pennsylvania in 1712 and located in Radnor, Chester county, removing to Hilltown in 1718, where he became a very large landholder and one of its most prominent residents. He was a Baptist preacher, and officiated in that capacity for the Baptists of Hilltown prior to the founding of the Hilltown church, the land for which was donated by him and the first church erected at his expense. Edward Mathew was a man of excellent parts and good standing in the community. He was for many years a deacon of the Baptist church of New Britain. The children of Edward and Eleanor (Thomas) Mathew were: Abel; Rebekah, wife of Charles Humphrey; Simon; and John, all of whom married and reared families in New Britain.

Simon Mathew, second son of Edward and Eleanor (Thomas) Mathew, was born in New Britain in 1781. At the death of his father he inherited sixty-three acres of the old homestead, on which he resided for some years, though he was at one time a resident of Montgomery county, and prior to the death of his father had resided in Roxborough, Philadelphia. He was a man of excellent character, and succeeded his father as deacon of the New Britain church. He died in New Britain in February, 1828.

He married his cousin, Isabella Stephens, daughter of William and Sarah Stephens, of Doylestown, formerly. New Britain township, and granddaughter of David and Ann Stephens, who were the parents of his grandmother Mary (Stephens) Mathew. Isabella was born and reared on the old homestead of the Stephens family in Doylestown (then New Britain township) which was purchased by her great-grandfather Evan Stephens, in 1729, and most of which remained the property of the family for four generations. Isabella (Stephens) Mathews died in 1833.

Dr. Charles H. Mathews, only son of Simon and Isabella, was born at Roxboro, Philadelphia, November 6, 1805. He received a liberal education and graduated from the medical department of the University of Pennsylvania in 1827, locating at Doylestown, Bucks county, where he practiced his chosen profession until his death, July 25, 1849. He was a man of fine intellectual ability, pleasing address and irreproachable character; a popular and skilled physician, who was loved and respected by all who knew him. He took an active interest in the affairs of the town and county, and filled many positions of trust. He was prothonotary of the county for the term 1836-9. He was for several years an officer of militia, and was commissioned major-general of the district composed of the counties of Bucks, Montgomery and Delaware, his commission being delivered to him by General W. W. H. Davis but a week prior to his death. Dr. Mathews married first Mary Meredith, of Doylestown township, and (second) Margaret Rodman, daughter of Gilbert and Sarah (Gibbs) Rodman, and a sister of his classmate, Dr. Lewis Rodman, who achieved high distinction in the practice of his profession in Philadelphia.

Mrs. Mathews was born January 29, 1797, and died January 12, 1875. She married Dr. Mathews on May 3, 1837. She belonged to a family that had been prominent in state and national affairs for several generations. Her grandfather, Richard Gibbs, was sheriff of the county of Bucks for the term 1771-2, and filled a number of other high positions. The pioneer ancestor of the Rodman family was John Rodman, who died in the Barbadoes in 1685. He is supposed to have been the same John Rodman, a Quaker, who for wearing his hat at the assizes at New Ross, Ireland, in 1665, was sent to jail for three months and later banished the country. See Rutty's "History of Quakers in Ireland." This theory is strengthened by the known fact that a great number of Quakers and other "dissenters" were transported to Barbadoes between the years 1669 and 1685. John Rodman died on his plantation in the parish of Christ Church,

11-3

Island of Barbadoes, in 1686, leaving a widow Elizabeth, sons Thomas and John, and daughters Ann Thwaite and Katharine Brandeth. The sons Thomas and John removed to Newport, Rhode Island, Thomas in 1675, and John in 1682.

Dr. John Rodman, the second son of John and Elizabeth, born in 1653, became a freeman of Newport, Rhode Island, in 1684, and was prominent in the affairs of that colony for five or six years. He later removed to Block Island, having purchased a three-sixteenth share of the Island. In 1691 he removed to Flushing, Long Island, but returned to Block Island later. He died September, 1731, at the age of seventy-eight years. He was a prominent physician, and a minister among Friends for forty years. In 1686 he purchased one thousand acres of land in Burlington county, New Jersey, where some of his descendants later lived. He married Mary Scammon and had twelve children, as follows: John, born in Barbadoes May 14, 1679, see forward; Mary, died at Newport in 1683; Samuel, died in New York city in 1720; Joseph, born August 11, 1685, died September, 1759, married (first) Sarah Lawrence, (second) Helena Willett; William, born May 20, 1687, died May 23, 1704; Anne, born August 11, 1689, died 1715, married Walter Newberry; Thomas, born 1692, died October, 1693; Mary, born December 20, 1693, married John Willett; Elizabeth, died young; Thomas, born January 9, 1698, married Elizabeth Scott; Hannah, born August 6, 1700, married (first) Jonathan Dickinson, and (second) Samuel Holmes; and Elizabeth, born at Flushing in 1702, married Thomas Masters, of Philadelphia.

Dr. John Rodman, eldest son of Dr. John and Mary (Scammon) Rodman, born in Barbadoes, May 14, 1679, was reared at Newport, Rhode Island, where he became a freeman in 1706, removed to Block Island, and from there to Flushing, Long Island, in 1712. In 1726 he purchased land in Burlington county, New Jersey, and settled there. He was, like his father, a prominent physician and a member of the Society of Friends. He was a member of provincial assembly 1727-9, member of governor's council 1738, and commissioner to treat with the Indians in 1741. He owned 1300 acres of land in Burlington county, and in 1703 purchased 3000 acres in Warwick township, Bucks county, comprising nearly the whole eastern side of the township, which at his death in Burlington county, July 13, 1756, was devised to four of his sons, John, William, Scammon, and Samuel. Dr. Rodman married (first) Margaret Grosse, daughter of Thomas and Elizabeth Grosse, of Boston, who died at Flushing, Lond Island, June 2, 1718. He married (second) July 7, 1719, Mary

Willett, daughter of William Willett, of Westchester county, New York, granddaughter of Thomas Willett, a native of Bristol, England, who married in 1643 Sarah Cornell, daughter of Thomas Cornell, of Cornell's Neck, Westchester county, New York. The children of Dr. John and Margaret (Grosse) Rodman were: John, born at Flushing, Long Island, 1714, died 1795; Thomas, born 1716, died in Burlington, New Jersey, 1796, married Elizabeth Pearson; Mary, married John Johnson, of Bucks county. The children of Dr. John and Mary (Willett) Rodman were: William, born May 5, 1720, see forward; Anna, born 1722, died 1763, married October 20, 1759, William Lister, of Essex county, New Jersey; Scammon, born March 8, 1723, died January 4, 1762, unmarried; Hannah, born July 4, 1726, died October 7, 1755; Samuel, born May 30, 1729, died July 4, 1761; and Margaret, born August 6, 1731, died October 18, 1752, married October 10, 1751, Charles Norris.

William Rodman, eldest son of Dr. John by his second marriage with Mary Willett, came to Burlington county, New Jersey, from Flushing at the age of six years. In 1744 his father sent him to Bucks county to take charge of six hundred acres of land in Bensalem township, called Rodmanda, later named by him after his birthplace, Flushing, where he lived until his death, January 30, 1794. He was one of the most prominent men of his day in Bucks county. He was a justice 1752-57, and a member of provincial assembly, 1763-76. He married Mary Reeve, of New Jersey, September 6, 1744, and they were the parents of eight children; Sarah, did at the age of four years; Mary, born July 23, 1747, died December 1, 1765, married, June 27, 1765, Phineas Buckley; Gilbert, born July 21, 1748, died August 21, 1830, married Sarah Gibbs, daughter of Richard and Margery Gibbs; Hannah, born 1751, died 1775, married John Howard; Margaret, born September 20, 1752, died February 22, 1781, married Dr. William McIlvaine; Elizabeth, died unmarried; William, born October 7, 1757, died July 27, 1824, married Esther West; and Rachel, born December 1, 1759, died September 1, 1783, married September 20, 1782, Samuel Gibbs.

Gilbert Rodman, born at Flushing, Bucks county, July 21, 1748, died in Bucks county, August 21, 1830. He was a maior in the continental forces during the Amboy campaign of 1776, and was disowned from the society of Friends for his military services. He inherited from his father, William Rodman, the farm on which the Bucks county alms house is now located in Doylestown township, it being part of the tract purchased by his grandfather of John Gray, alias Tatham, in 1703. He lived on this plantation until

1808, when he sold it to the county and, removed to Bensalem, whére he died. He married, June 3, 1784, Sarah Gibbs, and they,were the parents of eleven children: Mary, married Anthony McCoy, and was the mother of Dr. Gilbert Rodman McCoy, who succeeded to the practice of Dr. Charles Mathews at Doylestown, and was one of the most prominent physicians of the county; Margery, married Judge John Fox, president judge of the courts of Bucks county, 1830-40, and a leader of a powerful faction of the Democratic party in Bucks county for many years; Gibbs Rodman, born January 8, 1782, died December 18, 1812, unmarried; Sarah, married John S. Benezet; Elizabeth, married William Drinker of Philadelphia; Margaret, wife of Dr. Charles H. Mathews; Hannah, died unmarried; Gilbert, born August 25, 1800, died January 15, 1862, unmarriéd, studied law with Judge Fox, later with Judge Dallas at Philadelphia, located at Lancaster, was a clerk in the United States Treasury department under Samuel D. Ingham in 1829, later becoming chief clerk and filling that position until his death; Euphemia, born 1802, died 1807; Mary Ann, born 1804, died in 1827, unmarried; and Lewis, who graduated from the medical department of the University of Pennsylvania in the same class with Dr. Charles H. Mathews, located in Philadelphia, where he became a prominent physician, was censor of the Colleʒe of Physicians, consulting physician ror Preston's Retreat, etc.

CHARLES HENRY MATHEWS, only son of Dr. Charles H, and Margaret (Rodman) Mathews, was born at Doylestown, April 21, 1844. He was educated at the Doylestown English and Classical Seminary, the high school at Lawrenceville, New Jersey, and at the College of New Jersey, (now Princeton University) graduating in 1864. He studied law in the office of his cousin, Gilbert Rodman Fox, at Norristown, and was admitted to the bar of the Seventh Judicial District, comprising Bucks and Montgomery counties, in June, 1867 and to the Philadelphia bar in November of the same year. He located in Philadelphia, where he has since practiced his chosen profession, holding a high position in the legal fraternity, his present office being at 717 Walnut street. He married, March 1, 1881, Hannah Selena Black, daughter of William and Delia (Dimon) Black, of New York, and they have been the parents of three children; Charles Henry, Jr., born May 31, 1882, a graduate of Princeton University, class of 1905; Lewis Rodman died in infancy; and William Black, born April 12, 1887. Mr. Mathews is a member of the Bucks County Historical Society, and takes a lively interest in the affairs of his native county.

ATKINSON FAMILY. The family of Atkinson is an ancient and honorable one, whose representatives were found in different parts of Great Britain several centuries ago. Two distinct families of the name settled in Bucks county, Pennsylvania, in the latter part of the seventeenth century. Thomas Atkinson, of Sandwick, Yorkshire, was married to Jane Bond, at Knaresborough meeting of Friends in 1678, and four years later emigrated to America with his wife and three sons, Isaac, William and Samuel, settling first in Burlington county, New Jersey, but removing soon after to Bucks county. Both Thomas and Jane were ministers among Friends. The former died in 1687, and his widow married William Biles two years later. She travelled extensively in the ministry after her second marriage, both in the colonies and in England and Ireland. Thomas Atkinson was a son of John Atkinson of Newby, Yorkshire, and in his will in 1687 devises land in Bucks county to his brother John Atkinson, "should he come to Pensilvania." It is not known that the brother John ever emigrated to America. Isaac Atkinson, the eldest son of Thomas and Jane, died in Bucks county in 1721, leaving three children, John, Jane and Thomas. Most of the descendants of Thomas and Jane Atkinson eventually settled in New Jersey.

The present family of Atkinsons in Bucks county are descendants of John Atkinson, of Scotforth, near the city of Lancaster, England, who with his brother Christopher and their respective families embarked in the ship "Brittanica," in April, 1690, for Pennsylvania, where they had purchased of William Penn 1500 acres of land, to be laid out, etc., in March, 1690. Christopher Atkinson, the elder of the two brothers, was married at Lancaster Meeting, England, on 6 mo. 8, 1679, to Margaret Fell, daughter of Christopher Fell, of Newtown, Lancashire, and the records of that meeting show the birth of seven of their children, of whom at least four, William, Hannah, Margaret and Isabel, sailed with their parents, though only the two latter appear to have survived the voyage, the father, Christopher Atkinson, also dying on the way to America. John Atkinson, the other brother, had married at the same meeting, on 2 mo. 8, 1686, Susanna Hynde, daughter of Richard Hynde, of Scotforth, and the following children were born to them in Lancashire, viz.: William, 1 mo. 31, 1687; Mary, 7 mo. 25, 1689; John, 8 mo. 25, 1692, died 9 mo. 5, 1694; John, born 9 mo. 25, 1695. The three surviving children above named accompanied their parents on board the "Brittanica," and, both their parents dying on the voyage, were received by the Friends of Middletown Meeting, Bucks county, where the certificate from Lancaster Meeting, dated 2 mo. 30, 1690, was deposited.

The 1500 acres of land purchased by Christopher and John Atkinson was laid out in 1700 in Buckingham township, Bucks county; 1,000 acres in a parallelogram was surveyed in right of Christopher, lying between the present Mechanicsville road and the line of the land of T. Howard Atkinson, a lineal descendant of John, and extending from the Street road at Sands' Corner to the Greenville road at Beans' Corner. It was in two equal tracts of 500 acres each, and was patented to Margaret Atkinson, widow of Christopher, the upper half in her own right, under the will of her husband, proved on her arrival in Philadelphia, and the lower tract for the use of her children. The latter was conveyed by the widow and heirs to Joseph Gilbert, and the upper tract by Margaret Atkinson to William Cooper. The remaining 500 acres was surveyed for the use of the heirs of John Atkinson, and was laid out on the opposite side of the Street road, touching the upper tract of the 1,000 acres at Sands' Corner, and extending northwesterly from that point. It was resurveyed by Cutler in 1703 in the name of Alice and Mary Hynde, sisters of Susanna, wife of John Atkinson, who had taken out letters on the estates of John and Susanna, in Philadelphia, September 6, 1699. No conveyance appears of record by the Atkinson heirs or their representatives, the first actual settlers thereon being William George, and Alice his wife. Certain it is that none of the heirs of either Christopher or John Atkinson found homes on the land originally purchased by their respective parents.

John Atkinson, the youngest child of John and Sunsanna (Hynde) Atkinson, born in Lancashire, 9 mo. 25, 1695, is supposed to have spent his boyhood days among Friends in the neighborhood of Newtown, Bucks county. On 8 mo. 13, 1717, he was married at the house of Stephen Twining, Newtown, to Mary Smith, daughter of William and Mary (Croasdale) Smith, of Makefield. He immediately purchased 200 acres in the Manor of Highlands, now Upper Makefield, adjoining his father-in-law, and settled thereon and lived there until his death in January, 1752. The children of John and Mary (Smith) Atkinson were: John, born 1718; William, born 1721, married Mary Tomlinson, and remained on a portion of the homestead; Thomas, born 1722, see forward; Christopher, born 1725, married Lydia Canby; Mary, born 1725, married John Stockdale; Exekiel, born 1728, died on the homestead, 1768, married Rachel Gilbert; Cephas, born 1730, married Hannah Naylor; and Elizabeth, born 1732.

Thomas Atkinson, third son of John and Mary, was born and reared on the

Makefield homestead, but on his marriage in 1744 to Mary Wildman, located on 200 acres in Wrightstown township, near Penn's Park, the greater part of which is still owned and occupied by his descendants, part of it by his great-grandson, George G. Atkinson, and part by another great-grandson, Wilmer Atkinson Twining, Esq. Two children, Thomas and Mary, were born to him, but the latter died in infancy. He died in August, 1760.

Thomas Atkinson, only surviving child of Thomas and Mary (Wildman) Atkinson, was born on the Wrightstown homestead, 8 mo. 19, 1751. He inherited from his father the two hundred acre farm, and spent his whole life there, dying 8 mo. 19, 1815. He was a prominent man in the community, and an active member of Wrightstown Friends' Meeting. He married, 5 mo. 1, 1779, Sarah Smith, daughter of Timothy and Sarah (Kinsey) Smith, who bore him seven children, viz.: Mary, died young; Jonathan, born 5 mo. 9, 1782, married Esther Smith, and lived and died on the homestead: Timothy, see forward; Thomas, born 10 mo. 8, 1786, married Jane Smith, see forward; Mahlon, born 4 mo. 11, 1790, a physician, settled in Ohio, married Rebecca Babb; Sarah, born 2 mo. 25, 1793, married Jacob Heston; and Joseph, born 8 mo. 22, 1795, died 1815. Sarah, the mother of the above children, died 10 mo. 19, 1830.

Timothy Atkinson, second son of Thomas and Sarah, was born in Wrightstown township and spent his whole life there. He was a farmer and at his father's death purchased a considerable portion of the old homestead and lived thereon during his life. He married in 1807 Deborah, daughter of Edmund Smith, who bore him four children: Edmund S., born in 1808; Sarah, born 1815, died 1840; Elizabeth, born 1821, died 1836; and Timothy, Jr., born 1829, married Letitia Smith, daughter of Daniel and Hannah (Betts) Smith, died 1868. Timothy, the father, died in March, 1867.

Edmund S. Atkinson, born on the old homestead in 1808, lived his whole life thereon. He was twice married, first in 1831, to Ruth Simpson, who bore him three sons,—Robert, Thomas Ogborn and J. Simpson, the latter being now a resident of Springfield, Missouri. Edmund married (second) Ann L. Gillingham, and had children, Ann; Deborah, deceased; George G., now living on the old homestead in Wrightstown; Sarah E., single, residing in Wrightstown; and Lewis, deceased. Edmund S. Atkinson, the father, died February 16, 1895.

THOMAS OGBORN ATKINSON, son of Edmund S. and Ruth (Simpson) Atkinson, was born in Wrightstown township, Bucks county, October 12,

Thomas Ogborn Atkinson

T. Howard Atkinson

1834, on the homestead farm, and was reared thereon to manhood. He received an ordinary education in the public schools, and the school of Rev. Samuel Aaron, in Norristown, Pennsylvania, known as Tremont Seminary. In early manhood he taught school for several years, working on the homestead farm during vacation season. In August, 1858, he removed to Mound City, Linn county, Kansas, and engaged in the mercantile business in company with his brother, J. Simpson Atkinson, remaining until December, 1859, when he returned to Wrightstown and engaged in the same business at Penn's Park, where he did a large business until 1871, at which time he sold out and removed to Doylestown, his present residence, and engaged in the real estate business. He first formed a partnership with Andrew J. LaRue, under the firm name of A. J. LaRue & Co. After the death of Mr. LaRue in 1873 he formed a partnership with Samuel A. Firman, under the firm name of T. O. Atkinson & Co. The latter firm did a very extensive business in their line in Bucks and adjoining counties. In 1886 he quit the real estate business, and with the late Judge Richard Watson and others assisted in organizing the Bucks County Trust Company, and became its first treasurer and secretary, and has held that position until the present time. Mr. Atkinson is one of the best known business men in Bucks county, and has always stood deservedly high in the estimation of the people. He has held many positions of trust. Like all of his ancestors he is a member of the Society of Friends. In politics he is a Republican, but has never held other than local offices. He is now serving his third term as president of the town council of the borough of Doylestown.

He married in March, 1861, Mary B. Heston, daughter of Jacob and Sarah (Smith) Heston, who is also a member of the Society of Friends. Their only child, Edmund Russell, died in early manhood.

T. HOWARD ATKINSON, one of the most prominent farmers and business men of Buckingham township, Bucks county, was born in that township, May 14, 1848, being the son of Mahlon and Sarah (Smith) Atkinson of that township, both deceased. Thomas Atkinson, grandfather of the subject of this sketch, was born on the old Atkinson homestead in Wrightstown, 10 mo. 8, 1786. In early life he learned the blacksmith trade, which he followed for many years. He was an expert workman, and did a large and profitable business. He wrought the iron work for the jail built at Doylestown in 1812. On arriving at manhood he located in Buckingham, doing business for several years

at Pineville, and later at other points in lower Buckingham. He was also a farmer, and became a very large landowner, and prominent business man. He married 10 mo. 16, 1811, Jane, daughter of Thomas and Eleanor Smith, by whom he had nine children, viz: Mahlon, born 1812, died 11 mo. 6, 1879; Joseph S., born August 19, 1823, died 3 mo. 27, 1900; Sarah Jane, born 1825, died 10 mo. 9, 1899, who married Benjamin W. Smith; and Mary, Martha, Ogborn, Eleanor, Thomas and Timothy, who died young. Thomas, the father, died in 1864, and his widow Jane in 1867, aged seventy-eight years.

Mahlon Atkinson, eldest son of Thomas and Jane, was born in Buckingham township and received a good common school education. He had a special talent for business, and was one of the most successful business men of his day in Bucks county. On attaining manhood he settled on his father's farm in lower Buckingham, and married Sarah, daughter of Thomas and Anna Hicks Smith. He was one of the pioneer sausage makers and pork butchers in that section, hauling his product to Philadelphia. He was for very many years a director in the Doylestown National Bank, and did the banking business for his whole neighborhood. He became a large real estate owner, and conducted various business enterprises. He owned and operated for many years the agricultural machinery works at New Hope. He died at the home of his daughter-in-law, Anna C. Atkinson, in Buckingham, 11 mo. 6, 1897. His children were: Albert, died in infancy; Charles S., born March 30, 1841, married Matilda R. Magill; Silas C., born September 20, 1843, died October, 1876, married Anna C. Wollaston; T. Howard, the subject of this sketch; Anna Jane, born December 24, 1849, died 1902, married Charles H. Williams.

T. Howard Atkinson was born on his father's farm in Lower Buckingham, May 14, 1848. He received a good education, and on arriving at manhood assumed charge of the homestead farm, where he lived until April, 1882, when he purchased the Anderson farms, near Buckingham village, his present residence and moved thereon. He is a successful farmer and business man and holds many positions of trust. He was elected justice of the peace in 1890, and has served continuously high in that position since. He was elected a trustee and director of the Hughesian Free School in 1885; was a director of the public schools of Buckingham from 1886 to 1895; has been a director of the Bucks County Trust Company for many years; and is a director of the Buckingham and Doylestown and the Lahaska and New Hope Turnpike Companies. Politically he is a Republican, but has never held or sought other than local offices. He and his family are members of Buckingham Friends Meeting.

He was married in 1868 to Mary, daughter of Edward and Phoebe Ellen (Schofield) Williams. They have been the parents of seven children, viz.: Alvan W., born September 22, 1869, now a successful physician in Trenton, New Jersey; Ellen, born December 1, 1870, now wife of Edward A. Jenkins, of Swarthmore; Anna, born April 7, 1872, now the wife of Richard C. Sellers, of Swarthmore; Edith, born April 7, 1877, wife of Samuel P. Green, of Kennett Square, Chester county; Florence, born November 8, 1881, died November 22, 1886; Mahlon, born July 12, 1884, died November 15, 1885; and Emily, born July 28, 1888, residing at home.

MARY ATKINSON TURNER.

Charles S. Atkinson, eldest surviving son of Mahlon and Sarah H. (Smith) Atkinson, was born in Buckingham township, Bucks county, March 30, 1841, and was educated at the public schools of his native township and at the First Pennsylvania State Normal School at Millersville, and the Claverack Academy, on the Hudson, New York. In 1862 he located in Solebruy, where he has since followed farming in connection with various other business enterprises. In 1879 he purchased the agricultural works at New Hope and carried on the manufacture and sale of agricultural implements for many years. He married in 1862, Matilda R. Magill, daughter of Jonathan P. and Mary (Watson) Magill, of Solebury, and they have one child, Mary M. Atkinson, now the wife of H. W. Turner, a veterinary surgeon, who practiced his profession for a number of years at Lahaska, Bucks county, and for several years past has been engaged as veterinary surgeon for an equestrian establishment traveling through different parts of Europe and America. Dr. and Mrs. Turner have no children.

SILAS C. ATKINSON, Deceased, son of Mahlon and Sarah (Smith) Atkinson, was born in Buckingham township, on the old Atkinson homestead, September 20, 1843, and died on his farm near Bycot, in October, 1876. He was educated at the public schools of Buckingham, and at the Excelsior Normal Institute at Carversville. He married, October 17, 1867, Anna C., daughter of Thomas and Minerva (Pennoch) Wollaston, of Chester county, Pennsylvania, and settled on the farm where he died, and where his widow and family still reside. He was a man of fine qualities, and was universally esteemed in the community in which he lived.

Mrs. Atkinson was a lineal descendant of Jeremiah Wollaston, of New Castle county, Delaware, who married Catharine, daughter of George and Catharine (Hollingsworth) Robinson, at Newark, (now Kennett) Monthly Meeting of Friends, 9 mo. 21, 1716. Their son, James Wollaston, born 11 mo. 26, 1724, married Mary Chambers, 11 mo. 16, 1752, at New Garden Meeting, Chester county, was the great-grandfather of Mrs. Atkinson. The Wollastons were large landholders in Delaware. Thomas Wollaston, the father of Mrs. Atkinson, was born in Delaware, and died in Chester county at the age of eighty years.

Silas C. and Anna C. (Wollaston) Atkinson were the parents of four children: Alice M., residing at home; Sarah H., wife of Robert H. Engle, of Mt. Holly, New Jersey; Jane; and Susan W., the two latter named residing at home. All the children are graduates of Swarthmore College. The family are members of the Society of Friends.

WILLIAM H. ATKINSON, of Buckingham, son of Joseph and Eliza (Hibbs) Atkinson, and grandson of Thomas and Jane (Smith) Atkinson, some account of whom is given upon other pages of this work, was born at Pineville, Bucks county, Pennsylvania, August 10, 1850.

Joseph S. Atkinson, deceased, the father of the subject of this sketch, was born in Buckingham township, August 9, 1823, being a son of Thomas and Jane (Smith) Atkinson. He was a prominent farmer and large landholder in Bucks county. The first fifty years of his life was spent in Buckingham township. About 1879 he purchased the Shaw farm in Solebury township, near Lahaska, and lived thereon for several years. He later built a house in Lahaska and retired from farming. He died 3 mo. 27, 1900. His wife was Eliza, daughter of William and Margery (Kirk) Hibbs, of Pineville, by whom he had four children: William H., the subject of this sketch; Thomas, who died on the Solebury homestead in 1903; Mary, wife of George Watson, of Doylestown; and Albert, who died in infancy.

The subject of this sketch was reared on the farm in Buckingham, attended the public schools of the neighborhood, and later the Excelsior Normal Institute at Carversville and the Doylestown English and Classical Seminary. On arriving at manhood he took charge of the home farm, his father being occupied with the management of his other properties, and, on his marriage in 1879, his father removed to Solebury, and he took entire charge of the farm, which with six other farms he acquired at his father's death.

He married, in 1879, Elmira, daughter, of Jesse K. and Sarah (Headley) Harper, of Falls township. Mr. Harper was a prominent and highly esteemed farmer of Falls; he died in 1898, aged eighty-three years, and his wife died in 1893, aged seventy-seven years. Both were prominent members of the Society of Friends. Mr. and Mrs. Atkinson are the parents of two children, Eva W. and J. Harper, both residing at home. The family are members of the Society of Friends. In politics Mr. Atkinson is a Republican, but has never sought or held public office.

STEPHEN K. ATKINSON, Prothonotary of the county of Bucks, was born in Upper Makefield township, Bucks county, Pennsylvania, June 7, 1854, and is a son of Jesse H. and Martha B. (Stradling) Atkinson.

An account of the migration of John and Christopher Atkinson from Lancashire with their families, the death of the head of both families on the ill-fated "Brittanica" in 1692, and the subsequent marriage and settlement of John Atkinson, Jr., in Makefield, is given in the sketch of The Atkinson Family in this volume.

William Atkinson, second son of John Jr. and Mary (Smith) Atkinson, was born in Upper Makefield in 1721, and married, September 1, 1742, Mary Tomlinson, daughter of Joseph Tomlinson. He inherited from his father 120 acres of the homestead in Upper Makefield, and lived thereon until his death in April, 1800. He and his wife Mary were the parents of thirteen children, of whom eight lived to mature age. 1. Mary, married John Rose; 2. John, married Hannah Lee; 3. Sarah, and 4. Eleanor, both of whom married Lees; 5. Isaac, who moved to Maryland; 6. Phebe; 7. William; 8. Joseph.

John Atkinson, eldest surviving son of William and Mary (Tomlinson) Atkinson, inherited the homestead and lived thereon all his life, dying in 1831. He married his second cousin, Hannah Lee, in 1769, and had twelve children, nine of whom lived to maturity, viz: May, born 1770, married Joseph Gummere; Hannah, born 1772, married Joshua Burleigh; Esther, born 1774, married Joseph Randall; Jane, born 1775, married Charles Deeder; Elizabeth, born 1777, married Jacob Cooper; John, born 1778, married first Mary Atkinson, and second Elizabeth Harding; Phebe, born 1781, married William Neeld; William, born 1782, married Belinda Harvey; and Samuel, born 1789, married Mary Harding.

Samuel Atkinson, youngest son of John and Hannah (Lee) Atkinson, was born in Upper Makefield in the year 1789, and lived there all his life with the exception of four years spent in Doyles-

town. On April 28, 1821, his parents conveyed to him sixty-eight acres of the old homestead on which he lived until he became recorder of deeds in 1836, and which he conveyed to his son Samuel in 1842. He was commissioned recorder of deeds of Bucks county, January 23, 1836, and filled that position for four years, being recommissioned January 4, 1839, for one year, the constitutional convention of 1838 having made the office elective and to go into effect with the fall election of 1839. He also filled the position of deputy register of wills while an incumbent of the recorder's office. At the expiration of his second term as recorder he purchased a property in the village of Buckmanville, where he lived the remainder of his life, dying August 23, 1858. He was commissioned April 14, 1840, a justice of the peace of Upper Makefield township, and did a large amount of public business. He was a Whig in politics, and took part in the organization of the Republican party in 1856. Like all his ancestors for many generations, he was a member of Wrightstown Meeting of Friends. He married Mary Harding, of Southampton, and they were the parents of nine children, three of whom died young: Charles, Watson, and John. Those who survived were: Rachel, who married Kinsey Tomlinson, a prominent resident of Newtown; Samuel, who married Rebecca, daughter of Bezeleel Eastburn and lived and died on the old homestead; Silas L., who married Elizabeth Eastburn, and was a printer for several years in Doylestown, later of Langhorne, where recently died; Ralph L., who married first Sarah Ann Scarborough, and (second) Martha E. Johnson, and removed to Shelby county, Ohio; Jesse H., the father of Stephen K.; and Hannah, who married Stephen L. Kirk, a prominent merchant of Langhorne.

Jesse H. Atkinson, son of Samuel and Mary (Harding) Atkinson, was born in Upper Makefield, May 6, 1824, and was reared on his father's farm near Buckmanville, acquiring his education at the public schools. During his father's incumbency of the office of recorder of deeds he filled the position of transcribing clerk. He married, October 7, 1847, Martha B. Stradling, born August 12, 1828, daughter of William and Sarah (Carver) Stradling, of Newtown township. William Stradling was a son of Joseph and Hannah (Michener) Stradling, of Plumstead, grandson of Daniel, and great-grandson of Thomas and Lydia (Doan) Stradling, who were married at Middletown, October 5, 1719, and settled at Newtown township, where Thomas died in 1764. Sarah (Carver) Stradling, born February 19, 1794, was a daughter of William and Phebe (Worthington) Carver, granddaughter of William and Sarah (Strickland) Carver, and great-granddaughter of William and Elizabeth (Walmsley) Carver, the first of the family to settle in Buckingham, and William Carver, who came from England in 1682 and settled in Byberry, Philadelphia county.

Jesse H. Atkinson followed farming for a few years after his marriage in Upper Makefield, and later engaged in droving and dealing in western horses, residing in Newtown township. He was actively interested in local politics, and was elected to the office of register of wills of Bucks county in the fall of 1872, on the Republican ticket, and served the term of three years. He died January 4, 1876, one day after the expiration of his term of office. His wife, Martha B., still survives him, residing in Newtown, Bucks county. They were the parents of four children: Georgine T., who died at the age of thirteen years; William S., who died in his eighteenth year; Stephen K., the subject of this sketch; Sallie, born 1862, married Steward S. Crouse, of Riegelsville, Bucks county, and resided in Philadelphia, where he died in 1887, leaving three children,—J. Clyde, Mary and Fred.

Stephen K. Atkinson was educated at the Hughesian School, Buckingham, and at Doylestown English and Classical Seminary. At an early age he accepted a position as clerk in the general merchandise store at Holicong, and later worked on the farm for Josiah R. Pennington, in Buckingham, in the summer months, for three years attending school in winter. On the election of his father to the office of register' of wills he entered the office as his assistant and deputy. At the death of his father he engaged in farming for a few years, and then engaged in the clothing and gents' furnishing business at Doylestown, and later was employed as a traveling salesman for a wholesale house. He removed to Newtown, where he owned and conducted a livery stable for a few years, and later engaged in selling cigars for a large wholesale house. He has for several years taken an active interest in local politics, and was nominated and elected to the office of prothonotary of Bucks county in the fall of 1903.

He married May 24, 1877, Sallie M. Ruth, born in Buckingham, May 21, 1858, daughter of Jesse and Martha (Carver) Ruth. She is also a descendant of William Carver, the immigrant of 1682, her maternal grandparents being Izri and Mary (Hartley) Carver, the former of whom was a son of William and Martha (Addis) Carver, and a grandson of Joseph Carver, another son of William and Elizabeth (Walmsley) Carver before mentioned. On the paternal side Mrs. Atkinson is descended from early German settlers in Upper Bucks. The children of Stephen K. and Sallie M. (Ruth) Atkinson are: 1. Elmer H., born April

21, 1879, married Clara Sergeant, daughter of Charles Sergeant of Langhorne and resides in Newtown; they had three children, Ogden, Eugene, and Elmer R., the latter of whom died August 7, 1905; 2. Martha Ruth, born April 4, 1882, wife of Dr. George R. Doan of Newtown. They have one child, Ronald. Mr. Atkinson still retains his residence at Newtown, as well as an active interest in the affairs of that borough.

HOWARD W. ATKINSON, of Doylestown, is a descendant on both the paternal and maternal side from the oldest families in Bucks county. He was born at Davisville, Southampton township, Bucks county, November 22, 1853, and is a son of Mahlon and Mary Ann (Wood) Atkinson, and a grandson of Mahlon and Martha (Walmsley) Atkinson.

His paternal ancestor, John Atkinson, was born at Scotforth, Lancashire, England, 9 mo. 25, 1695, and came to this country at the age of four years. His father, John Atkinson, married Susanna Hynde, daughter of Richard, at Scotforth, 2 mo. 8, 1686, and in company with his brother Christopher and their respective families embarked for America in the ship "Brittanica" in April, 1699, bearing a certificate from Lancaster Meeting of Friends to Friends in Pennsylvania. John and Susanna Atkinson both died on the voyage, and their three children (William, Mary and John) were taken in charge by the Friends of Middletown Meeting in Bucks county on their arrival. John, the eldest, married 8 mo. 15, 1717, Mary, daughter of William and Mary (Croasdale) Smith, of Wrightstown, and the following year settled on a tract of two hundred acres of land in Upper Makefield, where their eight children were born, and where the father died in 1752.

Ezekiel, the sixth child of John and Mary, born in 1728, purchased a portion of the homestead tract and died there in June, 1768. He married in 1754, Rachel Gilbert, born 11 mo. 14, 1732, daughter of Benjamin and Sarah (Mason) Gilbert, of Byberry, granddaughter of Joseph and Rachel (Livezey) Gilbert, and great-granddaughter of John and Florence Gilbert, who came from England in the ship "Welcome," in 1682, settling first in Bensalem, Bucks county, but removing to Byberry in 1695, where his descendants resided for many generations. Ezekiel and Rachel (Gilbert) Atkinson were the parents of five children: Benjamin, Thomas, Watson, Rachel and Ezekiel, the latter born after the death of the father in 1768. After the death of her husband, Rachel Atkinson returned with her children to Byberry, and later married William Walton, of that place,

Henry G. Mayer

The Rembrandt Eng. Co. Phila.

known as "Jersey Billy," to distinguish him from his cousins of the name. Here the Atkinson children were reared. Benjamin, the eldest, married Jane Adams and died in 1816, leaving a family of six children. Thomas was a captain of a company in the war of 1812. Ezekiel, the youngest, married and removed to Drumore township, Lancaster county, where he purchased land in 1818, and died in 1842.

Mahlon Atkinson, the grandfather of the subject of this sketch, was born and reared in Byberry, but removed with his father to Drumore, where he purchased a farm of fifty-two acres in 1822. He died four years later, in August, 1826. His widow, Martha, returned to Byberry with her five children, Mary, Howard H., Violetta, Angelina, and Mahlon R., the latter born a few months after his father's death. Martha, the wife of Mahlon Atkinson, was a daughter of Daniel T. and Mary (Willett) Walmsley, and a granddaughter of General Augustin and Elizabeth (Hicks) Willett. General Willett was one of the first soldiers of the Revolution to enter active service; he was commissioned as a caption in the First Pennsylvania Battalion, raised under act of Congress of October 12, 1775, for the expedition against Canada, on October 27, 1775, and suffered the terrible privations and hardships of that disastrous campaign of nearly a year on the frontiers of Canada. Elizabeth Hicks, wife of General Willett, was a daughter of Gilbert and Mary (Rodman) Hicks, and a descendant of Robert Hicks, the Pilgrim Father, who came to Plymouth, Massachusetts, in the "Fortune" in 1621, from Southwark, London, England. He was a leather dresser in Bermonfdey street, Southwark, and had been twice married, his first wife being Elizabeth Morgan, by whom he had four children, Thomas, Elizabeth, John and Stephen. His second wife was Margaret Winslow, who with her four children, Samuel, Ephraim, Lydia and Phebe, followed her husband to Plymouth in the ship "Ann," arriving in June, 1722, and they settled at Duxbury. The sons John and Stephen removed to Long Island in 1642. The subsequent history of the descendants of John Hicks is given elsewhere in this work, under the title of "The Hicks Family."

Mahlon R. Atkinson was born at Byberry Cross Roads, where his mother had taken up her residence with her relatives after the death of her husband, on February 1, 1827. He learned the trade of a house painter, and early in life removed to Southampton township, Bucks county, near Davisville, where he followed his trade during the active years of his life, removing later to Ivyland. He died at the residence of his son, Lawrence Rush Atkinson, at Hatboro, October 17, 1904. His widow, who was Mary Ann Wood, survives him. They were the parents of ten children, viz.: S. Emma, who died unmarried in 1898; Charles S., of Doylestown; Howard W.; Violetta, wife of William Kline, of Philadelphia; Lawrence Rush, of Hatboro; Matilda, wife of Courtland Yerkes, of Willow Grove; Anna, deceased; Joshua J., and Harry B. of South Amboy; and A. Louisa, wife of Albert Hohensack, of Ivyland.

Howard W. Atkinson was born at Davisville, November 22, 1853, and at the age of eight years went to live at Huntingdon Valley, where he remained until the age of sixteen years, when he reurned home and learned the trade of a house painter, which he followed for fifteen years. In 1876 he removed to Doylestown, where he carried on painting, employing twelve to fifteen men. In 1884 he began the business of an undertaker, which he has since conducted at Doylestown with success. In 1891 he opened the summer resort known as Oakland, just outside the borough of Doylestown, formerly occupied by the Doylestown English and Classical Seminary, which has become one of the popular institutions of the neighborhood under the conduct of Mr. Atkinson and his excellent wife. Mr. Atkinson married, March 9, 1885, Emma Wilson, of Doylestown, and they are the parents of four children: Mary, Julia, Augustina, and Frances.

HON. HENRY G. MOYER, of Perkasie, Bucks county, Pennsylvania, for many years prominent in the business and official circles of Bucks county, was born in Hilltown, Bucks county, August 28, 1848, and is a son of the late Henry A. and Sarah (Gerhart) Moyer, of Hilltown, and is descended from early German settlers on the Skippack, nearly two centuries ago. The name of Moyer, Meyers. Myers. now almost as common in Bucks county as Smith, was originally spelled Meyer, and the present bearers of the name are descended from several German emigrants of that name who settled in what is now Montgomery county, in the first quarter of the eighteenth century, from whence their descendants migrated into Bucks county in the second and third generation.

I. Christian Meyer, the paternal ancestor of this sketch, was a landowner in Lower Salford township, Montgomery county, as early as 1719, and possibly some years earlier, and was one of the founders of the earliest congregations of Mennonites in that locality. All the earlier generations of the family belonged to that sect, though many of their descendants now belong to other denominations. Christian Meyer died in June, 1757, leaving three sons, Christian, Jacob and Samuel, the last of whom settled in Hilltown; and daughters Elizabeth, who married Nicholas Oblinger; Anna, who married Henry Funck, and Barbara, who married Abraham Reiff. The descendants of the two latter are now quite numerous in Bucks county.

II. Christian Meyer, Jr., son of the above, born in 1705, died 1787, was a farmer in Franconia, Montgomery county, and left sons, Christian, Jacob and Samuel, and daughters, Esther, wife of Christian Gehman; Anna, wife of John Kratz; Maria, wife of Martin Detweiler; and Barbara, wife of Abraham Kratz.

III. Rev. Jacob Meyer, second son of Christian and Magdalena, of Franconia, born January 28, 1730, married (second) Barbara Derstein, of Rockhill, and settled in Hilltown township, where he owned over three hundred acres of land. He was for many years a preacher of the Mennonite faith in Hilltown, and died there in 1782, leaving a family of nine children.

IV. Joseph Moyer (as the name then came to be spelled), second son of the Rev. Jacob and Barbara (Durstein) Meyer, was born in Hilltown, June 19, 1774, and died there June 21, 1815. He was a farmer and lived near Yost's, now Schwenk's mill, north of the present village of Blooming Glen. Joseph Moyer was quite a noted penman and more or less of an artist, several specimens of his artistic work with the pen being still extant. He married, April 7, 1795, Barbara Angeny, who was born in Bucks county, April 8, 1770, and died about the year 1857, and they were the parents of eight children, of whom seven lived to maturity, viz.: Jacob, who migrated to Canada; Samuel, who lived and died on the homestead; Joseph, who died in 1842; William A., who died in 1885; Henry A., see forward; Elizabeth who married Abraham Gerhart; and Mary, who married Abraham Hunsberger.

V. Henry A. Moyer, youngest son of Joseph and Barbara (Angeny) Moyer, was born in Hilltown, October 26, 1807, and died there August 4, 1875. He received a good education, and during his younger days taught school for a number of years, but on his marriage, December 8, 1833, to Sarah Gerhart, abandoned the life of a pedagogue and settled down as a farmer in Hilltown. He took a prominent part in local affairs, and filled a number of township offices, among others holding the office of assessor for many years. His wife, Sarah Gerhart, was born August 20, 1814, and died February 20, 1890. Their children were: Lydia, wife of Samuel M. Gerhart; Abraham G., deceased; Joseph G., a prominent business man of Perkasie; Barbara, wife of Samuel G. Kramer; Sarah Jane, wife of Henry O. Moyer, of Perkasie; Jacob G., of Perkasie; Isaiah G., deceased; and Henry G., the subject of this sketch.

VI. Henry G. Moyer, born and reared on his father's farm in Hilltown, attended the public schools, and later other institutions of learning, and closed his education with a course at Quaker City Business College, Philadelphia, from which he graduated with high honors in 1868, at the age of twenty. In 1879 he was elected justice of the peace, and since that time has done a large amount of public business, officiating as executor, administrator and agent in the settlement of estates, attending to the survey and transfer of real estate and other business of a public character. In 1882 he purchased a one-half interest in "The Central News," a paper published at Perkasie, with Mahlon Sellers, and conducted it under the firm name of Mahlon Sellers & Co., becoming one of its editors. Mr. Sellers dying soon after, his interest in the paper was purchased by Samuel R. Kramer, and the firm name became Moyer & Kramer, and that firm conducted the paper and a job printing office in connection therewith until 1904. Under their management "The Central News" became a successful weekly paper, and enjoys a circulation equal to that of any weekly paper published in upper Bucks. Mr. Moyer is an ardent Republican in politics, and has been for many years prominently identified with the local organization of the party in Bucks county, serving as delegate to a number of state and other conventions. In 1882 he was the party nominee for representative in the assembly, but was defeated though receiving much more than his party vote in his own locality, the county being then Democratic. In 1894 he was elected to the state senate by a majority of 1577 votes, and in the sessions of 1895 and 1897 served upon many of the important committees of the upper house. Mr. Moyer still does a large amount of public business. On the organization of Perkasie National Bank, he was elected president and still fills that position, giving much of his time to the affairs of the bank. On January 31, 1905, he was appointed postmaster at Perkasie, Pennsylvania, by President Roosevelt, which office he fills with satisfaction, and has established four rural free delivery routes from said office. He is a member of the United Evangelical Church, and has been for many years superintendent of the Sabbath School and class leader of the local church at Perkasie, rendering eminent and efficient services in that capacity. He is a member of the Masonic fraternity and affiliated with the Odd Fellows and O. U. A. M. He married Emeline Seiple, of Allentown, Pennsylvania, and they have been the parents of seven children, of whom but two survive Mabel Rebecca, born October 10, 1882, and Henry Clayton, born March 5, 1888.

WILKINSON COAT-OF-ARMS.

OGDEN D. WILKINSON. Lieutenant Lawrence Wilkinson, the ancestor of the Wilkinson family of Bucks county, belonged to a very old and respected family, one noted for its consistent adherence to the throne of England, and from time to time the recipient of its favors. He was a son of William Wilkinson, of Lancaster, county Durham, England, by his wife Mary Conyers, daughter of Christopher Conyers, of Horden, and sister of Sir John Conyers, Baronet; and a grandson of Lawrence Wilkinson, of Harpsley House, Lancaster, Durham. The arms of the family were confirmed and the crest granted to Lawrence Wilkinson, last mentioned, September 18, 1615, by Richard St. George Norrey, King of Arms, as shown by the following extract from the records of the College of Arms:

"Being now requested by Lawrence Wilkinson, to make search for the anciente coate Armor belonging to that name and Familye, which fynde to be Azure a fesse erminiois between three unicorns passant Argent, and for that I can fynde noe Crest proper or belonging thereunto, as unto manye anciente coates at this day there is wanting, he hath further requested me to confrme unto him such a one as he maye lawfullye beare—I hav likewise condescended and allowyde him the Crest ensvnage, (vide) a demy unicorne erazed erminoys standing on a murall crown gules, as more plainly appearth depicted in the margent hereof. All of which Arms amd Crest, I the said Richard St. George Norrey, doe give, grant, ratifye and confyrme unto sayd Lawrence Wilkenson and to the several descendants of hys bodye forever, bearing their due differences."

Lawrence Wilkinson, the younger, first above mentioned, was born in Lancaster, county Durham, at about the date of the confirmation of the arms to his grandsire as above recited. He became a lieutenant in the army of Charles I., and was taken prisoner by the Scotch and Parlimentary troops on the surrender of Newcastle-on-Tyne, October 22, 1644. In common with many others who fell into the hands of the enemies of the crown, he was deprived of his property. On the records of sequestrations in Durham we find the following item, in the period between 1645 and 1647: "Lawrence Wilkinson, of Lancaster, officer in arms, went to New England." His estate having been sequestered and sold, he obtained permission from Lord Fairfax to emigrate to America, and in 1652, with his wife and son, he settled in Providence, Rhode Island, where he had lands granted him. He was made a freeman in 1658, and in 1673 was chosen deputy to the general court. He was known as Captain Wilkinson, and was a soldier in the Indian wars. He was a member of colonial assembly which met at Portsmouth in 1659. He died May 9, 1692. This Lawrence Wilkinson had married Susannah Smith, daughter of Christopher Smith, who also settled at Providence, Rhode Island. The children of Lawrence and Susannah (Smith) Wilkinson, were six, viz: Samuel, Susannah, John, Joanna, Josias, and another Susannah. While we are chiefly concerned with the descendants of Samuel, the eldest of the above children, it might be pertinent to here state that John, the second son, married Huldah Aldrich, of Rhode Island, and their son, Ichabod Wilkinson, born in Rhode Island in 1720, removed to Bucks county, Pennsylvania, bringing a certificate from Smithfield, Rhode Island, to Wrightstown Meeting of Friends, 12 mo. 1, 1742, and married at that meeting, 7 mo. 7, 1743, Sarah Chapman, of Wrightstown, and settled at New Hope, where he erected a forge in 1753, and became the owner of extensive tracts of land in Solebury township. He died prior to 1780, leaving children: Joseph; Zibiah, wife of Peter Ink; Sarah, wife of John Prince; Huldah and Mary, some of whom have left descendants in Bucks county.

Samuel Wilkinson, eldest son of Lawrence and Susannah, married Plain Wickenden, daughter of Rev. William Wickenden, the second pastor of the first Baptist church in America. Samuel Wilkinson was commissioned a captain in the provincial militia of Rhode Island, April 4, 1697, and took part in the early Indian wars. He was a surveyor, and assisted in running the line between Massachusetts and Rhode Island in 1711. He was also a member of the provincial assembly, and a justice of the peace. He died August 27, 1827. He took a very active part in the Indian wars, and the old records of Providence give abundant evidence of the high position he held in provincial affairs. A summary of the positions he held, as taken from the original records, is, as follows: Samuel Wilkinson appointed constable July 12,

1683; swore allegiance to Charles I, May 1, 1682; chosen justice of the peace May 3, 1704; October, 1705, Captain Samuel Wilkinson, deputy to colonial assembly for Providence; February 25, 1708, reappointed deputy; October 27, 1707, Captain Samuel Wilkinson, deputy to assembly held at Warwick; October 31, 1716, deputy for Providence; May 14, 1719, Captain Samuel Wilkinson appointed to settle boundary dispute between Rhode Island and Massachusetts. (John and Josiah, brothers of Samuel were also in the Indian Wars, and the historians say "fought valiantly").

Samuel and Plain Wilkinson were the parents of six children, viz: Samuel, John, William, Joseph, Ruth, and Susannah. Of these Ruth married William Hopkins, and became the mother of two distinguished men, Stephen Hopkins for many years governor of Rhode Island, and a signer of the Declaration of Independence, and Essex Hopkins, the first commander of an American fleet in 1776.

John Wilkinson, second son of Samuel and Plain Wilkinson, was born on his father's homestead at Loquiessett, Providence, Rhode Island, on January 25, 1677-8. He left there when a young man and located in Hunterdon county, New Jersey, where he married Mary ————. He later removed to Wrightstown township, and in 1713 purchased three hundred and seven acres of land lying partly in the three townships of Wrightstown, Warwick and Buckingham, near what is now Rushland Station, on the Northeast Pennsylvania Railroad. In 1728 he returned to Providence and participated in the settlement of his father's estate, signing on July 3 of that year a power of attorney for his brothers and brothers-in-law, to sell his father's land. The deed for the land, dated July 6, 1728, and recorded at Providence, is signed by Josiah Wilkinson, of Providence, John Wilkinson of Wrightstown, in the county of Bucks and Province of Pennsylvania, William Hopkins and Ruth, his wife, James Angell and Susanna his wife, David, Samuel, and Huldah Wilkinson, Ichabod Comstock and Zabiah his wife, and Joseph Arnold and Patience his wife. John Wilkinson was one of the justices of the peace of Bucks county who were commissioned to hold the court of common pleas, quarter sessions and orphans' court for the county, and he became a large landowner on both sides of Neshaminy, and a prominent man in the community. He was an active member of Wrightstown Friends' Meeting. His will is dated February, 1751, and was proven April 23, 1751. He had seven children, viz: Mary, born July 17, 1709, married Joseph Chapman; Keziah, married Thomas Ross, and was the grandmother of Judge John Ross (see Ross family); Plain, married Peter Ball; Su-

sanna, married Adrien Dawes; Ruth, married Joseph Chapman; John, see forward; Josiah, who married Rosanna Kemble and (second) Mary Carver, daughter of William Carver and Mary Walmsley; and Joseph, who married Barbara Lacy. The last two removed to Chester county in 1762.

John Wilkinson, son of John above mentioned, was born in the year 1711. He became a very prominent citizen of Bucks county, serving in the colonial assembly for the years 1761, 1762-3, and in that of the commonwealth of Pennsylvania for the years 1776-1781, and 1782, and as a justice of the peace from 1764 to 1774 inclusive. At the organization of the committee of safety in 1774 he participated therein, and was one of the delegates from Bucks county to the conference held at Philadelphia July July 15, 1774; was selected on December 15, 1774, as one of the committee of observation; was again a delegate to the provincial convention at Philadelphia, January 23, 1775, and a member of the first constitutional convention, July 15, 1776. When, however, it became evident that war would ensue, he, with a number of other members of the Society of Friends, on July 21, 1775, "alleging scruples of conscience relative to the business necessarily transacted by the Committee, desired to be relieved from further attendance." Later, however, his patriotic feelings got the better of his religious feelings, and in spite of the protests of Wrightstown Meeting, of which he was a member, he again united himself with the defenders of the rights of his country, and continued to take an active part in that defence until his death on May 31, 1782, serving as lieutenant-colonel of militia, and filling other important positions. He was appointed lieutenant-cononel of the Third Bucks County Associators, August 16, 1775; and member of conference of delegates for all the counties at Philadelphia, July 18, 1776. He was constantly on important committees as representative of either the assembly or the committee of safety, in both of which he represented his district, during the most trying time of the Revolution. He was appointed justice of the peace and judge of the court of common pleas, September 3, 1776; committee and referee to Indian lands; one of committee to consider draft and report to the house what laws it will be necessary should be passed, at this season; (Journals of Assembly, vol. i, p. 133); was appointed by assembly one of committee to consider an act for emitting the sum of 200,000 pounds in bills of credit for the defence of the State, and providing a fund for sinking the same by tax on all estate, real and personal; as a member of the committee of safety he served upon the committee of observation and committee of cor-

LIEUT. COL. JOHN WILKINSON

respondence, and was a delegate to the second convention and conferences, and also, February 19, 1763, was appointed a committee to audit accounts of Benjamin Franklin. He died May 31, 1782. The Pennsylvania Gazette of June 19, 1782, has the following obituary article: "On Friday, the 31st ult., departed this life at Wrightstown, in the county of Bucks, John Wilkinson, Esq., in the seventy-first year of his age, after a long and painful illness, and on the Sunday following his remains were interred in the Friends' burying ground, the funeral being attended by a very large concourse of people of all denominations Mr. Wilkinson was a man of very reputable abilities and of a sound judgment, scrupulously just in all of his transactions, free from bigotry to religion or to party, and a friend to merit whenever it was found. As a companion, a friend, a neighbor, a master, an husband, a father, a guardian to the orphan and the widow, his life was amiable and exemplary. He served his people in several important offices with fidelity and applause, under the old constitutions as well as the new. His conduct in the present Revolution was such as entitled him to the peculiar esteem of all the friends of this country, but it drew on him the rage of enthusiastic bigots.

"He was born and educated among the people called Quakers, and was a member in full standing in the Wrightstown Meeting. His life was an ornament to the Society.

"He mingled not in idle strife and furious debates, but lived as became a Christian, studying peace with all men.

"His principles led him to believe that defensive war was lawful. He was strongly attracted to a republican form of government and the liberties of the people, and when Great Britain, by her folly and wickedness, made it necessary to oppose her measures from judgment and principle he espoused the cause of his country. He was unanimously chosen a member of our convention, and afterwards served in the Assembly with zeal and integrity, becoming a freeman and a Christian.

"This unhappily aroused the resentment of the Society with which he was connected, so that one committee after another were dealing with him and persecuting him to give a testimonial renunciation of what they were pleased to consider as errors of his political life, though there was no rule or order of the meeting which made his conduct a crime.

"This demand he rejected although as tending to belie his own conscience, but at length worried with their importunities, weakened by the growing infirmities of age, and fondly hoping that his country might dispense with his services, he consented to promise that he

would hold no other appointments under the constitution.

"This seemed to be satisfactory for a time, but, when Sir William Howe began his victorious march through Pennsylvania, a more pressing sense of duty urged his brethren to renew their visit, while his dear son lay dying in his house, and to demand an immediate and preemptory renunciation of his past conduct.

"Provoked by this indecent and unfeeling application he gave them a decisive answer, and preferred the honest dictates of his conscience to his membership in the meeting and was, for his patriotism alone, formally expelled as unworthy of Christian fellowship.

"The testimony of the meeting against him on this occasion was heretofore published in this paper. We trust he is now in those mansions where the wicked cease from troubling and the weary are at rest."

Colonel Wilkinson was twice married. By his first wife, Mary Lacy, married 3 mo. 21, 1740, who was a sister to General John Lacey, he had five children: Mary, born in 1741, married Stephen Twining; John, married Jane Chapman; Stephen, James and Rachel, all died unmarried. By his second wife, Hannah Hughes, (born 3 mo. 7, 1742, married 2 mo., 1770, died April 18, 1791), he had four children: Martha, who married a Bennett; Ann Lucy, married General Samuel A. Smith; Hannah, who married May 22, 1796, Abner Reeder, and removed to Trenton, and Colonel Elisha Wilkinson. Hannah Hughes, the second wife of Colonel John Wilkinson, was a daughter of Professor Mathew Hughes, Jr., (he was lieutenant-colonel of the Associated Regiment of Bucks county, 1747-8) and Elizabeth Stevenson, married March 17, 1733, the latter being a daughter of Thomas Stevensòn and Sarah Jennings, and granddaughter of Thomas Stevenson, of Newtown, Long Island, and Elizabeth Lawrence, daughter of Colonel William Lawrence. Sarah Jennings was a daughter of Governor Samuel Jennings, of New Jersey. Mathew Hughes, Sr., the grandfather of Hannah Wilkinson, was a very prominent man in Buckingham, Bucks county, a member of assembly, justice, etc. His wife was Elizabeth (Biles) Beaks, daughter of William Biles, provincial counsellor, and widow of Stephenson Beaks, the record of whom is noted elsewhere in this volume.

The Wilkinsons now residing in Bucks county are principally the descendants of John and Jane (Chapman) Wilkinson, who had children, John, Abraham, Elias and Amos. John, the father of these children, died in 1778, and on his deathbed received from his father a deed for one hundred and fifty acres of the old homestead, that part of his grandfather's purchase lying in Warwick township, and it has descended from father to son to the present day, being now occupied by Charles T. Wilkinson, a grandson of Abraham, the son of John and Jane (Chapman) Wilkinson. (See sketch of Charles T. Winkinson in this volume.)

Colonel Elisha Wilkinson, born 1772, died March 15, 1846, youngest son of John and Hannah (Hughes) Wilkinson, became a very prominent man in Bucks county. He was lieutenant-colonel of the Thirty-first Regiment Pennsylvania militia, as early as 1807, and filled that position and that of colonel for many years. He was sheriff of Bucks county for the term of 1809-1811. During the war of 1812-14 he was quarter-master of the Second Division, First Brigade, Pennsylvania militia, of which his brother-in-law, General Samuel A. Smith, was brigadier-general. He later became assistant quartermaster general of Pennsylvania Volunteer militia. He was proprietor of the inn at Bushington from 1805 to 1809, and from 1811 to 1836 of the popular hotel at Centreville, Buckingham township. He was a man of fine appearance and a great horseman. He introduced into Bucks county a very fine breed of Arabian horses, and maintained a track near his tavern, where his blooded colts were broken and trained. He was twice married, first on April 11, 1792, to Anna Dungan, daughter of Elias and Diana (Carrell) Dungan, of Northampton township, who bore him four children: John A., a member of the Doylestown bar, who died in 1830; Ogden D., see forward. Hannah, born March 22, 1794, married October 18, 1811, Crispin Blackfan, who was prothonotary of Bucks county in 1821-4, and later removed to Trenton, New Jersey. Hannah died May 8, 1818, and Blackfan married her sister, Eleanor, born August 14, 1796, died December 6, 1858. Anna (Dungan) Wilkinson died May 31, 1810, aged thirty-six years, and Colonel Elisha married (second) Maria Whiteman, by whom he had six children: 1. Sarah Ann, who died at Trenton, New Jersey, in 1880, unmarried; 2. Ross Wilkinson, who was educated at West Point, and served as a major during the civil war, and after its close purchased a plantation in Louisiana, where he died in 1880. He was United States marshal of the district at the time of his death. He married Hannah Ann Folwell, of Philadelphia, and had two children; his son, Henry Clay Wilkinson, was also educated at West Point, and was adjutant of Coloney Woodman's Forty-fourth Regiment Pennsylvania Volunteers during the civil war. 3. Samuel Smith Wilkinson left Bucks county and settled in Dallas, Texas, where he died, February 26, 1879. 4. Edward Blackfan Wilkinson, was a dentist, and located at Huntsville, Alabama.

He died of cholera, while on a visit to Paris, France, June 20, 1854, at the age of twenty-five years, and is buried at Mount Parnasse, Paris. 5. Elisha, died in infancy. 6. Algernon Logan Wilkinson, born October 22, 1821, settled in Huntsville, Alabama, in 1844, where he practiced medicine, married, and reared a family of children.

Anna (Dungan) Wilkinson belonged to one of the oldest families in Pennsylvania. Her father, Elias Dungan, was a soldier during the Revolution, and a prominent member and deacon of Southampton Baptist church. He was a son of Clement and Eleanor Dungan, and a grandson of Jeremiah and Elizabeth (Drake) Dungan, and a great-grandson of Rev. Thomas and Elizabeth (Weaver) Dungan, who came from Rhode Island in 1684, and established the first Baptist church in Bucks county. (See Dungan Family).

Ogden Dungan Wilkinson, second son of Colonel Elisha and Anna (Dungan) Wilkinson, was born in Bucks county, 1807; married, March 6, 1834, Sarah Snowhill Dill, born August 16, 1801, daughter of George Dill and Ann Redinger, who were married at Germantown, February 6, 1797, she being the daughter of John Redinger and Elizabeth Beker, who were married February 14, 1758. George Dill was the son of John and Elizabeth Dill; his father, John Dill, was an officer during the Revolutionary war. George Dill was born February 7, 1772, settled in Trenton, New Jersey, and April 2, 1798, purchased his homestead property. He was one of the largest real estate holders in Trenton, and did much to build up and improve the city. He was interested in numerous business enterprises, was one of the founders of the Mechanics' Bank and for some years its president. Ogden Dungan Wilkinson moved to Trenton, New Jersey, in 1832. He and his brother-in-law, Crispin Blackfan, built the Delaware and Raritan Canal, from Trenton to New Brunswick. They were many years in business together and opened up and built up much of the city.

Ogden Wilkinson (or Colonel Wilkinson, as he was known, he having been colonel of militia), was one of Trenton's most influential citizens. He was interested in many of the business enterprises and acted as director of several of the banks and filled other local as well as municipal positions of trust. He died August 24, 1866. His wife died February 16, 1891. They were the parents of several children, only one of whom, Frederick Redinger, survived infancy.

Frederick Redinger Wilkinson, only surviving child of Ogden D. and Sarah Snowhill (Dill) Wilkinson, was born in Trenton June 9, 1837; and graduated from Princeton, in the class of 1857. He married, January 24, 1860, Harriet Sarah

Folwell, born December 13, 1839, daughter of Robert Folwell and Harriet Graham. Robert Folwell, born April 5, 1800, died July 10, 1875, was son of Nathan and Rebecca (Iredell) Folwell; Harriet Graham, born April 24, 1815, died January 18, 1842, was daughter of Thomas and Sarah (Lasher) Graham. Thomas Graham was a son of Michael Graham, and Margaret Kittera, daughter of Thomas Kittera.

Frederick R. Wilkinson was a lawyer and resided in Trenton, New Jersey, but owing to his large real estate interests did not practice. He was actively interested in a number of financial enterprises, was for many years director of the Mechanics' Bank and the People's and Standard Fire Insurance companies, and held a number of important positions both in private and municipal affairs. He was one of the influential men of the city. He died December 30, 1883. They were the parents of three children, two of whom are now living. Ogden Dungan, the subject of the sketch; and Elizabeth Dill, wife of Louis Gompertz, now living in Paris, France; they are the parents of four children: Harriet, Helen, Ogden and Francisque.

Ogden D. Wilkinson, son of Frederick Redinger and Harriet (Folwell) Wilkinson, was born in Trenton, New Jersey, May 2, 1863, and now resides at 2031 Walnut street, Philadelphia. His early education was acquired at Cheltenhan Academy, and at Tivoli Military Academy. He later spent some time abroad, and attended Mr. Edward Foazy's school at Geneva, Switzerland. On his return to America he attended Phillips-Andover Academy and the University of Pennsylvania. At the conclusion of his University course he read law, but the care of the large family interests, most of which consisted of valuable real estate in the city of Trenton, have almost entirely engrossed his attention, and he has of late years devoted his entire attention to the improvement of the property there. He has built and owns some of the most valuable and important buildings in the business centre of Trenton, among them being the new State Street Theatre, said to be one of the most complete and attractive play houses in the State. The large department store opposite the postoffice; the Wilkinson building; the Hotel Sterling; and many others. Among the most extensive and attractive of Mr. Wilkinsont's building operations, is Wilkinson Place, a very attractive residence portion of the thriving city of Trenton, consisting of two large apartment houses and forty-five very attractive and stylish dwellings. While not a resident of Trenton, having large interests there, he is deeply interested in the affairs of the city, and in its improvement and development and spends much of his time there.

In Philadelphia he has been for many years quite actively interested in the patriotic societies of that city, and has from time to time acted as a member of the councils of most of them. He is a member of the Pennsylvania Society of Sons of the Revolution; the Founders and Patriots' Society; Colonial Society of Pennsylvania, of which he is a member of the council; Society of the War of 1812; member and secretary of Pennsylvania Commandery, Military Order of Foreign Wars; member of the Order of Albion; the Genealogical Society of Pennsylvania; Historical Society of Pennsylvania; Bucks County Historical Society; Society of Descendants of Colonial Governors; Union League Club of Philadelphia; New York Yacht Club; and of the Corinthian Yacht Club of Philadelphia, of which he was a founder and its first vice-commodore, and for several years commodore. He owned the schooners "Lydia" and "Speranza," and the steam yacht "Speranza."

During the Spanish-American war Mr. Wilkinson, after offering his services to the volunteer navy, assisted in organizing the Wetmore Regiment, which was tendered to the United States, but, not being accepted, was finally distributed among the several National Guard regiments, and was a great factor in bringing the old regiments up to the new standard of efficiency. Mr. Wilkinson was later first lieutenant and commissary of the Nineteenth Regiment, National Guard of Pennsylvania, which was formed as a provisional regiment for the Spanish American war, Colonel O. C. Bosbyshell, commanding, and was later commissioned captain and quartermaster of the same regiment, and was mustered out with the regiment after the close of the war. Mr. Wilkinson is a director of the Broad Street National Bank of Trenton, and of the Standard Fire Insurance Company of the same city.

He was married, April 4, 1883 to Sara Jane Taylor, daughter of Robert and Sarah Taylor, of Philadelphia, and they are the parents of two children: Sarah Dill, born December 30, 1883, and Elizabeth, born January 3, 1888.

SCARBOROUGH FAMILY. The family of Scarborough is an old one, and doubtless derived its name from the locality where its early progenitors resided when surnames first came to be used. Scarborough Castle, an old Norman fortress in Yorkshire, England, is built on a high, narrow, rocky promontory, extending seaward about a half-mile, at the foot o which the ancient seaport of the same name is nestled in a sheltered nook along South Bay. The modern town of Scarborough is now a noted watering place of about 40,000 inhabitants, and a few families of the name of Scarborough still reside there. The name is derived from its location, the word Scear, or Scaur, meaning a sharp rock or crag, and "burg,' or borough, meaning a town or fortress, the combination indicating and literally meaning a town or fort on or near the crags or rocks. The arms of the family consist of a castle by the sea, a beacon flaming on its turrets, the sun rising in the east, and a manned ship at anchor.

Several representatives of the family, at that time scattered over different parts of England, emigrated to America during the period of the early settlement of the colonies, one settling in Boston, Massachusetts, another in Connecticut, and still another on the eastern shore of Virginia. Edward Scarborough was the first surveyor general of Virginia. Charles Scarborough was the physician to King Charles I.

The earliest known progenitor of the Bucks county family of Scarborough was John Scarbrough, of the parish of St. Sepulchre's, London. He was known there as a blacksmith and coachmaker. He was a member of Peel Monthly Meeting of Friends, whose place of worship was in Peel Court, near 65 St. John street. He is referred to in the minutes of this meeting under date of 10 mo. 26, 1677. He signed his name "Scarbrough," as did his descendants until about 1800, although in the body of the papers executed by them the lawyers and conveyancers frequently wrote the name "Scarborough." The Scarborough, Scarboro, Scarbrough, Scardeburg and Scarburg families are probably of one descent.

On 7 mo. 4, 1682, he purchased of William Penn 250 acres of land to be laid out in Pennsylvania, and embarked for the Deleware to locate his purchase and prepare a home for his family in the new province. He left his wife in England, but took with him his only son John, then a youth. The 250 acres were surveyed to him in Middletown township, near the present site of Langhorne, where he was one of the first settlers. After remaining for two years and preparing a rude home in the wilderness, he embarked for England with the intention of bringing over his wife, leaving his son in the care of a Friend until he was able to take charge of his father's farm. His wife, not being a Quaker, declined to come to Pennsylvania, and, the persecution of Friends having somewhat abated, he decided to remain in England and never return to America. In 1696 he executed and sent to his son John a power of attorney to convey his lands in Bucks county. His early experiences among the Indians are mentioned on page 222 of vol. 1, of Proud's "History of Pennsylvania.'" He died 5, mo. 21, 1706, aged sixty years.

John Scarbrough, Jr., remained in Bucks county, when his father returned to England in 1684. His actual residence from that date until 1689, when he is shown to have been residing at Neshaminy, (the name by which Middletown Meeting was first known, as well as the locality), is somewhat a matter of conjecture. A sketch published at page 244, vol. 29, of "The Friend," states that he was born in London in 1667. Samuel Preston, a great-grandson, born in 1756, in a letter written in 1823, says that he ran away when a youth and resided several years among the Indians, learned their language, and later officiated at Indian treaties as interpreter. It is said that at one time he was instrumental in preventing an Indian war. He is known to have been a great friend of the Indians, and is said to have visited them on religious missions. He married about 1690, but, though he was an active member of Middletown Meeting, the maiden name of his wife Mary has never been ascertained. On the records of this meeting appear the dates of the birth of four of his children, his eldest child William being born 10 mo. 30, 1691. In pursuance of the power of attorney from his father, he sold the Middletown land and obtained a warrant of survey for 510 acres in Solebury, on which he settled about 1700, exchanging it later for 820 acres adjoining. The 510 acre tract is at the present time bounded as follows, viz: Beginning at the Five Points, and thence extending 250 perches along the road leading toward Lahaska, to the first right hand road, thence along the latter road 324 perches to the road leading from Carversville to Aquetong, thence along this road 250 perches to the Mountain road, thence along that road to the place of beginning. The 820 acre tract began at a point where the Lower York road crossed the eastermost boundary of the 510 acre tract, and thence extended northwestward 410 perches to the Upper York road, thence along that road 324 perches to a road located between the present Solebury Creamery and Centre Hill, thence along this latter road, southeast, 410 perches to a point and thence southwest 324 perches to the place of beginning. A sketch published on page 244 of Volume 29 of the "Friend" indicates that he was the first white man to settle in the Buckingham-Solebury valley. On 6 mo. 5, 1702, he and John Bye requested that a Meeting be set apart at Buckingham, and Falls' Monthly Meeting consented that a First Day Meeting be held at the house of Thomas Bye. The Quarterly Meeting records mention him as a minister and also in a list of "Friends eminent for their piety and virtue since their settlement in America." He was an elder of Buckingham Meeting prior to its establishment into a Monthly Meeting, and later one of its leading ministers. He died on his Solebury plantation, 1 mo. 27, 1727, devising it and the "Liberty Lot" at Fifth and Spruce streets, Philadelphia, patented to him in 1705, in right of his father's purchase of 250 acres, to his sons, William, John and Robert. He was one of the commissioners appointed by the Pennsylvania assembly in 1711 to lay out the York road from Reading's Ferry, now Centre Bridge, to Philadelphia. The children of John and Mary Scarbrough were as follows:

1. William, born 10 mo. 30, 1691; died 4 mo. 1727, married Mary; see forward.
2. Sarah, born 2 mo. 4, 1694, died 3 mo. 4, 1748, married (first), 9 mo. 28, 1710, George Haworth, and settled in Upper Buckingham, where Mr. Haworth died in 1730, and she married (second) Mathew Hall, a native of Staffordshire, by whom she had four children: David, Mahlon, Margery and Sarah. From Mahlon, who married Jane Higgs in 1757, is descended a numerous family of Hall in Bucks county. George and Mary (Scarbrough) Haworth had five children: Stephanus, George, Absalom, James, and Mary, who married John Michener. George married Martha —— and died in Solebury without issue. The other three boys moved to the Shenandoah valley, Virginia.
3. Mary Scarbrough, born 8 mo. 8, 1695, married 10 mo. 1712, Samuel Pickering. An account of their descendants is given elsewhere in this volume.
4. Susannah Scarbrough, born 5 mo. 19, 1697, married in 1718, Richard Brock, and died before her father, leaving children: John, Elizabeth, Mary and Susannah.
5. Elizabeth Scarbrough, married 10 mo. 29, 1719, John Fisher. They located on a farm adjoining the Haworths near Carversville, where were born their ten children: Robert; Sarah, married Mordecai Michener; John; Elizabeth, married Thomas Stradling; Hannah, married Paul Preston; Joseph, married Ann Cary; Deborah, married Joseph Burgess; Barbara; Samuel, married Margaret Dawes; and Katharine, married William Hartley.
6. Hannah Scarbrough, born 8 mo. 31, 1704, died 2 mo. 21, 1743, married Benjamin Fell. See Fell Family.
7. John Scarbrough married Jane Margerum in 1731, but died childless. He resided on the present farm of Wilson Pearson in Solebury, and was a very eminent minister among Friends from the year 1740 to his death, 5 mo. 5, 1769, in his sixty-sixth year, traveling extensively in the ministry in New Jersey, Virginia, and North Carolina. A sketch of him is printed on page 274 of Cruikshank's Memorials.
8. Robert, the youngest son of John and Mary Scarbrough, inherited from

his father a farm of 157 acres in Solebury, located opposite the present Solebury Creamery, on which he resided until 1737, when he sold it and removed with his wife Elizabeth and two children, John, born 11 mo. 28, 1734, and Elizabeth born 9 mo. 18, 1736, to the Shenandoah valley in Virginia, taking a certificate to Opeckon, now Hopewell Monthly Meeting, at Winchester, Virginia. Another son James was born in Virginia, and became prominent in the affairs of that section. His son John was an officer in different Virginia regiments throughout the revolutionary war. James and his children settled along the headwaters of Indian creek, a branch of the New river in Greenbrier county, now Monroe county, West Virginia. Some of his descendants still reside in Fayette county, West Virginia, and spell their names Scarbrough.

John Scarbrough, eldest son of Robert, returned to Solebury in 1757, and on 5 mo. 5, 1760, took a certificate to Wrightstown to marry Margaret Kirk, daughter of Isaac and Elizabeth (Twining) Kirk, and soon after removed with his wife to a tract of land owned by her father in Springfield township, where Margaret died, and her husband and children returned to Wrightstown in 1779. John Scarbrough married (second), 10 mo. 11, 1779, Johanna Cahoon, a widow. In 1791 he purchased of Crispin Pearson 103 acres of the land originally taken up by his grandfather, John Scarbrough, in 1700, in Solebury, and is still owned and occupied by his great-grandson, Isaac P. Scarborough.

The children of John and Margaret (Kirk) Scarbrough were as follows: 1. John, born 5 mo. 6, 1761, married Elizabeth Kelly, and settled in Cecil county, Maryland; Robert, born 3 mo. 9, 1763, married Ann Paxson; Rachel, born 5 mo. 8, 1765, married Ajax Osmond; Joseph, born 2 mo. 15, 1767, married Sarah Hartley, died 6 mo. 21, 1813; Isaac, born 5 mo. 8, 1769, married Amy Pearson; Elizabeth, born 11 mo. 30, 1772, married Thomas Hartley; Charity, born 11 mo. 5, 1774, married Mahlon Hartley, and settled at Quaker City, Guernsey county, Ohio. John Scarbrough died in Solebury in 1813, all the above named children surviving him.

Isaac Scarbrough, fourth son of John and Margaret (Kirk) Scarbrough, born 5 mo. 8, 1769, married 12 mo. 24, 1794, Amy Pearson, daughter of Crispin and Hannah (Willson) Pearson, who was born in Solebury, 10 mo. 10, 1769, and died 10 mo. 8, 1835. In 1809 his father conveyed to Isaac Scarbrough the Pearson farm purchased in 1791, where he lived through the active years of his life. He subsequently lived with his son Elijah Wilson Scarborough near Stony Hill school house, where he died 10 mo. 24, 1851, and is buried at Buck-

12-3

ingham Friends burying ground. Though he married "out of unity" he was subsequently forgiven this offense against their discipline, and remained a member of Friends' Meeting through life. In politics he was first a Federalist but later a Whig. The children of Isaac and Amy (Pearson) Scarbrough were: Crispin, born 10 mo. 31, 1795; John, born 2 mo. 13, 1797; William, born 4 mo. 23, 1799, married Martha K. Past; Asa, born 9 mo. 12, 1800, died 11 mo. 24, 1800; Cynthia, born 11 mo. 17, 1801, married Joseph Large; Isaac, born 7 mo. 1, 1804, married Mercy Pearson; Charles, born 10 mo. 6, 1806, died 11 mo. 26, 1839. He served under General Sam. Houston in the war between Texas and Mexico, was captured, and with eleven others drew black beans which meant that he was to be shot. They escaped at night and after being twelve days without food reached friends. His daughter, Mrs Dorothea Ann Burks, and her children reside at Kerrville, Kerr county, Texas. Amy, born 10 mo. 16, 1806, married Watson Smith; Pearson, born 4 mo. 7. 1813, married Hannah Worstall, died 2 mo. 7, 1874; and Elijah Wilson, born 10 mo. 7, 1817, married Sarah Adams. Crispin, the eldest son, married Mary Shaw, and they were the parents of Mrs. Isaiah Quinby, of Lumberville, Pennsylvania. John, married Hannah Reeder, and their children were: Reeder, of Wrightstown; Kirk, of Falls; Elizabeth, wife of Dr. George W. Adams; Cynthia, wife of Oliver H. Holcombe; Amy Ann, wife of William Buckman; Alfred, and Dr. John W. Scarborough, late of New Hope. William Scarborough settled in Buckingham adjoining the meeting house where he died in 1875; one of his daughters, Maria, married J. Watson Case, and is still living with her son, Edward G. Case, in Doylestown.

Isaac Scarborough, fourth son of Isaac and Amy (Pearson) Scarborough, born 7 mo. 1, 1804, married Mercy Wilkinson, daughter of Crispin and Elizabeth (Wilkinson) Pearson, of Solebury, who was born 7 mo. 3, 1810, and died 10 mo. 16, 1884. In 1853 he purchased the homestead farm and lived thereon during the active years of his life, retiring late in life to a lot adjoining the farm, at Canada Hill, where he died 3 mo. 22, 1883. In politics he was a Whig, and later a Republican, and boasted that he never missed a presidential election. Though neither he nor his wife were members of Friends Meeting, they always affiliated with the Friends, and used the plain language. The children of Isaac and Mercy (Pearson) Scarborough were: Amy Ellen, who died young; Watson, born 4 mo. 24, 1839, died 10 mo. 6, 1903; Elizabeth, born 10 mo. 11, 1840, married Richard C. Betts; Mercy Ellen, born 7 mo. 5, 1843, married Isaac C. Thomas, died

8 mo. 27, 1886; Isaac Pearson, born 7 mo. 24, 1846, married Emma Hampton, still living on the old homestead in Solebury; and Margaret, who died in infancy.

Watson Scarborough, eldest son of Isaac and Mercy (Pearson) Scarborough, married, 1 mo. 1, 1868, Anna M., daughter of Isaac and Elizabeth (Wismer) Stover, of Carversville, Pennsylvania, and took up his residence on one of his father's farms near Lumberville, known as "The Whittier Farm" from the fact that the poet, John Greenleaf Whittier, once spent a summer there. In the fall of 1890 he retired to Carversville, where he died 10 mo. 6, 1903. In politics he was a Republican. His wife was a member of the Christian church at Carversville. Watson and Anna (Stover) Scarborough were the parents of one child, Henry Wismer Scarborough.

Henry W. Scarborough was born in Solebury, 7 mo. 24, 1870. He received his preliminary education at the Green Hill school at Lumberville, entered the West Chester Normal School, from which he graduated in 1890. In 1894 he received the degree of B. S. from Haverford College, and in 1895 the degree of M. A. In 1896 he graduated from the law department of the University of Pennsylvania, and was admitted to the bars of Bucks and Philadelphia counties. He at once began the practice of his profession in Philadelphia, with offices at 522 Walnut street, and has met with marked success, being one of the rising young attorneys of the Philadelphia bar. He also practices at the bar of his native county. He is a professor of commercial law and the law of real property and conveyancing at the Temple College. He married 7 mo. 20, 1904, Clara Hagerty, daughter of ex-County Treasurer Jacob Hagerty, of Plumsteadville, Bucks county, by his wife Mary (Landis) Hagerty. A son, Jacob Watson Scarborough, was born in Germantown, Philadelphia, 4 mo. 30, 1905.

SCARBOROUGH FAMILY. William Scarborough, eldest son of John and Mary Scarborough, and grandson of John Scarborough, of St. Sepulchre parish, London, England, was born in Middletown, Bucks county, Pennsylvania, December 30, 1691, and removed with his parents to Solebury township, Bucks county, Pennsylvania, when a lad of ten years. He was a "turner" by trade, which probably implied a cabinet maker and all grades of local wood working, as well as that of a wheelwright, which latter trade he is known to have followed. On arriving at manhood he married and settled on a tract of sixty acres conveyed to him by his father in 1724, part of a tract of 520 acres taken up by the latter in 1701. He died a few months after his father, sometime between the date of his will, April 27, 1727, and the date of its proof, September 24 of the same year. His wife's name is unknown, and as she is not mentioned in his will, and a minor son is directed to reside with his uncle John during minority, it is presumed that she died shortly before her husband. His children were: William, who died without issue in 1783; Euclides, Lydia, Martha, and Sarah. The latter married a Stradling, and another daughter married a Smith.

Euclides Scarborough, second son of William, was born in Solebury, and was a minor at the death of his father. By the will of the latter he was directed to be apprenticed to John Heed "to learn the art of making German Wheels." Whether the parental direction was followed does not appear. He did learn the trade of a blacksmith, and followed it for many years in Solebury in connection with farming. He inherited from his father the homestead of sixty acres of land, but in 1746 sold it and purchased two tracts of over one hundred acres of his brother William. In 1762 he repurchased the sixty acre homestead, and probably resided thereon until 1770, although he later purchased one hundred and sixty acres in the present limits of New Hope borough of John Coryell, which he sold at different periods in tracts of forty-nine to seventy acres. In 1770 he closed out all his real estate and removed with his wife Mary and all of his children, except Isaac, the eldest, to Maryland, where he died in 1808. The children of Euclides and Mary Scarborough, were as follows, all of whom were born in Solebury: Isaac, born in 1745; Euclides, died unmarried; James, who was twice married, and removed with his family to Ohio; William, Samuel, John, Joseph, Thomas, all of whom married and lived and died in Maryland; Mary, who married Reuben Jones; Sarah, who married Joseph Rogers; and Hannah, who married John Richards, all of Maryland.

Isaac Scarborough, eldest son of Euclides and Mary Scarborough, was born on the old homestead where his grandfather, William Scarborough, had lived and died, in the year 1745. Like his father he was a blacksmith, and followed that occupation through life in Solebury and Upper Makefield townships, dying in Solebury in 1825. He married Susan Dean, and they were the parents of five children, viz: Enos Dean; Joseph; Elizabeth, married Joseph Hartley; Sarah, married Thomas Sands; Mary, married Abraham Gray. Susan, the mother, dying, Isaac married (second) Rachel Lewis and had three children,—Thomas, Isaac, and Rachel. Joseph, the second son,

was twice married, first to a Sutton and second to Sarah Dudbridge; he had three children,—Sutton, who removed to Maryland; Mary, who married Samuel Rose; and Eveline, who married Dr. George Twining.

Enos D. Scarborough, eldest son of Isaac and Susan (Dean) Scarborough, was born in Upper Makefield township, Bucks county, Pennsylvania, in 1771. Like his father, grandfather, and great-great-grandfather he was a blacksmith, and a very expert mechanic. He received a good common school education and was a proficient penman. He lived most of his life in New Hope, where he followed his trade. He was at one time deputy sheriff of the county, and during that period resided in Doylestown. He married in 1798, Meribah Jackson, of Buckingham, whose ancestors were among the earliest English settlers in Bucks county. Enos D. and Meribah (Jackson) Scarborough, were the parents of nine children, as follows: 1. Isaac, born 1799, died in Hunterdon county, New Jersey, 1849; married Eliza Howell. 2. Joseph, born 1801, died at Milford, New Jersey, in 1877, married (first) Sarah Shamp, and (second) Ann ———. 3. William, born 1804, married (first) Elizabeth Shamp, and (second) Elrania Potts; died in Lambertville, New Jersey, in December, 1884. 4. Hiram, born January 19, 1806; see forward. 5. Hannah, born 1808, died 1864, married Jacob Donaldson of Philadelphia. 6. John, born 1810, died in infancy. 7. Susan, born July, 1812, died unmarried at Centre Bridge, Bucks county, September 5, 1875. 8. Mary W., born December 12, 1815, married Samuel Hall, of Doylestown, and died in Doylestown, February 18, 1879. 9. John, born 1818, removed to Indiana; was twice married and had a family. Meribah (Jackson) Scarborough died in 1821 at the age of forty-three years, and Enos D. married (second) ——— Logan, by whom he had three sons; George W, and Andrew J. of Lambertville, New Jersey; and Enos D. Jr., who removed to Indiana.

Hiram Scarborough, fourth son of Enos D. and Meribah (Jackson) Scarborough, was born in New Hope, January 19, 1806, and resided there most of his life. He learned the blacksmith trade with his father and followed that occupation until 1851, when he lost his right arm by the accidental discharge of a gun. He then became collector of tolls at the Delaware Bridge, and filled that position for thirty-five years. He was the confidential agent of the owners and had charge of the repairs and entire control of the bridge. He was also the proprietor of the shad fisheries at New Hope. In politics he was a Democrat, and took an active part in the councils of his party. He served in the state legislature for the term of 1876-8. He was a man of good business ability and kindly disposition, and was widely and favorably known. He was a member of Lenni Lenape Lodge of Masons of Lambertville, New Jersey, and had taken most of the official degrees, and one of the oldest Odd Fellows in the state at his death. He was rectors warden in St. Andrews Episcopal church of Lambertville, New Jersey. He died in New Hope, March 12, 1888. His wife was Ann Jones, daughter of Joab and Elizabeth (Fisher) Jones, the former a cooper in Solebury township, and descendant of an old Bucks county family, and the latter a native of New Jersey. Ann Scarborough died in New Hope, April 5, 1904, at the age of eighty years. The children of Hiram and Ann (Jones) Scarborough are: Rutledge T., residing in Lambertville, New Jersey; Isaac; Catharine, wife of Robert J. Morris, of New York; Fletcher D., of Trenton, New Jersey.

Isaac Scarborough, of New Hope, is the second son of Hiram and Ann (Jones) Scarborough, and was born in New Hope, May 19, 1848, and acquired his education at the common schools there and at Trenton Business College. Almost from boyhood he has had charge of one of the fisheries formerly owned and operated by his father, and is still engaged in the fishery business. In politics he is a Democrat, and has always taken an active part in local and county politics, filling many local offices and serving as delegate to district, county and state conventions. He is now serving his second term of five years as justice of the peace. He is a member of Castle No. 136, Knights of the Golden Eagle. Mr. Scarborough married in 1871, Mary O'Brien of Lambertville, and they have been the parents of seven children, five of whom survive; Frank, of Lambertville, New Jersey; Hiram, of Philadelphia; Anna, at home; Andrew, telegraph operator for the P. & R. R. R. at New Hope; and Albert, a farmer in Solebury.

Mrs. Robert James Morris, of New Hope, Bucks county, formerly Miss Catharine Scarborough, is the only daughter of Hon. Hiram and Ann (Jones) Scarborough, an account of whose ancestry and life is briefly sketched in the preceding pages. She was born and reared in New Hope. In 1875 she married Albert Wills Taylor, an eminent journalist, who for several years prior to his death, held a responsible position on the staff of the Philadelphia Times. He died March 4, 1894. Mr. and Mrs. Taylor were the parents of two children; H. Ross Taylor, residing with his mother in New Hope; and Albert Wills Taylor, Jr., who was a member of Battery O, First U. S. Artillery, in the Spanish-American war.

Mrs. Taylor married (second) November 17, 1898, Robert James Morris, also a journalist by profession, who is employed in Philadelphia.

THE LA RUE FAMILY. The LaRue family is of French origin, the name being originally Le Roy, and the immediate ancestors of the members of the family who came to New York province about 1680 were probably among the millions of French Huguenots who fled from their mother country about 1666 and took refuge in Switzerland and the Palatinate, many also migrating direct to America and England. About 1680 Franz, Jacques, and Abraham Le Roy, probably all, and at least the last two brothers came from Manheim "In the Palz" and located in the Province of New York; Franz at or near the present site of Albany, New York, where there was a considerable colony of Huguenots under the leadership of Lois Du Bois, otherwise "Louis the Walloon," who had himself fled from France to Manheim in 1658 and from there to America in 1660; Jacques, on the Hackensack, in Bergen, later Essex county, New Jersey; and Abraham, on Staten Island.

Franz Le Roy married Celia Janse Damen, and his sons, Jonas and George went with the Ferrees to the Conestoga valley, and later located in York and Lebanon counties. He was also probably the father of Abraham LaRue, who settled near Mifflinburg, in 1754, though tradition makes him a brother of Jean Jacques Le Roy, who was killed by the Indians in 1755, and his daughter Barbara carried into captivity as related by her and made part of the state archives. This Jean Jacques Le Roy came direct from Switzerland to America in 1750. Some of the descendants of Franz Le Roy Germanized the name into "Koenig" and later Anglicized it to "King." Bergen in his "Early Settlers of Kings County" makes the curious mistake of supposing that Franz Le Roy's wife Celia Janse Damen was twice married, first to Franz Koenig and later to Franz Le Roy, because his name is given in the two forms on the Dutch records of baptisms of his children.

The marriage of Jacques Le Roy, at Bergen Dutch Reformed church, January 2, 1681, to Wybregh Hendricks, states that he was "of Manheim in the Palz," as does also that of his sister Susanna to Thones Hendricks, May 20, 1683, at the same church. This might mean that he was born at Manheim, or that he had recently arrived from there; the common practice with the Dutch being to give the place of birth. About the time of his marriage, with other Huguenots, he helped to organize a "French Church" at Bergen, but later affiliated with the Dutch church where his six children were baptised. He died in 1730, leaving ten children, all of whom seem to have remained in Bergen and Essex counties, New Jersey, and in New York.

Abraham La Roe, as both he and his brother Jacques came later to spell their name, located on Staten Island where he was still residing when he made his will in 1702, though prior to 1712, when it is first offered for probate, he had removed to the neighborhood of Hopewell, then Burlington county, later Hunterdon, and now Mercer county, New Jersey. His will mentions his children, but not by name. From contemporary records we learn that his sons were: Peter, Abraham, Daniel, David and Isaac. The witnesses to the will, William Tillyer, Francis L'Roe, Louis DuBois, and William Grassett, being all either deceased or removed to such distance that their testimony could not be obtained, his will failed of probate and letters of administration were granted on June 14, 1712, to his widow Olshe (Alice) who had been named as executrix and almost sole legatee in the will. Olshe, Alshe, or Alken, the wife of Abraham La Roe, was prior to her marriage to him the widow of Joshua Cresson, youngest son of Pierre Cresson, a native of France, who had come to America from Holland, where he had married a Dutch woman, and located on Long Island. Joshua Cresson was baptised in 1658, and died prior to 1690, which later date is approximately that of the marriage of his widow to Abraham La Roe. The names of Peter, Abraham, Isaac and David La Rue appear on the tax lists of Hopewell township, in 1722, and the first and last were contributors to a fund to purchase a plantation as a home for the pastor of Hopewell Presbyterian church in 1731. Abraham died in Hopewell "in the corporation of Trenton" leaving a will dated February 26, 1747, and proved February 15, 1749. It mentions his wife Harmeke, and children; Abraham, Isaac, Susannah, wife of Cornelius Slack; Altie, Catren (Catharine); another daughter, without giving her name, and Jacob. It devises his plantation in Hopewell to his sons, Abraham and Isaac, jointly at the death or marriage of his wife. Isaac was yet a minor. These sons, Abraham, Isaac and Jacob, are doubtless the three brothers referred to by Stapleton in his "Memorial of Huguenots," page 136, as the ancestors of the southern family of the name of La Rue; the first and last of whom he states were "pioneers in Kentucky, where LaRue county commemorates their name." If this be true, however, the date of their removal was considerably later than there given, as Isaac was still a minor and all were residents of Hunterdon county at the death of

their father in 1747. "Isaac," he states, "born in Hunterdon county, New Jersey, in 1712, removed in 1743 to the Shenandoah valley and established the Virginia family of the name." David LaRue died intestate in Hopewell township, and letters of administration were granted on his estate to Abraham La-Rue, February 18, 1732; nothing is known of his descendants. The remaining three brothers; Peter, Daniel, and Isaac LaRue, all settled, at least for a time, in Bucks county. "Peter La Row," of Hopewell in the western division of New Jersey Yeoman, on December 11, 1738, purchased of Abel Janney 288 acres in Makefield, and settled thereon, later purchasing 216 acres adjoining. On May 16, 1749, he conveyed 258 acres, part of both tracts, to Nicholas Larzelere, the ancestor of the Bucks county family of that name, who at that date removed from Staten Island to Bucks county. No further record appears in Bucks county of Peter LaRue. Isaac LaRue evidently located in Bucks county at about the same date as his brother Peter. On October 6, 1743, he married, at Abington Presbyterian church, Rebeckah Vansant, daughter of Jacobus Vansant, of Middletown. (See Vansant Family). He purchased land in Bensalem in 1745, and died there about 1760, leaving children: Rebecca, who married James Van Arsdalen; Abraham, Isaac and David, all of whom left descendants.

Daniel LaRue, with whose descendants this narrative is chiefly interested, was without doubt a son of Abraham and Alshe (Alice) Cresson LaRoe, or Le Roy, of Staten Island, later of Hopewell, New Jersey. He was born on Staten Island in the year 1697, and was reared at Hopewell, where, as before stated he contributed to the support of Hopewell Presbyterian church in 1722. On June 15, 1751, the executors of Mark Watson. convey to "Daniel La Roe. of Hunterdon county, Province of West Jersey," 300 acres in Falls township, Bucks county, Pennsylvania, and on January 26, 1763. John Plumley conveys to "Daniel La Roe, of Falls township, Bucks county" 200 acres in Middletown township. He died in Middletown township, February 1, 1795, at the age of ninety-eight years, and is buried in the old Presbyterian burying ground in Bensalem. His wife was Ann Praul, who died October 23, 1776. at the age of sixty-two years, and is buried in the same cemetery. The will of "Daniel Larrew, the elder. of Middletown township, dated March 19, 1786, and proven February 16. 1795, devised to son Abraham, five pds. "he already having had his share" Son Daniel the plantation where the testator then lived. 200 acres "bought of John Plumlev;" Son Moses the northeasterly part of the plantation in Falls, 212 acres; Son Peter and Daughter Mary

Stillwell the balance of the Falls plantation; Daughter-in-law Apama, widow of son David, 200 pounds if she have issue. The children of Daniel and Ann (Praul) LaRue were: I. Peter LaRue, eldest son of Daniel and Ann, was born in 1732, and died August 3, 1797, is buried at the Larzelere burying ground near Hulmeville, now Beechwood cemetery. He lived and died on the homestead in Falls township, was probably never married, at least had no children. II. Abraham, born 1734, died March 26, 1790, married Alice, daughter of Folekert Vandegrift, born April, 1731, died died September 24, 1801. They had children: Abraham; Anna, baptized at Southampton church in 1757, married John Larzelere; Elizabeth, married Garret Vansant; and Eleanor, married Joseph Sackett. III. Mary LaRue, married, April 25, 1769, Captain Richard Stillwell, of the revolution, and had son Daniel. IV. Daniel LaRue, born 1737, died February 27, 1819, married, May 21, 1763, Elizabeth Sutton, daughter of Daniel Sutton, of Burlington county, New Jersey, no issue. V. Moses La Rue, born 1744, died February 28, 1795, less than a month after the death of his father. He lived on a part of his father's plantation in Falls long before the decease of his father; probably from the date of his marriage, October 19, 1769, to Catharine Larzelere, daughter of Nicholas, before referred to as coming from Staten Island to Makefield. They were the parents of six sons: Jesse, Daniel, John, Moses, Nicholas and Aaron. See forward. VI. David LaRue, died late in 1785 or early in 1786 as his unborn child is referred to in the will of his father, March 19, 1786. He was a private in the company of his brother-in-law, Captain Richard Stillwell, Bucks county militia, in 1781. His widow Apama, married a Parsons. He had one child, Rebecca, born after his death.

Of the children of Moses and Catharine (Larzelere) LaRue, Elizabeth, the only daughter, married a Mr. Carlile. Jesse, the eldest son, lived on the homestead in Falls, where he died in 1814, leaving a widow Barbara, and eight children: Catharine, wife of John W. Vandegrift; Elizabeth, wife of Jonas Cox; Samuel; Mary Ann, wife of William Doble; Sarah Vandegrift; Julianna; Jesse and Martha. Daniel, the second son, was born September 9, 1774, and died April 29, 1853. He was a carpenter, and a considerable land owner in Falls township. He married, February 8, 1798, Elizabeth Vandegrift, born October 16, 1777, died June 30, 1871, in her ninety-fourth year. They were the parents of eleven children. William, who married Sarah Palmer and is still living; John, who married Rebecca Burton and died at the age of ninety years; Sarah, who married William Biles; Ann Eliza, died

December 9, 1867, at the age of sixty-four years; Mary, who married Jonathan Burton and died at the age of eighty-eight years; Moses, who married Elizabeth Russell and is living in Philadelphia at the age of ninety-seven years; Harriet, died at the age of nineteen years; Caroline, who married Abraham English, of Trenton, New Jersey; Elizabeth, who married Jesse Hellings and is living at the age of eighty-eight years. Susan, who married Tunis Hellings, brother of Jesse, and is living at the age of eighty-six years; and Catharine, who married Abraham Howell and is living at the age of eighty-five years. John, third son of Moses and Catharine LaRue, was a stone mason and lived in Byberry. He had children: Daniel, Marmaduke, Mary, wife of Joseph Knight, Ezra, Carey, Moses and Ann. Moses, the fourth son, mentioned hereinafter; Aaron, the fifth son, resided at Yardleville; he was county treasurer of Bucks county in 1827. Nicholas, the yongest son, married Elizabeth Kinsey, and also resided at Yardley; they had children: John Kinsey, and Mary.

Moses La Rue, fourth son and fifth child of Moses and Catharine (Larzelere) LaRue, was born in Falls township, Bucks county, November 11, 1779, and died at Newportville, Bristol township, August 7, 1860. He learned the trade of a coach maker early in life, and carried on an extensive business in carriage building at Newportville for many years. He was a prominent man in the community, serving for many years as a justice of the peace and filling the office of county treasurer in 1838. He married Rachel Johnson, born June 6, 1785, died July 19, 1852, and they were the parents of ten children as follows: 1. Mary, born August 28, 1803, married Lewis Reeder and removed to Muncy, Pennsylvania. She died at Bridesburg, Pennsylvania, July 5, 1879. Children: Kate, Annie and Sarah. 2. Catharine, born August 5, 1805, married 1864, John Wright, of Tullytown, died August 31, 1883. No children. 3. Nicholas, born October 14, 1807, died Philadelphia, August 9, 1849, married Catharine M. Bunting, see forward. 4. Daniel, born August 25, 1809. 5. Peter Johnson, born January, 1812, died young. 6. George, born September 15, 1813, died March 8, 1890, succeeded his father as carriage maker at Newportville, but later removed to Bristol where he died. He married first Christiana Headly, one child, John H., of Bristol township. Married second, Sarah A. White, one child, Mary Elizabeth, who married Dr. James Osman. 7. Sarah, born February 14, 1816, died February 10, 1896, married J. Hibbs Goforth, of Hulmeville. One child, Catharine, single. 8. Rachel Ann, born April 22, 1819, died

May 30, 1865, married Kinsey Krewson. Children, Rachel Florence, William Emley, single, and Kate L., wife of James V. Randall, of Newtown. 9. Edward W. born May 30, 1822, died Virginia City, Nevada, married Mary Lemon, no surviving issue. 10. Aaron, born March 30, 1827, died March 5, 1879, was a merchant in New York.

Nicholas La Rue, third child and eldest son of Moses and Rachel (Johnson) LaRue, was a tailor by trade and followed that vocation at Newportville and later in Philadelphia. He and his wife, Catharine Moon Bunting, were the parents of six children, as follows: 1. Albert G., born July 18, 1836, married, December 3, 1857, Annie H. Jackson and resided in Philadelphia. 2. Eugene, born September 17, 1838, died unmarried at Jefferson City, Missouri. 3. Moses, born May 26, 1841, died young. 4. Ruth A., born June 4, 1843, wife of John M. Hartman, of Mt. Airy, Philadelphia. 5. Rachel, born January 13, 1846, of Philadelphia, is unmarried. 6. George S., born February 1, 1848, married in 1868, Emeline Getz, and died in Philadelphia. The paternal ancestry of Catharine (Bunting) LaRue will be found in the sketch of the Bunting family in this volume.

WILLIAM H. LA RUE, deceased, who throughout his entire life followed farming, was born in New Jersey, February 19, 1823, his parents being Uriah and Elizabeth (Rockafellow) LaRue, in whose family were six children, namely: Asa, whose wife's name was Rachel; Hackett; William H.; Jonathan, who married Miss Kiphart; Calvin, who married Miss Ruth Tice; and Rebecca, who married Charles Kiphart.

William H. LaRue was reared in Huntington county, New Jersey, pursuing his education in its public schools. A portion of his boyhood was spent in the home of his uncle, William Heis. At an early age he engaged in farming and followed that vocation throughout his entire life. Mr. LaRue was married twice, his first union being with Jane Parks, by whom he had three children: George H., who married Mary Moore; Susanna; and Elizabeth, who became the wife of Nathaniel Briton. For his second wife Mr. LaRue chose Margaret Thompson. Her ancestry can be traced back to Mrs. Mary Thompson, who came to this country with her four sons: John, Hugh, William and Robert. Of this family John settled in Wrightstown, making his home near Chain Bridge, in Northampton township. His house, an old hiproofed one, is still standing, but some of it was torn down and rebuilt in later years. He was treasurer of the colonies at that time, and while holding the office was robbed, the

bullet holes being seen in the house until repaired. He married and had seven children: Hugh, born in 1764; William, who was a doctor, married and settled in Chester county, Pennsylvania; Thomas, who married Elizabeth Wilson; James; Elizabeth, who became Mrs. McClellen, and had a son, Charles, who died in the south; Robert, who married Jane Wilson, and settled near Chain Bridge, Bucks county; and John, who wedded Mary Wilson.

Hugh Thompson, son of John Thompson, was born in 1764, and died in August, 1847. He wedded Mary Houston and they had five children: Elizabeth, born December 2, 1791, died April 25, 1843, was the wife of James Gaine; John, born January 17, 1795; Charles, born August 11, 1797, married Ann Johnson; Samuel, a physician, born February 15, 1800, died February 21, 1863, was married twice; his first wife was Martha Burson, and his second wife was Hannah Thomas; and Maria, born September 26, 1803, died August 11, 1865, was the wife of William Poole.

John Thompson, son of Hugh and Mary Thompson, was born January 17, 1795, and married Ann Lefferts, a daughter of Abraham and Margaret Lefferts. Her father was born February 17, 1754, and died March 18, 1863, while Mrs. Margaret Lefferts was born February 9, 1761, and died August 4, 1831. Abraham Lefferts was married twice. By the first marriage there were two children, John and Alice. The former, born March 14, 1784, married and had children: Susan, who married Isaiah Delaney and had two children: Mary Helen, who married Lambert Cornell, and Annie wife of Peter Dyer; 2. Simon, married Susanna States and had a son, John, who married Helen Rich and had two children: Walter and Helen; 3. Mary Ann, became the wife of Harry Search and had two children: Susannah and Theodore; 4. Jonathan, married a Miss Cornell and had three children, one of whom was Helena, wife of Jacob Cornell; 5. Charles, married a Miss Cornell, and had two children: John and Julia; 6. Mary Catharine, became the wife of John C. Fetter and had one child, Emma, wife of Joseph M. Cornell. Alice Lefferts, daughter of Abraham Lefferts, was born October 28, 1790, and married Samuel Winner. Abraham and Margaret Lefferts had the following children: Simon, born April 14, 1793, died August 11, 1805; Abraham, born July 17, 1794, died August 24, 1862; James, born September 26, 1797; and Ann, born October 7, 1800, became the wife of John Thompson.

John and Ann (Lefferts) Thompson had nine children. 1. Albert, born November 21, 1822, married Susan W. Carey and their children were Warner C. and Amos, the latter now deceased. 2.

Abraham L., born March 28, 1824, died February 17, 1902. He married Letitia Collins and their children were: Edward, who married Ella Ingall; Clara, John, who married Miss Worthington; Emma, who became the wife of Charles Cope; and Hugh, who is living in Doylestown. 3. Mary Ann, born February 26, 1826. died September 12, 1903. 4. Benjamin Franklin, born October 3, 1827, married Emeline Johnson, and had two children, Harry and J. Wesley. 5. Charles, born July 18, 1829, married Emily Van Horn and they have two children: George H. and Anna Mary. 6. John Praul, born January 15, 1831, died in the winter of 1882. His wife was Lydia Knipe and they had the following children: Albert, deceased, and who married Sarah Holland, now deceased, and their children were: Albertta and Lydia; Kate, deceased, who was the wife of James McGrath; Charles, who married Henrietta Russel, and three children were born to them: Charles R., Warner C., deceased; and Norman, deceased; Annie, who married Herbert Alrich. 7. Henry, born May 2, 1833, married Mary Elizabeth Mathews and their children were: Alice, who married William Sacket; Bertha, unmarried and Harry, who married Marietta Carter and their children are: Elizabeth, John and Alice. Henry Thompson died April 15, 1901. 8. Margaret, born May 6, 1837, is the wife of William H. La-Rue and they have a daughter, Jennie. 9. Elizabeth, born August 16, 1840, is the wife of Charles Bemis. John Thompson and his cousin, Hugh Thompson, son of Robert Thompson, were each captains of the militia and went to escort General Lafayette from Briston to Philadelphia when he visited this country in 1824. John was captain of the Wrightstown militia and Hugh of the Northampton; each rode a white horse, and the blue plume tipped with red worn by John Thompson is still in the possession of his descendants.

BUNTING FAMILY. The pioneer ancestors of the Bunting family of America were three sons and a grandson of Anthony and Ellen Bunting, of Matlock, Derbyshire, England, the former of whom was born in Derbyshire, A. D. 1600, and died at Matlock, January 4, 1700, at the age of one hundred years, his wife following him to the grave on September 1, 1700. They were the parents of six children, four sons and two daughters. The daughters married and settled in Nottinghamshire. The sons were: John, born 1655, came to New Jersey in 1678, and married there in 1679, Sarah Foulke, and reared a large family of children, some of whom later settled in Delaware; William, married May 6, 1683, Mary Stevenson, and had five children, the youngest of whom, Samuel, born November 9, 1692, came to Pennsylvania in 1722, married Sarah Fearne, and is the ancestor of the Darby Buntings; Samuel, came to New Jersey and married, November 18, 1684, Mary Foulke, and is the ancestor of the New Jersey family of the name.

Job Bunting, see forward, youngest son of Anthony and Ellen, born in Matlock, Derbyshire, also came to Crosswicks, New Jersey, and married there Sarah Perkins, in 1685. She and her infant daughter died in 1687, and Job married at Falls Meeting, Bucks county, June 27, 1689, Rachel Baker, daughter of Henry and Margaret (Hardman) Baker, who was born in Hindley, West Darbye, Lancashire, April 23, 1669, and came to Bucks county with her parents in 1684. Her father, Henry Baker, was a prominent Friend in Lancashire, and suffered persecution there for his principles. After coming to Bucks county he became one of the most prominent men in the colony, and served as provincial councillor and member of assembly for several years, as well as filling many other high official positions in the county and province. He married a second time, in 1692, Mary Radcliffe, widow of James, and had ten children, nine by the first marriage and one by the second. His son Samuel, also a prominent man in Bucks county, was the ancestor of Johns Hopkins, founder of the University that bears his name. Job Bunting on his second marriage, located in Bucks county, on land conveyed to him by his father-in-law, and later purchased considerable other land in Bucks and Chester counties. He died in 1703, when comparatively a young man, and his widow married John Cowgill. The children of Job and Rachel (Baker) Bunting were: Rebecca, born March 1, 1691, married December 16, 1709, Joseph Wildman, born March 23, 1683, son of Martin and Ann Wildman, who came from England and settled in Middletown in 1682. Of the four daughters of Joseph and Rebecca only Rebecca, born January 9, 1715, survived infancy. 2. Samuel, born October 4, 1692, see forward. 3. Sarah, born 1694, died 1699; 4. Job, born March 26, 1696. 5. Rachel, born March 4, 1698.

Samuel Bunting, eldest son of Job and Rachel, settled in Falls township, and was a member of Falls Meeting. He died December, 1759. He married Pricilla Burgess, and they were the parents of thirteen children, viz: Rachel, born August 25, 1717; Samuel, born August 3, 1718, married Hannah Stock-'dale; John, born September 26, 1720; Priscilla, born July 22, 1722, married, 1747, Thomas Buckman; Sarah, born May 11, 1724; Phebe, born March 2, 1726; Joseph, born May 4. 1728, married 1753, Sarah Bidgood; Rebecca, born April 2, 1730, married, 1754, David Headley; Daniel, born February 1, 1733-4, married, 1754, Marry Bartholomew; David, born February 15, 1735-6, married, 1757, Martha Hough; Timothy, born July 4, 1736, married Elizabeth Headley; Isaac, born January 28, 1738; Benjamin, born September 7, 1740.

John Bunting, second son of Samuel and Priscilla, born September 28, 1720, married, January 16, 1745, Christiana Headley, born May 3, 1723, daughter of Joseph and Hannah (Palmer) Headley, of Middletown, and granddaughter of John and Christiana Palmer, the pioneer ancestors of that family in Bucks county. The children of John and Christiana (Headley) Bunting were: Joshua, born March 16, 1746, married Mary Brown; Samuel, born September 18, 1748, married, May 11, 1775, Ann Moon; Hannah; Joseph, see forward; John, born 1755; Sarah; Lydia, and Asa.

Joseph Bunting, son of John and Christiana, married November 27, 1783, Phebe Moon, daughter of William and Elizabeth Moon, of Falls, and a descendant of one of the oldest families in Bucks county, and later located in Lower Dublin township, Philadelphia county, where they resided until 1808, when he purchased a farm in Bristol township, between Nawportville and Bristol, where he resided until his death in April, 1830. He joined the Associated Company of Falls township in 1775, under Captain Thomas Harvey, of which his uncle, Daniel Bunting, was ensign, and was disowned by Falls Meeting the same year. The children of Joseph and Phoebe (Moon) Bunting were: William, born June 17, 1784; Ann, born August 6, 1785, died February 27, 1786; Solomon, born August 9, 1786, see forward; James, born January 11, 1788; Joshua, born December 17, 1788, married Elizabeth Wright; Christiana, born December 2, 1789, married Walter W. Baldwin; John, born May 12, 1792, never married; Timothy, born June 9, 1793, died young; Samuel, born July 4, 1795, died young; Charles, born October 1, 1796, married Isabella Hood; Phoebe, born December 23, 1797, died young; Lydia, born January 20, 1799, married Joshua Wright; David, born January 20, 1802, died August 11, 1802. Joshua, the fourth son, married Elizabeth Wright, daughter of James and Rebecca (Patterson) Wright, January 13, 1820, and they were the parents of the following children: James W. 2., born October 30, 1831, married Sarah Swart; Joseph, born October 26, 1823, married Beersheba Rue; Joshua E., born October 16, 1825, married Lucy Smith; John, born March 3, 1827, married Matilda Boate; Lydia, who married Joshua Wright, son of James and Rebecca, and has Phoebe Ann, James H. and Elizabeth; residence, Bristol, Pennsylvania.

Solomon, second son of Joseph and Phoebe (Moon) Bunting, born August 9, 1786, lived for several years on the old homestead in Bristol township, was later a farmer at Andalusia, and finally removed to Philadelphia, where he died. He married, January 17, 1811, Ruth Mathias. Solomon and Ruth (Mathias) Bunting were the parents of eight children: Eliza, born 1812, married Aaron MacDonald, a car builder, of Philadelphia, and died at St. Joseph, Missouri; Lydia, born 1814, married (first) Samuel Osler, a merchant of Philadelphia, and (second) Jacob Rambo, a cooper of the same city; Catharine Moon, born in 1816, married Nicholas La Rué, see LaRue family in this volume; Mary, born 1818, married Thomas I. Meyers, a saddler of Philadelphia, and died in that city; Spencer, born 1820, married Susan Noble, and was a carpenter in Philadelphia; Joseph, born in 1822, married Malvina Kessler; John, born 1824, died young; Solomon, born 1829, married Annie Steele, and was a saddler in Philadelphia for some years, removing later to the south, where he died. Solomon, the father is buried at the Hanover street cemetery, Philadelphia.

Joseph Bunting, second son of Solomon and Ruth (Mathias) Bunting, born on the old homestead in Bristol township, was a farmer and lived for a time on the old homestead, and later farmed near Bridgewater, Bensalem township, where he died in November, 1891. He married Malvina Kessler, and they were the parents of seven children: Edwin M., see forward; Elwood, a farmer in Bensalem township; Anna, wife of Joseph Preston, who died in Philadelphia twenty years ago; Ruthanna, wife of Edward T. Jenks, a prominent resident of Bensalem; Eliza, wife of Johnson Minster, of Bensalem; Catharine, wife of Theodore Lippincott, of Bensalem; and John S., a farmer in Bristol township, a sketch of whom appears in this volume.

The Buntings have been members of the Society of Friends, almost since George Fox began his ministry, but some of the family early drifted out of membership through marriage to non-members, though retaining their associations with the Society, whose meeting they attended. The branch of the family above noted lost their membership in the Society, through the patriotism of their ancestor, Joseph Bunting, Jr., son of John and Christiana, who violated the rules and principles of the sect by joining the Associated Company of Falls township, in 1775, under Captain Thomas Harvey, for the defense of the rights of his country. His uncle, Daniel Bunting, was ensign of the company.

Edwin M. Bunting, eldest son of Joseph and Malvina (Kessler) Bunting, born August 25, 1847, was reared in Bensalem township and educated in the public schools of that township. He followed farming and trucking in Bensalem until the spring of 1894, when he was appointed steward of the Bucks County Home, a position he has since filled to the satisfaction of the people of Bucks county, being several times successively reappointed by the different boards of directors of the poor. He has always affiliated with the Republican party politically, and had for many years been active in local politics prior to his appointment as steward, representing his district on the county committee. He served as supervisor of Bensalem township for three years, being elected by a handsome majority in a Democratic district. He married, March 16, 1872, Ellen Powell, daughter of David and Mary Ann (Moore) Powell, of Bensalem, and a representative of one of the oldest families in that locality, and they are the parents of two children: Wesley, born November 8, 1875, and Bertha, born November 10, 1879. Wesley, the son, was educated at the public schools of Bensalem and the Doylestown high school, of which he is a member of the alumni. He studied law in the office of the Hon. Robert M. Yardley, and was admitted to the Bucks county bar, April 23, 1902. On January 1, 1903, he formed a partnership with John C. Swartley, Esq., assistant United States attorney for the Eastern District of Pennsylvania, under the firm name of Swartley & Bunting, and the firm are enjoying a good practice in the several courts of Bucks county. Bertha, the daughter, resides with her parents.

John S. Bunting, youngest child of Joseph and Melvina (Kessler) Bunting, was born in Hulmeville, Middletown township, Bucks County, Pennsylvania. November 5, 1860. When five years of age he removed with his parents to Byberry, Pennsylvania; in 1874 removed to Penn's Manor; and in 1876 to Croydon, Bensalem township, where he purchased a farm in 1889, which by intelligent labor has been brought to a high state of cultivation. Mr. Bunting has served as supervisor two years, and is now a member of the school board. He is a Republican in politics, and is regarded as a citizen of influence and worth in the community in which he resides.

March 25, 1888, Mr. Bunting married Emeline Virginia Otto, of Bristol, Pennsylvania, daughter of Lewis and Ann (Hall) Otto, and a descendant of a German ancestry. She was educated in the public schools of Byberry and Bristol. Their children are: Marion Louisa, born March 15, 1889; Albert John, born July 12, 1890; Frederick, born April 27, 1892; and Katharine F., born September 24, 1896, who died in infancy. The children were educated in the public schools of Bristol township, and reside with their parents on the home farm.

JOHN A. FELL, M. D., of Doylestown, was born in Buckingham township, Bucks county, October 21, 1850, a son of Jesse and Priscilla Sands Fell, and is a descendant in the sixth generation from Joseph Fell, of Longlands, Cumberland, England, and Bridget Wilson, his wife, who came to Bucks county in 1705 and settled in Buckingham two years later.

Benjamin Fell, born in Cumberland, England, 9 mo. 1, 1703, married 6 mo. 27, 1728, Hannah Scarborough, daughter of John Scarborough, of Solebury, and had by her six children, four of whom grew to maturity: John, born 4 mo. 1, 1730; Asa, born 1732, married Elizabeth Mitchell; Phebe, who married Stephen Kirk; and Benjamin, who married Rebecca Casner. Benjamin settled on land in Buckingham conveyed to him by his father in 1726, where Charles Carwithen now lives, and later purchased considerable land adjoining. He was married three times, and has left a large number of descendants. His wife Hannah was born 8 mo. 31, 1704, and died 2 mo. 21, 1743. He died 9 mo. 12, 1758.

John Fell, eldest son of Benjamin and Hannah, born 4 mo. 1, 1730, was also a farmer. He purchased of his cousin, Isaac Fell, the farm upon which his great-grandson, Preston J. Fell still lives, soon after his marriage, and spent his whole life thereon. He married, 10 mo. 30, 1753, Elizabeth, daughter of Thomas and Elizabeth (Paxson) Hartley, of Solebury, and had thirteen children, eleven of whom lived to maturity, viz: Mahlon; William; Nathan; Seneca; Miriam, who married David Carr; Jonathan; Hannah; George; Rachel, who married John Paxson; John and Jonas.

Jonas Fell, youngest son of John and Elizabeth, was born on the old homestead 8 mo. 17, 1777, and died there 1 mo. 8, 1854. He married 3 mo. 28, 1802, Sarah, daughter of Joseph and Mary (Comfort) Church, and great-granddaughter of Joseph Fell, Sr., and his second wife, Elizabeth Doyle, through the marriage of their daughter Sarah to Richard Church, the father of Joseph. Sarah Church Fell was born 8 mo. 20, 18—, and died 5 mo. 25, 1857. They had five children, viz.: Hannah, born 1803, married Charles Kirk; Jesse, born 3 mo. 1806; Lydia, born 1811, married Jesse Dean; Jonas, born 1813, married Mary Louderborough; Sarah, born 1816, married Isaac Mathews.

Jesse Fell, born 3 mo. 8, 1806, was the father of the subject of this sketch. He married 2 mo., 1828, Priscilla Sands, daughter of William and Jane Sands, of Buckingham, born in 1808, and died 12 mo. 7, 1884. Jesse Fell died in 1858. The children of Jesse and Priscilla Fell were ten in number, viz.: Lydia Ann, born 1829, married Samuel Frankenfield, and is still living in Buckingham; Sarah

Jane, born 9 mo. 27, 1830, married Joseph Mathias Flack, died 1902; Preston J., born 2 mo. 1, 1836, a sketch of whom will be found in this work; Rachel S., born 10 mo. 31, 1837, married John M. Gray, a sketch of whom will also be found in this work; Isabella, born 1840, married John R. Rapp, died 1903; Henry C., born 1842, a soldier in the One Hundred and Ninety-fourth Pennsylvania Volunteers, died 5 mo. 31, 1862, from typhoid fever contracted in the army; Louisa, born 1846, married Amos Randall, died 1890; Adaline, born 1848. died 1903; and John A., the subject of this sketch.

Dr. John A. Fell, the youngest of the ten children of Jesse and Priscilla Fell, received a rudimental education at Church's public school, after which he attended the Doylestown English and Classical Seminary. He spent two years teaching school in Buckingham, one and a half years of which he was principal of Hughesian Free School. The next two years were spent at Lafayette College. He then entered the University of Pennsylvania and graduated in the class of 1874. In the same year he accepted a position as resident physician at the Bedford Street Mission Hospital, where he remained until January 1, 1875, when he began the practice of his profession at Centreville, Buckingham. He practiced at Buckingham until April 1, 1888, when he removed to Doylestown and forming a partnership with John B. Livezey, opened a drug store. At the end of one year the partnership was dissolved, and Dr. Fell went to attend lectures at the Philadelphia Polyclinic and College for Medical Graduates, during the next fourteen months attending the whole thirty-four courses; he passed a successful examination in all of them, and was elected on' June 23, 1890, the first Fellow of the College. In the same year he opened an office on Oakland avenue, Doylestown, where he now resides, and resumed the practice of medicine. Dr. Fell is considered one of the leading physicians of Bucks county, and has a large practice. He has devoted especial care to study of the defects and diseases of the eye, and has considerable local fame as an oculist. He is a member of the County, State and American Medical Associations. He has been a member of the board of health from its organization; was assistant surgeon of the Sixth Regiment National Guard, from 1884 to 1895, has been a member of the Doylestown school board since 1891, now serving his fifth term. He is a member of Doylestown Lodge, No. 245, F. and A. M.; of Aquetong Lodge. No. 193. I. O. O. F.; Doylestown Encampment. No. 35; and Sciota Tribe, No. 214, I. O. R. M. He was married, May 18, 1887, to Clara, daughter of Henry D. and Anna (Wambold) Livezey, and is the father of two daughters,—Anna, born February 17, 1888; and Dorothea, born January 4, 1896.

PRESTON J. FELL, eldest son of Jesse and Priscilla Sands Fell, was born February 1, 1836, on the farm owned and occupied by his father, grandfather and great-grandfather, and still owns and occupies a part of it. The farm, as owned by his grandfather, Jonas Fell, included the farm of Mrs. Joseph Ellis, on the opposite side of the Buckingham and Doylestown turnpike, and he lived and died there. Jesse Fell, the father of the subject of this sketch, took up his residence on the farm now occupied by the subject of this sketch upon his marriage, and his children were all born there, and Preston J. has resided there all his life. He was educated at Church's Public school and at the Hughesian Free School of Buckingham. As the eldest son, the responsible care of the farm devolved upon him at an early age, his father having died when he was but twelve years of age. He conducted the farm until the youngest child was of age, and then purchased it, and has conducted it together with the nursery business ever since. He married, November 3, 1870, Cassie H., daughter of Joseph and Elizabeth Stover. The Stovers came to Bucks county from Switzerland about 1727. They were residents of Bedminster for several generations. Joseph Stover lived for a time on the old homestead of his father, Henry Stover, but later removed to Buckingham and purchased the farm and mill property still known as the Stover Mill.

Preston J. Fell is a Republican in politics, and has always taken an active part in the affairs of his township and county. He was director of the poor for three years; has been a member of the township school board for many years, serving as secretary of the board for five years; and he is also a trustee of the Hughesian Free School, and president of both the Buckingham and Doylestown Turnpike Company and the Centreville and Pineville Turnpike Company, and is supervisor and director of the former company. He is a prominent man in the community, and has held many positions of trust.

DR. FRANK SWARTZLANDER, physician and surgeon, of Doylestown, was born in Southampton township, Bucks county, February 9, 1842, being a son of Joseph and Abigail (Rankin) Swartzlander. the former of German and the latter of English descent, though both were descended through several generations of American birth. On the paternal side the Swartzlanders are descended from Philip Schwartzlander, who came from Steinhardt, in Schwarzwald, arriving in Philadelphia on November 8, 1752, in the ship "Snow Louisa," Captain John Pitcairn, from Rotterdam. The voyage had been a long and perilous one, and many of the passengers had died on the way. Among these was the wife of Philip Schwartzlander, leaving on his hands two children, Gabriel, aged seven years, and Barbara, aged five. Soon after his arrival in Pennsylvania, Philip Schwartzlander found a home in New Britain township, Bucks county, where he married Margaret Angel, by whom he had two children, Conrad and Philip, descendants of whom still reside in that locality. Philip Schwartzlander, Sr., died in 1784, and is buried in the New Britain churchyard.

Gabriel Schwartzlander, born in Steinhardt, March 31, 1747, spent his boyhood days in New Britain township, where he learned the trade of a miller. At the age of twenty-seven years he married Salome, the widow of Abraham Freed, and daughter of Jacob and Anna (Leisse-Miller) Stout, an account of whose ancestry is given on another page of this volume. Abraham Freed, the first husband of Salome Stout, had purchased of his father-in-law the Pine Run mill property, one mile north of Doylestown, and also owned about two hundred acres of land adjoining the mill and extending over into Plumstead township. He died in 1773, leaving three infant daughters, and a year later the widow married Gabriel Schwartzlander. By proceedings in the orphans' court the mill and about fifty acres of land were sold for the payment of debts, and were purchased by Gabriel Schwartzlander. The remaining 150 acres of Freed descended to his two surviving daughters, one of whom married John Kratz, whose descendants still own and reside on a portion of the land on the Plumstead side of the line. John Kratz later found a second wife in a daughter of Gabriel and Salome Schwartzlander, and half-sister to his first wife. Jacob Stout owned considerable other land adjoining the mill on the west, which on his death in 1779 descended to his daughter Salome, and was later transferred to her husband, Gabriel Schwartzlander. He operated the mill until his death July 17, 1814. The children of Gabriel and Salome Swartzlander were: John, Magdalen, Jacob, Margaret, Catharine, Abraham, Joseph, Philip, and David. Of these, Abraham and Philip died young. A number of the descendants of Joseph and the daughters still reside in the neighborhood of Pine Run. At the death of Gabriel Swartzlander in 1814, his extensive real estate holdings were partitioned among his children by pro-

ceedings in the orphans' court, the mill property falling to Joseph, who owned and operated it until his death, the title remaining in the family for nearly a century.

Jacob Swartzlander, the grandfather of Dr. Swartzlander, was the second son of Gabriel and Salome, and was born at the old Swartzlander mill property in New Britain, now Doylestown township. He learned the trade and assisted in operating the mill until 1808, when he removed to Southampton township, where he purchased a mill property which he operated until his death in 1845. He was twice married; by his first wife, Elizabeth Cope, of Hilltown, he had four children: Abraham, Gabriel, Joseph and Salome. He married (second) Elizabeth Moode, of Southampton, by whom he had four daughters: Emily, Clara, Wilhelmina and Harriet. His widow survived him many years. Abraham, the eldest son, was also a miller and operated and owned a mill in Middletown. He was killed in May, 1839, by the falling of a wall of a barn which workmen, under his direction, were tearing down. He left a widow Rebecca, and three daughters, Elizabeth, Jane and Sarah.

Joseph Swartzlander, the father of the subject of this sketch, was born in Southampton township, Bucks county, January 1, 1812, and ended an eventful and useful career at Yardley, Bucks county, in May, 1903. He obtained the rudiments of an education at the public schools of his native township, and later attended the academy of Rev. Samuel Aaron, at Burlington, New Jersey. He learned the milling trade with his father at the Rocksville mill. In 1834 he started on a memorable trip through what was then our western states. Traveling by stage coach, canal boat and on foot, he reached Zanesville, Ohio, where he was stricken with smallpox. A stranger in a strange land, and having a contagious disease, he was fortunate in securing the services of an aged negress who had known the family in Bucks county. She nursed him back to health in her hut in the woods, and received for compensation his gold watch, which was returned to him several years later. On his recovery he continued his journey, taking passage on a flatboat down the Ohio and Mississippi to New Orleans. After a brief stay in this cosmopolitan southern city he returned by steamer to St. Louis, from which point he and a companion tramped overland to Detroit, Michigan, a distance of five hundred and sixty-four miles. Crossing the swamps and lagoons where Chicago now stands, they stopped at Fort Dearborn, the nucleus of the now famous "Windy City," and proceeded on their way to Detroit. From Detroit the travellers went to Buffalo, thence down the Erie canal to

Rochester, New York, from there to Albany, and thence overland to Boston, Massachusetts, from which point Mr. Swartzlander returned to his home in Southampton, where he resumed the occupation of a miller. Prior to his father's death in 1845 he removed to Yardley, where he operated a grist and saw mill. At the time of the Irish famine he was one of the largest grain dealers and millers in Bucks county, operating at one and the same time the Rocksville, Bridgetown, and Yardley mills, handling, grinding and kiln-drying immense quantities of corn and cornmeal which he shipped to New York and Philadelphia for exportation to Ireland. Through the dishonesty or default of a firm of commission merchants to whom he shipped his product he lost over $12,000, an immense sum in those days, and was ruined financially, but by industry and a close application to business succeeded in paying off his indebtedness and acquiring a competence. In 1860 he practically abandoned the grain business and devoted himself almost exclusively to the lumber business, buying native timber in the woods and sawing it into ship timber which he shipped to the shipyards at Williamsburg, New York, and Philadelphia. He was a very active business man, and continued to personally conduct his business in connection with his son Harry until within a few months of his death at the age of ninety-one years. Joseph Swartzlander married, in 1837, Abigail Rankin, a daughter of William Rankin, a well known merchant at Huntingdon Valley, Montgomery county. Their children were: Mary, wife of Daniel Beans, of Newtown; Dr. Frank, the subject of this sketch; Albert, a lawyer at Omaha, Nebraska; Laura, Harry and Ella, residing at Yardley; and Fred, a physician at Omaha, Nebraska.

Dr. Frank Swartzlander, the eldest son, was born in Northampton, February 9, 1842, and was therefore a mere child when the family removed to Yardley, where he attended the public schools and was later a student in Philadelphia. He began the study of medicine in 1860 with Dr. Joseph Smith, of Yardley, and was later under the preceptorship of Dr. Rufus Tryon, of Philadelphia, late surgeon-general of the United States Navy. Dr. Swartzlander entered the medical department of the University of Pennsylvania in 1861. Showing a remarkable aptitude for surgery, he was appointed in 1862, while still a student, anatomist at the Military Hospital, located at Twenty-fourth and South streets, Philadelphia, where he made all the post mortem examinations until his graduation at the University in 1863. In March, 1863, he was appointed assistant surgeon of the Seventy-fourth Regiment Pennsylvania Volunteers, and went with his

regiment to the front, passing through many trying scenes during the civil war. He was at the battles of Chancellorsville, Gettysburg, John's Island, S. C., and many other sanguinary engagements. At Gettysburg he was surgeon of the operating staff of the field hospital of the Third Division of the Eleventh Army Corps. When the Seventy-fourth Regiment was mustered out he accepted a commission as assistant surgeon of Volunteers and was sent south to meet Sherman's army on its march from "Atlanta to the Sea." General Sherman had just arrived at Savannah when Dr. Swartzlander reached the army, and he was assigned the charge of the Military Hospital at the Marshall House, and later had charge successively of the hospitals at the Scriven House and Pavilion House, and remained in the hospital service until the close of the war. After attending special lectures at the University he located at Doylestown in 1866, and began the practice of his profession. He soon built up a large practice, and enjoys an enviable reputation as a physician and surgeon.

Dr. Swartzlander was married in October, 1872, to Susan, daughter of John S. Bryan. She died February 4, 1884. Their children are: Dr. Frank B. Swartzlander, a practicing physician at Doyles town; Dr. Joseph Swartzlander, a practicing physician of Forest Grove, Buckingham township, Bucks county, Pennsylvania; and Susan, who resides with her father. Dr. Swartzlander was for twenty consecutive years physician of the Bucks County Almshouse, and later filled the same position for three years. He is a member of the County and State Medical Societies, and of the Grand Army of the Republic, and the Loyal Legion of the United States. He is also a member of the Masonic fraternity.

DR. FRANK B. SWARTZLANDER, Doylestown (son of the preceding) was born December 19, 1873. He was educated at public and private schools in Doylestown, and spent three years in the Germantown Academy. He entered the Medical Department of the University of Pennsylvania, and graduated in the class of 1894. In the same year he accepted the position of resident physician at the Children's Hospital, Philadelphia, which he filled until January, 1895, filled the same position in the Pottstown Hospital from January to August, 1895, and was then appointed a resident physician in the Episcopal Hospital at Philadelphia, which position he filled until August, 1897 He then came to Doylestown and began the practice of his profession.

Dr. Swartzlander was married May 4, 1899, to Florence R. Evans, of Pottstown, and has two daughters: Mary, and Ellen Bryan Swartzlander.

DR. JOSEPH RANKIN SWARTZLANDER, Forest Grove, Buckingham township, Bucks county, son of Dr. Frank and Susan (Bryan) Swartzlander, was born in Doylestown, August 23, 1875. He acquired his education at the public and private schools of Doylestown, studied medicine under his father, and in 1893 entered Jefferson Medical College, graduating in class of 1897. He served as resident physician in the Jersey City Hospital for eighteen months, and in the summer of 1899 located at Forest Grove and began the practice of medicine. With inherited ability and careful training and experience, he started well equipped in his chosen profession and has met with merited success. He is still single.

GEORGE C. WORSTALL, one of the most prominent business men of Newtown, is one of the representatives of a family that have been prominent in the business affairs of Newtown for four generations, and extending over a period of one hundred and thirty years. He was born in Upper Makefield, October 25, 1839, and is a son of Edward H. and Maria E. (Smith) Worstall.

The family is said to have been of Welsh origin, but nothing definite is known of the ancestry of John Worstall or of his whereabouts until his proposal of marriage at Middletown Friends Meeting in 7 mo., 1720, to Elizabeth Wildman, daughter of Martin and Ann Wildman, who was born in Settle, Yorkshire, England, 9 mo. 19, 1689, and came with her parents to Bucks county, and they settled in Middletown township. John and Elizabeth Worstall were the parents of three sons: John, born 7 mo. 4, 1722; Edward, born 5 mo. 21, 1724; and James, born 12 mo. 26, 1726-7. The mother died when James was but two weeks old, and the children were reared by their maternal relatives in Middletown. Nothing is known of the descendants of Edward Worstall. James married Esther Satterthwaite and removed to Makefield in 1759, and has left numerous descendants in Bucks county.

John Worstall, eldest son of John and Elizabeth (Wildman) Worstall, born in Middletown, 7 mo. 4, 1722, married 8 mo. 2, 1746, Mary Higgs, daughter of James and Elizabeth (Andrews) Higgs, of Bristol, who were married in 1719. James Higgs died in 1736, leaving a son James and four daughters: Mary; Elizabeth, who married Thomas Hutchinson; Jane, who married Mahlon Hall; and Ann. Mary Higgs Worstall was born in 1720, and died at the residence of her son

Joseph, in Newtown, 8 mo., 1808, at the age of eighty-eight years.

Joseph Worstall, son of John and Mary (Higgs) Worstall, was born in Middletown, 1 mo. 13, 1750, and married, in 1778, Susanna Hibbs, daughter of William and Anna (Carter) Hibbs of Middletown. In 1774 he purchased of General Francis Murray a tract of land on Penn street, in Newtown, part of the old court house grounds, and erected thereon a tannery which he operated for fifty-five years. He subsequently purchased considerable other land adjoining, and erected houses and other buildings and carried on an extensive business. In addition to the tanning business he carried on the manufacture of shoes on a large scale, and employed a number of workmen. He also ground and shipped an immense amount of bark. The bark after being cured and ground was packed in hogsheads and hauled to the Delaware, where it was loaded on the Durham boats then plying on the Delaware, and carried to Philadelphia, where it was shipped to France and other parts of the old world. It is related that George Washington, while he had his headquarters at Newtown, had a pair of boots made at the shops of Mr. Worstall, from leather tanned on the premises, which he wore during the revolutionary war. Mr. Worstall also owned about fifty acres of land adjoining his business place on the south, and carried on farming in connection with his other business enterprises, in which he was assisted by his sons Joseph and James. The successful business career of the family was suddenly wrecked in February, 1829, when his large currying shops, bark mill house, wagon house, barns and an immense amount of bark, implements and farm produce were consumed by fire. There was no insurance on the property, and Mr. Worstall was financially ruined, and in his old age saw the savings of a life-time of industry and business activity swept away in a single night. He sacrificed the greater part of his real estate for the payment of his debts, retaining the tannery and his residence and some of his other houses. Being unable to carry on the tannery, however, with his limited means, he sold that also in 1831, and it remained out of the family until 1842, when it was purchased and remodeled by his grandson Edward H. Worstall. Joseph Worstall, Sr., died 1 mo. 13, 1841, at the age of ninety-one years, having lived a long life of extraordinary business activity. His children were:

, 1. Elizabeth, born 9 mo. 3, 1779, married in 1807, James Sleeper.

2. Sarah, born 6 mo. 1, 1781, married in 1803 Edward Hicks, the eminent minister among Friends.

3. Joseph, born 2 mo. 8, 1783, see forward.

Geo C. Worstall,

4. James, born 2 mo. 20, 1786, married (first) Jane Eastburn and (second) Sarah Smith; died 10 mo. 7, 1839, without issue.

5. John, born 2 mo. 10, 1790, died unmarried.

6. Mary, born 6 mo. 19, 1791, died unmarried late in life.

7. Amos T., born 4 mo. 25, 1793, married Ann Chambers.

8. Susanna, born 11 mo. 25, 1797, married Amos Phipps, of Plymouth, Montgomery county.

Joseph Worstall, eldest son of Joseph and Susanna (Hibbs) Worstall, was born and reared in Newtown, and was actively associated with his father in the business enterprises established by the latter. He was one of the proprietors of the tannery at the time it was burned in 1828, and suffered heavily in the financial wreck. His remaining days were spent in Newtown township on a farm he purchased, and where he died April 1, 1856. He married in 1808 Jane Heston, daughter of Colonel Edward Heston, the founder of Hestonville, Philadelphia, who was a native of Makefield township, Bucks county, being a son of Jacob and Mary (Warner) Heston, and a grandson of Zebulon Heston, an early settler in Wrightstown. He was captain of the Sixth Company, Seventh Battalion, Philadelphia County Militia, in 1777, and later was commissioned lieutenant-colonel.

The children of Joseph and Jane (Heston) Worstall were as follows: Sarah Ann, who married Jacob Hibbs; Edward H., see forward; Hannah C., who married (first) Pearson Scarborough, of Solebury, and (second) Henry Magill; Joseph, who married Mary Ann Van Buskirk, and lived and died in Warrington; and Isaac H., of Solebury, who married (first) Sarah Jane Ely and (second) Amy Ely.

Edward H. Worstall, eldest son of Joseph and Jane (Heston) Worstall, was born at the old homestead on Penn street, Newtown, October 19, 1811, and was reared and educated in Newtown. He married November 1, 1838, Maria E. Smith, daughter of Joseph and Mary (Betts) Smith of Upper Makefield. The descent of George Worstall in the Smith line is as follows: 1. William Smith, 1684, Wrightstown, formerly of Yorkshire, England, married Mary Croasdale, 9 mo. 20, 1690, and had nine children; his second wife was Mercy ———, by whom he had seven children. 2. Thomas Smith married Elizabeth Sanders, 6 mo., 1727, and they had eight children; they were the first settlers on the Windybush farm. 3. Samuel Smith married Jane Schofield, 1750, and they had ten children. 4. Thomas Smith married Elanor Smith. 4 mo. 15. 1778, and they had six children. 5. Joseph

Smith married Mary. Betts, 1808, and they had five children. 6. Maria Smith married Edward H. Worstall, 11 mo. 1, 1838, and they had five children. 7. George C. Worstall.

After his marriage Edward H. Worstall located at the Smith tannery at Windy Bush, in Upper Makefield, where he resided until April 1, 1842, when he purchased the old tannery property in Newtown, formerly his grandfather's, that had been recently sold by the sheriff as the property of Thomas H. Buckman, and revived the old industry so long conducted by his father and grandfather. He purchased the following year the house where his grandfather lived and died, and subsequently purchased much of the property that had belonged to his grandfather, as well as thirty-five acres of land, the greater part of which had belonged to his uncle James Worstall. He operated the tannery and farm until 1882, during the last eleven years of the time having associated with him his youngest son, Willis G. Worstall. During the last ten years of his life he lived retired in Newtown. He died February 18, 1891, and his widow Maria E. on January 11, 1898, Their children were: George C., the subject of this sketch; Lavinia, wife of George C. Blackfan, of Newtown; Josiah S., born September 7, 1843, died March 3, 1883; Willis G., born July 9, 1846, married Lydia Croasdale, and is now a member of the firm of Worstall Brothers & Co.; and Lettie, born February 28, 1850, wife of William Eyre, of Newtown. Josiah was for a number of years associated in business with his brother George C., in Newtown; he married Sarah J. Uber, and left two daughters, now residing in West Chester, Pennsylvania.

George C. Worstall was born in Upper Makefield, but his parents having removed to Newtown when he was two and a half years old he was reared in that town and has spent his whole life there. On his marriage in 1865 he settled on a farm on the Yardleyville turnpike, purchased for him by his father of Nicholas Willard, and resided there until 1893. In 1868 in connection with his brother Josiah, he started a brick and coal yard thereon, which they conducted until 1880, when they removed to the present location of the firm of Worstall Brothers, where they had started a hay press in connection with their younger brother Willis G. a year previous. The old tannery was abandoned in 1882 and torn down in 1887, and the land laid out in building lots and built upon. In 1880 the firm erected a feed mill, and eight years later built a full roller process flour mill. which with the brick making. feed and coal business they still conduct. The hay business was abandoned in 1893, being burned out in February.

George C. Worstall has been one of the pioneers in practically every public improvement and corporate enterprise in and about Newtown since his arrival at manhood. Edward H. Worstall & Sons owned a twentieth interest in the Newtown and Philadelphia Railroad, and were among the most active promoters of that enterprise. George C. was chairman of the meeting that organized the Newtown Artesian Water Company in 1888, that now supplies the town with water, and has been its president from its organization to the present time. He was one of the organizers and an officer of the Newtown Building Association in 1867, and is a director in the present Association, organized in 1887. He was one of the organizers of the Newtown Electric Light and Power Company, and a director since its organization. He was one of the active promoters and secretary of the Newtown, Langhorne & Bristol Railway Company, and of the Newtown Electric Railway Company, that built the trolley line from Bristol to Newtown and to Doylestown, and is still secretary and director of the latter company. He was one of the organizers of the Standard Telephone Company, as well as of the Newtown & Yardley Street Railway Company, of which he is president. He is president of the Newtown Canning Company, secretary of the Excelsior Bobbin and Spool Company, a director of the Newtown Cemetery Company, director of the Bridgetown & Newtown Turnpike Company, and president of the Newtown Reliance Horse Company. During the Civil war he twice responded to his country's call, first in 1862, when he went to Harrison's Landing, Virginia, as a nurse, and assisted in caring for the sick and wounded, and second in 1863 as a member of an emergency regiment. He is a member of T. H. Wyncoop Post, G. A. R., of Newtown.

He married, March 22, 1865, Hulda A. Price, daughter of Samuel and Sarah (Betts) Price of Buckingham, who died January 1, 1899. They were the parents of two children,—Edward A., who died in his seventh year, and Emma L., residing with her father in Newtown. He married (second) February 19, 1902, Mary W. Barnsley, daughter of John and Mary (Hough) Barnsley, of Newtown, who died September 24, 1904.

In politics Mr. Worstall is a Republican. He has served several terms in town council, and filled other local offices. He was appointed postmaster of Newtown in February, 1901, and was reappointed in February, 1905. He is a member of the Bucks County Historical Society, and actively interested in its work.

DU BOIS FAMILY. The family of DuBois is of French origin, the name being derived from two French words signifying "of the forest." The family is an exceedingly old one, several representatives having achieved distinction there over five centuries ago.

The ancestor of the American branch of the family was Louis DuBois, who fled from France to the Palatinate to escape religious persecution, in 1658, residing for two years in Manheim on the Rhine, then the capital of the Palatinate. He emigrated to America, with his wife and two children in 1660. He located at Kingston, Ulster county, New York, with a number of other French Huguenots, and became a very prominent character there. His wife and three children were carried into captivity by the Indians on July 6, 1663, and he led a company of the enraged settlers, who rescued them and dealt summary vengeance on their savage captors. With his two sons, Abraham and Isaac, and nine other French refuges, known as the "Twelve Patentees," he organized the settlement of New Palz, on the Hudson, opposite Poughkeepsie, in 1677, on 36,000 acres purchased of the Indians and patented to them by Edmund Andros, governor-general under the Duke of York. The other nine patentees were Christian and Pierre Deyou, Abraham and Jean Hasbrouck, Andre and Simon LeFevre, Louis Bevier, Antoine Crespel and Hugh Frere.

Louis DuBois was the first elder of the New Palz Church, organized in 1683, and the first records of the church are in his handwriting. He returned to Kingston in 1686, and died there ten years later. His wife was Cathrine Blancon, whom he married in France, where he was born, near Lyons, in 1630. They had ten children, viz: 1. Abraham, born in France in 1656, died in New Palz, October 7, 1731, married Margaret Deyou, and had seven children, the youngest of whom Mary married Philip Veree, and they settled on the Conestoga, in Lancaster county, on land purchased by Abraham in 1717. 2. Isaac, born at Manheim in 1658, married Maria Hasbrouck, and died at New Palz in 1690. 3. Jacob, born in Kingston, New York, October, 1661, married Gerritje Van Newkirk, died 1745. 4. Sarah, married Joost Jansen. 5. David, whose descendants settled and lived in Ulster county, New York. 6. Solomon, born 1669, died 1759, married Trintje Van Newkirk. 7. Rachel, died young. 8. Rebecca, also died young. 9. Louis, born 1677, married Rachel Hasbrouck. 10. Mathew, born 1679, married Sarah Mathewsen. Of these children—Jacob and Solomon—have descendants in Bucks county.

Jacob DuBois, third son of Louis and Catharine (Blancon) DuBois, was the first of the family born in America, being baptised at Kingston, Ulster county, New York, October 9, 1661, when but a few days old. He married at New Paltz about 1690, Gerrite Van Niuwkirk, daughter of Gerrit and grand-daughter of Cornelius Van Nieuwkirk, one of the earliest emigrants from Holland, and with those other descendants later generations of the DuBois family married in New Jersey. Solomon, fifth son of Louis, married Trintje, another daughter of Gerrit, and his eldest daughter Jacomyntje became the wife of Barent, the eldest son of Jacob, her double first cousin, and they were the parents of the Rev. Jonathan DuBois, who became pastor of the Dutch Reformed church of North and Southampton in 1748, married Eleanor Wynkoop, and has left numerous descendants in Bucks county. Jacob DuBois settled on a farm of his father's at Hurley, Ulster county, New York, and spent his whole life there, dying in June, 1745. By his Dutch wife Gerritje, otherwise Margaret Van Newkirk, he had eleven children: Magdalena, Barent, Louis, Isaac, Sarah, who married Conrad Ermendorf; Gerritje, Gerrit, Catharine, who married Petreus Smedes; Rebecca, Neeltje, and John. Jacob DuBois purchased in 1714 1,200 acres in Salem county, New Jersey, upon which three of his sons settled on arriving at manhood, viz.: Barent, Louis and Gerrit, though the latter returned to Ulster county on the death of his father. Barent was an elder of Pittsgrove Presbyterian church, and a prominent man in Salem county: he died there January 22, 1750, leaving eight children. The other children of Jacob DuBois remained in Ulster county, New York.

Louis DuBois, second son and third child of Jacob and Gerritje, was born in Hurley, Ulster county, New York, January 6, 1695. He married, May 20, 1720, Margaret Jansen, and settled in Pittsgrove township, Salem county, New Jersey, where he became the owner of 1,091 acres of land. He and his wife were among the first members of Pittsgrove Presbyterian church, of which he was an elder and trustee. He died in 1784. He had eleven children, viz.; Jacob, born 1720, died 1768; Mathew, born 1722; Anna, born 1724, married Rev. Marenus, of New York, later pastor of Freehold church; Gerritje, born 1726; John, born 1728, died at New London, Chester county, Pennsylvania, while a student for the ministry with his cousin, Jonathan, in July, 1746; Elizabeth, born 1739, died 1785, married Garret Newkirk, born 1732; Peter, born 1734; Joseph, died young; Benjamin, born 1739, an eminent minister of the Gospel, pastor of Freehold Presbyterian church for sixty-three years, 1764 to 1827; Samuel, born 1741, died 1811. All except two of these have

left descendants who are now scattered over the United States.

Peter DuBois, eighth child of Louis and Margaret, was born in Pittsgrove, Salem county, New Jersey, April 10, 1734. He was an intelligent and thrifty farmer and a pious and consistent Christian gentleman. He was a lieutenant in the company of his cousin, Jacob DuBois, and later a captain during the revolution. He died August 21, 1795. He married in 1758 Amey, daughter of Jeremiah and Sarah (Blackman) Greenman, and sister to Rev. Nehemiah Greenman, pastor of the Pittsgrove church. She was born October 24, 1727, and died June 2, 1807. They had five sons and two daughters, viz.: 1. Joel, born October 22, 1759, died June 29, 1805. Jeremiah, born November 22, 1760, died December 29, 1844, an eminent justice and legislator for many years; Sarah; Thomas; Samuel; Uriah; and Amey.

URIAH DU BOIS, youngest son of Peter and Amey (Greenman) DuBois, born in Pittsgrove township, February, 1768, became one of the most prominent preachers and educators in Bucks county. He received his academic education near the home of his ancestors in Orange county, New York, entered the University of Pennsylvania in 1787, and graduated in 1790. While a student there he boarded in the family of Robert Patterson, professor of mathematics and natural philosophy at the University, whose daughter Martha he later married. On his graduation he accepted a position as teacher in an academy at Charleston, South Carolina, where he spent one year. Returning to New Jersey he taught at Woodbury and Bordentown for three years, and then returned to Philadelphia to pursue his studies for the ministry under the Rev. Ashbel Green, D. D., afterwards president of Princeton. He was licensed to preach in 1796 and preached as a licentiate at Allentown, and at Deep Run and Red Hill in Bucks county. The Presbyterians of the latter two churches were pleased with him and he was elected their pastor in 1798. On June 20, 1798, he married Martha Patterson, and in December of the same year took up his pastoral labors in Bucks county, residing for one year at Dublin, and then removing to the parsonage farm near the Deep Run church, and preaching alternately at Red Hill and Deep Run. In 1804 the inhabitants of the growing village of Doylestown built an academy and invited Rev. DuBois to become its principal instructor. The congregations at both churches had decreased by the removal of the English settlers from that locality, and he decided to accept the offer and removed to Doylestown, meanwhile continuing his pastorate. He built a house, still standing at the north corner of State and Broad streets, in what was then a "two acre blackberry patch" and removed into it in 1805. He later built the house adjoining the academy and lived there from 1807 to 1814, and then removed back to the first home where he spent his remaining days. The builders of the academy had provided that religious services were to be held therein, and Mr. DuBois frequently preached there. This was the nucleus of the present Presbyterian church at Doylestown, which was organized in 1814 and the building dedicated in August, 1815. Rev. DuBois was a fine classical scholar and an excellent instructor. He was an assiduous worker, and the infant academy and church both prospered under his guidance. He continued his work in both institutions as well as at Deep Run until his death, September 19, 1821. He was also clerk of the Orphans court of Bucks county for the last six years of his life, his eldest son Charles E. performing the clerical work. His wife Martha Patterson was also a native of New Jersey, being born in Carltown, Cumberland county, July 30, 1779, from whence her father moved to Philadelphia when she was a year old. She was a very estimable woman and a fitting helpmeet for the enthusiastic and struggling divine in a sparsely settled community, and a heroic wife and mother. She survived him many years, dying October 25, 1856. The children of Rev. Uriah and Martha (Patterson) DuBois were: Charles E., the grandfather of the subject of this sketch; Emilia, who married the Rev. Samuel Aaron, born 1803. and died 1830; Robert P., born, 1805, for many years pastor of the Presbyterian church at New London, Chester county, Pennsylvania, married Jane H. Latta; Samuel, born 1808,, a noted local photographer and artist; William, born 1810, married Susanna Eckfeldt; Matilda, wife of the Rev. Silas M. Andrews, who succeeded his father-in-law as pastor of the Doylestown church and filled the pastorate for a half century; Louis, born 1814, married Henrietta Cox; and Mary, who married S. H. Thompson.

Charles E. DuBois, eldest child of Uriah and Martha, was born at the Deep Run parsonage, July 16, 1799. His family removing to Doylestown when he was five years of age, his youth and manhood was spent there. He was educated at the Union academy under his father's tuition, studied law under Abraham Chapman, Esq., and was admitted to the bar August 28, 1820. In 1823 he was commissioned clerk of the orphans' court and filled that position for six years, and in 1832 was appointed district attorney. He was an able and successful lawyer, and practiced in the Bucks county courts for forty years. In 1847 he was elected president of Doylestown

National Bank, and filled that position until his death which occurred March 5, 1865. He was married to Mary S. Latta, daughter of Rev. John E. Latta, of New Castle, Delaware, by whom he had eleven children: John L., born April 16, 1832, died February 20, 1903; Samuel M., died 1859; Emma P., married Edward P. Flint, a merchant of San Francisco, California, died 1899; Helen M., living in Doylestown; James L., died in California in 1897; Charles, died in infancy; Louis P., died 1889; Mary L., living in Doylestown; Charles E., died 1867; Henry M., a practicing attorney in Philadelphia; and Edward M., died 1857.

JOHN L. DU BOIS, Esq., eldest son of Charles E. and Mary S. DuBois, was born in Doylestown, April 16, 1832. He attended school in Doylestown until 1847, when he went to Norristown, and attended an academy conducted by Rev. Samuel Aaron. He next attended a boarding school at New London, Chester county, kept by William F. Wyers, where he remained for one year, when he entered LaFayette College and graduated in 1852. Returning to Doylestown he read law with his father, and was admitted to the bar on February 4, 1856. He entered into partnership with his father, which continued until the death of the latter in 1865. He contiued the practice of law during the remainder of his life, handling many important civil and criminal cases, and settled some of the largest estates in Bucks county. He was an elder in the Presbyterian church and one of its most earnest workers for many years. He also held very many positions of trust, was president of the town council for three years, a director in the Doylestown National Bank, secretary and treasurer of the Doylestown Improvement Company, treasurer of the Doylestown Cemetery Company, and president of the Bucks County Bar Association. He was superintendent of the Presbyterian Sunday School for thirty-four years. He died at his home on Court street, Doylestown, on Friday, February 20, 1903. He married, June 11, 1863, Emma Rex, of Montgomery county, Pennsylvania, who survives him. His only surviving child is John L. DuBois, Junior.

JOHN L. DU BOIS, Jr., was born in Doylestown, June 30, 1873. He was educated at the public schools, Doylestown Seminary and at the William Penn Charter School, Philadelphia. He read law with his father and was admitted to the bar January 13, 1896; entered into partnership with his father, which continued until the death of the latter, and is one of the young enterprising members of the bar. He was married December 18, 1900, to Christiana, daughter of Dr. Samuel G. and Rachel Ann (Cad-

John L. DuBois

wallader) Price, of Doylestown. Their only child—John L., was born December 5, 1903.

JOSEPH DE BENNEVILLE ABBOTT, burgess of Bristol, Bucks county, Pennsylvania, is a native of the state, born in Philadelphia, (Tioga), June 28, 1866, eldest son of Francis and Julia (Churchman Shewell) Abbott. He is descended on his father's side from John Abbat (subsequently spelled by this ancestor, "Abbott") who came to America from Farnsfield, Nottingham, England, in 1684, and "settled a plantation on Crosswicks Creek," between Bordentown and Trenton, New Jersey, consisting at the time of his death in 1739 of eight hundred and ten acres. An active Friend, he took a prominent part in all that concerned the Chesterfield Meeting at Crosswicks, Burlington county, New Jersey. He was constable of Nottingham and surveyor of highways. In 1695 he married Anne Mauleverer, daughter of Edmund and Anne (Pearson) Mauleverer. She, like her husband, was an active Friend, an elder of the meeting, and prominent in all meeting interests, as the records indicate. She died in 1754. John and Anne (Mauleverer) Abbott had, with other issue,

Timothy Abbott, born in 1717, died 1776. He married Anne Satterthwaite. He succeeded to his father's estate in part, and was prominent like his parents in the Society of Friends. He was a merchant as well as farmer, and had vessels plying up and down the Delaware river to Philadelphia from the plantation on Crosswicks Creek, then a navigable stream for boats of, for those days, considerable draught. Timothy and Anne (Satterthwaite) Abbott had, with other issue,

John Abbott, born 1748, died 1809. He married Susannah Bulloch. He succeeded to his father's estate and was actively engaged in the business instituted by his father, continuing the mercantile phase of it until 1800, when his large land-holdings demanded all his attention. He took an active part in local public affairs and in those of the religious body to which he belonged. John and Susannah (Bulloch) Abbott had, with other issue,

Joseph Abbott, born 1779, died 1861. He married Anne Rickey. In his father's lifetime he moved to a portion of the original "Watson plantation," east of the Abbott homestead, and was a farmer. Joseph and Anne (Rickey) Abbott had, with other issue,

Timothy Abbott, born 1809, died 1882. He married Susan Conrad. In early life he was a merchant, then was long associated with Peter Cooper, and later with Cooper, Hewitt & Co., in the iron business. He was president of the Mechanics' National Bank, Trenton, New Jersey. Timothy and Susan (Conrad) Abbott had, with other issue,

Francis Abbott, born 1840. He married (first) Julia Churchman Shewell. Mr. Abbott entered the banking house of the late F. M. Drexel in February, 1857, and at this date (November, 1904) still holds an important position in the same house. Francis and Julia C. (Shewell) Abbott had, with other issue, Joseph de Benneville Abbott, mentioned at length hereinafter.

Through the pioneer ancestor, John Abbat, Dr. Abbott is descended from the Ingrams, Colvilles and Mauleverers, who successively, as named, were owners of Ingleby Arncliffe, Yorkshire, England, an estate in existence as such since the middle ages. Through the Maulevers the descent may be traced back to nearly all of the Barons of Magna Charta, 1215. The ancestry of Anne Mauleverer Abbott is of unusual interest because of this fact. Edmund Mauleverer, the father of Anne, became a Quaker, and was apparently the only member of the family who changed his faith. The Mauleverers have been Church of England folk since the time of Henry VIII, and were previously Roman Catholics. Edmund's father was James, who married Beatrice, daughter of Sir Timothy Hutton. James' father was William, who married Eleanor, daughter of Richard Oldborough. William's father was Sir Edmund, who married Mary, daughter of Sir Christopher Danby. Sir Edmund's father was Robert, who married Alice, daughter of Sir Niman Markenfield. Robert's father was Sir William, (knighted at Flodden in 1513) who married Anne, daughter of Sir William Conyers, and through this line the descent from Edward III is readily traced. Sir William's father was Robert, who married Joan, daughter of Sir Henry Vavasour. Robert's father was Edmund, who married Alionara, daughter of Sir James Strangwayes. Edmund's father was Robert, who married Joan ——, and his father was Sir William Mauleverer, who married Joan de Colville, and succeeded to the Ingleby Arncliffe estate. The marriage of Robert Mauleverer and Alice Markenfield linked the family to descent from eighteen of the Magna Charter barons, the descent having intermarried between 1215 and 1500. This descent in all its details is traced in the beautiful Marsshall-Clement chart published in 1904, to which the reader is referred. (Vide "Ingleby Arncliffe and its Owners," by William Brown, Esq., Secretary of the Yorkshire Archaeological and Surtees Societies, Leeds, John Whitehead & Son, 1901.)

On his mother's side Dr. Abbott is descended from Walter Shewell, born near the village of Painswick, Gloucestershire, England, in 1702. He came to Philadelphia, June 7, 1722, and purchased from the Penn estate a tract of land in New Britain township, Bucks county, Pennsylvania, near Doylestown. He founded Painswick Hall, of which an account will be found elsewhere in this volume. Dr. Abbott is the sixth in descent from Walter and Mary (Kimber) Shewell, who had with other issue, Robert Shewell, born 1740, died 1825. He was a merchant in the West India trade. He married Sarah Sallows, and they had, with other issue, Thomas Shewell, born 1774, died 1848. He was a merchant. He married Sarah B. Linnington, and they had, with other issue, Linnington Daniel Shewell, born 1808, died 1873. He married Martha R. Roberts, and they had, with other issue, Julia Churchman Shewell, born 1843, died 1882. She was the wife of Francis Abbott, and mother of Joseph de Benneville Abbott.

Dr. Joseph de Benneville Abbott was educated at the famous Germantown Academy, and subsequently studied medicine in the Hahnemann Medical College of Philadelphia, from which he was graduated in April, 1887. In October, 1890, he entered upon the practice of his profession in Bristol, Pennsylvania, in which he has been usefully engaged to the present time. February 20, 1903, he was chosen burgess for a two year term, ending in 1905. In 1897 Dr. Abbott married his second cousin, Helen Shewell Keim, who is a descendant on her mother's side of the Rodman family, prominent in Bucks county since early in the eighteenth century. (Vide "Autumn Leaves from Family Trees," by Theo. Francis Rodenbough, New York, 1892. Privately printed.) Two children have been the issue of this marriage: Charles Shewell, born February 17, 1899; Helen Rodman, born August 20, 1900.

MARY S. ABBOTT. The paternal ancestors of Mrs. Abbott were among the earliest German settlers in Pennsylvania, her first American ancestor being Johannes Keim, who emigrated from Germany in 1698, and after a short stay in Pennsylvania returned to the fatherland, where he married in 1706, and returned to Pennsylvania the following year. He located soon after on the Manatawny, in Oley township, Berks county, and took up land. He was probably one of "those adventurous Germans" who settled beyond the limits of the land purchased by Penn of the Indians, and referred to in the correspondence between James Logan, Penn's famous secretary, and the founder. He obtained a patent for his land in 1720 and further patents for additional land in 1737. He died in Oley in December, 1753. A manuscript in his own writing gives an account of his first marriage in 1706, (without mentioning the name of his wife) and the birth of his six children by that marriage, and his second marriage in 1731. By the second marriage he had ten children. The children by the first marriage were: Katharina, born 1708, died 1793; Johannes, born 1711; Stephen, born 1717; Johan Nicholas, born April 2, 1719, died at Reading, Berks county, Pennsylvania, in 1803; Elizabeth, born 1723; and Jacob, born 1724.

Nicholas Keim, the third son, became a merchant in Reading, and his son John, born at Oley in 1749, was the ancestor of Mrs. Abbott. At the age of twenty-eight years, in 1777, John Keim enlisted in the Fourth Battalion of Berks county and served through the Revolutionary war. He was a captain in the Fifth Battalion in 1778. At the close of the war he returned to Reading and resumed his position with his father in the mercantile business, and remained in that business until his death on February 19, 1819. The "Berks and Schuylkill Journal," in referring to his death, says: "The remains of John Keim, merchant, were interred in the Episcopal burial ground this afternoon. * * * * He had resided in this borough sixty-four years, during which time he amassed a large fortune which never caused a widow's tear or an orphan's execration. What he left behind was justly his own. As a creditor he was ever lenient and his numerous tenantry can testify to his goodness as a landlord." His wife was a daughter of George de Benneville, of Bristol township, near Germantown, Philadelphia county.

Daniel De Benneville Keim was captain of the Berks county "Washington Blues," attached to the First Regiment of Pennsylvania Volunteers in the war of 1812. General George de Benneville Keim, grandfather of Mrs. Abbott, was born in Reading in 1778, and died there in 1852. He married Mary May, daughter of James and Bridget (Douglass) May, of Reading. James May was born May 2, 1749, in Coventry township, Chester county, Pennsylvania, and removed to Reading prior to the Revolution, dying there March 13, 1819. He was a descendant of John May, born in Mayfield, Sussex, England, in 1590, and emigrated to New England in 1635, Robert May, the grandfather of James, coming from New England in 1700 and settling at Limerick, now Montgomery county. Bridget Douglass was a daughter of George Douglass and granddaughter of Andrew Douglass, of Scotland, the latter of whom settled at what is now Douglassville, Berks county.

Major Daniel May Keim, son of George De Benneville and Mary (May) Keim, was born at Reading, in 1806, and

Daniel May Keim,

died in Bristol, Bucks county, February 12, 1867. He was a man of much more than ordinary intellectual ability and of scholarly tastes and extensive learning. He had an antiquarian turn of mind, and made extensive researches in almost everything pertaining to history, and made many valuable contributions to the Historical Society of Pennsylvania, of which he was one of the most active and distinguished members. He was for many years engaged in mercantile business in Philadelphia, and during the later years of his life held a responsible position in the custom house at Philadelphia. He was a prominent member of the Masonic fraternity, and at the time of his death was affiliated with Bristol Lodge, No. 25, A. Y. M., and that lodge and the grand lodge of the order adopted resolutions commemorative of his worth as a man and his distinguished services in the order. He married, November 17, 1829, Mary Linnington Shewell, born in Philadelphia, June 5, 1805, daughter of Thomas and Sarah B. (Linnington) Shewell. The former was born at Painswick Hall, New Britain township, Bucks county, July 13, 1774, and was a son of Robert and Sarah (Sallows) Shewell, and a grandson of Walter Shewell, of Painswick Hall, the founder of the family. Thomas at the age of eighteen years went to Philadelphia and entered mercantile pursuits. In 1796 he went to the West Indies, and from thence to England, where he entered the house of Bonsfield & Co., woolen staplers and army contractors, London. He returned to Philadelphia and became a merchant there in 1802, and was a member of the board of managers of the House of Refuge, and held many other positions of honor and trust. He retired from business in 1832, and died in Philadelphia, March 23, 1848. He was three times married. His first wife was Sarah B. Linnington, born March 10, 1784, whom he married March 10, 1802. She was a granddaughter of Dr. George de Benneville, of Bristol township, Philadelphia county, near Germantown. She died February 11, 1819.

Daniel May, and Mary L. (Shewell) Keim, were the parents of eight children, the two eldest of whom died in infancy. Those who survived were: Thomas Shewell Keim, born January 3, 1834, in Philadelphia, died at Bristol, Bucks county, November 9, 1866; Joseph D. (Brown) Keim, (so signed as administrator of father and brother) born November 26, 1835, married April 17, 1868, Lillie Paxson; Esther de Benneville Keim, born November 26, 1835, died January 24, 1874, married James P. Wood; Augusta Shewell Keim, born September 6, 1840; Mary Shewell Keim, the subject of this sketch, born December 1,

1843, married January 22, 1884, Francis Abbott; Anetta Faber Keim, born December 29, 1845, died December 20, 1860.

MARTIN LUTHER SNYDER, wholesale dealer in rubber goods, at Fourth and Market streets, Philadelphia, was born at Farmersville, Northampton county, Pennsylvania, July 2, 1850, and is a son of John H. and Anna (Groover) Snyder, both of whom were natives of Bucks county.

Andreas Von Schneider (or, as he signed himself in America, Andreas Schneider), the great-grandfather of the subject of this sketch, was born in the year 1739, in Zweybrucken, or Deux Ponts, Rhenish Bavaria, and is said to have belonged to the nobility of that cosmopolitan town, but, having taken part as a mere youth in an uprising against the government, was stripped of his nobility and property and forced to flee from the country. He sold himself to the captain of a sailing vessel bound for the port of Philadelphia, where he arrived some time in the year 1759. He bound himself to a merchant in Philadelphia whose name has not been ascertained, by whom it is said he was employed in the capacity of a farmer in the neighborhood of Germantown for some years, and that later his employer sold him sufficient stock and farming implements with which to embark in the farming business for himself, taking his note without security for the same. It is probable that his employers and benefactors were Abel James and John Thompson, of Philadelphia, prominent merchants on whose plantation in Richland township, Bucks county, we find Andrew Schneider in 1775, and five years later they conveyed to him 140 acres thereof, on which he lived and died. He was a member of the first Associated Company of Richland township in 1775, and is said to have rendered active service in the defense of the rights of his adopted country during the Revolution and served as an officer under Washington when he crossed the Delaware to attack the Hessians on that memorable Christmas night. It is related of Mr. Schneider that he was in such haste to join the army in the time of his country's urgent need, that he left his team in the field hitched to the plow. After service in the army of five years he settled on his farm in Richland, and devoted his energies to the tilling of the soil, meanwhile rendering such service to the public as the needs of the community in which he lived demanded. In the latter part of the war he served as a collector of militia fines, and, having in his hands at different periods considerable public funds, he kept the money hid in places known only to himself in order to protect his family from the depredations of the Doane outlaws, who did not hesitate to maltreat and torture the families of tax collectors in order to ascertain the hiding place of the public money. In religion Andreas Schneider was a member of the Lutheran church. He had received more than the ordinary advantages in the way of education, and took an active interest in the establishment of schools in the community in which he lived. He spoke the French language fluently, and while living in the neighborhood of Germantown was generally referred to as "the Frenchman." He died on his Richland farm about the year 1816. He married in 1765 Margaret Jacobi, whose parents were also early settlers in upper Bucks county, and they were the parents of eleven children, viz.; Frederick, who married a Miss Eckhart and had seven children; Elizabeth, who married Stephen Knizeley and had five children; Catharine, who married Isaac Bean and had five children; Andrew Jr., who married Mary Mickley and had five children; Margaret, who married John Weisel and had ten children; Magdalena, who married Jacob Bean; Henry, who married a Miss Messimer and had one child; George, who married Mary Mickley and had ten children; John, who married Elizabeth Hinkle and had eleven children; Mary, who married Philip Rumfield and had four children; and Susanna who never married.

John Snyder was the seventh child of Andreas and Margaret (Jacobi) Schneider, and was born and reared in Richland township, Bucks county. He was a farmer and lived and died in Richland township, his death occurring about August 1, 1844. His wife was Elizabeth Hinkle, daughter of John Hinkle, who owned and occupied a farm adjoining that of Andreas Snyder, in Richland. The children of John and Elizabeth (Hinkle) Snyder were as follows: William H., who married Catharine Heist and died before his father, leaving two children, Charles and William; John H., the father of the subject of this sketch, who married Anna Groover; Tobias H., who died unmarried; Lydia, who died young; Sarah, who also died unmarried; Amos H., who married Mary Blank; Andrew H., never married; Caroline, who married George Brong; Thomas H., who married Sarah Erdman; Catharine, who married Samuel Cressman, and Joseph H., who never married.

John H. Snyder, son of John and Elizabeth (Hinkle) Snyder, was born in Richland township, May 20, 1816, and died in Philadelphia, September 30, 1875. When a lad he was apprenticed to the shoemaker trade but was obliged to relinquish it on account of ill health. He entered the famous academy of Professor Blech, at Bethlehem, and fitted

himself for teaching school, and taught for twelve years, 1839 to 1851, part of the time at Rufe's school in Durham township, later at Hellertown, Northampton county, where he resided at the time of his marriage, and the last three years, 1848 to 1851, at Farmersville, Northampton county, Pennsylvania. In 1851 he removed with his family to Richlandtown, Bucks county, where he conducted the village hotel until March 21, 1861, when he removed to a farm formerly owned by his wife's father, John Groover, in Durham township. In 1873 the family removed to Philadelphia, where Mr. Snyder died September 30, 1875. Mrs. Snyder is still living. Anna (Groover) Snyder, wife of John H. Snyder, was born in Nockamixon township, Bucks county, Pennsylvania March 29, 1821, and was a daughter of John and Catharine (Miller) Kruger, (that being the original spelling of the name). Her grandfather, Nicholas Kruger, is said to have been born in Germany, and died in Nockamixon township in 1842. His grandfather, Nicholas Grouger (or Kruger) was one of the earliest settlers on the Tohickon, in Tinicum township, and died there in 1773, leaving a widow Ulfronica and children Nicholas, Philip, Mary Barbara and Anna Elizabeth. Nicholas Kruger, first above mentioned, married Catharine Wolfinger and had five children; Henry, who married Mary Trauger; Elizabeth, who married Nicholas Younkin; Margaret, who married a Fenner; John, who married Catharine Miller; and Nicholas, who married Susan Rufe. John Kruger and Catharine Miller were the parents of five children: Anna, the wife of John H. Snyder, and the mother of the subject of this sketch; William, who died in infancy; Charles, who married Hannah Frankenfield; Sarah, wife of George Harwick; and Samuel, who died in childhood.

John H. Snyder was a member of the Lutheran church, and in politics was a Democrat. He was a master mason of Philetus Lodge, No. 527, F. & A. M., at the time of his decease. He had five sons,—Martin L., John A., and Charles A., who are living, and Robert J. and Marcus F., who died in infancy.

Martin L. Snyder was born in Northampton county, where his father was at that time teaching school, but his parents removing to Richlandtown, Bucks county, when he was less than a year old, his earliest education was acquired in the public schools there; he later attended the Monroe school in Durham township, and finished his education at the Excelsior Normal Institute at Carversville, Solebury township, Bucks county, Pennsylvania. At the age of sixteen years he began teaching school and taught in the public schools of Bucks county for three years. At the age of nineteen years he went to Philadelphia and was employed there as a clerk until 1878, when he embarked in business for himself as a wholesale dealer in rubber goods, in which he has since been successfully engaged. In politics he is a Republican, with a decided leaning toward clean politics as exemplified by the Committe of One Hundred and the Municipal League. In 1901 he was the candidate of the Municipal League, endorsed by the Republican party, for common councilman from the thirty-seventh ward of Philadelphia, but failed of election. He is an active member of the Protestant Episcopal Church of the Incarnation, Broad and Jefferson streets, and for the past seven years has been a vestryman of that church, and is the present secretary of the vestry. He is a Master Mason of Shekinah Lodge, No. 246, F. and A. M.; past regent of Apollo Senate, No. 6, Order of Sparta, and Great Ephor of the Great Senate of Sparta for the last twelve years, also secretary of the Great Ephori of the Great Senate of Sparta; past master workman of Quaker City Lodge, No. 116, Ancient Order of United Workmen of Pennsylvania, and an ex-supervising deputy grand master workman of the order in Pennsylvania; and a member of Pennsylvania council, No. 342, Royal Arcanum. Mr. Snyder was married in Philadelphia, January 28, 1880, by the Rev. Francis L. Robbins, D. D., to Eliza Hunter Cassin, daughter of Isaac Sharpless and Emily (Hunter) Cassin, of Philadelphia, and they have been the parents of two sons, the elder of whom died in infancy. Their son, Cassin Snyder, born February 27, 1885, received his education in the public schools of Philadelphia, graduated from the North East Manual Training School, and until recently was connected with the engineering department of the Philadelphia Rapid Transit Company in the construction of the subway and bridge work for the depression and elevation of the car tracks on Market street; but is now associated with his father in business.

Isaac S. Cassin, father of Mrs. Snyder, was born in Delaware county, Pennsylvania, July 29, 1826, and is of English and Irish lineage, Joseph Cassin, his great-grandfather having emigrated from Queen's county, Ireland, in 1725, and settled in Philadelphia. He had among other children sons John and Luke, the former of whom became famous as Commodore John Cassin during the Revolution, was a warm personal friend of Washington, who presented him with an oil portrait of himself, which was destroyed by fire in the home of his no less distinguished son, Commodore Stephen Cassin, at Washington. Commodore Stephen Cassin commanded the Ticonderoga in McDonough's famous victory on Lake Champlain in the war of 1812-14, and was awarded a medal by Congress for bravery in that action, a replica of which is now in possession of Cassin Snyder, above mentioned. Luke Cassin, brother of the first Commodore, was the great-grandfather of Mrs. Snyder. He was born in Philadelphia in 1763, and followed the trade of a silversmith. He married Ann Worrall, of an old Delaware county family, and had one son, Thomas W. Cassin, who married Rachel Sharpless, daughter of Isaac and Hannah (Wright) Sharpless, and had children: John, the distinguished naturalist and ornithologist; Lydia, Luke, Thomas W., Rebecca S., William V., Isaac S., Ann Eliza, and Susanna S.

Isaac S. Cassin was educated at the famous Friends' school at Westown and under private tutors, and early manifested a talent for mechanics. He served an apprenticeship with Messrs. I. P. Morris & Co., of Philadelphia, and subsequently became, successively, engineer of the Spring Garden Water Works, of Philadelphia Gas Works, chief engineer of the Philadelphia Water Works, and chief engineer of the United States Mint in Philadelphia. Relinquishing for a time public office, Mr. Cassin reorganized the Union Hydraulic Works, and was one of the most eminent water and gas engineers in the country, having built not less than fifty water works in prominent cities throughout the country. His services as an expert in the construction of water works, were in great demand, and he had a distinct and unique reputation in the valuation of water and gas properties. He was a life member of the Franklin Institute, and of the Engineers' Club, and for more than twenty years prior to his death was a member of the Public Buildings Commission, which had charge of the erection of the city hall of Philadelphia. He was a member of the Society of Friends, at the Race Street Meeting. In politics he was an uncompromising Democrat, and besides filling numerous public offices was frequently a delegate to state and national conventions. He married, October 10, 1850, Emily Hunter, daughter of John Morgan Hunter, of Delaware county, and they were the parents of six children: Thomas; Eliza H. (now Mrs. M. L. Snyder); Edward, John, Emily, and Isaac S. Cassin.

The maternal ancestors of Mrs. Snyder were no less distinguished than her paternal ancestors. John Hunter, the progenitor of the family in America, was a strong churchman, and was in the Protestant army, under William of Orange in the battle of the Boyne, where he commanded a troop of horse and was wounded in the hip. He was a native of Durham, England, and a descendant of the Hunter family of Madomsley Hall, Gateshead, where many of his ancestors are buried. Upon the accession of James II, he fled to Rathdrum, county Wicklow, Ireland, where he married Margaret Albin, who bore him ten children. He came to America in 1722, and a year later settled in Newtown township, Delaware county, where he died in 1734 at the age of seventy years, and lies buried at old St. David's, Radnor, of which church he was one of the founders and a member of the first vestry. He was accompanied to America by Anthony Wayne, the grandfather of Mad Anthony Wayne, of the Revolution, the former being his superior officer in the battle of the Boyne, and the two families were closely associated. John Morgan Hunter, the grandfather of Mrs. Snyder, was a descendant in the fifth generation from John Hunter, the pioneer. His mother's sister, Elizabeth Edwards, married Peter Penn-Gaskill, who claimed descent in the sixth generation from William Penn, the founder. John Morgan Hunter married Eliza Rhodes, by whom he had five children,—Rachel, Hannah, Samuel, Emily, (the mother of Mrs. Snyder), and Sarah.

JOSEPH W. SHELLY, for the past five years District Attorney of the county of Bucks, was born in Milford township, Bucks county, March 26, 1864, on a farm that had been the property of his ancestors for a century and a quarter. The family of Shelly, now very numerous in Upper Bucks, is descended from Abraham Shelly, who emigrated from the Palatinate, Switzerland, or northern France, about 1730. On January 29, 1739, Thomas and Richard Penn, proprietaries of Pennsylvania, conveyed to him fifty acres of land in Milford township, adjoining other land on which he was already settled, showing that he was already located in Milford at that date. In 1740 he purchased of Morris Morris 260 acres additional, a portion of which was occupied by his descendants, the lineal ancestors of the subject of this sketch, until 1873. In February, 1761, he and his wife Elizabeth entered into an agreement to convey to their son Michael Shelly 135 acres of this tract, but Abraham died before the conveyance was completed. They also conveyed a portion of their land to their son Jacob in 1760. Abraham and Elizabeth Shelly were the parents of six sons,—Abraham, Jacob, Joseph, Christian, John and Michael, from both the first and last of whom the subject of this sketch is descended through the inter-marriage of a grandson of the former with a granddaughter of the latter.

Abraham Shelly, Jr., purchased land adjoining his father in 1753, which he later conveyed to his son Joseph. The date of the death of Abraham Shelly and Eve his wife has not been obtained, nor a full list of their children, though it is known that their two sons were Joseph and Christian.

Joseph Shelly, son of Abraham, Jr., as above related, received from his father a portion of the homestead. He was a farmer, and followed that vocation in Milford township until his death in November, 1818. He married Jannie Yoder, and they were the parents of the following children: Jacob, Abraham, Joseph, John, Mary, wife of Michael Landis; Eve, wife of Peter Moyer; Anna, wife of Jacob Moyer; Barbara, wife of Peter Schneider; and Fannie, wife of John Fretz.

Jacob Shelly, son of Joseph and Anna (Yoder) Shelly, married Barbara, only child of Michael and Elizabeth (Musselman) Shelly, and granddaughter of Micheal Shelly, youngest son of Abraham the emigrant. The land purchased by Michael, Sr., of his father, in 1761, was devised by Michael to his son John, who, dying without issue in 1770, devised it to his brother Michael, the father of Barbara, and he, dying in 1790, devised it to his only daughter, who later married Jacob Shelly, her second cousin. Elizabeth, the mother of Barbara Shelly, died in 1793, while her daughter Barbara was yet a minor. Jacob Shelly died in September, 1847, and his wife Barbara in February, 1852. They were the parents of ten children, viz.: Michael; Fannie, wife of William H. Oberholtzer; Joseph S.; Elizabeth, who became the wife of Rev. Samuel Moyer; David; Susanna, who married Samuel K. Harley; John and Mary, who died young; Jacob; and Barbara, who married Levi S. Shelly.

Joseph S. Shelly, second son of Jacob and Barbara, was born in Milford township, Bucks county, December 20, 1809, and died there in 1872. By proceedings in the orphans' court in 1848, the property which had descended to his mother was adjudged to him, and he continued to own it until his death. He married Elizabeth Bauer, daughter of Andrew and Elizabeth (Bechtel) Bauer, who was born in Douglas township, Montgomery county, Pennsylvania, October 30, 1809, and they were the parents of four children,—Andrew B.; Susanna, wife of David Stauffer; Mary, wife of John Bleam Bechtel; and Elizabeth, who died in childhood.

Rev. Andrew B. Shelly, the father of the subject of this sketch, was born in Milford township, September 23, 1824. He received his early education at the public and parochial schools of that vicinage, and at the age of eighteen years began teaching school in the winter months, devoting the summer to study in connection with assisting his father on the farm. In 1854 and 1857 he was a student at Freeland Seminary (now Ursinus College) at Collegeville, Montgomery county. In 1864 he entered the ministry and became the pastor of East Swamp, West Swamp, and Flatland, Mennonite congregations, to which he has since ministered. He has from a youth been one of the active leaders and teachers in the doctrine of the Mennonite church, bringing to bear upon this work, as upon all that he has undertaken, an energy, earnestness and fidelity to principle that has characterized his whole life. He has filled many prominent positions in the church, being for many years president of the general triennial conference, and a prominent member of the foreign missions and publication boards of the church. He was for fifteen years editor of the "Mennonitche Friedensbote," a church paper published at Milford Square, and for many years associate editor of the "Christliche Bundesbote," a paper published in the interest of the Mennonite church at Berne, Indiana. He has also been for many years one of the editors of "The Mennonite," an English church paper published in Philadelphia.

He married, October 16, 1858, Fannie Weinberger, born March 11, 1834, daughter of Joseph and Mary (Shelly) Weiberger, and also a descendant of Abraham Shelly, Sr., her mother being a great-granddaughter of Jacob Shelly, son of the pioneer, Abraham. This union was blessed with the following children: Mary Elizabeth, wife of Isaiah T. Clymer, of Quakertown; Adeline, wife of Uriah S. Stauffer, editor of "Quakertown Free Press"; Joseph W.; Menno and Oswin.

The Shelly family have nearly all been farmers and from their arrival in America, have nearly all been adherents of the Mennonite church, and true to the tenets of that faith, have taken little part in active politics or affairs of State, though taking an active interest in local affairs, in their respective neighborhoods. They have almost invariably given their political support to the old Whig and later to the Republican party.

Joseph W. Shelly was born on the old Michael Shelly homestead (purchased by his great-great-great-great-grandfather in 1740) March 25, 1864. He received his early education at the public schools of his native township, and the Quakertown High School, and finished his elementary education at Ursinus College. On leaving college he taught school at Quakertown, in the meantime entering himself as a student at law in the office of the late Charles F. Meyers, Esq., at Doylestown. He was admitted to the Bucks county bar December 1, 1890, and formed a partnership with his preceptor, which continued for five years, since which time he has practiced alone. He was admitted to practice in the supreme court of Pennsylvania in 1893. Mr. Shel-

ly is a Republican in politics, and has from the time of attaining his majority been actively identified with the organization of his party, serving as secretary of the county committee for several years, and as its chairman for six years. He is also a member of the Union Republican Club of Philadelphia. He was elected to the office of district attorney of Bucks county in 1900, and was re-elected in 1903, being the only living member of the bar to serve two terms in that office, the only other instance of a re-election being that of the late Nathan C. James, re-elected in 1857. As prosecuting attorney of the county, Mr. Shelly has made a good record, and he enjoys the confidence and esteem of the court and his fellow members of the bar. In religion he conforms to the faith of his ancestors for many generations, and is a member of the Mennonite Church.

DR. OLIVER STOUT. Jacob Stout, the pioneer ancestor of the subject of this sketch, was born in Germany, Rhine Province, in the year 1710, and came to Pennsylvania in the ship "Samuel," arriving in Philadelphia on August 30, 1730. He was accompanied by two brothers, John and Abraham Stout, of whom little is known. Jacob Stout located in Bucks county near the present site of Perkasie, where John Lacey (who had emigrated from Germany with his wife Anna, nee Miller, in the ship "Adventurer" in 1732) had purchased a tract of two hundred acres in 1735. Lacey died in 1738, and in 1739 Jacob Stout married the widow Anna. He probably remained on the Perkasie plantation with his wife and her two sons by Lacey, for the next ten years and later came to what became Williams township. Northampton county, where he purchased a tract of 243 acres on September 9, 1750, which remained the property of his descendants for several generations, descending through his son, Isaac Stout, the father of the famous physician and surgeon, Dr Abraham Stout. Jacob Stout was a potter by trade, and seems to have followed that vocation both at Durham and at Perkasie. How long he remained at the former place does not appear, but in 1753 he purchased a mill property and tract of land at Church Hill, in Rockhill township. In 1759 his step-sons, John and Henry Lacey, having come of age, Jacob Stout conveyed to them 266 acres in Hilltown, which he had purchased in 1757, and they in turn conveyed to him the 200 acres in Rockhill, originally taken up by their father. This tract embraced a large part of the present borough of Perkasie, and it remained the residence of the ancestors of the subject of this sketch for at least three generations. Here Jacob Stout resided the remainder of his life, becoming a prominent man in the community and an extensive landowner. In 1767 he purchased the Pine Run mill property, one mile north of Doylestown, which in 1770 he conveyed to his son-in-law, Abraham Freed. In 1774 he purchased 150 acres in New Britain, on which he settled his daughter Catharine, who had married Jacob Schlieffer. Jacob Stout died April 30, 1779, at the age of sixty-eight and one-half years, and is buried beside his wife and several of their children and grandchildren in a neat little family burial lot within a few rods of Perkasie station on the N. P. R. R. on a part of the old plantation. The children of Jacob and Anna (Miller-Lacey), Stout were as follows: 1. Abraham, an account of whom follows: 2. Isaac, who settled on his father's Northampton county tract and reared a family, among whom were Dr. Abraham Stout. 3. E. Salome, who married first Abraham Freed, and after his death, in 1773, Gabrielle Swartzlander, and lived and died at what was known for a century as "Swartzlander's Mill" one mile north of Doylestown, and left many descendants, among whom is Dr. Frank Swartzlander, of Doylestown. 4. Catharine, who married Jacob Schleiffer, and lived and died in New Britain.

Abraham Stout, eldest son of Jacob and Anna, born at Perkasie, August 17, 1740, was probably the most prominent and best educated Pennsylvania German of his day. Most of his education was acquired at the famous Germantown Academy, for years the rival of the College of Philadelphia, later the University of Pennsylvania, under the tuition of Hilarius Becker, professor of German, and David J. Dove as instructor in English. Abraham Stout thus acquired a thorough knowledge of the English language, an accomplishment exceedingly rare at that date and for a century later among the descendants of the German colonists of upper Bucks, as well as a thorough scientific training. He was an excellent accountant and penman, a surveyor and conveyancer, as well as an excellent business man, and transacted practically all the public business for his German neighbors far and near. Most of the deeds, wills, petitions to the courts, etc., on file among the papers of the several county offices from 1770 to 1812, are in his handwriting, as well as numberless account of administrators and executors, (he having served very frequently as auditor in estates) and are models of brevity, neatness and execution. At the death of his father his brothers and sisters conveyed to him the old Perkasie homestead, and his whole life was spent thereon. At the begin-

ning of the protest against the oppressive acts of the mother country in 1774-75, he was foremost in the neighborhood in organizing for the protest, and was named as the member of the committee of safety from Rockhill in 1775. When, however, it became apparent that a resort to arms would follow, he resigned from the committee and thereafter held aloof from active participation in the struggle. The reason for this was, no doubt, owing to religious convictions on the subject of the war, as there is evidence to show that his sympathies were with the patriot side. Though later generations of the family were members of the German Reformed church, it is probable that he was reared in the Mennonite faith. When his father, Jacob Stout, took the oath of allegiance in 1751, his name appears among the list of "Quakers and others who from religious conviction conscientiously scruple to take the Oath on the Holy Evangelists and having complied with the terms required by the Act of Parliament took and subscribed the qualifications required." Again, the Germantown Academy was in its inception a Mennonist institution, and he probably imbibed ideas of non-combativeness that prevented his participation in a sanguinary struggle. The war having ended, he became, however, a prominent figure in public affairs. He was one of the delegates from Bucks county in the constitutional convention of 1790, and took a prominent part therein. His career of usefulness ended with his death on the eve of the second struggle with the mother country, June 8, 1812, and he is buried beside his father in the old burying ground at Perkasie. He married, October 21, 1773, Mary Magdalen Hartzell, daughter of Henry Hartzell, another prominent Pennsylvania German in Rockhill township. She died November 8, 1811. Abraham and Magdalen (Hartzell) Stout were the parents of seven children, viz.: 1. Nancy, who married Jacob Hartman. 2. Jacob, the grandfather of Hon. Mahlon H. Stout, president judge of the courts of Bucks county. 3. Henry H., the great-grandfather of the subject of this sketch. 4. Abraham. 6. Margaretta, who married Tobias Ruhl, and 7. Magdalen, who married John Gearhart.

Henry H. Stout, second son of Abraham and Magdalen (Hartzell) Stout, was born on the Perkasie homestead, June 3, 1776. He was a lifelong farmer and resided for some years after attaining manhood on a portion of the old homestead, but later settled in Hilltown, where he owned considerable land. He was a member of the German Reformed church at Tohicken and an influential man in the community. He married, May, 1798, Elizabeth Kern, daughter of Christian Kern, of Hilltown. She was born May 10, 1778, and died June 5,

1871. Henry H. Stout died January 12, 1854. Both are buried at Tohincon. Their children were: Catharine, born 1798; 'Mary, born 1800; Samuel, 1802; Magdalene, born 1805; Hannah, born 1807; Elizabeth, born 1809; Enos, born April 17, 1813; Lydia, born January 18, 1815; and Annie, born 1821.

Enos Stout, only son of Henry H. and Elizabeth (Kern) Stout, was born and reared on the Hilltown homestead, a part of which he purchased on attaining manhood, and erected buildings thereon. At the death of his father he purchased the remainder and lived thereon, during life. He was a prominent and influential man in the community, and a memebr of the German Reformed church. He married, November 13, 1834, Catharine Kratz, daughter of John and Magdalena (Swartlander) Kratz, of Plumstead, his cousin, her mother being a daughter of Gabriel and Salome (Stout) Swartzlander. Catharine was born May 2, 1809, and died March 31, 1890. Enos Stout died December 6, 1886. Their children were: Lewis K., born December 22, 1835; John Henry, born July 22, 1838; Reuben, born March 28, 1841; Allen K., born May 21, 1843; Edward Clayton, born March 3, 1846; died January 28, 1862; and Wilhelmina, born 1850, died 1862.

Lewis K. Stout, eldest son of Enos and Catharine (Kratz) Stout, and the father of Dr. Oliver Stout, was born on the Hilltown farm, and educated at the public schools. He taught school in Hilltown, Bedminster and Rockhill townships, in all eight years. He was a justice of the peace of Rockhill township for five years, 1874-1779. In April, 1886, he removed to Philadelphia, where he resided until May 1, 1903, when he removed to Perkasie, Bucks county, Pennsylvania, where he still resides. He married, October 28, 1865, Lavina M. Althouse, born August 23, 1844, daughter of Samuel and Sarah (Mitman) Althouse, of Bedminster, Bucks county, and they are the parents of seven children, viz.: Henry Erwin, born September 15, 1866, died April 8, 1874; Annie A., born January 14, 1868, unmarried; Oliver A., the subject of this sketch; Edward Clayton, born August 12, 1872, graduate of the College of Pharmacy, Philadelphia, a druggist at 4628 Woodland avenue, Philadelphia; Charles A., also a graudate of the College of Pharmacy and now a druggist at Eighth and Diamond streets, Philadelphia; Philip Samuel, born August 20, 1877, graduated at the College of Pharmacy, Philadelphia, class of 1899, graduate of University of Pennsylvania, class of 1904, now demonstrator in pathology in the University; Benjamin Franklin, born January 18, 1880, a graduate of the College of Pharmacy in 1903, a druggist at Tonopah, Nevada.

DR. OLIVER A. STOUT, second son of Lewis K. and Lavina M. (Althouse) Stout, was born in East Rockhill township, Bucks county, Pennsylvania, November 11, 1869. He was reared in Rockhill, and received his elementary education in the Rockhill public schools, supplemented by two years at the Perkasie high school, entered the College of Pharmacy, and graduated from the three years' course in 1891. He entered the medical departnfent of the University of Pennsylvania, from which he graduated in 1893. He was drug clerk for J. Howard Evans, at Sixth and Venanga streets for one year; then located at Twentieth and York streets, where he practiced medicine for two years. In 1896 he purchased the drug store at Fifth street and Glenwood avenue, of J. Howard Evans, where he is still located. He is a member of Welcome Lodge, No. 453, F. and A. M., of Philadelphia, of the Jr. O. U. A. M., the Foresters of America, and the P. O. S. A. He married, June 11, 1902, Gail Louise Simpkins, daughter of Samuel Robert and Louise (Patterson) Simpkins, and they are the parents of one child, Louise Martindale, born June 11, 1903.

ANNIE COMFORT. The ancestry of Annie Comfort can be traced back to John Comfort, the first of the name known in Bucks county. He brought a certificate from the Friends of Flushing, Long Island, to the Friends' monthly meeting held in Falls township, December 15, 1719. Pleased with this portion of the country he settled in Amwell, Hunterdon county, New Jersey, where he continued to follow farming throughout his active life. On the sixth day of August, 1720, he married Miss Mary Wilson, and they had three children: Stephen, Sarah, and Robert.

(II) Stephen Comfort, eldest son of John Comfort, was married August 25, 1744, to Mercy Croasdale, and they had nine children: John, Ezra, Jeremiah, Stephen, Grace, who became the wife of Jonathan Stackhouse; Mercy, who became the wife of Aaron Phillips; Moses, Robert, and Hannah.

(III) John Comfort, eldest son of Stephen Comfort, removed from Mount Holly, New Jersey, in 1793, and settled upon, the farm where his descendants are still living. He married Miss Mary Woolman, a daughter of John and Sarah (Ellis) Woolman, and six children were the issue of this marriage: Samuel, John, Stephen, Mary, who became the wife of Moses Doan; Ellis, and Joseph. John Comfort was the father of another child, Ezra, by a second marriage. John Woolman, father of Mrs. Comfort, was a very noted man in his day in the Society of Friends, also a well known anti-slavery man, and it was largely through his efforts that the Friends Society took strong steps against slavery and gave up the slaves that were in their possession. He spent a considerable portion of his time in religious work and writing. His book, "The Journal of John Woolman," is a representation of the man; it has a very lengthy introduction by John Greenleaf Whittier, the celebrated poet, and Charles Lamb, an Englist poet and essayist, is of the opinion that every one should memorize the words of John Woolman.

(IV) Samuel Comfort, the eldest son of John and Mary (Woolman) Comfort, was born near Mount Holly, New Jersey, in 1776. When fourteen years of age he removed to the home now occupied by his granddaughter, Annie Comfort, whose name heads this sketch, in Falls township, Bucks county, Pennsylvania, and there he remained until his decease, giving his entire attention to agricultural pursuits. His influence was a recognized factor for good in the community in which he resided for so many years. He was a preacher in the Society of Friends, as was also his second wife, and when his son, George Comfort, took possession and management of the old homestead, he devoted most of his time to religious work, traveling and preaching throughout many states, being accompanied by his second wife, and in this way they were enabled to perform a large amount of good work. Mr. Comfort married Miss Rebecca Moon, and they were the parents of six children: Martha, who became the wife of Mark Wright; Mary, who died unmarried; Sarah, who became the wife of Ezekiel Combs; George, mentioned hereinafter; Rebecca, who became the wife of James Lawrence; and Ann, who became the wife of John Simpson. Three years after the death of Rebecca (Moon) Comfort, which occurred in 1836, Samuel Comfort married Mrs. Elizabeth Cox, who was a minister in the religious society of Friends. She survived him a number of years.

(V) George Comfort, son of Samuel and Rebecca (Moon) Comfort, was born on the old family homestead in Falls township, Bucks county, Pennsylvania, in 1808. For a few years after attaining manhood he taught a private school in the city of Philadelphia, but later returned to Bucks county and took possession of the old homestead, giving his entire attention to the quiet but useful calling of agriculture until his death. He was a man of the strictest integrity and took an active part in everything that tended to the betterment of the neighborhood, rendering efficient aid in every enterprise, whether of a religious, educational or social character. He was held in peculiar honor by his fellow citizens for his many noble and manly

characteristics, and his daily walk and conversation was well worthy of emulation. He was a true friend to all who were in distress, giving liberally of his substance, and throughout his lifetime followed and obeyed the scriptural proverb "It is more blessed to give than to receive." He was one of the directors of the Fallsington Library, and for the long period of thirty-five years served in the capacity of school director of Falls township. He was a regular attendant and stood high in the Friends Society. In politics he was an adherent to the principles of the Republican party. Mr. Comfort married Miss Susan Lower, of Philadelphia, Pennsylvania, and their children are: Rebecca, who became the wife of Joshua Palmer; Samuel, who has spent many years abroad; Annie, whose name heads this sketch; Susan E., deceased, was the wife of the late Milnor Gillingham; and Georgina, who became the wife of Charles Satterthwaite. George Comfort, father of these children, died at his home in Falls township, in 1887, leaving behind him the memory of a good name and an untarnished reputation.

SAMUEL COMFORT, son of George and Susan (Lower) Comfort, grandson of Samuel and Rebecca (Moon) Comfort, great-grandson of John and Mary (Woolman) Comfort, was born at the Comfort homestead near Morrisville, Bucks county, Pennsylvania, May 5, 1837. He was educated under private instructors and at the Trenton Academy. At an early age he developed special talents in mathematics and sciences, and attained considerable distinction as an inventor of improvements in mowing and reaping machines, sewing machines, counting machines, etc., for which he received numerous patents.

Samuel Comfort joined the union army in October, 1861, and served in Captain Palmer's "Anderson Troop," the bodyguard of General D. C. Buell, in Kentucky, Tennessee, Mississippi, and Northern Alabama, and was present at the battle of Pittsburg Landing. After eleven months' service in this command he was honorably discharged from the service on account of physical disability contracted in the service. In June, 1863, under special authority from Governor Curtin, of Pennsylvania, he recruited an independent company of cavalry in Bucks and Montgomery counties and the city of Philadelphia which was mustered into the service of the United States for a term of six months under the name of "Captain Samuel Comfort, Jr.'s Independent Company of Cavalry, the Bucks County Troop." This company served on escort and provost guard

duty at the headquarters of General Cadwallader at Philadelphia. In January, 1864, Captain Comfort re-enlisted his company for a further period of three years, or during the war, and was mustered into the service as captain of company "F" of the 20th Pennsylvania Volunteer cavalry, One Hundred and Eighty-first Pennsylvania Volunteers, commanded by Colonel John E. Wynkoop. The regiment was ordered to join the army in West Virginia, and Captain Comfort was never absent from his command when any important operations were in progress from that time until the end of the war. Captain Comfort was promoted to be major of the Twentieth regiment Pennsylvania Volunteer Cavalry in March, 1865. He was mustered out and honorably discharged from the service as major of the first Provisional Pennsylvania Cavalry, July 25, 1865. Major Comfort was present in nearly fifty battles or skirmishes of more or less importance, chiefly in and near the Shenandoah valley and in other parts of Virginia and West Virginia. His last campaign was with General P. H. Sheridan from the Shenandoah valley to Appomattox Court House. At this time his regiment was in General Deven's Second Brigade of General Merrit's First Division of General Sheridan's Cavalry Corps, and he was actively engaged in the battles of Five Forks and Sailer's Creek, and at the surrender of General Lee's army at Appomattox Court House. He was wounded in the right arm while in command of the skirmish line in the battle of New Market, in the Shenandoah valley, in 1864.

After the close of the war Major Comfort engaged in manufacturing and mercantile pursuits, and travelled extensively in foreign countries. He resided in India ten years and was United States vice consul at Bombay from 1894 to 1896, consul at Bombay from 1896 to 1898, and United States vice and deputy consul general at Calcutta from 1900 to 1903. Major Comfort was a member of the Union League Club of New York, the Army and Navy Club of New York, the military order of the Loyal Legion of the United States, the Grand Army of the Republic and other clubs and societies in the United States, and in foreign countries. He accumulated a comfortable fortune and retired from active business in 1904. On October 16, 1866, he married Elizabeth Jenks Barnsley, daughter of John and Mary Hough Barnsley, of Newtown, Bucks county, Pennsylvania, a second cousin of General U. S. Grant. One child was born of this marriage, Emma Walraven Comfort, who was educated at Vassar College and married Harry M. Crookshank, Pacha, a British official temporarily residing in Cairo, Egypt.

HOWARD OLIVER FOLKER, of Philadelphia, was born at Davisville, Bucks county, Pennsylvania, March 15, 1857, and is a son of David and Elizabeth (Wilson) Folker. David Folker, the father, was born in Buckingham, Bucks county, July 17, 1826, and was a son of James and Mary (Hurlinger) Folker. He learned the trade of a harnessmaker, which he followed in Southampton township, Bucks county, for many years. During the civil war he was an uncompromising friend of the Union, and stood shoulder to shoulder with the loyal and earnest men of that section in measures tending to the support of the government and the prosecution of the war. He was an industrious and exemplary citizen who had the respect of all who knew him. He died February 23, 1892. He married Elizabeth Wilson, born September 4, 1826, died November 11, 1882. She was a daughter of Ezekiel Wilson, who was born July 11, 1789, and died April 28, 1854. He was a private in Captain William Purdy's company in the war of 1812-14, serving at Camp Dupont, Marcus Hook, under Colonel Thomas Humphrey. His wife was Elizabeth Dungan, born May 31, 1794, died August 17, 1850, youngest daughter of John and Mary (Hyle) Dungan, and great-granddaughter of Rev. Thomas Dungan, of Cold Spring. The children of David and Elizabeth (Wilson) Folker were: Mary, died in infancy; Charles White, now a resident of Camden, New Jersey; Howard Oliver, and Horace Conard, deceased.

John Dungan Wilson, second son of Ezekiel and Elizabeth (Dungan) Wilson, born August 28, 1817, died September 1, 1875, was a man of fine parts and varied accomplishments. He was a jeweler and watchmaker, gunsmith, machinist and carpenter, and a thorough mechanic in all that the word implies. He was also an expert dancing master and a professor in the manly art of self-defense. He married Lucy Ann Lewis, daughter of Elias Lewis, and was a model husband and indulgent father. His wife still survives him, living in 1905 at Hatboro, Pennsylvania. No children now living. He is interred at Davisville Baptist church.

Howard O. Folker was educated in the common schools and at the First State Normal School at Millersville, Pennsylvania. He taught school for a short time, and in 1873, during the Cuban imbroglio, entered the United States navy and assisted in returning to the United States the filibustering steamer "Virginius," after the massacre of American citizens at Santiago. A year later he was transferred to the Mediterranean squadron, and visited all the different countries of Europe as well as those of Asia and Africa. In 1877, under the new naval apprentice system, he was appointed naval schoolmaster by Commodore Schufeldt, and sent to Port Royal, South Carolina, to take charge of the cadets at the training station there. Two years later he was transferred to the U. S. S. "Kearsage," of Alabama fame, and in her made several cruises in the West Indies and to South American ports; was at the occupation of Shepherd's Island, United States of Colombia, and assisted in the establishment of a coaling station there. He· left the navy in 1881 and entered the service of the Philadelphia & Reading Railroad Company, filling the position of traveling car agent for twelve years. He is at present connected with the transportation department as chief car distributor, with offices in the Reading Terminal, Philadelphia, Pennsylvania. Since leaving the navy he has taken great interest in veteran associations, and has assisted in the formation of a number of these patriotic associations. He is a past commander of the John A. Dahlgren Garrison, No. 85, Army and Navy Union, and is its present adjutant. He is also an active member of Farragut Association, U. S. Naval Veterans. Mr. Folker is a member of the Bucks County Historical Society, and has prepared a number of papers for its archives on local and family history. He has devoted several years to investigations in reference to his distinguished ancestors, the Dungan family, and from his "Chronicles of the Dungan Family" the brief sketches of some of its distinguished members which follow this sketch are derived. Mr. Falker married Annie M. Forney, daughter of Peter and Mary Ann (Henning) Forney, of Annville, Lebanon county, Pennsylvania, and they are the parents of six children: Lucy Wilson, now a teacher in the Philadelphia schools; Marian Henning; Alma Forney; Judson La Barre; and Irene Stine, deceased. Their eldest child, Amos Franklin, is also deceased.

WALLACE DUNGAN, one of the successful and active business men of Doylestown, was born in Doylestown township, Bucks county, July 8, 1845. John Dungan, son of Thomas (4) and Mary (Drake) Dungan, and grandson of Rev. Thomas Dungan, was the ancestor of Wallace and Mahlon K. Dungan, of Doylestown. He had sons Thomas, John, Joseph and Jesse. Thomas Dungan, son of John, above mentioned, married Deborah Doan, daughter of Daniel and and Sarah, born March 25, 1757, died December 7, 1829. Thomas Dungan died intestate August 30, 1803. He had issue James, born January 22, 1778, died January 20, 1840; Isaac, see forward; and Daniel, born December 30, 1784,

married Catherine Adams, of Warminster.

Isaac Dungan, son of Thomas and Deborah (Doan) Dungan, born July 14, 1779, died January 27, 1844, married Mary Dyer, daughter of Joseph and Christine Dyer, born May 10, 1781, died June 23, 1849. Their sons were: 1. Thomas, born September 30, 1803, died January 13, 1869; married Rebecca U. Montanye; he was county treasurer in 1847; and lived late in life in Plumstead. 2. Jesse, see forward; 3. John, born May 5, 1805, died July 18, 1868; married Eliza Reed, and lived and died in Northampton township, Bucks county; had children: Harman Y., Dyer C., and John T., deceased, and Mary, wife of David S. Fetter.

Jesse Dungan, son of Isaac and Mary (Dyer) Dungan, born February 5, 1802, died May 4, 1892, married Adriana Cornell. He was a successful farmer, and a man much esteemed by his neighbors. He filled the office of director of the poor of Bucks county for the term 1866-68, and a few years later retired from active life, and lived to the age of ninety years. Religiously he was a Presbyterian and politically was a staunch Democrat of the old school. He died at Churchville and is interred in the churchyard there. Jesse and Adrianna (Cornell) Dungan, were the parents of four sons and five daughters, viz.: Isaac, George, John K. David, Mary Jane, Ann Eliza, Louisa, Sarah and Adelaide.

Isaac Dungan, son of Jesse Dungan, was born on his father's farm in Northampton township and spent practically all his life in that and the adjoining township of Southampton. He was a farmer, and an active and prominent man in the community, holding at different times different township offices. Politically he was a Democrat, and took an active part in the councils of his party. He was an earnest and consistent member of the Davisville Baptist church. He died in Southampton township in 1887, at the age of sixty-five years. His first wife was Rebecca Boos, by whom he had two sons Wallace, to be further mentioned, and Mahlon K., of Doylestown. The mother died at Richboro in 1849, and Isaac Dungan married (second) Cynthia Ann Doan, and two children were born to them that grew to maturity: Sarah, wife of Albert Fesmire of Hartsville, and William Dungan, of Southampton.

Wallace Dungan, son of Isaac and Rebecca (Boos) Dungan, though born in Doylestown township, removed with his parents to Northampton township when a child. At the age of thirteen years he went to Tinicum township, where he lived for three years. Returning to Southampton, he lived with his father until twenty-one years of age. He re-

Wallace Dunsan

ceived a fair common school education in the schools of the neighborhood, and at the age of twenty-two years he began farming on his own account and followed that vocation for five years. In 1872 he engaged in the hide and tallow business in a building near the Doylestown flour mill, and in the following year built a factory near the present Doylestown electric light plant. By strict attention to business he built up a prosperous business, and prospered in spite of repeated reverses. His factory was totally destroyed by fire June 29, 1880. Undismayed by this untoward disaster, he at once erected another factory near his present residence, just east of the borough line, and equipped it with the most improved machinery for utilizing the several products of dead animals. In 1892 he purchased a tratt of seventy-five acres, one mile west of Doylestown, and moved his factory thereon and added a fertilizer plant, both of which he conducted on a large scale. He now experienced another great loss in the destruction of his plant by fire on April 8, 1897, but he again rebuilt it immediately, and has since conducted the business with entire success, assisted by his son-in-law, William Worthington. Mr. Dungan erected his present residence on Maple Avenue in 1878, and has resided there ever since. In 1899 Mr. Dungan had the misfortune to lose his left arm by having it drawn into the machinery in his factory, necessitating an amputation near the shoulder. He has, however, accustomed himself to the loss and continues to personally conduct his business. In politics Mr. Dungan is a Democrat. He is a deacon of the First Baptist Church of Doylestown. He is a member of Doylestown Lodge No. 245, F. and A. M., Doylestown Chapter No. 270, R. A. M., and Mary Commandery, No. 36, Knights Templar, of Philadelphia. He was married February 21, 1867, to Rachel Heaton, of Moreland, Montgomery county, Pennsylvania, and the union was blessed with one child, Effie F. H., now the wife of William Worthington. Rachel Heaton Dungan died December 22, 1898, aged fifty-eight years, and Mr. Dungan married, March 11, 1903, Anna, daughter of George Martin, of Doylestown township.

DUNGAN FAMILY. R e v e r e n d Thomas Dungan, the great-grandfather of John Dungan, mentioned in the preceding sketch, was born in London. England, about the year 1632. His father, William Dungan, was a merchant of London, and was of a cadet branch of the Dungans of Dublin, Ireland, ennobled by Queen Elizabeth. The senior branch ended under the following circumstances: William Dungan, Earl of Limerick, died in 1698, without leaving issue, in consequence of the death of his son, Lord Walter Dungan, colonel of dragoons at the Boyne, in 1690. The title of Earl of Limerick then came to Colonel Thomas Dungan, brother of the Earl of Limerick. Thomas, under the will of his father, Sir John Dungan, baronet, inherited an estate in the Queen's county, and served in the army of Louis XIV till 1678 as colonel of an Irish regiment, worth to him about £5,000 per annum. He had from Charles II a life pension of £500 a year; was made lieutenant-governor of Tangier, in Morocco, and subsequently governor of New York in America. The title of Earl of Limerick ceased in the Dungan family on the death of Colonel Thomas Dungan in December, 1715, he leaving no heirs. William Dungan died in London in 1636, leaving four children, Barbara, William, Frances, and Thomas. The mother of Rev. Thomas Dungan was Frances Latham, daughter of Lewis Latham, sergeant falconer to Charles I. She had married (first) Lord Weston and (second) William Dungan, and soon after the latter's death married Captain Jeremiah Clarke, and with him and her children emigrated to New England and settled in Newport, Rhode Island, where Captain Clarke became prominent, serving in the provincial assembly and filling other official positions. He died in 1651, and his widow married (fourth) Rev. William Vaughan, pastor of the first Baptist church in America. Mrs. Vaughan died in September, 1677, at the age of sixty-seven years.

Thomas Dungan came to Newport, Rhode Island, in 1637, with his mother and stepfather, Captain Clarke, and was reared and educated in that colony, probably receiving his education in a school established there by Roger Williams. His second stepfather being a Baptist clergyman he imbibed that faith and became an eminent Baptist preacher. He was a representative in the colonial assembly of Rhode Island, 1678-81, and a sergeant in the Newport militia. He became one of the patentees of East Greenwich, Rhode Island, but sold his real estate there in 1682 and removed with a colony of Welsh Baptists from Rhode Island to Cold Spring. Falls township, Bucks county, and established the first Baptist church in Pennsylvania. He died in 1688. He married in Newport, Rhode Island, Elizabeth Weaver, daughter of Sergeant Clement and Mary (Freeborn) Weaver. Clement Weaver was a member of colonial assembly in 1678, and his father-in-law, William Freeborn served in the same body in 1657. Elizabeth (Weaver) Dungan, died at Cold Spring, Bucks county, in 1690. The children of Rev. Thomas and Elizabeth (Weaver) Dungan were as follows:

1. William, born 1658, preceded his father to Bucks county, died there 1713; married Deborah Wing of Newport and left five children.

2. Clement, died in Northampton township, Bucks county, in 1732, without issue.

3. Elizabeth, married Nathaniel West and had four children, one of whom, Elizabeth, married Joseph Hough of Warwick, and has numerous descendants in Bucks.

4. Thomas, born about 1670, died June 23, 1759, married Mary Drake and had nine children, Thomas, Joseph, James, John, Jonathan, Elizabeth, who married John Hellings; Mary, married Thomas Barton; and Sarah married ———— Stevens.

5. Rebecca married Edward Doyle, who died in 1703, leaving sons Edward and Clement, who were the ancestors of the Doyles for whom Doylestown is named.

6. Jeremiah, born about 1673, died in Bucks county, April 6, 1766, married Deborah Drake and had eight children.

7. Mary, married a Richards and had three children.

8. John, who died without issue.

9. Sarah, who married James Carrel, and had six children.

The sons and sons-in-law of Thomas and Elizabeth Dungan became large landowners in Bucks county, and they and their descendants were prominent in the affairs of the county, province and state.

James Dungan, son of Thomas and Mary (Drake) Dungan, of Northampton township, Bucks county, Pennsylvania, was the great-great-grandfather of Howard O. Folker, the historian of the family, and a full account of him is given in his "Levi Dungan, the Pioneer," among the archives of the Bucks County Historical Society. He married Rebecca Wells, daughter of Samuel Wells, a farmer in Lower Dublin township, near the present site of Bustleton, Philadelphia county, and lived and died on a farm in Lower Dublin township.

JOHN DUNGAN, the great-grand-father of Mr. Folker, was a son of James and Rebecca (Wells) Dungan, and was born in 1753, died March 22, 1798. He was a lieutenant in Captain Andrew Long's company, Pennsylvania Rifle Regiment, Colonel Samuel Miles. This company was in the disastrous battle of Fort Washington, November 16, 1776, under the command of Lieutenant John Spear, and was almost annihilated. Lieutenant John Dungan was a farmer in Northampton township, Bucks county, and is buried at Southampton. He married Mary Hyle, and had four children—two sons: Uriah and Jonathan; and two daughters: Esther, who married William Hibbs, Jr., and Elizabeth, who married

Ezekiel Wilson. Another daughter, Rebecca, died young. Uriah, born 1777, died October 4, 1822, had children: Mary, who married Edmund Van Artsdalen, of Springville, Northampton township, whose daughter Elizabeth married Elias Hogeland, (see Hogeland Family); and John and Martin. Mary, the widow of Uriah, married (second) ———— Everett, and (third) Jonathan Knight. John, son of Uriah, had four sons: William, now living at Ringoes, New Jersey; Edmund B., who died at Harlingen, New Jersey, in 1900, leaving five children; Charles, deceased; and Thomas A., now a resident of Chicago. Nelson Y. Dungan, son of Edmund B., is a practicing attorney at Somerville, New Jersey, ex-district attorney, state senator for two terms and major of Second Regiment National Guards of New Jersey.

COLONEL THOMAS DUNGAN.

Joseph Dungan, son of Thomas and Mary (Drake) Dungan, born 1710, died 1785 married Mary Ohl, born 1710, died 1788, and had children: Thomas, Joshua, Sarah (wife of Benjamin Corson) and Hannah, (wife of Benjamin Marple). Both Joseph and his wife are interred at Southampton churchyard.

Thomas Dungan, eldest son of Joseph and Mary (Ohl) Dungan, was born in Warwick township, Bucks county, Pennsylvania, March 16, 1738, entered the University of Pennsylvania (then "College of Philadelphia,") in 1762 and graduated in 1765. Was a tutor there 1764-66; professor of mathematics 1766-69; and Master of Arts 1767. On May 2, 1767, he was called to preach at the Southampton Baptist Church, but declined. In 1774, March 18th, he was chosen principal of the Germantown Academy. Soon after this date, however, he entered the continental army, and was commissioned paymaster of the Twelfth Regiment, Continental Line, April 29, 1777; was transferred to Sixth Pennsylvania, and commissioned ensign June 2, 1778; made paymaster of Sixth Regiment, September 1, 1778; promoted to Lieutenant January 1, 1781, and transferred to Second Pennsylvania, January 1, 1783. General Washington in refering to the deplorable condition of the troops while suffering from smallpox in their winter quarters at Morristown, New Jersey, mentions the special efforts made by Paymaster Dungan to ameliorate their conditon and his persistent importuning of Robert Morris, the financier of the Revolution, for money for necessary clothing and medicine. He served until the close of the war and then returned to the charge of the Germantown Academy, where he remained until about 1800. He died at Germantown, April 26, 1805, aged sixty-seven years, and is buried in Hood's cemetery at that place. He married, May 19, 1793, at Neshaminy Presbyterian Church, his cousin Elizabeth Dungan, daughter of Jeremiah and Ann (Whitton) Dungan, of Northampton township, Bucks county, and three children were born to them: Thomas, died in infancy; Elizabeth, who married George Taylor Stuckert, and had one child Elizabeth, the wife of Dr. William Wilby Burnell of Philadelphia; and another Thomas.

Another prominent descendant of Rev. Thomas Dungan was General Mahlon Dungan, born April 23, 1780, died December 8, 1848, seventh child of David and Sarah (Newell) Dungan, grandson of David and Rachel Dungan, and great-grandson of Jeremiah, fourth son of Rev. Thomas Dungan. He married, October 7, 1802, Phoebe Addis, daughter of John and Mary of Northampton, and lived for many years at "Lakeside," the ancestral home of Thomas Yardley, at Yardley, Pennsylvania, built in 1728. He was a prominent Democratic politician, and a Mason of high degree. He was elected in January, 1824, brigadier-general of Bucks county militia and had command of the military escort that accompanied Marquis Lafayette across Bucks county on his visit to America in 1824. In 1827 he was a candidate for the nomination for sheriff, and was defeated by General John Davis. He left three children, viz.: John A., born August 11, 1803, married Amelia V. Bailey, and left one son Mahlon, died 1849, Methodist minister at Yardley, and three daughters; Levi, born March 23, 1805, died August 5, 1824, unmarried; and Mary Ann, died 1831, unmarried.

HENRY W. GROSS, of Doylestown, Bucks county, Pennsylvania, was born in New Britain township, Bucks county, Pennsylvania, February 4, 1842, and is a son of Joseph N. and Sarah (Wismer) Gross.

Rev. Jacob Gross, the great-grandfather of the subject of this sketch, was a native of Germany and came to this country about 1763, locating in Hatfield, now Montgomery county, Pennsylvania, from whence about the year 1780 he removed to Bedminster township, where he purchased a farm and resided until his death, December 12, 1810, at the age of sixty-seven years. He was for many years a minister of the Mennonite congregation at Deep Run, and later a bishop of that denomination. His wife Mary nee Krall, survived him and died in Bedminster, February 10, 1816, at the age of sixty-five years. They were the parents of six children: Isaac, Christian, Mary, wife of Abraham Nash, Jacob, Daniel and John.

Daniel Gross, son of Jacob and Mary, was born May 24, 1784, and was a farmer

14-3

in Bedminster, and later in Doylestown township, where he died in 1875. He married, June 20, 1809, Elizabeth Nash, born June 25, 1788, died November 9, 1823. She was a daughter of Joseph and Elizabeth (Wismer) Nash, and granddaughter of William Nash, an early German settler on the Skippack, who later settled in Bedminster township. Joseph Nash was born January 18, 1753, and died May 31, 1830, was a farmer and weaver in Tinicum township, Bucks county. He was a member of the Mennonite congregation at Deep Run and a deacon for many years. His wife, Elizabeth Wismer, was a native of Bedminster and was born September 1, 1753, died September 9, 1837. Daniel Gross was a deacon of the Doylestown Mennonite congregation for thirty years. His children were: Mary, born May 20, 1812, died September 12, 1813; Joseph N., born August 3, 1816, see forward; Elizabeth, and Sophia, married Samuel Kaisinger.

Joseph N. Gross, eldest son of Daniel and Elizabeth (Nash) Gross, born in Bedminster township, August 3, 1816, was a lifelong farmer. On his marriage he located on a farm in New Britain township, on which he resided for forty-four years. He was a Mennonite, and politically was a Republican. He took an active interest in local affairs, and served for a number of years as a school director, also filled the position of county auditor. He died April 13, 1902. He married, March 16, 1841, Sarah Wismer, born April 30, 1819, daughter of Samuel and Susanna Wismer, and they were the parents of five children: Henry W., the subject of this sketch; Susanna, born June 4, 1843, died December 11, 1873, married William J. Leatherman, of Plumstead; Daniel W., born June 3, 1846, died February 12, 1880, unmarried; Levi N., born October 24, 1854, removed to Oakland, California; and Isaiah W., born January 10, 1861, living in Philadelphia.

Henry W. Gross was born and reared on the farm in New Britain township, and attended the public schools there, later entering the First State Normal school at Millersville, Pennsylvania, from which he graduated in 1873. He taught school in Bucks and Allegheny counties for sixteen years; was principal of the Etna borough schools, Allegheny county, for five years. Since 1880 he has been connected with the creamery business. In politics Mr. Gross is a Republican, but has never sought or held other than local office. He has served as school director of Doylestown township for two terms. He is interested in several local institutions, and is president of the White Hall Mutual Fire Insurance Company, and of the Chalfont Mutual Wind and Storm Insurance Company. Religiously, he is a member of Doylestown Presbyterian church, of which he hàs been a ruling elder since 1890. He joined the Forest Grove Presbyterian church, Allegheny county, in 1869, and was superintendent of the Sharpsburg, (Allegheny county) Presbyterian Sabbath School for two years. He has been superintendent of the Danboro (Bucks county) Sabbath School since 1890, except for an interval of less than a year. He has served for several years as secretary of the Bucks County Sabbath School Association and as president of the Sabbath School Association, second district of Bucks county, and superintendent of the normal department of the Sunday schools in that district.

In June, 1905, Mr. Gross asked to be relieved from the Sunday School superintendent duties at Danboro. In doing so the school presented him with a beautiful combination couch, and the following resolutions signed by the one hundred and thirty members:

Dear Mr. H. W. Gross:

It is with the deepest regret, that we, the officers, teachers and members of the Danboro Union Sunday School, accept your resignation as superintendent.

We lose 'a superintendent whose life has been marked by the most genial companionship and devoted Christian character.

In you we have recognized a worker whose individual fidelity has been the means of inspiring the young people and adding endurance and courage to the older ones.

In you we have seen the Christian in belief, in experience and in example.

In you we have noticed a church member in profession, in loyalty and in work.

In you we have seen a Bible student in teachableness and in thoroughness.

You have been a teacher in knowledge and a teacher in tact and we will be grateful for continued services.

All have profited by your sympathy and helpfulness.

The members of your family deserve their share of credit for the help they have been. Those were happy Sunday School days when the entire family gathered in the chapel from Sabbath to Sabbath. Every man, woman and child have felt for you all in the sad affliction which has overtaken one of your children and one of our scholars.

God be praised that He gave you the talent to do so much for us, and may He continue to give you and us strength to bear what lies before us.

And we would not be forgetful of your helpmate who has stood so faithfully by you.

Again, we desire to express our grateful appreciation of the services you have so faithfully and conscientiously rendered, and may our relationship cease with Mizpah.

July 1, 1905.

Mr. Gross married at Line Lexington, Bucks county, Pennsylvania, June 17, 1875, Susan Elizabeth Funk, of Hilltown, daughter of Jacob and Susanna (Fretz) Funk, the former a native of Springfield, and the latter a daughter of Martin Fretz, for many years a miller at the old Yost mill near Bloomington Glen, and a granddaughter of Christian and Barbara (Oberholtzer) Fretz, of Bedminster. Mr. and Mrs. Gross have been the parents of four children: Sarah Ella, Emma Laura, Esther F. and Walter Gross. The latter died at the age of eight months. S. Ella Gross attended the West Chester Normal school, and has taught in the public schools of Bucks county for two terms. Emma Laura is an invalid and resides at home. Esther F. Gross attended the State Normal school at Stroudsburg, Pennsylvania, for one year, graduated from the West Chester Normal school, and is now a teacher in the public schools of Quakertown borough, Bucks county.

HON. WEBSTER GRIM, of Doylestown, representative of Bucks county, in the upper house of the state legislature, was born in Nockamixon township, Bucks county, Pennsylvania, August 11, 1866, and is a son of Dr. George W. and Elizabeth P. (Koons) Grim. On the paternal side his ancestors were early German settlers in what is now Montgomery county, the pioneer ancestor being doubtless Adam Greim, who emigrated from Rhenish, Bavaria, arriving in Philadelphia in the ship "Anderson," Captain Hugh Campbell, August 25, 1751. The family of Grimm, though for several generations, residents of Prussia or Rhenish Bavaria, trace their descent to early Franks who were residents of that part of Gaul which became later Normandy, whose descendants became allied with those of their Norse conquerors before their migration to the Rhine provinces about the tenth century.

The earliest American ancestor of Senator Grim of whom we have any definite record was George Grim, who was a resident of Upper Salford township, Montgomery county, Pennsylvania. He married Elizabeth Favinger, also of German origin, and they were the parents of three children, one son Adam and two daughters. Adam Grim, son of George and Elizabeth (Favinger) Grim, married Christina Desmond, daughter of Daniel Desmond, who was of English and Irish extraction. Adam Grim was killed on the Reading railroad in 1846, when his son George W. was fourteen years of age.

Dr. George W. Grim was born in Montgomery county, March 13, 1832. He was educated at Washington Hall, Trappe, Pennsylvania, and received a

good academic education. His father dying when he was fourteen years of age, he was cast upon his own resources, and learned the trade of a stove moulder, which he followed for some years. An accident, by which his foot was badly burned in the discharge of his duties, decided him to prepare himself for the medical profession. He resumed his studies at Washington Hall, where he also taught for a short time, and began his preparation for his chosen profession under the preceptorship of Dr. Gross, of Harleysville. He later entered Jefferson Medical College, from which he graduated in 1859. He located in Nockamixon township, Bucks county, and soon built up a large practice, becoming one of the leading physicians of upper Bucks, and was engaged in professional work there for thirty-three years, dying March 6, 1892. Dr. Grim was a man of good business qualifications and strict integrity, and always held the esteem and confidence of his community. He was the owner of a fine farm near Revere, the work of which he superintended in connection with his professional duties. In politics he was a Democrat, and he and his family were members of the Reformed church. Dr. Grim married in 1857 Elizabeth P. Koons, who survives him, and they were the parents of nine children, as follows: F. Harvey, who succeeded his father as a practicing physician at Revere; George W., a physician at Ottsville, Bucks county; A. Florence, wife of Oscar H. Bigley, of Doylestown, transcribing clerk in the recorder of deeds office; Webster, the subject of this sketch; Frank S., a physician at Baptisttown, New Jersey; Harry E., law partner with his brother Webster, under the firm name of Grim & Grim, with offices at Perkasie, Pennsylvania; Cora B., wife of William H. Rufe, a merchant at Riegelsville; Nora E., wife of Asher K. Anders, Esq., a successful attorney of Doylestown; and James S., professor of natural science at Keystone Normal School, Kutztown, Pennsylvania.

Hon. Webster Grim, the third son, was reared in Nockamixon and attended the public schools of that township and the Riegelsville high school, and later entered the Keystone normal school at Kutztown, Pennsylvania, from which he graduated in 1887. Prior to his graduation he taught school in Bucks county for five years. Immediately after his graduation he began the study of law in the office of Nathan C. James, Esq., and was admitted to the bar of Bucks county in September, 1889. Locating in Doylestown, he at once began the practice of his chosen profession and built up a lucrative practice. He was the Democratic nominee for district attorney in 1894, but was defeated by a small majority, receiving a much larger vote than the other nominees on the ticket. He has been active and prominent in the councils of his party for many years, and has served as delegate to several state conventions, and was permanent chairman of the state convention of 1903. He filled the office of justice of the peace for Doylestown borough from 1890 to 1900, and did a large amount of official business. He was elected a member of the school board in 1900 and re-elected in 1903 and is at present the treasurer of the board. In the fall of 1902 he was elected to the state senate, and in the sessions of 1903 and 1905 took an active part in the proceedings of the upper house, introducing a number of meritorious bills and serving on important committees. In the latter session he was chairman of both Democratic caucuses, and was the recognized leader of the minority party in the legislature. He was at all times the uncompromising foe of vicious legislation and extravagant appropriations, and his course met with the approbation of his constituents without reference to party. Among the important bills introduced by him was one for the regulation of the speed of and registration of automobiles, which was passed at the session of 1903, and amended upon his motion at the session of 1905; a bill for freeing the toll bridges over the Delaware river between the states of Pennsylvania and New Jersey and New York; and a bill for more adequate punishment of the crime of criminal assault. He was also instrumental in securing liberal appropriations for Bucks county educational institutions. He was one of the prominent candidates before the Democratic state convention of 1905 for the nomination for judge of the superior court, and only the decision to nominate but one candidate defeated his nomination.

Being possessed of a natural musical talent he has given much time to the organization and perpetuation of musical organizations. He was for five years musical director of the choir of the Doylestown Presbyterian church, and has since filled the position of choir master and organist at the Salem Reformed church, of which he is a member. He also had charge of the musical part of the program at the Bucks County Teachers' Institute for many years, and has been the director of the Arion Glee Club for many years, furnishing vocal music for entertainments in all parts of Bucks county. He was superintendent of the Sabbath school of the Salem Reformed church for twelve years, and introduced a uniform and graded course of study that has since been adopted by a number of other Sabbath schools in the county and elsewhere. He has been one of the most active members of St. Tammany Castle, No. 173, Knights of the Golden Eagle, served as its clerk of the exchequer for several years, and has been a member of the grand castle of Pennsylvania for twelve years and in May, 1905, was installed as grand chief of the order in the state. He arranged, codified and published a digest of the laws of the order which has been in use for several years. He is a past grand /of Aquetong Lodge, No. 193, I. O. O. F., of Doylestown, and has filled the position of musical director and degree master of that lodge for several years. As such he organized and instructed a degree staff that has the reputation of being one of the best in the state, taking second prize in a competition this year before a Committee of the Sovereign Grand Lodge, in which were entries in all parts of the United States. He has been the collector of Lenape Council, No. 1117, Royal Arcanum, since 1890, and is treasurer of the fraternal accident order, known as the "True Blue." He has served as a director of Eastern Union Building and Loan Society of Philadelphia since 1890, and is connected with a number of other business enterprises. He has prepared and published two directories of Bucks county, and is at work upon a third edition. In August, 1904, he purchased a controlling interest in the Doylestown Publishing Company, the proprietors of the "Doylestown Democrat," daily and weekly, which he has since personally conducted as president of the company, and has greatly improved the standard of the paper.

Senator Grim was married August 9, 1890, to M. Alice Sassaman, daughter of Jacob and Emeline (Wildonger) Sassaman of Bucksville, Bucks county, and they are the parents of two children, Ruth S. and George W.

MOON FAMILY. James Moon and Joan Burges were married near Bristol, England, and with a family of children were among the early emigrants to settle in Pennsylvania. By deed dated 10 mo. 13, 1688, he purchased of James Hill 125 acres of land in Falls township, one and a half miles west from Morrisville, and largely covered in 1905 by the classification yard of the Trenton branch of the Pennsylvania Railroad. On 12 mo. 11, 1706, he conveyed the same by deed in fee to his son Roger. James Moon's will mentions six children: Sarah, James, Jonas, Jasper, Mary and Roger. James married Mary Wilsford, 1 mo., 1696, and afterward Agnes Priestly, in 1714; he deceased 4th mo. 6, 1755.

Jonas, born 10 mo., 24, 1671, married Alice Chissum, about 1707, and deceased 10 mo. 4, 1732; Mary married a Curtis. Tradition says that Jasper went to Virginia and was the progenitor of the Moon family of that state. He married Susanna ———. Among the earmarks of cattle recorded at the clerk's office in a book preserved in the Library of the Bucks County Historical Society are those of James Moon. He was a member of Falls Monthly Meeting of Friends, and was buried in the old graveyard at Fallsington. His wife Joan's English relatives sent her money with which she purchased a farm near the river Delaware, two miles north of Yardleyville, since owned by Zachariah Betts. She resided with her son Roger at the homestead until her death, at nearly ninety, having survived her husband twenty-six years. She was an active member of Falls Monthly Meeting, and frequently preferred to walk to meeting when in advanced years.

Roger Moon, son of James and Joan Moon, born about 1680, married Ann Nutt, of England, at Falls Meeting of Friends, 8 mo. 23, 1708; they had seven children: James, born 1 mo., 1713, died 5 mo. 9, 1796; John, born 5 mo. 27, 1717, died 9 mo. 24, 1732; Elizabeth, born 10 mo. 16, 1719, died aged eighty-five and one-half years, 1805; Roger, born 1 mo. 20, 1722, died 12 mo. 4, 1759; Isaac, born 11 mo. 6, 1724, died 6 mo. 23, 1748; William, born 3 mo. 6, 1727, died 10 mo. 4, 1795; Ann, born 4 mo. 7, 1730, died 3 mo. 28, 1764. Roger Moon's second marriage was to Elizabeth Price (daughter of Reese and Mary Price), 1 mo., 1734. Their children were: John, born 12 mo. 28, 1734, died 1 mo. 6, 1788; Mary, born 3 mo. 8, 1736, died 11 mo. 20, 1815; Sarah, born 10 mo. 29, 1737; Timothy, born 10 mo. 15, 1739, died 7 mo. 5, 1813; Samuel, born 7 mo. 1, 1744; Jasper, born 1 mo. 12, 1748; Hannah, born 8 mo. 29, 1749.

Roger Moon said he had lived seventy years in the same place, and had never discharged a gun or quarrelled with any man. He deceased 2 mo. 16, 1759, on the ancestral acres, at the ripe old age of seventy-nine years; eleven of his children surviving him.

James Moon, eldest child of Roger and Ann Nutt Moon, married three times, and one child of each marriage lived to grow up; first to Hannah Price, 11 mo. 18, 1737; their son James married Sarah Dowdney, and had two children, James and Mary. James married and had several children, lived and died on the same farm his father did near the river two miles above Morrisville. Mary married John Thornton, had a large family of children. James, son of Roger and Ann Nutt Moon's second marriage was to Elizabeth, daughter of Edward and Bridget Lucas, 3 mo. 18, 1742; she deceased 6 mo. 14, 1748. One daughter survived her mother, who married Yeomans Gillingham, at Falls Meeting, 1 mo. 13, 1768, and had nine children. James Moon's (son of Roger and Ann Nutt Moon) third marriage was to Ann Watson, widow of Mark Watson, and daughter of John and Mary (Lofty) Sotcher, at Falls Meeting, 3 mo. 28, 1753. One child, Moses Moon, survived this marriage. On 1 mo. 29, 1749, James Moon purchased of Robert Lucas, for £480, two hundred and eighteen and one-quarter acres of land in Middletown township, now known as "Woodbourne," where he resided the remainder of his life, and in 1905 it is owned and occupied by his descendants. Beside ordinary farming he was a nurseryman, as entries in his cashbook testify, one reading thus: "11th mo. 22nd 1775. Joseph Lovett bought six Newtown pippins and two grafted pear trees for eight shillings." He thus started a business which his descendants have followed to a greater or less extent for over one hundred and thirty years.

Moses Moon was born 10 mo. 9, 1754. Beside following the occupations of his father as farmer and nurseryman, he also was a noted surveyor. He married Rachel Burges, at Falls Meeting of Friends, and deceased 4 mo. 19, 1822, having resided his entire life at Woodbourne, which he inherited from his father and bequeathed to his only son James, who adhered more closely to farming than did his predecessors. James Moon married Jane Haines, at Evesham Meeting, N. J., 5 mo. 13, 1813, and continued to reside at the homestead until his death in 1855. He left six children: Mahlon, Eliza, Charles Rachel, James H. and Jane C.

Mahlon, the oldest son of James and Jane (Haines) Moon, followed the nursery business for quite a period of time, after which his brother James H. Moon purchased the greater part of the land. Charles Henry Moon, son of Charles Moon, is a prominent surveyor and engineer, and lives on the western portion of the place, he being the fifth generation of the family to occupy these ancestral acres.

James H. Moon, the third son of James and Jane (Haines) Moon, married Elizabeth Balderston, in 1853, and settled two miles west of Fallsington, where they still reside with their son, Alfred H. Moon. Of their nine children five are still living: Everett, LL. D., Alfred H., Willett B., M. D., Elizabeth Laetitia, Ph. D., and Rachel, M. D.

Of James and Jane Haines Moon's daughters, Eliza married Morton A. Walmsley, of Byberry, Pa.; Rachel married William Tatnall, of Wilmington, Delaware, and Jane C. married Hon. Jonathan Chace, of Rhode Island.

Of the eleven children which survived Roger Moon, we have partially traced but one line, that of his eldest son James. The descendants of the five sons who survived him are scattered in all directions, although there is proof that many remained near home, the name occurring frequently in this vicinity and in New Jersey. His son William married Elizabeth Nutt; and settled on Moon's Island in the Delaware River. An account of his descendants is given later. Ann married Jonathan Pursell; Elizabeth married William Janney, 7 mo., 1739, at Falls Meeting and they moved near Waterford, Loudoun county, Va.; John, Roger and Isaac died without issue. Of the second wife's children; John married and left descendants; Mary married John Linton; Sarah married Daniel Burges; Timothy married Martha Richie; Hannah married Mahlon Hartley, and removed to Ohio; Jasper, unknown.

PRICE FAMILY. Elizabeth Price, second wife of Roger Moon, was of Welsh origin and a daughter of Reese and Mary Price (or Preese), who settled in Bucks county about the year 1700.

The ancestors of Mrs. Samuel C. Moon, of Morrisville, were Nathaniel and Sarah (Briggs-Shaw) Price, who emigrated from Rhode Island and settled in Middletown township, Bucks county, near the present site of Langhorne about the middle of the eighteenth century. They were the parents of three children; Nathaniel, of whom a more particular account follows: Elizabeth, married Edward Worstall; and Susanna, married Thomas Jones. Sarah (Briggs-Shaw) Price died 10 mo. 22, 1808, in her eighty-seventh year.

Nathaniel Price, son of Nathaniel and Sarah, born February 8, 1759, was received into membership with Friends and married October 18, 1786, Ann Bailey, daughter of Edward and Ann (Satterthwaite) Bailey, of Bucks county, and had three children: (1) William, born September 14, 1787, died June 4, 1852, married April 18, 1808, Mary Mahan, and had nine children: Cornelius, Mary, John, Deborah, Ann, Amos, Susan, Catharine and William. (2) John, born November 23, 1788, died April 5, 1867, married Rachel Burgess, daughter of Joseph and Sarah (Matson) Burgess, and had children: Daniel B., of whom an account follows; Lydia B., Sarah Ann and Phebe B., none of whom married, living and dying near Fallsington, Bucks county. (3) Edith, born 1790, died 1792. Ann (Bailey) Price died January 8, 1791, and Nathaniel married (second) December 13, 1792, Mary Spicer, daughter of James and Rachel Spicer, and they were the parents of four children: (4) Joseph, born March 10, 1793, married October 14, 1821, Eliza Wildman, and had children, Mary and Elizabeth. (5) Ann, born February 23, 1795, married, 1819, Israel Burgess, and had two children, William and Mary, both of whom married into the Longshore family. (6) Isaiah, born December 20, 1798, married May 20, 1824, Margaret Burges, daughter of William and Rachel Burges, and had four children: Rachel, married Benjamin Woolston; Ann, married a Hance; Jane, married a Croshaw; Martha, married Dr. William E. Case, and has two sons, William and Philip of Morrisville. (7) Rachel, born December 4, 1800, lived to an advanced age at Langhorne, but never married. Mary (Spicer) Price, the mother of the above named four children, died December 8, 1829.

Daniel B. Price, only son of John and Rachel (Burges) Price, was born December

3, 1823. He was a successful farmer and died at his residence, Brookdale farm, two miles from Fallsington, Bucks county, March 26, 1891, at the age of sixty-seven years. He married, first, May 18, 1848, Hannah B. Childs, of Le Raysville, New York, and they were the parents of four children: Rachel Anna, married Samuel C. Moon; Clinton, died young; Elizabeth, married John W. Tatum, of Wilmington, Delaware, and has three children—Anna P., Lucy R. and John W. Tatum, Jr.; Mary C., remained single.

THE BURGES FAMILY, with whom the Moon and Price families are much intermarried, are descended from Samuel and Eleanor Burges, who came from England in 1685 and settled in Falls township, on 200 acres of land purchased of William Penn, for one silver shilling per acre, the original deed for which is still in possession of their descendants. This land joined that on which James and Joan (Burges) Moon settled, and Samuel was probably a brother of Joan Moon. On this tract lying on both sides of the road now leading through the village of Fallsington, all the Friends' meeting houses of Falls Meeting have been built. In 1689, when the Friends decided to build a meeting house, Samuel Burges gave them six acres on which the first meeting house and graveyard were located. The first building was of logs and the second of brick. In the latter a school was kept for many years in which the great-grandchildren of Samuel Burges, living in 1855, remember attending, being used as a school after the erection of the third meeting house, a little distant from the first site and now (1905) used as a dwelling house. The fourth meeting house was erected in 1789 on the first location, north of the graveyard and Newportville road, and is still used by one branch of the society. The fifth meeting house was built in 1840, when a stone school house erected in 1799 was removed to make room for it, the present school house being erected in 1817. The will of Samuel Burges, made in 1713, mentions wife Eleanor, sons Joseph, Samuel, John and Daniel, and daughters Priscilla and Sarah. Priscilla became the wife of Samuel Bunting, and an account of her descendants is given in this volume. Sarah married John Hutchinson and an account of her descendants is also given in the Rickey family. Samuel, the son, a member of assembly in 1712, married Ann Snowden, and had three children—Margaret, married Joseph Jackson; Rebecca, married Joseph Church; Ann, died single.

Joseph Burgess married Hannah Wilson, and had five children: Daniel, of whom a more particular account follows; Joseph, married Deborah Fisher and removed to Buckingham, later to Baltimore, Maryland, and subsequently to Virginia; had children; Thomas, Sarah, John, Tacy, Martha and Daniel, of whom Thomas married Elizabeth Hendricks, and removed to Highland

county, Ohio, about 1813; John, Sarah, and Hannah. John, son of Samuel and Eleanor, married Mary Duer, and had six children, Samuel Ellen, Jonathan, Mary, Susanna, and Martha.

Daniel Burges, son of Samuel and Eleanor, was twice married, but left no issue, devising his farm, part of 600 acres purchased by Samuel, the pioneer in 1695, to his brother Joseph's son Daniel.

Daniel Burges, son of Joseph and Hannah (Wilson) Burges, married 6 mo. 17, 1750, Lydia Sisom, and had eight children: Joseph, born 3 mo. 31, 1752, married, 11 mo. 8, 1780, Sarah Matson; Rachel, born 11 mo, 14, 1753, married Moses Moon; Hannah, born 12 mo. 23, 1755, married Joseph Child; Sarah, born 9 mo. 17, 1758, died at the age of ninety-six years; Rebecca, born 10 mo. 26, 1763, married John Burton; Edith, born 3 mo. 15, 1766, married Joseph Headley; Phebe, born 6 mo. 20, 1769, died single in 1839; Amos, born 10 mo. 11, 1772, married Sarah Boulton. Daniel Burges married (second), Sarah Moon and had two children; Daniel, born 10 mo. 15, 1780, married Deborah Wood, and lived on the homestead for some years and then removed to New York state; and Elizabeth, born 11 mo. 28, 1784, died at the age of eighteen years.

Joseph Burges, eldest son of Daniel and Lydia, married Sarah Matson, and had eight children: Moses, born 8 mo. 17, 1781, married Ann Hancock; Lydia, born 8 mo. 28, 1783, and Amy, born 11 mo. 28, 1785, both died single; Daniel, born 4 mo. 30, 1787, also died single; Rachel, born 7 mo. 26, 1789, married John Price; John, Joseph and Aaron, died young. Joseph Burges married, second, Deborah Bailey and had one child, Mary born 12 mo. 24, 1803, died young. Moses and Ann (Hancock) Burges had eight children, Joseph, Sarah, Phebe, Moses, Rebecca, Robert, Ann, and George, of whom Robert and Phebe still reside on the ancestral homestead, and are nearing the sunset of life. Anna Price Moon, Elizabeth Price Tatum, and Mary C. Price, daughters of Daniel B. and Sarah (Burges) Price, with their children are the only living descendants of Joseph and Sarah (Matson) Burges.

OWEN MOON, JR., of the Trenton (New Jersey) Times," is a descendant of James and Joan (Burges) Moon, the pioneer ancestors of the family, as shown by the preceding narrative, throughout the following line: '

William Moon, fifth son and sixth child of Roger and Ann (Nutt) Moon, was born March 6, 1727, and died October 4, 1795. He married his cousin Elizabeth Nutt, and was treated with therefor by the Friends' Meeting at Falls, the marriage of first cousins being "against the good order maintained among Friends." Among the children of William and Elizabeth (Nutt) Moon were Ann, married, May 17, 1775, Samuel Bunting; and William Moon, born February 5,

1765, died May 30, 1827, at the age of sev-, enty-two years. He was twice married; first to Sarah ———, who died about 1749, and (second) to Phoebe Mott, born May 26, 1754, died July 23, 1847, aged ninety-three years. The children of the first marriage were as follows: 1. Daniel, see forward; 2. Phoebe, married Benjamin Kelly, son of Joseph and Phoebe (Buckman) Kelly, and had three children: Benjamin; Elizabeth, married Thomas Miller; and Sarah, married John Miller. 3. Elizabeth, never married. 4. Mary, born March 19, 1794, died January 22, 1866, married John Stackhouse, and had two children, one of whom, Phoebe, married 1847, Joseph Brown, of Fallsington, and has two children: Charles and Edward.

Daniel Moon, eldest child of William and Sarah, born July 5, 1789, died August 21, 1869, aged eighty years. He married Mercy Lovett, born July 17, 1789, died December 23, 1840, daughter of Evan Lovett and Sarah Neeld (nee Stackhouse) and they were the parents of eleven children: 1. William L., born August 25, 1810, died 1900; married in 1839, Elizabeth Y. Williamson, born July 1, 1819, died July 26, 1891, daughter of Mahlon and Charity (Vansant) Williamson, and had eleven children, five of whom survive: Daniel H., born October 15, 1843; Mary Jane, widow of Andrew Crozer Reeves, whose only child 'Andrew C. Reeves, is prominent in the business interests of Trenton, New Jersey; Mercy Ann, wife of Frank W. Muschert, senior member of the wholesale grocery firm of Muschert, Reeves & Company, Trenton, New Jersey, and has one child, William M. Muschert; Georgiana Watson of Langhorne, Pennsylvania, who has three children, Elizabeth W., Thompson, Elwood Watson, and Margaret Watson; and Anna Elizabeth, wife of William B. Parry, of Langhorne, who have two children. 2. Evan L. Moon, born August 8, 1812, died April 19, 1898; married (first) Ann Palmer, March 12, 1835, and had one child, Owen, a more particular account of whom is given below. Evan L. Moon married (second) Mary Atchley, and had two children, Jesse and Daniel, the latter of whom married Mary Fell, daughter of Henry R. and Rachel W. Fell, of Trenton, New Jersey, and has four children; Arthur E., Elizabeth F., Rachel W., and Ridgway. 3. Sarah, born July 9, 1814, died September 7, 1883, married George Thompson, who died in 1864, and had four children, three boys and one daughter, Mercy Ann, who married B. Woolston Watson, in 1862, and has three children. 4. John Moon, died in infancy. 5. Owen, born 1817, died at the age of thirteen. 6. Daniel, died in infancy in 1819. 7. John Hutchinson Moon, born October 5, 1820, married in 1848, Sarah Ann Crozer, daughter of Robert and Grace (Wright) Crozer, and had six children. 8. Andrew Moon, born October 16, 1823, died January 2, 1897; married, February 20, 1845, Anna Mary Watson, daughter of Miles and Ann (Kelly) Watson, and

had three children; M. Watson Moon, of Fallsington, who married Charlotte Green Mull, daughter of Ebenezer and Sarah (Green) Mull, and has three daughters, Emma, wife of Willets B. Farley; Jennie and Annie, unmarried. 9. 'Phoebe Ann Moon, born October 5, 1825, married (first) January 20, 1848, William Kelly, who died in 1862, leaving one child, Daniel Edward, who married Mary F. Gilkyson, and had six children; she married (second) in 1865, John Hellings, and had no children. 10. Benjamin, born September 1, 1827, died 1864; married Rebecca B. Miller, and had one child Ella. 11. Anna Mary, born July 11, 1829, married, October 24, 1861, William Penn Crozer, son of Robert and Grace (Wright) Crozer, and has one child, Mercy.

Owen Moon, only child of Evan L. and Ann (Palmer) Moon, born January 1, 1836; married December 14, 1859, Elizabeth Buckman, daughter of Spencer W. and Sarah (Williamson) Buckman, and their only surviving child is Owen Moon, Jr., of the "Trenton (New Jersey) Times." The maternal ancestry of Mr. Moon is given under the heading of the Williamson Family.

Owen Moon, Jr., son of Owen and Elizabeth (Buckman) Moon, was born at Penn Valley, Bucks county, Pennsylvania, December 6, 1873. He received his primary education at local schools and graduated at Swarthmore College in June, 1894, with the degree of B. Sc., and is a member of the national college fraternity of Delta Upsilon. In the fall of 1894 he removed to Trenton, New Jersey, and in conjunction with a course at Trenton Business College, took up the study of law, but relinquished it a year and a half later to devote himself to a number of business interests. From 1896 to 1901 he was interested in the construction of a number of electric railways in Philadelphia, Trenton, Bucks county and elsewhere, as director and official of the various organizations having them in charge.

He was perhaps more largely interested in trolley development in and about Trenton than any other individual. He was president of the Trenton, Morrisville and Yardley Street Railway Company, who constructed a line of six miles connecting those towns; was a director and financial agent of the Trenton, Lawrenceville and Princeton Railroad Company, which constructed a trolley line of ten miles connecting those towns; a director and treasurer of the Trenton City Bridge Company, the owners of the only Delaware river bridge at this point not controlled by the Pennsylvania Railroad Company, and which bridge was purchased from the former (Bucks county) owners, on account of it being the key to any trolley connection between Pennsylvania and Trenton. These two trolley lines, upon their completion, together with the bridge, were sold to the Lehigh Valley Traction Company interests, represented by Mayor Tom L. Johnson, of Cleveland, Ohio, and are now successfully operated by that company. Mr.

Moon is also a director and an official in the syndicate which owned the old turnpike extending across lower Bucks county, connecting Trenton with Bristol and Philadelphia, as well as of a half dozen or more railroad corporations, whose object was the completion of a trolley line from Philadelphia to Trenton, which was initiated by General Morrell in 1891. The history of the construction of this line represents one of the most stubborn fights between the trolley interests and the railroads ever before the courts of Pennsylvania or any other state, a right-of-way fight of ten years duration, on the line between Bristol and Bridgwater, being ultimately won by the syndicate securing an elevated trolley charter, at Harrisburg, which permitted track connections across the disputed right of way and assured the completion of the Philadelphia and Trenton line. This road was later sold to a Baltimore syndicate which now operates its cars direct from Philadelphia, over the tracks of the Trenton, Morrisville and Yardley street railway and the Trenton city bridge into Trenton. Mr. Moon became a director of the Yardley (Penna.) National Bank in 1895, at the age of twenty-two years. He is a director and secretary of the Philadelphia firm of the Scott Paper Company; a director of the Reeves Engine Company of Trenton, and also a director in a number of other corporations and industrial and business organizations. In 1901 he became one of the proprietors and treasurer of the "Trenton (New Jersey) Times," and in 1902 became the active business manager of the establishment. Under his capable management the circulation of "The Times" has nearly doubled, and it is becoming one of the popular and strong newspapers of the state. Mr. Moon is a member of the Historical Society of Pennsylvania and the Bucks County Historical Society. He is also a member of the Young Men's Christian Association of Trenton, the Republican Club of Trenton, and the Trenton Country Club. He married, November 8, 1899, at Swarthmore, Pennsylvania, Margaret Scott, born October 20, 1876, daughter of Mr. and Mrs. E. I. Scott, of that place.

THE WILLIAMSON FAMILY. The history of this family takes us back to the period prior to the grant of Pennsylvania to William Penn and possibly to two or three decades prior to that date when the representatives of three Eureopean nations were battling for supremacy on the shores of our middle states. The Swedes made the first organized settlement on Pennsylvania soil in 1638 under Peter Minuit. The Dutch began almost immediately to contest their supremacy there, and from the time of the conquest of the Swedes by the Hollanders, two decades later, until the subsequent conquest of the latter by the English, representatives of the Anglo-Saxon and Celtic races began to make their appearance on the Delaware. The earliest records of the court at Upland (now Chester) under English jurisdiction in 1676, show a number of names of undoubted English origin, though the first justices were all Swedes. Dunck Williames, as his name is usually spelled in the earlier records, though it appears in various forms both as to first and surname, during his whole life was the founder of the family of Williamson in Pennsylvania. He is claimed by his descendants to have been of Swedish or Holland origin, but many circumstances in connection with his first appearance on Pennsylvania soil strongly indicate to the writer of these lines that he was of English or Scotch origin. The most significant of these is the fact that he was associated in his first purchase of land with Francis Walker, whose name clearly indicates that he was of neither Dutch or Swedish origin. Again, hereditary surnames were unknown in either Sweden or Holland until late in the sixteenth century and their representatives in America were known by their father's given name, with the addition of "es" or "se" and "sen." Had he therefore been of Dutch origin his name would have been more probably Gulliamse, if his father was named William, and the name William was practically unknown among the Swedes. The name Dunck or Dunk was doubtless a contraction of Duncan, and in neither form has ever been found among the Swedes or Dutch Just when Dunk Williamson arrived on the Delaware is a matter of some conjecture. As early as 1667 Dunk Willims and eight others secured from Governor Richard Nicolls a patent for a tract of land of one thousand acres, known as Passayunk, indicating that he was one of the first settlers to secure title to land in what is now Philadelphia, from the English rulers who conquered the territory in 1664. His grant of land, in connection with Francis Walker, under patent from Sir Edmund Andross under date of July 18, 1676, comprehended 450 acres on the Neshaminy in the present limits of Bensalem township, comprising the present site of Dunks Ferry, named for him. "Franck Walker," first appears of record at Upland as the custodian of goods belonging to Captain Edward Cantwell, who administered the oaths to the first justices at Upland in 1676. On a "List of Tydable persons under the jurisdiction of ye Court," made November 13, 1677, the names of "Dunk Williames" and "Franck Walker" appear in the district of Taokanink (Tacony), and on November 12, 1678, Dunk Williams petitioned to take up one hundred acres of land "on the lower syde of Nieshambenies (Neshaminy) creek, 50 acres thereof att ye river syde & ye other 50 acres up in the woods;" this was therefore at the mouth of Neshaminy in Bensalem. He also served on a jury at the same date. On March 12, 1678-79, he petitioned to take up four acres of marsh back of his "plantaceion." On the latter date Edmund Draufton brought suit against him for the tuition of his children, showing that at that early date the Pennsylvania colonists were interested in the education of their youth. The title of Williamson and Walker to the tract of land in Bucks county was confirmed by Penn, and the former became a large landowner. The will of Dunck Williamson, dated February 12, 1697-8, and probated March 1, 1699-1700, mentions his wife, Wallery, sons William and John Williamson, and daughters, Hanna, wife of John Gound, and Margred, wife of John Johnson. To John he devises 500 acres of land in the bounds of Cohanset. (Cohansey, Salem county, New Jersey), to Hanna Gound, one hundred acres in the county of Kent; to Margred Johnson, five pounds or its equivalent; and to William, all his estate in Pennsylvania.*

William Williamson, born 1676, died 1721, married Elizabeth Claessen, of Dutch or Swedish origin,‡ and had five sons: Jacob, who is said to have died without issue; Abraham, who married Rachel ——, and had two sons and two daughters; John who married Elizabeth ——, and had eight sons and two daughters, who resided in Philadelphia county, see forward; William, married and had a son John and a daughter; Peter, married Leah ——, and had seven children: Jacob, Isaac; Peter; Elizabeth, who married a Moore of Burlington, New Jersey, and after his death removed to Virginia; Sarah; Rebecca; and Jane, who married Abraham Heed.

Peter Williamson, third son of Peter and Leah Williamson, born in Bucks county, January 17, 1735, settled in Falls township, Bucks county, and died there June 11, 1823, at the age of eighty-nine years. He was twice married; first to Sarah Sotcher, daughter of Robert and Mercy (Browne) Sotcher of Falls, and granddaughter of John and Mary (Lofty) Sotcher, the last named being William Penn's steward and stewardess at Pennysbury for many years. They were married at Pennsbury in the presence of William Penn, October 16, 1701, Falls Meeting having held a special session in order that they might be married before

Penn left for England at the conclusion of his last visit to his province in America. John Lofty became a prominent man in the colony and served many years in colonial assembly, 1712 to 1722. He died November 19, 1729. John and Mary (Lofty) Sotcher were the parents of four children: Hannah, born January 25, 1702, married October 26, 1720, Joseph Kirkbride; Mary, born September 15, 1704, married November 12, 1724, Mahlon Kirkbride; Ann, born March 27, 1710, married April 23, 1729, Mark Watson; Robert, born November 3, 1706, married in 1731, Mercy Browne, youngest daughter of George and Mercy Browne, who came from England in 1678 and settled in Falls township, Bucks county. George Browne was the first Englishman to serve as justice of the court at Upland, being returned as a justice at the June sessions, 1680, but not being present was sworn and took his seat as a justice, in accordance with his commission, October 13, 1680, and served until the establishment of the courts by Penn after his arrival. George and Mercy Brown reared a large family who have left numerous descendants. General Jacob Brown, commander-in-chief of the United States Army, was a great-grandson.

Peter and Sarah (Sotcher) Williamson were the parents of eight children, as follows: Letitia, born June 12, 1765, died August 5, 1847, married Jonathan Burton, of Falls; Mercy, born June 12, 1766, died March 10, 1830, married William Crozer, of Falls, and had ten children; Parmelia, born January 16, 1768, died October 23, 1813, married Thomas Crozer and had three children; Jesse, born September 21, 1769, died October 23, 1852, married Sarah Williamson, daughter of Josephus, see forward, and had three children; David, born March 14, 1773, died August 10, 1799; Mahlon, born March 15, 1777, died July 8, 1848; John, born February 24, 1778, was lost at sea March 4, 1798; Sarah, born November 28, 1781, married Nov. 30, 1799, Jesse Kelly, son of Joseph and Phoebe (Buckman) Kelley, and died July 18, 1862. Sarah (Sotcher) Williamson died November 3, 1799, and Peter married a second time Elizabeth Banes, but had no children by her.

Mahlon, sixth child and third son of Peter and Sarah (Sotcher) Williamson, born March 15, 1777, settled near Fallsington, Bucks county, and lived there all his life, dying July 8, 1848. He married Charity Vansant, born November 16, 1781, died April 29, 1848, daughter of Cornelius and Ann (Larzelere) Vansant, and whose paternal and maternal ancestry is given elsewhere in this volume. Mahlon and Charity were the parents of eight children, as follows: John, born December 21, 1800, died July 28, 1802; Isaiah V., born February 4, 1803, died March 7, 1889, unmarried, was the founder of the Williamson Industrial School in Delaware county, Pennsylvania; Peter, born September 4, 1805, died February 21, 1880, married May 26, 1831, Eliza Martin, and had six children; John B.

---

*In the Williamson (sometimes called the Johnson graveyard situated in Bensalem township, near Bridgewater, a tablet has been erected with this statement: "In memory of Duncan Williamson, one of the original settlers of this township, who died about the year 1700."

‡Members of the Claessen family, children of Jan Claassen, who was of Dutch or Swedish origin and a grantee in 1666, are as follows: Henricka, eldest daughter of Jan Claassen, married Matthias Kyn (Keen) born 1687, died 1714, eldest son of Hans and Willemka Kyn, and grandson of Joran Kyn, an original Swedish settler near Chester about 1644. Gertrude, second child of Jan Claassen, married Hans Laican, eldest son of Peter Nilsson Laykan, a native of Sweden. Of the Kyn family, one Jonas Keen (the third son of Hans and Willemka Kyn and grandson of the original Swedish settler, Joran Kyn) married in 1697 to Frances Walker, only daughter of Francis Walker (Walcker), a grantee in Bucks county on the Neshaminy Creek with Dunck Williams and others in 1676. Catherine, third child of Jan Claassen, married Erie Kyn (Keen second son of Hans and Willemka Kyn, and grandson of the original Swedish settler Joran Kyn. Elizabeth, another daughter of Jan Claassen, married William Williams, a son of Dunck Williams.

born January 4, 1808, died October 24, 1874, moved to New Albany, Indiana, about 1833, married and had nine children; Jesse, born May 13, 1810, died October, 1892, married first Margaret Buckman, and second Elizabeth Albertson, (had five children: Edward C., of Morrisville; Henry D., of Lancaster; Franklin, of Lancaster; Ida, wife of Headley Harper; and Ella, wife of J. D. Tantum); Sarah Ann, born May 14, 1812, died July 22, 1891, married December 14, 1836, Spencer W. Buckman of Falls, Bucks county, see forward; Mahlon, born March 9, 1815, died May 1, 1871, married Mary Ann Stiles and settled in Philadelphia, had seven children; Eliza Ann, born February 1, 1819, died July 26, 1891, married William J. Moon, son of Daniel and Mercy (Lovett) Moon and had eleven children. Spencer W. Buckman, born December 18, 1814, was a son of Zenas and Mary (Worthington) Buckman. He married December 14, 1836, Sarah Ann Williamson above mentioned, and they were the parents of seven children, as follows: Mary, born December 11, 1837, married Charles A. Parsons, see Parsons Family in this volume; Elizabeth, born January 2, 1839, married Owen Moon, son of Evan and Ann (Palmer) Moon, see preceding sketch; Isaiah, born May 26, 1841, died May 9, 1842; Charles, born July 13, 1842, married Henrietta Anderson and has eight children; William A., Spencer W., Engene, Anna Mary, George, Ida, Sarah, and Macre; Wallace, born April 26, 1845, married Elizabeth Hart, and has two children: Edwin H., and Williamson; George, born 1846, died 1848; Sarah, born March 5, 1854, died April 24, 1883, married Mahlon Wharton and had two children: Caroline and Albert.

John Williamson, third son of William and Elizabeth (Claessen) Williamson, and grandson of Dunck and Wallery Williamson, born 1698, died August 31, 1761, married Elizabeth ————, who survived him. They lived on the homestead (inherited from his father) and are buried in the old family burying ground on the banks of the Neshaminy. They had nine sons and two daughters, as follows: William, born June 14, 1727; John, born May 10, 1730; Joseph, born September 16, 1731, removed to Philadelphia; Abraham, born November 16, 1733; Elizabeth, born April 25, 1736, married Joseph Vandegrift, Katharine, born November 17, 1738, married Benjamin Walton, of Byberry; Jesse, born June 25, 1741, removed to Philadelphia; Josephus, born December 3, 1743; died April 28, 1817, married Mary Bush, who died July 28, 1843, aged 87 years, both buried at St. Peter's churchyard, Philadelphia, see forward; David, born September 21, 1748, died April 22, 1794, married Ann Bennett and had eight children, see below; Jeremiah, born March 8, 1751, removed to Philadelphia; Benjamin, born July 8, 1752, also removed to Philadelphia.

Josephus and Mary (Bush) Williamson had nine children, as follows: Jeremiah; David, died September 7, 1803, aged 33; Joseph (none of whom married); Rebecca, born 1774, died July 5, 1831, married December 3, 1797, David Fleckmire, of Philadelphia and had seven children; Sarah, born September 22, 1776, died May, 1868, in her ninety-second year, married November 2, 1794, Jesse Williamson, son of Peter and Sarah (Sotcher) Williamson, before mentioned; Ann, born 1779, died April 21, 1839, married her cousin David Williamson, of Philadelphia, a son of David and grandson of John, see forward; Elizabeth, died 1840, married May 3, 1804, John Burns, lived on a farm adjacent to Pennsbury until 1825, and then removed to Wayne county, Indiana; John, born May 15, 1786, died April 1, 1791; John G., married Harriet Shardon, and after her death removed to St. Louis, Missouri, had three children.

The children of David and Ann (Bennett) Williamson were as follows: Catharine, born April 20, 1777, died August 30, 1798; Thomas, born May 5, 1774; Joseph, born September 15, 1779, had one son; Jesse, born January 24, 1782, died September 2, 1798; David, born June 18, 1785, died June 10, 1851, married his cousin Ann Williamson, and had three children: Joseph, Bennett, and David E.; Benjamin, born June 5, 1788, married Ellen Fitzmaury; Ann; and Samuel, who died in infancy.

LEWIS W. FELL, of Buckingham, merchant, was born in Buckingham township, near Mechanicsville, on a farm that had been the property of his ancestors since 1723. He is only son of David and Margaret (Atkinson) Fell, of Buckingham, and of the sixth generation in descent from Joseph Fell, who came from Longlands parish, Rockdale, Cumberland, England with Bridget Wilson, his wife, in 1705.

Joseph Fell, eldest child of Joseph and Bridget, born in Cumberland, England, 4 mo. 29, 1701, was reared on his father's farm near Pool's corner, where H. Clay Large now lives, and on his marriage in 1735 received from his father a deed of gift of 125 acres of land on the Durham road, above Mechanicsville, purchased by Joseph, Sr., in 1723, and lived thereon until his death, 2 mo. 22, 1777. He married, 1 mo. 4, 1735; Mary Kinsey, daughter of Edmund and Sarah (Ogborn) Kinsey, the former an eminent preacher among Friends. The children of Joseph and Mary Fell were seven in number, five of whom grew to maturity, viz.: Joseph born 8 mo. 31, 1738; Sarah, never married; Rachel, born 1744, married William Lownes; David, born 1750, married Sarah

Kinsey; and Martha, born 1756, married Edward Rice. Mary (Kinsey) Fell, was born 2 mo. 29, 1715, and died 12 mo. 29, 1769.

Joseph Fell, eldest son of Joseph and Mary, born 8 mo. 31, 1738, on the homestead farm in Buckingham, married 10 mo, 21, 1767, Rachel Wilson, born 4 mo. 5, 1741, died 3 mo, 8, 1810, daughter of Samuel and Rebecca (Canby) Wilson, of Buckingham, and removed to Upper Makefield, where he purchased a farm. He died there 3 mo. 26, 1789. He had eight children, six of whom grew to maturity, viz.: Joseph, born 1768, married Esther Burroughs; John, born 1770, married Edith Smith; Martha, married Benjamin Schofield; David, married Phebe Schofield; Jonathan, born 5 mo. 5, 1776; Rachel, born 1783, married John Speakman.

Jonathan, son of Joseph and Rachel, was born in Upper Makefield township, 5 mo. 5, 1776, and married 1 mo. 2, 1799, Sarah Balderston, and removed to Northampton township. Two years later he removed to Falls township, near Morrisville, where he lived until 1831, and then removed to the old homestead of his ancestors in Buckingham, where he died 7 mo. 27, 1849. His wife Sarah died at Morrisville 11 mo. 23, 1802, and he married 10 mo. 11, 1809, Jane Buckman, born 12 mo. 12, 1784, died 3 mo. 25, 1874, daughter of James and Sarah (Burroughs) Buckman. By his first wife he had two children—Jane, who married Seth Davis; and Rebecca, who died an infant. By his second marriage he had six children, viz.: James, born in 1810, married (first) Mary Cadwallader, and (second) Mary Holcombe; Sarah, who never married; Joshua, born 2 mo. 22, 1814, married Mary Watson, has been postmaster and merchant at Mechanicsville for many years; Elizabeth, born 1817, died 1853, unmarried; Hannah, born 2 mo. 22, 1820, married Thomas Story Smith, of Upper Makefield; David, born 11 mo. 13, 1823, married Margaret Atkinson.

David Fell, the father of the subject of this sketch, born in Penn's Manor, near Morrisville, 11 mo. 13, 1823, was the youngest child of Jonathan and Jane Buckman Fell. As he was but eight years old when the family moved to the old homestead in Buckingham, his boyhood days were spent on the farm that remained his home during the rest of his life. He was a man of high character, much esteemed in the neighborhood, and held many positions of trust. Like his ancestors for many generations, he was a member of the Society of Friends, and a regular attendant at Buckingham Meeting. He died on the old homestead 8 mo. 9, 1887. He had married 1 mo. 3, 1850, Margaret, daughter of Abner and Sarah Atkinson, who bore him three children; Sarah Jane, born 11 mo. 7, 1850, married Horace Michener, living in Doylestown; Mary Lester, born 9 mo. 26, 1853, married Thomas B. Claxton. and died; and Lewis, the subject of this sketch. Margaret (Atkinson) Fell is still living in Doylestown.

Lewis W. Fell was born on the homestead of his ancestors in Buckingham, 6 mo. 2, 1857, and remained thereon until 1881. He was educated at the public school of the neighborhood and at the Doylestown English and Classical Seminary. In the spring of 1881 he accepted a position in the store of his brother-in-law, Evan T. Worthington, at Buckingham, and two years later acquired an interest in the business, forming a co-partnership under the firm name of Worthington & Fell, which lasted for six years, when he purchased the entire interest in the store and has since conducted it with marked success. The store has the reputation of being one of the best country stores in the county and does a large trade. Mr. Fell was appointed postmaster of Buckingham on February 18, 1890, and has held the position continuously since. In 1896 Mr. Fell was one of the organizers of a local telephone company in Buckingham, which was later purchased by the Standard Telephone Company, who established their exchange in his store, which is also the exchange for the Bell Telephone Company. Mr. Fell is a member of Aquetong Lodge, No. 193, I. O. O. F., of Doylestown, and was an original member of Buckingham Castle, No 208, A. O. K. of the M. C., and has been its treasurer since 1893. He is a member of Buckingham Friends' Meeting. Politically he is a Republican.

Mr. Fell was married on January 20, 1881, to Emma Clara Worthington, daughter of Elisha and Harriet (Lukens) Worthington, who has borne him two children: Arthur D., who assists his father in the business; and Ashton W., who is private secretary to John Shreeve, publisher of the "Atlantic City Review," Atlantic City, New Jersey. Mr. Shreeve is also secretary for Congressman Gardner, and secretary of the Congress of Labor. Both the sons are graduates of Friends Central School, Philadelphia, and of Pierce's Business College.

ALLEN G. MOYER belongs to one of the old and honored families of Bucks county. The name was variously spelled bv the ancestors, some using the form of Meyer, while others continued the spelling used by the subject of this review and his immediate branch of the family.

His father, Christian Moyer, was born near Sumneytown, Montgomery county, about 1814. In early life he followed milling, but later engaged in merchandising at New Galena, Pennsylvania, for many years one of the enterprising representatives of commercial interests in that place. He conducted his store with good success until his death, and was also the promoter of other business enterprises which proved of direct value to the community. In 1860 he discovered the lead mines at New Galena, which were on the property owned by himself and his brother-in-law, Daniel Barnes. His political views were in accord with the principles of the Republican party, which he always supported by his ballot. He held the office of school director, and at one time was postmaster of New Galena for your years. He belonged to the Old Mennonite church, and died in that faith in 1867. His wife was Miss Barbara Godshalk in her maidenhood, a daughter of John Godshalk. They had eight children, one of whom was drowned in a mill race when only two years of age, while another died at the age of six years. The surviving six members of the family are: Enos, who is now connected with mining interests in British Columbia; Isaac G., a butcher, residing in Dover, New Jersey; Allen G.; Mahlon G., of North Wales, and who for the past thirty years has been in the employ of the Western Union Telegraph Company; Lydia, the wife of Samuel Leatherman, of Doylestown; and Amanda, the wife of H. Erwin Fritz, of Bedminster.

Allen G. Moyer, son of Christian Moyer, was born in New Britain township, Bucks county, August 5, 1848, and at the usual age entered the public schools, where he completed his literary education. In the school of experience, however, he has learned many valuable lessons. He clerked in his father's store until seventeen years of age, and following his father's death was employed for a year as a salesman in the store of R. J. Hillier, at Line Lexington. He afterward followed house painting and paper hanging for a number of years, and since 1884 has been engaged in butchering hogs in Hilltown and Plumstead townships. In 1888 he purchased the place which is now his home at Danboro, and has made extensive and modern improvements there. This property is an evidence of his life of business activity and energy, for he started out with little capital, and all that he has acquired has been won through his own efforts. Mr. Moyer is a leading member of the Doylestown Presbyterian church, and has been particularly active in Sunday-school work.

He wedded Miss Mary Brand, a daughter of John and Margaret Brand, and in 1902 was called upon to mourn the loss of his wife, who died on the 11th of December of that year. They were the parents of fifteen children, seven of whom died ere reaching the age of ten years. The others are Wannita,

born January 6, 1871, and is the wife of J. P. Leatherman; J. Arthur, born March 9, 1872; Purdy B., born December 27, 1873, and was ordained as a minister of the Baptist church in 1900, now occupying the pulpit of the Hepzibah Baptist church near Coatesville, in Chester county, Pennsylvania; Carey, born July 10, 1877, and is engaged in the butchering business in Danboro; Harvey K., born April 28, 1878, and is engaged in merchandising at Doylestown; Margaretta B., born February 28, 1880, now the wife of Wilson Fretz; Jesse, born June 1, 1882; and Nellie, born December 1, 1887.

ABRAHAM GEORGE MOYER. A type of the well-informed and energetic business man who is essential to the well-being of any community is Abraham George Moyer, of Quakertown. He belongs to a well known family, the various branches of which are scattered through Bucks county.

He is a grandson of Samuel Moyer, who was a resident of Hilltown. Joseph Hunsicker Moyer, son of Samuel Moyer, before mentioned, was born May 22, 1840, on the homestead in Hilltown township, and until his eighteenth year attended the public schools of his district. His life was devoted to agricultural pursuits. He married Elizabeth Yoder, daughter of Abraham and Mary (Yoder) George, the former a farmer of Milford township, who had obtained his education in the subscription school. The other children born to himself and his wife were: 1. Charles, who married a Moyer. 2. Jacob, who married and lives at Milford Square. 3. Benjamin, who married and is a resident of Spinnerstown. 4. Daniel, who is a farmer at Milford Square and has been twice married, his second wife being Mary, daughter of Jacob Shelly, of Milford township. 5. Anna, who is the wife of Abram Leatherman, of Plumsteadville.

Mr. and Mrs. Moyer were the parents of the following children: 1. Mary, who married Jacob Rush, son of William and Mary (Moyer) Rush, of Bedminster township, and lives on the Moyer homestead, near Plumsteadville. 2. Emma, born May 24, 1865, became the wife of John Bergstresser, of Haycock township, and died in 1904, leaving four sons: Abel B., Howard, Daniel, and Elton. 3. Abraham George Moyer mentioned at length hereinafter. 4. Daniel born in May, 1870, married Maggie, daughter of Henry Souder, of Souderton, and lives at Perkasie. 5. Elizabeth, born in 1872, became the wife of John, son of William and Maria (Moyer) Stauffer. 6. Catharine, born in 1874, married Henry C., son of the Rev. John and Mary Beidler, of Rosedale Valley, and lives at Allentown. 7. Adeline, who is the wife of John Fluck, and lives at Lansdale. 8. Joseph Wilson died in infancy. Mr. Moyer, the father of the family, died at the comparatively early age of forty-six, passing away February 20, 1886, on his own farm in Plumstead township.

Abraham George Moyer, son of Joseph Hunsicker and Elizabeth Yoder (George) Moyer, was born April 4, 1867, on his father's farm in Hilltown township. When he was one year old his father purchased a farm of fifty-eight acres near Plumsteadville, and there the family took up their abode. On this farm, which had previously been the property of Tobias Rickert, Abraham George rendered valuable assistance, at the same time attending the district school. He left school in his eighteenth year and was not yet nineteen at the time of the death of his father. The farm was then sold, and Mr. Moyer became a pupil in the West Chester State Normal School After teaching for a time in a school near Dublin, he went to Plumsteadville, where for four years he was engaged in the creamery business. He then devoted four years to a mercantile business at Milford Square, and at the end of that time purchased the Milford Square creamery which he conducted for five years. His next venture was to build a creamery in Milford township, which he still owns. In 1900 he purchased from Enos R. Artman the store which he now occupies, and which was then conducted by his brother-in-law, Henry Beidler. On this site he is now doing a thriving business. The confidence reposed in Mr. Moyer by his fellow-citizens is demonstrated by the fact that he has been chosen by them to fill the office of committeeman for Shelly district, and that while a resident of Milford township he served for one year as school director, resigning his position when he moved to Quakertown. In his political principles he is a Republican. He and his family are members of the Mennonite church at West Swamp, in which he served as superintendent of the Sunday school from 1896 to 1900.

Mr. Moyer married, November 26, 1887, Hannah Oberholtzer, daughter of Levi and Mary (Oberholtzer) Fretz, the former a native of Plumsteadville. Mrs. Moyer received her education in the district school. The family of Mr. and Mrs. Moyer consists of the following children: 1. Willis, born April 23, 1891. 2. Pearl, born February 12, 1893. 3. Edna, born November 28, 1895. 4. Elizabeth, born November 27, 1898. 5. Joseph, born June 16, 1901. It is to be believed that these children will prove worthy heirs of the good qualities as well as of the good name of their ancestors, and that they will live to do credit to their native county.

HARVEY W. MOYER. Among Chalfont's progressive and public-spirited citizens must be numbered Harvey W. Moyer. Mr. Moyer is a son of Levi S. Moyer, who learned the trade of a miller at Diehl's mill near Hellertown, Pennsylvania, and afterward purchased the property and the business. Subsequently he engaged in business as a butcher. He married Caroline, daughter of Shelly Weinberger, of Milford, and the following children were born to them: Clinton W.; Mary A.; Joseph W.; Emma W.; and Harvey W., mentioned at length hereinafter. The parents of these children were, as their names would indicate, of German descent.

Harvey W. Moyer, son of Levi S. and Caroline (Weinberger) Moyer, was born June 21, 1868, in Bingham, Northampton county, Pennsylvania, and was educated in the public schools of his birthplace. There also he was trained by his father to the occupation of a butcher, and followed the business for four years. Beginning in a small way and on borrowed capital, his efforts were crowned with success, and he was enabled to discharge his obligations and build up a flourishing trade. In 1894 he moved to Chalfont, and is now at the head of a large establishment, his connections extending throughout the adjacent country. He is a successful business man and has built for himself a comfortable and attractive home. He is active as a citizen, and has been chosen by his neighbors a member of the town council, an office which he still holds. In politics he is a Republican, and in religion a member of the Mennonite church. Mr. Moyer married, December 29, 1892, Lizzie S., born November 23, 1871, daughter of Abram and Ellamina (Sleifer) Kulp, and three children have been born to them: Florence, who was born January 30, 1894; Grace Lorene, born October 14, 1896; and Ray K., born November 23, 1898, and died July 19, 1900.

———

H. WATSON JOHNSON, a prosperous agriculturist, son of Charles and Esther (Strawn) Johnson, was born November 11, 1832, on the farm where he now resides, it being part of the original tract acquired by Casper Johnson (great-grandfather), the first of that family to come to the colony of Pennsylvania, emigrating from his home in Holland early in the eighteenth century. Casper Johnson (grandfather), son of the emigrant ancestor, was born on the farm now owned by Henry Johnson, the farm owned by H. Watson Johnson being a part of that tract. Charles Johnson (father), son of Casper and Geborah Johnson, was born on the homestead farm. He attended the subscription schools of his community, and followed farming. He was a man of considerable fame as a farmer and man of affairs in northern Bucks county, and in 'his immediate neighborhood was looked upon as a leading agriculturist. His employes always received recognition and their just dues for faithful services, and his home was always a resort for neighborly intercourse. He was a member of the Whig party, and took an active interest in its affairs. He married Esther Strawn, daughter of Abel and Elizabeth Strawn, of Haycock township, and had issue: H. Watson, Mary Ann, wife of Aaron Walp,¹of Quakertown; Oliver James married Maria Stover, and they reside in Haycock township; Anna Maria, wife of Louis N. Shelly, of Quakertown.

H. Watson Johnson attended the subscription schools of Richland township until the free school system was introduced, and later the public schools, completing his studies at the age of eighteen years, and in the meantime assisted on the home farm. For one year after leaving school he clerked in the general store of Mr. H. Buchacer, at Richlandtown, but, his parents being insistent upon his returning home, he complied with their request and thereafter remained at home. After his marriage he assumed charge of his father's farm, working the same on shares, and continuing thus until the death of his father, February 28, 1879, and at the settlement of the estate he became the owner, purchasing the interest of the other heirs. Since attaining his majority Mr. Johnson has taken an active part in the affairs of his community. In politics he is a Republican, and has served his party in local, county and state conventions as delegate, and has also served for fifteen years as director of the local school board. In the campaign of 1874 Mr. Johnson, at the solicitation of his party, stood as candidate for the state legislature, and, although the county was at that time strongly Democratic, he, with no special effort on his part, came within twenty-two votes of being elected, which was an unmistakable proof of his popularity. Of recent years Mr. Johnson has not taken so active a part in political affairs as of yore, devoting his time and attention to the care of his estate, he being of the fourth generation to reside there.

Mr. Johnson married, November 15, 1855, Margaret Kratz, daughter of Jacob and Eliza (Fretz) Kratz, of Plumstead township. Five children were the issue of this union: 1. Erwin Thomas, now a practicing physician and surgeon at Leidytown, Hilltown township; he married Martha, daughter of Leidy Sheip. 2. Charles Jacob died in 1878. 3. Oliver Kratz died in 1893. 4. Harvey Ellwood, who attended the township schools, and is now at home, assisting his father with

the duties of the farm. 5. Jennie, who married November 7, 1894, Wilson Erdman, M. D., son of Owen and Mary Ann Erdman, of Richland township; Dr. and Mrs. Erdman reside in Richlandtown. Mr. Johnson and his family attend the Union Reformed church at Richlandtown.

LEVI SWARTLEY, of Chalfont, Bucks county, is the only surviving child of John and Mary (Moyer) Swartley, and was born in New Britain township, April 5, 1832. Philip Schwardley, the grandfather of the subject of this sketch, was born in Eppingen, in Necker, grand duchy of Baden, Germany, October 28, 1764 and is supposed to have come to this country with his elder brothers John and Jacob in the ship "Minerva," arriving at Philadelphia on September 30, 1772. As, however, the list of passengers does not include the names of the two younger brothers, it is possible they may have followed their brother to Pennsylvania some years later.

Philip was probably a resident for some years of Franconia township, Montgomery county, where he married Sarah Rosenberger, born January 24, 1765, daughter of Rev. Henry and Barbara (Oberholtzer) Rosenberger, and a sister to Magdalena, the wife of his brother John Schwardley. About 1790 Philip Schwardley settled in New Britain township, Bucks county, where he became a large landowner. He died September 23, 1840, and his wife Sarah died April 6, 1849. They were the parents of nine children, viz.: Elizabeth, married Jacob Krout; Henry; John; Jacob; Mary, married Jacob Hafner; Philip; Abraham; Samuel; and Sarah, who married John Price.

John Swartley, second son of Philip and Sarah (Rosenberger) Swartley, was born in New Britain township June 8, 1792, and was reared on his father's farm. In 1814 he married Mary Moyer, born in Springfield township, Bucks county, October 9, 1795, and died in New Britain, on April 10, 1872, daughter of Jacob and Magdalene (Moyer) Moyer, of Springfield, and settled in Plumstead township, where they resided for one year. April 3, 1816, his parents conveyed to him a farm of ninety-one acres in New Britain, where he lived from that date until his death, March 14, 1856. John and Mary (Moyer) Swartley were the parents of eight children, viz.: 1. Jacob M., born April 15, 1816, died December 20, 1885, married Anna Ruth and left a number of children. 2. Sarah, born September 28, 1818, died January 7, 1901, married Abraham Kratz. 3. William, born June 25, 1821, died April 17, 1875, was blind for thirty-eight years. 4. Magdalena, born September 28, 1824, died April 7, 1893, married in 1844

JOSEPH THOMAS

Henry Ruth; 5. Joseph M., born December 7, 1826, married three times; lived on the old homestead, where he died March 26, 1892. 6. John M., born September 18, 1829, died September 24, 1900; Levi M., the subject of this sketch; and Mary, born May 5, 1835, died January 2, 1888, married William G. Moyer.

Levi M. Swartley, youngest son of John and Mary, was born and reared on the New Britain homestead and remained there with his mother until he was twenty-seven years old. After a residence of a year and a half in Hilltown he purchased the old homestead and returned to it, and resided thereon until 1890, since which time he has lived a retired life in the borough of Chalfont. He is a member of the Mennonites, and politically is a Republican. He married December 2, 1860, Lydia H. Myers, daughter of Isaac Myers, of Plumsteadville, and they have been the parents of three children: Mary Ann, born September 22, 1862, married Abraham L. Garges, of New Britain, and has children: Anna, Howard and Lydia. Isaac M., born January 16, 1865, died May, 1892, married Mary L. Moyer, daughter of Abraham Moyer, and left one child, Bertha. Ella M., born August 3, 1873, married Henry Rosenberger, and has one child, Laura Elizabeth.

JOHN SWARTLEY, postmaster of Chalfont, was born in New Britain township, Bucks county, November 19, 1862, and is a son of John M. and Mary (Moyer) Swartley, and a grandson of John and Magdalene (Moyer) Swartley, whose ancestry is given in the sketch of Levi Swartley.

John M. Swartley was born in New Britain township, September 18, 1829, and was educated at the local schools. He followed the life of a farmer, near the little village of Newville, and was a member of the Mennonite church. He was an active and progressive farmer, and filled the office of supervisor of New Britain township for a number of years. He married on October 18, 1853, Elizabeth M. Moyer, daughter of Rev. Abraham and Anna Moyer, of Bedminster, the ancestors of the former having borne the name of Christian for four generations, the first of whom was Christian Meyer, who came to Pennsylvania about 1712 and settled in Franconia township. His grandson, Christian Moyer, born in Franconia, March 27, 1763, married Mary Landis, and settled in Bucks county. Rev. Abraham Moyer, of Bedminster, above mentioned, was the ninth of their eleven children; he married Anna Moyer, and Elizabeth M., who married John M. Swartley, was the youngest of their five children. John M. and Elizabeth M. (Moyer) Swartley

were the parents of eight children, viz.: Mary Ann, born January 5, 1855, died July 12, 1873; Amanda, born April 19, 1856, died June 22, 1878, married November 13, 1877, A. G. Ruth; Oliver J., born November 15, 1857, died August 30, 1885; William M., born September 24, 1860; John, the subject of this sketch; Emma Jane, born November 24, 1863, died April 19, 1878; Elizabeth M., born May 11, 1865, died February 15, 1884; Elmer M., born June 25, 1873, died April 29, 1899. John, the father, died September 24, 1900.

John Swartley, the subject of this sketch, was reared on the farm near Newville, and was educated at the local schools. In 1882 he entered the general merchandise store at Chalfont as clerk, and filled that position for sixteen years. In 1898 he entered into the mercantile business for himself, and carried it on for five years and then sold out. He was appointed postmaster of Chalfont in February, 1897 and still fills that position. He is a member of the Methodist church, and politically a Republican.

He married April 7, 1891, Laura Scholl, daughter of Leidy L. and Lucilla (Diehl) Scholl. They have no children.

DR. JOSEPH THOMAS, of Quakertown, Bucks county, one of the best known public men of Upper Bucks, was born in New Britain township, June 15, 1829, and is of Welsh, English and German descent. His paternal ancestor, Alban Thomas, a native of Wales, located in Plumstead township about 1720, purchasing of Richard Hill 125 acres of land west of Danboro, and in 1749 adding fifty acres more, most of which remained in the family for four generations, Danboro itself being named for his son Daniel. Alban Thomas died June, 1776, his wife Jane surviving him a few years. Their children were Joseph, Daniel, and Isaac. Isaac, the third son, inherited the homestead, purchased other land adjoining, and lived there all his life, dying in 1825. He left several children, among them a son Alban, who was the grandfather of Dr. Thomas. Elias Thomas, son of Alban and grandson of Isaac, was born at Danboro, Plumstead township, and on attaining manhood married Sarah Snyder, daughter of Frederick Snyder, of German ancestry, and settled on a farm in New Britain township, near the present village of Levin, where his son, Dr. Joseph Thomas was born.

Dr. Joseph Thomas received a good English education, and at the age of seventeen began teaching school, which vocation he followed for eight years. In 1854 he began the study of medicine, and, entering the medical department of the University of Pennsylvania, graduated in 1856. He located at Applebachsville, where he practiced his profession until the breaking out of the war in 1861, when he organized a company of which he was commissioned captain, and it was assigned to the Pennsylvania Reserve Corps. In the autumn of 1862 he was appointed surgeon of the 118th Corn Exchange Regiment, Pennsylvania Volunteers, and subsequently became surgeon-in-chief of the field hospital and filled that position to the close of the war.

At the return of peace he again located at Applebachsville and resumed his professional work. In 1866 he was appointed assistant assessor of internal revenue and removed to Quakertown, Bucks county, where he has since resided. In 1870 he organized the Quakertown Savings Bank, was made its cashier, and filled that position until the bank closed out its successful career in 1877, by paying out to its stockholders four dollars for every one dollar invested. The Quakertown National Bank was then organized, and Dr. Thomas became its president, and has filled that position ever since. Like its predecessor, the Quakertown National Bank, with Dr. Thomas 'at its head, has been one of the most successful banks in Bucks county, and has always stood in the first rank of financial institutions. In 1904 the Quakertown Trust Company was organized, and the veteran financier Dr. Thomas was one of its prominent promoters and sponsers, and is still intimately identified with the conduct and management of this institution. Jonas S. Harley is its president.

Though he has not been in active practice of his profesion for many years, he is still considered one of the able physicians of Upper Bucks, and is frequently called in as a consulting physician. Politically Dr. Thomas is an ardent Republican, and has always taken an active interest in the success of the party in whose principles he believes. In 1878 he was elected to the state senate by a handsome majority, though at that time the county was strongly Democratic. He has served as delegate to state and national conventions, and has filled a number of local positions. In the midst of an extraordinary busy life Dr. Thomas has found time to devote to science and literature, and is one of the best versed men in the county on ornithology and natural history. In connection with his former colleague, Dr. I. S. Moyer, of Quakertown, he prepared the catalogue of the flora, birds and mammals of Bucks county for General W. W. H. Davis's first edition of the History of Bucks County. He is past master of Quakertown Lodge, No. 512, F. and A. M., and is also a member of the chapter, commandery and other high branches of the Masonic fraternity, as well as a member of Quakertown Lodge,

No. 714, I. O. O. F. He belongs to Peter Lyle Post, G. A. R., No. 145, and to the Loyal Legion of the United States. Dr. Thomas married, April 3, 1860, Sarah Ott, daughter of Samuel and Eliza (Fluck) Ott, and they are the parents of one son, Byron, who has been for many years teller of Quakertown National Bank. Dr. Thomas is one of the best known and most highly respected men in Bucks county.

CHRISTIAN M. MYERS. Among the descendants of the early German settlers on the virgin land of Bedminster, Bucks county, Pennsylvania, when it was still a wilderness and the haunt of the red men, is Christian M. Myers, still a resident of the township where his ancestors settled over a century and a half ago.

Hans Meyer, the pioneer ancestor and great-great-grandfather of Christian M. Myers, emigrated from Germany or Switzerland, about the year, 1718, and in 1729 purchased a plantation in Skippack township, Philadelphia (now Montgomery) county, in that part later incorporated into Upper Salford township, still in the occupancy of his great-grandson. Hans Meyer was a Mennonite and one of the pioneer settlers in that locality. He was married before emigrating to America, and brought with him his eldest son Henry, then but a year old. Six other children were born to him in Pennsylvania, viz.: John, the great-grandfather of the subject of this sketch; Barbara, who married John Fretz, another pioneer in Bedminster; Jacob, who enlisted in the colonial war of 1756, and never returned; Elizabeth, who married Christian Stover; Anna, who married Jacob Beidler, and became the ancestress of Mrs. Christian M. Myers; and Hester, who married Nicholas Lear.

John Meyer, born about 1720, settled in Bedminster township soon after attaining manhood, on land owned by William Allen, Esq., which he later purchased. In 1762 he purchased a farm of two hundred acres in Plumstead township where he resided the remainder of his life. He was a farmer and blacksmith by occupation, and a member of the Mennonite congregation at Deep Run. He married a widow Nash, whose maiden name was Sensenich, and they were the parents of six children, Henry, Abraham, and Christian, all of whom learned their father's trade and followed it in connection with farming in Plumstead: Hester and Mary, who lived to an advanced age, but never married; and Barbara, who married Charles Dyer.

Christian Myers, son of John, and the grandfather of the subject of this sketch, was born on the old Plumstead homestead, April 24, 1772, and later purchased it, and lived there all his life, He followed blacksmithing for many years in the old, smith-shop built by his father. He married Hanna Derstein, of Rockhill, where her ancestors were early settlers, born January 12, 1778, died August 27, 1848, and they were the parents of seven children, viz.: Amos, born 1800, died 1825, unmarried; John, died in infancy; Catharine, born February 14, 1803, married Abraham Wismer; Michael, born May 9, 1804, removed to Fairfield county, Ohio, where he died in 1889; Samuel, the father of the subject of this sketch; Abraham, born 1807, died 1834, unmarried; Charles, who married Susan Myers and left several sons still residing in Bucks county; and Isaac, who died in 1845, leaving an only daughter, Hannah Wolfsberger, of Philadelphia. Christian Myers, the father, died November 15, 1850.

Samuel Myers, son of Christian and Hanna (Derstein) Myers, was born on the old homestead in Plumstead, December 27, 1805, and lived there all his life, dying February 4, 1879. He probably learned the blacksmith trade with his father, but never followed it further than to do his own work in that line. He was a mechanical genius, doing his own shoe and harness making, and manufacturing most of the implements of husbandry needed on the farm. Those were the days when the farmer was almost independent of the outside world except for the luxuries of life. Mr. Myers raised and prepared the flax and wool for the spinning wheel, and the clothes of the family were exclusively the product of the spinning of Mrs. Myers, and the weaving of the father. Samuel Myers married December 24, 1835, Susanna Nash, born December 30, 1810, daughter of Jacob and Elizabeth (Meyer) Nash, the latter being also a descendant of Hans Meyer, the emigrant, through his eldest son Henry, who married Barbara Miller, and their son Henry, born 1750, (died in Plumstead) who married Susan Smith. Elizabeth (Meyer) Nash, the daughter of the last named Henry, was born August 16, 1786, and married Jacob Nash, of Tinicum, son of Joseph Nash, and grandson of William Nash, another pioneer of Bedminster. Samuel and Susanna (Nash) Myers were the parents of eight children, viz.: Hannah, died in infancy; Tobias N., married Rosanna Kratz, and lived for a time in Plumstead, now a resident of Philadelphia; Jacob, married Maria Myers, and resides in Hilltown, Bucks county; Christian M., the subject of this sketch; Amos, married Hilda Myers, and resides on the homestead in Plumstead, being the fourth generation in the township; Elizabeth, died at the age of nineteen years; Anna, widow of David Kratz; and Charles, deceased. Samuel Myers was a member of the old

Deep Run Mennonite congregation, and a man much respected in the community. He never held or sought office.

Christian M. Myers, son of Samuel and Susanna (Nash) Myers, who born April 29, 1841, on the old homestead in Plumstead, and educated at the public schools. He inherited the mechanical genius of his father, and made the first hay rake and hay drag used on the home farm, as well as a number of other implements of husbandry, and, in the earlier years of the conduct of the mill where he now resides, he dressed his own mill picks and did the necessary millwrighting about the mill. On his marriage in 1863 he took charge of the Stover mill, on Tohickon creek, in Bedminster township, near Pipersville, Pennsylvania, belonging to his father-in-law, Samuel Stover, and conducted it until 1904, keeping in pace with the times in the installation of improved machinery, having in 1885, equipped the mill with the latest improved roller process for the manufacture of flour, and again in 1903, installed the Gyrator system of bolting and other improvements. In 1904 he retired and turned the business over to Norman L. Worman, who had been his foreman and head miller for many years, and who is now doing a flourishing business there. Mr. Myers is a strong advocate of higher education, and has given each of his sons a college education. He and his wife are not members of any church, but are liberal supporters of church, Sabbath school and charitable work, and to which and the temperance cause they have devoted much time and labor. Mr. Myers married, February 7, 1863, Eliza Beidler Stover, born February 22, 1844, daughter of Samuel and Anna (Beidler) Stover, an account of whose ancestry follows, and they are parents of three sons, viz.: 1. Samuel Horace Myers, born May 9, 1864, a graduate of Lafayette College, class of 1888, and of the law department of the University of Pennsylvania, July 17, 1892. He was admitted to the Philadelphia bar in 1892, and has since practiced there with success. He married; February 22, 1893, Eleanor Matilda Stover, daughter of Isaac S. and Ellen A. (Capner) Stover, and they are the parents of one daughter Roberta Eliza Myers, born October 9, 1897. 2. Hugh Ely Myers, born August 30, 1871, graduated at Lafayette College June 21, 1893, took a two years post-graduate course there in chemistry and is now employed as chemist with the United Engineering and Foundry Company, at Pittsburg, Pennsylvania. 3. Ira Stover Myers, born August 3, 1876, educated at Germantown Academy and Lafayette College, graduated at College in class of 1898, is now in the office of his brother, Samuel Horace in Philadelphia.

15-8

Eliza B. (Stover) Myers, the wife of Christian M. Myers, is descended from pioneer settlers in Bucks and Montgomery counties, who have been prominently identified with the settlement and development of the native resources of the county. Henry Stauffer, (as the name Stover was then spelled) Mrs. Myers' paternal ancestor, was born and reared in Alsace or Manheim, Rhenish Prussia, and married there in 1749, Barbara Hockman, and accompanied by Christian, Daniel and Ulrich Stauffer, probably his brothers and Ulrich Hockman, his wife's brother, sailed for Pennsylvania in the ship "St. Andrew," Captain James Abercrombie, from Rotterdam, arriving in Philadelphia on September 9, 1749. He located in Bedminster township on the Allen tract, where he purchased 213 acres of land June 12, 1762, having previously resided for a time among his compatriots on the Skippack in Montgomery county. The Bedminster homestead remained the property of his descendants for nearly a century, having been sold by Reuben Stover, a greatgrandson, in 1860 to Joseph Sine. The children of Henry and Barbara (Hockman) Stauffer, were: 1. Ulrich, born July 16, 1750, married Barbara Swartz, and died on the homestead November 2, 1811. 2. Barbara, died young. 3. Henry, born July 10, 1754, married Elizabeth Fretz, and settled near Bursonville, Springfield township. 4. Jacob, see forward. 5. Ralph, born June 10, 1760, died November 7, 1811, married Catharine Funk; was a very prominent man, justice of the peace, member of assembly and one of the first board of directors of the poor of Bucks county.

Jacob Stover, third son of Henry and Barbara, born May 13, 1757, was reared in Bedminster township. During the war of the Revolution his father's team and wagon was pressed into the service of the continental army under General Sullivan, and Jacob, a lad of sixteen years, accompanied it in the Jersey campaign, and endured many hardships. He purchased the mill property now owned by the subject of this sketch, December 27, 1784, and resided there the remainder of his life, dying April 28, 1844. He married (first) Elizabeth Swartz, and had by her one daughter, Elizabeth, who married Philip Kratz. He married (second) Catharine Stauffer, daughter of Mathias and Anna (Clemens) Stauffer, who kept an inn in colonial times on their farm in Lower Salford, Montgomery county, where officers of Washington's army were entertained and sheltered by them after the battle of Germantown. Mathias Stauffer was a son of Christian Stauffer, Jr., who died in Lower Salford in 1781, and a grandson of Christian Stauffer, a pioneer emigrant, who purchased 150

acres at the present site of Harleysville, Montgomery county, and died there in 1735, leaving a large family of children of whom Christian, Jr., was the eldest, and settled in Lower Salford in 1736. Jacob and Catharine Stover were the parents of eight children: Henry S., born October 17, 1786, died at Erwinna, August 19, 1872, married Barbara Stout; Mathias, born April 28, 1789, died June 4, 1807; Anna, born 1791, married David Worman, a tanner, at Parkerford, Chester county, Pennsylvania; Jacob, born July 12, 1794, died March 30, 1856, married Sarah Treichler; Abraham, died young; Catharine, born August 12, 1799, married Henry Funk and removed to Northumberland county; Jonas, born February 27, 1802, died 1855, a miller at Church Hill, Bucks county; Samuel, see forward; and Isaac, born March 13, 1806, died January 21, 1876, miller at Carversville, married Elizabeth Wismer.

Samuel Stover, father of Mrs. Myers, was the seventh child of Jacob and Catharine, and was born on the homestead, near Pipersville, November 25, 1804, and died there February 18, 1888. In 1836 he purchased of his father the brick dwelling erected in 1832, the mill and fifty acres of land, and in the same year rebuilt the mill. He continued to operate the mill during his active days, and lived there all his life. He was a successful business man, and upright and conscientious in all his dealings. He married in December, 1836, Anna Beidler, born near Plumsteadville, September 12, 1808, died March 2, 1893, daughter of Jacob Beidler, and great-granddaughter of Jacob and Anna (Meyer) Beidler, the latter daughter of Hans Meyer, the paternal ancestor of the subject of this sketch, C. M. Myers. Samuel and Anna (Beidler) Stover were the parents of two children: Susan, born June 19, 1839, died March 25, 1842; and Eliza Beidler Stover, born February 22, 1844, the wife of Christian M. Myers. She was educated in the public schools of the township, both English and German, and at Excelsior Normal Institute at Carversville, in 1861, Rev. Dr. F. R. S. Hunsicker, principal, where Hon. D. Newlin Fell was also a pupil.

ISAAC PARRY. The name of Parry is closely interwoven with the history of eastern Pennsylvania, having been established in this part of the state when the country was still numbered among the colonial possessions of Great Britain. The ancestors of Isaac Parry were in comfortable financial circumstances, and at the time of the Revolutionary war the homestead farm was foraged by both armies. On one occasion some British scouts made their way to the farm and seeing some fat sheep caught and killed one, compelling Mrs. Parry to cook it for them in the Dutch oven, but before their feast was prepared some American troops arrived on the scene and the British fled, so that the Continental troops enjoyed the meal instead. The ancestry of the family is traced back through several generations to Thomas Parry, Sr., who emigrated from Radmanshire, Wales, settling in America in colonial days. He became one of the pioneer residents of Montgomery county, and assisted materially in promoting its substantial development and moral improvement. He lived a straightforward, honorable life, leaving an example for his descendants that is well worthy of emulation. He was a consistent member of the religious Society of Friends, and successive generations of the family have always adhered to that faith, living lives of simplicity without vanity. They have been conservative to a considerable degree, and yet they have won success and gained the respect of all with whom they have been associated. The family has largely been represented in the great department of agriculture, and yet certain of its representatives have entered professional and commercial life. Samuel Parry was a broadminded, intelligent business man, whose ability was often sought by people of the neighborhood who wished him to write wills, settle estates or act as guardian to minors. Thomas Parry, Sr., the progenitor of the family in America, obtained a large tract of land near Baronhill, Montgomery county, where he improved an extensive farm, being one of the prominent and successful agriculturists of his day. Upon the home place he reared his family and continued to reside until his death.

His son, Thomas Parry, Jr., was reared to manhood on the old homestead, and after his marriage located in Warminster township, Bucks county, where by purchase he became the possessor of large landed holdings. Settling thereon he improved the property, and a part of it is yet in possession of his descendants. He continued to reside thereon until his death.

Jacob Parry, son of Thomas Parry, Jr., was reared on the home farm in Warminster township, and at the time of his marriage took his bride to that farm and reared his family there.

Isaac Parry, son of Jacob Parry, inherited the old homestead and he, too, reared his family there.

Isaac Parry, son of Isaac Parry, in turn inherited the old homestead, reared his family thereon, and died on the farm. Isaac Parry was born in June, 1774, and passed away in October, 1857. He first married Sarah Hopkins, and they became the parents of three children: Rebecca, Jacob, and Richard H.

After the death of his first wife Isaac Parry wedded Mary Nixon, a daughter of Samuel and Susan (Roberts) Nixon, also of a prominent early family of Bucks county. By the second marriage there were six children: Tacey, who died unmarried; Thomas, Samuel, Isaac C., Susanna, and Mary, who was the wife of Joseph Saunders, of Philadelphia.

Thomas Parry, second child of Isaac and Mary (Nixon) Parry, was born at the Parry homestead in Warminster township, was reared upon the farm there and at the time of his marriage took his bride to the old home place. He wedded Lydia Conard, a native of Horsham township, Montgomery county, and a daughter of Josephine and Hannah (Nixon) Conard. In his younger days her father was engaged in the lumber business at Philadelphia, but afterward removed to Horsham township, Montgomery county, where he purchased land and carried on farming. He also built a mill known in after years as Walker's mills. This is still in use, being operated by Eugene Blair. Jonathan Conard spent the remainder of his life at that place and died upon his farm near the mill. He was a member of the religious Society of Friends, and was highly respected. His children were: John; Charles, a carpenter and builder of Philadelphia; Susanna, the wife of W. Folk; Deborah, the wife of N. Cleaver; Mary, the wife of B. Brown, of Byberry; Ann, the wife of B. Morgan; Lydia, who became Mrs. Thomas Parry; and Rebecca J., who died unmarried. All were members of the religious Society of Friends. Following his marriage Thomas Parry lived on a farm which he purchased from Jonathan Conard, now the property of Isaac Parry. He remodeled this farm, made substantial improvements, and continued to carry on agricultural pursuits there throughout his remaining days, passing away in 1857 at the age of forty-five years. He followed general farming and also attended the city market, and was practical and successful in all his business dealings. He was a devoted member of the Friends Society, ever active in church work and was a generous contributor toward the erection of the Warminster Meeting, which was built on one corner of his farm and is yet standing as a monument to the religious enterprise of its promoters. Politically he was an Abolitionist in early life. He at all times commanded the respect and confidence of those with whom he was associated because of his upright life and honorable purpose. To him and his wife were born eight children: Edward H., who served in the First New Jersey Cavalry during the war of the rebellion, joining the army with the rank of corporal and returning with the rank of lieutenant, is now proprietor of a hat store in Philadelphia. Rebecca C., who became the wife of J. Tyson, of Abingdon, but both are now deceased; Isaac is the third of the family; Oliver, is a farmer of Warminster township; William is a practicing physician of Haynesport, New Jersey; Charles C. is a farmer of Wrightstown township; Thomas E. is living in California; Joseph S. is an attorney-at-law of Hoboken, New Jersey.

Isaac Parry was born upon the home farm, June 30, 1844, and under his father's instructions learned the various methods of tilling the soil and caring for the crops. In 1869 he was married, after which he rented the homestead and continued its cultivation for two years. In 1872 he purchased the Hart homestead, including the town site of Ivyland. He removed to this farm, remaining thereon for five years, and then sold forty acres of the land to Edwin Lacey, who desired to build the town of Ivyland there. Later he sold the remainder of the farm to Comly Walker, and in 1877 removed from the place. In 1878 he took up his abode upon the old Parry homestead, and in 1886 purchased the interest of the other heirs in the property, making his home thereon continuously. In 1877 he bought the interest of L. W. Damenhower in a coal and feed business at Bradyville, and continued in the business twenty-eight years. He secured an extensive patronage throughout the surrounding country, and gave his personal attention to his mercantile interests, while his farm is operated under his personal supervision. He is both a practical and successful agriculturist and business man. In his political views Mr. Parry has always been a stanch Republican, and has filled some township offices, including those of auditor and supervisor, yet he has always preferred to give his undivided attention to his business affairs. In addition to his agricultural and commercial interests, he is a stockholder in the National Bank and in other corporations. He has a wide and favorable acquaintance, is known for his reliability and enterprise, and stands to-day as one of the representative men of his community. Mr. Parry was married March 11, 1869, to Miss Elizabeth Logan, who was born at Jenkintown, Pennsylvania, and is a daughter of George and Jane (Shoemaker) Logan, belonging to one of the old and honored families of eastern Pennsylvania. The children of the Logan family were Elizabeth; Theodore, now deceased; and Albanus. To Mr. and Mrs. Parry have been born three children: Samuel D., who is principal of the Olney public school in Philadelphia, Pennsylvania; George, a practicing dentist of Jenkintown; and Charles K., who is engaged in the lumber business of Philadelphia as a member of the Righter, Parry Lumber Company. The children have been provided with good educational privileges, thus fitting them for the responsible and practical duties of life.

JOHN BURTON, of Tullytown, dealer in coal and general merchandise, was born in Tullytown, Pennsylvania, August 12, 1864, and is a son of Elwood and Anna H. (Bailey) Burton, of Tullytown, and a representative of a family that have been prominent in the settlement and development of Bucks county for six generations.

Anthony Burton, the emigrant ancestor of the family, was a native of England, and was among the earliest settlers in Bristol township, where he owned land as early as 1684. His name appears among those who registered the "ear marks" for their cattle in the old book kept for that purpose by Phinehas Pemberton in 1684. On March 16, 1695, he and Thomas Burk purchased the tract of land on which the town of Bristol was subsequently built, and laid it out in streets and building lots, and laid the foundation of the present metropolis of Bucks. It was incorporated by the provincial council of Pennsylvania at a meeting of that body held at the house of Phinehas Pemberton in Falls township, Bucks county, on the petition of "severall in that countie for a Market Town, viz: att the Ferry agt. Burlington, within the said township of Buckingham, and that the sd persons have projected the same Into ways & streets, Haveing regard to the divisions of divers men's Land by the sd streets in the sd Town as now laid down," whereupon, "It was resolved by the Gouvernor & Council, that a town be there erected and the ways & streets to be according to ye model ye agreed upon." The town being erected, grew to such importance that Mr. Burton and other lot holders on October 17, 1718, petitioned the council to erect it into a borough, which was done, and its charter as engrossed was agreed to by the board of provincial councillors at a meeting held July 19, 1720. The name of Buckingham, first selected for the new town, was soon dropped, and it retained the name of Bristol.

Anthony Burton was a man of liberal education and wielded a wide influence in the community. He was commissioned a justice of the peace on May 13, 1715, and was regularly re-commissioned until 1733, and probably held the position until his death in 1739, the records for the intervening period merely stating "Justices now acting, re-commissioned." He was a member of the established church, and donated the land upon which St. James Episcopal church of

John Buxton

Elwood Burton

Bristol was erected, and contributed liberally to its erection in 1712. From the records of this old church it appears that his lineal descendants are entitled to occupy two pews therein forever. Anthony Burton married, December 18, 1687, Sarah Gibbs, a widow. She died June 28, 1718, without issue. On July 28, 1720, he married Susan Keene, by whom he had two children; Martha, who died unmarried; and Anthony, Jr., born July 17, 1721. Anthony Burton, Sr., died in 1739, and is buried in St. James churchyard at Bristol.

Anthony Burton, Jr., son of Anthony and Susan (Keene) Burton, was a farmer and a large landowner in Bristol township, residing on the road from Bristol to the "Falls of the Delaware." He married, February 12, 1752, Mary Hough, daughter of Richard Hough, of Falls, and, she being a member of the Society of Friends, he also became affiliated with that society, as have been his descendants to this day. He died February, 1798. Anthony and Mary (Hough) Burton were the parents of eight children, four of whom died in infancy; those who survived were: John, born September 17, 1753; Martha, born July 25, 1756, married John Minster; Anthony, born August 9, 1758; and Jonathan born August 21, 1765.

John Burton, eldest son of Anthony and Mary (Hough), born September 17, 1753, was the great-grandfather of the subject of this sketch. He was a farmer and resided for many years on the old homestead in Bristol township, but removed late in life to Falls township, where he died September 3, 1835. He was twice married, first in February, 1778, to Rachel Wilson, nee Sotcher, widow of Henry Wilson and daughter of Robert and Mercy (Brown) Sotcher. She died in 1781, leaving two sons, Joseph and John. On October 9, 1789, he married Hannah Watson, by whom he had five children: Benjamin, Mary, Rachel, Anthony, and Charles.

Anthony, the second son of Anthony and Mary (Hough) Burton, born August 9, 1758, married Jane, daughter of John and Deborah (Watson) Gregg, April 27, 1781, and had children: John G., Amos, Deborah, and William. The latter became a successful merchant in Philadelphia and afterwards a physician. He was a remarkably brilliant man. His wife was Susan Hallowell, of Philadelphia, belonging to an old Bucks county family, who died in Penns Manor, Bucks county. Jonathan, the other son of Anthony and Mary, married Letitia Williamson, March 11, 1790, and died in 1840. His children were William, Sarah, Peter, Ann L., and Elizabeth. His grandson, Jonathan Burton, was a large manufacturer of iron, and died in Ohio. Joseph Burton, son of John and Rachel (Wilson) Burton, was a large landhold-

er in Bristol and Falls township, and a justice of the peace for over thirty years. He married Sarah Watson, and died in 1858. Many descendants of the three sons of Anthony and Mary (Hough) Burton still reside in Bucks county, where they have intermarried with other families that have been prominent in the development of the county.

Anthony Burton, grandfather of the subject of this sketch, born in 1796, was a son of John and Hannah (Watson) Burton. In his younger days he was a school teacher, but later became a farmer, and he was also identified with various business enterprises, operating for several years an extensive shad fishery on the Delaware. He was for twenty-four years the president of the Farmers' National Bank of Bucks county, at Bristol, and was also president of the Upper Delaware River Steamboat Company, and filled many other positions of trust. He was a prominent member of the Society of Friends, and a man much esteemed in the community. He died near Tullytown in 1874, at the age of seventy eight years, lamented by all who knew him. He was twice married, his first wife and the mother of his children being Mary Headley, and his second wife was Anna Paxson. His children were Caroline, Hannah, John, Anna, and Elwood. John, born August 3, 1829, was a soldier in the war of the rebellion, serving in the Anderson Cavalry, and participating in eighteen engagements. He was a prominent business man in Falls township, holding many positions of trust and honor, being a director of the Farmers' National Bank of Bucks county, president of the Bristol Improvement Company, and director of the Delaware River Steamboat Transportation Company, and of the Cape May and Delaware Bay Navigation Company. He was also president of the William Penn Mutual Loan and Building Association. He married, February 7, 1867, Elizabeth Headley, daughter of William and Eliza, and had children, Franklin, Elwood, Horace H. and A. Russell. Caroline Burton, daughter of Anthony and Mary Headley Burton, married Pierson Mitchell, of Middletown. Hannah never married, and Anna married John W. Paxson, of Philadelphia.

Elwood Burton, father of the subject of this sketch, was the youngest son of Anthony and Mary (Headley) Burton, and was born on the old homestead farm near Tullytown, February 28, 1836. He obtained his elementary education in the public schools of Falls township, and finished at the academy at Langhorne. On leaving school he entered the store of his brother-in-law, John W. Paxson, at Tullytown, as a clerk, and filled that position until arriving at his majority, when with his brother John he purchased the plant of Mr. Paxson. Two years later he purchased his brother's interest, and successfully conducted the business until his death in 1896. He was a man of much more than ordinary business ability, and h' many positions of honor and trust. He was a director of the Farmers' National Bank of Bucks county from 1874 until his death, also a director of the Bristol Rolling Mill Company, the Bristol Improvement Company and the Standard Fire Insurance Company of Trenton, New Jersey, and was frequently called upon to act as executor, administrator, agent and guardian in the settlement of estates. He was a consistent member of the Society of Friends, and was highly respected and esteemed in the community. He married, September 8, 1859, Anna H. Bailey, daughter of John W. and Phoebe (Brown) Bailey, of Falls township, and a descendant of two old and prominent families of Bucks county, and they were the parents of five children; Ida C., wife of A. Brock Shoemaker, a prominent merchant of Tullytown; John, the subject of this sketch; Pierson, who died in infancy; Raymond A.; and Lilian C., wife of Allen Corson, of Philadelphia. Anna (Bailey) Burton resides in Philadelphia. The maternal ancestors of the subject of this sketch were also among the most prominent people of Bucks county. Richard Hough, the father of Mary, the wife of Anthony Burton (2) was the son of Richard and Margery (Clowes) Hough, of Makefield, the former of whom came from Macclesfield, in the county of Chester, England, arriving in the Delaware river in the "Endeavor," 7 mo. 29, 1683, and settled in Makefield township. He was a member of provincial council, and was drowned in the Delaware in 1706, while on his way to attend a meeting of the council. His wife, Margery Clowes, was a daughter of John and Margery Clowes, who also came in the "Endeavor" and settled in Makefield. Rachel Sotcher, who became the wife of John Burton (1) was the daughter of Robert and Mercy (Brown) Sotcher, and granddaughter of John and Mary (Lofty) Sotcher, the latter of whom were William Penn's trusted stewards at Pennsbury, and John Sotcher was for many years a member of colonial assembly. George and Mercy Brown, the parents of Mercy, the wife of Robert Sotcher, was the youngest child of George and Mercy Brown, who came from Leicestershire, England, together in 1679, and were married at New Castle on their arrival, and later settled in Falls township, where they reared a family of eight sons and three daughters. General Jacob Brown was a great-great-grandson of George and Mercy Brown. Phoebe (Brown) Bailey, the maternal grand-

mother of the subject of this sketch, was of the same lineage. The Headleys and Baileys were also among the earliest settlers in Lower Bucks, where they have left numerous descendants.

John Burton was educated at the Friends' Central School in Philadelphia, and later took a course in Trenton Business College, after which he assisted his father in the conduct of the general merchandise and coal business at Tullytown, and succeeded his father in 1893. He is a director of the Farmers' National Bank of Bucks county at Bristol, and a director of the Bristol Improvement Company, treasurer of the William Penn Mutual Loan and Building Association, of Tullytown, and a director of the Standard Fire Insurance Company, of Trenton, New Jersey. In politics he is a Republican. He married, September 1, 1893, Sarah G. Eastburn, daughter of Thomas C. and Abi (Crozer) Eastburn, who was born in Bucks county, Penn's Manor, in 1866, and is a descendant of Robert and Sarah (Preston) Eastburn, who came from Yorkshire in 1714, their son Samuel settling later in Solebury, from whence Samuel Eastburn, a grandson of the above named Samuel, removed to Penn's Manor in 1803. The Eastburns were members of the Society of Friends. John and Sarah G. (Eastburn) Burton have one son, Pierson Mitchell Burton.

JACOB H. SWARTZ. The name which introduces this record is that of an honored veteran of the civil war, and one of the enterprising agriculturists of Plumstead township, and was also borne by his paternal grandfather, who lived and died in Bucks county, where he followed farming for many years. The family, although its earlier history has not been preserved, was undoubtedly one of the first established in Bucks county. Jacob Swartz, the grandfather, who served in the war of 1812, purchased of Nicholas Swartz in 1812 the farm upon which his grandson and namesake now resides, and the property has since been continuously in the family. Jacob Swartz was united in marriage to Miss Ann Black, and they became the parents of six children: Sarah Ann, Thomas B., Catherine, wife of Lewis Horn; Henry, Cyrus, and Sophia, who married Abraham Garis, and after his death Josiah Tomblin.

Thomas B. Swartz, the eldest son of Jacob and Ann (Black) Swartz, was born April 16, 1813, upon the farm now owned and occupied by his son Jacob, and his boyhood days were quietly passed in the usual manner of farmer lads of that period. He learned the blacksmith's trade in his youth and followed it for a number of years, but about

1840 resumed agricultural pursuits, purchasing the old homestead farm from his father. He then gave his entire attention to farming until his retirement from active business life, about two years prior to his demise, which occurred April 22, 1895. In all business transactions he was thoroughly reliable and he won the respect and confidence of his fellow men. In politics he was a Republican, and held the office of school director at one time. He married Miss Emily Ann Beans, born October 29, 1814, died May 15, 1899, and they became the parents of four children: 1. Levi B., born 10 mo. 26, 1837, married, 1 mo. 10, 1860, Elizabeth Nash, and their children were: Mary Alice, born 4 mo. 6, 1863; Abraham Thomas, born 10 mo. 19, 1865; and Emily Ann, born 9 mo. 2, 1867. 2. Jacob H., born 9 mo. 23, 1842, married, 12 mo. 5, 1867, Caroline P. Meginnis, mentioned at length hereinafter. 3. Anna Mary, born 8 mo. 29, 1847, married, 10 mo. 30, 1871, Cephas W. Michener, and their children are: Evan W., born 10 mo. 8, 1872; Frank P., born 11 mo. 18, 1875; Hiram M., born 1 mo. 28, 1878; and Thomas Swartz Michener, born 6 mo. 8, 1880. 4. Laura F., born 11 mo. 11, 1855, married, 6 mo. 6, 1881, Stacy B. Emmons, and they are the parents of one child: Stella Alice Emmans, born 1 mo. 6, 1885.

Jacob H. Swartz, the second son of Thomas and Emily Ann Swartz, first opened his eyes to the light of day on the old family homestead September 2, 1842. At the usual age he enterd the public schools and acquired therein a good knowledge of the fundamental branches of English learning. He remained at home with his father on the farm until 1862, when his patriotic spirit being aroused by the continued attempt of the south to overthrow the Union he enlisted as a member of Company D, Forty-fifth Pennsylvania Infantry, from which command he was honorably discharged on August 29, 1863. Following his return from the war he again began work for his father, with whom he remained until 1868. He then purchased the home farm, on which he remained for three years, when he sold it back to his father. He then removed to Lumberville, where he engaged in the coal and feed trade for a year and also conducted a general mercantile store. After a year he purchased the Hellyer farm in Plumstead township, where he remained until 1897. His son then took charge of the farm, and for two years Jacob H. Swartz carried on agricultural pursuits and also engaged in the commission business. In 1899 he purchased the interest of the other heirs in the old homestead property, where he now resides, giving his undivided attention to agricultural pursuits. He follows progressive methods of farming, utilizing the latest improved machinery and the scientific methods of rotating crops in order to secure good harvests, and his fields now annually return to him a bountiful product. Mr. Swartz votes with the Republican party, and while he has never sought nor desired public office he has held the position of school director for two terms. Fraternally he is connected with the Knights of Pythias Lodge, No. 221, at Carversville, Pennsylvania. Mr. Swartz has been married twice. He first married, 12 mo. 5, 1867, Caroline P. Meginnis, and to them were born three children: Flora May, 5 mo. 7, 1869, wife of Thomas S. Michener; Henry, 4 mo. 26, 1874, a resident farmer of Plumstead township; and Emily Ann, 4 mo. 4, 1880, wife of Harry Vassey. For his second wife Mr. Swartz chose Mrs. Emma Meginnis, nee Stout.

SAMUEL SNYDER HILLPOT. Samuel Snyder Hillpot, a prosperous farmer and old resident of Bucks county, Pennsylvania, was there born in Tinicum township, November 20, 1802, the son of Barnard and Barbara (Snyder) Hillpot, and grandson of Barnett Hillpot. Samuel received what education the subscription schools of that period afforded, leaving school at the age of twelve years. He then turned his attention to farming and has since followed that occupation with considerable success. He was born and reared in Tinicum township. He was a Democrat in politics, and although he took a lively interest in the affairs of that organization, and always advocated its principles with great enthusiasm, he never aspired to public office. He was a regular attendant of the Lutheran church in Lower Tinicum.

March 9, 1830, Mr. Hillpot was united in marriage to Christena, daughter of George and Catherine (Hager) Shive, weavers of cloth and blankets, of Nockamixon township. The following named children, eight in number, were born to Mr. and Mrs. Hillpot: William Barnett, July 2, 1831, died October 10, 1879; 2. Elizabeth Shive, born May 26, 1833, died May 19, 1855; 3. Thomas Shive, born June 4, 1835, married Amanda, daughter of Jonas and Lydia (Landis) Landis; 4. Jonas George, born July 16, 1837, died October 15, 1865; 5. Mary Ann Shive, born June 6, 1840, married, June 6, 1865, William Keep, of Allentown, who died in February, 1884, and had the following children: 1. Anna, born February 25, 1866, died March 12, 1889; 2. Samuel George, born October 9, 1874, resided at Salt Lake City, Utah, where he was instructor in bookkeeping in Brown's School of Correspondence. He died in Salt Lake City in February, 1905. 6. The sixth child born to Mr.

and Mrs. Samuel Hillpot was Leah Shive, born April 11, 1844, married John King, a wheelwright of Plumstead township; 7. Fannie B., born December 1, 1846, married May 12; 1870, to Lewis, son of John and Mary Fluck, farmers of Richland township. He was a Democrat in politics and was postmaster of Richland Center during Grover Cleveland's second administration. He died February 20, 1888, and Mrs. Fluck married, August 28, 1890, William H. Mininger, son of Joseph and Mary Mininger, a carpenter and builder at Zion Hill, Bucks county, Pennsylvania, and lives in Quakertown. By her first husband Mrs. Mininger had two children: John Samuel, born April 16, 1878, married Addie Moyer. He is engaged as car tracer for the Reading railroad, and lives at Lansdale, Pennsylvania; Arthur Fluck, born March 28, 1881, lives at home, unmarried, and is assistant freight agent to the North Pennsylvania Railroad of Quakertown. The eighth child born to Mr. and Mrs. Hillpot was Clarissa, born October 6, 1849, died November 17, 1857.

THOMAS STINTSMAN. The good business men and useful citizens of the county have a worthy representative in Thomas Stintsman, of New Hope. Mr. Stintsman is a grandson of Samuel Stintsman, who emigrated from Germany and settled in Bucks county, where his son, also named Samuel, spent his life on the homestead, dying at the advanced age of ninety-two. The Stintsman homestead is situated near Point Pleasant, in Plumstead township.

Silas Stintsman, son of Samuel, second bearer of the name, mentioned above, was born in Plumstead township, and on reaching manhood engaged in boating on the canal, owning and controlling two canal boats. He married Elizabeth Solomon, and they were the parents of a son and two daughters: Annie A., who is the widow of Edward McNutt, of Philadelphia; Thomas, mentioned at length hereinafter; and Laura J., deceased. While boating on the Hackensack, Mr. Stintsman was accidentally killed by the cars in consequence of delay in opening a bridge through which his boat was to pass.

Thomas Stintsman, son of Silas and Elizabeth (Solomon) Stintsman, was born October 20, 1854, in Plumstead township, and was about ten years old at the time of his father's death. After that event he went on the canal with an uncle and until his seventeenth year was employed in boating on the Lehigh, Delaware, Raritan and Morris canals. He then went to New Hope to learn the boat-building business under his uncle, A. J. Solomon. In four years he finished his apprenticeship and then worked two years as a journeyman. His uncle being elected county commissioner, Mr. Stintsman took charge of the yards and during two years built many boats on his own account. The times, however, being unfavorable to the business, he accepted a position with C. S. Atkinson in his agricultural implement shops, where he remained fifteen or eighteen years, holding during the latter four or five years the position of superintendent of the shops. After resigning this position he was engaged for a short time in contracting and house building. July 3, 1896, he was appointed postmaster of New Hope, taking his place August 1, following, and served a full four years' term under President Cleveland's administration. On the expiration of his term he engaged in the hardware business in partnership with John W. Kooker, and the firm conducted a flourishing trade. In May, 1903, Mr. Stintsman sold his interest in that firm and established a general notion store. Mr. Stintsman has served six years as a member of the borough council, the same length of time as treasurer of the borough, for eighteen months held the office of deputy coroner, and for three years was a member of the school board. He belongs to Delaware Castle, No. 196, Knights of the Golden Eagle, and since 1888 has been secretary to the order. He is also a member of the Order of Heptasophs. In politics he is a Democrat. Mr. Stintsman married in 1880 Laura, daughter of Moses L. Fryling, of New Hope, and of the eleven children born to them nine are now living: Catherine, who is engaged in her father's store at New Hope; Elizabeth; Moses, who has the newspaper route in the borough; Harold; Samuel; Frank; Charlotte; Howard; and Harry. All these children are at home with their parents.

FRANKLIN BUCKMAN. Prominent among the old residents of Bucks county is Franklin Buckman, of Upper Makefield township. Mr. Buckman is a son of Zenas Buckman, who was a farmer in Newtown, and married Mary Worthington. Of their nine children four survive: Spencer, who lives in Trenton; Amos, who is a resident of Newtown; George, who lives in Wrightstown township; and Franklin, mentioned at length hereinafter. Mr. Buckman, the father, died on his farm at Newtown at the comparatively early age of forty-five years.

Franklin Buckman, son of Zenas and Mary (Worthington) Buckman, was born October 9, 1823, and when a child was taken by his aunt, Margaret Worthington, who lived in Warwick township, where he remained until reaching his eighteenth year. He then began to work for farmers, and after three years became a tenant farmer. In 1857 he purchased the farm which has since been his home. He also owns two other farms in Upper Makefield township, where he is one of the leading citizens. He affiliates with Newtown Lodge, No. 225, F. and A. M., and is a Republican in politics. He is a member of the Society of Friends. 'Mr. Buckman married in 1845 Martha, daughter of Joseph Hampton, of Buckingham township, and the following children have been born to them: Edward H., who resides in Wrightstown township; Joseph, deceased; Walter, who lives in Upper Makefield; E. Smith, who is also a resident of Upper Makefield; Anna, who is the wife of Lemuel Hendrycks; Mary, who married Wilbert Trego, of Upper Makefield; Frank, who lives in Kansas; Sallie, who is the wife of John F. Adams, of New York state; Benjamin, deceased; Richard J., and Henry H. Buckman.

EDWARD HAMPTON BUCKMAN, one of the best known citizens of Newtown township, was born December 25, 1845, and was educated in the common schools. When about twenty years old he began to work by the year as a farm hand, and at the end of two years hired the "Gus Taylor farm," near Taylorsville. Seven years later he purchased his present farm of eighty-one acres, in Newtown township, where he has since resided. He is a good citizen and votes with the Republicans. Mr. Buckman married, June 6, 1867, Sarah H., daughter of Joshua Heston, of Upper Makefield township, and they are the parents of one son, Jesse, who is a blacksmith at Wood Hill, Upper Makefield.

ELIHU SMITH BUCKMAN. One of the progressive men of Upper Makefield township is Elihu Smith Buckman, son of Franklin and Martha Hampton Buckman. He was born February 4, 1852, on the homestead in Upper Makefield township, and received his education in the common schools. For twenty-three years he was a tenant farmer on different estates, and in 1898 bought the "Moses Van Horn farm" in Upper Makefield township. The property consists of ninety-five acres, and it is there that Mr. Buckman has resided since its purchase. For eight years he was a member of the school board, and has also served at different times as inspector of the electoral board. He is a member of Newtown Lodge, No. 427, F. and A. M., and endorses the principles of the Republican party. Mr. Buckman

married in October, 1875, Maggie, daughter of Joseph and Mary Ann (Young) Phillips, and they have four children: Harry, who is a farmer in Upper Mekefield; Mary, who is the wife of Albert File, of Stoops Corner; Raymond; and Ethel. The two last named reside at home.

WALTER BUCKMAN. A type of the active, enterprising citizen is found in Walter Buckman, of Upper Makefield township. He is a son of Franklin and Martha (Hampton) Buckman, and was born June 4, 1857, at Dolington, Bucks county, and obtained his education in the common schools. He worked on the home farm until the spring of 1880, when he moved to Taylorsville and there engaged in the coal, lime, and lumber business, which he conducted until 1894. In that year he disposed of the business and turned his attention to farming, to which he has since devoted himself. For several years he served as school tax collector and for eight years was supervisor of the township. He is an adherent of the Republican party and a member of the Society of Friends. Mr. Buckman married in 1878, Ida, daughter of Joseph Phillips, of Trenton, New Jersey, and they are the parents of the following children: Charles, who lives in Upper Makefield township; Ambrose, who is also a resident of that township; Eva, Lela, Watson, Willard, Lulu, Edward, and Laura. Of these, all but the two eldest are at home with their parents.

LEVI S. MOYER. The pioneer ancestor of the branch of the Moyer family to which belongs Levi S. Moyer, a prosperous agriculturist of Chalfont, was the Rev. Peter Moyer, a native of Switzerland, who came to American in 1742, accompanied by his widowed mother, sister, and three brothers, William, Jacob and Henry. Peter, William and Henry settled in Springfield township, Bucks county, and Jacob at Center Valley, Lehigh county. They all became farmers, and were active members of the Mennonite church. The supposition is that Peter was a minister in Switzerland, and he was one of the early ministers of the church in Springfield township; Jacob was also a minister and preached in Saucon township. The year prior to their emigration to America they were the guests of friends who resided in the vicinity of Kerlock, Germany, whither they removed from their native land, Switzerland, during the persecution of the Mennonites by the Calvinists, or State Reformed church.

Rev. Peter Moyer (aforementioned) was born in Switzerland in 1723. He purchased a farm of one hundred and seven acres in Springfield township, formerly the property of Joseph Green, which he cultivated to a high state of perfection, and whereon he resided. By his marriage to ———— ————, which occurred May 28, 1752, the following named children were born; John, Jacob, William, Abraham, Henry, Isaac, Mary, and Barbara. William Moyer, son of the Rev. Peter Moyer, was born in Springfield township, Bucks county, Pennsylvania, June 7, 1764. His occupation was that of farmer, and in connection therewith he preached the gospel. He married Mary Overholt, who was born December 27, 1767, and who bore him six children, as follows: Magdaline, Nancy, Hannah, Kate, Mary, and Abraham D. The deaths of Mr. and Mrs. Moyer occurred February 12, 1848, and September 1, 1850, respectively.

Abraham D. Moyer, son of William and Mary (Overholt) Moyer, was born on the old Peter Moyer farm in Pleasant Valley, June 6, 1798. He followed in the footsteps of his forefathers, devoting his time and attention to the tilling of the soil. He was the possessor of a fine voice, and was the leader of the choir in the Monnonite church. In 1832 he married Mary Geisinger, a native of Upper Milford, Lehigh county, born September 18, 1811, daughter of Philip and Fanny (Hestand) Geisinger. Four children were born to them: William G.; Fanny, who became the wife of Nathaniel Bechtel; Mary; and Abraham. Abraham D. Moyer (father) died September 15, 1871; his wife survived him many years, passing away December 9, 1900.

William G. Moyer, eldest son of Abraham D. and Mary (Geisinger) Moyer, was born in Springfield township, Bucks county, February 14, 1834. His first occupation was that of teacher, which vocation he followed for ten years (1855 to 1865) and from the latter year until 1872 he was engaged in farming in Springfield township, after which he removed to New Britain township, and purchased a farm in the borough of Chalfont. He was the recipient of several public offices which were in the gift of his fellow-citizens, and during his incumbency of the same rendered valuable service. He was township auditor for six years, secretary of the school board for a similar period, jury commissioner for Bucks county, and first president of the council of Chalfont. For a number of years he served as correspondent and reporter for the government agricultural department. He is an active and consistent member of the Monnonite church, in which faith he was reared, and his political allegiance is given to the Republican party. In 1860 he married Mary Swortley, born in New Britain township, 1835, daughter

of John Swortley. Their children were as follows: Emma, born December 17, 1861, died January 9, 1881; Levi S., born May 22, 1864, mentioned hereinafter; Abraham S., born November 7, 1866, married Susie M. Fretz, and they are the parents of one child, Alvin, born October 18, 1900; William, born November 29, 1868, a merchant of Chalfont; Menno S., born November 18, 1870, a member of the firm of Moyer Bros., merchants of Lansdale; he married Annie Souder, and their children are: Evelyn and Elizabeth; Harvey, born March 16, 1877, married Mary Johnson. The mother of these children died January 2, 1888. Mr. Moyer married for his second wife Mrs. Hannah (Sleifer) Weis, who was born near Quakertown, Bucks county, daughter of Philip Sleifer.

Levi S. Moyer, eldest son of William G. and Mary (Swortley) Moyer, was born in Springfield township, Bucks county, Pennsylvania, May 22, 1864. He obtained a practical education in the public schools of New Britain township, and since the completion of his studies has devoted his time and attention exclusively to agricultural pursuits. He is an active and public-spirited citizen, keenly alive to everything that pertains to the welfare of the community in which he resides, a faithful member of the Mennonite church, and a stauch Republican. January 6, 1887, Mr. Moyer was married to Anna B. Detwiler, daughter of Enos and Sarah (Sherm) Detwiler, whose family consisted of five other children, namely: John F., William H., Irvin S., Alfred S., and Lizzie S. Detwiler. Eight children were the issue of the marriage of Mr. and Mrs. Moyer; William D., born December 25, 1887; Sarah Amelia, born July 27, 1889; Theresa, born October 23, 1891; Mary, born April 17, 1894; Irene, born February 2, 1897; Enos, born July 5, 1898; Eva, born February 9, 1900; and Norah, born June 25, 1901.

———————

WILLIAM BAUM, deceased, one of the best known and respected citizens of Bedminster township, was born in Springfield township, Bucks county, Pennsylvania, March 30, 1841, and was a descendant of early German settlers in that township. Heinrich or Henry Baum, the great-grandfather of the subject of this sketch, was one of a family of five brothers and two sisters, born in Wurtemberg, Germany, of which four of the brothers and one sister emigrated to America and settled in Bucks county, viz.: Carl or Charles, Heinrich, Michael, Susanna, and Philip Baum. Carl and Heinrich came together in the ship "Hero,' arriving in Philadelphia, October 27, 1764, and settled in Springfield township. Carl, the eldest of the fam-

ily, married Barbara Youngken, and after a residence of several years in
Springfield, removed with his family to
Carlisle, Cumberland county, Pennsylvania, and later removed to what was
then Northumberland county and from
thence, in 1798, to Northwestern Territory, now the State of Ohio, where he
died. His son Samuel, born in Springfield, Bucks county, August 16, 1769,
died in New Berlin, Union county, Pennsylvania, October 2, 1842. His other
eight children, most of whom lived and
died in Felicity, Ohio, were: Elizabeth,
wife of Peter Emery; Catharine, wife
of Benjamin Sells; Mary, wife of Peter
DeWitt; Susanna, wife of Thomas
Jones; Margaret, wife of Conrad Metz-
ger; Barbara, wife of Leonard Metz-
ger; Michael and Charles Baum. Michael, the third of the emigrant brothers,
also settled in Bucks county and reared
a family of ten children, as follows:
Samuel, who settled in Montgomery
county; Elizabeth, the wife of John
Trumbore, of Milford; Mary, wife of John
Trumbore; Ann, wife of John Gregg;
Catharine, wife of Jacob Werhold, of
Rockhill; Susan, wife of Jacob Willauer;
Michael, of Milton, Pennsylvania; Henry, of Montgomery county; Hannah,
wife of William Grafley; and Sarah, Phil-
lip, the youngest of the emigrant brothers, married Mary Moyer, settled in
New Britain township, where he died
at an advanced age, on March 1, 1841,
without issue. Susanna, the sister, married John Landis, of Milford township,
and had two sons: Samuel and Henry.
Another brother Samuel and a sister
lived and died in Wurtemberg.

Heinrich Baum, the second of the emigrant brothers, as before stated, arrived
in this country in 1764, and almost immediately after his arrival located in
Springfield township, where he took up
a tract of land on which he resided until his death in 1803. His wife's name
was Elizabeth, but her maiden name is
unknown by her descendants. They
were the parents of eleven children, all
of whom were born and reared in
Springfield, viz: Abraham, Anna, who
married John Landis and removed to
Warren county, New Jersey; Susanna,
who married Isaac Meyer, of Springfield; Elizabeth, who married Henry
Ackerman; Henry, the grandfather of
the subject of this sketch; Catharine,
who married Samuel Bleam; Hannah,
who married John Shelly; Margaret,
who married Henry Bleam; Barbara,
who married Michael Huddle; Philip,
who died in 1814, without issue; and
Mary, who married Joseph Moyer, and
died in 1815.

Henry Baum, second son and fifth
child of Heinrich and Elizabeth Baum,
was born and reared in Springfield township, Bucks county, and spent his whole
life there, dying in 1823. He married

Magdalene Moyer, daughter of William
Meyer, born in Springfield, June 17, 1767,
died there February 12, 1848, son of the
Reverend Peter Meyer, one of the early
Mennonite ministers of Bucks county, who
was born in Switzerland about 1723 and set-
tled in Springfield in 1752. The mother of
Magdalene (Moyer) Baum was Barbara
Overholt, who was born December 27, 1767,
and died September 1, 1850. The children
of Henry and Magdalene (Moyer)
Baum were: William, Joseph, Henry,
Elizabeth, wife of Henry Focht, of Le-
high county; and Mary, who married
Samuel Detweiler. After the death of
Henry Baum, his widow married John
Shantz and had three children: Abra-
ham, Lydia and Sarah.

Joseph Baum, second son of Henry
and Magdalene, was born in Springfield,
September 26, 1810. Left an orphan at
the age of thirteen years, he learned the
trade of a shoemaker with Christian
Moyer, of Hilltown township, and followed that trade until his marriage,
when he settled in Springfield township.
After a few years spent in agricultural
pursuits in Springfield he removed to
Bedminster township, where he resided
for a few years; returned again to
Springfield, but later again removed to
Bedminster where he purchased the
farm on which his son William lately
resided and passed the remainder of his
life there, dying April 28, 1892. He was
an active and prominent man in the
community, filling the office of school
director in Springfield township, and
that of supervisor for eighteen years in
Springfield and ten years in Bedminster.
He also served as township auditor. He
was a member of the New Mennonite
church. He married in 1828 Esther
Moyer, born August 3, 1808, daughter
of Christian and Barbara (Landis)
Moyer, and they were the parents of six
children: Hannah, widow of Jacob K.
Overholt, of Bedminster; Sarah, who
married Christian F. Meyers; Henry,
who married Hannah Moyer and resides
in Philadelphia; Joseph, who died in the
army in 1863; William, the subject of
this sketch; and Magdalena, who died at
the age of seven years.

William Baum, third son and fifth
child of Joseph and Esther (Moyer)
Baum, born in Springfield township,
March 30, 1841, received his education
at the public schools. Reared to the life
of a farmer he took charge of the home
farm at his marriage and cultivated it
for his father until 1873, when he purchased the farm; his parents continuing
to reside with him until their death. He
was one of the directors of Souderton
National Bank at the time of his decease, and had been for ten years a director of the Bucks County Fire Insurance Company. He was also a director
of the Dublin Mutual Insurance and
Protective Company from its organi-

zation in 1892 to the time of his death. He served a number of years in different local offices, filling the position of assistant assessor for nine years, and was census enumerator in 1890. He was elected to the office of director of the poor for Bucks county in 1897, and reelected in 1900, serving in all six years. He was a member of the Mennonite congregation at Deep Run, and politically was a Republican. Mr. Baum stood deservedly high in the regard and confidence of the people of Bucks county, and of the community in which he lived. He was a faithful and conscientious public servant, an earnest patriotic citizen, a devoted husband and father and an honest consistent Christian gentleman. His loss is keenly felt in the community. He died June 7, 1905, buried at Deep Run. Mr. Baum married, October 5, 1865, Maria Hunsicker, daughter of Jacob and Barbara (Moyer) Hunsicker, of Hilltown, Bucks county, granddaughter of Rev. Isaac and Anna Hunsicker, great-granddaughter of Jacob and Elizabeth Hunsicker, who came from the Skippack to Hilltown township in 1757, and a great-great-granddaughter of Valentine Hunsicker, who emigrated from Switzerland in 1717, and settled in Montgomery county. She is also a descendant through her mother, Barbara Moyer, born July 26, 1813, died August, 1890, from Heinrich Baum, the pioneer ancestor of her husband, her grandmother Susanna Bleam, wife of Samuel Moyer, of Hilltown, being a granddaughter of Heinrich and Elizabeth Baum. The children of William and Maria (Hunsicker) Baum are: Hannah, wife of Samuel H. Moyer, of Blooming Glen; Harvey H., who married Mary Shaddinger, and lives in Perkasie; Ida, wife of Edwin F. Stover, of Blooming Glen; Jacob, deceased; Joseph H., who married Lizzie Detweiler and lives on the homestead; Edwin, deceased; William Garfield married Mary Overholt; and Nora, who resides at home.

CHRISTIAN TREICHLER CLYMER. Bucks county has no more useful citizen than Christian Treichler Clymer, of Quakertown. The Clymer family is of German origin, the name having been formerly spelled Klemmer. It was brought to this country by two brothers, one of whom was Christian Clymer, or Klemmer. He was born in 1697 in Germany, and is thought to have emigrated to America prior to 1730. He settled in what is now Lower Milford township, and in 1734 his name appeared on the record as a petitioner to divide the township. His wife was Barbara ———, and they were the parents of seven sons and five daughters. Among the sons was Jacob, mentioned at length hereinafter. Christian Clymer died in 1759, and some of his descendants are yet living on the land which he settled. His wife passed away January 14, 1776.

Jacob Clymer, son of Christian and Barbara Clymer, was born in 1729, and was the father of a numerous family, among whom was Henry, who married Maria, daughter of Peter and Maria (Zeingenfus) Shaffer, of Northampton county. They were the parents of seven sons and two daughters. Among the sons was Henry Shaffer, mentioned at length hereinafter. All the descendants of Christian Clymer were born in the region in which that pioneer ancestor made his home.

Henry Shaffer Clymer, son of Henry and Maria (Shaffer) Clymer, was born in 1819, on his father's farm, near Milford Square. He attended the subscription school, also the Friends Richland Meeting, and learned the shoemaker's trade, which he followed in connection with farming. In politics he was an old line Whig, and later became a Republican. He was a member of the Lutheran church, which he served as deacon and was active in religious work. He married Lavina, daughter of Jacob and Sarah (Trumbauer) Treichler, and ten children were born to them, among whom was Christian Treichler, mentioned at length hereinafter. Mrs. Clymer, the mother of the family, died in 1859, and her husband passed away in January, 1863.

Christian Treichler Clymer, son of Henry Shaffer and Lavina (Treichler) Clymer, was born February 10, 1846, on his father's farm, near Milford Square, Milford township. He attended the public schools of his native place, and remained on the farm until his eighteenth year, when he was apprenticed to learn the shoemaker's trade with Isaac Groff, near Quakertown. At the end of two years he became a journeyman, and for six months worked near Zion's Hill. In the autumn of 1866 he moved to Quakertown, where he engaged in business as a custom shoemaker on Main street, near the Friends' meeting-house. He carried on a flourishing trade until April, 1903, when he retired from business. Mr. Clymer has always taken an active interest in local political affairs, and for thirteen years was a member of the board of education, serving two terms as president and two as treasurer. He has also acted as delegate to the county convention. On March 18, 1903, he received the appointment of postmaster of Quakertown, an office which he still holds, discharging its duties with credit to himself and satisfaction to the government. His political principles are those advocated and upheld by the Republican party. Since 1864 he has been a member of St. John's Lutheran church, to

John R. Johnson

which his family also belong. He is a member of the choir, and has served ten years as treasurer of the Sunday school, in which he has been a teacher since 1864.

Mr. Clymer married, January 29, 1869, Andora, daughter of Samuel and Catharine (Trumbauer) Troxel, of Montgomery county, and they have one son, Benjamin Franklin, who was born September, 1870, attended the Quakertown public schools, and is now a commercial traveller, residing in Wilmington, Delaware. C. T. Clymer married in 1884, for his second wife, Margaret, daughter of David and Rachel (Kulp) Kulp, of Skippack township, Montgomery county, and they have one son, William Kulp Clymer, who was born June 20, 1886, and was educated in the Quakertown public schools, graduating in 1903. He holds the office of assistant postmaster.

JOHN R. JOHNSON. Martin Johnson was the emigrant ancestor of the family to which John R. Johnson, of Lumberville, belongs. He came from England, where his birth occurred on the 5th of May, 1755, and located on Bools Island, now Raven Rock, Hunterdon county, New Jersey, where he acquired extensive farming lands and other property, becoming one of the wealthy citizens of his community.

John Johnson, son of Martin Johnson, was born and reared on the old homestead secured by his father, and he, too, followed the occupation of farming. He married Sarah E. Bray, and their son, Albert R. Johnson, became the father of John R. Johnson. He was born on the old homestead in Hunterdon county, New Jersey, August 3, 1833, was there reared, and in later years acquired possession of the old home property, upon which he resided until 1844, when he retired and removed to Stockton, where he now resides. He was very successful in his agricultural pursuits, and acquired a very desirable competence. He has long been a member of the Presbyterian church. He married Margaret A. Dilts, who died April 8, 1893, at the age of sixty years, six months and twenty-two days. She was a member of the Dunkard church. They had six children, of whom five are living: John R.; Clark B., who occupies the old homestead; Catherine, wife of Wilmot Quinby, of Solebury township; Rachael, wife of Theodore L. Green, of Union county, New Jersey; and Sarah, wife of Eden B. Hunt, of Stockton, New Jersey.

John R. Johnson was born in Hunterdon county, New Jersey, April 22, 1854, and the first nineteen years of his life were spent upon his father's farm, during which time he acquired a public school education. In 1873 he went to Lambertville, New Jersey, where he accepted a position in a mercantile establishment and there laid the foundation for his later successful mercantile career. He remained there for two years and in 1875 came to Lumberville, accepting a position in the store of Reading & Shaddinger, acting as clerk in the establishment for two years, when he purchased the interest of Mr. Shaddinger, and the firm name was changed to Reading & Johnson, this connection being maintained until 1892, when Mr. Johnson became sole owner of the business. He has developed an enterprise of considerable importance, and his annual sales now bring a good financial return, his business principles being based upon the rules which govern strict, unswerving integrity and unabating industry. Politically Mr. Johnson is a Democrat. He belongs to Black City Lodge, No. 391, I. O. O. F., of Black City, and he and his wife are active members of the Baptist church, to the support of which he contributes generously.

In 1879 Mr. Johnson married Miss Marietta Bodine, of Stockton, New Jersey, a daughter of William and Mary (Bellis) Bodine. Her brother, Wesley Bodine, now deceased, was for many years sheriff of Hunterdon county, New Jersey. Mr. and Mrs. Johnson had three children, but lost their elder son, Raymond D. Bessie K. and Wilmot Q. are at home. The daughter is a graduate of the George school, has been a close student since the completion of her course there, now holds a state certificate and at the present writing (1904) is teaching in Solebury township.

JOHN S. CORNELL, who has now passed the seventy-seventh milestone on life's journey, and throughout his business career has followed farming, is a representative of one of the old families of Pennsylvania, a son of John and Elizabeth (Vandegrift) Cornell, and a grandson of Gilliam and Janetje (Suydam) Cornell. His grandfather, Gilliam Cornell, had a brother, Remsen Cornell, who had two children, a son, Adrien, and a daughter.

Gilliam Cornell had eight children: 1. Adrien married Rachel Feaster and had four children, David, William, Henry and Jane. 2. Lambert married a Miss Feaster, and their children were: Gilliam, David, James and Aaron. 3. James married a daughter of Remsen Cornell, and his second wife was Margaret Vandergrift, by whom he had four children, Jacob, Remsen, Cornelia Ann and Jane. 4. John was the father of John S. Cornell, of Northampton township. 5. Gilliam married Elizabeth Krewson. 6. Jane married Christopher

Van Artsdalen, and their children were John, Simon, Jane, Johanna and Elizabeath. 8. Abbie married Henry Dubois, and had six children: Christian, Susan, Ellen, Nancy, Jane and Mary Ann.

John S. Cornell, Sr., son of Gilliam and Janetje Cornell, was born in 1782, baptized at the Dutch Reformed church of North and Southampton. He was devised by his father a farm purchased by the latter of Henry Dyer in 1793, containing 105 acres, near Holland, and lived there until he died, December 15, 1851. He was married twice. His first wife was Mary Krewson, by whom he had two children. Matilda, the younger, born October 21, 1813, died in childhood. Elizabeth, the elder, was born March 6, 1811, and became the wife of Thomas Purdy, by whom she had six children: Mary Jane, John, Elizabeth Ann, Matilda, Mrs. Catherine Lingerman, and Amanda. For his second wife John S. Cornell, Sr., chose Elizabeth Vandegrift, (daughter of Jacob and Cornelia (Vanartsdalen) Vandegrift, of Northampton and sister to Margaret, the second wife of his brother, James Cornell. The children of John S. and Elizabeth (Vandegrift) Cornell were: 1. William, born August 4, 1818, remained on the homestead; he married Cornelia Krewsen, and their children were Edmond and Anna Mary. 2. Mary, born October 8, 1819, married James Craven and their children were Annie, Charles, Elizabeth and Matilda. 3. Alfred, born September 27, 1822, married Jane Van Buskirk, and their children were: Elizabeth, Johanna, Samuel, Matilda, Allen, Frank, John, Albert, Mary and Susannah. 4. John S., the subject of this sketch. 5. Louisa, born July 9, 1825, married Isaac Rightley.

John S. Cornell, Jr., youngest son of John S. and Elizabeth (Vandegrift) Cornell, is descended in the maternal line from Jacob Vandegrift, who served in the Revolutionary war and afterward removed to Northampton county, Pennsylvania, settling in the southeastern part. It was his daughter who became the mother of John S. Cornell, of this review.

John S. Cornell, who was born July 16, 1827, was reared to farm life, and was educated near Holland, in Northampton county, Pennsylvania. He engaged in farming at an early age and has followed this occupation to the present time. He resided near the Bear Hotel, at Richboro, until 1877, when he removed to his present farm, purchasing eighty acres of land in Northampton township, which his labors have placed under a very high state of cultivation, and although now well advanced in years he still gives his personal supervision to its cultivation.

Mr. Cornell wedded Ellen Bennett, a daughter of William and Sarah (Wynkoop) Bennett, and through long years they have been held in favorable regard in Northampton township. Mrs. Cornell's ancestors in both paternal and maternal lines were, like those of her husband, of Holland descent, and among the earliest settlers in Northampton and Southampton counties. Mr. and Mrs. Cornell have had no children.

JACOB SCHEERER, of Buckingham, was born in Hilltown township, Bucks county, August 29, 1850, the son of Christian and Lovina (Cassel) Scheerer. Christian Scheerer was born in Wurtemberg, Germany, in November, 1813, and came to this country when a young man. As a youth he had learned the trade of a dyer, and was employed in the Manayunk mills of Ripka & Co., in Montgomery county, Pennsylvania, for about twenty-five years. On April 2, 1850, he purchased of his father-in-law, Jacob Cassel, a small farm in Hilltown township, Bucks county, and lived thereon until his death in 1897. In 1847 he married Lovina, daughter of Jacob and Elizabeth (Oberholtzer) Cassel, of Hilltown. The Cassels emigrated to this country about 1740, and have been residents of Montgomery county for several generations. Jacob Cassel was a farmer in Hilltown township from the time of his marriage. Christian Scheerer was a man of fair education, and took an active interest in the affairs of his adopted country. In early life he was a Whig, but later a Democrat. In religion he was a member of the Lutheran church. He was a member of the I. O. O. F. His wife was born in Hilltown in 1821, and died in 1900. She was a member of the German Reformed church.

The subject of this sketch was the second of the three children of Christian and Lovina Scheerer, his elder brother John is still living and a younger brother, Charles, is deceased. He was reared on the farm and received his education at the public schools. At the age of seventeen he apprenticed himself to learn the shoemaker's trade at Hockertown. Finishing his apprenticeship in 1869, he worked as a journeyman shoemaker for seven years in Hilltown, Hatfield, Pennsburg and Line Lexington. In 1876 he came to Buckingham and opened a shop, where he now resides. In 1875 he married Ann Rebecca, daughter of Aaron and Letitia (McDowell) Carver, of Buckingham, by whom he has three children: Carrie, residing at home; Walter, a trainman on the P. & R. R. R.; and Evan T., a printer, now foreman of the composing room of the "Doylestown Democrat," at Doylestown. In politics Mr. Scheerer is a Democrat. He is a member of Doylestown Lodge, No. 94, I. O. O. F.

DR. NOAH S. NONAMAKER, a well-known physician of Bedminster, Bucks county, Pennsylvania, was there born March 23, 1854. He is a descendant of Adam Nonamaker, a native of this county and of foreign parentage. His parents came to this country about 1747. Adam Nonamaker was born April 21, 1759, lived in Hilltown township, and was a farmer throughout the active years of his life. He married Miss Barbara Kramer, born March 5, 1763, died April 27, 1821. They had one child, Henry, the grandfather of Noah S. Adam Nonamaker died August 28, 1843, and is buried at the Tohickon church burying ground.

Henry Nonamaker was born in Hilltown township, July 31, 1786. He carried on for many years the business of undertaker and cabinetmaker very successfully in Bedminster. He, with all his family, was noted for skill as workers in wood. He married Miss Elizabeth Rosenberger, born November 25, 1785, died in Bedminster township, April 7, 1845. There were seven children born of this union, four sons and three daughters: Charles, died at the age of about seventy-two; Henry died at the age of seventy-five; Maria died at the age of seventy-five, was the widow of Peter Stout; Elias, died at the age of about seventy-two from injuries sustained from a falling tree; Rebecca died at the age of sixty-five; Elizabeth died in early childhood; and Aaron, father of Noah S., died March 17, 1885, in the seventy-first year of his age. Henry Nonamaker, father of these children, died in Bedminster township, September 16, 1871.

Aaron Nonamaker, the father of Noah S., was born in Rockhill township, June 26, 1814. He was brought up to farming and for fourteen years after his marriage farmed the home place in Bedminster township, and then purchased a small place near Perkasie, where he lived for nearly thirty years. He was an honest and upright man and though without education enjoyed the confidence and respect of the entire community. His wife was Anna Shutt, of Horsham township, Montgomery county. She was born March 5, 1815, and died in 1894, in the seventy-ninth year of her age. Their children are: 1. Debaroh, widow of Charles Wise, resides in Perkasie; 2. Elizabeth, deceased; 3. Jacob, a resident of Perkasie; 4. Noah S. Aaron Nonamaker laid down the burden of life at his home in Perkasie, March 17, 1885, in the seventy-first year of his age.

Noah S. Nonamaker attended the district school until he was thirteen years old, then worked at farming and later engaged in mechanical pursuits for ten years. He was a great reader and student, and while working in the vicinity of Doylestown attracted the attention of Dr. F. Swartzlaider, who enabled him to satisfy his love for the study of medicine, and while continuing to work industriously he began reading for the profession under the instruction of Dr. Swartzlaider. He began his collegiate course in 1877, graduating from the Jefferson Medical School, Philadelphia, Pennsylvania, in 1879. He at once came to Bedminster, where he has built up for himself a large and enviable practice. Dr. Nonamaker is identified with the Doylestown lodge No. 245, F. and A. M., the Bucks County Medical Society, and the State Medical Society. He is emphatically a self-made man, starting in life without advantages of any kind, supporting himself by industrious work in the daytime, and with assiduous study at night. With rare energy, perseverance and indomitable courage he has become a well read and successful member of the honored profession. March 15, 1883, Dr. Nonamaker married Lizzie, a daughter of Abraham Beans, of Sellersville. She was born September 8, 1857. Six children were born of this union: Annie Lucretia, deceased; Edgar Vasco, who graduated from Perkiomen Seminary in 1905, and is going to prepare for the ministry at Muhlenburg College; Claudius Howard, deceased; Bessie Gertrude, deceased; Mattie Pauline, deceased; and Celia Helen. The mother of these children died June 26, 1895.

ROBERT BROWN, late of Lower Makefield, deceased, was born on the old homestead where he spent most of his life and where his widow and two daughters still reside. This homestead is a part of a plantation that has been in the family for two hundred and twenty-five years, having been originally taken up by George Brown, who came from Leicestershire, England, and landed at New Castle in 1679, proceeding thence up the Delaware to Bucks county. His wife Mercy came over on the same ship with him and they were married at New Castle on their arrival. Tradition states that he had been courting her sister in Leicestershire, but that on her refusal to accompany him to America, he proposed to Mercy to accompany him. They were members of the Society of Friends, and among the first members of Falls Meeting. They were the parents of fifteen children, several of whom died in infancy. Eight sons and three daughters survived; of the latter one married a Titus, another a Stackhouse, and the third, Mercy, married Robert Sotcher, son of William Penn's trusted steward, John Sotcher, many years a member of colonial assembly. George Brown was born in 1644, and died in 1726.

Samuel Brown, son of George and

Mercy, was born 9-11-1694, and married, 5-9-1717, Ann Clark and had five children, viz.: George, who married (first) Martha Worrell and (second) Elizabeth Field; John, see forward; Mercy, who married Joshua Baldwin; Ann, who married Joseph Lovett; and Esther, who married Daniel Lovett, Samuel Brown died 10-3-1769.

John Brown, second son of Samuel and Ann (Clark) Brown, was born 8-29-1724. He was known as "Fox Hunting John Brown" to distinguish him from his cousins of the same name, and was a prominent man in the community. He settled on the Newport road, near Emilie, where he died 1-1-1802. His wife was Ann Field, daughter of Benjamin Field, a trustee of the loan office in 1743 and a member of colonial assembly 1738-1745. John and Ann (Field) Brown were the parents of nine children: Samuel, the eldest, born 11-1-1751, died 1813, married Abi White and was the father of General Jacob Brown; 2. John, born 1753, died 1821, married Martha Harvey; 3. Benjamin, born 1754, married Jane Wright; 4. David, born 1756, died 1777; 5. Sarah, born 6-11-1758, married Samuel Allen; 6. Mary, born 1761, died 1777; 7. Charles, born 3-27-1762, see forward; 8. William, born 1764, died 1764; 9. Elizabeth, born 12-11-1765, died 1824, married Mahlon Yardley in 1787.

Charles Brown, the seventh child of John and Ann, resided on the Milford road, two miles from Fallsington. He married in 12 mo., 1784, Charlotte Palmer. He was a farmer and a member of Falls Meeting. He died 9-20-1834. Charles and Charlotte were the parents of thirteen children, five of whom died in infancy and three daughters, Mary, Martha and Mercy, died in early life, unmarried. Those who survived were: Joshua, born 1785, married Sarah Lovett; Benjamin, born 8-18-1787, see forward; Joseph, born 1789, never married, was drowned in the Neshaminy in 1863; Alice, born 1792, married John Moon.

Benjamin Brown, second son of Charles and Charlotte, born 8-18-1787, married 6 mo., 1811, Mary, daughter of Isaac Barnes and Martha Brown, his wife, the latter being a daughter of George Brown (3), above mentioned, who had married Elizabeth Field. After his marriage Benjamin Brown went to live on the old homestead which for two generations had been in the branch of the family to which his wife belonged, and died there 9-10-1879. Benjamin and Mary (Barnes) Brown were the parents of nine children, three of whom died young. Isaac, the eldest son, born 2-5-1815, married Sarah C. Smith, and is still living in Newtown; William, born 10-25-1817, married Huldah Pettit, of Philadelphia, and died 4-17-1877; Robert,

see forward; Joseph, born 12-28-1824, died in 1903, he married Phebe Stackhouse; Joshua, born 2-3-1831, is still living in Philadelphia, he married Sarah Hance; Charlotte, born 1834, married Herbert Galbraith, of Philadelphia, and died in 1879.

Robert S. Brown, the third son of Benjamin and Mary (Barnes) Brown, was born on the old homestead, 1-24-1820. He married, 10-19-1871, Caroline Barnes, daughter of John R. S. and Mary D. (Loud) Barnes, and granddaughter of Isaac Barnes, who was a cousin to Isaac Barnes, the grandfather of her husband. Her maternal grandfather, Thomas Loud manufactured the first upright piano ever built in this country; it is now on exhibition at Memorial Hall, Philadelphia. Before his marriage Robert S. Brown removed to Philadelphia and carried on the milk business for some years, and then returned to the old homestead, where he died February 17, 1903. His widow and children still reside there. His children are: Mary, born 9-7-1872, and Charlotte, born 1-19-1876. The latter married, 6-12-1900, Nicholas Brewer Davis; they have two children: Lynn David, born August 1, 1901, and Dorothy Wayne Davis, born May 17, 1904. The family are members of the Society of Friends.

PHILIP C. SWARTLEY, of Line Lexington, Bucks county, belongs to a family that has been prominent in the affairs of the section in which he resides for five generations. His paternal ancestor, Philip Schwartley, was born in Eppingen, in Necker Grand Duchy of Baden, Germany, October 28, 1764, and accompanied his elder brothers John and Jacob to America in the ship "Minerva," arriving in Philadelphia September 30, 1772. The Schwartley brothers located for a time in Franconia township, Montgomery county, Pennsylvania, where Philip married Sarah Rosenberger, born January 24, 1765, daughter of the Rev. Henry and Barbara (Obenholtzer) Rosenberger, and granddaughter of Henry Rosenberger, the pioneer ancestor of the family in America. Philip Schwartley about the year 1790 settled in New Britain township, and became a large landholder and prominent citizen of that township. He died September 23, 1840, and his wife Sarah died April 6, 1849. They were the parents of nine children, the sixth of whom, Abraham Swartley, was the grandfather of Philip C. Swartley. He was born in New Britain township and resided there all his life, becoming a large landholder and a prominent and useful citizen. He died November 17, 1879. He was twice married, his first wife being Anna Delp, daughter of John Delp, of New Britain, also of German descent, whose family,

like that of her husband, were of the Mennonite faith. Abraham and Anna (Delp) Swartley were the parents of four children: Henry D., Philip, Abraham, and Sarah, who died young. Abraham Swartley married (second) Barbara Hunsicker, who survived him, and had four children; Isaac, who died young; John; Anna, wife of Levi Henge; and Sarah, who married Joseph Hyer.

Henry D. Swartley, eldest son of Abraham and Anna (Delp) Swartley, was born in New Britain township. Soon after his marriage he settled in Hilltown township, where he followed the life of a farmer. He married Sarah Clymer, daughter of Henry and Elizabeth (Kulp) Clymer, and they were the parents of five children: Annie, wife of Milton D. Alderfer; Abraham C., who married Sallie Detweiler; Philip C., the subject of this sketch; Henry C., who married Elizabeth Myers; and Sarah, who married David B. Beidler, of Philadelphia.

PHILIP C. SWARTLEY, a son of Henry D. and Sarah (Clymer) Swartley, was born in Hilltown, Bucks county, Pennsylvania, July 15, 1860. He acquired his education at the public schools of Hilltown township, the North Wales high school and at Perkiomen Seminary. He worked on his father's farm until sixteen years of age, and then taught school in Hilltown during the years 1876, 1877 and 1878. He then began farming, which he has since followed in connection with the vocation of an auctioneer. He also does an extensive business in the sale of live stock on commission. In 1900 he purchased his present farm at Line Lexington, which he has since conducted. In politics he is a staunch Republican, and is one of the local leaders of his party in that section, serving for several years as a member of the county committee. He has filled the position of township assessor for four years, and has occupied other township offices. In religion he is a Mennonite. He is a member of the Order of Knights of Maccabees, and is affiliated with other beneficial organizations. He married Helen Leidy, daughter of Isaiah and Elizabeth (Swartz) Leidy, and they have been the parents of six children: Warren, deceased; Elizabeth; Raymond; Margaret; Edmund; and Paul, deceased.

LOUIS AUGUSTUS HOGUET, for sixty years a public-spirited and influential citizen of Bristol, Bucks county, Pennsylvania, was born May 5, 1822, in the city of Philadelphia, a son of Francis Augustus and Mary (Collins) Hoguet, who were the parents of six children: Josephine and Francis (twins), Louis Augustus, Adelaide, Lucien and Mary. Francis A. Hoguet (father) emigrated to America and located in Philadelphia, Pennsylvania, where he engaged in business as a jeweler on a large scale. He is a descendant of a French ancestry, and was born and died in France.

Louis A. Hoguet attended the schools of Philadelphia, and after completing his studies learned the drug business, being employed in a wholesale and retail drug house, and at the age of twenty-two came to Bristol, Bucks county, and opened the first drug store in that section of the county. This was in the year 1844, and he conducted that business very successfully from that date to the time of his decease, June 23, 1904. He was a man of excellent judgment, a careful adviser, and one who had the full confidence of his business and social associates. He occupied a prominent position among the business men of the town of his adoption. He was one of the oldest directors of the Farmers' National Bank, his term of service in this capacity being the longest of any in its history. He was treasurer of the Bristol Water Company, and sometimes called "its father;" was president of the Bristol Gas Company; and an ardent friend to all measures that in his judgment would improve the borough or be helpful to his fellow-citizens. He was for many years an active member of Bristol Fire Company, No 1, having been a charter member of this organization. He was a member of the Masonic fraternity, affiliating with Bristol Lodge, No. 25, Ancient York Free and Accepted Masons, and a member of the Independent Order of Odd Fellows, of Bristol. He was one of the originators and for many years the treasurer of the first Building and Loan Association in Bristol, the first meeting for organization being held in his store. He was a painstaking methodical man of business, his characteristics winning for him the confidence and esteem of the entire community.

On March 9, 1844, Mr. Hoguet married Mary Louisa Murphy, of Philadelphia, and the issue of this union was the following named children: Thomas Henry, deceased, who was educated at Louisburg Seminary; Clara became the wife of J. Ross Calhoun, whose father was Admiral Edwin Calhoun, of the United States navy, deceased; Albert, deceased; William, deceased; Clifford, deceased; Ellen, who received her education at Chelton Hills, and became the wife of Winfield Scott Wintermute, of Mauch Chunk, Pennsylvania, and they are the parents of five children: Louis Hoguet; Clara, who became the wife of William R. Pierce, of Philadelphia; Edith, who became the wife of Louis Conant, of Montevista, California, and they are the parents of one child, Emily; and Helen. Mrs. Hoguet, the mother of these children, died about 1860. On February 26, 1862, Mr. Hoguet married Maria Hellings, of Bristol, Bucks county, daughter of Joseph A. and Susan (Richards) Hellings. The issue of this union was one child, Annie, born September 19, 1869, who was educated at St. Mary's Hall, Burlington, New Jersey, and on October 23, 1894, became the wife of Richard Henry Morris, of Bristol, Pennsylvania, son of Captain Richard Henry and Alice (Vanuxem) Morris, now living at Germantown, Pennsylvania, and they are the parents of three children: Charlotte, born December 1, 1895; Richard Henry, born May 14, 1897; and Margaret, born September 1, 1898. This family is now living in Germantown, Pennsylvania.

JOHN JOSEPH KILCOYNE, the genial proprietor of the Closson House at Bristol, Bucks county, Pennsylvania, was born at Holmesburg, Philadelphia. September 30, 1864, and is a son of Michael and Margaret (McGinnis) Kilcoyne, the former of whom was a well-known contractor and builder of Holmesburg.

John J. Kilcoyne was educated at the Holmesburg Academy, and at the close of his school days learned the trade of a mason with his father and worked at the same for about twelve years. In the spring of 1897 he came to Bristol and assumed the management of the old and popular ‘hostelry, known as the Closson House, and on April 3, 1900, became its proprietor and has since conducted it in an efficient manner, maintaining its old-time reputation as one of the leading hostelries of lower Bucks. Mr. Kilcoyne is the Exalted Ruler of the Elks Lodge of Bristol.

Mr. Kilcoyne married, September 20, 1894, Theresa Marie Antoinette Farley, daughter of James and Elizabeth Jane (Leslie) Farlev, of Bristol, and granddaughter of Thomas and Ann (Brady) Farley, and two children were the issue of this union: John Leslie, born July 30, 1895, now a student at St. Dominic's, Holmesburg, and Anita, born July 26, 1897, now attending the Sacred Heart Academy at Torresdale. James Leslie, maternal grandfather of Mrs. Kilcoyne, who was a well-known resident of Bristol, Pennsylvania, for many years, was a native of Ireland, from whence he came to America and settled at Mauch Chunk, Pennsylvania, later locating in Bristol, and becoming the owner of boats on the Lehigh Valley canal. He was also the owner of the "Exchange Hotel," in Bristol. James Leslie married Mary Boyle, who bore him a family of six children, four of whom attained years of maturity, as follows: Elizabeth J., Henry, a physician and druggist; James,

an attorney; and Mary A., who became the wife of John W. Closson. John W. Closson, now deceased, was born near Point Pleasant, Tinicum township, June 16, 1839, a son of George W. and Charlotte (Wyker) Closson, natives of Bucks county, and a grandson of William and Sarah Closson and Henry and Mary Wyker. John W. Closson was educated at Point Pleasant, and clerked in stores for his father and brother until the outbreaking of the civil war, when he joined the Doylestown Guards, April, 1861. Upon his return home he engaged in mercantile business for himself at Point Pleasant, continuing the same until his marriage to Mary A. Leslie, above mentioned, after which he moved to the "Exchange Hotel" in Bristol, which he purchased in 1872 of his father-in-law, James Leslie, and in 1875 remodeled, and which has since been known as the Closson House. In 1872 Mr. Closson was elected coroner, and by a special act of the legislature he was empowered to appoint deputies throughout the county of Bucks, and served six years, when his health failing him, he gave up political life and turned his attention to his hotel, where he died November 8, 1882. Mrs. Closson took charge of the hotel at once, and being a lady of excellent mind and business talent, she made the house one of the most popular in the state. Owing to the increase in trade, she erected a fine three-story brick building with pressed brick front and all the most modern improvements; the chambers of the house are spacious, handsomely furnished, well ventilated and comfortable, and the parlors and reception rooms are attractive and elegant. Mrs. Closson, who was an aunt of Mrs. John J. Kilcoyne, reared Mrs. Kilcoyne to womanhood and at the death of the former she left the Hotel Closson to her, which is now being managed by her husband, John J. Kilcoyne.

ELMER L. JOHNSON, a representative of that class of men whose active careers are spent in the quiet but useful calling of agriculture, was born on the old Johnson homestead in Bensalem township, Bucks county, Pennsylvania, February 8, 1860. His parents were Jesse L. and Anna P. (Levis) Johnson, and his grandparents were Clark and Rachel (Grim) Johnson.

Clark Johnson (grandfather) was born on the old Johnson tract, which consisted of between six and seven hundred acres, owned by his father, who divided it among his five children, and the farm of one hundred and fifty acres farmed by Elmer L. Johnson, whose name heads this review, is all that remains in the family at the present time

(1904). Clark Johnson followed farming as a means of livelihood, his products finding a ready market. He was a vestryman of the Episcopal church, and his political affiliations were with the Democratic party. He married Rachel Grim, who was a native of Delaware county, Pennsylvania, and their children were: John, who was a merchant of Hulmeville; Adaline, who became the wife of C. M. Henry; Ann, who became the wife of Frank Wood; and Jesse L., who is mentioned hereinafter. Both Mr. and Mrs. Johnson lived many years beyond the allotted scriptural age of three score years and ten, he dying at the age of eighty-four, and she at the age of eighty-six.

Jesse L. Johnson (father) was born on the old homestead in Bensalem township, September 5, 1822. He attended the district school at Eddington, and after completing his education settled on the old homestead, where he followed agricultural pursuits successfully during his lifetime. Like his father, Mr. Johnson served in the capacity of vestryman of the Episcopal church, and cast his vote for the candidates of the Democratic party. He was a member of the Independent Order of Odd Fellows. He was united in marriage to Anna P. Levis, a daughter of Robert Levis, a tanner of Mt. Holly, New Jersey, later of Maryland. Mrs. Johnson was reared by her aunt, Eliza Renshaw, of Eddington. Ten children were the issue of this marriage, namely: Lizzie, Elmer L., Mary, Josephine, Clark, deceased; Louisa, deceased; Clara, John, Jesse, deceased; and Annie. Jesse L. Johnson (father) died September 25, 1901; his wife passed away May 12, 1895, after one day's illness.

Elmer L. Johnson attended the public schools at Eddington, thereby acquiring a practical education which qualified him for the many duties and responsibilities of life. He engaged in farming pursuits, having become familiar with that line of work by assisting his father, and in due course of time succeeded to the old homestead of one hundred and fifty acres, which is one of the best cultivated and most productive farms in that section of Bucks county. The neat and thrifty appearance of the property bespeaks the careful supervision of one thoroughly versed in the details of farm work. Mr. Johnson follows in the footsteps of his forefathers in religious and political affairs, being a vestryman of the Episcopal church, and a Democrat. He is interested in all matters pertaining to the welfare of the community, and in every relation of life has proved himself an honorable and conscientious man. On April 2, 1890, Mr. Johnson was married to Elizabeth I. Schaffer, who was born in Bucks county, Pennsylvania, a daughter of Godfrey Schaffer. Their children are: Jessie A., born April 30, 1894; Helen I., born January 1, 1899; and Elizabeth V., born December 3, 1903.

J. HERMAN BARNSLEY. Thomas Barnsley, major in "His Majesties 60th Royal American Regiment of Foot," came with his regiment to America during the French and Indian War of 1756. At the close of the war he resigned his commission and returning to England brought over to Bucks county his wife Bersheba and his nephew John Barnsley. In 1763 he purchased six hundred acres in Bensalem, part of the Tatham tract, and erected thereon a handsome and commodious mansion house, the bricks for which were brought from England. He died in 1771, and his wife died some years earlier. The property was sold by his executors to John Swift in 1772, and remained in the Swift family until 1883, when it was purchased by Sallie B., wife of Dr. Richard Dingee. The mansion house is still standing.

John Barnsley inherited a fourth interest in his uncle's estate, but it was paid him in Continental money and became practically worthless. He was one of the committee for driving off cattle in Bensalem to prevent them from falling into the hands of the British, and was with Washington's army in January, 1777, in the march from Trenton to Princeton, his team having been impressed to haul ammunition. He purchased a farm in Newton township, where he lived until his death, February 2, 1796. His wife was Elizabeth Van Court, who was born at Huntingdon Valley in 1751, and died in 1824. The children of John and Elizabeth (Van Court) Barnsley were: Thomas, born January 21, 1774, removed to Maryland; WILLIAM, born November 8, 1775; Mary, born March 21, 1778; Elizabeth, born August 3, 1780; George, born November 8, 1783; Moses, born February 23, 1788; Sarah, born March 10, 1791; and Ann, born October 14, 1795.

William Barnsley, second son of John and Elizabeth, married Jane Van Horn, born in Makefield, July 25, 1784, and died July 25, 1861. They were married January 21, 1808. Their children were: Mary, born 1809, died unmarried January 16, 1889; John, born August 26, 1811; Thomas C., born October 21, 1815, died September 5, 1866, and Joseph Barnsley, born June 9, 1820, died near Hartsville, January 12, 1888. William Barnsley died at Newtown, August 21, 1848.

John Barnsley, eldest son of William and Jane, resided on the homestead at Newtown until his death, January 11, 1880. He was a justice of the peace for thirty-five years, and transacted a great deal of business in settlement of estates and in transfers of real estate. He was a man of more than ordinary ability and very much respected in the community. He was county treasurer about 1848. He married October 27, 1835, Mary Hough, born October 15, 1814, in Doylestown township, daughter of Benjamin and Hannah (Simpson) Hough, and a first cousin to the mother of General U. S. Grant. She died at Newton, September 25, 1895. Their children are: Anna J., born 1836, married Captain Henry Y. Pickering; William, born February 17, 1838, died October 27, 1902, married Mary Ellen Paff, and has one daughter, Lily H., the wife of Edward P. Hicks, of Newtown. Hannah H., born 1839, married October 16, 1860, Captain Thomas P. Chambers. Elizabeth J., born July 4, 1844, married Major Samuel Comfort. Wilhelmina, born 1847. Mary, born 1850, married George C. Worstall. John Herman, born December 12, 1854, married April 23, 1902, Elizabeth, daughter of Colonel E. A. L. Roberts, of Titusville, Pennsylvania.

J. Herman Barnsley, son of John and Mary (Hough) Barnsley, was born in Newtown, December 12, 1854. He was educated in the public schools and Newtown Academy and later took a course at a business college. He has traveled extensively in this country and abroad and spent several years in Kansas. He filled for some time a clerical position with the Standard Oil Company at Titusville, Pennsylvania, and later opened an office in Newark, New Jersey, and conducted a brokerage business. He married April 23, 1902, Elizabeth C. Roberts of Titusville. He purchased the old homestead, "Sharon," near Newtown, Pennsylvania, which he remodeled, and resided there one year when he sold the property to Mr. John J. Tierney, of West Virginia, the present owner, and the following year erected a handsome residence on North Chancellor street, Newtown, where he now resides. His only child, John, was born March 15, 1903.

HOWARD P. WHITE, of Doylestown, coroner of Bucks county, was born in Warrington township, Bucks county, Pennsylvania, September 2, 1859, and is a son of the late Jonathan and Mary Anna (Brunner) White. The paternal ancestors of Mr. White were residents of Solebury, Bucks county, for several generations. William White having purchased a farm of 125 acres on the Carversville road below Peters Corner in 1729.

William White, the grandfather of Howard P. White, was a lifelong resident of Solebury, residing near Carversville, and a shoemaker by trade. He married Mary Delaney, and they were the parents of several children, among whom was Jonathan White, the father of the subject of this sketch.

Jonathan White was born in Solebury, September 2, 1825, and was reared in that township. He learned the shoemaker's trade with his father, and followed that vocation for a few years. In 1857 he was appointed deputy sheriff by Albert Phillips, the sheriff of Bucks county, and served during the three years' term of Sheriff Phillips, closing with the year 1853. In the fall of that year he was elected to the office of clerk of Orphans' court, and served in that office for three years. On his retirement from office he became proprietor of the Frog Hollow Hotel in Warrington township, Bucks county, which he conducted until the breaking out of the war, in 1861, when he enlisted in Company D, One Hundred and fourth Pennsylvania Volunteers, Colonel W. W. H. Davis, Captain Jacob Swartzlander, and was commissioned sergeant of his company. He served during three years of arduous service, participating in many hard fought battles, the record of the gallant One Hundred and Fourth being too families to the people of Bucks county to be recounted here and was mustered out September 25, 1864. He returned home badly broken in health, and never fully recovered from the effects of the hardships endured in the service of his country. After a few months rest he became the proprietor of a hotel at No. 1220 Market street which he conducted for three years; he then returned to Bucks county and kept a restaurant at Buckingham at the present location of the "Ottaway House," where he died in 1868. He married Mary Anna Brunner, daughter of Thomas and Theresa (Fredericks) Brunner, the latter a native of Germany, and the former of German descent, his ancestors having emigrated from Germany and settled in New Britain several generations back. Thomas Brunner was proprietor of the Willow Grove Hotel for two years, and then purchased the mills at Bridge Point, now Edison, Bucks county, of which he was the proprietor for many years, residing in Edison in all over fifty years. Mary Anna (Brunner) White resides with her son in Doylestown. Jonathan and Mary Anna (Brunner) White were the parents of two children: Howard Phillips and Arthur Cernea White, the latter of whom died in 1896.

Howard P. White resided with his parents to the age of seventeen years, and then became a clerk in the store of E. H. Worthington, at Edison, and filled that position for four years. In 1881 he went to Philadelphia and filled various positions there for two years. In 1883-4 he was employed at Cresson Springs, Pennsylvania. He then accepted a position as steward on Jay Gould's yacht and later was bookkeeper of the Philadelphia Art Club of Philadelphia for several years, resigning in 1897, since which time he has been engaged in the mercantile business at Doylestown. In the fall of 1904 he was elected to the office of coroner of Bucks county, and is now filling that position. In politics he is a Republican, and is one of the well known men of the county seat. He is a member of Aquetong Lodge No. 193, I. O. O. F., St. Tammany

Wm G. Moyer

Castle, K. G. E.; and the Doylestown Mannaerchor Society.

He married, May 12, 1889, May Emma Roberts, born May 12, 1861, daughter of John and Susanna (Kratz) Roberts, of Doylestown. On the maternal side she is descended from John Valentine Kratz, who was born in the Palatinate in 1707, and came to Pennsylvania at the age of twenty years in the ship "Friendship," arriving at Philadelphia, October 15, 1727, and settled in Upper Salford, now Montgomery county. The grandparents of Mrs. White are Isaac H. and Sybilla (Duke) Kratz; her greatgrandparents Abraham and Elizabeth (Fretz) Kratz; and her great-great-grandparents Isaac and Mary (Yellis) Kratz, Isaac being a son of John Valentine, the emigrant. The only child of Howard P. and Mary Emma (Roberts) White is Edward Earle, born February 18, 1890. The family are members of the Presbyterian church.

WILLIAM G. MOYER, a venerable and eminently esteemed resident of the borough of Chalfont, for many years an active and potent factor in the agricultural, political and social interests of New Britain township, was born at Pleasant Valley, Springfield township, Bucks county, Pennsylvania, February 14, 1834, a son of Abraham D. and Mary (Geisinger) Moyer.

The founder of the American branch of the family was the Rev. Peter Moyer, who with his brothers William, Jacob and Henry, and their sister and widowed mother, came to America in 1741. The family were natives of Switzerland, and were forced to flee from their native country during the fierce persecution of the Mennonites by the Calvinists, or State Reformed church, to the Palatinate in Germany, where they remained with friends in the vicinity of Kerbach for about one year, when they emigrated to America. The mother married Nickey Schaafroth; no issue. Of the brothers, Peter was the oldest and Henry the youngest. Peter, William and Henry settled in Springfield township, Bucks county, and Jacob settled at Center Valley, Saucon township, Lehigh county. They all became farmers, and were active members of the Mennonite church. The supposition is that Peter was a minister in Switzerland, and he was one of the early ministers of the church in Springfield township; Jacob was also a minister and preached at Coopersburgh.

Rev. Peter Moyer, great-grandfather of William G. Moyer, was born in Switzerland about 1723, married ———. He settled in Springfield township, Bucks county, Pennsylvania, near Pleasant Valley, where on May 28, 1752, he purchased his farm consisting of 107 acres (old measure) from Joseph Green. The property was bounded by lands of William Bryan, Joseph Unthanks, and James Green, and is owned now by Mary Moyer Geissinger, wife of Charles A. Geissinger, daughter of Abraham G. Moyer, a great-grandson. Rev. Peter Moyer was one of the early ministers of the Mennonite church of Springfield. Children: Christian, John, Jacob, William, Henry, Isaac, Mary (Mrs. Kulp), Barbara. Two daughters married Kulps, and three children died young.

William Moyer, grandfather of William G. Moyer, was born in Springfield township, Bucks county, June 7, 1764. His occupation was that of a farmer. He was united in marriage to Mary Overholt, who was born December 27, 1767, and their children were: Magdalena, Nancy, Hannah, Kate, Mary and Abraham D. The death of William Moyer occurred February 12, 1848; he was survived by his wife, who passed away September 1, 1850.

Abraham D. Moyer, father of William G. Moyer, was born on the old Peter Moyer farm in Pleasant Valley, June 6, 1798. He was reared on the homestead, received a good common school education, and throughout his active career followed farming as a means of livelihood. He was the leader of the singing in the Mennonite church. In 1832 he married Mary Geisinger, who was born in Upper Milford, Lehigh county, September 18, 1811, a daughter of Philip and Fanny (Hestand) Geisinger. Their children are: William G., mentioned hereinafter; Fanny, who became the wife of Nathaniel Bechtel, of Berks county; Mary and Abraham. The father of these children died September 15, 1871; the mother passed away December 9, 1900. They were honest and industrious people, and in every relation of life performed their duties conscientiously.

William G. Moyer spent his childhood and early manhood years on the farm owned by his father, and his education was obtained in the schools of Springfield and Quakertown. For ten years, from 1855 to 1865, he served in the capacity of teacher, achieving a fair degree of success in this vocation owing to the fact that he was able to impart to others clearly and concisely the knowledge he wished them to receive. From the latter named year until 1872, a period of seven years, he engaged in farming in Springfield township, after which he removed to New Britain township, where he owns a fine farm in the borough of Chalfont. He is practical and progressive in his methods, and, being familiar with all the details of this branch of industry, derives a goodly income from his labor. He has been active and prominent in political affairs, and has been chosen the incumbent of several offices of trust and responsibility. He was township auditor for six years; secretary of the school board for a similar period and jury commissioner for Bucks county, having been elected in June, 1903; and was first president of the council of Chalfont, serving three years. For many years he has served as correspondent and reporter for the United States Agricultural Department. He is a prominent member of the Mennonite church, and a Republican in politics.

In 1860 Mr. Moyer was married to Mary Swartley, who was born in New Britain township, in 1835, a daughter of John Swartley. Their children are: 1. Emma, born December 17, 1861, died January 9, 1881. 2. Levi, born May 22, 1864, married Anna Detwiller, and they are the parents of the following named children: William D., born December 25, 1887; Sarah Amelia, born July 27, 1889; Hannah Theresa, born October 23, 1891; Mary Maria, born April 17, 1894; Irene, born February 2, 1896; Enos, born July 5, 1898; Eva, born February 9, 1900; Nora, born in June, 1901. 3. Abraham S., born November 7, 1866, married Susie M. Fretz, daughter of Eli Fretz, of Bedminster, and one child is the issue of this union, Alvin, born October 18, 1900. 4. William, born November 29, 1868, a merchant of Chalfont. 5. Menno S., born November 18, 1870, was educated in the State Normal School at West Chester, and Haverford College. After his graduation he taught school for a number of years, and now is a member of the firm of Moyer Brothers, merchants of Lansdale. He married Annie Souder, and their children are: Evelyn Elizabeth and Margarette, born February 2, 1904. 6. Harvey, born March 16, 1877, married Macie Johnson. The mother of these children died January 2, 1888. Mr. Moyer married for his second wife Mrs. Hannah Slifer Weis, who was born near Quakertown, Richland township, Bucks county, October 6, 1837, a daughter of Joseph Slifer.

WILSON B. McKINSTRY. Nathan McKinstry, the founder of the McKinstry family in this country, was a native of the north of Ireland. He was born in the year 1712 and came to this country when a youth. In connection with a brother-in-law, Hugh Young, they purchased in 1744 a tract of 195 acres in Wrightstown, which they subsequently divided. Ten years later he sold his Wrightstown farm and removed to that part of Buckingham township now included in Doylestown township, where he purchased a farm of 202 acres and resided thereon until his death, April 15, 1790. He and his wife Mary were active members of Neshaminy Presbyterian church of Warwick township, of which he was a trustee. Their children were John, born 1736, died 1791; Jane, born 1745, married James Kerr, died 1797; Samuel, born 1748, died January 24, 1796; Henry, born 1750, died November 28, 1804; William, born 1752, died ——; Robert, born 1756, died July 25, 1834.

Robert McKinstry, youngest son of Nathan and Mary, was born on the Buckingham homestead in 1756, and remained there until his father's death in 1790. He married in 1783 Mary Weir, daughter of James Weir, of Warrington. Her sister, Rebecca Weir, married John Simpson and became the grandmother of U. S. Grant. The distinguished soldier and statesman, shortly after his graduation at West Point, paid a visit to his cousins, the McKinstrys of Warrington. On the marriage of Robert McKinstry, his father built a house for him on the old homestead, but at the settlement of his father's estate he did not elect to retain any of the paternal farm, and took up his residence in New Britain. He died July 25, 1834. His wife Mary died April 6, 1846, at the age of eighty-nine years.

Robert and Mary (Weir) McKinstry were the parents of seven children, viz: Jane, born 1784, died unmarried April 24, 1869; John, born November 1, 1786, died unmarried September 24, 1863; Nathan, born January 29, 1791, died December 23, 1862; Robert, born 1793, died September 5, 1871; William, born 1796, settled in Ohio; James, born 1799, died 1877; and Henry, born 1805. Robert McKinstry, wife and their five sons and one daughter who remained in Bucks county were all active and consistent members of Neshaminy Presbyterian church; John was for a long period a trustee; and Henry and Nathan were elders. In their later days services were frequently held in their houses. John, Nathan, James and Henry lived in Warrington, and Robert lived and died on the homestead in New Britain; he left no issue.

Henry McKinstry, the youngest son of Robert and Mary, was reared on the homestead, and early in life learned the trade of a carpenter, which he followed for several years. In April, 1832, he purchased of Anthony Robinson a farm of ninety acres, and erecting an entirely new set of buildings thereon settled down to agricultural pursuits. He married, November 29, 1838, Amanda Brady, daughter of Alexander Brady, of Philadelphia, but for many years a resident of Warrington, where she died in 1863. Henry McKinstry was an elder in the Neshaminy Presbyterian church for a number of years. He was active and prominent in social and political matters of his community, and served several years as school director. After a long and useful life, he died in 1885 at the age of eighty years. His wife Amanda died in August, 1902. The children of Henry and Amanda (Brady) McKinstry were five in number viz.: Sarah, Mary, Wilson Brady, Henry Martyn, and Franklin Pierce. Sarah married David Cornell; Mary married Samuel McNair; and Franklin married Jennie Boileau. He is now a prominent physician of Washington, New Jersey.

Wilson Brady McKinstry, eldest son of Henry and Amanda (Brady) McKinstry, was born March 1, 1846, on the farm where he still resides. On arriving at manhood he assumed the conduct of the home farm which he purchased at the death of his mother. In politics he is a Democrat, but has never sought or held other than local office. He has been a member of the local school board for nine years, serving both as treasurer and president of the board. He and his family are members of Neshaminy Presbyterian church, with which the family has been connected for four generations. He married in 1876 Matilda Breuhl, born in Philadelphia, in 1855, a daughter of John Breuhl, a native of Alsace, who came to this country when a youth and settled in Bucks county. To Wilson and Matilda (Breuhl) McKinstry have been born four children, viz: Mary, died in infancy; William, Henry and Herbert. William and Henry are electricians and are both actively interested in the telephone business. William married Mary Stocker, and lives in West Chester.

H. MARTYN McKINSTRY was born June 25, 1849, on the farm in Warrington township where his brother, Wilson B. McKinstry, now resides. He is the second son of Henry and Amanda (Brady) McKinstry, the children of whom are five in number: Sarah B., wife of the late David Cornell, Southampton; Mary, wife of Samuel MacNair, Mt. Pleasant, Pennsylvania; Wilson B., Warrington, Pennsylvania; H. Martyn, Warrington, Pennsylvania; Frank P., (M. D.) Washington, New Jersey.

Henry McKinstry was born in 1805. He was a stanch Presbyterian and was a member of the Neshaminy Presbyterian church of Warwick. For many years and up to the time of his death, he was an elder in the church and although living six miles distant, he was always in his place unless hindered by something over which he had no control. If the condition of the roads were such that he could not drive he quite often walked the whole distance to be able to be in his place. On November 29, 1838, he was married to Amanda Brady, daughter of Alexander and Achsah (Appleton) Brady, who helped and encouraged him in all duties, both spiritual and domestic. After his marriage he moved to the farm, which he had purchased a short time before, and which his son, Wilson B., now owns. He was a good, practical and prosperous farmer.

H. Martyn McKinstry obtained his education at the local school and remained on the home farm, being associated with his brother in its management until 1893. On January 19, 1893, he married Mattie L., daughter of John B. and Adeline E. (Hoover) Walter, born March 9, 1862. Her father, John B. Walter, was born and reared where his daughter was born, in Warrington township, February 14, 1835, and was a son of Samuel and Deborah (Brunner) Walter, and grandson of George Walter. He was a practical and active business man and a prominent member of the Reformed church. He died June 14, 1900, aged sixty-five years. He married on December 2, 1856, Adeline E., daughter of Frederick and Maria (Fleck) Hoover, and

granddaughter of Philip and Mary (Conrad) Hoover, of one of the oldest and most prominent Pennsylvania German families of the vicinity.

After his marriage H. Martyn McKinstry purchased a farm belonging to his father's estate, about one mile north of the village of Warrington, where he still resides and on which he has since made many improvements. It is now one of the most convenient and comfortable homes in the neighborhood, the house and barn being supplied with water and the house heated throughout. Another of the modern conveniences of this home is the telephone of the local telephone company, of which Mr. H. Martyn McKinstry is the president. He is a member of the Neshaminy Presbyterian church and in 1890 was elected a trustee and in 1904 he was elected an elder, which offices he still fills. H. Martyn and Mattie L. (Walter) McKinstry have been the parents of three children: Frank R., born November 3, 1893; and Adeline W. and Amanda B., twins, born January 5, 1895. Adeline died at the age of two weeks.

LINFORD R. CRAVEN. Among the men who have achieved local eminence in their chosen profession is Linford R. Craven, photographer, Doylestown, Pennsylvania. He was born March 26, 1864, in Hilltown, Bucks county, Pennsylvania, the son of Joseph and Ann (Ritchie) Craven.

The family of Craven are of Holland descent, and have been residents of Bucks county since the first quarter of the eighteenth century. Jacobus (James) Craven was one of the trustees of Neshaminy Presbyterian church of Warwick in 1743. He was a large landowner in Warminster township and in Moreland township, Montgomery county. He died about 1760 at an advanced age. His children were: Thomas, Giles, James, Alice, wife of Harman Vansant; Elinor, wife of Clement Dungan; Hannah, wife of William McDowell; Esther, wife of William Gilbert; and Mary, wife of Anthony Scout. Giles died without issue in 1798, and James removed to Virginia.

Thomas Craven married Lena, daughter of William and Janet (Suydam) Bennett, and settled in Warminster township, where he died August, 1799, leaving sons: William, James, Giles, Isaac and Thomas, and daughters: Christiana, wife of Thomas Beans; Edith, wife of Charles Vansant; Ann, Catharine and Helena.

Isaac Craven inherited from his father the "Mansion House" and 103 acres of land in Warminster that had been his grandfather's, whereon he died in May, 1835, at an advanced age. His children were William, Isaac, Abraham, and Elenah, wife of John Finney. Only the last two survived him and inherited his lands. His son Abraham married Hannah Finney and settled on a farm in Moreland, but returned to Warminster some time after his father's decease. He died in 1882, aged about eighty-five years, leaving seven children, four sons and three daughters.

Joseph Craven, son of Abraham, and father of the subject of this sketch, was born near Hatboro, in Moreland township, in 1823. He married Ann, daughter of Thomas Ritchie, and great-granddaughter of James Ritchie, a Scotch-Irish settler of Warwick township, Bucks county. In 1869 he removed to Hatboro, where he conducted a store for four years. In 1873 he purchased a farm in Moreland, upon which he resided until 1883, when he removed to North Wales, Montgomery county, where he lived a retired life.

His children are: Edwin, residing in Scranton, Pennsylvania; Sue, wife of Frank McVeagh, of Philadelphia; Joanna, wife of Lewis K. Hall of Upper Makefield; William of Bridgeport, Pennsylvania; Linford R.; Robert, of Ashbourne, Pennsylvania; and Mary deceased, who was the wife of Elmer Smith.

Linford R. Craven, the subject of this sketch, was educated at the public schools of Hatboro and Upper Makefield, and at the age of fourteen years began his business career as a clerk in a store at Frankford, Philadelphia. In 1880 he removed to North Wales, where he was employed in making shirts, came to Doylestown three years later and followed the same business for one year, when he began photographing in connection with Samuel F. Dubois, a local photographer, and William Boyce of Philadelphia. In 1885 he opened a portable studio in Doylestown, and a year later purchased the old spoke factory at the junction of Court and State streets and erected his present residence and studio. In politics Mr. Craven is a Democrat. He and his family belong to the Doylestown Presbyterian church. He is a member of Doylestown Lodge, No. 94, I. O. O. F., Doylestown Encampment, No. 35, I. O. O. F., St. Tammany Castle, No. 173, K. G. E., and of Lenape Council No. 1117, Royal Arcanum. He has served three years in Doylestown borough council, and held other local offices. He was married February 14, 1883, to Fannie H., daughter of Gibson Johnson.

CHARLES D. BIGLEY, the genial proprietor of the North Main Street Bakery, Doylestown, Pennsylvania, and for many years an officer in the Bucks county courts, was born in Nockamixon township, Bucks county, Pennsylvania, December 14, 1844, and is a son of Isaac and Mary (Deemer) Bigley, both of German extraction.

Adam Bigley, the grandfather of Charles D., was a saddler by trade, and a lifelong resident of Nockamixon township, having purchased a small farm there in 1807, which he conducted in connection with his vocation as a harness maker. He died in Nockamixon in 1839. He and his wife Sarah were the parents of four children: Isaac, Solomon, Ann, wife of David Haring, and John.

Isaac Bigley, eldest son of Adam and Mary, was born in Nockamixon township, September 5, 1798, and died there October 12, 1883. He was a limeburner in Durham township and in Hunterdon county for several years, but during the last forty years of his life resided in Kintnersville, Nockamixon township, on the line of Durham township, on a small lot conveyed to him in 1842. He married Mary Deemer, daughter of Solomon and Mary Deemer, of Nockamixon, and a granddaughter of Michael Deemer, an early settler in Nockamixon. (See Deemer Family). They were the parents of nine children, viz: Elizabeth, who married James Lewis; Sarah, who married Jesse Moser; Catharine, wife of William Cyphers of Riegelsville, Pennsylvania; Hannah, wife of Frank Laubenstaine; Susan, wife of Owen Gares; Adam, who married Mary Bellis of New Jersey; Lydia, wife of William Nicholas; Solomon and Charles D. All three of the sons served in the Union army during the civil war; Adam in a New Jersey regiment; Solomon D. in the First Pennsylvania Regiment and later as recruiting sergeant; and Charles D. in the One Hundred and Seventy-fourth regiment.

Charles D. Bigley was born and reared in Nockamixon township, and acquired his education in the public schools. In early life he followed the trade of a cigar maker, and was also engaged for some time in limeburning. In October, 1862, he obtained the consent of his father and enlisted for nine months service in the One Hundred and Seventy-fourth Pennsylvania Regiment, under Colonel John W. Nyce, and at the organization of the regiment in Philadelphia on November 1, 1862, was appointed corporal in Company F under Captain Thomas W. Harris. November 19, 1862, the regiment proceeded to Washington, D. C., and from there to Suffolk, Virginia, where it reported to General Peck and was assigned to General Ferry's brigade, and on December 31, was ordered to Newbern, North Carolina, where it arrived January 6, 1863. In the same month it was ordered to reinforce the army operating in front of Charleston, South Carolina, and sailed from Beaufort, arriving at Hilton Head on February 5, and was stationed on Helena Island for about a month. It then proceeded to Beaufort, where it was engaged in provost duty until June, 1863, when it was again transferred to Hilton Head. Towards the close of July, the term of enlistment being about to expire, the regiment was ordered north, and, returning to Philadelphia, was honorably mustered out of service August 7, 1863. Mr. Bigley returned to Nockamixon, where he resided for the next twenty years, being employed for fourteen years at Durham furnace. Politically Mr. Bigley is a Democrat, and has always taken an active part in the councils of his party, as well as in the affairs of the community in which he lived. He was a member of the school board of Nockamixon township for a number of years, and also filled other local offices. In the fall of 1884 he was elected on the Democratic ticket to the office of clerk of quarter sessions of Bucks county, and removed with his family to the county seat. He filled the office of clerk of courts for three years with eminent ability, and since the expiration of his term of office has filled a number of official positions. He was a member of borough council for seven years, resigning the position during his third term by reason of his removal to a different ward. In 1896 he was appointed a tipstaff of the court, and in 1901 was advanced to the position of court crier, which he since filled to the satisfaction of the court. In 1890 he purchased the North Main Street Bakery of Enos Weiss, and is still engaged in conducting it. He is a member of Peace and Union Lodge, No. 456, I. O. O. F., of Rieglesville, Pennsylvania; of Pakonet Lodge, No. 158, I. O. R. M., of Kintnersville; and of General Robert L. Bodine Post, G. A. R., of Doylestown. He and his family are members of Salem Reformed church.

Mr. Bigley has been twice married. His first wife was Mary Jane Fluck, daughter of Amos Fluck, of Springfield township, Bucks county, and they were the parents of two children; Oscar H., now transcribing clerk in the office of the recorder of deeds; and Minnie, wife of Reuben C. Stever. Oscar H., married A. Florence Grim, daughter of the late George W. and Elizabeth (Koons) Grim, of Nockamixon, and sister of Hon. Webster Grim of Doylestown, and they have been the parents of six children, three of whom survive, viz: Grace, a teacher in the public schools of Bucks county, Ethel, and Dorothy. Reuben C. and Minnie (Bigley) Stever are the parents of three children: Charles B., Helen and Frank, deceased. Mrs. Mary Jane Bigley died July 11, 1894, and Mr. Bigley married (second) December 3, 1896, Mrs. Ella (Harrold) Haldeman, widow of Jacob Haldeman, of Doylestown township, and daughter of William Harrold, of Doylestown.

JAMES S. HARRAR, descended from an honored early family in Montgomery county, Pennsylvania, and now following farming in Warminster township, Bucks county, was born April 30, 1866, in the former county, his parents being Joel J. and Wilmina (Haupt) Harrar, who were likewise natives of Montgomery county. The father was a son of James S. Harrar, also born in Montgomery county, while

the great-grandfather, John F. Harrar, Sr., was a native of Wales and emigrated to America during the colonial epoch in the history of the United States, settling in Montgomery county. He was a Baptist in religious faith. In early manhood he learned the shoemaker's trade, and in addition to that occupation followed farming. James S. Harrar was reared in Montgomery county, and after his marriage settled upon a farm there, carrying on agricultural pursuits throughtout his remaining days. He, too, was a Baptist in religious faith and was of a leading and influential family of the county. He had a brother, Nathan Harrar, who was twice a representative of the district in the state legislature of Pennsylvania. The children of James S. Harrar, grandfather of our subect, were five in number: Lydia, Joel J., Martha, Elwood and Mary.

Joel J. Harrar, father of James S. Harrar, was married and settled near the old home farm, where he remained for five years. He afterward removed to the Thomas Folk farm, upon which he lived for thirteen years, when he purchased the William Shae farm in Horsham township, Bucks county, where he remained until his death, which occurred January 29, 1904. He lived the quiet life of a farmer, and his upright and honorable career gained for him the respect of his fellow men. His political support was given the Democracy. His wife survives him and finds a good home with her son James. She was a daughter of John and Susan (Fell) Haupt. The Haupt family, residents of Berks county, were of German descent, while the Fells lived in Buckingham township, Bucks county, and were of Quaker faith. John Haupt was an agriculturist, actively identified with farming interests in Montgomery county, and he died upon the old family homestead near Montgomeryville. In his family were four children: Seneca, a farmer; Wilmina, who became Mrs. Harrar; Nathan; and Elizabeth. To Joel J. and Wilmina (Haupt) Harrar were born four children: John, a farmer; James S.; Elwood; and Wilmar, a farmer for the McKean estate.

James S. Harrar was reared to farm life and remained at home until his marriage, when in 1890 he rented the old historic farm known as the Isaac Parry property in Warminster township, Bucks county. He has since purchased this place and yet resides thereon, carrying on general farming and also attending the Philadelphia market. He has repaired and remodeled the barn, placed all of the buildings in good condition, has his fields under a high state of cultivation and, in fact, has made his farm one of the best improved properties of the locality. He uses modern machinery in its development and cultivation, and everything about his place is kept in excellent condition. He also has a herd of cows and sells milk and he also keeps good horses, both for the farm work and driving. Mr. Harrar was reared in the Democratic faith, and has always supported the party, but has never sought or desired office.

He has been married twice. His first wife died August 8, 1898, leaving a son, Carrell, who was born May 3, 1893. December 4, 1901, Mr. Harrar wedded Miss Susan C. Parry, belonging to one of the old and prominent families of Pennsylvania. Her parents were Isaac C. and Sarah B. (Hicks) Parry, both natives of Bucks county, descended from ancestors who have long been identified with the development and progress of the state. The mother was a daughter of Edward and Sarah (Worstel) Hicks, of Newtown. Edward and Elias Hicks were cousins, and both were highly educated and became eminent preachers, being the founders of the Hicksite branch of the Friends society. Edward Hicks was an eminent divine of that denomination, and was well known throughout the world by the representatives of the Society of Friends. He resided in Langhorne and at Newtown, Bucks county, but he preached the gospel according to his interpretation in many places in America and thoroughly established the faith in which he believed. The children of Edward Hicks were: Mary, Mrs. Susan Carlac, Isaac W., Mrs. Elizabeth Plummer, and Mrs. Sarah H. Parry.

In the paternal line the ancestral history of Mrs. Harrar can be traced back through many generations to Thomas Parry, Sr., who came from Radmanshire, Wales, to America during colonial days and settled in Montgomery county, being one of the early promoters of development and progress in eastern Pennsylvania. He assisted in laying broad and deep the foundation for the present development and progress of his part of the state, and was a leading and influential resident of Pennsylvania. He and his descendants have been consistent members of the Society of Friends, to which they yet adhere. They have lived lives of simplicity and of honesty, and have ever commanded the respect of those with whom they have come in contact. Thomas Parry, Sr., was the father of Thomas Parry, Jr., and he was the father of Jacob Parry, whose son Isaac Parry, Sr., was the father of Isaac C. Parry, who was Mrs. Harrar's father. Isaac Parry, Sr., was a broad-minded, intelligent business man and farmer, who was often called upon to write wills, settle estates and acts as guardian for heirs. None of the family have ever aspired to elective offices or public notoriety of any kind. They have mostly followed farming, but others have been concerned with industrial and commercial interests. Thomas Parry, Sr., obtained a large tract of land at Edgehill, where he improved an extensive farm, becoming very successful. There he reared his family and spent his remaining days. Thomas Parry, Jr., his

son, was reared to manhood upon the old homestead and after his marriage removed to Bucks county, Pennsylvania, where he purchased an extensive tract of land, including the farm upon which James S. Harrar now resides. Thomas Parry improved a large portion of his property and thereon reared his family. His son Jacob married and settled upon the old homestead, continuing the work of further development and there he, too, lived and died. His son, Isaac Parry, Sr., obtained the old homestead, which in turn was inherited by his son, Isaac C. Parry, and both reared their families and died upon that place. During the period of the revolutionary war the Parry family was often molested by the contending armies, who foraged upon their place. On one occasion a scouting party of English came to the homestead farm and found there some fat sheep, one of which they killed, compelling Mrs. Parry to cook it for them in the Dutch oven. Before the cooking process had been completed, however, a party of American scouts appeared and the British fled, so that the American troops got the meal which had been prepared for the other soldiers. The Parry family, from Thomas Parry, the progenitor in America, down to the present generation, has always been distinguished for simplicity of living, purity of morals, untiring industry and high principles. Isaac Parry, Sr., grandfather of Mrs. Harrar, was born upon the old family homestead in June, 1774, and died there in October, 1857. He was married twice, his first union being with Sarah Hopkins, by whom he had three children: Rebecca, Jacob and Richard H. His second wife was Mary Nixon, a daughter of Samuel and Susan (Roberts) Nixon, also of a prominent family of Bucks county, and their children were: Tacey, who died unmarried; Thomas; Samuel; Isaac C.; Susanna; and Mary, who became the wife of Joseph Saunders, of Philadelphia, and is the only one now living.

Isaac C. Parry, father of Mrs. Harrar, was born and reared on the old family homestead in Bucks county, and became one of the prominent farmers of the locality, carrying forward the work of agricultural development that had been instituted by his ancestors. He was a man of sterling integrity and honor, his name being above reproach, and he lived a life in harmony with the principles of Friends, in which he reared his family and they have never departed from that faith. He married Miss Hicks, and they became the parents of five children: Elizabeth H., who married Isaac Warner; J. C., of Philadelphia; Tacey M., the wife of R. Willetts; Mary S.; and Susan C., the wife of J. S. Harrar. The father died upon the old family homestead July 12, 1893, passing away at the age of seventy-seven years, while his wife's death occurred February 23, 1895.

ABRAHAM M. MYERS. Six generations of the Myers family to which Abraham M. Myers belongs, have resided in Bucks county. His great-great-grandfather was the first of the name to locate here, settling in Bedminster township, near Pipersville, whence he removed to Plumstead township. He was a farmer and blacksmith, following those pursuits throughout his entire life. He married a Miss Nash and they had children: Henry, Abraham, Christian, Esther, Mary and Barbara.

Henry Myers (2) son of John Myers, also learned the blacksmith's trade, which he followed in connection with agricultural pursuits. He lived near Smith's corner, in Plumstead township, on land which had hitherto been in possession of his father. He married Margaret Geisinger, and they had children: Abraham G., Joseph G., Mary, Nancy, Esther and Henry G.

Abraham G. Myers (3) son of Henry and Margaret (Geisinger) Myers, was born on the old home farm in Plumstead township, October 27, 1800, and died January 27, 1881. He, too, followed the occupation of farming, and lived near Pipersville. He was married in 1834 to Sarah Fritz, and their children were three in number: Francis F., Mary, who was born April 23, 1840, and died June 7, 1893; and Aaron F., born May 4, 1846.

Francis F. Myers (4), elder son of Abraham G. and Sarah (Fritz) Myers, was born in Bedminster township, April 22, 1838. He was a farmer, and lived all his life in the township of his nativity. His wife bore the maiden name of Rachel Myers, and they had the following children: Abraham M., Sarah Ann, the wife of Allen Zetty; Mary Ellen, wife of Levi Myers; Minerva, wife of Henry Myers; Huldah; Rachel, Amanda; Ida; and Livvie, deceased.

Abraham M. Myers (5), the eldest child of Francis Myers, was born in Bedminster township, July 19, 1861, and was reared upon his father's farm, while his education was acquired in the district schools of the neighborhood. At the time of his marriage he settled in Skippack township, Montgomery county, where he conducted a farm for two years and then returned to Bedminster township, where he worked in a mill for three years. On the expiration of that period he purchased the Jacoby farm, on which he still resides, and to the further development and improvement of which he still directs his energies, making it an excellent property. He has also been active in community affairs, and in 1892 was elected a school director, which position he has since continued to fill. His political allegiance is given to the Republican party, and he is a

member of the Lutheran church. On January 13, 1883, Mr. Myers was united in marriage to Miss Sarah Ann Gruver, a daughter of John and Hannah (Hillpot) Gruver, and they now have seven children, who are representatives of the Myers family in the sixth generation in Bucks county. These are: Ervin G., born April 7, 1884; Eva G., born May 9, 1885; Francis G., born August 17, 1887; Jerome G., born September 19, 1894; Hannah G., born March 6, 1896, died April 15, 1897; Aaron G., born September 14, 1898; and Norman, born June 21, 1902.

WILLIAM PENN ROBERTS, a member of the firm of Roberts, Winner & Co., manufacturers, of Quakertown, Pennsylvania, was born August 16, 1843, near Perkiomen Junction, Schuylkill township, Chester county, Pennsylvania, a son of Lewis and Harriet (Brooke) Roberts and grandson of Israel and Anna (Foulke) Roberts. who resided near Trumbauersville, Pennsylvania, where Israel Roberts was engaged in agricultural pursuits.

Lewis Roberts (father) was born December 21, 1791, in Milford township, Bucks county, Pennsylvania. He attended the subscription schools of his district, and received some instruction from the Friends' school at Richland Monthly Meeting, Quakertown. He then learned wheelwrighting and ploughmaking, which trades he followed throughout the active years of his career. On May 24, 1821, Mr. Roberts married Harriet Brooke, daughter of Isaac and Susan (Jones) Brooke; her father was a miller of Conshohocken, Montgomery county, and settled at Perkiomen Junction, Chester county. Their children were as follows: Clementina Brooke, became the wife of Samuel Lee, of Leesport, Berks county. Anna Foulke became the wife of Evan Vanderslice, of Schuylkill township, Chester county; they now reside at Valley Forge. Sarah Emily became the wife of Joseph Fussell, of Chester Springs, Chester county. Mary became the wife of Charles Fish, and they now reside at Reading. Charles Brooke, born September 13, 1829, died February 5, 1885, married Rebecca Rossiter; they lived in Perry county, Pennsylvania. Lewis Ellwood, born February 26, 1835, married Jane Foulke, of Quakertown, and they reside in the city of Philadelphia. Joseph Jones, died at Relay Station, Maryland; he was a member of the One Hundred and Twenty-eighth Pennsylvania Volunteers during the Civil war. William Penn, mentioned at length hereinafter. David Brooke was killed in the battle of Petersburg, April 1865; he was first lieutenant of Company H, Two Hundred and Fifth Pennsylvania Volunteers, Ninth Army Corps, during the civil war.

William Penn Roberts attended the district school, and at the same time assisted with the work at home until the death of his father, in 1861, when the family moved to Port Kennedy, Montgomery county. He attended the school of that section for one winter, 1861-62, and in the spring of the latter named year went to Philadelphia and entered an apprenticeship to learn stoveplate molding with Cox, Weightman & Cox, founders. Here he remained for one year, but on account of labor troubles was compelled to give up learning the trade at that place. He went to Stuyvesant, New York, and entered the employ of the Columbia Company, where his brother, Lewis E. Roberts, was engaged as moulder, and here completed his term of apprenticeship, serving one and one-half years with this firm. He worked as a journeyman for the same company until the fall of 1865, when he was employed by his brother, Lewis E. Roberts, who had established a stove plate foundry at Quakertown, Pennsylvania, in 1864, in conjunction with David H. Thomas, who had erected a small shop near Strawn's Mill. In 1867 the firm felt the necessity of enlarging their facilities to meet the demands of their constantly increasing business, and accordingly located on Broad street, near Third street, Quakertown, where they erected a large foundry and stove fitting room, taking possession of the same in that year. William P. Roberts continued with them as a floor worker until 1875, in which year he was engaged as foreman of the molding department, and continued in that capacity until the destruction of the plant by fire in 1880. The firm then leased the American Stove Foundry, at Second and Mifflin streets, Philadelphia. In 1881 William P. Roberts joined with several other former employes of Roberts & Thomas and purchased the ruins of that firm at Quakertown, and under the title of Rogers, Roberts, Ecypes & Co. started the plant in February, 1882. Since then there have been some changes in the personnel of the firm, but Mr. Roberts has kept his place. and together with William P. Winner and Francis Cavanaugh form the firm of Roberts, Winner & Co., master mechanics in their lines, all of them, and during this latter partnership the business has gained in volume and importance until at the present time (1905) the stoves of Roberts, Winner & Co. can be found at the homes of people from the Atlantic to the Pacific. The firm gives employment to about one hundred hands in its various departments, and is thus an important factor in the industrial life of the town. Mr. Roberts is actively interested in local political affairs, has served on the Quakertown board of education, and also in other positions of usefulness to the citizens of that town. His views coincide with those of the Republican party.

Mr. Roberts was twice married. His first wife was Anna Rawlings, daughter of Franklin and Martha (Roberts) Rawlings, of Quakertown, who died March 24, 1882. Their children were: Rachel, born May 23, 1871, attended the public schools

of Quakertown, is unmarried. and resides at home. Warren, born September 1, 1873, died December 6, 1873. Thomas, born August 12, 1876, died August 12, 1876. William Arthur, born June 13, 1879, attended the public schools of Quakertown, also the George School, at Newtown, Bucks county, and then entered the dental department of the University of Pennsylvania, graduating with the class of 1902. He practiced for a time at Ambler, Pennsylvania, but is now traveling through the south, west and Mexico. In 1884 Mr. Roberts married Letitia K. Kinsey, daughter of Nathaniel and Elizabeth (Morgan) Kinsey, of Quakertown. Their children are: Linford Brook, born December 15, 1885, attends the Quakertown public school. Nathaniel Joseph, born October 25, 1888, attends the Quakertown public school. Marian Elizabeth, born September 7, 1890, also attends the Quakertown public school. The family are members of the Society of Friends.

JAMES VANSANT RANDALL, of Newtown, one of the best known and largest carriage manufacturers in Bucks county, was born in Byberry, Philadelphia county, December 10, 1831, and is a son of Eber and Rachel (Vansant) Randall.

The Randall family have been residents of Bucks county for over two centuries, and are of English descent. Nicholas Randall, a carpenter by trade and a native of England, settled in Southampton township, Bucks county, where he purchased 250 acres of land in 1698. His son, Nicholas Randall, Jr., married in 1738 Agnes Comly, daughter of Henry and Agnes (Heaton) Comly, of Middletown, and later removed to Moreland township. George, Joseph and William Randall, supposed to be sons of Nicholas, became members of Buckingham Meeting of Friends in 1722. They lived for a time near Newtown, removing later to Southampton. Joseph removed to York county with his family in 1755. Both George and Joseph married Doans, daughters of Daniel Doan and Mehetabel his wife, who came to Middletown, Bucks county, from Sandwich, Massachusetts. George married (second) Mary Harding, widow of Thomas Harding, Jr., and another daughter of Henry and Agnes (Heaton) Comly.

The paternal grandfather of the subject of this sketch was Amos Randall, said to have been a grandson of Jacob Randall, eldest son of George by his second marriage with Mary (Comly) Randall. Jacob was married in 1753 to "a woman of another persuasion" and was disowned by the Friends. Amos Randall was a carpenter by trade and lived from early life in Buckingham township. He was born in the year 1779, and was married December 11, 1804, before John Wilson, Esq., of Buckingham, to Jane Hartley, daughter of Anthony and Sarah (Betts) Hartley, of Buckingham, granddaughter of Thomas and Elizabeth Hartley, and great-granddaughter of Edward Hartley, who settled in Buckingham in 1702, and was the ancestor of all the Hartleys of Bucks county. Edward was the father of three sons—Thomas, John and Roger, all of whom had large families and were large land-owners in Buckingham and Solebury. Thomas and Elizabeth had twelve children, of whom Anthony was the fourth. He was twice married; by his first wife, Elizabeth Smith, he had seven children, and by his second, Sarah Betts, six more, Jane, born 4 mo. 1, 1779, being the fourth. Her mother, Sarah Betts, was a daughter of Thomas and Elizabeth Betts, of Buckingham, and was born 4 mo. 14, 1747, and died in 1797. Her grandfather, Thomas Betts, was a native of Long Island and died at Newtown, Bucks county, in 1747.

Amos Randall purchased in 1810 a small farm in Buckingham, which he conducted in connection with carpentering until his death on April 14, 1854, at the age of seventy-five years. Amos and Jane (Hartley) Randall were the parents of eight sons: Aaron, Eber, David, Levi, Ralph, Isaac, Jesse and Edward. Jane, the mother of these children, was a member of Friends' Meeting; the father was not a member, though frequently attending their meetings. All of the eight boys were reared to mechanical trades, and five of them eventually engaged in the manufacture of carriages in Bucks county. Aaron and Levi never married; David removed to the west; Isaac and Jesse married sisters by the name of Lambert, the former settling in Makefield and the latter in Solebury; Ralph married Deborah Firman, and died in 1883; Edward never married.

Eber Randall, the father of the subject of this sketch, was born in Buckingham township in the year 1807, and was educated at the local and Friends' schools. He remained on the farm until the age of sixteen years, when he became an apprentice to the shoemaker's trade, which he followed for a number of years. He later purchased and moved to his father-in-law's farm in Middletown, and followed farming until 1858, when he removed to Newtown, and later to Princeton, New Jersey, where he resided for a short time, and then removed to Bristol, Bucks county, where he died in 1887, at the age of eighty years. His wife was Rachel Harrison Vansant, daughter of Garret Vansant, of Middletown township, Bucks county, whose

ancestors had been residents of Bucks county, for several generations, being of Holland descent and settling originally on Long Island, from whence his great-grandfather, Garret VanSandt, removed to Bucks county in 1699. Garret Vansant, the maternal grandfather of Mr. Randall, was the father of six children, three sons and three daughters— Rachel, the mother of Mr. Randall; Jane, who married Isaac Randall, a cousin of Eber; and Mary, who married Jonathan Hunter. Eber and Rachel (Vansant) Randall were the parents of five children: 1. James V. 2. Wilson, who married Caroline Harding, and was for a number of years associated with his brother James in the carriage business, and some time afterwards in the same business at Bristol, Bucks county. Their children were: Clarence, who married Hannie L. White, one son, Clifford W. Randall; James Merton, who married Martinette Patterson, daughters, Helen and Marian; Clara, who married William Broadnax, issue: Clara, Wilfred and Wilson. Clara married for second husband Thomas Ivins, issue: Charles; Rachel, who married Samuel Roberts, issue: Samuel Ralph and Wayne Walton. 3. Mary Jane. 4. Anna L., who married Penrose Wilson, one son, George R. 5. Isaac, who died at the age of four years.

James V. Randall was educated in the public schools of Bucks county, and at an early age learned the carriage manufacturing business with his uncle Isaac Randall, at Dolington, Bucks county, serving an apprenticeship of five years and working as a journeyman for his uncle one year. In 1854 he located at Newportville, Bucks county, and engaged in the manufacture of carriages. In the fall of the same year he took his brother Wilson into partnership and they did a small business there until 1857 under the firm name of J. V. & W. Randall. In the latter year they removed to Newtown, having purchased the plant of J. E. Woolsey, who had established a carriage manufacturing business there in 1852. This firm continued the business at Newtown until 1865, doing a large business. In that year James V. purchased the interest of his brother and continued the business alone until 1895, when his nephew, Clarence Randall, became a member of the firm, under the firm name of J. V. & C. Randall, which has continued to the present time. This firm do a large business in the manufacture and repair of carriages and wagons of all kinds used in this part of the country, and have built up an enviable reputation for the character of the work they turn out, and for fair and reliable methods of doing business with their home people. Their plant is thoroughly equipped with the best up-to-date machinery, and by a careful study of the wants and needs of the people they are able to keep in their large warerooms and sell at reasonable prices every variety of wagon and carriage used in this part of the country. The plant is one of the valuable institutions of Newtown, and employs several hands. In politics Mr. Randall is a Republican, but is a man of unassuming manners and retiring disposition, devoted to his business, and has never sought public office. He has served one term in the town council of Newtown. He is a strong advocate of temperance principles, and from boyhood has lived a moral, upright and temperate life, and devoted time and money to the cause of temperance. As an employer of a large number of hands over a period of fifty years, he has never permitted intemperance, profanity or the inordinate use of tobacco among his employees. His support and sympathy have always been with the Society of Friends, and all others whose teaching makes men better citizens and fits them for the whole of life's duties. He takes little interest in dogmatic theology, but much in the discoveries of science in the nineteenth century relating to the problems of the universe and man's place in nature.

He was married in 1858 to Mrs. Hannah L. Stradling, a daughter of Thomas Harding, and they were the parents of two children: George, who died at the age of four years; and William E., who is a photographer at Newtown, and is married to Meta Schisler, of Germantown, Pennsylvania. Mrs. Hannah Leedom Randall, the mother of his children, died in 1886, and Mr. Randall married in 1894 Kate Larue Krewson, daughter of Jonathan K. Krewson, of an old and highly respected family of lower Bucks. Her father devoted most of his life to school teaching and was for many years one of the prominent educators of Bucks county.

WILLIAM JOHNSON, of South Perkasie, Bucks county, Pennsylvania, was born February 6, 1847, at White Marsh, Montgomery county, on the old homestead where his ancestors had lived for several generations. Henry Johnson, the father of William, was a son of Henry, and was born and reared on the old homestead at White Marsh. He was a farmer and lime burner, carrying on for many years an extensive business in lime burning. He died on the old homestead in 1901. His wife was Deborah DeWees, of an old family in the nieghborhood of Valley Forge, and they were the parents of six children, Henry; the subject of this sketch; Samuel; Rachel; Emma, wife of Joseph Nyce; and Annie, wife of Daniel Hallman.

William Johnson was reared and educated in White Marsh township. He was for several years engaged in the lime business, and also was an extensive contractor in the building of macadam roads. He built the macadam road from Philadelphia to Chestnut Hill, and also filled other large contracts. In 1902 he came to South Perkasie and purchased the hotel property there, which he has since conducted. He is a member of the Masonic fraternity, being affiliated with Thompson Lodge, No. 340, F. and A. M.; and Thompson Chapter, No. 360, R. A. M., of Philadelphia. Mr. Johnson was for ten years a resident of Chester county, where he did an extensive business in lime burning, stone crushing and road building. In 1870 he married Sarah Leisinger, of Montgomery county, and they have been the parents of four children: Henry, who married Rebecca Schultz, of Norristown, and is engaged in the lime and stone business at Reading, Pennsylvania; Howard and Alfred, both of whom are deceased; and Mary.

HESTON WALTON, who was born December 31, 1845, on the home farm near Hatboro, where he yet resides, traces his ancestry back through several generations to William Walton, who was the youngest of four brothers of the Walton branch who came from England to America in 1678 and settled at Wilmington, Delaware, whence they found their wary to Byberry, in Philadelphia county, locating on land as a temporary place of residence. Later two of the brothers went on foot to Wilmington for supplies, and each carried a half bushel of wheat home with him. It is supposed that this was the first wheat seeded in eastern Pennsylvania. The brothers concluded to remain in the vicinity of their first location, and there they became valued settlers, promoting in large measure the early development and progress of the locality. William Walton, the youngest of the brothers, became the progenitor of the branch of the family to which Heston Walton belongs, and his descendants are now numerous in Montgomery and Bucks counties. The brothers were consistent members of the Friends' meeting in England, and became early representatives of the denomination in Pennsylvania. They were allied with the farming interests, and lived exemplary lives, contributing in large measure to the moral development as well as material upbuilding of the localities in which they lived. William Walton married Sarah Howell, and their son

(II) Jeremiah Walton, wedded Elizabeth Wamsley, and continued farming in eastern Pennsylvania.

(III) Jacob Walton, son of Jeremiah, Walton, was a farmer of Montgomery county, and his son

(IV) Isaiah Walton was born in Montgomery county, and wedded Mary Harding, whose birth occurred in Bucks county, and who belonged to a prominent old family founded in America in early colonial days. She was descended from Henry Harding, of Churchville, Bucks county. The children of Henry Harding were: Thomas, Joseph, Jonathan, Isaac, Abram, and Sarah, who married Jesse Gilbert. Thomas Harding was a farmer by occupation, and was a member of the Friends' meeting. His children were: Thomas, Henry, and Mary, the last named the grandmother of Heston Walton and the wife of Isaiah Walton. Isaiah Walton settled near York Pike, below Hatboro, where he reared his family and remained until his death. His children were: Seth, Sarah, Joseph, Jacob, Thomas, and Mary.

(V) Thomas Walton, son of Isaiah and Mary Walton, was born in Montgomery county, and wedded Mercy Heston, also a native of Bucks county. Thomas Walton was reared to the occupation of farming and afterward learned the stone-mason's trade, which he followed for twenty years. He then engaged in agricultural pursuits, and at the time of his marriage settled upon the farm which is now occupied by the son, Heston, taking up his abode there about 1842. He reared his family upon that place, and died December 14, 1882, at the advanced age of eighty-two years. He lived the quiet life of a mechanic and farmer, attending strictly to his business without active participation in public affairs, save that he never neglected his duties of citizenship. He was a faithful adherent of the Friends' meeting. His wife survived him and died March 26, 1888, in the eighty-seventh year of her age. She was a daughter of John and Rachel (Warner) Heston, who also belonged to colonial families that were identified with the Friends' meeting and were highly respected people. John and Rachel (Warner) Heston had four children: Rebecca, who died unmarried; Esther, who became the wife of A. Michner; Mercy, who became Mrs Walton; and Hannah, the wife of C. Stackhouse.

(VI) Heston Walton, the only child of Thomas and Mercy (Heston) Walton, was born and reared on the old family homestead, where he yet resides, early becoming familiar with the labors necessary for the cultivation and development of the fields and the care of the crops. He pursued a public-school education, and largely assisted his father in the farm work during the period of his youth, while later he has engaged in farming and marketing on his own ac-

count. In his work he has prospered, owing to his close application and careful management, and he now has a well improved farm on which is a commodious stone residence, large barns and other outbuildings, and groves of forest and fruit trees. He keeps the entire place under a high state of cultivation and uses the latest improved machinery in operating his land. He is an enterprising and public spirited agriculturist, and in addition to his home place owns a well improved farm in Montgomery county. Mr. Walton exercises his right of franchise in support of the Republican party, takes an active interest in the questions of the day and frequently attends the party conventions, but has never sought or desired office. He was reared in the Friends' faith, and although not a member of any church has lived a life in consistent harmony with high principles.

In 1874 Mr. Walton was married to Elizabeth Eastburn, who was born in Makefield township, and is a daughter of John and Sarah (Smith) Eastburn, representatives of families long connected with eastern Pennsylvania. The father, John Eastburn, was a well known farmer of Bucks county, and throughout his entire life remained on the old homestead, where he died January 27, 1878, at the age of seventy-seven years. His wife had passed away August 18, 1863, at the age of sixty-three years. They were the parents of three children: Hettie A., the wife of C. Williams; Elizabeth, now Mrs. Walton; and one that died unmarried. Mr. and Mrs. Walton had a daughter, Hettie A., who was born May 10, 1875. Mrs. Walton's death occurred September 9, 1888.

JOSHUA RICHARDSON. The Richardson family of Attleboro, Pennsylvania, the members of which have been noted for sterling integrity and indomitable courage and patriotism, was founded in America in 1724 by Joseph Richardson, who upon his arrival here from his native land, England, located near Oxford, where he commenced work on the farm of William Paxson. October 21, 1732, he married Mary Paxson, daughter of William Paxson, and shortly afterward moved to Four-Lanes-End, where he engaged in business for himself in a country store. The line of descent from the pioneer ancestors is as follows: Joshua, who married Sarah Preston; Joseph, who married Mary Dixon; and Joshua, whose name appears at the head of this sketch.

Joshua Richardson, son of Joseph and Mary (Dixon) Richardson, was born in Attleboro, Pennsylvania, (now Langhorn borough) March 6, 1803. After completing his studies in the Friends' school at Attleboro he assisted in the farm work, as was the custom with the boys of that period, on his father's estate, and this occupation proving congenial to his tastes and also highly remunerative he followed the same throughout the active years of his career.

October 15, 1835, Mr. Richardson married Mary Carpenter Hunt, who died July 18, 1836, leaving no issue. On March 15, 1838, he was united in marriage to Mary Knight, of Lower Makefield, Bucks county, daughter of Joshua and Jane (Bunting) Knight, the former named having been a son of John and Margery (Paxson) Knight, and the latter a daughter of William and Margery (Woolston) Bunting. Three children were the issue of the second marriage, namely:

1. Joseph, born March 14, 1839, attended the Friends' school, Bucks County Academy at Langhorn, and Foulk's boarding school at Gwynedd. He is now retired from active agricultural pursuits. February 16, 1865, he married Hannah Gillingham Rowland, of Middletown township, daughter of William D. and Margaret G. Rowland, and their children are as follows: Margaret, born February 3, 1866, attended the public schools of Middletown township and the Friends' school at Langhorne, and January 23, 1890, became the wife of Newton May Comly, of Philadelphia, and their children are: Rowland Richardson, born December 23, 1890; Bessie May, born February 11, 1892; Edith Bosler, born July 17, 1894; John Byron, born June 17, 1896; Mary Richardson, born July 14, 1897; and Helen Maud, born February 18, 1899. These children attended the public schools of Bustleton, and the eldest, Rowland Richardson Comly, is completing his studies at the Manual Training School in Philadelphia. Mary Rowland, born July 13, 1867, attended the public schools of Middletown township and the Friends' school at Langhorne. Samuel, born February 25, 1869, also acquired his education in the same institutions. Joshua, born November 12, 1872, attended the same institutions of learning as his brothers and sisters, and the knowledge thus obtained was supplemented by attendance at Pierce's Business College, Philadelphia, from which he was graduated.

2. Edward, born April 21, 1841, attended the Friends' school and the Bucks County Academy at Langhorne, and he is now one of the representative agriculturists of Bucks county, his prosperity being the direct result of capability and efficiency.

3. Mary, born March 7, 1844, acquired her educational advantages at the Friends' school and Bucks County Academy, and is widely known and highly esteemed throughout the section in which she resides for her many estimable traits of character.

SIPRON C. KEITH, the genial proprietor of the popular hostelry known as the White Hall Hotel in Newtown, was born in Kings county, province of New Brunswick, Domonion of Canada, where his paternal ancestors had resided for several generations, on October 1, 1854. He is a son of Noah and Catharine (Alward) Keith, the ancestors of the latter having resided in the state of New York for several generations. He was educated at the parish schools of his native county, and early in life learned the trade of a plasterer, which he followed in his native county until 1883, when he removed to Minneapolis, Minnesota, where he remained for three years. After a year spent in Chicago he removed to Philadelphia in the spring of 1886 and was employed there until the spring of 1891, when he came to Newtown and purchased the White Hall Hotel, which he has since successfully conducted, making it one of the popular hostelries of lower Bucks. Mr. Keith married in Philadelphia, July 18, 1889, Kate E. Salter, daughter of Charles Burleigh and Anna E. (Sperry) Salter, of that city. Their only child is Ruth Marion, born at Newtown, May 10, 1892.

The White Hall Hotel, while not one of the old colonial inns, is nevertheless of historic interest. At the time of the revolutionary war and for many years after it was kept as a store, the proprietor at that time being a man by the name of Campbell. During a great part of the war it was occupied by a government quartermaster as a store house for supplies for the American army, and was raided by the Doan outlaws, who carried off a lot of government stores. It was later occupied as a store by a man by the name of Evans, who Josiah B. Smith, the historian of the town, referred to as "one of the noisy storekeepers." In 1796 it was purchased by Isaac Hicks, Esq., and was occupied by him as a residence and justice's office for the next forty years. The "Old Squire," as he was known, was a character in his day, and did an immense amount of public business, and could the old timbers of the White Hall be given a tongue they could probably recite for our edification many amusing legal tilts held within its walls. After the death of the "Squire" it was purchased by his grandson, Dr. Edward H. Kennedy, who soon after built a new house, and the old White Hall was occupied as a school, the title being vested in about a dozen of the prominent citizens of the town at that time. It was

James Conrad

Henry Gage

first licensed as a tavern in 1852 to Daniel Y. Harman, on the petition of about one hundred residents of the town and vicinity, and against the remonstrance of about half that number and was re-licensed the following year. For the next five years the license was refused by the court. In 1858 a license was granted to Amos W. Buckman, and it has remained a regularly licensed place every since. Mr. Buckman conducted the tavern until 1864, and was succeeded by Samuel Thatcher, and he in turn three years later by Mahlon S. Harding, who remained for two years, and then sold out to James Wesley Hellings, who in less than a year sold the tavern to Samuel L. Ettenger, who owned the property for many years, and was its proprietor at three different periods during the next ten years, it being conducted in the intervals by his tenants, Burtis Magill, George W. Shinn, Mrs. Alice Shinn, and Frederick Schiefer. From February, 1880, to May, 1891, it was conducted by Edward A. Tomlinson, who was then succeeded by Mr. Keith. During the year 1904 Mr. Keith made extensive improvements, practically renewing and remodeling the whole structure.

JAMES CONRAD, for many years the popular funeral director of Mozart, Buckingham township, Bucks county, was born in Warwick township, July 12, 1835, and died January 20, 1905. He was a son of Charles and Mary (Patterson) Conrad, and grandson of William and Hannah (DeCoursey) Conrad. Both the father and grandfather were farmers and lifelong residents of Buckingham and Warwick townships. Charles Conrad was born in Buckingham in 1800, and died there in 1873. He was the father of four children, three of whom survive, John Conrad, of Rushland; Robert, of Philadelphia; and the subject of this sketch.

James Conrad was reared in Buckingham and received his education at the public schools. At the age of eighteen years he apprenticed himself to the carpenter trade, and after finishing his apprenticeship, followed the trade for several years, erecting many buildings in that section of Bucks county. He also engaged for some time in the manufacture of pumps. In 1870 he began the business of an undertaker, which he followed up to his decease, conducting a large number of funerals in central Bucks county during the last thirty years. Mr. Conrad was a man of high standing in the community, and filled many positions of trust. He served as a school director, and was one of the trustees and directors of the Hughesian free school. In politics he was a Republican. He was a member of Doylestown

17-3

Lodge, No. 245, F. and A. M., and Doylestown Chapter, No. 270, R. A. M. He was married March 13, 1862, to Martha C. Worthington, daughter of William and Seraphina (Taylor) Worthington, of Buckingham. She was a native of Wrightstown, but her girlhood days were spent in Buckingham. She died in April, 1902. Their only child Minnie Jane died at the age of twenty-one years.

HENRY GARGES. Among the men who have achieved financial success in the management of their farming interests, and have thus been enabled to retire from active business pursuits during the latter years of their life, is Henry Garges, who was born on the old homestead near Doylestown, Bucks county, Pennsylvania, August 19, 1830.

John Garges, grandfather of Henry Garges, lived and died near Doylestown, Bucks county, where he followed farming as a means of livelihood during his entire active career. He owned the farm adjoining that of Henry Garges, now in the possession of the County Historical Society. He was a member of the old Mennonite church. His family consisted of four sons and five daughters, namely: William, Henry, John, Abraham, Mary, wife of Abram Gile; Sarah, wife of John Myers; Elizabeth, wife of Philip Gile; Percilla, wife of William Borrows; and Margaret, wife of William Fritz.

Abraham Garges, father of Henry Garges, was born on the old homestead near Doylestown, Bucks county, in 1784. In early life he served an apprenticeship at the trade of blacksmith, which occupation he worked at in connection with farming for a number of years, thereby providing a comfortable home for his family. He was one of the first school directors of Doylestown township after the free school system was inaugurated, this giving evidence of the appreciation in which he was held by his fellow citizens. In 1845 he removed to Warwick township, and also served as school director there for a number of years. He held membership in the old Mennonite church, and his political views were in accord with those of the old Whig party. He was united in marriage to Leah Ruth, and eight children were born to them: William, deceased, who was a farmer of New Britain township; Mary, wife of James C. Fell; Rebecca, wife of Joseph Funck; Henry, mentioned hereinafter; Sarah Ann, wife of Oliver P. Shutt; Prucilla, wife of Henry Haines; Amy L., who died in early life; and Lewis, a farmer of Doylestown township. Abraham Garges (father) died in Doylestown township, May 5, 1861, aged seventy-seven years.

Henry Garges spent the years of his

boyhood in the same fashion as the majority of boys reared on a farm—attending the common schools and assisting with the duties pertaining to farm life. He remained at home with his father—cultivating and tilling the farm —until the death of the latter in 1861, when he inherited the property, on which he continued his operations until 1900, since which time he has lived retired. He served as school director of Doylestown township for three years, and the cause of education has always found in him an active and willing supporter. He is staunch in his advocacy of Republican principles, contributing materially to the success of that party in his community. He is a member of the Presbyterian church of Doylestown. Mr. Garges was united in marriage to Mary Elizabeth Roberts, daughter of George and Anna Roberts, and three children were the issue of this union: Annie Leah, born March 16, 1864, wife of B. Frank Bodine; Edward, born April 6, 1865, a farmer of Warrington township; and Isaac B., born February 9, 1867, a grocer of Philadelphia. Mrs. Garges, the mother of these children, died June 9, 1901.

CHARLES H. RHOADES, liveryman, Doylestown, was born near Brick Tavern, Milford township, Bucks county, June 4, 1860, a son of Jacob B. and Mary (Hockman) Roth. The family of Roth (the original form of the name) is a German one, many of the name emigrating to Pennsylvania between the years 1730 and 1800. One branch of the family settled in Rockhill, where their descendants still reside. The name being pronounced "Rote," came to be spelled Rhoad, and in various other forms. The subject of this sketch was, however, descended from a later emigrant. Johan Jost Roth, with wife, Louise Rodepiller, (later Reedmiller), and children, John Heinrich, Ludwig, and Herman, migrated from Germany in the ship "Fortune," from Hamburg, and settled in Bedminster township. Ludwig Roth, the great-grandfather of the subject of this sketch, purchased a small farm near Bedministerville in 1806, and died there in 1824, leaving wife Elizabeth, sons Mathew and George, and grandsons John B. and Jacob B., sons of his deceased son Christian.

Jacob B. Roth settled in Milford township in 1841, where he followed the trade of a stone mason. As early as 1841 he purchased land near Brick Tavern on the Bethlehem road. He was twice married, his first wife being Roselna Groude, by whom he had one child that died young. He married (second) Mary Hockman, who survives him, living with her daughter in Doylestown. Jacob B.

Roth died at Brick Tavern, Milford township, November 6, 1866. His chilren were: Sallie, who married Eliab Ritchie; and Charles H., the subject of this sketch.

Charles Hockman Rhoades, the subject of this sketch, was but six years old at the death of his father, and his sister Sallie was but two years his senior. As soon as the estate of his father was settled, the widow Roth, with her two children, removed to Doylestown, where her brother Peter Hockman had a livery stable, and about a year later removed to Warrington, where his mother was housekeeper for Joseph Paul, Esq., for two years. The family then removed to Fox Chase, Montgomery county, where the boyhood of the subject of this sketch was spent. He was educated at the Abington Friends' school, and on arriving at his majority in 1881 he came to Doylestown, and, in connection with his brother-in-law, Eliab Ritchie, opened a livery stable near the railroad depot, where he still has his stand. A year later he bought out the interest of his brother-in-law, and has since conducted the business alone. In politics Mr. Rhoades is a Republican. He has served three years as a member of town council, and has filled other local offices. He is a member of Aquetong Lodge, No. 193, I. O. O. F., and of St. Tammany Castle, K. G. E., of Doylestown. He was married February 6, 1886, to Ella, daughter of George and Anna Maria Burgstresser, and has one daughter Edith, now fifteen years of age.

JOHN PHILLIPS BLACK. Among the active business men of Langhorne, Bucks county, is John Phillips Black, who was born in that town March 16, 1839, and is a son of John and Rachel Shaw (Wells) Black.

John Black, the father, born in 1807, was a cooper by trade, and followed that trade for several years in Langhorne, where he purchased a home in 1850. He also assisted in building a number of the older buildings in that vicinity. He was a native of Bucks county, and a son of James and Judith (Searle) Black, the latter being a granddaughter of Arthur Searle, an early settler near the Neshaminy in Southampton, who married a daughter of John Naylor of Southampton. John Black married Rachel Shaw Wells, born 1814, daughter of Valentine (born 1784) and Phoebe (Shaw) Wells of Middletown (born 1785) the latter being a daughter of Gideon Shaw. John and Rachel S. (Wells) Black were the parents of nine children: John P., the subject of this sketch; Elizabeth, wife of William Gillingham; Margaret, wife of Barclay Wildman; Franklin S., of Tullytown; Emma T., wife of Byran Wright; Phebe W.; William G., George D., and Catherine, died young.

John Black, Sr., died in July, 1859, and his widow survived him many years, dying August 6, 1904, at the age of nearly ninety years.

John Phillips Black was reared in Langhorne, and obtained his education in the public and Friends' schools of that town. At the age of twelve years he hired out on a farm, where he remained for four years. In 1856 he went to Newtown to learn the trade of a carriage blacksmith, which he finished at Langhorne. He found employment at Hulmeville as a journeyman, and later located at Bridgetown, where he remained for five years. He then bought the T. W. Boileau property in Langhorne, and later the wheelwright shops and business adjoining, thus uniting under one ownership and management a complete carriage building establishment which he has since successfully conducted, doing a large and profitable business, making his establishment one of the largest of its kind in lower Bucks. Mr. Black is an enterprising and active citizen, and takes an active interest in the affairs of his town. He has served several terms in the town council, and has filled other local offices. He is a member of Orionto Lodge, No. 177, I. O. O. F., of Langhorne.

On February 5, 1863, Mr. Black married Rachel Pyle Boyce, daughter of Samuel and Jane (Stevens) Boyce, of Philadelphia county, the former a native of Delaware, and a son of Robert Boyce, whose father was a large tobacco planter and snuff manufacturer in that state; and the latter a native of Southampton township, Bucks county, and a daughter of Benjamin Stevens, whose ancestors had been residents of that locality for several generations. Mr. and Mrs. Black are the parents of three children, viz: Wilmer Stevens, born April 18, 1865; Emma Elizabeth, born August 15, 1869; and Clarence Randall, born June 6, 1873, all of whom were born and reared in Langhorne, and were educated in the local schools.

Wilmer Stevens Black at an early age became associated with his father in the conduct of the carriage building establishment, and has been a valuable assistant in the work. He married April 17, 1890, Anne Bentley Candy, daughter of James B. and Mary Jane (Moser) Candy, of Langhorne, an account of whose ancestry is given elsewhere in this work. Wilmer S. and Anne C. Black are the parents of two children: Edith Holbrook, born September 13, 1898; and Cyrille Kershaw, born July 29, 1904.

Emma Elizabeth Black, only daughter of John P. and Rachel (Boyce) Black, married August 21, 1890, Samuel Mills Myers, and they are the parents of five children, viz: Elenore Kruger, born October 12, 1893; John Harold, born October 8, 1895; Boyce Mills, born October 7, 1897; Inez May, born December 4, 1899; and Dever, born April 15, 1902.

CLARENCE RANDALL BLACK, son of John Phillips and Rachel Pyle (Boyce) Black, was born in Langhorne, June 6, 1873, and was educated in the public and Friends' schools of Langhorne. At the age of sixteen years he entered the wood working department of his father's carriage building establishment, where he was employed for about two years, when, having an inclination towards the painting department, he learned that branch of the work and now has entire charge of the carriage painting department of the works as superintendent of the entire force of men employed therein. He also acts as salesman, and has a general oversight over the whole establishment. In politics Mr. Black is a Republican, and takes an active interest in local affairs. He is a member of Langhorne Castle, Knights of the Golden Eagle. He and his family attend the Langhorne Methodist Episcopal church, both Mr. and Mrs. Black being members of the choir of that church. He married, May 26, 1898, Elizabeth Davis Duffield, daughter of the late Thomas Hart Benton and Rebecca (Search) Duffield, granddaughter of Alfred Torbert and Rebecca Miles (Davis) Duffield, and great-granddaughter of General John Davis, of Davisville, Bucks county. Her maternal grandparents were James and Susanna (Hall) Search, the former a son of Samuel and Katharine (Puff) Search, and grandson of Christopher and ———— (Torbert) Search, and the latter a daughter of John and Eleanor (Comly) Hall, all early and prominent residents of lower Bucks.

SAMUEL G. PRICE, V. S., of Doylestown, was born in Solebury township, Bucks county, Pennsylvania, May 25, 1846, and is a son of John N. and Christianna (Godshalk) Price, of Solebury. The paternal ancestors of Dr. Price were early settlers in New Jersey, but were probably descendants of John Price, who came from England to Philadelphia, in 1683.

James Price was a considerable landowner in Maidenhead township, near the present site of Lawrenceville, New Jersey, as early as 1698, and was a prominent man in that section. He was commissioned lieutenant of provincial militia, March 19, 1714, and his son John was a captain in the provincial service during the colonial wars, and died at Hopewell in 1773, leaving sons: John,

James, and David and several daughters, one of whom, Elizabeth, married James Slack, of Hunterdon county in 1732. James Price, above mentioned, married Elizabeth Ely, daughter of George Ely, of Trenton, in 1737, and had one son George.

David Price, supposed to have been a son of James of Maidenhead, was the direct ancestor of Dr. Price. He was a large landholder in the neighborhood of Hopewell, New Jersey, and in 1756 purchased 200 acres of land in Middletown township, and died there in 1765, leaving two sons, Nathan and James, and four daughters, Rebecca, who married Daniel Price of Kingwood, Hunterdon county, New Jersey, and doubtless a descendant of Benjamin Price, who settled at Elizabethtown, New Jersey, in 1677, whose son Daniel was sheriff of his county in 1692; Eleanor, who married Benjamin Stackhouse of Bucks county in 1761; Sarah, who died single in Merion, Philadelphia county, in 1767; and Susannah, who married Joseph Mahr, of Northampton county. James Price, the second son, married Sarah Huddleston, of Middletown, and lived and died on the old homestead there.

Nathan Price was for some years a resident of Bucks county, but removed to Kingwood, Hunterdon county, New Jersey, prior to 1775, where he became a prominent citizen, and served as sheriff of the county, 1806-8. He is said to have married a daughter of Timothy Smith, sheriff of Bucks county, 1728-30, and 1737-9. The children of Nathan Price in 1767 as shown by the will of his sister Sarah were: John, Rebecca, Smith, Elizabeth, Sarah, Phebe, James and David.

Smith Price, second son of Nathan, was born September 11, 1748. Both he and his brother John were residents of Plumstead township during the revolution, the latter serving as first lieutenant of militia. Smith was a wheelwright by trade and followed that line of work for a number of years in Plumstead. He later became a storekeeper at Gardenville, and was a considerable land owner in Plumstead. He married, September 1, 1776, before Isaac Hicks, Esq., of Newtown, Martha Carver, born December 21, 1756, died April 11, 1793, daughter of Joseph Carver, of Buckingham, and had one son John, born May 15, 1779. He married (second) Hannah ―――― and had children: Jonathan, Joseph, Samuel, Smith, Mary and Burroughs. He died October 17, 1816, at the age of eighty-eight years.

John Price, only surviving child of Smith and Martha (Carver) Price, born in Plumstead township May 15, 1779, was a lifelong resident of Plumstead. On his marriage in 1798 he settled on his father's farm on the Durham road,

below Gardenville, which he inherited later under his father's will, and lived there until his death, November 2, 1828, in his fiftieth year. He married, January 21, 1798, Elizabeth Kirk, born October 19, 1773, died January 11, 1849, daughter of Stephen and Phebe (Fell) Kirk, and granddaughter of Isaac and Elizabeth (Twining) Kirk, and of Benjamin and Hannah (Scarborough) Fell, the former of whom was born in Cumberland, England, in 1703. (See Fell, Kirk, and Scarborough families in this work). The children of John and Elizabeth (Kirk) Price were: Phebe, born 1799, died 1802; Charles M., born June 29, 1801, married Susan Rich; Martha, born February 8, 1804, married Yeamans Paul Jones; Kirk J., born September 24, 1805, married Sarah Brown; Stephen K., born October 30, 1807, married (first) Rebecca Carey and (second) Nancy Flack; Sarah B., born October 7, 1809, married James Meredith; John N., born September 19, 1811, married Christianna Godshalk; Hannah Brock, born January 20, 1814, married Eleazer F. Church, of Newtown; Smith, twin to Hannah B., married Harriet Opp; and Preston, born September 30, 1816.

John N. Price, son of John and Elizabeth (Kirk) Price, born in Plumstead, September 19, 1811, resided the greater part of his life in Solebury township, where he owned and operated a small farm. After the death of his wife he resided for a number of years with his son Samuel G., in Plumstead and Doylestown, dying at the later place August 8, 1888, in his seventy-seventh year. He married, December 27, 1832, Christianna Godshalk, daughter of Samuel and Sidney Godshalk, born April 20, 1811, died February 19, 1865. Samuel Godslalk was born November 11, 1778, and died June 26, 1860, and his wife Sidney, whom he married in February, 1801, was born December 17, 1780, and died May 30, 1850. The children of John N. and Christianna (Godshalk) Price were: Edmund M., born November 7, 1833, died at Lahaska, Bucks county, August 12, 1893, was for many years a veterinary surgeon in Buckingham; Elizabeth H., born July 1, 1836, died April 2, 1856, married Walker Booz, of Carversville; Sidney G., born August 16, 1840, married Joseph Mathews, of Solebury, and is still living; John Beatty, born April 17, 1842, died in a military hospital at Mound City, Illinois, August 19, 1863, from sickness contracted in the army in the civil war, in Durell's Battery; Mary P., born November 26, 1843, married Harvey Fretz; and Samuel G., born May 25, 1846.

Samuel G. Price was born and reared in Solebury township, and acquired his education at the public schools and at Carversville Excelsior Normal Institute. On leaving school he filled the position of clerk in the store of Richard R. Paxson, at Lahaska, for two years. He then taught school in Warwick township for one term, in the meanwhile studying veterinary surgery under Dr. Joshua C. Smith, of New Hope. He began practice as a veterinary surgeon in Plumstead, in 1869, and followed his profession there for seventeen years, most of which time he was located at Danboro. In 1886 he removed to Doylestown, where he has since conducted a large practice. He takes an active interest in local affairs, has served for three years as a member of the Doylestown school board, and is serving his second term of three years each as a member of borough council. At Danboro he was affiliated with the local lodges of I. O. R. M. and the Golden Eagles. He is a member and past master of Doylestown Lodge, No. 245, F. and A. M., and a past high priest of Doylestown Chapter, No. 270, R. A. M. He is also a past officer of Aquetong Lodge, No. 193, and Doylestown Encampment, No. 35, I. O. O. F., and takes a leading part in the degree staffs of both lodge and encampment.

Dr. Price married, at the Doylestown Presbyterian manse, November 29, 1872, Rachel A. Cadwallader, daughter of James and Christianna (Fell) Cadwallader, of Buckingham, and granddaughter of Eli and Rachel (Morris) Cadwallader. On the maternal line Mrs. Price is descended from Joseph Fell, who came from Cumberland, England, in 1795, and settled in Buckingham two years later, through his son Benjamin, before mentioned. To Dr. and Mrs. Price have been born two children: Beatty, July 2, 1876, died May 8, 1877; and Christianna, February 24, 1879, wife of John L. DuBois, Jr., a member of Bucks county bar. To Mr. and Mrs. DuBois have been born two children: Rachel, who died September 29, 1901, and John Latta DuBois, born December 5, 1903.

WILMER KRUSEN, M. D., was born in Bucks county, Pennsylvania, May 18, 1869, a son of John and Elizabeth A. (Sager) Krusen. He is of Holland-Dutch descent, and his father was a farmer of Bucks county.

He was educated in the public schools of his native county, and read medicine for a year with Dr. Charles B. Smith, of Newtown, Pennsylvania, before entering Jefferson Medical College, from which he was graduated in 1893, with the degree of Doctor of Medicine. For a year following he was resident physician in the Jefferson Hospital. He then opened a practice in Philadelphia, his specialty being gynecology, and since 1894 has been instructor in gynecology

at Jefferson College. He has been assistant gynecologist in the Jefferson Hospital, the St. Joseph Hospital and the Samaritan Hospital. He is chief of the Gynecological Dispensary of St. Joseph's Hospital, and a fellow of the College of Physicians. He is at present (1905) chief gynecologist of the Samaritan Hospital, and professor of gynecology in the Temple Medical College. He is a member of the American Medical Association, of the Philadelphia County Medical Association, of the Philadelphia County Medical Society, the Philadelphia Medical Club, the Philadelphia Obstetrical Society, the Northwestern Medical Society, and the Philadelphia Pathological Society. He is a collaborator on "American Medicine," and has written many articles in the line of his specialty. In politics he is a Republican. In 1895 Dr. Krusen married Elizabeth W. Gilbert, and his three children are: Edward M., Francis H., and Carolyn A.

JOHN H. VANSANT, whose extensive agricultural pursuits have brought to him a large degree of prosperity as a result of his reliable and progressive methods, is a native of the community in which he resides, Eddington, Bensalem township, Bucks county, Pennsylvania, born October 31, 1840, a son of John F. and Mary (Boozer) Vansant.

John F. Vansant (father) was also a native of Bucks county, Pennsylvania, born in 1806. He was a blacksmith by trade, which line of work he followed in Cornwells, opposite the old tavern where the stage horses were changed, and, being an expert mechanic, his trade increased steadily both in volume and importance from year to year, becoming a lucrative means of livelihood. In 1840 he purchased the farm at Eddington where his son John H. now resides, and in connection with his farming pursuits conducted a blacksmith shop at that place, continuing until his death. By his marriage to Mary Boozer, of Bensalem township, Bucks county, nine children were born, seven of whom attained years of maturity, as follows: Charles, Jesse, Thomas, Margaret, Elizabeth, John H., and James. The family attended the Episcopal church, in the work and to the support of which they were liberal contributors. Mr. Vansant died in 1866, in the sixty-seventh year of his age; his wife died September 29, 1889, having attained the advanced age of eighty-six years.

John H. Vansant was reared on his father's farm, whereon he has resided during his entire lifetime, and thus became thoroughly familiar with all the details of the quiet but useful calling of agriculture, to which he has since devoted his entire time and attention. His land is under a high state of cultivation and therefore produces goodly harvests, and, the products being of a superior quality, find a ready sale in the nearby markets. Mr. Vansant has always taken a keen interest in township affairs, and has been the incumbent of several local offices, including that of assessor, in which capacity he served for a number of years. His political views coincide with those advocated by the Democratic party, whose candidates and measures he has upheld since attaining his majority. He and family attend the Episcopal church.

Mr. Vansant married, September 11, 1867, Ella Van Horn, daughter of Thomas Van Horn, of Philadelphia county, Pennsylvania, and two children were the issue of this union: 1. William N., born February 5, 1869, educated in the public schools, and at the Naval Academy, at Annapolis, Maryland, graduating at the head of his class in 1888. He was sent by the government to The Royal Naval College, Greenwich, England, studying three years as a naval constructor, and ranked as lieutenant His death occurred January 1, 1893. 2. Charles H. born February 19, 1871, attended the Lehigh University, and is now a civil engineer. He is connected with the Berlin Construction Company, and he assisted in the construction of the New York Subway.

HARRY F. MOLLOY, recorder of deeds of the county of Bucks, was born in Wrightstown, August 14, 1856, and is a son of Nicholas E. and Frances Jenks (Stradling) Molloy.

Nicholas E. Molloy, for many years a well known farmer and highly respected citizen of Wrightstown, was born on the Atlantic ocean when his parents were on their way to America from Ireland in 1817. At the age of six he was taken charge of by David Shipps of Northampton township, and was reared in his family. Soon after arriving at manhood he purchased a farm in Northampton, near Richboro, on which he resided for a number of years, and then sold it and removed to Wrightstown where he resided for two years, and then removed to the old Lacey farm in Buckingham, on the Wrightstown line, the birthplace of General John Lacey, living in the house erected by the Lacey family about 1706, now torn down. He purchased this farm in 1878, but had previously purchased and removed upon an adjoining farm, now occupied by his son Harry F Molloy, where he died in August, 1880, aged sixty-three years. Mr. Molloy was an industrious and successful man, and was highly respected in the community. For over thirty years he ran a commission wagon to Philadelphia, carrying his own and his neighbors' country produce to the Philadelphia market. He was a member of the I. O. O. F. lodge and encampment. Frances J. Stradling, the mother of the subject of this sketch, was a daughter of Thomas Stradling, and a descendant of Thomas Stradling who married, October 5, 1715, Lydia Doan, daughter of Daniel Doan, who came to Middletown from Massachusetts in 1699. Thomas Stradling settled in Newtown township, where he died in 1761, leaving two sons: Daniel, of Plumstead, and Joseph, who died on the homestead in 1810, without issue, and the children of his second son Thomas who died in Newtown in 1757. Thomas, Jr., the ancestor of Mrs. Molloy, married, December 13, 1744, Elizabeth Fisher, born June 13, 1727, daughter of John and Elizabeth (Scarborough) Fisher, who, after his death, married, December 4, 1759, Joseph Lee. The children of Thomas and Elizabeth (Fisher) Stradling were: Sarah, Elizabeth, John, Thomas, and Daniel, of whom Thomas was the grandfather of Mrs. Molloy. Nicholas E. and Frances J. (Stradling) Molloy were the parents of three children: Harry F., the present recorder of deeds of Bucks county, and popular merchant at Pineville; Anna, wife of W. Harry Rockafellow, of Buckingham; and John B. Molloy, of Wycombe, a sketch of whom appears in this work.

Harry F. Molloy was born and reared in Wrightstown and has always lived in that vicinity. He was educated at the public schools, and continued to reside on his father's farm until 1875, when he became a clerk in the store of Jesse P. Carver, at Pineville, of which he is now proprietor. On Mr. Carver's retirement in 1877 he continued with his successor, Seth Cattell Van Pelt, until 1879 when he went back to the farm. In 1888 he purchased the store at Mozart, Buckingham township, where he conducted the mercantile business for five years. Having purchased the store stand at Pineville, he removed there April 1, 1893, and has since conducted a large and successful business there. In politics Mr. Molloy is a Democrat, and in the fall of 1902 was elected on the Democrat ticket to the office of recorder of deeds. He continued to conduct his store at Pineville, spending a portion of each week in the office in Doylestown, which is mainly conducted by his son J. Carroll, a young man of much promise. Mr. Molloy takes an active interest in local affairs, and is well and favorably known in his native township. He is a member of Doylestown Lodge No. 245, F. and A. M.; Doylestown Chapter No. 270, R. A. M.; of Northern Star Lodge No. 54, I. O. O. F. at Richboro; Newtown Council, K. of P.; and Wycombe Castle No. 125, K. G. E.

Harry F. Molloy

He married in 1883 Anna M. Leedom,, daughter of John and Sarah (Harrold) Leedom, of Wrightstown. She died October 5, 1902. On the paternal side she was descended from Richard Leedom, an early English settler in Southampton, the ancestor of a numerous and prominent family in Lower Bucks and elsewhere, and on the maternal side from Samuel Harrold, who came from Ireland in the early part of the eighteenth century and settled in Buckingham, where he became a large landholder and prominent man. He was twice married and reared a large family, who have left numerous descendants in Bucks, though few of the name now reside here. The children of Harry F. and Anna M. (Leedom) Molloy are: J. Carroll and William H.

JOSEPH L. SMITH connected with the farming interests of Warminster township, was born in Lower Makefield township, Bucks county, June 8, 1860. The family is of German lineage and was established in America at an early epoch in the history of this part of the state. The paternal grandfather, Andrew Smith, was a native of Bucks county, following the occupation of farming and was widely known and highly respected. He gave his political allegiance to the Democratic party. His sons and daughters were as follows: Elias A.; William; Andrew; James; Jessie H.; Alfred R.; Mary, the wife of J. B. Tumbleson; Elizabeth, the wife of George Slack; and Jane and Etta, who are still living. The parents were consistent and faithful members of the Episcopal church.

William Smith, father of Joseph L. Smith, was born in Makefield township, and was reared to the occupation of farming in Bucks county. He followed that pursuit throughout his entire life, remaining upon the old homestead farm up to the time of his marriage, when he settled upon a tract of rented land, which he continued to operate for a few years or until his industry and economy had brought him capital sufficient to enable him to make purchase of land. He then bought a farm, which he conducted for a number of years; he then sold that and purchased a larger tract of land whereon he spent his remaining days. He followed general farming and sold his produce in the Philadelphia market. In all of his business interests he was practical and energetic, and his well conducted affairs brought to him deserved success. He left to his family an untarnished name because of his integrity and honor in all life's relations. His political views were in harmony with Democratic principles, and he kept well informed on all the questions and issues of the day. He belonged to the Friends' Meeting, and died in that faith in April, 1904. In early manhood he wedded Sarah A. Linton, who died May 25, 1902. She was a daughter of Thomas and Hannah Linton, descendants of old families of Bucks county. Her father was a leading and influential farmer, whose political support was given to the Whig party and afterward to the Republican party, and who in his religious faith was a Friend. In his family were two sons and a daughter: William and Joseph, who follow farming; and Sarah, who became Mrs. Smith. To Mr. and Mrs. William Smith were born six children: Anna, who married Joseph R. Comly; Emma, the wife of S. D. Tomlinson; William A., who follows farming on the old homestead; Joseph L.; Sarah H., who married Joseph W. Ross; and Jennie E.

Joseph L. Smith remained in the home of his parents up to the time of his marriage, which occurred in 1888. He had been reared to the occupation of farming, and he chose that pursuit as a life work. At the time of his marriage he settled on the farm where he now resides, one mile east of Ivyland, and there he carries on general agricultural pursuits, attending the Philadelphia market, where he places his farm products on sale. He has many regular patrons, and his business has become profitable. His farm is productive and is kept in a high state of cultivation. There is a commodious residence, splendidly situated on a building site that commands an excellent view of the surrounding country. There are beautiful trees about the place and everything is neat and attractive in appearance. There is a large barn, commodious outbuildings and, in fact, the entire property is well improved. He uses the best farm implements in conducting the labor of field and meadow, and he raises some stock for the support of the farm. He is a fancier of fine horses and always has some splendid ones upon his place. He is now raising some colts, having two fine thoroughbreds which will undoubtedly develop into superior roadsters if not race horses. Mr. Smith is a stanch advocate of Democratic principles, and uses his influence to further the growth and success of his party. He is well qualified for public office, but the Democracy is in the minority in Bucks county, and Mr. Smith belongs to that class of men who would never surrender a principle for an office within the gift of the people. He has served as school director, however, for nine years and the cause of education has found in him a warm friend. He is a man of social nature, of pleasant address, public-spirited and highly respected.

Mr. Smith married Miss Martha H. Spencer, who was born in Northampton township, in 1864, a daughter of Cameron and Rachel B. (Hart) Spencer, both natives of Bucks county, their ancestors having located here in early days. In fact the name of Spencer is closely associated with the history of the material and moral development of this part of the state. The early representatives of the name here were of Irish birth and of Presbyterian faith. John Spencer was enrolled with the volunteers in the war of 1812, and afterward received a pension in recognition of his services. His son, Samuel Spencer, was a reliable farmer, successfully conducting his business affairs. He voted with the Whig party in early life, and upon its dissolution joined the ranks of the new Republican party. His religious faith was that of the Presbyterian church. He married Sarah A. Harmon, and died in March, 1889. Their only son, Cameron G. Spencer, was born in Bucks county and reared and educated there, remaining upon the old homestead as his father's assistant until 1859, when he married and brought his bride to the farm, of which he then took charge, making a home for his father during his remaining days. Cameron Spencer was born in November, 1836, and was but five years of age when he lost his mother in 1841. He was reared by his father and the latter's housekeeper, and his life developed into that of a man of remarkable strength of character and sterling purpose. He never used tobacco or liquor in any form, and he was popular and prominent in the community, receiving the unqualified trust and respect of those with whom he was associated. After his marriage he conducted the home farm for eleven years, and then sold that property, removing to Philadelphia, where he rented a hotel property in Spring Garden street. He made it a temperance house and to the astonishment of all his friends prospered in this undertaking, although those who knew him predicted that he could not win success unless he sold liquors there. However, he conducted a temperance house for ten years after which he purchased a farm near Jacksonville, Bucks county. He then resumed farming, in which line of activity he continued until his death. He was a Republican, and although he was never an aspirant for office he served for one term as assessor, while residing in Philadelphia, discharging the duties of the office with credit to himself and satisfaction to the general public. He was widely known and commanded the confidence and good will of the people of every community in which he lived. His death occurred in May, 1882. His wife still survives him and makes her home with her two children, Mrs. Smith, and a son who resides upon the homestead farm. She was born in Northampton

township in 1837, and is a lady of culture and intelligence; she is a daughter of Joshua and Martha (Bonham) Hart, both connected with early colonial families. Her father was a son of John and Sarah (Dungan) Hart, also of Bucks county. John Hart followed farming and merchandising, making his home in Jacksonville, and he became widely known as a highly respected citizen. He was of Irish lineage, affiliated with the Baptist church, and his political allegiance was given to the Democracy. His children were: Joshua, William, Rachel, Joseph, John, Elizabeth, Sarah, Humphrey, and Rebecca.

Joshua Hart, who was born in 1802, was reared to farm pursuits, and after his marriage settled in Northampton township, while later he took up his abode upon the farm now occupied by Mrs. Smith. Throughout his entire life he carried on agricultural pursuits, and died in Buckingham township. In politics he was a Democrat, but had no political aspirations. In an early day he served as captain in a militia company. His wife was born in 1809, and was a daughter of Joseph and Letitia (Kinsey) Bonham, both of Bucks county, her father being a prominent and well known farmer. In politics he was a Whig. The members of the Bonham family were Jonathan, Isaiah, Charles, Kinsey, Samuel and Martha. The children of Joshua Hart were: Sarah, the wife of John Spencer; Letitia; Charles, who died in the civil war; Rachel B., who became the mother of Mrs. Smith; Elizabeth, the wife of Josiah Thompson, of Philadelphia; and John, also of Philadelphia. To Mr. and Mrs. Cameron Spencer were born three children: Horace G., who was reared upon the home farm, and was later employed by the Presbyterian board of publication; died in September, 1888, leaving a wife but no children; Martha H., who became Mrs. Smith; and A. Lincoln, who is now farming the old homestead; he is a stanch Republican in his political views; he has a son, Cameron, born January 23, 1895.

FRANK F. BELL, deceased, who was elected the first treasurer of Philadelphia under the new city charter, popularly known as the "Bullit Bill," having been the youngest incumbent upon whom this responsible office had ever fallen, was of old and honored German origin. His paternal grandparents were natives of Wurtemberg, Germany. His grandmother died when her son, John Bell, father of Frank F. Bell, was about eleven years of age, and subsequently her husband and son emigrated to America, the former named dying during the voyage at sea.

John Bell (father) came to Philadelphia, Pennsylvania, an orphan, and subsequently became a well known and respected citizen of Old Northern Liberties, having established an extensive business as caterer and confectioner. He was united in marriage to Mary Langenstein, who was born in Gros-Glattbach, Wurtemberg, Germany, daughter of Frederick and Anna Mary (Weingartner) Langenstein, whom she accompanied to America in 1839, settling in Philadelphia, Pennsylvania. Frederick Langenstein was a son of Michael and Eva Dorothea (Schaefle) Langerstein, both of Gros-Glattbach, Wurtemberg, Germany, and grandson of Michael Langenstein, who served in the capacity of burgomaster of the aforementioned place. John Bell (father) died at the early age of thirty-six years, his son Frank F. being then only two years of age.

Frank F. Bell was born in the city of Philadelphia, May 26, 1855. Upon reaching the qualified age he was entered as a pupil at Girard College, from which institution he was graduated with high honors at the conclusion of the eight years' course. After his graduation he entered upon the study of architectural drawing in the office of Professor Richards, of the University of Pennsylvania, and later he accepted a position in the manufacturing firm of W. C. Allison & Sons. He had a special aptitude for accounts which rapidly brought him to promotion in the counting room of this great firm. Not long after, however, an opportunity arose which promised him an opening in the political arena, and served to afford opportunity for the study of law, which he had already decided to follow as a profession. He was offered a position of trust in the office of the receiver of taxes, which he accepted, and at the same time became a law student in the office of Hampton Todd. Shortly after his acceptance of this new office an investigation of its affairs was ordered by the city comptroller, which proved to be prolonged and exhaustive, and Mr. Bell acquired a reputation in this investigation which led directly to his future advancement. Shortly after its conclusion William B. Irvine was elected city treasurer of Philadelphia, and he, having a knowledge of the executive ability of Mr. Bell, tendered to him the important office of chief of the department for the collection of revenue due the commonwealth. The successful efforts of Mr. Bell in this position brought him prominently into public favor, and resulted in making him the nominee of his party to succeed Mr. Irvine. The public confidence in his fitness for the office was expressed by a popular majority of 21,106 votes, and he met the responsibilities of the position and fulfilled the duties of the position in a highly creditable manner. In his business and political relations he was eminently consistent and reliable. His matured capabilities had received ample and thorough training in the great trusts and in all the departments of activity to which he had been called, and in his handling of the millions of dollars in the city treasury there was not the slightest whisper of the innuendos and scandals so frequently alleged of men in public life.

Mr. Bell was a member of the Union League Club of Philadelphia; of the Philadelphia Athletic Club; of the Algonquin Club of Bristol; and of the Stock Exchange of Philadelphia and New York.

In 1881 Mr. Bell was made a Mason in Oriental Lodge, No. 385, and four years from that date was chosen worshipful master, and this rapid rise in Masonry and in the affections of the craft was but a reflex of his walks in life. The following is an extract from the eulogy paid to Frank F. Bell by Past Master Z. Taylor Rickards: "Acquaintance with him elicited admiration, intimacy was to love him; to contribute to his ambitions was but to do right and receive his gratitude always. To-morrow we shall look for the last time at the face of our dear friend and brother, stilled, no longer to respond to the cheerful greeting he had for all who knew him. We shall not look again into those soul-lit eyes. He is dead—and what is this condition we call death? What of it? It has come to Frank F. Bell at forty-eight. When it will come to each of us, no man can tell, but of him we know that in this preparing room he leaves a record so good that we believe it is well with him now. Let us emulate his virtues and remember him for his ever kindly walks with us here."

On January 18, 1888, Mr. Bell was married to Helen Geneva Edwards, of Philadelphia, daughter of James and Elizabeth (Atmore) Edwards, paternal granddaughter of James and Mary Edwards, maternal granddaughter of William Penn and Caroline (Stowe) Atmore, maternal great-granddaughter of William and Mary Magdalene Stull, and maternal great-great-granddaughter of George and Caroline Lausatte, who were born in Alsace or Lorraine, France. William Penn Atmore came to America in the same ship with William Penn and settled in Philadelphia. George Stroup, maternal great-great-grandfather of Mrs. Bell, served with Washington during the revolutionary war, as did also his son. The children of Frank F. and Helen G. (Edwards) Bell are as follows: Frank Frederic, born September 25, 1888, is being educated at Swarthmore preparatory to entering the Institute of Technology at Boston, Massachusetts; Helen Florentine, born January 29, 1891, is a student at the Holman School, Philadelphia; Dudley Edwards, born October 4, 1894, attends the Friends' Central School, Philadelphia. Frank F. Bell, father of these children, died August 31, 1903. His widow resides in a beautiful home, elegant in its appointments, is devoted to her children, and prominent in the social life of Bristol, Pennsylvania.

ROBERT M. JOHNSON, one of the energetic business men of Chalfont, is a son of William Johnson, who was reared on a farm, and upon the breaking out of the civil war enlisted in the Union army from New Britain township. He married Hannah Lutz, and their children were: Franklin L., Emma E., and Robert M., mentioned at length hereinafter. Franklin L. married Anna Lister. Emma E.. became the wife of Abraham Clymer, of Line Lexington, and after his death married John Lewis, of Hilltown.

Robert M. Johnson, son of William and Hannah (Lutz) Johnson, was born July 13, 1859, in New Britain township, and was educated in the public schools of his birthplace. He acquired a knowledge of plumbing, heating and ventilation with David E. Hebner, of Chalfont, and after the expiration of his time he worked for five years as journeyman at Line Lexington. In 1887 he purchased the store of William Bruner, at Chalfont, where he now conducts an extensive plumbing and heating business, carrying a large stock of stoves, heaters, ranges and similar articles. His patronage is not limited to Chalfont, but includes the surrounding towns. His political connections are with the Democratic party, and he is a member of the Pleasantville Reformed church. Mr. Johnson married Lillie I., daughter of Dr. Louis C. and Lucilla (Ely) Rice, and they are the parents of the following children: Marion, who was born January 1, 1882; Florence, born October 31, 1891; and Chester, who was born December 3, 1898.

BYRON M. FELL, D. D. S., of Doylestown, was born in Buckingham township, Bucks county, Pennsylvania, December 21, 1872, being a son of James B. and Josephine B. (Conard) Fell, and of the sixth generation in descent from Joseph and Bridget (Wilson) Fell, of Longlands, Cumberland, England, who settled in Buckingham in 1707.

Benjamin Fell, son of Joseph, born in Cumberland, England, 9 mo. 12, 1703, died in Buckingham 9 mo. 12, 1758, was thrice married, first 6 mo. 27, 1728, to Hannah Scarborough, by whom he had six children, second to Hannah Iredell, who bore him four children, and third to Sarah Rawlins, by whom he had one son.

John Fell, eldest child of Benjamin and Hannah (Scarborough) Fell, was born in Buckingham, 4 mo. 1, 1730, and married Elizabeth, daughter of Thomas and Hannah (Paxson) Hartley, 10 mo. 30, 1753, and had by her thirteen children. Among them were Seneca and Nathan, twins, born 4 mo. 5, 1760.

Seneca Fell married Grace Holt, of Horsham, Montgomery county and settled in Buckingham on a farm purchased by his grandfather in 1753, part of which has remained in the family to the present time, the late residence of E. Hicks Fell. Seneca and Grace had eight children, viz.: Sarah, married John Stockdale; Eli, see forward; Martha, married Jacob Michener; Rachel, married Charles Wilson; Jesse, died unmarried; Seneca, married Sarah Cress; and Grace, married Benjamin Buckman. In 1817 Grace Fell, the widow of Seneca, removed with her son Jesse and son-in-law Jacob Michener to Harrison county, Ohio, and died at the residence of her son-in-law Jacob Michener, in Morgan county, Ohio, about 1845.

Eli Fell, eldest son of Seneca and Grace, was born on the homestead above referred to in 1787, and died there 3 mo. 6, 1859. He married 5 mo. 4, 1808, Rachel Bradshaw, daughter of William Bradshaw, and had thirteen children, nine of whom grew to maturity; Jane, wife of Cornelius Shepherd; Ruth, died unmarried; Eunice, married Charles M. Shaw; Uree, married Abraham Geil; Eli; Rachel, widow of Wilson Pearson; Martha, married John Burgess; James B.; and Elias Hicks; and Hulda Ann, married John M. Kirk.

James B. Fell, the eleventh child of Eli and Rachel (Bradshaw) Fell, was born on the old homestead in Buckingham 8 mo. 17, 1827, and died in Buckingham 5 mo. 19, 1880. He was a farmer, and lived all his life in Buckingham. He married 1 mo. 1, 1857, Josephine B. Conard, daughter of Jacob and Martha Conard, of Buckingham, who died 5 mo. 28, 1891. They were the parents of seven children, five of whom lived to mature age; Clara M., late wife of Elmer W. Kirk, of Doylestown; J. Conard, of New Hope; Eli H., of New York; Marian V., wife of Earl Peters, of Mt. Holly Springs, Pennsylvania; and Byron M., the subject of this sketch.

The subject of this sketch was reared on the farm in Buckingham, and acquired an elementary education at the public schools. In November, 1891, he entered Trenton Business College, from which he graduated in 1892, and accepted a clerical position with the Pennsylvania Railroad Company, which he filled until October, 1893, when he entered Philadelphia Dental College, from which he graduated March 5, 1896. On his

Byron W. Fell,

graduation he at once located in Doyles-town, opening an office in the Rhoads building on Main street, and began the practice of his profession. He soon built up a lucrative practice, and four years later purchased his present residence and offices on Court street.

Dr. Fell was married February 17, 1897, to Catharine E. Kenney, of Philadelphia, daughter of William R. and Savilla Kenney. Four children have been born to them: Foster Flagg, born December 2, 1897; Earl Garretson, born May 26, 1899; Margaret Gaskill, born September 29, 1902; Max Kenney Fell, born December 12, 1904.

ABRAHAM M. SWARTLEY. Among the old German families of Pennsylvania is that of which Abraham M. Swartley, of Chalfont, is a representative. Mr. Swartley is a great-grandson of Philip Swartley, who was born in 1764 in Baden, Germany, and in 1782 emigrated to America. He married Sarah Rosenberger, and they were the parents of nine children, six sons and three daughters. Among the sons was Philip, mentioned at length hereinafter. Mr. Swartley died September 2, 1840, and his wife passed away in April, 1847, at the advanced age of eighty-four years.

Philip Swartley, son of Philip and Sarah (Rosenberger) Swartley, was born February 28, 1799, in New Britain township, and followed the calling of a farmer. He married Mary Smith, and their family consisted of the following children: George, born July 12, 1820, married Catharine Funk; Henry S., mentioned at length hereinafter; Levi, born April 7, 1824, married Catharine Haldeman; Philip, born November 12, 1825; Susanna, born March 23, 1827, married Jacob Alderfer; Sarah, born November 11, 1830, married John Alderfer, whom she survived but one day and whose grave she shared; Mary, born December 9, 1833, married David Rosenberger; Elizabeth, born August 15, 1838, became the wife of Louis Schleier, and Aaron, born February 7, 1841, married Maria Leidy.

Henry S. Swartley, son of Philip and Mary (Smith) Swartley, was born March 24, 1822, on the homestead. He married Sarah Myers, and the following children were born to them: Lavinia, who married Isaac, son of Joseph Funk; Abraham M., mentioned at length hereinafter; Anna Eliza, who became the wife of Henry F., son of Abraham Moyer; and Sallie J., who married David, son of Joseph Funk.

Abraham M. Swartley, son of Henry S. and Sarah (Myers) Swartley, was born November 6, 1854, on the homestead in New Britain township. He re-ceived his primary education in the Newville public school, and graduated at the Millersville high school. His youth and early manhood were passed in assisting his father in the cultivation of the paternal acres, and on reaching the age of twenty-eight years he settled on the farm which is now his home. For a number of years he conducted a large dairy, disposing of its products in the markets of Philadelphia, but is now engaged exclusively in general farming. He is a Republican in politics, and is a member of the Mennonite church at Line Lexington.

Mr. Swartley married, March 28, 1885, Anna M., daughter of Oliver K. and Mary Jane (Stever) Myers. The latter was the daughter of Reuben Stever, who built the Dublin Hotel. Mr. and Mrs. Swartley are the parents of the following children: Mary M., who was born December 15, 1886, and died August 5, 1887; Harry M., born December 9, 1890; Sadie M., born March 9, 1892; Viola Mae, born April 18, 1900; and Minnie Isabella, born August 20, 1903, and died February 2, 1904.

WILLIAM SHIMMEL TAYLOR, a manufacturer, of Quakertown, was born on a small farm near Passer Post Office, in Springfield townhsip, Bucks county, Pennsylvania, July 31, 1854, son of Thomas and Maria (Shimmel) Taylor. Thomas Taylor (father), son of Joseph and Nancy Taylor, was born in Springfield township, July 19, 1827. He acquired the limited education afforded by the subscription schools of that place and day, and afterwards learned the trade of shoemaking, which he followed in conjunction with farming. He was industrious, economical and thrifty, and was one of the representative citizens of the community. September 24, 1850, he married Mary Shimmel, daughter of John and Hannah (Oberholtzer) Shimmel, farmers, of Springfield township, and had issue: Emeline, born June 23, 1853, died September 30, 1853; William S., born July 31, 1854, mentioned hereinafter; Joseph S., born March 15, 1856, married Kate Johnson, and resides at Sedgwick Park, Fordham Heights, New York; he is an educator; Elemina, born November 9, 1859, became the wife of Louis Link, and they reside at No. 1925 North Eleventh street, Philadelphia.

When William S. Taylor was nine years of age his father died, leaving him a small patrimony, and in the care of a guardian, Louis Slifer, with whom he resided for two years. He then went to Philadelphia to work with an uncle, a brother of his mother, with whom he proposed making his home. Finding the work too difficult and arduous for a boy of his years, he returned to Bucks county and hired out with a farmer, a Mr. Geisinger, but, not taking very well to the strenuous life of the farm, after being there for six months, during which time he worked for his board and also attended school, he left the place and entered as an apprentice to learn shoemaking with Christian Musselman, near Steinsburg, in Milford · township, and remained there for two years. He then went to live with a farmer, Henry Moyer, near Line Port, Bucks county, and later purchased a farm in Springfield township, which he cultivated and whereon he resided up to 1887, when he disposed of the same. He then purchased the property where he now resides, at Sixth and Juniper streets, Quakertown, where he is a manufacturer of ice cream, and has established an extensive trade throughout northern Bucks county, from which he realizes a goodly income. Mr. Taylor adheres to the Republican party, but takes no interest in local affairs outside the casting of his vote for the candidates of the party of his choice.

While a resident of Line Port, August 23, 1873, Mr. Taylor married Sarah Roth, daughter of David and Lydia (Musselman) Roth, of Rockhill township, where Mr. Roth followed agricultural pursuits. Their children were as follows: Elmer M., born May 2, 1875, married Sarah Rissmiller, daughter of Josiah and Elenia Rissmiller, of Richland township, farmers, and they reside in Quakertown, Pennsylvania. Addie R., born November 3, 1876, became the wife of Harvey Benner, of Lansdale. The mother of these children died February 5, 1881, aged twenty-seven years, four months and five days. Mr. Taylor married for his second wife, Mary Roth, a sister of his first wife, and had issue: Joseph Warren, born October 24, 1885, died August 23, 1886. Katie, born June 15, 1887, died July 1, 1901. Elsie, born January 28, 1895, resides with her parents. The family are members of the Bathany Mennonite church of Quakertown, in which body Mr. Taylor is serving as trustee.

HENRY M. KRATZ. The Kratz family, of which Henry M. Kratz is a representative, is of German origin, and was established in America in the early part of the eighteenth century, its progenitor in the new world being John Valentine Kratz, a son of John Philip Kratz, who was born in Germany, October 8, 1665, died in 1746, aged eighty years; his wife died in 1710. John V. Kratz emigrated from the Palatinate in Germany to Pennsylvania in the year 1727, and he married Ann Clemmens, whose death occurred in 1793.

Abraham Kratz, son of John Valentine and Ann (Clemmens) Kratz, was born in Montgomery county, Pennsylvania, in 1741, and resided for many years in New Britain township. He purchased the Williams homestead in that township and continued its cultivation through a long period. He married Barbara Moyer, and they became the parents of ten children: Anna, Mary, Valentine, Susanna, Barbara, Veronica, Magdaline, Elizabeth, Abram and Catherine.

Valentine Kratz, son of Abram and Barbara (Moyer)' Kratz, was born April 22, 1773, in New Britain township, and in his youth learned the weaver's trade, which he followed throughout his entire business career. He also engaged in farming in connection with his other occupation, and died September 18, 1830. His wife bore the maiden name of Anna Overholt, and they were the parents of six children: Simeon, Elizabeth, Jacob, Abram, Barbara and Mary.

Jacob Kratz, son of Valentine and Anna (Overholt) Kratz, was born on the old homestead in New Britian township in a house which was built in 1795. He was educated in the public schools of his home locality, and afterward engaged in teaching school in New Britian and Hilltown townships, following that profession for several years. He also engaged in farming, and for a long period served as a school director in Hilltown township and took an active and helpful interest in public affairs. He died February 23, 1903. November 28, 1838 he married Mary Myers, a daughter of Christian Myers, and they had four children: Salome, who was born August 30, 1839, and was married January 19, 1864, to John F. Funk, by whom she has six children; Henry M.; Anna, who was born July 22, 1850, and was married July 22, 1899, to Joseph D. Bishop; Isaiah, who was born May 7, 1856, and died on the 31st of August of the same year.

Henry M. Kratz, elder son of Jacob and Mary (Myers) Kratz, was born at Naces Corner in Hilltown township, Bucks·county, July 23, 1845. He pursued his education after attending the public schools in the New Britian Seminary and at the North Wales Normal Institute at Carversville, and following his graduation he engaged in teaching for three terms, being thus occupied successively at Hilltown, Bedminster and Milford. He has since followed farming at his present home at Naces Corner, where he was born and has always lived. He is a member of the Mennonite church, and his political allegiance is given to the Republican party. He was married January 4, 1868, to Sophia L. Shaddinger, a daughter of Jacob L. and Mary (Leatherman) Shaddinger. They have one child, Mary Emma, born September 23, 1868.

HENRY O. MOYER.

Among the well known and enterprising business men of upper Bucks is Henry O. Moyer, of Perkasie. He is a native of Hilltown township, and was born November 27, 1845. He is a descendant of that sturdy, frugal, truth-loving race of German Mennonites who peopled upper Bucks and Montgomery counties in the early part of the seventeenth century, and have probably added more to the wealth and prosperity of our country than any other nationality or sect.

Christian Meyer, supposed to have been a native of Switzerland, founded an asylum from religious persecution in the Netherlands prior to 1700, and some time after that date emigrated from Amsterdam to Pennsylvania and settled in Lower Salford township, Montgomery county, where he was a landowner prior to 1719. He was an ardent Mennonite, and one of the founders of the earliest Mennonite congregation in that locality. He died in June, 1757, leaving children, Christian, Jacob, Samuel, Elizabeth, Ann and Barbara.

Christian Meyer, Jr., was born in the year, 1705, probably in Holland, and was reared in Lower Salford. On attaining manhood he settled in Franconia township, Montgomery county, where he purchased 170 acres of land in 1729, most of which is still owned and occupied by his descendants. He was the first deacon and one of the founders in 1738 of the Mennonite meeting at Franconia, and was later a minister there. He died in May, 1787. By his wife, Magdalena he had children: Christian, Jacob, Samuel, Anna, Maria, Fronica, Esther, Barbara, all except one of whom married and raised families.

Samuel Meyer, third son of Christian Jr., and Magdalena, was born in Franconia, June 10, 1734, and became a widely known Mennonite preacher. He settled in Hilltown township, Bucks county, early in life, and spent his remaining days there, living to a venerable and highly respected old age. He married Catharine Kolb, and reared a family of nine children, as follows: 1. Fronica, born 1757, died 1818; married Abraham Wismer, of Plumstead township, where they have numerous and worthy descendants. 2. Isaac, born 1758, married a Landis and reared a large family. 3. Elizabeth, died young. 4. Christian, born 1763, married Mary Landis and settled in Bedminster township. 5. Samuel, born 1765, died 1847, married Susanna Bleam, and lived and died in Hilltown. 6. .Rev. Jacob Moyer, born 1767, married Magdalena Bechtel and removed to Canada. 7. Abraham, see forward. 8. Dilman, born December 20, 1772; married Barbara Latshaw, and emigrated to Canada in 1801. 9. Heinrich, born October 27, 1774, died October 19, 1857; was a farmer and weaver in Hilltown; married Salome Stover; was a deacon of the Mennonite meeting at Blooming Glen. Samuel Moyer, the father of the above children, was devised by his father the homestead in Franconia, but having already settled in Hilltown he never returned to his native county. The homestead he conveyed to his sons Isaac of Franconia, and Christian of Bedminster. The latter conveyed his portion to his son Rudolf in 1810, and it is now the property of Abraham F. Moyer, son of Rudolph.

Abraham Moyer, seventh child of Samuel and Catharine (Kolb) Meyer, was born in Hilltown, November 19, 1770, and was reared to the life of a farmer. He married Elizabeth Bechtel, and reared a family of ten children as follows: 1. Susan, married John Bergy. 2. Anna, married Samuel S. Yeakel. 3. Abraham B. married a Delp and left one son, Francis. 4. Samuel B., see forward. 5. Rev. Henry B., removed to Westmoreland county, Pennsylvania, where he was ordained a Mennonite minister, and returned to Hilltown and preached for some years at Blooming Glen. 6. Martin, died unmarried. 7. Catharine died unmarried. 8. John B., moved to Canada, married there; later moved to Michigan and had children. He died in Michigan. 9. Mary married George Swartz, and removed to Illinois. 10. Elizabeth, married Rev. Isaac Overholt (or Oberholtzer).

Samuel B. Moyer, fourth child of Abraham and Elizabeth (Bechtel) Moyer, was born in Hilltown in February, 1815, and died there November 7, 1852, leaving a family of five small children, the youngest but a year old. He was a farmer and a consistent member of the Mennonite congregation at Blooming Glen. He married October 31, 1841, Hannah Overholt, who was born in Plumstead, January 1, 1819. Their children were: Abraham, who died young; Isaac, born December 5, 1843, died April 12, 1854; Henry O., the subject of this sketch; Samuel, born August 2, 1847; Mary Ann, born September 23, 1844, died October 12, 1877, married Peter Yoder; Enos, born 1851, died 1873.

Henry O. Moyer was born and reared on his father's farm in Hilltown. In early life he learned the blacksmith trade, which he followed for ten years in Hilltown. In 1881 he started in the creamery business and successfully operated a creamery at Bedminsterville for thirteen years. In 1894 he removed to Perkasie, where he conducted a clothing and gents' furnishing store until 1899, when he sold out, and in the autumn of the same year entered into the real estate business with his son Theodore, of Uhlertown, Bucks county, and they still conduct that business. At the organization of the National Bank of Perkasie he was selected as one of the directors of that successful financial institution, and has served as such ever since. He is one of the active and successful business men of the thriving borough, and is interested in all that pertains to the best interest of that growing business town. He is a member of the German Reformed church, and politically is a Republican. He is a member of Bedminster Castle, Knights of the Golden Eagle, and was for many years its keeper of records. He married October 6, 1866, Sarah Jane Moyer, daughter of Henry A. and Sarah (Gearhart) Moyer, and a sister of Hon. Henry G. Moyer, of Perkasie. She was born in Hilltown, October 15, 1845.

Mr. and Mrs. Moyer are the parents of eight children, as follows: Theodore M., born February 10, 1868, a prominent justice and business man in Nockamixon, Bucks county; married Belle Mills, and has seven children. Hannah M., born February 14, 1871; married Joseph H. Gulden, a prominent creamery man. Ida Jane, born July 25, 1873, wife of Charles M. Meredith, editor of the "Perkasie Central News." Henry Clinton, born June 25, 1876. Samuel Linford, born April 19, 1879. Sarah Alice, born July 25, 1882; Florence Mabel, born March 13, 1885. Marian Viola, born April 4, 1888.

ELI L. CLYMER. At the time that the United States formed a part of the colonial possessions of Great Britain the Clymer family was established in Bucks county. The progenitor of the family in America came from Germany, and most of his descendants have been tillers of the soil, recognized in the various generations as men of prominence and influence in the community and of unquestioned honor, integrity and worth. Henry Clymer, Sr., grandfather of Eli Clymer, was born and reared in Bucks county, and married Elizabeth Kulp, also a native of this county. They became the parents of eleven children: Abram, Henry, William, Hannah, wife of Jonas Clymer; Polly, wife of C. Moyer; Elizabeth, wife of B. Kulp; Mrs. Ann S. Haldeman, Valentine, John, Fannie, who became the wife of John Kulp; and Sarah, the wife of H. Swartley. All were reared in the faith of the Mennonite church, and continued adherents of that denomination.

Henry Clymer, Jr., son of Henry and Elizabeth (Kulp) Clymer, was born in New Britain township, and remained with his parents up to the time of his marriage, when he purchased a farm in Warrington township, whereon he settled and reared his family. He carried on general farming and also attended the market, and was practical, enterprising and therefore successful in his labors. His political support was given to the Republican party. Reared in the faith of the Mennonite church, he was always a faithful member thereof and was widely known and highly respected in his township. He was a man of medium size, but of strong constitution and did much hard work in his younger years. He married Mary Benner, a native of Hatfield township, Bucks county, and a daughter of John Benner, a farmer and a member of one of the pioneer families of this county. He, too, was a devoted member of the Mennonite church. He married a Miss Haldeman, also connected with one of the leading families, and their only child became the wife of Henry Clymer. She survived her husband about twelve years. They were the parents of eight children: John, a farmer; Eli L., Ann, who became the wife of Joseph Sapp; Valentine, a mechanic; Daniel, a farmer; Henry, a carpenter; Kate, the wife of E. Kratz; and Abram, who is an assessor and auctioneer in Warrington township.

Eli L. Clymer was born in Warrington township on his father's farm, June 5, 1841, and acquired his education in the public schools. He began earning his own living as a farm hand and afterward rented land for a year. Subsequently he purchased a house, but sold this property in the fall of 1868, and bought the farm where he now resides, comprising seventy-one acres, which was originally the John Grove farm. This was but partly improved, but he at once began its further development and cultivation, and made it a splendid property. He has erected all the present substantial buildings, including a commodious two story frame residence, which is built in modern style of architecture and is one of the attractive features of the landscape. There is also large barn and substantial outbuildings. He has set out a good orchard and follows general farming, sending his products to the city where they are sold to the commission merchant. In all of his business transactions he is active and energetic, and whatever he undertakes he carries forward to successful completion.

On May 6, 1865, Mr. Clymer was married to Miss Magdalena Detweiler, who was born in New Britain township, March 12, 1844, a daughter of Joseph and Hannah (Burdy) Detweiler, the former a native of Bucks county, Pennsylvania, and the latter of Montgomery county. Her paternal grandfather, Jacob Detweiler, of New Britain township, represented an old colonial family of German lineage. They became prominent and progressive citizens of this part of the state and were faithful adherents of the Mennonite church. Jacob Detweiler was a farmer and also owned and operated a sawmill. His children were: Elizabeth, who became Mrs. Rosenberger; Jacob and John, farmers; Mary, the wife of M.

MRS. LEVI CASSELL   MISS ELMANDA BIEHN

LEVI CASSELL

JOHN C. HILLEGASS   MRS. JOHN C. HILLEGASS

Kindy; Joseph, father of Mrs. Clymer; and Magdalena, wife of J. Knise. At the time of his marriage Joseph Detweiler purchased a farm in New Britain township, where he spent his remaining days, living a quiet and uneventful life, yet commanding the good will and confidence of all by reason of his fidelity to honorable, manly principles. He married Hannah Burdy, and died in 1849 at the age of forty-seven years, while his wife, long surviving him, passed away in 1890. He had left but a small estate, and in her later years she made her home with her older children. Both Mr. and Mrs. Detweiler were members of the Mennonite church. Their children are: Isaac, a practicing physician of Lancaster, Pennsylvania; Mary, the wife of M. Rosenberger; Sarah, who married Eli Yoder; Jesse, a farmer; Elizabeth, who married E. Rosenberger; Magdalene, wife of Eli L. Clymer; Joseph, a farmer and tailor to the trade; and Hannah, who died at the age of forty years.

Mr. and Mrs. Clymer have become the parents of eight children: Ellen, wife of William Swartley, a farmer; Adda, wife of L. McCune, a farmer; Hannah, who married William Worth; Frank, who died at the age of thirteen years; Elmer, a farmer; Flora, the wife of Frank McNare; Oliver, at home; and Emma, a school teacher. All were given good educational privileges, and the daughters have become successful teachers. The parents and children are members of the Mennonite church, and Mr. Clymer is a Republican, who has filled the office of school director for ten years, and takes an active interest in public affairs. He is a typical American, alert and enterprising in business, loyal in citizenship, and interested in everything pertaining to the welfare and progress of his county, state and nation.

LEVI CASSEL, deceased, was born on the old Cassel homestead farm in Hilltown township, Bucks county, February 24, 1816, and died in Richland township, September 1, 1879. The paternal grandfatehr, Hoopert Cassel, was a joiner by trade, and lived in Franconia township, Philadelphia county, Pennsylvania. In 1758 he purchased a tract of land, one hundred and six acres, adjoining Perkasie Manor. He married Susan Swartz, a daughter of Abram Swartz, a minister of the Mennonite church and a man of considerable influence and ability in his day.

Isaac Cassel, son of Hoopert Cassel, was born April 20, 1776, in Hilltown township, on the farm purchased by his father. Throughout his entire life he carried on agricultural pursuits, and was one of the leading citizens of his

neighborhood, active in business affairs, reliable and energetic in business, and highly esteemed in social circles because of his hospitality and of his genuine worth. He succeeded his father in the ownership of the old home farm, and there lived for many years. He was married to Catherine Trumbore, who was born February 8, 1776. His death occurred July 3, 1856, while his wife passed away several years earlier. Their children were: Susan B., born March 2, 1804, died May 11,, 1889; Polly, married Michael Kulp; Kate, married Jacob Fillman; Elizabeth, married Philip Hood; Sallie, married Joseph Schull; Joseph, deceased; Enos, married Marie Gerhart; Samuel, married Susan Mann; and Levi, married Sarah Ann Biehn.

Levi Cassel was born on the old homestead farm in Hilltown township, where two generations of the family had previously lived, and there he was reared in the usual manner of farmer lads of that period. He attended the subscription schools of his district, although his advantages for an education were somewhat limited owing to the primitive conditions of the schools of that period. He worked with his father on the old home farm until his marriage, and later became proprietor of a hotel at Sellersville, where he remained for two years. He then removed to Hagersville, and later to Dublin, while subsequently he lived at Richlandtown, where he conducted a hotel for fourteen years, and it was while thus engaged that his death occurred. He was energetic in his business affairs, carefully watching every indication that pointed to success, and by his keen discernment and strong purpose he won a comfortable competence. September 17, 1848, Mr. Cassel was united in marriage to Mrs. Sara Ann Beihn, a daughter of Abraham and Hanna (Fluck) Beihn, who were living people living at Ridgehill, in Rockhill township, Bucks county. Her father was born August 5, 1800, and died December 5, 1875. He was descended from one of the old families of this country, long connected with the material upbuilding of eastern Pennsylvania. He was married July 18, 1823, to Hanna Ott Fluck, born May 29, 1801, died April 12, 1891, at the advanced age of ninety years. Her parents were Jacob and Elizabeth Ott Fluck. The children of Mr. and Mrs. Beihn were as follows: Sara, born September 17, 1826, became the wife of Levi Cassel; Maria, born July 8, 1829, married John Louright, of Richlandtown; Elizabeth, born July 9, 1837, married Leno Kile, a veterinary surgeon of Perkasie; Hanna, born August 28, 1839, married John C. Hillegoss, who was born February 19, 1839, and died May 25, 1893, his parents being William and Eliza (Carver) Hillegoss, farming people of Milford township;

Elmanda, born July 12, 1843, living with Mrs. Cassel at Quakertown.

In his political affiliations Mr. Cassel was a stalwart Republican, and although he never aspired to office he took deep and active interest in the welfare of his party, and assisted materially in its growth and upbuilding. He and his family were members of the Reformed church at Richlandtown, and he lived an upright, honorable life. Passing away in September, 1879, his remains were interred in the cemetery adjoining the Reformed church. He was always liberal in his support of the church and of every worthy object, and his entire life was actuated by high manly principles. He was well liked by all who knew him, the circle of his friends being almost coextensive with the circle of his acquaintance.

FRANK HEADMAN FLUM, of Bristol, Bucks county, Pennsylvania, who has won and retained an enviable reputation in the community for integrity and probity, and whose career has been one of marked enterprise, was born in Bensalem township, Pennsylvania, April 2, 1868, a son of Frederic and Catherine (Barth) Flum.

Frederic Flum (father) was born in Wurtemberg, Germany, March 18, 1823. He came to America about the year 1850, followed some years later by his wife and children, and settled in Bensalem township, where they resided for many years, and where Mrs. Flum is residing at the present time (1904), Mr. Flum having passed away May 5, 1875. Mrs. Flum, whose maiden name was Catherine Barth, was born in Wurtemberg, Germany, June 15, 1826, and was the mother of the following named children: 1. John, born September 27, 1847, married Emma Page, and they were the parents of three children: Fred, John, and George. 2. Fred, born December 2, 1849. 3. Hannah, born October 10, 1853, widow of George Thackara. 4. David, born August 31, 1859, 5. Frank H., born April 2, 1868, mentioned hereinafter. 6. Lizzie, died in infancy. 7. Daniel, born October 3, 1869, married Annie Kilpatrick, June 5, 1880, and three children were born to them: Catharine, Bessie and Helen.

Frank H. Flum was educated in the public schools of Bensalem township. He then worked at farming with his father, remaining until 1880, when he took up his residence in Bristol, Bucks county, and at once engaged in the butchering business, which he has followed ever since, and in which he has achieved a large degree of success. Mr. Flum stands well in the community, as is evidenced by the fact that he has served two terms in the borough council. He is a charter member of the Good Will Fire Company of Bristol, serving in the capacity of its treasurer, a member of the Improved Order of Red Men, and a member of the Knights of Friendship. He is a Republican in politics. Mr. Flum was married August 18, 1890, to Elizabeth Rotta Guyon, of Bristol, a daughter of Robert and Eleanor (Murray) Guyon, and granddaughter, on the paternal side, of John and Elizabeth (Thomas) Guyon, and on the maternal side of Lewis and Martha (Wolohon) Murray. Their children are: Edith Guyon, born May 8, 1893; and Frank Leslie, born May 8, 1902. Mr. and Mrs. Flum are Presbyterians in religion.

JOHN S. WILLIAMS, a public-spirited citizen of Solebury township who has given generous and helpful support to many movements fostering progress and improvement in the county, was born in Buckingham township, March 21, 1831. The first ancestry of whom the family has definite record was Jeremiah Williams, of English descent, who wedded Mercy Stephenson.

(II) Benjamin Williams, son of Jeremiah and Mercy (Stephenson) Williams, was a resident of Nockamixon township, where he followed the occupation of farming. He wedded Mercy Stevenson October 11, 1744, in Huntington township, New Jersey.

(III) Samuel Williams, son of Benjamin and Mercy (Stevenson) Williams, was born July 20, 1762, and reared in Tinicum township, where he resided until after his marriage, when he removed to Buckingham township and continued to engage in farming there up to the time of his death, which resulted from typhus fever when he was about forty-five or fifty years of age. His political allegiance had been given to the Whig party, and he was a man of local prominence, highly respected throughout his community. He wedded Sarah Watson, who was also reared in Tinicum township.

(IV) Edward Williams, son of Samuel and Sarah (Watson) Williams, was born on the old homestead farm in Buckingham township, and he, too, devoted his entire life to agricultural pursuits, becoming not only one of the leading farmers of his community, but also a man of prominence in community affairs, whose integrity stood as an unquestioned fact in his career. He was frequently called upon to serve in positions of public trust, was president of a turnpike company and one of the trustees of the Hughesian free school. His political allegiance was given first to the Whig and afterward to the Republican party. He was married twice, his first union being with Phoebe Esther Schofield. They had three children, but John S. Williams, whose name introduces this record, is the only one now living. A second marriage resulted in the birth of seven children: Charles

H., deceased; Esther S.; Mary E.; William, deceased; Marshall, who resides in Florida; Frank H., a practicing physician of Trenton; and Harriet F. The father, Edward Williams, died at the age of seventy-two years.

John S. Williams, son of Edward and Phoebe Esther (Schofield) Williams, was reared under the parental roof, acquired his early education in the common schools and afterward attended the Friends' school in Buckingham, also in Langhorne as a student in a boarding school conducted by James Anderson, and in the boarding school at Abington conducted by Samuel Smith, and in the Tremont Seminary at Norristown, Pennsylvania, of which Samuel Aaron was principal. When twenty-one years of age he assumed the management of the farm in Solebury township, which was the ancestral home of the Schofield family and descended to him through his maternal grandfather, John Schofield. He has since been actively and prominently identified with agricultural interests along progressive lines, and his splendidly improved property is an indication of his unflagging thrift and enterprise. He has been vice president and director of the Bucks County Trust Company since its organization, has for thirty years been a director of the Farmers' and Mechanics' Insurance Company, and for twenty years its treasurer, and is secretary and treasurer of the New Hope and Delaware Bridge Company, in which capacity he has served for several years. His interest in public progress and the material upbuilding and improvement of his county has found tangible evidence in the hearty co-operation which he has given to many measures for the benefit of his community. In politics he is a Republican, and for several years served as school director, but otherwise has declined public office. He belongs to the Friends' Society, and stands today as one of the best known and honored men of Solebury township.

Mr. Williams was married to Miss Rachel R. Magill, a daughter of Jonathan Paxson and Mary (Watson) McGill, of Solebury township, one of the early families of the county. Mr. and Mrs. Williams have three children: Carroll R., the eldest, was graduated from Swarthmore College in 1877 and completed the latter course in the University of Pennsylvania with the class of 1880. He was admitted to the bar the same year, began the practice of his profession in Philadelphia, and is today one of the most successful lawyers of that city. He was elected a member of the common council from the twenty-fourth ward, serving thereon from 1835 until 1839. On January 23, 1890, he married Eleanor (Boyd) Palmer, of Baltimore, Maryland, and they have three children: Catherine B., born September 26, 1891; John S., born April 8, 1893; and Carroll R., born September 3, 1903. Agnes Blackfan, the only daughter of John S. and Rachel Williams, is at home. Edward Newlin, the younger

18-3

son, died when but twenty-six years of age. He was a graduate of the medical department of the University of Pennsylvania, and was acting as physician and surgeon on the American Line steamship plying between London and New York.

THE WILLIAMS FAMILY of Nockamixon and Tinicum, and other parts of Bucks county, trace their ancestry to Joseph Williams, of Boston, Massachusetts. He and his wife, Lydia, had ten children, namely: Joseph, born 12 mo., 14, 1670 (O. S.); William, 10 mo., 13, 1671; Richard, 12 mo., 8, 1673; Hannah, 3 mo., 20, 1674, died in infancy; Daniel, 10 mo., 25, 1676; Hannah, 3 mo., 26, 1679; Jeremiah, 6 mo., 22, 1683 (referred to hereafter); Elizabeth, 7 mo., 22, 1686, died in infancy; Elizabeth, 10 mo., 9, 1688; and Mary, 9 mo., 6, 1869.

Jeremiah at an early age was bound to a ship carpenter to learn the trade. During his apprenticeship he left the church of England and joined the Friends or Quakers. 1 mo, 28, 1706-07 (O. S.), he presented a certificate to the monthly meeting of Philadelphia from the Monthly Meeting of Rhode Island. 1 mo., 1707-08, he requested a "Certificate of Clearness" from the Philadelphia Monthly Meeting to Flushing Monthly Meeting to marry Philadelphia, daughter of George and Mary (Willis) Masters. In 1680 or '81 George Masters, a tailor of New York, married Mary, daughter of Henry Willis, of Flushing, Long Island. Henry was fined for allowing his daughter to be married by Friends ceremony. After their marriage they went to England, where their first child, a daughter named Mary, was born in 1682. Upon their return to this country they must have been in Philadelphia for a time, as their second child, a daughter, was born there in 1684. She was the first white female child born in the city, and was named Philadelphia for the city in which she was born. Jeremiah and Philadelphia Williams lived in the city of New York. They had two children. Joseph, born 3 mo., 15, 1710, died in infancy; and Hannah, born 9 mo., 8, 1711, married Benjamin, son of Charles and Elizabeth (Jackson) Doughty, of Long Island, in 1737. Philadelphia Williams died 3 mo., 16, 1715, and the same year, 5 mo., 5, he bought a mill property at Hempstead Harbor, Nassau Island, Queens county, New York, of John Robinson. The following year, 7 mo., 11, 1716, Jeremiah married Mary, daughter of Walter and Anne (Collins) Newbury, of Newport, Rhode Island, and widow of Jedediah Howland. This is a copy of their marriage certificate.

Marriage Certificate—Whereas, Jeremiah Williams, late of New York, but now of Hempstead in Long Island, and Mary Howland, widow and relict of Jedediah Howland, of Newport, in Rhoad Island, Having declared their intention of taking each other in Marriage before severall Public Meetings of the people commonly called Quakers in said Rhoad Island, according to the Good order used among them whose proceedings therein after a deliberate consideration thereof with regard unto the righteous law of God and example of his people recorded in the Scriptures of Truth in that case were approved by the said Meetings, they appearing clear of all others and Having consent of parents and others concerned.

Now these are to certifie all whom it may concern that for the full accomplishing of their said Intentions this eleventh day of the Seventh month called September in the year according to the English, one thousand seven hundred and sixteen they the said Jeremiah Williams and Mary Howland appearing in a publick assembly of the People and others met together for that purpose in their Publick Meeting place at said Newport and in a solemn manner, he the said Jeremiah Williams taking the said Mary Howland by the hand did openly declare as followeth:

Friends, in the fear of God and before this assembly whom I desire to my witnesses I take this my friend Mary Howland to be my wife promising through the Lord's assistance to be to her a faithful and loving husband till death separate us. And then and there in the said assembly the said Mary Howland did in like manner declare as followeth; Friends, in the fear of God and before this assembly whom I declare to be my witnesses I take this my friend Jeremiah Williams to be my husband promising through the Lord's assistance to be to him a faithful and loving wife till death separate us. And the said Jeremiah Williams and Mary Howland as a further consideration thereof did then and there to these presents set their hands.

And we whose names are hereunto subscribed being present among others at the Solemnizing of their said Marriage and subscription in manner aforesaid as witnesses hereunto have to these presents subscribed our names the day and year above written.

JEREMIAH WILLIAMS,
MARY WILLIAMS.

Witnesses—Johannah Mott, Elizabeth Whartenby, Jacob Mott, Mary Wing, William Barker, Hannah Brinley, Bethia Folger, Ann Kay, Clarke Rodman, Susanna Freeborne, Ephraim Hicks, Katherine Hull, Thos. Leach, Hannah Hull, Samuel Collins, Thomas Rodman, John Headly, Thomas Borden, Ruth Fry, Peter Easton, John Stanton, Junr., Dorcas Easton, Samuel Buffum, Johannah Leach, Thomas Hicks, Susannah Hicks, John Hull, Junr., Mary Caine, Deliverance Cornell, Abigail Hicks, Elizabeth Borden, Rebecca Bennett, Hope Borden, Ann Redwood, Alice Borden, Sarah Redwood, Mary Borden, Mary Stanton, Thomas Rodman, John Easton, Walter Newberry, William Anthony, Ann Cranston, John Wanton, Justice, Elizabeth Bordens, George Cornell, Leah Newberry, Joseph Borden, Ann Richardson, John Borden, Martha Cornell, Thos. Richardson, Patience Anthony, Patience Redwood, Hannah Fry, Sarah Newberry, Sarah Borden, Ann Newberry, Blenham Stanton, A. Redwood, Catherine Clarke, Ann Clarke, Hannah Rodman, Katherine Sheffield.

At the time of her marriage to Jeremiah, Mary had one son, Joseph Howland, born 10 mo., 25, 1710 (O. S.) The children of Jeremiah and Mary Williams were: Anne, born 4 mo., 17, 1719, married, first, Fortunatus Woods, second, Ebenezer Carter; Walter, born 10 mo., 17, 1720, married out of meeting, 1744; Benjamin, born 9 mo., 4, 1722 (referred to hereafter); Mary, born 9 mo. 26, 1724; Jeremiah, born 3 mo. 18, 1726; Lydia, born 12 mo., 6, 1729; and Martha, date of birth unknown, married Benjamin Hill, at Kingwood, 8 mo., 3, 1753 (N. S.). In the year 1743 or '44 Jeremiah and his two sons, Walter and Benjamin, and daughter Martha moved to Kingwood, Hunterdon county, New Jersey. His daughter Mary came in 1758. Jeremiah, at the establishment of the Monthly Meeting at Kingwood, was made with Joseph King the first elder of that meeting. Some years after this his health failing he, with his wife and daughter Mary, moved to their son Benjamin's, he having moved some years before to Nockamixon township, Bucks county, Pennsylvania. He remained with his son until his death, 3 mo., 15, 1766 (N. S.), and was buried in the old grave yard at Quakertown, New Jersey. His will was written in Nockamixon, 1 mo., 23, 1760, proved 6 mo., 6, 1766. His wife died in 1774. Her will is dated Nockamixon, Pennsylvania, 6 mo., 12, 1766, proved 3 mo., 20, 1774.

Benjamin Williams, son of Jeremiah and Mary (Newbury) Williams, was born 9 mo., 4, 1722 (O. S.). He married Mercy, daughter of John and Margaret Stevenson, of Kingwood, New Jersey, in 1744. Their children were: John, born 1 mo., 29, 1745, married Hannah Pursell; Mary, born 10 mo., 11, 1747; Jeremiah, born 5 mo., 9, 1749 (referred to hereafter); Margaret, born 4 mo., 4, 1751, married John Iliff; Lydia, born 4 mo., 18, 1752 (N. S.), married David Burson; Benjamin, born 10 mo., 30, 1756, married Dorothy Leiper; Anne, born 7 mo., 15, 1758, married Jacob Ritter; William, born 9 mo., 20, 1760, married Rachel Leiper; Samuel, born 7 mo., 20, 1762, married Sarah Watson; Susanna, born 7 mo., 30, 1765, married a Mr. Stroud; Benjamin and his family moved to Nockamixon township, Bucks county, Pennsylvania, some time prior to 1760, and must have lived there some considerable time before receiving a deed for the property. It was finally deeded to him in 1769. There were 515 acres and 31 perches, the boundaries reaching from near the Narrows to the village of Upper Black's Eddy along the river, and extending over the hill regions for a considerable distance. This was the land once owned and controlled by the

Chief Nutimus and his tribe, and this chief was always an honored guest of Benjamin Williams, Sr., whose home was nearly on the site of the mansion built by Jacob Stover soon after purchasing in 1818. Benjamin Williams, Sr., and his family lived here during the time of the raids by the Doans, and having a valuable horse of which he was very fond, and hearing of the approach of the Doans, he quietly stabled his favorite horse in his kitchen and it was thus saved from falling into the hands of the lawless gang. Soon after taking possession of the land in Nockamixon the young Indians roaming over it at will, gathered the apples from the trees and took them away, and disturbed the water in the spring until it was unfit for use for a time. Benjamin expostulated with Nutimus, and asked why they did it. Nutimus replied it was true the Indians had sold the land, but not the apples and spring. Benjamin asked them how much they wanted for the apples and spring, and the chief replied, five bushels of Indian corn, five bushels of buckwheat and five loaves of rye bread. After that the spring and the apples were not disturbed. In 1778 or '79 Benjamin bought about 500 acres of land in Tinicum township, Bucks county, Pennsylvania, and built the house on the river road now owned by Clinton Haney, near the little hamlet of Lodi. The little creek which empties into the Delaware was the northern boundary of this tract. His son, Jeremiah, took possession of this tract in 1779. Some time after this Benjamin bought about 500 acres in the beautiful Buckingham Valley, which was occupied by his youngest son Samuel.

In his will, which was dated Nockamixon township, Bucks county, Pennsylvania, 3 mo., 16, 1809, and probated 5 mo., 30, 1809 he mentions "a general arrangement of my estate," in which, on the '4th d of the 1st m. in the year one thousand eight hundred and three" he deeded to his three sons, Jeremiah and Benjamin the land on which they were living, and on the "3rd of the first m. in the year one thousand eight hundred and four" he deeded the land in Buckingham to his son Samuel, who was then residing there. Benjamin died at the home of his son Samuel in Buckingham and was buried in the grave yard at the Buckingham Meeting House. He died in 1809, probably in the early part of the fifth month.

Jeremiah, son of Benjamin and Mercy (Stevenson) Williams, born 5 mo., 9, 1749, married 4 mo. 25, 1779 (N. S.), Mary, daughter of Thomas and Elizabeth Blackledge, of Richland township, Bucks county, Pennsylvania. Their children were: John, born 1 mo., 27, 1780; Thomas B., born 4 mo., 11, 1781, married Rebecca Arndt; Benjamin, born 12 mo., 18, 1782, married, first, Mary (Meredith), widow of ———— (?) Burson, second, Rachel, daughter of Benjamin and Dorothy (Leiper) Williams; Susan, born

6 mo., 10, 1785, never married; William, born 6 mo., 12, 1789, married Hannah Whiting; Samuel, born 6 mo., 18, 1792, died 1812; Isaac B., born 4 mo., 23, 1794, married Martha Shelton White; Margaret, born 4 mo., 28, 1796, married Abel Lester; Jeremiah, born 12 mo., 28, 1798, married Elizabeth Lake.

John, son of Jeremiah and Mary (Blackledge) Williams, born 1 mo., 27, 1780, married July, 1804, Christiana, daughter of John and Anne (Kimple or Kimball) Moore. Christiana was born 3 mo., 5, 1781. Their children were: Mary, born 5 mo. 20, 1805, married Nathan Whiting; Newbury Davenport, born 5 mo. 9, 1807, married Lucy Adelaide Gould; was made the first cashier of the Frenchtown, New Jersey, National Bank, when that institution was established; James, born 8 mo. 23, 1809, married first Phoebe Treichler, second, Josephine Krause (widow). He died March 14, 1903, at the age of nearly ninety-four years; Ann Eliza, born 7 mo. 30, 1812, married Jonas Smith, at this writing, August 26, 1905, she is still living in possession of all her faculties, and enjoying a ripe old age in the home of her only child, John W. Smith, at Stockton, New Jersey. Barzilla Newbold, born 7 mo. 4, 1814, referred to later; and Caroline, born 1 mo. 18, 1821, married Thomas W. Harris. John and Christiana Williams built a home on the estate of his father, at Lodi, at the intersection of the river road and a road leading back to the western part of the township. The place is now owned by a Mr. Adams. After the death of his father, Jeremiah Williams, in 1834, John bought land, in Tinicum township, of the William Erwin estate, about 300 acres, and moved there in the spring of 1837. In the settlement of his father's estate, Thomas was the only purchaser of any part of the original estate; his purchase being about one-half of the land on the north and west side of the tract. His three brothers, Benjamin, Isaac and Jeremiah, with their sisters, Margaret Lester and Susan Williams moved to Ohio with their families about 1840. John died 6 mo. 6, 1858. Prior to his death he sold the middle portion of the tract, bought of the Erwins, to Conrad Wyker and at the sale, after his death, the northern portion was bought by his son Barzilla and the remaining portion by his daughter Caroline. There had been a few lots sold to others for building purposes, and these together with three houses on the south side of the public road comprise the little village of Erwinna.

Barzilla Newbold Williams, born 7 mo. 4, 1814, married first, in 1839, Mary, daughter of Azariah and Anna Cummings Davis, of Sussex county, New Jersey, and had two daughters: Stella, born 6 mo. 13, 1841, died 10 mo. 4, 1843; and Anna M., born 1 mo. 4, 1844, married 2 mo. 15, 1877, William H., son of Rev. Samuel and Katherine (Wolfinger) Stahr. William and Anna lived in Philadelphia; he died 3 mo. 9, 1903; they have one daughter, Francelia Williams, who resides with her mother in Philadelphia. She was born 1 mo. 10, 1878. In September, 1847, he married Sarah S., daughter of William L. and Elizabeth (Large) King, by whom he had two children: Josephine King, born 10 mo. 4, 1852, referred to hereinafter, and Sarah Francelia, born 3 mo. 4, 1855, married 3 mo. 7, 1878, Evan Thomas, son of Elisha and Harriet (Lukens) Worthington. Their children were: Elisha, born 2 mo. 27, 1879; Helen born 6 mo. 15, 1881, died 9 mo. 30, 1881; Eleanor F., born 12 mo. 7, 1887, died 6 mo. 15, 1888. Evan T. and Sarah F. Worthington resided in Buckingham, Pennsylvania, where he had a general store until the spring of 1890 when they moved to Newtown, Pennsylvania, where he conducts the middle store purchased by him before his removal to Newtown. Barzilla's second wife died 1 mo. 26, 1856, and in March, 1858, he married Mary, daughter of George and Maria (Davis) Morrow, by whom he had one son, Samuel Silvey, born 2 mo. 1, 1859; he married Harriet May, daughter of William and Mary Ann (Hagenbuck) Hendricks, of Chicago. They were married 12 mo. 10, 1888, have one child, Marion Francelia, born 6 mo. 7, 1897. Samuel Silvey and his family reside in Chicago, he is the associate manager of the Detroit Stove Works, whose main office is located in Chicago. On 6 mo. 1, 1875, Barzilla married his fourth wife, Hannah, daughter of Ralph and Martha Harrison, and widow of a Mr. Johnson, of Camden, New Jersey, who still survives him. They had no children. He died 6 mo. 1, 1901, and was buried in the Pursell burying ground at Upper Black's Eddy, Bucks county, Pennsylvania.

Josephine King Williams, daughter of Barzilla and Sarah (King) Williams, and the compiler of this record, was born at Erwinna, Bucks county, Pennsylvania, 10 mo. 4, 1852. She married, 4 mo. 22, 1885, Stacy B., son of Bruce M. and Martha (Poore) Pursell, of Upper Black's Eddy, Pennsylvania, a record of whose ancestry on both sides is embraced in this work. At the time of their marriage Stacy was a druggist in Portland, Northampton county, Pennsylvania. In the spring of 1888 he sold his drug store in Portland and they removed to Bristol, Pennsylvania, their present place of residence. In the settlement of the estate of Barzilla Williams, the administrator, Stacy B. Pursell, sold the farm to Readen Tettemer, and thus, excepting a store property in Erwinna, owned by Joseph Williams, and a house and lot at Lodi, owned by Mrs. Alice (Williams) Winter, all the ancestral estate in Tinicum has passed out of the name, as it has also in Nockamixon; only a few acres of the hill regions of that tract are now owned by the descendants of Benjamin Williams, the original purchaser.

REUBEN ORLANDO SWOPE, at present prinicpal of Glen Rock High School, Glen Rock borough, Bergen county, New Jersey, was born in Bedminster township, Bucks county, Pennsylvania, November 17, 1868. The ancestors of Mr. Swope were of German extraction and have been residents of Bucks county for many generations. But little is known of the earlier generations of the family further than that they belonged to the solid substantial yeomanry of Upper Bucks, and filled their places in the history with honor and integrity. The grandparents of the subject of this sketch were John and. Mary (Wildonger) Swope, whose son Joseph Swope, born in Tinicum township, Bucks county, August 6, 1831, was reared and educated in that and Bedminster townships, and followed the occupation of a farmer in Bedminster and Plumstead townships—and he, as well as his immediate ancestors, was a member of the Lutheran church, and politically he was a Democrat, though he never sought or held political office. He married Mary Overholt, daughter of Abraham and Hannah (Shutt) Overholt, and granddaughter of Martin and Elizabeth (Nash) Overholt. She was born in Plumstead township, Bucks county, Pennsylvania, October 6, 1833.

Reuben Orlando Swope was educated in the common schools of Bucks county, and. later took a course at the West Chester State Normal School, and followed the profession of teacher for eight years in the public schools of Bucks county, two of which he was principal of the high school at Richlandtown. He is now principal of the high school at Glen Rock, Bergen county, New Jersey. Thoroughly devoted to his profession, he has taken little part in public affairs. He is a member of the Lutheran church of Hilltown, and filled the position as organist there for some time. He also served as superintendent of the Sunday school for two years. Mr. Swope is unmarried.

THE NATIONAL FARM SCHOOL. In the summer of 1894 the Rev. Dr. Joseph Krauskopf, of Philadelphia, visited Russia in an effort to secure data concerning the condition of the Jews in that country and to urge means for its amelioration. While there he observed the astonishing zeal with which Jews pursued agriculture within the limits allowed by the Russian Government. He saw a people yearning, not as common prejudice has assumed, for a life of trade, but for opportunities to work out their existence from the soil. He further visited, at the suggestion of Count Tolstoi, the Jewish Agricultural School at Odessa, the end and aim of whose activity was the graduation of practical working farmers, and instructors and managers of agricultural colonies. The avidity with which the Jewish lads avail themselves of the facilities thus given them convinced him that the agricultural instincts, fostered in Bible times, still lingered, and needed but opportunity for their manifestation. On his return to America, Dr. Krauskopf proceeded to formulate plans for the institution of a Farm School, which, while welcoming all students regardless of creed, might satisfy the demand of large numbers of Jews for agricultural opportunities. After months of agitation sufficient funds were procured for the purchase of a farm and the erection of adequate buildings thereon. On April 10, 1896 the National Farm School was incorporated. The Watson farm, situated a mile from Doylestown, the county seat of Bucks, was purchased, where school buildings were erected, and the school opened with fifteen pupils in its first class. The school is a purely technical institution which has for its purpose the education of young men in both practical and scientific agriculture. The course of instruction continues for four years. The entrance requirements are those ordinarily demanded of candidates to enter a good high school. The grade of instruction is somewhat higher than that of a high school, because the length of the school year is 11 months. The academic studies consist of instruction in many of the different branches of agriculture and horticulture, general, analytical and agricultural chemistry; general and agricultural physics, animal hygiene, United States history, English, mathematics and surveying. The technical or practical agriculture is required of each pupil every day for three hours, and during the summer months the time is extended to seven hours per day. All of the work on the farm is performed by the pupils. The young men graduating from the school are sufficiently proficient to take positions in the United States Department of Agriculture at Washington and with different Experiment Stations, and some have full charge of farms, other conduct dairies, while others go into farming for themselves.

The facilities for instruction consist of a home farm of 122 acres, well stocked with fifty head of cattle, fifteen horses, sheep, swine and poultry. There is donated or loaned to the school from the manufacturers for use and instruction every kind of a farm implement that is considered of practical use on a Pennsylvania farm. There is also a well equipped dairy where the pupils are taught how to make butter. In addition to these advantages the school possesses two farms of about forty acres each, which are equipped as model farms, and which are used for post-graduate instruction, upon which the graduates of the school have practice in superintendence. One also finds at this school well equipped laboratories of chemistry and physics with surveying instruments and a good greenhouse, together with orchards and vineyards and small fruit gardens, for instruction in horticulture. A library consisting of over 2,000 well chosen books adds greatly to the equipment of all departments. A comfortable dormitory provides a home for forty-five pupils, which is the number enrolled for January 1, 1906. A large number of names are on the waiting list due to the school's limited accommodations.

The president of the board of managers is the Rev. Dr. Joseph Krauskopf, of Philadelphia; the secretary is Mr. Harry Felix; the director of the school is John H. Washburn, Ph. D.

HENRY CLAY STUCKERT, of Warrington, Bucks county, is the eldest son of William H. and Rachel (Scarborough) Stuckert, and one of the prominent farmers of Warrington township. Henry Stuckert, the father of William H., and grandfather of H. Clay Stuckert, was born and reared in Germany, where he learned the trade of a baker. He came to Philadelphia when a young man and followed his trade there until 1811, first as a journeyman but for many years afterwards carrying on business for himself. On April 6, 1811, he purchased the farms now occupied by his two grandsons, 213 acres, in Warrington township, Bucks county, and turning over his baker business to his eldest son George removed to Bucks county. He was an intelligent, practical and successful business man, and was highly respected in the community. He married soon after coming to America, Elizabeth Bennett, of Philadelphia. He died in 1836, at the age of seventy years, and his wife died in 1843. They were the parents of six children: 1. George, who succeeded his father as baker in Philadelphia, but later removed to Northampton township, Bucks county, married Anne Hough, of Warrington, but returned to Philadelphia where he died. 2. Louisa, married George Jamison. 3. John, who remained in Philadelphia. 4. William H., the father of the subject of this sketch. 5. Anna Maria, who married A. Jackson Beaumont, of Solebury. 6. Jacob, who purchased a portion of the home farm in 1845, but some years later removed to Trenton, New Jersey, where he died.

William H. Stuckert, third son of Henry and Elizabeth (Bennett) Stuckert, was born at Warrington, October 2, 1816, and was reared on the farm. At his father's death in 1836 he took charge of the farm for his mother and conducted it for seven years. At the death of his mother he purchased that part of the homestead now occupied by his son, H. Clay Stuckert, and made substantial improvements. Several years later he purchased the homestead of his brother Jacob and lived there until his death with the exception of a few years spent on a farm in Doylestown township, in 1874, returning to the homestead at the death of his wife in 1880, and residing with his son Amos. He was an enterprising and successful farmer and business man, and held many positions of trust. He and his family were members of the Presbyterian church, of which he was a trustee. He died in November, 1896. He married in 1841 Rachel Scarborough, of Wrightstown, daughter of Amos and Elizabeth (Cooper) Scarborough, both natives of Bucks county and of English Quaker descent. Both the Cooper and Scarborough families were among the earliest settlers in Bucks county. William H. and Rachel (Scarborough) Struckert were the parents of five children, viz.: 1. Henry Clay, born August 7, 1842, see forward; 2. Sarah, wife of Dr. A. H. Clayton, of Richboro, Bucks county; 3. Amos, born March 19, 1846, see forward; 4. William, a prominent lawyer of Doylestown; 5. John C., a prominent lawyer of Bristol, Bucks county.

Henry Clay Stuckert, eldest son of William H. and Rachel (Scarborough) Stuckert, was born on the farm where he still lives, August 7, 1842. He was reared on the farm and acquired his education at the common schools and at a normal school at Upland, Chester county, Pennsylvania. On reaching manhood he took charge of the home farm, which he eventually purchased of his father, and this he has greatly improved and beautified; he is an enterprising and successful farmer. He married in 1875, Emma J. Harman, born in 1849, daughter of Daniel Y. and Elizabeth K. (Bennett) Harman, and granddaughter of John and Elizabeth (Addis) Harman, both of Holland descent. John Harman was an early settler in Upper Makefield township. Daniel, the ninth of his ten children, married first Hannah, daughter of Benjamin and Hannah (Simpson) Hough, of Doylestown township, by whom he had six children. He married second Elizabeth K. Bennett, daughter of Miles and Hannah (Kroesen) Bennett, both of Holland descent, and representatives of early Knickerbocker families that settled first on Long Island and removed later to North and Southampton, Bucks county. Daniel Y. Harman was in early life a farmer, but later was a hotel keeper at Newtown; he was for several years a justice of the peace. He died in 1855. By his second wife, Elizabeth K. Bennett, he had three children: Emma J., the wife of the subject of this sketch; Lewis C., a merchant of Philadelphia; and Franklin P., who died at the age of seven years. The children of Henry Clay and Emma J. (Harman) Stuckert are: Frederick, an attorney at law at Bristol, Bucks county, Pennsylvania; William R., see forward; Louis H., a bookkeeper at Trenton, New Jersey; Henry, a student at Jefferson Medical College, Philadelphia; and Anna P., residing at home. Mr. Stuckert and family are members of the Presbyterian church.

AMOS STUCKERT, of Warrington, the second son of William H. and Rachel (Scarborough) Stuckert, was born on the Warrington farm March 19, 1846, and on his marriage in 1873 took up his residence where he still resides, on the original homestead, buying the farm of his father. He is an enterprising and successful farmer, and has introduced all the latest improvements in farm machinery. He married in 1873 Esther N. Fesmire, daughter of H. C. and Sydonia (Chappelle) Fesmire, of Moreland township, Montgomery county, Pennsylvania, where Mrs. Stuckert was born December 6, 1852. Her grandfather, Peter Fesmire, was a native of Germany, who settled in Montgomery county in early life, was a successful farmer. His son, Henry C., the third of seven children, settled in Moreland township, where he lived for a number of years and then removed to Delaware, where he lived for three years on an experimental farm, and then returned to Glenside where he died in 1900. His widow still survives, residing at Glenside at the age of seventy-eight years. She is of French Heugenot descent, and a daughter of John Santell, a life-long resident of Montgomery county.

Mr. and Mrs. Stuckert have been the parents of eleven children, viz.: George J., died at the age of eighteen years; Esther B., wife of Professor William H. Black, who was captain of a company in the Spanish-American war, and is now principal of a school at High Bridge, New Jersey; Elizabeth, wife of Albert Reed, a machinist; John C., a farmer, married Eva Jamison; Grace, wife of H. J. Worthington; William H., residing at home; Sarah, married B. R. Yerkes; Sidney, residing at home; Clarence, who died young; Anna and Claud, who reside at home. Mr. Stuckert and his family are members of the Presbyterian church.

WILLIAM R. STUCKERT, second son of Henry Clay and Emma J. (Harman) Stuckert, was born on the old homestead in Warrington township, March 23, 1877. He was educated in the public schools of Warrington, the Doylestown High School and Ursinus College. After completing his course of study at college in 1899, he taught school for one year in Bucks county, and then entered upon the study of the law in the offices of his uncles, William and John C. Stuckert, and was admitted to practice in the Bucks county courts in December, 1902. In March, 1903, the law firm of William and J. C. Stuckert was dissolved, and William R. Stuckert was taken into partnership by his uncle, William Stuckert, under the firm name of William & William R. Stuckert, with offices at Doylestown and Newtown, and he at once took charge of the Newtown office and entered upon the active practice of his profession. Mr. Stuckert is the present borough solicitor of the borough of Newtown, and has already built up a remunerative business, and established a reputation for careful and painstaking service in behalf of his clients.

GEORGE W. HARTLEY, JR., of Pineville, Buckingham township, Bucks county, was born in New Hope borough, Bucks county, December 28, 1867, and is a son of William H. and Sarah Ellen (Girton) Hartley, and a grandson of Levi and Rachel (Heaton) Hartley. The pioneer ancestor of the Hartley family was Edward Hartley of English Quaker stock who settled in Buckingham about 1700, and has left numerous descendants in various parts of the union, although few of the name now reside in Bucks county.

William H. Hartley, the father of the subject of this sketch, was born in Buckingham, July 4, 1836. At the age of sixteen he left the paternal roof and learned the trade of a blacksmith, which he followed in connection with farming until 1886, when he retired from active life. He resided in Pineville from 1877 until his decease on April 10, 1904. He married Sarah Ellen Girton, daughter of James and Diadama Girton, who was born at Dolington, Bucks county, November 18, 1841, and died at Pineville, January 6, 1900. Their children were as follows: J. Howard; Mary, widow of Pierson Eddowes of Hartsville; George W., the subject of this sketch; Eli of Doylestown; and Dr. William K. Hartley of Doylestown.

George W. Hartley, Jr., acquired his education at the public schools and remained on the farm with his father assisting in the operations during the summer months, and during the winter months followed various other occupations. After the death of his father he moved to his present residence where he has since lived a retired life. He married November 1, 1894, Margaret Ann Kelley, daughter of Isaac and Martha E. (Mathews) Kelley, of Solebury, and they are the parents of one child, Walter Sickle, born March 28, 1899. In politics Mr. Hartley is a Republican, and is a member of the Methodist Episcopal church. He is a member of Wycombe castle, No. 125, Knights of the Golden Eagle.

CYRUS T. VANARTSDALEN, of Newtown township, Bucks county, was born in Northampton township, April 5, 1823. He is a son of Isaac and Ann (Torbert) Vanartsdalen, the former a descendant through seven generations in an unbroken line from as many Dutch ancestors who emigrated from Holland to New Netherlands in the first half of the seventeenth century, while the latter's ancestry traces back to at least four Ulster Scots who found homes in Bucks county a century later. The paternal ancestor of the Van Artsdalens, who bore their patronymic, was Simon Jansen Van Artsdalen, who emigrated from Holland in 1656 ,and settled in Flatlands, Long Island, where he married Pieterje Claesen Wycoff, who had accompanied her brother to New Netherlands in 1636. Simon Jansen Van Artsdalen was a magistrate of Flatlands, 1661-1686, and a deacon of the Dutch church there. He died in 1710, leaving several sons and daughters; among the former was Cornelis Symonse Van Artsdalen, born in Flatlands in 1665, and died there in 1745. He was thrice married, first to Tlletje Reinerse Wizzelpenning, second, on March 16, 1687, to Aeltje Willemse Couvenhoven, born December 14, 1665, daughter of Willemse Gerretse Covenhoven and Altie Brinckerhoff, and granddaughter of Gerret Wolfertse Couvenhoven, who had emigrated from Holland with his father in 1630, having been born in Holland in 1610. Cornelis Symonse Van Artsdalen married third, Maretje or Mary Dirckse, on May 2, 1691. By the three wives he had ten children: Aeltje, Jacobus, Dirck, Petronella, Maria, Abraham, Jannetje, Jacobus, who married Alice, daughter of Jacob Hogeland, of New Jersey, Philip, John, and Simon, born August 16, 1697. Cornelis Symonse Van Artsdalen purchased a farm of his father at Gravesend, May 7, 1700, and is supposed to have lived thereon until 1726 when he sold it to his brother John and removed to Somerset county, New Jersey. He was active in building the Dutch church there, and was prominent in the affairs of the community. It is possible that he returned to Long Island prior to his death, as his will is registered at the surrogate's office at New York in 1745, though dated at Somerset in 1738.

SIMON VAN ARTSDALEN, son of Cornelis and Mary (Dirckse) Van Artsdalen, was born at Flatbush, Long Island, August 16, 1697, and married there, October 30, 1716, Jannetje Romeyn, whose father and his two brothers had emigrated from Holland about 1650. Simon removed with his father to Somerset county, New Jersey, and prior to 1730 removed with his family to the Dutch colony in Southampton township, Bucks county, Pennsylvania, where he was one of the early elders of the Dutch church, lived a long and useful life, and reared a family of seven children, five sons and two daughters. He died in the winter of 1770, and is buried at "The Buck." The children of Simon and Jane (Romeyn) Van Artsdalen were as follows: 1. John, born at Flatlands, Long Island, June 27, 1718, died in Northampton in 1777. 2. Lammetje, born August 21, 1720, married first Derick Kroesen, and second Cornelius Wyckoff. 3. Christoffel, born April 15, 1722, married, October 26, 1748, Elizabeth Kroesen, daughter of Henry Kroesen. Died 1765, leaving children, Simon, born 1752; Else, born 1754; Jane, born 1757; Henry, born 1759; and Jacob, born in 1762. 4. Simon, born April 18, 1726, married, January 24, 1751, Elsie Kroesen. Died 1795, leaving nine children, Cornelia, wife of Jacob Vandegrift; Simon, married Joanna Hogeland; Jane, married Joshua Praul; Derrick; Margaret, married Abraham Lefferts; Jacob; John; Elizabeth, married Thomas Fenton; and Mary, married Joseph Fenton. 5. Margaret, born January 12, 1729, married Derick Kroesen, and had several children. 6. Jacobus or James, born January 25, 1732, married Rachel LaRue, daughter of Isaac LaRue. 7. Nicholas, born July 14, 1736, died 1805, married December 29, 1759, Jane Vansant. 8. Peter, born March 2, 1739, probably died young, not mentioned in father's will.

John Van Artsdalen, born January 29, 1718, accompanied his father to Bucks county and settled on a farm in Northampton township, containing 250 acres, where he lived and died. He married, April 30, 1742, Elizabeth Kroesen, daughter of Garret, granddaughter of Dirck Kroesen and Elizabeth Kregier, and great-granddaughter of Gerret Dirckse Kroesen, who emigrated from Holland about 1650 and settled in Brooklyn, where he died in 1680. John and Elizabeth (Kroeson) Van Artsdalen had seven children, as follows: 1. Jane, born November 17, 1744, died of smallpox, January 30, 1756, unmarried; 2. Ariantje, born May 25, 1746, married, February 18, 1767, Arthur Lefferts; 3. Lammetje, born April 2, 1748, married, January 11, 1770, Peter Lefferts; 4. Elizabeth, born September 1, 1750, died at the age of two years; 5. Simon or Simeon, born July 10, 1753, was pastor of the Dutch church at Readington, Hunterdon county, New Jersey, died 1788, married Magdalen Hogeland; 6. Elizabeth, born May 7, 1756, married John Cornell, left no issue surviving; 7. Garret, born May 8, 1758, died 1848, married, November 29, 1781, Euphemia Hogeland, born October 24, 1761, died February 19, 1829, daughter of George and Maria (Scheneck) Hogeland, a lineal descendant of Dirck Hogeland, the emigrant. (See Hogeland Family in this work.)

Garret Van Artsdalen purchased the interest of his brother and sisters in the old homestead and resided thereon. He and his brother Simon were members of Captain Henry Lott's company of associators in Northampton in 1775. The children of Garret and Euphemia (Hogeland) Van Artsdalen were: 1. John, born January 17, 1784, married, April 17, 1806, Jane Kroesen, died 1844; 2. Simon, born November 10, 1786, married Deborah Dyer, had twelve children; 3. Isaac, born September 23, 1791, married, September 1, 1814, Ann Torbert. 4. Garret, born May 5, 1797, died September 20, 1799. 5. Maria, born May 2, 1794, married Joel Carver.

Isaac Van Artsdalen was reared on the old plantation in Northampton, and in 1831, his father conveyed to him ninety acres thereof, and a year later he acquired by his brother Simeon another tract, part of the same, and he spent his whole life on the farm of his ancestors. He died in 1860. Ann Torbert, the mother of the subject of this sketch, was a daughter of James and Margaret (McNair) Torbert, of Makefield, and a granddaughter of James Torbert and Hannah Burley, and of James and Martha (Keith) McNair. Her four great-grandfathers Samuel Torbert, Samuel McNair, John Burleigh and William Keith emigrated from the north of Ireland and settled in Makefield, Bucks county, about the year 1730. Samuel Torbert came from Carrick-Fergus on the northeast coast of Ireland in 1726. He was a tanner, and located in Newtown where he lived for many years. Late in life he became a farmer in Upper Makefield, where he died in 1778. Isaac and Ann (Torbert) Van Artsdalen had eight children, as follows: 1. Garret, born 1816, died 1881, married Harriet E. Warne and had seven children; 2. James Torbert, born in 1818, married Catharine Naglee; 3. Theodore Milton, born 1821, died 1904, married, 1843, Cornelia M. Cornell; 4. Cyrus Torbert, born April 5, 1823, married Jane E. Cornell, see forward; 5. Margaret Ann, born 1825, married, 1846, David Wynkoop McNair. 6. Alice Elizabeth, born 1828, married James Anderson; 7. Maria, born 1831, married, 1850, James L. Torbert; 8. Isaac Keith, born 1834, married Sarah Matthiea.

Cyrus T. Vanartsdalen was born and reared on the old homestead in Northampton, and remained on the farm with his father until twenty-five years of age. He then followed farming in Northampton until 1859, when he purchased the farm in Newtown township, where he still resides. He married, December 15, 1847, Jane Eliza Cornell, daughter of Jacob and Maria Cornell, of Northampton, who bore him three children: Mary, born December 18, 1850, died January 25, 1875, was wife of George C. Fetter. Alice, born November 22, 1853, died February 11, 1880, was wife of Murray Gardner. Isaac T., born March 28, 1757, married Addie C. Camm. Mr. Vanartsdalen has been a member of the Presbyterian church since his eighteenth year, served several years as deacon and has been an elder of the Newtown church since 1868. In politics he is a Republican, but has never sought or held office except that of school director.

HENRY H. VAN ARTSDALEN, of Feasterville, Southampton township, Bucks county, was born near Feasterville, November 1, 1842, and is a son of James and Rachel (Hough) Van Artsdalen. He is a lineal descendant of Simon Jansen Van Artsdalen, who emigrated from Holland in 1653 and settled on Long Island, his great-grandfather being Nicholas Van Artsdalen, mentioned in the preceding sketch, who was born July 14, 1736, son of Simon and Jane (Romeyn) Van Artsdalen, the pioneer ancestor of the family in Bucks county. Nicholas Van Artsdalen married, December 29, 1759, Jannetje or Jane Vansant. Being the youngest surviving son, he remained upon the old homestead which was devised to him at the death of his father, and died there in November, 1805. His widow Jane survived him, dying in August, 1813. They were the parents of seven children, four sons, Simon, James, John and Christopher, and three daughters, Anna, married Garret Stevens, Jane, who married John Kroesen, and Margaret, who married Jesse Willard.

James Van Artsdalen, son of Nicholas and Jane, was the grandfather of the subject of this sketch. He was born on the old homestead and inherited a portion of it at his father's death, and died there August 29, 1834. His wife was Elizabeth Staats, daughter of Daniel and Mary (Praul) Staats, and a granddaughter of Peter Praul. They were the parents of eight children, as follows: Silas, who married Effie Cox and had children, Silas and Elizabeth. Nicholas, who married Louisa Knight and had children, Joseph, Cursey and James. Cornelius, who married and had children, Daniel, Truxton, and Mrs. Silas Twining. Daniel, who married Maria Clayton and had children, George, Jonathan, Elizabeth, and Lucinda. Jesse, who married and had a family. James, father of subject of this sketch. George, who married and had children, Walter, Emanuel and Lydia. Phebe, who married Allen Dyer, and had children. Peleg and James.

James Van Artsdalen, Junior, was born on the old homestead in 1803, and received his education at local schools. He learned the trade of a wheelwright and followed it at Feasterville, until succeeded by his son in the seventies. He purchased a house and lot in Feasterville of Aaron Feaster in 1834, and died there in 1891. He married, about 1828, Rachel Hough, who was born in 1805 and died in 1888. They were the parents of six children, as follows:

Charles, born November 3, 1830, married Mary Elizabeth Cornell, and had one daughter who married James Cornell, and has a son, Charles Cornell. Martha, born 1832, married Christopher Clayton and has three children. Spencer, died young. Mary Elizabeth died at age of seventeen years. Eliza Ellen, married Michael Irwin and had two children, both deceased. Henry H., born November 1, 1842.

Henry H. Van Artsdalen was reared at the Feastersville home purchased by his father in 1834, and acquired a common school education at the local schools. He learned the trade of blacksmithing and has carried on the business for upwards of forty years. In politics he is an ardent Democrat, and has always taken an active interest in the councils of his party. He served one term as auditor of the county, and has filled local offices at different periods. He was his party's candidate for director of the poor in 1902, but was defeated. He married Annie, daughter of Benjamin and Mary (Clayton) Worthington, and they have been the parents of three children: Minnie, born March 26, 1867, died October, 1900, married Israel Stack and had one child, Anna: Henry, who died young, and Benjamin, born November 14, 1880.

WILLIAM JOHN COOLEY, Esq., of the Philadelphia bar, though not a native of Bucks county was reared from childhood within its borders and still retains his residence at New Hope, where his grandfather was a prominent manufacturer many years ago. Mr. Cooley was born at Trenton, New Jersey, July 9, 1877, and is a son of John P. and Catharine Young (Umbleby) Cooley. On the paternal side he is descended from an old New Jersey family, and on the maternal side his grandfather, William Umbleby, came from England at the age of eight years and located in Chester county, Pennsylvania. He was a manufacturer of cordage, and later removed to New Hope, Bucks county, where he owned and operated the flax or cordage mills for many years. He was a man of a high sense of honor and of a deep religious nature, and was for many years a local preacher of the Methodist Episcopal church. He had one son, John, and two daughters, Mary, the wife of William H. Closson, and Mrs. Cooley. On the death of Mrs. Cooley, in Trenton, New Jersey, the subject of this sketch was reared by his uncle, William H. Closson, of New Hope.

William J. Cooley was educated at the New Hope high school, Pennington (New Jersey) Seminary, and at the University of Pennsylvania. He graduated from the law department of the latter institution in the class of 1898, and was admitted to the bar of Philadelphia county in the same year. He has since practiced his profession in that city, with offices at the Hale Building, 1328 Chestnut street. He is a member of the Law Association of Philadelphia, and of the Law Academy. He is a member of the Methodist Episcopal church, and a local preacher of that faith.

ALBERT C. LARUE, one of the young enterprising farmers of Buckingham, was born in Southampton township, in which vicinity his paternal ancestors have been residents for two centuries, on November 10, 1874; he is a son of John B. and Eva (Cadwallader) Larue. His father, John B. Larue, was born on the same farm as his son in the year 1850, being a son of Marmaduke Larue of Southampton. He was a farmer for several years in Southampton, and then removed to Buckingham, purchasing a farm near Pineville, where he still resides with his son-in-law. He is a member of the Methodist Episcopal church, and in politics is a Republican. The family of La Rue is of French descent, the American progenitors being Huguenots who came to America about the middle of the seventeenth century, and became residents of Bucks county early in the next century. John B. and Eva (Cadwallader) Larue are the parents of four children: viz.: Albert C., the subject of this sketch; Harry C., Alice, wife of Fred Worthington, and Edgar J., all of whom are residents of Buckingham.

Albert C. Larue was reared on the farm in Southampton. From his twelfth year he lived in the family of his uncle, Samuel K. Tomlinson, of Southampton. On February 10, 1897, he married Sarah Rhoads, daughter of Nathan and Rebecca Rhoads, and removed to his present farm in Buckingham, previously purchased by his uncle. He and his family are members of the Methodist Episcopal church. To Mr. and Mrs. Larue have been born three children: Horace Raymond, Earl Stanley and Edith May.

ROBERT L. CYLMER, the successful merchant of Doylestown, Bucks county, was born in Bethlehem, Pennsylvania, June 20, 1872, and is a son of John H. and Maria (Kiser) Clymer. The Clymer family is of German origin, but has figured in the history of Pennsylvania for nearly two centuries, Richard Clymer having come to Philadelphia in 1795, and engaged in ship building until his death in 1734. From his sons, Christian and William, have descended a numerous progeny that have been more or less prominent in the affairs of Pennsylvania, many of them holding high official position. George Clymer, signer of the Declaration of Independence, was a son of Christian, and was born in Philadelphia in 1838, and died in Morrisville, Bucks county, in 1813, leaving two sons: Henry and George. Another branch of the family now numerous in Bucks and Montgomery counties are descendants from Valentine Clemmer, a bishop of the Mennonite church, who came to this country from Germany or Switzerland in 1717, and settled in what is now Montgomery county, most of his descendants becoming known later by the name of Clymer. Tradition connects the subject of this sketch with the former family, but there is absence of authentic records to prove the connection.

Christian Clymer, the great-grandfather of Robert L. Clymer, was an extensive landowner in Milford township, and died there in 1802, leaving seven sons, Jacob, Christian, Isaac, Gerhard, John, David and Samuel, and three daughters, Esther, wife of Adam Scheetz, Ann, wife of Henry Souder, and Mary, wife of Henry Beidler.

John Clymer, the grandfather of Robert L. Clymer, born March 31, 1793, located in Nockamixon township soon after arriving at manhood, married Margaret Pearson, daughter of Lawrence Pearson, of that township, and purchased a small farm, part of his father-in-law's homestead. He followed the vocation of a weaver for some years, and was also a merchant at what is now Ferndale prior to 1826. He later purchased considerable other land in that vicinity, and his later days seem to have been devoted to agricultural pursuits. He died in Nockamixon, March 11, 1868. His wife, Margaret Pearson, was born in Nockamixon, near Ferndale, November 22, 1794, and died September 30, 1863. They were the parents of the following children: Sarah Lavina, wife of Ephraim Yost; Caroline, wife of Frederick Horn; Sybilla, wife of William Loudenberger; Catharine, wife of Franklin J. Shick; Esther, wife of Jacob Sumstone; Elwood; Margaret, who died unmarried; and John H., the father of the subject of this sketch.

Lawrence Pearson, great-great-grandfather of Margaret (Pearson) Clymer, was a native of Yorkshire, England, and came to Pennsylvania with his father, Edward Pearson, in 1683, and settled in Falls township, Bucks county, from whence he removed to Buckingham in 1701, and later to Plumstead, where he died in 1756, and his wife Ann in 1760. They were members of the Society of Friends and their children were reared in that faith. They were the parents of two sons: Enoch, who died in 1748, unmarried, and Joseph, and daughters:

Hannah Fenton, Elizabeth Allen, Martha Shrigley, Priscilla McKinstry, and Mary Jewell. Lawrence Pearson, son of Joseph and grandson of Lawrence and Ann, was born about the year 1720, and in 1744 purchased of Bartholomew Longstreth 250 acres of land in Nockamixon, including the site of Nockamixon German Lutheran and Reform church, a portion of which he conveyed to the trustees of the church in 1797 to enlarge their graveyard. Lawrence Pearson died in 1803, leaving a widow, Elizabeth, and eight children, viz.: Christian, Henry, Philip, Lawrence, Peter, Mary, wife of John Kohl; Catharine, wife of Jacob Saassaman; and Susanna, wife of John Easterling. Kohl and Sassaman were trustees of Nockamixon church. Lawrence Pearson, son of the above named Lawrence, was the father of Margaret Clymer. He married Margaret ———, of German ancestry, and became a member of the Nockamixon church, where his children were baptised. Lawrence, the eldest, born August 27, 1782; William, June 27, 1784; Abraham, November 28, 1790; Margaret, November 22, 1794; John, about 1800; and Elizabeth, January 4, 1807. The latter married Jesse Algart. Lawrence, the father, died in 1810. Though of English ancestry on the paternal side, the children of Lawrence Pearson (3) imbibed the language and customs of their maternal ancestors, and both spoke and wrote in the German language.

John H. Clymer, youngest son of John and Margaret (Pearson) Clymer, was born in Nockamixon, November 3, 1836. On arriving at manhood he located for a time in Durham township, but on the death of his father in 1868 purchased of the other heirs a portion of his father's real estate in Nockamixon and lived thereon for some years, removing later to Tinicum township, where he died August 5, 1881. He married Maria Kiser, daughter of Jacob and Ann (Selner) Kiser, of Nockamixon, granddaughter of Frederick and Gertrude (Hoffman) Kiser, and great-granddaughter of Frederick and Anna Barbara (Stein) Kiser, who emigrated from Bretzinger, in the grand duchy of Baden, and settled in Durham township, Bucks county, prior to 1770. Maria (Kiser) Clymer is living with her son in Doylestown. The children of John H. and Maria (Kiser) Clymer are: Robert L., the subject of this sketch, and Idella, wife of Edward Steely, of Tinicum.

Robert L. Clymer was reared in Nockamixon and Tinicum townships, and acquired his education at the public schools. At the age of fifteen years he began his mercantile career as a clerk in the general merchandise store at Kintnersville, where he was employed for eight years. In 1897 he came to Doylestown and purchased the stock and fixtures of the general merchandise store at the corner of Clinton and Ashland streets, of Kohn K. Benner, where he has since successfully conducted the business. He has taken an active interest in the affairs of the town and is a well known and popular business man. Mr. Clymer is a member of the Reformed church, and is affiliated with Aqueton Lodge No. 193, I. O. O. F., of Doylestown, the Junior O. U. A. M., Ferndale Council No. 685, and the F. and A. M., of Doylestown. He married October 18, 1894, Stella Rufe, daughter of Josiah and Mary Jane Rufe, of Nockamixon, where her ancestors had been prominent landowners and business men for several generations.

F. M. MARPLE. The Marple family has been connected with Bucks county through various generations. N. David Marple, grandfather of F. M. Marple, was born in Bucks county and became an influential and leading farmer of his community. His early political support was given the Democracy, but at, the time of the civil war he joined the ranks of the Republican party, and upon that ticket was called to offices of honor and trust. He held office as a Democrat long before the war. He served as county commissioner and prothonotary of Bucks county, and acted as clerk for General John Davis when the latter was serving as collector of customs for the United States. N. David Marple was a man of superior education and was closely identified with the educational interests of his county at an early day, having been a competent school teacher. He served as a colonel in his regiment in the war of 1812, and was thus prominent in business, political and military circles, a man whose life was above reproach, and who in consequence commanded the entire respect and confidence of those with whom he was associated. His last days were spent in Kansas, to which state he removed in his later years. He belonged to the Baptist church, and all of his relations with his fellowmen exemplified his Christian faith. His wife, who bore the maiden name of Eliza Hart, was born in Bucks county and was descended from an old colonial family of Pennsylvania. Their children were: Eliza A., Mary P., Clara, Virginia, Ellen, Alfred, Joseph, Silas, Nathan, Warren, and Eugene.

Alfred Marple, born in Bucks county, was reared upon his father's farm, acquired a liberal education and became a capable teacher in the public schools. At the time of his marriage he located upon a farm, but later turned his attention to merchandising at Langhorne. He also served as postmaster there for a number of years, and at one time was principal of the Soldier's Orphan's schools of Quakertown. He served for three years in the war of the rebellion, becoming a member of the One Hundred and Fourth Pennsylvania Infantry, Colonel W. H. Davis commanding. He performed his full duty as a valorous soldier and on the expiration of his term of service was honorably discharged. Politically he was a Democrat until the time of the war, when he espoused the cause of the Republican party that stood so loyally by the Union in the darkest hour of our country's history. Following the war he engaged in farming, and in his later life lived retired, making his home in Langhorne, where he died in 1896, when seventy-four years of age. In early manhood he married Anna A. Van Sant, a native of Bucks county, who died in 1871, and later he wedded Sarah Aaron. His first wife was a daughter of Garrett Van Sant, of Bucks county, who was a blacksmith by trade, for many years closely identified with the industrial life of his community. His political views accorded with the principles of Democracy, and he filled the office of county commissioner. His religious faith was that of the Presbyterian church. The children of Mr. and Mrs. Van Sant are: George, William, Maria, Elizabeth, Anna, and Jane. The children of Mr. and Mrs. Alfred Marple are: Frank H.; William W., a prominent farmer; Mary, deceased; Florence; and Ida, wife of Dr. Heritage, a physician of Langhorne.

Frank H. Marple, son of Alfred Marple, was born in Langhorne township, Bucks county, December 31, 1849, and was reared to farm life, while in the public schools he acquired his education. He remained under the parental roof until he had attained his majority, and in 1876 he was married and settled on the old Hart homestead, where he remained for four years. He then returned to the township of his nativity and rented his father's old homestead, there carrying on agricultural pursuits until 1902, when he purchased the old Hart homestead on which he had resided immediately after his marriage. Hereon he has since made his home, his farm lying partly in Warminster and partly in Southampton townships. He carried on general farming and marketed his own produce, and for two years also operated a creamery, but is now devoting his entire time and attention to the production of vegetables and cereals and to the sale of his products in the Philadelphia markets. His business affairs are capably managed and his enterprise and unremitting diligence form strong and basic elements for a successful career. Mr. Marple was married to Miss Laura Tomlinson, a native of Bucks county, and a daughter of William Tomlinson, also of Bucks county. He was

a carpenter by trade, and was killed while serving his country in the civil war, being for three years a member of the Union army. In his political views he was a Republican. His wife long survived him, passing away in 1882. Their children were: Charles, Elizabeth, and Laura, the last named the wife of Mr. Marple. To Mr. and Mrs. Marple were born three children: William, who is clerking; Grace, at home; and Alfred, who is a stenographer in California. After the death of his first wife, Mr. Marple married Mrs. Susan Johnson, a cultured lady, whose parents were William B. and Mary A. (Alford) Kitchen, of Philadelphia. Her father, a tailor by trade, followed that business throughout his entire life, and died at Center Hill in 1869. In his political views he was a Republican, and he held some local political positions. He belonged to the Baptist church, of which his wife, who now makes her home with her children, is also a member. In the Johnson family were six children: Victor, Florence, Orville, Claude, May and Burleigh. In his political views Mr. Marple is a Republican, but the honors and emoluments of office have had no attraction for him, and although he is never remiss in the duties of citizenship, he prefers to devote his time and energies to his business affairs, which are now bringing him a desirable financial return.

A. J. MILLER, following farming near Neshaminy, was born in Philadelphia, February 18, 1845, and in the maternal line comes of German ancestry. His father, A. J. Miller, was born in Allentown, Pennsylvania, and after acquiring a good education went to Philadelphia as a young man, there engaging in mercantile pursuits. He made for himself an excellent place in business circles in that city, becoming a member of the firm of Miller, Weber & Hand, conducting an extensive and profitable business as dealers in dry goods at the corner of Fourth and Market streets. Mr. Miller remained a member of the house until 1847, when his death occurred at the age of forty years. While business affairs claimed much of his time, he yet found opportunity to devote to movements effecting the general interests of society. He was a leading member of the Presbyterian church, and served as an elder and as superintendent of its Sunday-school. He contributed generously to the work of the church, and did all in his power to advance the cause of Christianity. He was also generous to those who needed assistance, sympathetic with those in sorrow, and at all times kind and considerate. Having prospered in his business he was able to leave his family in comfortable circumstances. In 1831, in Philadelphia, he married Miss Catherine Helffenstein, a cultured and intelligent lady, a granddaughter of John C. Helffenstein, of honored Germany ancestry, belonging to a distinguished family of that country, connected with the nobility and possessing a coat-of-arms. Her parents were Rev. Samuel and Ann (Stitle) Helffenstein, both of German descent. Her father, who was born April 17, 1775, was regularly ordained as a minister of the German Reformed church in 1796, at which time he took charge of the old Bean church in Bluebell, Montgomery county, Pennsylvania. In 1799 he became pastor of the congregation of that denomination at Fourth and Race streets, in Philadelphia, where he remained for thirty-two years, preaching in both the German and English languages. Later in life he retired to his farm near North Wales, where he spent his remaining days. He still continued preaching, taking charge of a church in Northampton county, to which he rode twenty miles in order to deliver the gospel message. He preached his last sermon at North Wales when ninety years of age. He was a fine musician, and his musical talent added greatly to his services. He passed away on his home farm at the age of ninety-three years, after a long, useful and honorable career. He had likewise prospered in his material affairs, and became possessed of a large estate. In his family were twelve children, eleven sons and a daughter, all of whom are now deceased. Three of the sons became ministers of the gospel, and all were professional men or merchants. Seven sons and a daughter survived him, the latter being Mrs. Catherine Miller. A. J. Miller, Sr. died in 1847 and his wife, long surviving him, passed away in 1884. She remained at the old home in Philadelphia throughout that period, and both were buried in one of the cemeteries of that city. They had five children: Samuel H., a merchant, now deceased; Lavina G.; Mary M., the wife of Joseph Linton; Annie M., the widow of E. D. Wakeling, who was an attorney of Philadelphia; and A. J., of this review.

A. J. Miller, whose name introduces this record, spent his boyhood days in the manner of most city lads, his time being largely given to his school work as a student in the grammar and high schools of Philadelphia. He thus obtained a good education. He was but a young lad when his father died, but the mother kept her children together, carefully rearing them. When he had attained the proper age he was employed as a clerk in his brother's store, and later engaged in he real estate business in Philadelphia, which he continued to follow for many years. At length he turned his attention to general merchandising at Bethayres, and subsequently expanded the field of his labors by establishing a coal and lumber business in connection with his real estate operations, continuing therein until 1890. He then bought the farm upon which he now resides; it is one of the old historic places of the county, and the house is a commodious three story stone residence, which was occupied at the time of the revolutionary war and is yet in a good state of preservation. Many additions have since been made and modern improvements added, but one of the old doors yet swings with its latch string that always hung out in the olden times. In 1774 the Rev. N. Erwin resided here, and ministered to the spiritual wants of the people of the locality for many years as pastor of the Neshaminy Presbyterian church. In 1800, however, he built the residence that Joseph Dobbins now occupies and there he remained until his death, his remains being then interred in the Neshaminy cemetery. Since taking up his abode upon the farm Mr. Miller has devoted his entire attention to its further cultivation and improvement, and he annually harvests good crops and markets the products of the gardens.

A. J. Miller was married to Miss Ellen V. Sickel, who was born in Quakertown, Bucks county, Pennsylvania, June 13, 1844. She was a devoted wife and helpmate to him, and was the only daughter of General H. G. Sickel, of national fame. Her mother, who bore the maiden name of Eliza Van Sant, was a daughter of William Van Sant, a representative of one of the oldest families of Bucks county. Mr. and Mrs. Sickel had but two children: Jane, who became the wife of Joseph Hart; and Eliza, the mother of Mrs. Miller. General Sickel was reared in the vicinity of Mechanicsville, and being left an orphan when quite young was entirely a self-made man. He learned the wheelwright's and blacksmith's trades, which he followed for many years. He was married at Davisville and later settled at Quakertown, where he followed his pursuits, conducting an extensive business. About 1846 he removed to Philadelphia, where he became connected with mercantile interests as a dealer in lamp and gas fixtures, continuing in that line until 1857. He afterward held various public positions by appointments of the governor, and was prominent and influential in community and state affairs. At the time of the outbreak of the civil war he raised a company for service in defense of the Union, was made its captain and was promoted from time to time, being brevetted major general at the close of the war. He served throughout the entire period of hostilities with honor and distinction, his promotion coming in realization of meritorious conduct on the field of battle. He was several times wounded, and on one occasion it was thought that he would lose an arm because of injuries. Following the cessation of hostilities he was appointed revenue collector and health officer of Philadelphia, filling these positions for a number of years. He was also appointed pension agent at Philadelphia by appointment of the president, and he occupied many positions of official preferment, discharging the duties of all in a most creditable and honorable manner. His last position was that of pension attorney, in which capacity he was serving at the time of his death, which occurred April 17, 1889, when he was seventy-two years of age. He was a consistent and worthy member of the Presbyterian church, taking a most active and helpful part in its work and contributing generously to its support. Broad-minded, liberal and charitable, he was ever found fearless in conduct, honorable in action and stainless in reputation. As the years have passed he had made investment in different public enterprises, becoming a stockholder in some paying business concerns. He was president and one of the promoters of the Newtown railroad. His military service and the influential position he occupied in political circles of Pennsylvania won him national fame. His wife died prior to his demise, passing away at the age of sixty-two years. They were the parents of five children, all of whom are living: Howard V., who entered the pension office during his father's service and yet holds a position in that department in Washington, D. C.; Ellen, the wife of A. T. Miller; Charles A., who is a pension attorney in Washington, D. C.; William V., a pension attorney in Philadelphia; and Horatio, who is a major in the United States army in the Philippines. All are married, and this circle constitutes an interesting family.

Mr. and Mrs. Miller have become the parents of three children: Randolph H., a structural engineer, who married Miss Catherine Darrah; Clarence, who is foreman for the Kittarlinus Lithographic Company of Philadelphia, and married Miss Helen Warner; and Augustus J., an architect of Philadelphia. The parents and their children are members of the Presbyterian church. Politically Mr. Miller is a Republican where national issues are involved, but at local elections is independent, casting his ballot for men and measures rather than for party. He is active in the church work, serving as superintendent of the Sunday school at Warrington. He has also been connected with several federal organizations, but has now withdrawn from these and his time and energies

are devoted in more undivided manner to his business affairs, which, capably conducted, are bringing him desirable success.

B. FRANK COPE. Among the active and efficient business men of Lower Buckingham is B. Frank Cope, for many years a director and superintendent of the Forest Grove Creamery. Mr. Cope was born in Doylestown township, Bucks county, August 14, 1859, and is a son of Amandus F. and Anna Elizabeth (Funk) Cope. His father, who is a son of Franklin S. and Magdalena (Urfer) Cope, was born near Pennsburg, Montgomery county, Pennsylvania, and soon after his marriage purchased a farm in Doylestown township, where he resided until 1870, when he removed to Montgomery county, near Bryn Mawr. He was a farmer during his active life, but now resides with a daughter at Atlantic City, New Jersey.

The subject of this sketch was born and reared on the farm, and received a good education at the schools of Doylestown township and Bryn Mawr. At the age of twenty-one he accepted a position as assistant in the Pine Run creamery, Doylestown township. On June 4, 1882, he took charge of the Forest Grove creamery, and was superintendent and salesman, as well as a member of the board of directors, for many years, and giving entire satisfaction to the patrons and stockholders. Mr. Cope was for many years an ardent Democrat and took an active part in the councils of his party. He was the party nominee for director of the poor in 1898, and received the highest vote of any on the ticket, running far ahead of other candidates in his home township. In 1902 he was nominated for the assembly, but a fusion was later effected by the local leaders, and he was forced off the ticket. He is a member of Doylestown Lodge, No. 245, F. and A. M.; Warrington Lodge, No. 447, I. O. O. F., of which he has been secretary and representative for ten years; Neshaminy Castle, No. 139, K. G. E.; and Paunacussing Lodge, No. 221, K. of P. In the spring of 1904 he purchased a farm in Lower Buckingham, upon which he now resides. He was married, in 1883, to Rose Ella Barton, daughter of Joel and Phoebe (Carver) Barton, of Solebury. Her parents now reside in Warwick township. Mr. and Mrs. Cope have been the parents of four children: Linford W., deceased; Edmund B.; Anna E., deceased; and Harman Yerkes.

The brothers and sisters of Mr. Cope are as follows: Mary J., widow of Samuel Eckstein, of Philadelphia; Samuel E., of Telford, Pennsylvania; Edwardine, wife of Harry L. Riley, of Atlantic City; Clinton B., of Buckingham; James

R., of Egg Harbor; John A., of Atlantic City, and Daniel, who has been an employe of John Wanamaker for several years.

HENRY CRAWFORD PARRY, one of the best known citizens of Langhorne, Bucks county, Pennsylvania, retired business man, president of the People's National Bank, is of Welsh descent. His earliest ancestor in America was Thomas Parry, who was born in Caernarvonshire, North Wales, in 1680, and came to Pennsylvania when a young man, married Jane Phillips, in 1715, and settled in Moreland, near the present site of Willow Grove. The family of Parry is one of the most ancient in the United Kingdom, and their coat-of-arms is registered in Burke's General Armory.

Thomas Parry, above mentioned, was a grandson of Colonel Geoffrey Parry, of Caernarvonshire, who married Margaret Hughes, of Cefn Llanfair, and son of Love Parry, of Wanfour, who was high sheriff of Caernervonshire in 1685, and his wife Ellen, daughter of Hugh Wynn of Penarth. Thomas and Jane (Phillips) Parry were the parents of ten children, eight sons and two daughters. He died in 1751, aged seventy-one years.

Philip Parry, born in the "Manor of Moorland," now Moreland township, Montgomery county, 11 mo. 18, 1716, married 2 mo., 1740, Rachel Harker, daughter of Adam Harker, one of the most prominent Friends of his day in Pennsylvania, and settled in Buckingham township, where he purchased March 11, 1746, 170 acres of land near Holicong. He died on this plantation, the late residence of E. Watson Fell, in 1784, leaving three sons: John, Philip, and Thomas; and five daughters: Hannah, Jane, Grace, Rachel and Mary.

John Parry, son of Philip and Rachel (Harker) Parry, born in Moreland, 9 mo. 10, 1743, married 4 mo. 17, 1771, Rachel, daughter of Titus and Elizabeth (Heston) Fell, and granddaughter of Joseph Fell, who came from Longlands, in Cumberland, England, in 1705, by his second wife, Elizabeth Doyle, daughter of Edward and Rebecca (Dungan) Doyle. John Parry died in Buckingham 11 mo. 13, 1807, and his wife Rachel, 2 mo. 18, 1818. They were the parents of nine children: Elizabeth, who married George Shoemaker; Joyce, who married Jacob Shoemaker; Mercy; Charity; Tacy; Rachel; and John, who died unmarried; David, who married Elizabeth Ely, and (second) Lydia Richardson, and settled in Drumore, Lancaster county, and Thomas Fell Parry.

Thomas Fell Parry, youngest child of John and Rachel (Fell) Parry, was born in Buckingham 7 mo. 8, 1791. He married 12 mo. 17, 1829, Mary, daughter of

Moses and Rachel (Knowles) Eastburn, of Solebury, who was born 9 mo. 13, 1800. Mr. Parry was for many years a resident of Philadelphia, where he was engaged in mercantile pursuits. In 1846 he purchased property at Langhorne and two years later removed to that locality, where he spent the remaining years of his long and useful life. He died 3 mo. 27, 1876. His wife, Mary E., died 6 mo. 5, 1872. They were the parents of five children: Rachel, born 9 mo. 20, 1830, married Gilbert Shaw; Eliza beth, born 4 mo. 16, 1832, married Wilson Croasdale; Henry C., born 3 mo. 23, 1834; John E., born 11 mo. 22, 1836, married 2 mo. 14, 1861, Mary Jane Livezey; Charles, born 11 mo, 24, 1839, died 12 mo. 19, 1842.

Henry C. Parry, the subject of this sketch, eldest son of Thomas Fell and Mary (Eastburn) Parry, was born in the city of Philadelphia and received his primary education at private and public schools in that city. He was fifteen years of age when the family removed to Middletown, Bucks county, and then entered Pennington, New Jersey, Seminary, where he finished his education. On arriving at manhood he engaged in farming in Middletown township, which vocation he followed successfully for sixteen years. In 1876 he engaged in the coal and lumber business at Langhorne station, which he conducted for twenty-one years, building up a fine and profitable business. He sold out the business in 1887, and has since lived retired. Mr. Parry has always been actively interested in the local affairs of his neighborhood, and has held many positions of trust. He has served as chief burgess of the borough for two terms, and two terms as a member of council. He was for many years a director of the First National Bank of Newtown, has been for eight years a director of the People's National Bank of Langhorne, and was unanimously elected president of the latter institution in 1899, a position he still fills. Mr. Parry has been actively interested in the improvements in and around Langhorne, and is one of the solid substantial business men of that section. He and his family are members of the Society of Friends. Politically he is a Republican.

He was married November 13, 1856, to Susan Gillam Blakey, daughter of William Watson and Anna (Gillam) Blakey, and granddaughter of William and Elizabeth (Watson) Blakey. On the maternal side she is a granddaughter of William and Susanna (Woolston) Gillam, and great-granddaughter of Simon and Anna (Paxson) Gillam, and of Jonathan and Elizabeth (Harvey) Woolstore. There of her lineal ancestors were members of the colonial assembly at one time—Thomas Watson, William Paxson and John Sotcher, all of them serving a number of years. Her great-great-grandfather Mazry Watson, was also a member of colonial assembly for very many years. Henry C. Parry is also a descendant of John Sotcher, through his grandmother Rachel (Knowles) Eastburn. (See Eastburn sketch in this work.) William Blakey Parry, only child of Henry C. and Susan G. (Blakey) Parry, was born in Middletown township, 5 mo. 18, 1858. He was educated in the schools of Middletown and in Philadelphia. He married September 27, 1883, Elizabeth, daughter of William and Elizabeth (Williamson) Moon, who was born 7 mo. 27, 1857. Two children have been born to this marriage: Laura Elizabeth, born July 28, 1891; and Henry Crawford, Jr., born November 2, 1895.

PROFESSOR ALLEN S. MARTIN. County Superintendent of Public Schools, was born in Lancaster county, Pennsylvania, April 7, 1868, and is a son of the late Henry K. and Anna (Sahn) Martin, both natives of Lancaster county. He was reared on his father's farm, and attended the public schools until the age of sixteen years, when he began teaching in the public schools of his native county, teaching in all in that county for five years. He graduated at the State Normal School at Millersville, Lancaster county, and later took a course in arts and sciences in the University of Pennsylvania, receiving the degree of Bachelor of Sciences. In June, 1893, he became principal of the high school of Sellersville, Bucks county, Pennsylvania, and two years later accepted the position of principal of the Doylestown high school, which latter position he filled with eminent ability for seven years. In 1902 Prof. Martin was elected to the office of Superintendent of Public Schools of the county, and was unanimously reelected to the same position in 1905. Superintendent Martin is deeply interested in the cause of popular education, and has done much to improve the efficiency of our public schools. He has a superior talent for organization and one of his plans that has proved eminently successful, is the holding of frequent "educational meetings" of teachers and directors in different parts of the county, where subjects that are of direct interest to teachers and directors are discussed, whereby the interest of both in the work of bettering the schools is stimulated and strengthened, and the best methods of imparting knowledge are brought within the reach of all. Professor Martin is president of the Bucks County Natural Science Association, and a member of the Academy of Natural Science of Philadelphia. He takes a deep interest in botany and zoology, and is considered an authority on the flora and mammals of the section in which he lives. He is a member of the State Teachers' Association, and has been frequently called upon to aid in educational work in different parts of the state.

Professor Martin was married, in Lancaster county, to Mary Magdalena Kauffman, of an old family in that county, and they are the parents of four children—Edith and H. Clay, born in Lancaster county; and Lenore and Mildred, born in Doylestown.

GULICK FAMILY. Joachim Gulick, or, as he signed his name, "Jochem Guyllyck," the pioneer ancestor of the Gulick family of Hilltown, Bucks county, emigrated from the Netherlands in 1653, and settled in Gravesend, Long Island, removing later to Staten Island. He married Jacomyntje Van Pelt, daughter of Teunis Janse Lanen Van Pelt, who emigrated from Liege, Belgium, in 1663, with wife Grietje Jans and six children and settled at New Utrecht, Long Island, from whence his grandson, Joseph Van Pelt, migrated to Staten Island and later to Byberry, Philadelphia county, Pennsylvania, and has numerous descendants in Bucks county. Jochem Gulick was an ensign at Gravesend in 1689, and about 1691 purchased land on Staten Island, and is said to have removed later to New Jersey, though of this there is no proof. Jochem and Jacomyntje (Van Pelt) Gulick were the parents of four sons,— Hendrick; Samuel, born 1685; Joachim, born 1687; and Peter, born 1689. Of these, Joachim and Hendrick located on Three-Mile-Run, Somerset county, New Jersey, in 1717, and left numerous descendants.

Hendrick Gulick, eldest son of Joachim, the founder, married Cantje Dirckse Amerman, who was baptized on Long Island, April 2, 1677. He located in Somerset county, New Jersey, where he died in 1757, leaving eleven children: Joachim, Derrick, Jacomyntje, Samuel, Alshe, Catrin, Mary, Grrebrantje, Hendrick, Peter and Antje or Anna.

Hendrick (or Henry, as he later signed himself), son of Hendrick and Cantje (Amerman) Gulick, settled in Alexandria township, Hunterdon county, New Jersey, near the present site of Milford, where he died in April, 1798, leaving nine children, Samuel, Nicholas, Charity Hoagland, Minnor, Catharine Buckalew, Mary Duckworth, Ranshea Allen, Abraham and Rachel. His wife, Mary Williamson, whom he married September 26, 1754, survived him.

Samuel Gulick, eldest son of Henry and Mary (Williamson) Gulick, settled in Northampton county, where he married and reared a family.

Jonathan Gulick, son of Samuel, born in Northampton county, Pennsylvania, in 1795, removed to Towamencin township, Montgomery county, Pennsylvania, in 1818, where he followed farming until 1837, when he removed to Hilltown, Bucks county, where he located on a small farm adjudged to him in right of his wife as part of the real estate of her father, Obed Aaron, and later purchased other land adjoining. He died in Hilltown in 1873, at the age of seventy-seven years. He married Urey Aaron, daughter of Obed Aaron, and granddaughter of Moses and Elizabeth (James) Aaron, the former a native of Wales, settled in New Britain about 1725, and died there in 1765. Thomas James, the father of Elizabeth Aaron, was also a native of Wales, and came with his father, John James, from Pembrokeshire in 1712. Obed Aaron was born in 1761 and died in 1837. The children of Jonathan and Urey (Aaron) Gulick were Merari, Harriet, Sybilla and Urey, all of whom are deceased.

Merari Gulick, only son of Jonathan and Urey, was born on his father's farm in Towamencin township, Montgomery county, Pennsylvania, in 1819, and removed with his parents to Hilltown in 1837. In 1843 he purchased a farm in Hilltown of 117 acres, which he conducted during the active years of his life. He was an active and prominent farmer of that section, and followed the Philadelphia markets for some thirty years. He married, in 1841, Christina Swartz, who was born in New Britain township in 1819, and died in Hilltown in 1888. She was a daughter of Christian Swartz, a prominent farmer of New Britain township, of German ancestry. He married Margaret Funk, daughter of Rev. John and Elizabeth (Lewis) Funk of Line Lexington, the former a son of Martin Funk, who came from Germany in 1737 and settled in Hatfield, Montgomery county, and the latter a native of Wales and a daughter of Henry Lewis of New Britain. John Funk was the founder of a branch of the Mennonites known as Funkites. He is said to have preached at Germantown while residing in Hilltown, making the journey back and forth on horseback. Christian and Margaret Funk Swartz were the parents of eight children: John, died young; Andrew F.; Elizabeth, wife of John Rosenberger; Margaret, wife of Enos Gehman; Christina, wife of Merari Gulick; Lydia, wife of John Heckler; Amelia, wife of John Hunsberger; and Mary, wife of Samuel Rosenberger.

The children of Merari and Christina (Swartz) Gulick were: Mary, wife of William D. Yocum, a farmer of Hilltown; Urey, wife of Joseph B. Allabaugh, also a farmer in Hilltown; Jonathan, of Hilltown; Obed Aaron, a gro-

cer in Philadelphia; Merari, who died at the age of two years; Samuel S., of South Perkasie; Christopher S., of Blooming Glen; and John S., born February 17, 1861, died September 28, 1878.

SAMUEL S. GULICK, son of Merari and Christina (Swartz) Gulick, was born in Hilltown township, October 10, 1856, and was educated at the public schools. He was reared on his father's farm and remained there until his marriage in 1886, when he located at what is now South Perkasie. In 1890 he was elected a justice of the peace of Rockhill township, and was re-elected in 1895, and served until 1900. He is an auctioneer, which business he has followed for many years, crying hundreds of sales in a single year. Since his election as justice of the peace he has conducted a general business agency in connection with his official duties, and has settled a great number of estates and has done a large amount of public business. He is the owner of several private properties at South Perkasie, a small farm located within the limits of Perkasie borough, and his present residence in South Perkasie. He is director of the Quakertown Trust Company, and one of the progressive and prominent business men of the growing town of Perkasie. He is a member of McCalla Lodge, No. 596, F. and A. M., of Sellersville, and of the brotherhood of the Union. Politically he is a Republican. He and his family are members of the German Reformed church. He married, March 13, 1886, Mary E. Shellenberger, daughter of Jacob S. and Catharine (Rudy) Shellenberger, and they have been the parents of eight children: Paul, Katie, deceased; Ella, Herman, Esther, Emma, Samuel and Robert, deceased.

CHRISTOPHER S. GULICK, ex-register of wills of Bucks county, now (1905) deputy treasurer of the county, was born in Hilltown township, Bucks county, Pennsylvania, June 11, 1859, and is the youngest son of Merari and Christina (Swartz) Gulick, whose ancestry is given in a preceding sketch.

He was reared in Hilltown township, and has resided there all his life with the exception of the three years, 1896-98, during which he filled the office of register of wills, when he resided in Doylestown. He received his elementary education at the public schools of Hilltown township, later attending Sellersville high school, from which he graduated at the age of nineteen years, and began teaching in the public schools of the county. He taught for one year in Bedminster and ten in his native township, eight of which were spent in conducting the school at Blooming Glen, where he now lives. In politics Mr.

19-3

Gulick is a Republican, and has always given an unfaltering support to the principles of that party, and done effective service in its behalf in his home locality, and keeping himself well informed as to the questions and issues of the day. In 1885 he was elected to the office of justice of the peace in Hilltown township, and filled that position for five years, doing a large amount of official business and assisting in the settlement of estates. He also took up the business of auctioneering, and did considerable business in that line. On the termination of his term as justice, in 1889, he was appointed, under President Harrison, deputy collector of internal revenue for the district in which Bucks county is included, and served in that capacity for four years. In 1894 he embarked in the mercantile business at the thriving village of Blooming Glen, in partnership with M. H. Leidy, under the firm name of Leidy & Gulick, which continued until his election to the office of register of wills, in the fall of 1895. On assuming the duties of this office in January, 1896, he transferred his interest in the store to Abram M. Moyer, and removed with his family to Doylestown. Thoroughly diligent and conscientious in the transaction of his official duties, and courteous to all with whom he came in contact, he made a very popular and efficient official, and made many friends throughout the county. On the termination of his term of office in 1899, he returned to Blooming Glen, and in August of that year purchased his former store of the firm of Leidy & Moyer, and conducted the business until February, 1904, when he sold out to the present firm of Apple & Shaddinger, and, purchasing a residence of his former partner, M. H. Leidy, followed farming and auctioneering until May, 1905, when he was appointed deputy county treasurer, under John B. Poore, and assumed the duties of that office. retaining his residence at Blooming Glen.

Mr. Gulick is a member of McCalla Lodge, No. 596, F. and A. M., of Sellersville; of Doylestown Chapter, No. 270, R. A. M.; of Perkasie Lodge, No. 671, I. O. O. F., and of Doylestown Encampment, No. 35, I. O. O. F., of which he is a past chief patriarch. Mr. Gulick has always taken an active interest in all that pertains to improvement and development of the material interest of the community in which he lived, and has filled a number of positions of trust. At the organization of the Perkasie National Bank he was elected one of the original board of directors, and has served continuously in that position since. He is a member of the Reformed church.

He married, February 28, 1885, Emma H. Moyer, daughter of Rev. Abraham and Hester (Hunsberger) Moyer, of Hilltown. She was born in Hilltown, October 1, 1864, and was the tenth of eleven children. Her father, Rev. Abraham F. Moyer, was born in Upper Salford, Montgomery county, Pennsylvania, September 19, 1822, and was a son of Abraham and Elizabeth (Fretz) Moyer, grandson of Christian Meyer, great grandson of Henry Meyer, who came to Pennsylvania about 1725, at the age of one year, with his father, Hans Meyer, from Germany or Switzerland, who settled in Skippack, now Salford township, Montgomery county, and purchased land there in 1729, which is still in the tenure of his great-great-grandson, Jacob L. Moyer. Henry, the son of Hans, married Barbara Miller, who came from Germany at the age of eighteen years, and inherited the homestead at the death of his father, in 1748. He reared a family of seven children, many of whom have left descendants in Bucks county. Rev. Abraham F. Moyer came to Bucks county when a lad, and lived with his maternal uncle, Martin Fretz. From the age of sixteen to twenty-one he was a clerk in a store, but later became a farmer in Hilltown. He was ordained minister of the Mennonite congregation at Blooming Glen November 6, 1855, and continued to minister to that flock until his death. He was an active and faithful Christian teacher, and much respected in that community. He was twice married. His first wife, and the mother of his eleven children, was Hester, daughter of Jacob and Mary Hunsberger, of Hilltown, who died February 28, 1873. He married, in 1874, Anna, widow of Henry M. Hunsberger, of Montgomery county, and daughter of Abraham L. Moyer.

The children of Christopher S. and Emma H. (Moyer) Gulick, are: Arnon M., born July 8, 1886; Mabel M., born April 13, 1889; Gertrude Hester, born December 3, 1891; Blanche M., born February 15, 1894; Russel Blair, born March 5, 1898; Howard M., born January 6, 1901; and LeRoy M., born April 12, 1904.

SAVACOOL FAMILY. The paternal and pioneer ancestor of the Savacool family of Hilltown and South Perkasie was Jacob Savacool (or Sabelkool, as the name was then spelled), who was born in Germany in the year 1713, and emigrated to Pennsylvania at the age of eighteen years, arriving in Philadelphia on board the ship "Brittania," Michael Franklin, master, September 21, 1731. Like all the other early German settlers of Upper Bucks he made his way into Bucks through the present county of Montgomery. The earliest record of him is his purchase on June 14, 1742, of 102½ acres of land in Rockhill township, near the present site of Sellers-ville, of Michael Durstine, the pioneer ancestor of that family, whose descend-ants still reside on a part of the same tract, one mile south of Sellersville, at the station bearing their name. Here Jacob Savacool lived and reared a fam-ily of six children,—two sons, William and Isaac; and four daughters,—Cath-arine, Eleanor, Susanna, and Elizabeth. He was a member of the Mennonite congregation of Rockhill, to whom he devised a legacy of ten pounds. His widow, Elizabeth, survived him. Will-iam Savacool, the eldest son of Jacob and Elizabeth, was born at Derstines, Rockhill township, but on his marriage located on a farm in Hilltown purchased for him by his father in 1772, and devised to him by his father in 1782, Isaac, the second son, being devised the Rockhill homestead. William married Eliza-beth Miller, and they were the parents of seven children: Michael; Catharine, wife of George Jenkins; Susanna, wife of John Cope; John; Henry; Maria, and Jacob. William, the father, lived to a good old age, dying in 1832.

Jacob Savacool, youngest son of Will-iam and Elizabeth (Miller) Savacool, was born on the old homestead in Hill-town in the year 1803. Early in life he learned the wheelwright trade, which he followed until after the death of his father in 1832, when he purchased the old homestead and conducted it until his death in 1878. He married Lydia Snyder, daughter of Jacob and Eliza-beth (Yost) Snyder, of Hilltown, (whose ancestry is given elsewhere in this work) and they were the parents of fourteen children, three of whom died in infancy; those who survive are: Enos B., born January 18, 1831, of South Perkasie; Aaron, a sketch of whom fol-lows; Elizabeth, wife of Leidy Scholl; William B., see forward; Lydia; Amelia, wife of Benjamin Althouse; Caroline, wife of John Sherm; Jacob A., see for-ward; Emma, who married Tobias Cuf-fel, of Lansdale, and is now deceased, leaving nine children; and Elias, de-ceased. The old homestead still remains in the family and is occupied by Jacob A. Savacool, the youngest son.

ENOS SAVACOOL, eldest son of Jacob and Lydia (Snyder) Savacool, was born in Hilltown, January 18, 1829, and was reared on the old homestead, acquiring his education in the public schools of that township. At the age of sixteen years he entered the general merchandise store of his uncle, C. A. Snyder, in Richland township. He later engaged in the business with his uncle in Rockhill township. In 1884 he pur-chased a farm at Bridgetown, now South Perkasie, where he still resides. He is a member of St. Andrew's Luth-eran church, and politically is a Demo-crat. He married, February 26, 1854, Hannah Moyer, daughter of Samuel M. and Barbara (High) Moyer, and they have been the parents of five children: 1. Susan, died at the age of fourteen years; 2. James Erwin, born January 1, 1856, died at the age of eight years; 3. William Henry, born February, 1858, now a resident of Philadelphia; has been twice married; by his first wife, Ella Stoneback, he has two children,—Lizzie and James Erwin; he married (second) Mrs. Lavinia (Clymer) Savacool, by whom he has three children; 4. Levi M., born January 15, 1860, died December 31, 1882; 5. Franklin M., born December 5, 1864, married Lydia Weigner, and has one child, Frank.

AARON SAVACOOL was born in Hill-town township, and reared on the old home-stead, acquiring his education at the lo-cal schools. Reared to the life of a farmer, he has never followed any other vocation. Until 1898 he was one of the active and progressive farmers of Hill-town township. In connection with the tilling of the soil he ran a commission wagon, carrying his own and his neigh-bors' lighter produce to the Philadelpnia markets. In the latter year he built himself a handsome and commodious residence in Perkasie, where he now re-sides, enjoying the fruits of a life of industry and usefulness. He is a mem-ber of St. Andrew's Lutheran church, and in politics is a Democrat, but has never sought or held other than local office, having served for four years as assessor of Hilltown township. He mar-ried, November, 1857, Esther Shetler, and to them have been born three chil-dren: Martha, wife of J. Howard Gear-hart, and has four children; Susan, de-ceased, the latter having been the wife of Milton L. Cope, and had two chil-dren, and one son, Jacob, who married a distant cousin, Lizzie Savacool, daugh-ter of Mahlon Savacool, and has one child, Esther.

WILLIAM B. SAVACOOL, son of Jacob and Lydia (Snyder) Savacool, whose ancestry is traced in a preceding sketch, he being a grandson of William and Elizabeth (Miller) Savacool, and a great-grandson of Jacob Savelkool, who came to Pennsylvania in 1731, and settled in Rockhill, was born on the old homestead in Hilltown, August 27, 1833. He was educated in the public schools of Hilltown, and remained on the farm with his parents until his marriage in 1856, when he removed to Sellersville, where he lived for five years. He then returned to the homestead and worked for his father for five years. In 1880 he settled at South Perkasie, and opened a flour and feed store, and also purchased calves for the New York and Philadelphia markets. He continued the business until 1904, when he leased the mill and feed store to his nephew, W. Elmer Savacool, and now lives retired in South Perkasie. He is a member of the Lutheran church of Perkasie, and in politics is a Democrat. Mr. Savacool married in November, 1858, Christiana Fulmer, daughter of Jacob and Mary (Kramer) Fulmer.

W. ELMER SAVACOOL, of South Perkasie, Bucks county, Pennsylvania, was born on the old homestead in Hilltown township, which has been the property of his ancestors for over one hundred and fifty years, and is still occupied by his parents, Jacob A. and Eva (Steeley) Savacool.

Jacob A. Savacool, the father of William Elmer, was born on the old homestead October 9, 1850, and is the youngest son of Jacob and Lydia (Snyder) Savacool, whose ancestry is traced in preceding pages.* He was reared on the old homestead where he still resides, and was educated in the public schools of Hilltown township. Being the youngest of the family, he remained with his parents on the homestead, and at the death of his father in 1876 he purchased the homestead of ninety-four acres, and has always followed the life of a farmer. He is a member of the Lutheran church of South Perkasie, and in politics is a Democrat. He married, May 10, 1873, Eva Steeley, of Tinicum township, Bucks county, Pennsylvania, and they are the parents of five children; William Elmer, the subject of this sketch; Stella; Emma, deceased; Ada and Jacob.

William Elmer Savacool was reared on the old homestead and attended the Red Hill school, later entering the Sellersville high school. He remained on the farm with his father until the age of twenty-two years, and then removed to Hagersville, Bedminster township, where he lived for two years. He then removed to South Perkasie and entered the employ of his uncle, William B. Savacool, in the mill and feed store, and five years later (in 1904) leased the plant of his uncle and now conducts the business for himself. He has always taken an active interest in local affairs, filling a number of local offices. He has been a member of the board of health of Perkasie borough and is now serving a term as school director of that borough. He is a member of Relief Circle, No. 57, Brotherhood of the Union, and religiously is affiliated with the Lutheran church of South Perkasie.

*For ancestry of Lydia (Snyder) Savacool see sketch of Henry H. Snyder.

He married, December 16, 1896, Clara Meyers, born August 6, 1877, daughter of Abraham F. and Susanna (High) Myers, the latter deceased; and granddaughter of Joseph F. and Barbara (Fretz) Myers. Her great-grandfather Henry Meyer, was born in Bucks county, February 23, 1780, and died in Plumstead township, Bucks county, October, 1847. His wife was Elizabeth Fretz, born March 24, 1807. John Meyers, the father of Henry, was also a resident of Plumstead township, and was born in 1756 and died in 1814. His wife was Catharine Souder. William Elmer and Clara (Meyers) Savacool are the parents of two children—Eva M. and William Russell.

SHELLENBERGER FAMILY. The paternal ancestors of Mary E. (Shellenberger) Gulick were early settlers in Hatfield township, Montgomery county, Pennsylvania, and were the descendants of Johannes Schellenberger, who emigrated from Germany and settled in that township, arriving in Philadelphia, October 4, 1751, in the ship "Queen of Denmark." He purchased 250 acres in Hatfield and became one of the prominent men of that section. By his wife Margaret he had at least five sons, Conrad, John, Philip, Jacob and Charles, all but the two last settling in Bucks county. In 1776 he purchased several tracts of land in Hilltown, which he soon after conveyed to his sons above mentioned.

Conrad Shellenberger, son of John of Hatfield, settled in Rockhill township, where he was living in 1779, when his father conveyed to him 120 acres of land in Hilltown. He eventually purchased several other farms in Hilltown, and became one of the prominent landholders there. He died in 1839 in Hilltown. His wife, Eve Leidy, died about 1828. They were the parents of seven children,—two sons, John L. and Jacob L., and five daughters: Hannah, who married a Trauger, and died before her father, leaving two daughters, Eve and Mary; Elizabeth, who married Jacob Datesman; Eve, who married John Wart, of Bedminster; Susanna, who married John Drumbore; and Anna, who married George Mumbauer. Jacob L. died on a portion of the old homestead in 1857.

John L. Shellenberger, eldest son of Conrad and Eve (Leidy) Shellenberger, was born in Hilltown township in 1792. In 1829 his father conveyed to him 102 acres of the old homestead, purchased by his grandfather in 1772, and at Conrad's death ten acres additional were adjudged to him. He lived on the old homestead all his life, dying April 26, 1882, at the age of ninety years. He was twice married, his first wife being Catharine Snyder, daughter of Jacob and Elizabeth (Yost) Snyder of Hilltown, whose ancestry is given elsewhere in this volume and they were the parents of eight children: Elias, late of Sellersville; Eve; Elizabeth; Catharine; John; Levi, of Hagersville; Jacob S., and Amelia. He married (second) Elizabeth (Harr) Savacool, a widow, and had by her one son, Henry H., who lives on the old homestead in Hilltown.

Jacob S. Shellenberger, son of John L. and Catharine (Snyder) Shellenberger, was the father of Mrs. S. S. Gulick. He was born in Hilltown in 1824, and died there in 1881. He married Catharine Rudy, born June 8, 1830, died June 6, 1898, and had seven children; Amanda, wife of Frank Alderfer; Mary E., wife of Samuel S. Gulick; Emma, wife of Dr. Milton Fretz, of Palmyra, Pennsylvania; Hiram R., of North Dakota, who married Sarah Rolfe; Ella, wife of Simon Snyder, of Swarthmore; Leidy R., a civil engineer in New York, who married Mary Stump, and Jacob, of Montana, who married Bertha Risk.

JACOB M. RUSH. The Rush family has been represented in Bucks county since an early period in its development. Jacob Rush, grandfather of Jacob M. Rush, was a son of Peter Rush, who lived and died in Bucks county. By trade he was a tailor and followed that pursuit for a number of years, but subsequently turned his attention to farming. He was a member of the Tohickon Reformed church. He married Miss Catherine Hofford, and they became the parents of six children: Charles, Hillary, Peter, William, Remandus, and Lucy Ann, the wife of Eleazer McCarty.

William Rush, father of Jacob M. Rush, was born in Bedminster township, Bucks county, Pennsylvania, where he has followed farming all his life. His religious faith is indicated by his membership in the Old Mennonite church. He married Miss Annie Myers, and they became the parents of nine children: Jacob M.; Lizzie, wife of Joseph Schuler; Catherine, the wife of Philip Musselman; Annie, wife of Newton Snyder; Isaac M.; Allen M.; William M.; Amanda, who died at the age of four years; and Mahlon M.

Rev. Jacob M. Rush was born in Bedminster township, Bucks county, Pennsylvania, April 4, 1862, and his education was acquired in the common schools near his home. In the periods of vacation he assisted in the work of the home farm, gaining practical knowledge of the best methods of conducting agricultural interests, so that he was well qualified to successfully carry on business for himself in the same line. He remained on the homestead farm until twenty years of age, and then entered the employ of the Plumsteadville Dairymen's Association in the capacity of foreman. He remained in that service for about four or five years, and in 1887 purchased the farm whereon he now resides. His attention has been chiefly given to agricultural pursuits and his property is now well improved, his fields being under a high state of cultivation. He was ordained on the 24th of October, 1895, a minister of the Old Deep Run Mennonite church by Bishop Andrew Mack, of Bucks county, since which time he has officiated as pastor of the Deep Run church, and was also a supply for the Plumstead church. His life consecrated to his holy calling has been a potent element in the moral development of his community, and by example as well as precept he teaches the living truths of the gospel. Rev. Mr. Rush was married on the fourth of August, 1883, to Miss Mary G. Moyer, a daughter of Joseph H. and Elizabeth (George) Moyer. Their union has been blessed with ten children: Nora Lizzie, born February 20, 1885; Anna M., April 16, 1889; Aquila M., June 30, 1891; William Norman M., November 4, 1892; Joseph M., April 22, 1894; Mary M., August 7, 1896; Jacob Paul, December 15, 1897; Raymond M., June 30, 1900; Isaac M., August 17, 1902; Theodore M., March 28, 1905.

THE PENROSE FAMILY. The Penrose family is an old one and was established in Yorkshire, England, many generations before Robert Penrose, the ancestor of the subject of the sketch left there in 1669. He was the son of Robert and Jane Penrose, and in that year removed to county Wicklow, Ireland, where in the same year he married Anna Russell. In 1673 he was imprisoned for refusing to take an oath. He was probably accompanied or preceded to Ireland by other members of the family, as Richard and John Penrose, of county Wicklow, suffered persecution in the same year for their religious faith.

Robert Penrose, a son of Robert and Anna (Russell) Penrose, born in county Wicklow, married in 1695 Mary Clayton, of Back Lane, Dublin, by whom he had thirteen children. On 3 mo. 2, 1717, Robert Penrose and Mary his wife of Ballykenny, county Wicklow, Ireland, with daughters Ann and Margaret and son Christopher, obtained a certificate from the Two Weeks Meeting at Dublin, which they produced at Philadelphia Monthly Meeting, 8 mo. 25, 1717. Another son Robert soon followed them to Pennsylvania, and the family settled first in Philadelphia and later at Marple, Chester, (now Delaware) county, where Christopher married at Middletown Meeting, 3 mo. 1719, Ann Hunter. Robert Penrose, son of Robert and Mary (Clayton) Penrose, born in Ireland, as before stated, followed his parents to Pennsylvania and located near them in Chester county. On September 13, 1733, he married at Springfield Meeting, Mary Heacock, and in 1734 obtained a certificate to Gwynedd Monthly Meeting. He located in the Great Swamp, later Richland township, becoming a member of Richland Monthly Meeting at its organization in 1742. Their children, all born in Richland, were: Jonathan, born March 1, 1736;· Joseph, born August 10, 1737; John, born January 19, 1740, married Ann Roberts; William, born April 15, 1742, married Mary Roberts; Robert, Jr., born May 6, 1744; Samuel, born August 21, 1748, see forward; Benjamin, born December 30, 1749; Mary, born June 5, 1753; and Jesse, born May 2, 1755. Of the above named children· of Robert and Mary Penrose Jonathan, Joseph, John and William remained in Richland and reared families. Jesse, the youngest son, removed to Warrington, York county, by way of Exeter, 1776.

Samuel Penrose, sixth son of Robert and Mary (Heacock) Penrose, born in Richland, August 21, 1748, remained there until April, 1801, when he removed with his wife and children, William, Eeverard, Benjamin and Margaret, to the Graeme Park farm in Horsham, Montgomery county, which he had just purchased. Graeme Park was established as the country residence of Sir William Keith, the last of the English provincial governors of Pennsylvania. The old historic mansion erected by him in 1721 and still standing, an illustration of which appears in these volumes, is replete with historic associations as narrated in a previous volume. He married at Richland, November 9, 1777, Sarah Roberts, born June, 1758, daughter of Abel and Gainor (Morris) Roberts, and granddaughter of Edward Roberts, born in Merionethshire, Wales. in May, 1687, came to Pennsylvania in 1699, and settled in Byberry, Philadelphia county. He married in 1714 Mary Bolton, daughter of Everard, and in 1816 removed to Richland, where he became an extensive landholder and reared a family of eight children. He was a minister among Friends for many years, and died on his Richland farm, November 25, 1768, in his eighty-second year. His widow died July 22, 1784, in her ninety-seventh year. Abel Roberts, their second child and eldest son, born October 23, 1717, married, April 17, 1744, Gainor Morris, daughter of Morris and Susanna (Heath) Morris. Morris Morris was also a native of Wales. His father, Evan Morris, born in Grikhoth, Caernarvonshire, Wales, in 1654, became

a convert to Friends' faith and suffered persecution therefor. He emigrated to Pennsylvania with his wife and family about 1690, and lived for a time in the present limits of Delaware, removing later to near Abington, now Montgomery county, where he died. His son Morris Morris, born 1674, was a farmer near Abington for a number of years but became one of the pioneers to the Great Swamp, where he died June 2, 1764. His wife Susanna was a daughter of Robert Heath; she died in Richland, June 8, 1755. The children of Samuel and Sarah (Roberts) Penrose, all but the youngest of whom were born at Richland, were as follows: Abel, born August 7, 1778, died in Richland, married (first) Keziah Speakman and (second) Abigail Foulke; Gainor, born March 4, 1780; William, born March 13, 1782; Everard, born October 7, 1784; Mary, born May 11, 1787, died young; Benjamin, born· September 16, 1791; Susanna, born August 21, 1793; Samuel, born August 10, 1796; Margaret, born September 20, 1798, and Morris, born June 15, 1801. Samuel Penrose, the father, on the marriage of his son William sold him the Graeme Park farm and removed to Warminster, where he died February 2, 1833.

William Penrose, second son of Samuel and Sarah, born in Richland, March 14, 1782, removed with his parents to Horsham, in 1801. In 1810 he married Hannah Jarret, daughter of William and Ann, of Horsham, purchased the home farm of his father, and erecting a commodious residence on a natural building site, lived thereon until a few years before his death, when he purchased a farm adjoining and there spent his remaining days. His seven children were:· Ann J., born September 25, 1811, married Abraham Iredell, of Horsham; Samuel, born April 18, 1813, died unmarried at the age of thirty-five years; Jarret, born April 1, 1815; Abel, born May 3, 1817, married Sarah Beisel, of Allentown, in 1856; Hannah, born February 28, 1820, married Isaac W. Hicks, of Newtown. (See Hicks Family); William, born 1822, died in infancy; and Tacy S., born October 14, 1823, married Morris Davis, of Warminster. William Penrose, the father, died November 20, 1863, and his wife in 1850. Both were consistent members of Horsham Friends' Meeting, and their children were reared in that faith.

Jarrett Penrose, second son of William and Hannah (Jarret) Penrose, born April 1, 1815, was reared at the Horsham homestead and lived all his life in that township. On his marriage he purchased the Abraham Iredell farm in Horsham and lived thereon until his death in 1889. His life was one of unfaltering industry and straightforward dealing. He and his wife were members of Horsham Meeting of Friends, and their children were reared in that faith.

In politics Mr. Penrose was a Republican, but while giving his unfaltering support to the principles of that party by his ballot he neither sought nor held public office. He married Tacy Ann Kirk, daughter of John and Tabitha Kirk, who still survives at the age of eighty-three years. Her great-grandfather, a mason by trade, born 1692, and a son of John and Joan (Elliot) Kirk, the pioneer ancestors of the family, erected for Sir William Keith, the last of the provincial governors of Pennsylvania, Graeme Hall, the home of her husband's ancestors in Horsham. The children of Jarrett and Tacy Ann (Kirk) Penrose were: Ellen S., born January 14, 1843, married Edward T. Betts, late of Buffalo, New York, deceased; Elizabeth H., born January 4, 1845, wife of Alfred Moore, of Horsham; William, of Warrington, Bucks county, born July 31, 1847, mentioned hereinafter; Alfred, born May 14, 1849, died in infancy; and Samuel, also mentioned hereinafter.

William Penrose, born in Horsham township, Montgomery county, Pennsylvania, July 31, 1847, spent the days of his childhood and youth upon the home farm and early became familiar with the duties and labors that fall to the lot of the agriculturist. After his marriage he began farming on his own account in Warrington township, Bucks county, upon the tract of land which is yet his home. He has attended market and is regarded as a practical and prosperous agriculturist. He has one of the extensive and valuable farms of Warrington township, comprising three hundred acres, upon which are two sets of farm buildings, houses, barns and outbuildings. The farm is well equipped in every way and its highly cultivated conditions indicates the careful supervision which he has given to it. He is now largely living retired, having given the management of the property over to his son. His present residence is situated on the Doylestown pike and trolley line, and is a commodious two story stone structure, built in modern style of architecture. It is surrounded by a fine stone fence, the gates being formed by heavy pillars, and beautiful forest and evergreen trees adorn the land, while in the rear are many fine fruit trees. He endorses Republican principles and is deeply interested in the success of his party, but has never sought or desired office for himself. He was reared in the Friends' meeting and has never departed from that faith.

William Penrose was married December 14, 1871, to Miss Hannah Paul, who was born in Warrington township, Bucks county, a daughter of Morris and Lydia (Hallowell) Paul. Joseph and Mary Paul, ancestors of Mrs. Penrose, came from Yorkshire, England, about 1682, and settled near the site of the present village of Fox Chase. Joseph Paul purchased the farm now occupied by William Penrose in 1727, and it descended to his son James, who married 2 mo. 25, 1737, Mary Worth, daughter of Judge Worth, of Maryland; she was a lady of education and culture and a warm friend of Lady Ferguson, who then lived at Graeme Park. Joseph Paul, first child of James and Mary (Worth) Paul, born 1739, became the next owner of the old Warrington homestead. He married his cousin, Hannah Paul, whose mother, Sarah Morris, was a daughter of Morris and Susanna Morris, the latter a prominent minister of the Society of Friends for forty years, and although the mother of twelve children she made several religious visits to various parts of the American colonies and three voyages over the sea, attending the Meetings of Friends, and the gracious arm of divine providence was evidently manifested in preserving and supporting her through divers remarkable perils and dangers, which she ever reverently remembered and gratefully acknowledged. Her paternal grandfather, Joshua Paul, was a descendant of an old colonial family connected with the Friends' meeting. Morris Paul was reared in Warrington township, where he settled on a farm after attaining man's estate, remaining one of the reliable and enterprising agriculturists of his community up to the time of his death, his life being in harmony with his profession as a member of the Society of Friends. His only child became the wife of Mr. Penrose. She was a lady of culture and intelligence, who proved a devoted wife and loving mother and was also a consistent Christian. She died of typhoid fever in 1900, and their daughter Lydia H. died on the 29th of April of the same year when twenty years of age, also from an attack of typhoid. The other children are J. Howard, born May 10, 1873; Morris P., born November 8, 1875; and William, born October 16, 1877. Howard married Miss Edith Chapman, and is in the office of the Reading Coal & Iron Company. Morris is connected with the extensive lumber, coal, and milling business in Pedricktown, New Jersey. William Penrose, Jr., is operating the old homestead farm. On the 16th of October, 1902, William Penrose married (second) Miss Anna Hallowell, who was born in Abingdon township, Montgomery county, September 28, 1865, her parents being Joseph W. and Hannah (Lloyd) Hallowell, the former born in Abingdon township and the latter in Moreland township, Montgomery county, where both were representatives of distinguished early families of this state. Her father, Joseph W., was a son of John R. and Ann (Jarrett) Hallowell, the former descended from John Hallowell and a native of Nottinghamshire, England. Emigrating to America he became one of the first settlers of Pennsylvania. John R. was one of the directors of the old York pike road. Joseph Hallowell was a brother-in-law of Edwin Satterthwaite. who was a grandson of Betsey Ross, who made the first American flag and who made the ruffles for General Washington's shirt fronts. The Satterthwaite family were among the oldest and most respected members of the Abingdon meeting. The children of John R. Hallowell were: William, Lydia, Mrs. Martha Satterthwaite, Joseph and Penrose. Joseph Hallowell was reared to farm pursuits and always carried on the work of an agriculturist. However, he extended his efforts to various other lines and was connected with many enterprises, his good management winning him desirable success. He was recognized as one of the substantial men of his county. After his retirement from the farm he resided at Jenkintown, becoming one of the incorporators of the Jenkintown Bank and a director thereof for many years. He was a man of plain deportment, but reliable and trustworthy at all times, and his freedom from self laudation and ostentation commanded the good will of all who recognized and appreciated true worth. He died at Jenkintown, April 3, 1904, leaving a wife and four children. His widow still occupies the residence at Jenkintown and she, too, is a member of the Friends' meeting. They were parents of four children: Edwin S., a prominent farmer of Abingdon, Pennsylvania; Emma L., who is living with her mother; Fanny, born August 12, 1856, died March 25, 1900; and Anna, the wife of William Penrose. Hannah (Lloyd) Hallowell, the mother of these children, was descended through Benjamin Lloyd and Sarah Child, whose marriage took place 6 mo., 1775, and is also descended from George and Sarah Shoemaker, of Warrington, who were married in 1662, and George and Sarah (Wall) Shoemaker, who were married at Abington Meeting, 12 mo. 14, 1694. Benjamin H. Shoemaker commemorated the two hundredth anniversary of the marriage of the latter named by a dinner, Sixth day evening, twelfth month fourteenth, 1894, at seven o'clock. George Shoemaker, Jr., and Sarah Wall, his wife, were the great-great-great-grandparents of Benjamin H. Shoemaker. Mr. and Mrs. Penrose have one son, Joseph Hallowell, born July 31, 1903. They are prominent socially in the community where they reside, and the circle of their friends is almost co-extensive with the circle of their acquaintance.

Samuel Jarrett Penrose, born at Horsham, May 5, 1852, was reared in that township and educated at the Friends' school, at Loller Academy, Hatboro, the Excelsior Normal Institute at Carver-

ville, and Swarthmore College. At the close of his school days he accepted a clerical position with the firm of Ellis P. Moore & Co., lumber merchants in Philadelphia, where he remained for eighteen months. He then returned to his father's farm in Horsham, and was engaged in agricultural pursuits until his marriage in 1881 with Mary C. Farren, daughter of John and Elizabeth (Fretz) Farren, of Doylestown township, whose ancestry is given under the title of "The Fretz Family" in this work. He continued as a farmer in Horsham until 1884, when he removed to his mother-in-law's farm in Doylestown township, where he has since resided, he and his wife having inherited it at the death of Mrs. Farren, and devotes his time to the care of his three farms comprising 278 acres. Mr. Penrose is now serving his second term as director of the poor of Bucks county, and is also a director of the Doylestown Trust Company, vice-president and director of the Philadelphia and Eastern Railway Company, and director of Fellowship Norse Company. Their children are: Cyril, Ralph F., and Norman, all of whom reside with their father. The mother of these children is deceased.

HON. HARRY J. SHOEMAKER, one of the prominent members of the Bucks county bar, and an officer of several of the important corporations of the county, was born in Horsham township, Montgomery county, Pennsylvania, December 25, 1855, and is a son of James and Phebe (Shoemaker) Shoemaker, of that township. He comes of a distinguished ancestry that have been potent in the affairs of their respective communities since the founding of Penn's colony on the Delaware.

His paternal ancestor, Peter Shoemaker, was born in Kreigsheim, a rural village on the Upper Rhine, "two hours ride from the City of Worms," in the year 1622. He was one of the earliest converts to the principles of George Fox, the founder of the Society of Friends, and suffered persecution for his religious faith as early as 1665 when he had goods to the value of two guilders taken from him in payment of a fine for attending a meeting of Friends at Worms. He was also imprisoned and fined at subsequent periods for his religious faith. He was one of the Friends seen by Penn on his visit to Kreigsheim early in 1683, and was induced to join a company of Palatines in founding a colony in Penn's new province of Pennsylvania. He was a carpenter by trade, and before leaving Kreighsheim entered into an agreement with Dirck Sidman, of Crefeld, on August 16, 1685, to proceed to Germantown, where the original thirteen families from Crefeld had already formed a settlement, and receive from Herman Op den Graef 200 acres of land upon which he was to erect a dwelling and pay therefore two rix dollars. This old agreement and the deed for the land is recorded in German at Philadelphia and has been seen by the writer. He embarked in the "Frances & Dorothy," with his son Peter, daughters, Mary, Frances, and Gertrude, and the widow of his cousin, Sarah Shoemaker and her children, and arrived at Germantown, October 12, 1685. He at once became one of the active men of the youthful colony, and is frequently mentioned in the old annals of Germantown. He was an active member of the Society of Friends, and one of the signers of the certificate to the Meeting at London in 1695 for Samuel Jennings, who carried the protest of Pennsylvania Friends against the schism of George Keith. He died in Germantown in 1707, aged eighty-five years. His daughter Frances married John Jacob Van Bebber, and another daughter married Rynier Herman von Barkelow and removed to Bohemia Manor, Maryland. A grandson Martin Kolb accompanied him from Germany and has left numerous descendants.

Peter Shoemaker, Jr., born at Kreigsheim, accompanied his father and sisters to Germantown in 1685 and became one of the prominent men of the colony, filling the office of burgess of Germantown in 1696, 1704 and 1707, and many other positions of trust. He was one of the committee appointed December 30, 1701, to organize a school at Germantown, erect a school house and arrange for a teacher. Through his efforts Francis Daniel Pastorius was induced to take charge of the school and it became one of the famous institutions of the infant province. Peter, Jr., was like his father a carpenter or "Turner," and had a part in the erection of most of the early buildings in Germantown. He was a prominent member of the Society of Friends, and was frequently the representative of his meeting in quarterly and yearly meetings. He married, at Germantown Meeting, 2 mo. 6, 1697, Margaret Op den Graef, daughter of Herman Op den Graef, one of three brothers who were among the first thirteen families to settle Germantown in October, 1683. He was a native of Crefeld on the Lower Rhine, and a son of Isaac and grandson of Herman Op den Graef, who was born at Alderkerk, November 26, 1585, and died at Crefeld, December 27, 1642. He was a delegate to the Mennonite council at Dordrecht in 1632 that formulated the creed of that sect. Herman Op den Graef and his brothers were the authors of the famous protest against human slavery presented

to Germantown Meeting in 1688 and by them forwarded to the Quarterly and Yearly Meetings of the Society. It was the first protest of its kind ever formulated in America. Peter Shoemaker died at Germantown, 4 mo. 1, 1741, and his widow Margaret on 7 mo. 14, 1748. They were the parents of ten children, as follows: 1. Sarah, born 5 mo. 22, 1698, married Daniel Potts; 2. Mary, born 7 mo. 15, 1701, married Thomas Phipps; 3. Margaret, born 6 mo. 8, 1704, married Benjamin Masin; 4. Peter, born 6 mo. 8, 1706; 5. Daniel, born 11 mo. 14, 1709; 6. Isaac, born 1 mo. 15, 1711, see forward; 7. Elizabeth, born 11 mo. 6, 1713, married Joseph Davis; 8. Agnes, born 3 mo. 9, 1716, married William Hallowell; 9. John, born 6 mo. 30, 1718; 10. Samuel, born 6 mo. 13, 1720, died young.

Isaac Shoemaker, son of Peter and Margaret, born at Germantown, March 15, 1711, on arriving at manhood settled in Upper Dublin township, Philadelphia (now Montgomery) county, where he purchased a tract of land and followed the life of a farmer. He was a member of Abington Meeting and took a certificate from there to Philadelphia Monthly Meeting, 5 mo. 27, 1741, to marry Hannah Roberts, daughter of John Roberts, of Philadelphia. They were members of Horsham Meeting at its organization. Isaac and Hannah (Roberts) Shoemaker were the parents of thirteen children, as follows: Margaret, born 10 mo. 3, 1742, died unmarried in 1788; Peter, born 4 mo. 12, 1744, married Hannah Norman; Elizabeth, born 4 mo. 23, 1748, married John Letchworth; Martha, born 7 mo. 14, 1750, married Jonathan Shoemaker; Daniel, born 12 mo. 9, 1752, married Phebe Walton, daughter of Thomas, of Byberry; Isaac, born 10 mo. 29, 1754; James, born 10 mo. 13, 1757, see forward; Rachel, born 3 mo. 26, 1759; David, born 6 mo. 15, 1761; Hannah and Mary, born 3 mo. 9, 1764; Thomas, born 3 mo. 22, 1766, and Rebecca, born 4 mo. 29, 1769.

James Shoemaker, seventh child of Isaac and Hannah, born in Upper Dublin, 10 mo. 13, 1757, was a farmer and lived all his life in Upper Dublin. He married in Horsham Meeting house, 6 mo. 1, 1781, Phebe Walton, daughter of William and Phebe (Atkinson) Walton, the original certificate of the marriage engraved on parchment, as well as that of the marriage of William Walton and Phebe Atkinson, which was solemnized at the same place, 9 mo. 26, 1741, are in the possession of the subject of this sketch. William Walton, father of Phebe Shoemaker, was a resident of Moreland, and a son of Jeremiah and Elizabeth (Walmsley) Walton, of Byberry. William Walton, father of Jeremiah, was one of the four Walton brothers who landed at New Castle in 1675 and subsequently located in Byberry. He was married at Byberry, 4 mo. 29, 1689, to Sarah Howell, and was the first minister at Byberry after the Keithian trouble and continued to preach there for many years. Phebe (Atkinson) Walton was a daughter of William and Phebe (Taylor) Atkinson, of Upper Dublin, and granddaughter of John and Susannah (Hinde) Atkinson, of Lancashire, England, an account of whom is given elsewhere in this volume.

William and Phebe (Atkinson) Walton were the parents of ten children, several of whom died young. Phebe, who married James Shoemaker, was the second of the name and was born 11 mo. 16, 1759. The children of James and Phebe (Walton) Shoemaker were as follows: William, born 3 mo. 16, 1782; Joseph, died an infant; Isaac, born 4 mo. 6, 1785; John, born 9 mo. 8, 1786; Hannah, born 2 mo. 24, 1789; Jesse, born 4 mo. 17, 1791, see forward; Jonathan, born 9 mo. 3, 1793, married in 1822 Margaret Rutter; Rebecca, died an infant; Rachel, born 2 mo. 28, 1798; and Phebe, born 9 mo. 2, 1802.

Jesse Shoemaker, sixth child of James and Phebe, was born and reared in Upper Dublin, and spent the active years of his life in that township, removing late in life to Horsham where he died in 1882, aged over ninety years. He married at Horsham Meeting, 3 mo. 8, 1821, Edith Longstreth, daughter of Isaac and Jane Longstreth, of Bucks county, a descendant of Bartholomew Longstreth, one of the earliest settlers in Warminster, who was born in Longstrothdale, Yorkshire, in 1679, came to Pennsylvania in 1698, and married Ann Dawson in 1727. The children of Jesse and Edith (Longstreth) Shoemaker were: James, the, father of the subject of this sketch, born 8 mo. 20, 1822; Charlotte L., who died in infancy; and John L., born 10 mo. 7, 1832. The latter became an eminent lawyer in Philadelphia and filled many important positions. He was a member of select and common council for a number of years, and took an active part in the management of the Centennial Exposition at Philadelphia in 1876.

James Shoemaker, eldest son of Jesse and Edith, was born in Upper Dublin, but on arriving at manhood settled on a farm in Horsham township, where he has since resided, following the life of a farmer during his active years. He married Phoebe Shoemaker, daughter of Jonathan and Margaret (Rutter) Shoemaker, and granddaughter of James and Mary Rutter. She died in April, 1896. James and Phoebe were the parents of eight children: Bella, residing with her father in Horsham; Adeline B., wife of Charles E. Chandler, of Germantown; Jesse, who died in infancy; Harry J., the subject of this sketch; Augustus Brock, an active business man of Tullytown,

Bucks county, who married Ida, daughter of Elwood and Anna Burton, and has one son Lester; Charlotte L., wife of Russel Twining, of Horsham; Emily P., wife of Edward B. Webster, of Philadelphia; and Mary G., wife of Isaac Warner, of Horsham.

Hon. Harry J. Shoemaker was born and reared in Horsham township and acquired his education at the public schools and at Doylestown Seminary. At the age of nineteen years he began teaching school in Bedminster township, Bucks county, and the following year was appointed principal of the Tullytown (Bucks county) school, which he taught for three years. In 1880 he embarked in the mercantile business at Tullytown, conducting a general merchandise store there until 1884. In politics he is an ardent Republican, and has always taken an active interest in the councils of his party and in everything that pertains to the best interest of the community in which he lived. He was postmaster of Tullytown for four years, and also filled the office of school director and other local offices in that district. In the fall of 1884 he was elected to the state legislature, being the only Republican elected from Bucks county, and served one term with marked ability, being appointed on several important committees. At the termination of his term he declined the renomination and became a candidate for congress in the seventh congressional district, but was defeated in the convention by two votes. He was a delegate to the National Rpublican Convention of 1884, and also to that of 1888, which nominated Benjamin Harrison to the presidency. During Harrison's administration he was confidential clerk to the second Comptroller of the United States treasury. In the meantime he entered himslf as a student at law in the office of the late Hon. B. F. Gilkeson, of Bristol, and was admitted to the bar of his native county, and also to the Bucks county bar on January 3, 1890. At the close of his term of four years as confidential clerk he located in Doylestown and began the practice of law, in which he has been successful in the building up of a lucrative practice. Later he was admitted to practice in the supreme courts of Pennsylvania and of the District of Columbia. In 1893 he was a judge of awards at the World's Fair at Chicago, and in that capacity served as secretary of the committee on food products. In 1896 he was again a candidate for the nomination for congress and received a majority of the vote from his home county, but was defeated in the joint convention. He was a charter member of the Doylestown Trust Company, and has served continuously as a director of that institution since it organization. He was one of the orig inal promoters of a trolley road from Doylestown to Easton, and was one of the most active and energetic in pushing the work to a completion, being one of the original directors of the Philadelphia and Easton Railway Company, who built the road, and is secretary and treasurer of the company. He is also solicitor and director of a number of other important corporations. He has served for a number of years as school director of Doylestown township, and fills the position of secretary of the board. He married, November 28, 1878, Ella B. Wright, daughter of John H. and Elizabeth (Harding) Wright, of Penn Manor, and they have been the parents of two daughters: Elsie C., who died November 30, 1898, at the age of eighteen years; and Edith E., who died in infancy.

EZRA PATTERSON CARRELL was born in Warminster township, Bucks county, Pennsylvania, November 25, 1857, on the Carrell farm (now owned by H. Warner Hallowell), on which he resided twenty-three years. His father was born and died on the same property, having lived thereon seventy-three years.

Ezra P. Carrell was educated until his thirteenth year in the public schools of the township. After a two years' course at the Excelsior Institute of Hugh Morrow, in Hatboro, Pennsylvania, his education was finished by a four years' course at the private school of Rev. George Hand of the same place. He is by occupation a farmer, as has been his ancestors for at least four generations before him. He was located first in Warminster, next at Willow Grove, and for the last fourteen years on his present farm near Jamison, Pennsylvania, which he purchased at that time. Although a Republican, he has always been very independent in politics and always ready to vote for a better man on the opposite side. He has never held a political office, never wanted nor would accept one, yet has always been ready and willing to serve his fellow citizens in any other capacity, and through their choice has served in many positions of trust, as manager and director in various associations and companies. A busy, progressive farmer, he has not allowed his occupations to dwarf his other attainments nor his educational advancement, but has kept himself abreast in all matters which tend to the betterment and enrichment of the lives of those about him. Interested in genealogy he has in later years devoted much time to research into the history of his family, and is the secretary and genealogist of the Carrell Reunion Association. In religion a Presbyterian, as has been his family for many gener-

ations, he has always interested himself in church work, taking an active part in it. At present he is a Sunday school teacher, Sunday school superintendent, and ruling elder in the Neshaminy Presbyterian church in Warwick. On December 22, 1881, he was married to Mary McCarter, daughter of James and Rebecca A. McCarter, of Ivyland, Pennsylvania. The McCarter family is an old English family which has lived in Cheltenham township, Montgomery county, Pennsylvania, for many generations. Rebecca Aikley (Shoemaker) McCarter, the mother of Mrs. Carrell, is of the well known Shoemaker family of Shoemakertown, (now Ogontz) also in Cheltenham township. Three children have blessed their union: Esther, died in infancy; Margaret L., and Edith.

Mr. Carrell is the son of Ezra Patterson Carrell and Margaret Long (Beans) Carrell. Mr. Carrell, Sr., who died a few years ago, was one of the substantial men of Warminster township, always taking an active interest in the affairs of the vicinity. A man of education and refinement, hospitable, generous and honored by his neighbors for his probity and integrity, he held for many years the office of ruling elder in the Neshaminy church in Warminster, and later in Neshaminy in Warwick. Always interested in church work, he served long and well in the capacities of teacher and superintendent in the Sunday school, and for many years as chorister in his church. He fully justified in his life the words of his pastor, who prefaced his remarks at his funeral by these words: "Before me lies the remains of an honest man. The world says that no man can be honest and successful, but the life of Mr. Carrel fully refutes this." Margaret Long Carrell, his wife, is the daughter of John C. Beans and Elizabeth Yerkes. The Beans family have been residents of Warminster for many years. Mrs. Carrell's grandfather, Thomas Beans, was the keeper of the old hotel at Warminster, then a post station on the mail line between Philadelphia and New York, and was a breeder of running horses, having a half mile track on the large tract of land which he owned. The holdings of the contiguous estates of the Beans and Yerkes families was the largest in this section, several hundred acres of which is retained in the families. The Beans family trace their genealogy back to Donald (Bane) of Scotland, immortalized by Shakespeare. Mrs. Carrell was educated by a private teacher, and later finished her education by a course at a young ladies' seminary in Wilmington, Delaware. She is still living at the home place in Warminster. Mr. and Mrs. Carrell had five children: Joseph, who is a farmer in Warminster township; John Beans, one of the leading physicians of Hatboro; Stacy Beans, in the wholesale and retail grocery business in Philadelphia, Pennsylvania; Ezra P., the subject of this sketch; and Emily, who died in infancy.

James Carrell, the pioneer ancestor of the family, settled in Bucks county about 1700 and possibly came from Rhode Island in 1683 with Rev. Thomas Dungan, whose daughter Sarah he married. Tradition, however, relates that he was a weaver, and had a mill or loom, in Philadelphia, where he wove linen and linsey-woolsey; some products of his loom remaining in the family until recently. He purchased one hundred acres of land in Southampton in 1704 and lived thereon until his death about 1730. In 1711 he purchased of his brothers-in-law, Thomas and Clement Dungan, a tract of land in Warminster which is still the property of his descendants, descending from father to son down to the present owner, Isaac Carrell. The children of Thomas and Sarah (Dungan) Carrell were six in number: James, the eldest son; Benjamin, who died in 1733; Elizabeth, who married Samuel Gilbert, of Warminster; Sarah, who married Silas McCarty; and Lydia, who married Robert Tompkins, of Warminster, later of Warrington, Bucks county; and another daughter of whom we have no record. In 1732 the other heirs of James Carrell conveyed the homestead in Southampton to the eldest son James and in 1734 he also purchased the Northampton homestead on which he settled and lived until his death in 1750, conveying the Southampton homestead on his purchase of the Northampton farm. The family were of Scotch-Irish Presbyterian stock, and are supposed to have emigrated from Scotland or Ireland in the seventeenth century. Tradition relates that James Carrell, Sr., was imprisoned in Londonderry during that memorable siege of one hundred and five days, and soon after came to America. The family is probably of the branch of the house of Carroll who were rulers in the northern counties of Ireland, which Dr. William Carrell in his history of the family traces back to the beginning of the third century.

James Carrell, Jr., married Diana Van Kirk, of Holland descent, daughter of Bernard and Rachel (Vandegrift) Van Kirk, and granddaughter of Jan Janse Ver Kirk or Van Kirk, who emigrated to Long Island in 1663 from the little town of Bueer Maetsen, in Gelderland, Holland, and settled at New Utrecht, where he died in 1688. His wife was Maykje Gysberts and they were the parents of the following children: Roelof Janse, born 1654; Aert Janse, born 1655; Geertje, married Jan Dirckse Von Vliet; Barentje, married Nicholas Vandegrift; Cornelis Janse; Jan Janse, Jr., and Bernard or Barnet, the father of

Diana, above mentioned, who married Rachel Vandegrift. The maternal ancestor of Diana (Van Kirk) Carrell is given in full in this work under the head of "The Vandegrift Family." James and Diana Carrell were the parents of eleven children, viz.: Rebecca, born May 25, 1725, married Robert Weir, of Warrington, and their descendants later migrated to Kentucky. Sarah, born September 25, 1726, married Robert Patterson, of Tinicum, whose descendants settled in Virginia, from whence they migrated to Ohio and Missouri. Bernard, married Lucretia McKnure and settled on one of his father's farms in Warminster purchased of the heirs of Rev. William Tennent, and including the site of the famous log college of which Tennent was the founder, and which remained in the tenure of the descendants of Bernard until quite recently. James, born March 26, 1730, married Sarah ———— and settled in Tinicum township, Bucks county, in 1765, on land purchased of his brother Solomon and died there leaving four children who have numerous descendants scattered over the whole union. He was a private in the associated company, of Tinicum, Nicholas Patterson captain, during the revolution. Jacob and Rachel (twins), born April 27, 1735; Rachel became the second wife of Robert Stewart, of Warwick, Bucks county, and after her husband's death settled with her son Robert in Tinicum, from whence the family migrated to New Jersey. Phoebe, born August 20, 1837, married Andrew Scout, of Warminster. Solomon, born May 25, 1740, died 1777, married Mary Van Kirk, and in 1761 purchased a farm of three hundred and five acres in Plumstead, one hundred and forty-three acres of which he conveyed to his brother James in 1765 and the balance of which he sold in 1774 and then settled in Kensengton, Philadelphia; he went with Washington to New York, dying of the fever on Staten Island, whence his body was never removed; his widow married Charles Ryan, and died in Wallingford, Chester county, in 1821. Descendants of Solomon now reside in Chester, Pennsylvania, and in Delaware. Elizabeth, born May 16, 1742. Diana married Elias Dungan, who was a soldier in the Revolutionary war, and has left numerous descendants; her daughter Rachel married Jesse Johnson.

Jacob Carrell, son of James and Diana (Van Kirk) Carrell, born April 27, 1735, was the great-grandfather of Ezra P. Carrell. He was born and reared on the old family homestead known as Carrellton and lived there all his life. He and his brother served in the Northampton company in the revolutionary war. He was a successful farmer and possessed of considerable means. He devoted himself to home and church affairs, taking little part in public mat-, ters outside his own immediate locality. He married Elizabeth Jamison, daughter of Daniel Jamison, of Nockamixon, Bucks county, of Scotch-Irish ancestry, and they reared a large family of children who by intermarriage with families in that vicinity brought the Carrells into relation with many of the leading families of Bucks county. His children were: Joseph; Benjamin, married Mercy Comfort; John; Mary, married Lot Bennett; Sarah, married Mahlon Banes; Jesse, married Mary Bennett; Isaac; Elizabeth, married John Cornell.

Joseph Carrell, the grandfather of Ezra P. Carrell, was born June 1, 1792, at Carrellton, the old family homestead near Richboro, Bucks county. When a young man he learned the trade of a carpenter under his uncle, Jesse Johnson, and followed it some years. About 1835 he purchased the Carrell farm in Warminster where he lived the remainder of his life, dying April 25, 1884. When quite a young man he served as corporal in the army during the war of 1812-14, and many were the anecdotes he used to tell of camp life at Camp Dupont, near Marcus Hook, where his regiment was then stationed, Philadelphia at that time only extending as far north as Vine street and south to Pine street. Those who knew him remember him as a portly, white-haired old gentleman, tall and erect, with a military bearing acquired in youth and never forgotten. He was one of the last survivors of the small coterie of veterans of the war of 1812-14 which included General John Davis, William Bothwell, and one or two others whose relations were very intimate. He was for many years an elder of Neshaminy Presbyterian church, with whose interests he was actively identified during his whole life. He was twice married, to Mary and Anna Gill, sisters, of an old English family who emigrated from London to Philadelphia and later settled in Northampton, Bucks county, where their descendants are now quite numerous. By the first marriage he had three children: Hugh Jamison, Emily, and Ezra Patterson; and by the second marriage two daughters: Sidney, who became the wife of Thomas B. Montanye; and Elizabeth, who married Robert Thompson Engart.

F. HARVEY GRIM, M. D., who for the past twenty-five years has been a prominent physician at Revere, Bucks county, Pennsylvania, was born at Revere, September 4, 1859, and is a son of the late Dr. George W. and Elizabeth (Koons) Grim, the former of whom was one of the prominent practicing physicians of Upper Bucks and for thirty-three years was located at Revere, being

one of the prominent men of that locality. His great-grandfather was a native of Rhenish Bavaria, and belonged to a family that were prominent in the affairs of Europe several centuries ago, tracing their descent from Frankish residents of that part of ancient Gaul that became later Normandy, where the family became allied with those of the Norse conquerors, and later migrated to the Rhine Provinces about the tenth century.

The American pioneer of the family located in Montgomery county, where George Grim, the great-grandfather of F. Harvey Grim, was born. He located in Upper Salford township and married Elizabeth Favinger, also of German origin, and they became the parents of three children, one son Adam and two daughters.

Adam Grim, son of George and Elizabeth (Favinger) Grim, married Christina Desmond, of English or Scotch-Irish extraction, and lived in Montgomery county. He was killed on the railroad in 1846.

Dr. George W. Grim, son of Adam and Christina (Desmond) Grim, was born in Montgomery county, March 13, 1832, and was educated at Washington Hall, Trappe, Pennsylvania, receiving a good academic education. His father dying when he was of the age of fourteen years, he learned the trade of a stove moulder and worked at the same for some years. Having badly burned his foot in the discharge of his duties, he decided to prepare himself for the medical profession, and resuming his studies at Washington Hall accepted a position as instructor in that institution, in the meantime entering himself as a student in the office of Dr. Gross, at Harleysville. He later entered Jefferson Medical College, from which he graduated in the class of 1859, and immediately located at Revere, Nockamixon township, Bucks county, where he soon built up a large practice. He purchased a fine farm near Revere, which he conducted in connection with his professional duties. He married in 1857 Elizabeth P. Koons, who survives him, and they were the parents of nine children, six sons and three daughters. Three of the sons are prominent physicians, two are members of the Bucks county bar, and one is an instructor at the Keystone State Normal school at Kutztown. The family are members of the Reformed church. Dr. George Grim died at Revere, March 6, 1892.

Dr. F. Harvey Grim is the eldest son of Dr. George W. and Elizabeth (Koons) Grim. He was reared in Nockamixon township and acquired his education at the local school, the West Chester State Normal school and the Keystone State Normal school at Kutztown. He studied medicine with his father and entered Jefferson Medical College, from which he graduated in the class of 1881. Returning to Revere he began the practice of his chosen profession in connection with his father, and after the latter's death continued the practice at Revere where he has a large and lucrative practice, and maintains the reputation of his father as a physician of superior merit. Dr. Grim has taken an active interest in the affairs of the community in which he lives, and has been identified with various local enterprises. He has served for twelve years as a member of the local school board in which he filled the position of secretary. He was a member of the medical board of pension examiners for four years, and is a member of the County and State Medical Associations. He was instrumental in the establishment of Revere postoffice, and was its first postmaster in 1885. Previous to that time it was known as "Rufe's" and earlier as "Kintner's." He is a member of Riegelsville Lodge, No. 567, F. and A. M.; a past chief of the K. G. E., and a member of the Jr. O. U. A. M. and I. O. R. M. of Ferndale and Kintnersville. Dr. Grim married Ella M. Rufe, daughter of Reden and Mary Ann (Hillpot) Rufe, of Nockamixon, whose paternal ancestors were among the earliest and most prominent residents of Nockamixon. Mrs. Grim died October 4, 1899, leaving seven children: Edna F., Mamie B., Lizzie E., George W., Clair F., Esther M., and Horace R. The family are members of the Reformed church.

Jacob Ruff, as the name was originally spelled, emigrated from Germany in the ship, "Snow Betsy," arriving in Philadelphia, August 27, 1739, at the age of twenty-one years, and soon after located in Nockamixon, Bucks county, where he became the owner of 180 acres of land. He was corporal of captain Jacob Shupe's company, Bucks county militia, in 1775 and 1777, and his sons, John, Jacob and Henry, were privates in the same company. This company was one of those stationed at Bristol, Bucks county, in 1777, under the command of Colonel Hugh Tomb, and probably saw active service in the New Jersey campaign. Jacob Rufe died on Christmas day, 1790, aged seventy-two years. His wife Elizabeth survived him. They were the parents of six sons, John, Jacob, Henry, Christian, George and Frederick, and one daughter, Sophia, who married George Fulmer.

George Rufe, son of Jacob and Elizabeth Rufe, was the great-grandfather of Mrs. Grim. In 1795 he became the owner of 181 acres of land near Kintnersville, and in 1798 of 176 acres near Revere. He was a blacksmith by trade and followed that vocation in connection with farming until his death in Decem-

ber, 1822. His wife Sarah survived him. They were the parents of four sons, Jacob, John, Frederick and Samuel, and four daughters, Elizabeth, Sarah, Susanna and Catharine.

John Rufe, son of George and Sarah Rufe, was born in Nockamixon, in 1797. He learned the trade of a blacksmith with his father, and followed that vocation for several years in connection with farming. He also owned and conducted the well known "Rufe's Tavern," one of the old hostelries of that section. He died in 1872 at the age of seventy-five years. His wife was Catharine Hager, daughter of Valentine Hager, and they were the parents of six children: Isaac, Reden, Amanda, wife of Hugh Kintner, who was recorder of deeds of Bucks county in 1854; Josiah, William and John H.

Reden Rufe, the father of Mrs. Ella M. Grim, was born in Nockamixon, June 20, 1824. He learned the carpenter trade at an early age and followed it for twenty-five years. He then purchased the homestead of ninety acres, where he still reside. He was twice married; first to Sarah Burgstresser, who died at the age of thirty-one years; and second to Mary Ann Hillpot, of an old Tinicum family, who bore him four children: Ella, who married Dr. F. H. Grim; Josiah; Seymour, who married Cora Kohl; and Annie, wife of Oscar Stone.

EDWARD LONGSTRETH. The late Edward Longstreth, for many years superintendent of the Baldwin Locomotive Works, and a retired member of the firm of Burnham, Williams and Company, who now operate that plant, though a resident of Philadelphia for the last forty years of his life, was a native of Bucks county. Throughout a long and busy life he kept in touch with the county of his nativity and took an active interest in all that pertained to her welfare and advancement. Mr. Longstreth was born in Warminster township, Bucks county, June 22, 1839, and was a son of Daniel and Hannah T. Longstreth, and a descendant of one of the oldest and most prominent families of Bucks county. His pioneer ancestor, Bartholomew Longstreth, settled in Bucks county in the time of William Penn and became one of the prominent men of his time. An account of the descendants of Bartholomew Longstreth is given in General Davis' narrative history of Warminster contained in these volumes. The Longstreths came of good old English Quaker stock and represented the solid, conservative and substantial elements of the county in the colonial days as well as down to the present time.

Daniel Longstreth, the father of Edward Longstreth, was born in War-

Edward Longstreth

minster, November 25, 1800, and died there March 30, 1846. He married (first) Elizabeth Lancaster, January 4, 1827. She was born July 5, 1803, and died September 19, 1829. They were the parents of two children: John L., born November 10, 1827, who has been for many years actively associated with the business life of Philadelphia and now resides at 556 North Eighteenth street; and Elizabeth L., who died April 23, 1848. Daniel Longstreth married (second) October 25, 1832, Hannah Townsend and they were the parents of seven children; Joseph T., born August 7, 1833, died July 12, 1834. Sarah, born September 4, 1834, died in Baltimore, March 14, 1881, married Charles R. Hollingsworth. Moses Robinson died April 2, 1838. Edward C., born June 22, 1839, died February 24, 1905. Samuel T., born August 2, 1837. Anna, born April 2, 1841, married Robert Tilney. David S., born October 26, 1844, died July 9, 1845.

Edward Longstreth, the fifth child, was reared on his father's farm in Warminster and received a good English education. On October 4, 1857, at the age of eighteen years, he went to Philadelphia. A month later he began his apprenticeship with M. W. Baldwin and Company at the Locomotive Works. Trained in the habits of industry, punctuality and strict integrity, he was in many ways a remarkable apprentice. During his five years of apprenticeship he was never known to be late in reporting for duty, and this trait characterized his after life. His energy, aptitude and punctuality were so marked that when less than three years of a five years' apprenticeship had elapsed, he was made assistant foreman of one of the departments and was advanced to the position of foreman of the second floor of the works. While filling these positions he applied himself to a study of an improvement in the gauge system with success, and his perfected system has long been in use and is one of the characteristic features of the Baldwin Locomotive Works. Mr. Baldwin also patented locomotive trucks and draft appliances of his improved pattern, which are still used in the works. On August 1, 1867, he became foreman of the erecting shop, and on January 1, 1868, superintendent of the entire works. He became a member of the firm January 1, 1870, and continued the control of the mechanical and construction department, superintending the work of three thousand men. By reason of impaired health he retired from the active business of the firm January 1, 1886. Mr. Longstreth was at one time vice president of the Franklin Institute, and a director of the Williamson Industrial School. In 1884 he was one of the most energetic and active members of the Committee of One Hundred, which de-

feated the corrupt organization in Philadelphia and aided Samuel S. King to the mayoralty. Until his death, Mr. Longstreth was a member of the Merchant's Fund, a charitable organization; director of the Delaware Insurance Company: a member of the Union League and the Engineers' Club. He was a life-long member of the Society of Friends, holding membership in the meeting at Fourth and Green streets, Philadelphia. He was a member and for several years one of the trustees and directors of the Bucks County Historical Society, and took an active part in the work of preserving the records and archives of the history of the county, in which his ancestors had resided for many generations. It was through his liberality that the tablet was placed on the old York road in Warminster to mark the place where John Fitch conceived the idea of steamboat navigation, and he was also instrumental in having many other historic places duly marked. The first tract of land owned by the Society upon which to erect a building for its archives and collections was a gift from Mr. Longstreth. He was a man much respected and loved by his Bucks county contemporaries, among whom he had a large acquaintanceship. He died at his home, 1410 Spruce street, February 24, 1905, lamented and honored by all who knew him. Mr. Longstreth married, June 7, 1865, Anna C. Wise, and they were the parents of two sons: Charles and Howard, and one daughter, Mrs. W. L. Supplee, all residing in Philadelphia. Mrs. Anna W. Longstreth, the mother, died September 18, 1899. His son Charles also served a five years' apprenticeship at the Baldwin Locomotive Works after his father had left the firm, and is now the head of the United States Metallic Packing Company, which conducts a very large business in that and other lines.

THE SIEGLER FAMILY. Mathew Siegler, for nearly thirty years a resident of Doylestown, Bucks county, Pennsylvania, was born in the province of Baden, Germany, January 6, 1812, and married there, in 1837, Antoinette Eckerly, who was born in Baden, June 16, 1812. Mathew learned the trade of a stone mason, which he followed in Baden until 1849, when he emigrated to Pennsylvania and located in Hilltown, Bucks county, at the present site of the borough of Silverdale. Having established a home in his adopted country, he sent for his wife and three children, who arrived in Bucks county in 1851. After following his trade in Hilltown for ten years in 1859 Mr. Siegler removed with his family to Doylestown, where he resided until his death, July 30, 1888, being killed at a railroad crossing west of the town, one year after the celebration of the fiftieth anniversary of his married life, at which all his children and grandchildren were present. His widow Antoinette survived him over ten years, dying November 1, 1898. They were the parents of five children, all of whom are still living: Augustus, of Philadelphia; Pauline, who married (first) Francis Roach, and is now the wife of Joseph Merkle, of Doylestown; Charles Louis, of Doylestown; Peter, of Doylestown; and Annie, wife of Bernard McGinty, the veteran job printer of Doylestown. Augustus, the eldest son, married Mary Taylor, and they are the parents of six children, all of whom reside in Philadelphia, except one. They are: Clara, wife of A. Fries Shive, of Doylestown; Nettie, wife of Harry Goldsmith; Julia, wife of John Friend; Mary, wife of Dr. Borger; Henry and Agnes, who are single. Bernard and Annie (Siegler) McGinty are the parents of five children: Antoinette, Katharine, Helen, Allen and Frank. The family are all members of St. Mary's Roman Catholic church.

CHARLES LOUIS SIEGLER, Sr., D. D. S., of Doylestown, second son of Mathew and Antoinette (Eckerly) Siegler, whose arrival in America from the fatherland is mentioned in the preceding sketch, was born in the province of Baden, Germany, July 17, 1845, and accompanied his mother to America at the age of five years. He was reared to the age of sixteen years in Hilltown, Bucks county, and attended the public schools there. Removing with his parents to Doylestown in 1860 he studied dentistry with the late Dr. Andrew J. Yerkes, and at the latter's death in 1868 continued his practice until 1872. On April 1 of that year he started to practice dentistry on his own account at his present location on State street, where he has since practiced and has built up a large and lucrative business. Dr. Siegler represents a fine type of German-American citizenship, and is one of the highly respected citizens of the town. He is deeply interested in local affairs and institutions, but takes little part in partisan politics. He is a member of St. Mary's Roman Catholic church, of St. Joseph's Beneficial Society, and an active member of the German Aid Society of Doylestown, of which he has been a trustee for many years. He is also a member of the Mannaerchor Society.

Dr. Siegler married, February 5, 1873, Catharine Kearns, of Hilltown, Bucks county, who was born in Norriton township, Montgomery county, Pennsylvania, May 15, 1852, and is a daughter of John and Catharine (Kennedy) Kearns, both natives of Ireland, he of Drogheda, county Lough, and she of Carrick-on-Suir, county Tipperary. John Kearns came to America in 1839, and was married to Katharine Kennedy at Norristown in 1844. She had accompanied her parents, John and Katharine Kennedy, from Ireland some years previously. Dr. Siegler and Katharine Kearns were married at St. Agnes' Roman Catholic Church at Sellersville by Reverend Father Hugh McLoughlin. Five children were born to this marriage, in Doylestown: Katharine and John, who died in infancy; and Estelle, C. Louis, and Frank, all of whom reside with their parents.

C. LOUIS SIEGLER, Jr., eldest surviving son of Charles Louis and Katharine (Kearns) Siegler, was born in Doylestown, Bucks county, Pennsylvania, October 2, 1878. His earliest education was acquired at St. Mary's parochial school, Doylestown. He later attended Doylestown seminary, and graduated from the Roman Catholic high school in Philadelphia in 1896. In the same year he entered the dental department of the University of Pennsylvania, and graduated with honors in the class of 1899. He located on Main street in his native town, where he has since practiced his chosen profession with success. He is a member of the State Dental Association, and stands high in his profession. He is a member of St. Joseph's Society and the German Aid Society of Doylestown.

PETER SIEGLER, youngest son of Mathew and Antoinette (Eckerley) Siegler, was born in Hilltown township, Bucks county, Pennsylvania, June 16, 1852, and came with his parents to Doylestown in his seventh year. He was reared in Doylestown and acquired his education at the Doylestown public schools. In 1871 he entered the employ of Louis Spellier, at that time an eminent jeweler and watchmaker in Doylestown, with whom he remained for three years. Having mastered the mysteries of the craft he went to Lambertville, New Jersey, and entered the employ of Rudolf Talcott. Mr. Talcott having sold his jewelry establishment at the end of three months, Mr. Siegler went to Trenton, New Jersey, where he was employed at his trade for a short time, and then returned to Doylestown and took charge of the jewelry and watchmaking department in the store of Henry Y. Moyer, on State street, where he remained for five years, the latter part of the time having an interest in the business. In the winter of 1883-4 he and his brother-in-law, Bernard McGinty, purchased the site of their present establishment and erected the present store and printing offices, Mr Siegler taking possession of his present jewelry store on June 6, 1884. By professional skill and close attention to business he has built up a nice business, and is one of the solid conservative business men of the county seat. He is a member of the German Aid Society, of St. Joseph's Society, Sciota Tribe, I. O. R. M., and the Mannaerchor Society. He married, October 31, 1884, Rosa E. Schmutz, daughter of John and Katharine Schmutz, who was born in Doylestown township, both her parents being natives of Germany, her

father of Baden, and her mother of Bavaria. Mr. and Mrs. Siegler are the parents of eight children, the eldest two, William and Katie, died in childhood, and those who survive are Marie, Catharine, Gertrude, Anna and Emma, twins, and Rose. The family are members of the Roman Catholic church.

WILLIAM S. ERDMAN, M. D., of Buckingham, Bucks county, Pennsylvania, was born in Richland township, Bucks county, Pennsylvania, October 5, 1869, and is a son of Owen and Mary Ann (Singmaster) Erdman, both of German descent, whose ancestors were among the early German settlers in Bucks and Montgomery counties. John Yost Erdman, the paternal ancestor of Dr. Erdman, was born at Pfungstadt, in Hesse-Darmstadt, in the year 1682, and emigrated to America with his son Andrew, arriving at Philadelphia on board the ship at "St. Andrew's Galley," John Stedman, master, September 24, 1737. Like nearly all the early German emigrants he probably made his home for a short time among his compatriots on the Schuylkill or its tributaries. In 1750, however, we find him settled in Upper Saucon township, near Centre valley, in what was then Bucks county, but became a part of Northampton county in 1752 and Lehigh county in 1812. He was the owner of 178 acres of land that descended to his son Andrew and has remained in the family ever since. John Yost Erdman died in 1760, at the age of seventy-eight years.

Andrew Erdman, son of John Yost Erdman, married Anna Maria Frederick and had nine children, viz.: John, Andrew, Jacob, Catharine, wife of Jacob Barnhart; Yost, Sybilla, wife of Henry Bittz; Abraham, George, and Anna Margaret, wife of George Sober. Of the above children John, Jacob and George remained in Lehigh county; Andrew settled in Montgomery county where he was living in 1833 at the age of seventy-eight; Abraham removed to Westmoreland county, and Yost settled in Milford township, Bucks county. The sons-in-law settled in Northampton and Bucks counties.

John Erdman, great-grandfather of Dr. Erdman, was born on the old Lehigh county homestead about the year 1760, and was probably the second son of Andrew and Anna Maria (Frederick) Erdman. He married Sarah Bitz and to them was born a family of six children, viz.: Jacob, Daniel, John, Henry, Kate and Levina.

Daniel Erdman, grandfather of Dr. Erdman, was born on the Upper Saucon homestead in Lehigh county, February 12, 1797, and spent his whole life there, living to a good old age. He married Anna M. Miller and had four children,

viz.: Sara Anna, Daniel, Owen and Anna Marie.

Owen Erdman, father of Dr. Erdman, was born on the old homestead in Lehigh county, November 11, 1828. He was reared to the life of a farmer and followed that vocation in his early manhood. His education was acquired in the district schools of his native township; he conducted his father's hotel prior to his moving to Steinsburg, ...is county, where he purchased a farm and entered the cattle business, eventually drifting into the commission business; moving to the city of Philadelphia, where he conducted a commission house. Returning to Bucks county he settled in Richland Centre, where he began making leather flynets and harness; he followed that until the civil war broke out when he enlisted in the army. He served three years and three months as a member of Company E, Third regiment, Pennsylvania Reserves and participated in several engagements, the most notable of which was the battle of Bull Run, where he received a wound which made it necessary for him to be sent to the hospital. He is still living in Richland township, near Quakertown, being engaged in the harness business. Mary Ann Singmaster, the mother of Dr. Erdman, was a native of Richland township, and comes of a well known Bucks county family of German ancestry that have been residents of Bucks county for several generations. Owen and Mary Ann (Singmaster) Erdman were the parents of four children: Dr. Milton S. Erdman, deceased, who was one of the most successful physicians in the county; Dr. Wilson S. Erdman, a prominent and successful physician of Richlandtown, Bucks county; Sarah O. residing at home; and Dr. William S.

Dr. William S. Erdman was born and reared in Richland township, and acquired his education at the public schools of that township and at the Quakertown high school. After his graduation from the latter school he spent two years in his father's harness shop, and in 1889 took up the study of pharmacy and served an apprenticeship of three years, and later began the study of medicine under his brother, Dr. Milton S. Erdman, to which he applied himself for four years. In 1893 he entered the Medico Chirurgical College of Philadelphia, from which he graduated with honors in the spring of 1896. After his graduation he spent the summer with Dr. E. S. Reed, of Atlantic City, and in the autumn of the same year located at Buckingham, Bucks county, where he has since practiced his profession with marked success, building up a large and lucrative practice. Among his friends and patrons are people who have graced the highest walks of life. It must be said for Dr. Erdman that with a brave and indomitable spirit combined with industry he has succeeded in life. He is the owner of a handsome colonal residence, which has been occupied continuously by physicians since 1832. Dr. Erdman is a lover of "antiques" and among his collection of "old china" and "antique furniture" are many pieces dear to him. He is a member of the Bucks County Medical Society, the Lehigh Valley Medical Association, the Pennsylvania State Medical Society and the American Medical Association. Dr. Erdman married on June 3, 1903, Clara Wendell Lovett, daughter of Edmund and Clara (Weaver) Lovett, of Penns Manor, Falls township, Bucks county, who is a descendant of one of the oldest English Quaker families in Bucks county, members of which have been prominent in the business, social and political life of Bucks county for nine generations.

GEORGE MELVIN GRIM, M. D., of Ottsville, Bucks county, Pennsylvania, is a son of Dr. George W. and Elizabeth P. (Koons) Grim, an account of whom is given in the sketch of his brother Hon. Webster Grim, and was born in Nockamixon township, Bucks county, Pennsylvania, March 8, 1863.

After attending the public schools of his native township, he attended the high school at Spring City, Chester county, and then entered the academic department of Muhlenburg College, Allentown, and graduated in 1880. He also took a course in the Keystone Normal school at Kutztown, Pennsylvania, graduating in 1884. After teaching three terms in Nockamixon township he entered Jefferson Medical College, Philadelphia, and graduated in the class of 1887, having previously read medicine with his father at Revere. He began the practice of his profession at Revere in 1887, and a year later located at Ottsville, where he has since practiced his chosen profession with success. He is a member of the American Medical, Lehigh Valley and the Bucks County Medical Associations, and stands high in his profession. He has always been deeply interested in the cause of education, has served for the past twelve years as a member of the local school board, and is one of the active and prominent members of the School Directors Association of Bucks County, before which he has delivered a number of addresses on school management, hygiene and kindred subjects. He is a member of the Knights of the Golden Eagle and the Shield of Honor Lodges. Religiously he is a member of the Reformed church, and politically a Democrat. He married, October 18, 1888, Sarah E. Fetter, daughter of B.

Frank and Mary Jane Fetter, of Southampton, Bucks county, and they are the parents of four children, Harold F., Helen K., Alma, and Sara Margaret.

WILLIAM B. LEIGH. Thomas Leigh, the ancestor of that branch of the Leigh family resident in Bucks county and vicinity, Pennsylvania, was born in Lancastershire, England, in the year 1775. He was a son of William Leigh, who it appears was in some way connected with Sir Walter Raleigh as the maiden name of that gentleman's wife was Ann Leigh. In early life Thomas Leigh married Alice ———— and he became the father of eleven children, all of whom were born in England. Thomas Leigh came to America in 1816, settling in Trenton, New Jersey, and shortly afterward his eldest daughter came over to keep house for him, his wife and remaining children coming in the year 1818. After a short residence in Trenton, the family removed to the vicinity of Fallsington in the old house on the farm now owned by Daniel Kelly. After residing in various places they settled on the farm of John Wildman in Lower Makefield, where his wife died in 1853. After this sad bereavement Mr. Leigh resided with his daughter Ellen about a mile west of Fallsington until his death, which occurred in 1856. Their remains were interred in the Friends' Yard at Fallsington. Their children were as follows:

1. Nany, born 5 mo. 7, 1795, died 1848; she was the wife of John Lonsdale and they were the parents of four children: Thomas, Ellen, Alice, and James, all deceased. 2. Catharine, born 1 mo. 3, 1797, died 1856; she was the wife of Joseph Radcliffe, no issue. 3. Alice, born 1 mo. 11, 1799, died young. 4. Ellen, born in 1801, died young. 5. Alice (second), born 7 mo. 30, 1802, was the wife of Samuel Morris, and they reared a large family of children. 6. William, born 11 mo. 4, 1806, died young. 7. Thomas, born 12 mo. 4, 1806, died in 1881; he married Esther Margerun, and they were the parents of several children. 8. Thomas, born 4 mo. 2, 1809, married Martha Van Horn, who bore him four children: Cynthia, Wallace, Augustus, and Edward. In 1843 he moved to western Illinois and died there in 1894. 9. Ellen (second), born 7 mo. 15, 1811, died in 1899; in 1845 she became the wife of William Brelsford, no issue. His death occurred in 1876. 10. William (second), born 2 mo. 1, 1814, died 9 mo. 15, 1875; in 1840 he married Louisa M. Schaffer, who is living at the present time (1905); their children were: John S., born 9 mo. 18, 1841, married Anna Clark; Thomas, born 4 mo. 14, 1843, married Elizabeth Foster; Eliza H., born 5 mo.

G. M. Grim M.D.

8, 1846, married John D. De Coursey;, William B., born 9 mo. 2, 1848, mentioned hereinafter; Edward L., born 2 mo. 7, 1851, married Margaret Leaman; Henry C., born 6 mo. 28, 1853, married Susan Smith; Anna Alice, born 4 mo. 6, 1859, married Elwood Lovett; and James L., born 7 mo. 12, 1862, died August 22, 1899. 11. Joseph, born 7 mo. 1, 1816, married Elizabeth Wharton, who bore him several children. He moved to western Illinois in the early forties.

William B. Leigh, third son of William and Louisa M. (Schaffer) Leigh, was born 9 mo. 2, 1848. By his marriage to Fannie Lovett the following named children were born: William Lovett, 5 mo. 6, 1873; Arthur H., 8 mo. 19, 1877; and Laurance R., 5 mo. 7, 1882. Samuel Lovett, the ancestor of Mrs. William B. Leigh, and the first of the family to arrive in this country, was one of the "Proprietors of West Jersey" and came in the ship "Kent," arriving in the Delaware in 1677. He settled in Burlington, New Jersey. They were people of good estate in England and came to this country to enjoy religious liberty, which was guaranteed to them before they sailed. The birth of his son Jonathan (1) was registered in the Friends' meeting. The christening of his son Jonathan (2) is recorded as having taken place in 1719 in St. Mary's church, Burlington, New Jersey. Jonathan (3) was christened in 1746 in St. Mary church, Burlington, New Jersey. He married (first) Mary Bates, of Penn's Manor, and moved to Falsington, Bucks county, Pennsylvania. He married (second) Acsah Moon. The family born in Bucks county consisted of twelve children. The children of his first marriage were: 1. William, who married Mary Bowman, mentioned hereinafter; 2. Jonathan, who married Rebecca Palmer; 3. John, who married Mary Woodruff; 4. Aaron, who went to sea with Billy Moon; and 5. Mary, who married David Munyon. The children by his second marriage were: 1. Mahlon, who married Phoebe Clark, and after her death Charlotte Mershon; 2. Samuel, who married Margaret Fitzgerald; 3. Sarah, who married Daniel Bowman; 4. Joseph, who married Susan Rue; 5. Elizabeth, who married Richard C. Winship; 6. Ann, who married Longstreet Poland; 7. Daniel, who married Buehla Fitzgerald.

William Lovett, son of Samuel and Mary (Bates) Lovett, and his wife Mary Bowman were the parents of eight children: 1. Henry, who married Sarah Margerum; 2. Mary, who married (first) Thomas Cheston, (second) Joseph Hutchinson, (third) Elijah Scattergood; 3. Rebecca, who married Joel Cheston; 4. Phoebe, who married Elijah Scattergood; 5. Jonathan, who married Mary Pullen; 6. Elizabeth, who married

Charles Smith; 7. Ann, who married George Brown; 8. William, who married Mary Ann Green.

Henry Lovett, eldest son of William and Mary (Bowman) Lovett, and his wife Sarah Margerum were the parents of twelve children: 1. Mary, who married Amos Shippy; 2. Adeline, who married Jonathan Brown; 3. Rebecca R., who married W. S. Winship; 4. William H., who married Harriet Dickel; 5. Phoebe, who died in infancy; 6. Richard R., who married (first) Ann Shippy, (second) Elmira Hibbs; 7. Charles E., who married Madge Barnes; 8. Aaron, who married Mary ———; 9. Biven, who died in infancy; 10. Elijah, who married Jennie ———; 11. George, who died without issue; 12. Frederick P., who married Mary E. Dean.

Jonathan Lovett, second son of William and Mary (Bowman) Lovett, and his wife Mary Pullen were the parents of eight children: 1. Anthony, who died in infancy; 2. Charles, who died without issue; 3. Sarah, who married a Mr. Appleton; 4. Rebecca, who married a Mr. Hazzard; 5. Lucy B., who died in infancy; 6. Amanda, died in infancy; 7. Mary Elizabeth, died in infancy; 8. Martha, died in infancy.

William Lovett, youngest son of William and Mary (Bowman) Lovett, and his wife Mary Ann Green were the parents of eight children: 1. George G., who died of wounds received at the Battle of the Wilderness; 2. Anna Mary, who married Joseph Wells; 3. Fanny B., who married William B. Leigh; 4. William, unmarried; 5. Andress, died in infancy; 6. Henry L., who married Eliza Myers; 7. Elwood, who married Alice Leigh; 8. Miranda, who died in infancy.

CLAYTON D. FRETZ, M. D., a son of Abraham and Sarah (Detweiler) Fretz, was born in Bedminster, Bucks county, November 16, 1844. His paternal ancestor, who with his brother Christian established the family in America, emigrated from near Manheim, in the Grand Duchy of Baden, Germany, in 1720. He spent his boyhood on the "old homestead" in Bedminster, attending the public schools, and later taught in the county four years. He chose medicine as a profession, and graduated from the medical department of the University of Pennsylvania, March 13, 1868. He commenced practice at Sellersville immediately thereafter, and in 1872 also opened a drug store. On November 16, 1871, he was married to Kate B. Everhart, a daughter of Charles W. Everhart, who was a graduate of Jefferson Medical College of Philadelphia. Four children were born to them, of whom a son and a daughter died in infancy. Alfred E. Fretz, M. D., a graduate of the medical department of the University of Pennsylvania, of the class of 1896, was born August 30, 1874. He served the appointment as resident physician at Mercy Hospital, Pittsburg, Pennsylvania, and returned to his native town to begin the practice of his profession. S. Edward Fretz, M. D., a graduate of the same institution in the class of 1900, was born August 30, 1878. He served as resident physician in Cooper Hospital, Camden, New Jersey, and two years as assistant physician to the Relief Association of the Pennsylvania Railroad Company. He is now in practice at Denver, Pennsylvania.

On September 1, 1898, Dr. Clayton D. Fretz's wife died, aged fifty-two years. He was married to his second wife, Annie M. Fackenthall, a daughter of Aaron Meredith, late of Doylestown, and the widow of Alfred Fackenthall, Esq., of the same town, on August 14, 1900.

The study of botany and the collection of plants and flowers has afforded Dr. Fretz much pleasure during his long career as a country practitioner. He has added many new and rare plants to the known flora of Bucks county, and about forty to the state flora. His herbarium contains a complete set of nearly all the plants in the county, and a large majority of the plants east of the Mississippi, including about 10.000 specimens, and 4,000 species and varieties. He has just completed a revision of Dr. I. S. Moyer's catalogue of the plants of Bucks county.

Politically Dr. Fretz is a Republican, and was a delegate to the state convention of 1895. He served as a school director for a period of fifteen years; is a member of St. Paul's congregation of the Reformed church, and has been president of the Sellersville National Bank since 1893. He is a member of the Bucks County Historical Association, the Bucks County Branch of the Pennsylvania Forestry Association, the Philadelphia Botanical Club, the General Alumni Association of the University of Pennsylvania, MacCalla Lodge No. 596, F. and A. M.; Doylestown Chapter, R. A. M.; Pennsylvania Commandery, Knights Templar, of Philadelphia; and Sellersville Lodge No. 658, I. O. O. F.

HEINLEINS AND MORGANS of Durham township, Bucks county. All the Heinleins in America are descendants of Matheis Heinlein, who with his wife, son George, and daughters Sarah and Eva, took passage in the ship "Bannister." Captain John Doyle, from Amsterdam, and qualified at Philadelphia, October 31, 1754. He settled in Durham township on a tract of land on the southern slope of Bucher Hill. A farm now belonging to B. F. Fackenthal was part of this tract, the other portion reaching over the hill into Northampton county. This entire tract became the property of his son George. Eva, the oldest daughter, became the wife of George Bernhard Horn. Sarah, the other daughter, became the second wife of James Morgan, ironmaster of Durham Furnace, and father of Daniel Morgan, the famous general of the Revolution.

Daniel Morgan's biographer, in a fit of romance, tells the story that the General, when a boy of fifteen, left his home solely by reason of his dislike to his stepmother. At the same time he sets Daniel's departure in the year 1752, which is the correct period, and just two years before Sarah Heinlein arrived in America. She was married to James Morgan in 1765, and, tradition says, "made an excellent wife for her husband, helping to rear the children from his first wife." These were Mordica, Abel, James, Samuel and Olivia. Abel became a noted physician in Philadelphia. Mordica, James and Samuel were lumbermen, and were purchasers of large tracts of land in the upper Delaware and Susquehanna river country. Mordica purchased four hundred acres in Monroe county in 1785, on which he erected extensive saw-mills, and also four hundred acres in Luzerne county as early as 1776. James and Samuel also purchased four hundred acres each in this same year. Mordica and James finally settled at a place called Morgan's Hill, in Wayne county, Pennsylvania, where their stepmother, Sarah Heinlein, passed her widowhood. General Daniel Morgan made a visit to his brother on one of his trips from the north, the place being about twenty miles from the Delaware river, along which the old mine road traversed, the road generally used by the troops in passing between the Delaware and Hudson rivers. Probably Daniel's cause for leaving home was more through the spirit of adventure than by any other reason. This same characteristic we find in his favorite cousin, Daniel Boone (Boone's mother was a sister of James Morgan). The Boone family lived about this time near the Lehigh river, in Allen township, Northampton county. Squire George Boone and James Morgan were close friends. Dr. Abel Morgan and Captain George Heinlein never forgot their friendship of their boyhood days, and were close friends during the entire period of the Revolutionary War. Dr. Morgan was surgeon of the Eleventh Regiment. Pennsylvania Line.

George Heinlein was a very popular man and became captain of the Durham township militia, served all through the war, and afterwards secured additional land and pursued farming. He always took an active part in public affairs, and at the time of his death, which occurred October 2, 1805, at the age of sixty-three, he was the possessor of the entire east end of Bucher Hill. He was buried with great honors in the famliy burying ground on the plantation. This quarter acre lot is along the road at the extreme end of Mr. Fackenthal's farm, and through neglect is fast becoming obliterated. In it are buried all the first generations of Heinleins, Longs, Buchers and others. His family consisted of eleven children: Margaret, wife of Nicholas Brotzman; Eleanora, wife of John Bucher; Sarah, wife of Abraham Bucher; Lawrence, James, George, William, Reading, John, Ann and Catharine. All the Heinleins living in the regions roundabout are descendants of James, who married Ann Bay, only daughter of Hugh Bay and his wife Elizabeth Bell, both of Philadelphia. After Hugh Bay's death Dr. Abel Morgan married the widow, and removed to what is now Morgan's Hill, in Williams township, about one mile below Easton. They had only one daughter, Hannah, who died while yet in her teens. James Heinlein is credited with changing the spelling of the name from Heinlein to Hineline, yet the baptismal records of his family show the former way of spelling. His children were George Bay Heinlein, Hugh Bay Heinlein, Abel Morgan Heinlein, Edward Bay Heinlein, Morgan Bay Heinlein, Jacob Bay Heinlein, John Bay Heinlein, Henry Bay Heinlein, Hannah Eliza, wife of William Raub. They all were born prior to 1820. The children of George Bay Heinlein are: Hugh Abraham, born 1823; Joseph, 1825; John William, 1829; Samuel Morgan, 1832; Susan, 1834; Daniel Edward, 1836; Ann Shultz, 1839. The children of Joseph Heinlein are: Mary, married Kemmerer; Emma, married Edelman; Charles, Frank and Clara, married Kleinhans, all of whom have children, and some grandchildren. Hugh, Abel, Jacob and John, with their entire families, about the year 1860 removed to Ohio, where their descendants are quite numerous. The descendants of Morgan and Edward are to be found in Warren county, New Jersey, and Bucks and Northampton counties, Pennsylvania. Henry died without issue.

WILLIAM JACOB HELLER, of Easton, Pennsylvania, manufacturer, has long been numbered among the patriotic citizens of the land, and his efforts were largely instrumental in instituting the movement that resulted in placing the flag upon the school houses of the United States. He comes of a family noted for loyalty and patriotic service in the colonial struggles and in the war for independence, and traces his descent from eleven patriots who served Pennsylvania in the revolution.

He is a direct descendant of Christopher Heller, who was born in Petershiem, near Bingen, along the Rhine, in the Province of Pfaltz, Germany, in 1688, and emigrated to America in 1738, arriving in Philadelphia with his six sons on the fifth of September of that year. He established his home in what is now Milford township, in the southern part of Lehigh county. He passed the last few years of his life with his son, Daniel, who lived along the creek a short mile below Hellertown, and where he died in the year 1778. Of his six sons, Joseph, in early life known as Joe Dieter, was the oldest, having been born in 1719, and died unmarried in 1800. He was buried at Plainfield church. The second son of Christopher Heller was Johan Simon Heller, born in 1721. On attaining his majority he purchased the 200 acre farm in Lower Saucon township, along the creek, where he built what is now Wagner's mill in 1746. He was one of the founders of the Reformed church in that township, and in the year 1763 removed to what is now known as the Woodley house, in the town of Wind Gap. Here he assisted in the organization of the Reformed church in Plainfield township, and later married a second time and removed to Hamilton township, and there organized Hamilton church. His patriotic spirit was manifested by active military service in the French and Indian war. He had sixteen children, of whom Jacob, John, Abraham, and Simon served in the revolutionary army. His death occurred in 1783, and he was buried at Plainfield church. Johan Michael Heller, the third son of Christopher Heller, was born in 1724, died in 1803, and is buried at the ancient burying ground of the Reformed church, now known as the Lime Kiln schoolhouse. Daniel, the fourth son, was born in 1726, and died in 1803. Daniel's children were Mathias, John, Jeremiah and Michael (the potter). He was buried in the ancient burial ground at what is now Lime Kiln schoolhouse. Ludwig, the fifth son, was born in 1728, and in early life removed to Bucks county, later to Hamilton township, Monroe county, where he died in 1807, leaving several children, of whom Andrew and John remained in Bucks county. He is buried in Hamilton township, at the church which he helped to organize. The sixth son, George Christopher, was born in 1731. He married in early life and settled on a farm adjoining that of his brother Michael. A few years later he purchased an adjoining property, on which was erected a grist mill and a hemp mill. He was the father of two boys, Joseph and Michael, who on attaining their majority were given the property, Joseph taking the grist mill, and Michael the oil mill. The father removed to Upper Mount Bethel where he died in 1805, leaving besides the two boys four children by a second marriage, Elizabeth, Magdalena, Solomon and Daniel. He was buried at Stone church in Mount Bethel township. After a few years Joseph sold his mill to Michael, and moved to a mill site along the Monocacy, in Hanover township. Milchael was now the possessor of his father's entire tract of land in Lower Saucon township, and which is now embodied in the entire east side of the main street in Hellertown. Michael was the father of a large family, all of whom died in infancy, with the exception of Paul and Tobias, who after their father's failure removed to what is now Lanark, Lehigh county, and built the hotel known as Heller's Tavern.

Johan Michael Heller, above mentioned, was a direct ancestor of William J. Heller, the subject of this sketch, and was known as Michael, the elder (Alt vater Mike). Early in life (1751) he purchased a farm on Saucon creek, in what is now the entire west side of the main street in Hellertown. In the same year he built a stone house which is still standing. He became the founder of Hellertown, and was an extensive land owner, prospering in all his business affairs, but lost very heavily through the depreciation of currency during the revolution, which, together with his contributions to the revolutionary cause, and his gift of several hundred-acre farms to each of his children, left him comparatively a poor man at the time of his death. His team was the first to leave Saucon Valley loaded with provisions for the starving army at Valley Forge. However, he gave not only assistance of this character, but rendered active service in behalf of the cause of liberty as a lieutenant in the army. His children were: David, born in 1751, served a period in the revolutionary war, and was a farmer in Lower Saucon township; Margaret, who married Jacob Kreeling; Heob (Job), born 1765, and was a farmer in Upper Saucon; Simon, born in 1758, was a farmer, and settled near Plainfield church; Michael, who was known as "Creek Mike," was born in 1757, and always remained at the homestead, where he died in the year 1828.

David Heller, son of Johan Michael Heller, was the great-great-grandfather of William J. Heller. He married Elizabeth, daughter of John Ladenmacher, and their children were: Catharine, born in 1773, died in 1776; Susanna, born in 1774, died in 1776; Elizabeth, born in 1775, married Jacob Roth, who became the owner of the homestead immediately east of Hellertown; Michael, born in 1777, died in 1816, leaving several children; his oldest son Michael lived and

died in Cunningham valley; David, born in 1778, learned the trade of a tanner, and afterwards removed to Lehighton, Carbon county; Job, born in 1780, died in 1822, unmarried; Catharine, born in 1780, died in 1786; Yost, born in 1783; Susanna, born in 1784; Maria, born in 1786; Joseph, born in 1788, and at the age of thirty years removed to Philadelphia, where he remained until his death; Rosanna, born in 1789, died in 1811.

Yost Heller, the great-grandfather, was reared upon the home farm, and in his early youth was full of life, fun and merriment. Many a laugh did he cause in the neighborhood by his merry pranks, but he also commanded the respect of friends and neighbors, and as the years advanced his attention was given to work that proved of benefit to the community along material and moral lines. He was the most popular man in Lower Saucon township, was the first deacon in Appel's church, and reared his family according to its teachings, while its principles formed the rule of his own conduct. He was married to Elizabeth Shaffer, of a prominent family of Lehigh county, and their children were: Jacob, Elizabeth, who became Mrs. Bachman, and later Mrs. Flexer, and Mary, who became Mrs. Weiss, and afterward Mrs. Rice.

Jacob Heller, the grandfather, was born in 1804, and died in Easton, in 1881. Brought up in the faith of the church according to its teachings, he also reared his family in the same way. He was the first elder in Appel's church. He married Sarah Bellis, of Lower Saucon, a descendant of one of the original owners of West Jersey, Lawrence Bellis, and their children were: Elizabeth, born in 1825; William, born in 1827; Josiah B., born in 1829; Jacob, Sarah, John, Susan and Emma.

Josiah B. Heller, the father of William J. Heller, was born in 1829, and pursued his education in a school at Hellertown, and under Dr. Vandervee at Easton. Subsequently he engaged in teaching in Easton and in surrounding townships, and he also was numbered among the music instructors of the Lehigh Valley on his day. After devoting a number of years to educational work he engaged in farming for a decade, and then returned to Easton, where he conducted a transfer freight line for many years. He was one of the early members of the Independent Order of Odd Fellows at that place, and took a helpful interest in promoting the lodge and its growth. His political allegiance was given to the Democracy, whch he continued to support until his death, December 5, 1898. He married Susan Heinlein, of Forks township, a descendant of George Heinlein, captain of the Durham township militia during the revolution and a great-granddaughter of Elizabeth

Morgan, of Morgan's Hills. Their chil-, dren were: George B., born in 1853; William J., in 1857; Arthur P., born in 1864, died in 1903; and Lizzie May, born in 1869, marred Chester Seip.

William J. Heller is indebted to various institutions of Easton, Pennsylvania, for the educational privileges he enjoyed in his youth. After putting aside his text books he followed various pursuits and became quite widely known because of his artistic talent and ability. In 1886, however, he established his present business, the manufacture of flags, opening the first exclusive flag factory in the United States. His business has constantly grown in volume and importance, and to-day he manufactures nearly one-half of the flags used in this country. While witnessing the decoration of a public school building for a celebration in the year, 1886, the idea occurred to him that the nation's emblem should be seen over school buildings of the country in order to foster a spirit of patriotism among the children of the land. He began discussing the idea with the prominent educators of America, and, in fact, was the founder of the movement which has embodied his ideas, and deserves great credit for instituting the patriotic movement which swept over the country in 1892. He is popular and well known among workers in patriotic circles, and was one of the first active members of the Patriotic League. He has had many honors conferred on him by the Woman's Relief Corps, the National Congress of Women, and other national patriotic organizations. He is a charter member of the George Washington Memorial Association, organized to promote the establishment of the University of the United States. He is an honorary member of the various leading women's clubs in many parts of the country. He has lectured in many of the principal cities of America upon patriotic occasions. His lecture on "The Evolution of Our National Ensign" is universally known. History has always been a most interesting study to him, and he believes in promoting every line of thought that will foster a love of country and its people. He has made a study of local Indian history during his leisure hours, and is now engaged in compiling data for a history of the Forks of the Delaware. He is a life member of the Historical Society of Pennsylvania, also the Pennsylvania German Society, a member of the Bucks County Historical Societies in this and adjoining states. He takes an active part in public affairs, and is a member of the board of trade and of the Municipal League of the city of Easton.

Mr. Heller married, May 5, 1877, Miss Tillie A. Lesher, a daughter of George Lesher, and a lineal descendant of George Loesch, of Tulpehocken, Berks county, Pennsylvania, who gave so generously of his means to assist the struggling Moravians when they first landed in this country. His memory is yet perpetuated by the record of his good deeds, preserved in the Moravian archives. Mr. and Mrs. Heller became the parents of three children, two sons and one daughter. The two sons, Ray and Harry, died in early childhood. The daughter, Bessie Evelyn Heller, is a lineal descendant of sixteen patriots who gave active service in the revolutionary war, and a great-great-great-granddaughter of Elizabeth Morgan, of Morgan's Hill, through her paternal grandmother, Susan (Heinlein) Heller, a daughter of George Bay Heinlein, who was the son of James Heinlein and his wife Ann Bay, a daughter of Mrs. Morgan by her first husband Hugh Bay.

Mrs. Morgan's maiden name was Lizzie Bell, or "pretty Lizzie Bell," as she was known by nearly every one in Philadelphia, where she was born and raised. She was the daughter of Jacob and Ann Bell, residing on Front street, Philadelphia, prior to the revolutionary war. Her parents were orthodox Quakers, and consequently frowned upon a certain young grocer, Hugh Bay, son of Rev. Andrew Bay, a chaplain in the provincial army, who was getting very intimate with Elizabeth, and who was not of their faith. They used mild methods to discourage intimacy, and when, a few years later, Hugh made his appearance dressed in the uniform of a noted artillery company in the revolutionary service, he was refused admittance to the Bell domicile, and Elizabeth was compelled to make closer application to her studies. All went seemingly well until the British army was reported coming toward Philadelphia, when its citizens prepared to repel the enemy by gathering all ammunition, collecting old lead and converting it into bullets, etc. Elizabeth, whether through born intuitiveness or from close application to study, at that opportune time developed character that was one remarkable feature in after life. She removed the leaden weights from her father's clock and converted them into bullets for her soldier lover, Hugh Bay. This not only caused a flurry in Quakerdom, but so enraged her father that he forthwith transported her to Europe to finish her studies. After the lapse of four years her father, thinking that she had outlived her infatuation, brought her home. Elizabeth, however, true to her first love, was married to Hugh Bay in the Swede's church, Philadelphia, August 16, 1781. This act so shocked the orthodox Quaker congregation that they immediately called a special meeting at which a resolution was passed expelling Elizabeth from the congregation for marrying a worldly man, and a certificate to that effect was given her. What effect all this had upon her parents is unknown. Her father died a few years later, and left the greater part of his wealth to Elizabeth and her mother. Hugh made a good husband and maintained a fine house on the fashionable street. After a marriage of three years he unfortunately died, leaving only one child, Anna. Elizabeth remained a widow six years, when, on September 2, 1790, she became the wife of Dr. Abel Morgan, a prominent physician of Philadelphia, and formerly a surgeon in the revolutionary army, and a brother of General Daniel Morgan. Two months later her mother died. With the exception of the birth of another daughter, nothing eventful transpired until 1793 when the great epidemic broke out in Philadelphia, when Dr. Morgan took precautionary measures and removed his family from Philadelphia to the Lehigh Hills, leaving his home in charge of the colored servants. Dr. Morgan selected for his retreat a hotel on the top of the hill overlooking the "Forks of the Delaware." This delightful locality was a favorite of Dr. Morgan's when he was surgeon in the revolutionary army and encamped with his regiment at Colonel Proctor's headquarters along the ravine to the south of what is now Kleinhan's green houses, which was then along the main road to Easton from the south. Dr. Morgan, after seeing his family comfortably settled, returned to Philadelphia to help stamp out the epidemic. Elizabeth, not receiving any communication from him for upwards of two months, and quarantine being removed from Philadelphia, concluded to make a trip there. On her arrival at her Philadelphia home she found that the servants had decamped, the house had been ransacked from garret to cellar, and everything of value confiscated. At a loss to know what had become of her husband, she made inquiry of the health officers and found that her husband had contracted the malady and died within a few days after his arrival, and was buried in the trench along with the rest. This double affliction required considerable fortitude to withstand. Finding herself the second time a widow, she disposed of her fine home and all her interests in Philadelphia and returned to the "Hills," with the purpose of living in quiet retirement with her two daughters. She never returned to Philadelphia, but purchased the hotel property in which she had taken up her abode, and lived there for upwards of fifty years. Mrs. Morgan made good use of her excellent education. She possessed a fine library, and her favorite pastime was reading law books, of which she had a complete set. These were kept on a bench in the public room,

where she would dispense law when occasion required. This. room, in time, became the popular retreat for those of her neighbors who could not settle their differences themselves. They would invariably refer their case to this improvised court. A request for her decision was never refused; both old and young respected her judgment, and seldom was there an appeal to a higher tribunal. This condition of affairs brought forth a protest from the legal fraternity of Easton, who endeavored by various methods to break up the practice. Reflections as to her character and the character of the place were made, bringing her name into ridicule with the unthinking. All this unkindness toward the "Widow" Morgan only increased her popularity. Few of these gentry of the bar could boast of a better legal education than Elizabeth Morgan, and none of a better university training. Her last will and testament (written by herself) for scholarly composition and legal construction is the peer of any instrument of any member of the legal fraternity of her day. Steeled to adversity, never showing resentment toward her traducers, living a good and true life, a kind and generous neighbor, ministering to the afflicted, adjusting neighborly disputes for many years, she died October 16, 1839, aged eighty years, and was buried in the Reformed cemetery on Mount Jefferson (now the site of the new library). Her obsequies were attended by people from far and near, her funeral cortege being nearly two miles long, reaching from the cemetery gates to a point along the Philadelphia road beyond Lachenour Heights, South Side. Her second daughter, Hannah Morgan, died at the age of twenty years. Her first daughter, Ann Bay, was married to James Heinlein, a son of Captain George Heinlein, of Durham township, Bucks county, a prominent figure in the revolution. Their children were: George, born 1799: Hugh, born 1802; Abel Morgan, born 1804; Edward, born 1806; Morgan, born 1808; Jacob, born 1811; John, born 1813; Henry, born 1814; Hannah Eliza, born 1815, became the wife of William Raub. Of the many descendants of these grandsons of Elizabeth Morgan living in the Lehigh Valley and the regions round about, there are very few bearing the name of Heinlein. Mrs. Morgan took great pride in her grandsons and gave all of them an advanced education. Three of these grandsons emigrated in company with several of the families of Hays from Lehigh county to Ohio, settling in and around Fremont. Mrs. Heinlein, the mother, married for the second time a Mr. Schultz. She was buried to the right of her mother, Mrs. Morgan, and Hannah, the other daughter, was buried on the left side. Their remains were not disturbed when the site of Easton's colonial burying ground was remodeled for the park surrounding the new library.

FRANCIS R. SWALLOW. Well known and valued in Bucks county is Francis R. Swallow, one of the summer residents of Lumberville. Mr. Swallow is a son of Charles R. Swallow, who was born about 1812, near Ringold, New Jersey, and was reared in Hunterdon county. He settled on a farm near Rosemont, where for many years he followed agricultural pursuits. About 1851 he moved to Lumberville and engaged in mercantile business, which he carried on for several years. About 1865 he removed to Lambertville, New Jersey, where for a number of years he conducted a mercantile business, which he finally sold and became a commercial salesman for a wholesale shoe house, a position which he continued to hold during the active years of his life. He married Eliza Robinson and five of the ten children born to them are now living: Harriet, who lives in Philadelphia; Emma, who is also a resident of that city; Hannah, who is the wife of A. H. Horton, of Philadelphia; Francis R., mentioned at length hereinafter; and Winfield, who lives in Philadelphia.

Francis R. Swallow, son of Charles R. and Eliza (Robinson) Swallow, was born September 29, 1846, in Rosemont, Hunterdon county, New Jersey, and from his early boyhood was in the store with his father. At twelve years of age he went to Lahaska, where he found employment in the store of William Balderston, a worthy member of the Society or Friends, with whom he remained until the second year of the civil war. In August, 1862, he enlisted in Company B, One Hundred and Twenty-Eighth Regiment for nine months' service. Two months after the expiration of his term he re-enlisted in Company B, One Hundred and Ninety-Sixth Regiment for three months' service, and after the expiration of this his second term was employed for some months in Philadelphia. In March, 1864, he again enlisted, this time in Company I, Two Hundred and Thirteenth Regiment for one year, serving until the close of the war. After Mr. Swallow's retirement from military service he went to Philadelphia and for nineteen years was employed by the old Carpenter Ice Company. In 1886, in partnership with Thomas C. Jenkins, he organized the Washington Ice Company, with offices at 13 Brown street, and a shipping wharf at the Brown street shipping market wharf. From a small beginning the business increased to large proportions, the company running thirty-five wagons, the first wagons and teams ever used in that business in

Philadelphia. In 1899 they sold out advantageously to the trust, and for five years Mr. Swallow and his partner served as officers of the company. In the autumn of 1903 Mr. Swallow again engaged in the ice business, confining himself strictly to the wholesale trade, with offices at Broad and Cumberland streets, Philadelphia. The title of the present company, of which Mr. Swallow is sole owner, is "The Washington Ice Company." The business is carried on principally by car-load lots and wagons are run as far from the city as Bristol. Mr. Swallow is also interested in the New Knickerbocker Ice Company. He is a member of Birney Post, No. 63, G. A. R., of Philadelphia, and also belongs to Gothic Lodge, No. 519, F. and A. M. In politics he is a Republican. Mr. Swallow married in 1876 Mary A. Diddleback, of Philadelphia, and nine children have been born to them, five of whom are living: Mamie E., who is the wife of Charles Krupp, of Philadelphia; Frank W., who is a student in Jefferson Medical College; Isabelle May; Florence H., and Lilliam Hazle. The four last-named are at home with their parents. In 1899 Mr. Swallow purchased the old Fretz residence in Lumberville, which he has since used as a country home, his city residence being at 2042 Mount Vernon street, Philadelphia.

JOSEPH JENKINS ERWIN, of Spokane, Washington, though his lot is now cast far from the place of his nativity, cherishes a love of the good old county of Bucks where his ancestors on both maternal and paternal lines lived, loved and labored. He was born in the year 1844, and is a son of John and Martha M. (Jenkins) Erwin, both of whom came of Bucks county ancestry and are descended from early settlers in and near Bucks county, of Scotch-Irish Welsh, Holland, and English extraction. His maternal ancestry is given fully in the sketch of his cousin, Zachary Taylor Jenkins, which appears elsewhere in this work.

John Erwin, his great-grandfather, was of Scotch-Irish origin, and a resident of Southampton township, Bucks county, Pennsylvania, where he died February 7, 1823, at the age of fifty-three years. The Erwin family were early Scotch-Irish emigrants to Bucks county, and took a prominent part in the founding of the Republic, many of them taking an active part in the revolutionary struggle. Hugh Erwin was a member of the associated company of Southampton in 1775, and doubtless the pioneer ancestor of John Erwin, and probably also a kin to Colonel Arthur Erwin, of Tinicum, who came to Pennsylvania about 1760 and was assassinated while serving in the state assembly in 1790. John Erwin, of Southampton, married Susan Tomlinson, of English Quaker ancestry, who was born in Bucks county, in 1775, and died February 5, 1856. She was a descendant of Ralph Dracott, an early Huguenot settler in Southampton. John and Susan (Tomlinson) Erwin reared a family in Southampton, among whom was Joseph Erwin, born December 23, 1792, died October 8, 1870.

Joseph Erwin married Hannah Morrison, born February 10, 1796, died December 10, 1860, daughter of John and Hannah (Yerkes) Morrison, and granddaughter of John Morrison, who came from the north of Ireland and settled on the Brandywine, and a descendant on the maternal side from Anthony Yerkes, one of the early burgesses of Germantown. (See "Morrison Family" in this work.) Joseph and Hannah (Morrison) Erwin lived for a time in Montgomery county, where was born to them a family, of whom two were as follows: John Erwin, the father of the subject of this sketch, and Martha Morrison Erwin, who married John Jenkins, brother ot Martha Merrick Jenkins, whom her brother married.

John Erwin, son of Joseph and Hannah (Morrison) Erwin, was born in Montgomery county, Pennsylvania. As before stated he married Martha Merrick Jenkins, daughter of Joseph and Tacy (Martindale) Jenkins, of Bucks county, whose distinguished ancestry is given in the account of the Jenkins family in this work, and they were the parents of six children: Joseph Jenkins, the subject of this sketch, born June 16, 1844; B. Frank, residing in Philadelphia; Preston, of Westport, Missouri; Tacy, wife of William Sutton, of Philadelphia; and James and Charles Erwin, also of Philadelphia.

THE BARNSLEY FAMILY. The late Joseph Barnsley, of Hartsville, Warminster township, Bucks county, was of English descent. He was born in Newtown, Bucks county, June 9, 1820, a son of William and Jane (Van Horn) Barnsley, and grandson of John and Elizabeth (Van Court) Barnsley.

John Barnsley emigrated from Yorkshire, England, about 1760. He was the first member of his line to found a family on American soil. His uncle, Thomas Barnsley, was a major of the British army in the "60th Royal Ameriman Regiment," and had fought in the French war under Lord Loudon in 1756. After the settlement of the "French and Indian trouble" in connection with Braddock's defeat, he resigned his commission, went back to England, whence he returned with his wife and nephew John, and bought an estate of five hun-

dred acres on the Neshaminy creek in what is now Bensalem township. Here he built a mansion, the bricks for which were brought from England. This house is yet standing, a fine representation of colonial architecture. Major Barnsley died in 1771, his wife surviving him several years. They had no children, and the executors being Tories, who were expatriated, the estate was not settled for several years.

John Barnsley, one of the four heirs, received his portion in continental money, and not investing it at once it became worthless. He was married about the time of his uncle's death and managed the estate until his aunt's demise. On the breaking out of the revolution he became one of a committee in Bensalem to drive off the cattle to keep them from the British. In January, 1777, he was with Washington's army in the night march from Trenton to Princeton. His team was impressed to haul ammunition, and in the battle of Princeton he was ordered by Washington in person to drive along the line to supply the soldiers. His time expiring shortly after, he came home suffering great hardships on the way. He followed farming in Bensalem for several years, finally buying property at Newtown, where he lived until his death, February 2, 1796. His wife was Elizabeth Van Court, whose ancestors were French Huguenots, originally called De la Court. She was born at Huntingdon valley, Montgomery county, in 1751, and died in 1824.

Their son, William, father of the subject of this sketch, was born in Bensalem township, November 8, 1775, and removed with his parents to Newtown township when a boy. He married, January 21, 1808, Jane Van Horn, born in Lower Makefield, March 25, 1784, who died July 25, 1861. Their children were: Mary, John, Thomas and Joseph. He lived in Newtown until 1831, when he bought a farm at Huntingdon valley, Moreland township, where he resided until his death in 1848. He was a successful farmer and financier, acquiring three farms, besides other property. His son John remained on the homestead farm in Newtown, where he lived until his decease, January 11, 1880. He followed surveying and held the office of magistrate for thirty-five years. Mary, died unmarried January 16, 1889. Thomas lived on the homestead at Huntingdon valley until his death, September 6, 1866.

Joseph Barnsley was reared at Newtown and Huntingdon valley, and in 1845 located on the farm in Warminster which he later inherited. He resided there until 1868, when he was appointed United States revenue collector for fifth district and transferred his home to Doylestown. On the expiration of his

Joseph Barnsley

Geo. K. Wildman

term of office in 1870, he did not return to his farm which he had rented, but purchased a new home, the beautiful "Roseland" property at Hartsville, where he lived until his sudden death from heart trouble in full vigor of mind and body January 12, 1888. He married, January 21, 1847, Lydia Harper Walton, who was born in Horsham township, November 28, 1826, and at this writing, September, 1905, survives him, living in Hatboro, Montgomery county, Pennsylvania. They had no issue. Mr. Barnsley was a man of clear-cut principles and staunch integrity, of strong mental powers with a philosophical bent, brightened by a rich vein of humor. He had a tender heart and generous nature, becoming a public benefactor within the circle of his influence. He was further an individual of intense public spirit and patriotism. A Republican in politics he took a lively interest in the success of his party. One of the best known citizens of the township, his personal popularity led to his election to the state legislature in 1858, 1859, and 1860, up to that time the first nominee of his party to serve three successive terms from this county. From early manhood he had been called to fill various public offices and positions of trust and confidence. He was president of The Farmers' Hay Market Company, of Philadelphia for eleven years prior to his death, and director of Hatboro National Bank from its organization. He lies interred in the graveyard of St. Luke's Protestant Episcopal church in Newtown. In his will he bequeathed an ample trust fund for the erection and maintenance of a memorial library and reading room in this town, the home of his boyhood and last resting place of his parents and family.

GEORGE KNORR WILDMAN. Prominent among the representative citizens of Bensalem township, Bucks county, Pennsylvania, who follow the quiet but useful calling of agriculture, is George K. Wildman, a native of that township, born on the homestead farm, February 22, 1859. The founder of the Wildman family in America was Martin Wildman, who came from Yorkshire, England, in 1683, accompanied by his wife, Ann Wildman, and settled in Bucks county, Pennsylvania, where he followed farming as a means of livelihood. They were honest and God-fearing people, members of the Society of Friends, and at their decease left to their children the legacy of an untarnished name and reputation. The line of descent is traced through their son, John Wildman, who was the father of a son, John Wildman, who married Marjorie Knight, and among their children was a son, John Wildman, who was born in Bensalem

township, Bucks county, March 28, 1771, married Mary Knight, and died May 21, 1842. Among their children was a son, Joshua Wildman, who became the father of George Knorr Wildman.

Joshua Wildman (father) was born in Bensalem township, Bucks county, Pennsylvania, August 3, 1819. He was reared on the homestead farm, and in the common schools of the day obtained a good English education. He devoted his attention to farming, and the income thus derived provided his family with the necessaries of life. On August 28, 1844, Mr. Wildman married Hannah Johnson, who was born in Philadelphia, Pennsylvania, August 28, 1823, daughter of William and Catherine (Knorr) Johnson, and granddaughter of John and Rachel (Liozne) Johnson. Four children were the issue of this marriage: Catherine, deceased; Caroline, deceased; Lavina, wife of Edward Comly, of Byberry, Philadelphia county, Pennsylvania; and George Knorr, whose name heads this sketch. Edward and Lavina Comly are the parents of four children, as follows: Joshua K. Comly, who died in infancy; Edward Comly, who died at the age of eleven years; Hannah Wildman Comly, and Deborah Ann Comly, who died at the age of ten years. Joshua Wildman, father of George K. Wildman, died February 26, 1867.

George K. Wildman pursued his studies at the Friends' school in Byberry and at the Friends' Central School at the corner of Fifteenth and Race streets, Philadelphia. Having been reared on a farm he naturally chose that occupation for his life work, and in following the same has acquired a large degree of financial success as a result of his practical and progressive methods and painstaking labor. Upon the death of his father he succeeded to the fine old homestead in Bensalem township, upon which he now resides. His political affiliations are with the Republican party. Mr. Wildman was united in marriage, June 9, 1881, wth Rachel Ridge Comly, who was born in Philadelphia county, near Bustleton, was educated at Swarthmore College, and is a daughter of John and Emeline (Ridge) Comly, and granddaughter of Robert and Esther (Shallcross) Comly, who were the parents of ten children. Robert Comly was a successful business man, and his only brother, Samuel Comly, was one of the earliest to engage in the tea trade with China, owning his own ships, and became very wealthy. He, like his brother Robert, was the head of a large family. Esther (Shallcross) Comly was a daughter of Leonard Shallcross, who was a son of Leonard Shallcross. Both father and son were prominent in the business circles of Philadelphia in their day. Five children were born to Mr.

and Mrs. Wildman: Edith, born May 23, 1882, died in infancy. Allen Comly, born June 8, 1883. Clara Wilson, born January 22, 1886. Emma Comly, born October 18, 1888. John, born September 14, 1891, died in infancy. The children are bright and intelligent, and the family are highly esteemed in the community in whch they live. The family are members of the Society of Friends.

JOHN L. KULP, whose enterprising spirit has prompted him to fill many public positions resulting in benefit to his community and who is well known as proprietor of a hotel in the village of Plumsteadville, was born in Bedminster township, Bucks county, November 13, 1857, and is a representative of one of the old families of this part of the state. His paternal grandfather, Henry Kulp, lived and died in Bucks county, where for many years he followed the occupation of farming. He was a member of the Old Mennonite church. His children were: Jacob, David, Abraham, Hannah, who married John Porter; Mary, the wife of Isaac Gross; and Elizabeth, the widow of Samuel Wismer.

Abraham Kulp, son of Henry Kulp, was born in Bedminster township, in 1816, and in early life learned the shoemaker's trade, which he followed for many years in connection with general agricultural pursuits. He was a member of the Mennonite church and a law-abiding citizen, whose upright life won the respect of all. He wedded Miss Nancy Leatherman, a daughter of John Leatherman, and his death occurred in August, 1900. To them were born six children: Mary, wife of Aaron M. Kulp; Annie, wife of Isaac S. Yothers; Barbara, who died in childhood; John L., Henry, who died in childhood; and Abraham.

John L. Kulp acquired his education in the common schools of Bucks county and in the State Normal schools at Millersville and Westchester, Pennsylvania. He afterward engaged in teaching through the winter months, while in the summer seasons he worked at the carpenter's trade, giving his attention to the dual pursuits for about ten years. In 1887 he began farming in Bedminster township and while carrying on the work of cultivating the fields through the summer months he continued as a teacher for about ten years. He was thus closely identified with the educational development of his locality, and was acknowledged as one of the competent instructors in the common schools of Bucks county. In 1897 he purchased the hotel at Plumsteadville, and has since given his undivided attention to its conduct, making it a popular hostelry with the traveling public. Politically a Republican, Mr. Kulp is now filling the office of township auditor, and while he has never been very active as an office seeker he has always kept well informed on the questions and issues of the day. He belongs to the Odd Fellows Lodge, No. 678, now of Plumsteadville, where he has passed all of the chairs, and he likewise belongs to the Order of United American Mechanics, No. 75, at Plumsteadville, in which he has also filled all of the offices. His religious faith is indicated by his membership in the Old Mennonite church. John L. Kulp was married to Miss Hannah E. Barndt, a daughter of Henry and Elizabeth Barndt, and they became the parents of nine children, of whom one died in infancy. The others are: Henry B., born July 29, 1884; Isaac Newlin, December 7, 1886; Eleanora, July 2, 1888; Anna Mary, September 20, 1889; Estella May, December 20, 1891; Abram Lincoln, September 12, 1893; Aaron Freeman, February 13, 1895; and John Walter, born April 29, 1897.

EDWARD GARGES. The Garges family came from Germany and was planted on American soil in colonial days. Almost continuously from the time that the white race had dominion over the district embraced in Bucks county, representatives of the name have been connected with its history. The family in more recent generations is represented by descendants of Abraham and John Garges. Abraham was grandfather of Edward Garges, learned the blacksmith's trade and lived a life of a mechanic and farmer. He held membership in the Mennonite church, and was interested in public affairs to the extent that he gave hearty support to all movements which he believed would contribute to the general good. He married Leah Ruth, and died in the year 1860. His children were William, a farmer; Henry, father of Edward Garges; Lewis, a farmer; Rebecca, who became the wife of Joseph Funk; Mrs. Mary J. Fell; Sarah A., wife of O. P. Shutt; Priscilla, wife of H. Hines; and Amy and Abraham, both deceased.

Henry Garges, son of Abraham and Leah Garges, was born in Doylestown, Bucks county, August 19, 1830, and reared upon the old family homestead, which is now owned by Joseph Rich. He was but sixteen years of age when his father and uncle John, who jointly owned the above property, dissolved partnership by drawing sticks, and it fell to his father's lot to leave, so he removed to another farm in Bucks county. At the time of his marriage he settled upon a tract of land in Doylestown township, near Edison, which he yet owns, although he is now living retired from active farm labor. His business career was characterized by unfaltering diligence and perseverance, and was crowned with a very gratifying measure of success. He sold his farm products to wholesale dealers, and in connection with general farming engaged in the raising of stock. As the years passed, his financial resources increased until he has become the possessor of a good estate. A Republican in his political views, Henry Garges has filled a number of township positions. He belongs to the Presbyterian church at Doylestown, and is a man of charitable spirit, kindly nature and genial disposition, qualities which have won him the high regard and good will of those with whom he has been associated. March 13, 1862, Henry Garges married Mary E. Roberts, a native of Bucks county, whose father died during her infancy, so that little is known concerning the history of the Roberts family. Her people, however, were identified with the Friends. Mrs. Garges was an only child. She became a member of the Presbyterian church and passed away July 7, 1901, at the age of sixty-eight years, but Mr. Garges is still living, at the age of seventy-five years. Their children are Anna L., the wife of Frank Bodine; Edward; and Isaac Buckman, a merchant of Philadelphia.

Edward Garges, the elder son of Henry and Mary E. (Roberts) Garges, was born in Doylestown township, April 6, 1865, and his elementary education acquired in the common schools was supplemented by study in the high school of Doylestown. Under his father's direction he gained practical and comprehensive knowledge of farm methods and in April, 1889, he settled upon the homestead farm, which he cultivated for thirteen years. He then purchased the old homestead property of John B. Walter, deceased, and since 1902 has operated this tract of land, giving his undivided attention to the cultivation of field and garden and to the sale of his products on the markets. He is a practical and successful business man, watchful of opportunities, and by the careful conduct of his business affairs has gained a very desirable competence. He raises stock for the support of his farm. Mr. Garges usually exercises his right of franchise in support of the men and measures of the Republican party, but is somewhat independent in his political views, and does not consider himself bound by party ties. He belongs to the Presbyterian church of Doylestown, and investigation into his life record shows many points worthy of commendation.

Edward Garges married Miss Maria F. Walter, who was born on the farm which is now her home, her parents being John B. and Adeline E. (Hoover) Walter, both natives of Bucks county. Her ancestry can be traced back to George Walter, who was a blacksmith of Doylestown in early manhood. He worked at his trade on the Garges homestead before mentioned, now occupied by Joseph Rich, while his wife run a saw mill on the same place. It is said he came there from Skippack, Montgomery county, to operate these trades for Mrs. Garges after her husband's death. He afterward became a resident of Warrington township, where he purchased a tract of land of one hundred and thirty-one acres, developing this into a very productive farm, where he also conducted his blacksmith shop. His son, Samuel Walter, grandfather of Mrs. Garges, was born on his father's farm in Warrington township, and where he spent his remaining days, his death occurring before the death of his father, George Walter. He passed away in 1851. His wife, who bore the maiden name of Deborah Brunner, was a daughter of John and Elizabeth Brunner, her father being proprietor of a hotel in Philadelphia. He was also a farmer and miller at Bridge Point, Bucks county, now called Edison, where in 1800 they boarded the hands who built the stone bridge which still spans the Neshaminy at that place. Mrs. Samuel Walter died in 1874. By her marriage she had become the mother of six children: John B., father of Mrs. Edward Garges; George, a plasterer; Catherine, the wife of W. A. Smith; Elizabeth, the widow of John Marks; Anna M., the wife of Joshua W. Scott; and Frances, the wife of Preston Bissy.

John B. Walter was born February 14, 1835, on the farm now owned and occupied by Edward Garges. This had been purchased by his grandfather, George Walter, in 1805, and after his death John B. Walter bought the property at the sale. There were but meager improvements upon it then, but Mr. Walter began its further development, and in due course of time made it a splendidly improved farm. He repaired the house and erected a barn, added many modern equipments, and altogether developed a farm whose value was hardly second to none of the size in the county. He tilled the fields and raised stock, having some very valuable horses and cattle. He was particularly fond of horses, and many specimens of the noble steed were seen upon his place. He was also a market man, and secured a large patronage in the Philadelphia markets. In matters relating to his county he was public-spirited and progressive, and at all times his business integrity was above reproach. He was devoted to his home and family, and held friendship inviolable. Politically a Democrat, he filled many township offices, and also served on the election board. The moral development of the community was likewise of deep interest to him, and he was a consistent member of the Reformed church, taking a very active part in its work, and serving as trustee for a long period. He died June 14, 1900, at the age of sixty-five years. He was prominent in fraternal circles, belonging to Doylestown Lodge, No. 245, A. F. and A. M.; Doylestown Chapter, R. A. M.; Pennsylvania Commandery, No. 70, K. T., of Philadelphia; and Warrington Lodge, No. 447, I. O. O. F. He filled the position of school director for nineteen years and held other township offices.

John B. Walter was married December 2, 1856, to Miss Adeline E. Hoover, who was born in Warrington township, September 10, 1831, and died February 4, 1905. She was a lady of intelligence and culture. Her parents were Frederick W. and Maria (Fleck) Hoover, both descendants of early settlers of Bucks county. Her paternal grandparents were Philip and Mary (Conrad) Hoover, who were born in this county and were of German descent, the Hoover family having been established in Pennsylvania at an early epoch in the colonization of the state. Frederick W. Hoover, father of Mrs. John B. Walter, was reared on the home farm, and after his marriage engaged in merchandising in Pleasantville, Pennsylvania, for a number of years. Subsequently he purchased a tract of land and continued to make his home upon the farm, which he there developed until his life's labors were ended in death. When he was at Pleasantville he became one of the founders and organizers of the Reformed church and one of its pillars, taking a most active part in its work and serving as elder. His home was always open for the reception of the ministers and the church people. Possessing marked musical talent, he was a leading singer in the church and also played upon different musical instruments. His ability in this direction also added to the attractiveness of his home. He voted with the Democracy and held different township offices, while his father and grandfather were prominent in political circles of the state, each representing his district in the general assembly. Frederick W. Hoover was married to Maria Fleck, a daughter of Adam Fleck, who died from camp fever contracted while serving in the war of 1812. He was a farmer of Montgomery county prior to entering the army. He and his brothers, Daniel and Jacob, were representatives of an old Pennsylvania family. Adam Fleck had six children: Charlotte; Samuel; Maria, who became Mrs. Frederick W. Hoover; Eliza; Benjamin; and Adam. The children of Frederick W. and Maria (Fleck) Hoover were Tilghman A.; Adeline E., who became Mrs. John B. Walter; Philip W., of Philadelphia; F. Lyman, deceased; Samuel, of North Wales;

Truman and William L., both of Philadelphia; Frank, who is living at Bluebell; and Andrew, who died at the age of fourteen years. They were reared in the Reformed church, but some of the family became identified with other religious denominations.

The children of John B. and Adeline E. (Hoover) Walter are: Mary H., a school teacher; Ida E., the wife of Frank Larzelere; Mattie L., the wife of H. M. McKinstry; Maria, the wife of Edward Garges; Andrew J., pastor of the Dutch Reformed church at Harlingen, New Jersey; and William, who died at the age of nineteen years; Samuel, who died at the age of two years; and Gertrude, at the age of six years. The children of Edward and Maria Garges are Ethel F., born March 8, 1893; John W., born October 1, 1894, died March 8, 1903; Mary E., born November 7, 1896; Mildred A., May 17, 1898; Henry W., December 16, 1900; and Anna M., January 12, 1903.

JOHN HART, president of the Doylestown Trust Company, and his brother Frank Hart, of Doylestown, retired banker, are the sons of Josiah and Sarah (Brock) Hart. The former was born in Doylestown township, February 3, 1846, and the latter February 24, 1851. On the paternal side they are of Scotch-Irish descent.

Among the thousands of Ulster Scots who migrated to Pennsylvania in the first half of the eighteenth century were those who formed two distinct settlements within the present limits of Bucks county, one on the banks of the Neshaminy in Warwick, Warrington and New Britain, and the other on the banks of the Tohickon in Plumstead, Tinicum and adjacent townships. In the latter settlement were the Stewarts, Harts, Means, McGlaughlins, Pattersons, Armstrongs, Erwins, Davies and a host of others, more or less united by ties, consanguinity, and common interest, whose names are found on the earliest lists of military companies organized for the defense of the frontiers against their hereditary enemies, the French and their savage allies.

Among these early settlers on the Plumstead side of the Tohickon about 1735 was Samuel Hart and his family, consisting of wife and nine children, the eldest of whom, James, was born in the year 1717, and the second son William was probably three or more years younger. Samuel Hart obtained a warrant of survey for 100 acres of land on March 9, 1737, and settled thereon. Ten years later in 1747 when the first clouds of war appeared on the horizon, companies were formed in the several townships for the defence of the frontiers. The Plumstead company had for its captain the veteran Charles Stewart, lieutenant, James Hart, and ensign, William Hart, both of the latter being ancestors of the subjects of this sketch through the marriage of a grandson of the latter with a granddaughter of the former many years later. Across the Tohickon in Tinicum the captain of the company was James McGlaughlin, who had married Mary, the eldest sister of the Hart brothers, and the lieutenant was James Davies, whose son William was a brother-in-law to them, all three having married daughters of William Means or Main, a neighbor and compatriot. Samuel Hart, the elder, died in April, 1750, devising his plantation to his sons James and William. His other children than the three above mentioned were: Joseph, John, Jean, who married Samuel Mathers and removed to North Carolina, Elinor, Samuel and Elizabeth.

James Hart, born 1717, died May 4, 1766, was an innkeeper in Plumstead, near Wismer, where he had purchased a tract of about 400 acres of land in 1751 adjoining the plantation of his father. He married Jean, daughter of William and Mary Means, and their children were: Samuel, born August 30, 1746, died January 21, 1831, unmarried. William, born March 24, 1748, died January 2, 1830, married Elizabeth Means, his cousin. John, born March 24, 1748, died February 24, 1803, married Mary McCalla. Elizabeth, born February 13, 1750, died in infancy. Mary, born January 15, 1752, married James Ruckman. James, born December 27, 1753, died young. Joseph, born February 16, 1755, married Elinor Wilson and removed to New Jersey. Elizabeth, born February 28, 1757, married John Johnston and removed to New Jersey. James, born March 17, 1759, married Ann Hankinson, removed to New Jersey. Solomon, born August 30, 1762, died April 27, 1810, married Isabel Long, daughter of Captain Andrew Long, of Warrington, and settled in Warrington. Jane, born August 4, 1765, married Samuel Opdycke, of Hunterdon county, New Jersey. Jean (Means) Hart was born August 30, 1726, and died January 31, 1799.

William Hart, second son of James and Jean Hart, married in 1776 his cousin Elizabeth, daughter of John and Grizelda (Patterson) Means. He purchased in 1783 of his brothers and sisters the whole of his father's plantation in Plumstead, but a few years later removed to Hartsville, then known as "Warwick Cross Roads" and purchased the old tavern property, where he served as "mine host" for many years. He died January 2, 1830, and his widow died January 10, 1841. She was born March 15, 1753. Their children were: Jane, born June 28, 1779, married Joseph Carr, of Warwick. John, born December 17, 1780, died January 27, 1811. Mary, born February 19, 1783, married Samuel Hart,

son of Joseph Hart, January 6, 1806. James, born March 6, 1785, married Jane Baird, of Warwick. Grizelda, born March 19, 1787, never married, died October 5, 1868. William, born January 4, 1789, married Martha Carr, daughter of Adam and Frances Carr, of Warwick. Joseph, born November 9, 1790, died 1872, unmarried. Elizabeth, born April 14, 1794, married her cousin William Hart, son of John and Mary Hart. William Hart, father of the above children, was commissioned major of second battalion of Bucks county militia, May 6, 1777, and rose to rank of colonel. Both James and William Hart, the two eldest sons of Samuel, the pioneer, died comparatively young, whether in the service of their country or not is not known.

Of the children of William and Margaret (Means) Hart we have record of but one, Joseph Hart, born November 20, 1745, died August 31, 1797. His mother, Margaret (Means) Hart, married a Beatty. His early manhood was spent in the neighborhood of Hartsville. He was a member of the Associated Company of Warminster in 1775, was commissioned a captain, May 6, 1777, and rose to the rank of colonel of militia. He married, January 1, 1770, Elizabeth, daughter of Nicholas and Esther (Craven) Gilbert of Warminster. She was born July 9, 1748, and died January 26, 1841. In 1772 the 173 acre farm of which Nicholas Gilbert died seized in Warminster on the Street road and Warrington line was adjudged to Joseph Hart in right of his wife Elizabeth and they settled thereon. Joseph Hart later sold the Warminster farm and removed to the mill on the York road in Warwick, near Hartsville, now owned by John M. Darrah, where he died August 31, 1797. His children were: Josiah, born October 15, 1770, died May 20, 1850, unmarried. Levi, born August 16, 1773, died young. Mahlon, born March 11, 1775, died young. Elizabeth, born November 2, 1777, married first Jonathan Conrad, second, Samuel Croasdale. Samuel, born November 1, 1783, died November 25, 1863, married first Mary, daughter of William and Elizabeth Hart, born February 19, 1783, died February 28, 1828.

Samuel Hart, grandfather of the subject of this sketch, was but fourteen years of age at the death of his father, and Robert Loller, Esq., of Hatboro, who was appointed his guardian, took him to his home and superintended his education. He studied surveying and conveyancing and assisted his guardian in these pursuits, and at the death of the latter succeeded to his business and was employed in settling a number of estates. He was for many years a justice of the peace and surveyor. He married, January 6, 1806, Mary, daughter of Colonel William and Elizabeth (Means) Hart, and had by her seven children as follows: Mary, born October 9, 1808, married June 17, 1834, William C. Jamison, of Warwick. Elizabeth, born January 22, 1810, died unmarried. Josiah, born September 15, 1811, died 1898, married November 24, 1842, Sarah Brock. William, born August 24, 1813, married April 19, 1844, Isabella Mann. He died February 25, 1867. Irwin, born December 9, 1815, died young. George, born April 4, 1817, died February 7, 1871. Nathaniel, born October 15, 1819, died November 14, 1862, married December 10, 1843, Susan L. Cox. Samuel Hart was a member of Neshaminy Presbyterian church, of which he was trustee for thirteen years—1810 to 1823. In 1829 he joined the Society of Friends. He married Amy, widow of John Mathews, and daughter of Benjamin Kinsey, of Buckingham. His only child by the second marriage was Samuel Hart, of Doylestown township, born in 1832, married Ellen Eastburn.

George Hart, son of Samuel and Mary Hart, studied law and was admitted to the Bucks county bar November 16, 1843. He was a man universally admired and respected for his many good qualities. He was thrice married; (first) February 1, 1842, to Zallida, daughter of James and Amelia (Brockway) Goff; (second) January 22, 1846, to Sarah, daughter of Nathan and Sarah (Callender) Cornell; and (third) February 1, 1854, to Martha, daughter of John and Martha (Duncan) Watson, a sister to Judge Richard Watson.

Josiah Hart, son of Samuel and Mary Hart, was born in Warwick township, September 15, 1811. He received a liberal education and on June 18, 1834, was appointed a clerk in the Doylestown Bank and December 8, 1847, was promoted to the position of cashier, which position he filled for ten years, being succeeded by John J. Brock, November 19, 1857. In the following year he organized a banking institution in connection with his brother, George Hart, Richard Watson, Willam M. Large and Jonas Fretz, under the name of J. Hart & Co. During the civil war Messrs. Fretz, Large and Watson retired, and after the death of George Hart, John and Frank Hart became partners with their father and sole proprietors of the bank. Josiah Hart died October 16, 1885, and the sons continued the business until 1896, when the business was closed out. Josiah Hart married, November 24, 1842, Sarah, Daughter of Stephen and Mary (Jones) Brock. John and Frank were their only children. On the organization of the Doylestown Trust Company, March 24, 1896, John Hart became its president. Both John and Frank Hart received a liberal education and early in life became clerks in their father's bank and later proprietors as above stated. At the closing of the

bank Frank retired from active business. John married Grace Vansant, and has one child, Rebie. Frank married Lizzie Pallett, who is now deceased, and he has one son George.

MARY HOLCOMBE, of Newtown, is a native of Plumstead township, Bucks county, being a daughter of Charles and Hannah Robinson Holcombe, and a descendant of John and Mary (Green) Holcombe, an account of whose descendants is given in the preceding sketch.

Richard Holcombe, the grandfather of Mary Holcombe, was the second son of John and Mary (Closson) Holcombe, of Amwell township, Hunterdon county, New Jersey, where he was born in 1767. On November 20, 1792, he married Elizabeth Closson, daughter of Cornelius and Jennet Closson, of Solebury, and settled on his father's farm in Amwell, where he spent his whole life, dying in 1827. He was a carpenter by trade, and was distinguished from his cousins of the same name by the appelation of "Carpenter Richard Holcombe." Richard and Elizabeth (Closson) Holcombe were the parents of nine children: John C., who resided on the old Amwell plantation, dying at the age of ninety years; Thomas; Charles; Mary, married Absalom Phillips; Allen; Elizabeth, married Wilson Moore, and Aaron.

Charles Holcombe, son of Richard and Elizabeth, was a wheelwright by trade, but for many years prior to his death was a farmer in Plumstead township, Bucks county. He married (first) Mary Roberts, who bore him seven children, only one of whom grew to maturity, Elizabeth, who married Charles P. Fenton. He married (second) Hannah Robinson and had four children: Mary, the subject of this sketch; Allen, and Sarah Ellen, both of whom died young; and Charles, who married Phebe Ellen Betts, and is now deceased, leaving three children: Reuben, who married, September 15, 1898, Amy Cooper, daughter of George and Sarah (Miller) Cooper, of Avondale, Chester county, Pennsylvania; Rachel B., and Charles, who is a local minister of the Methodist church; he married, February 22, 1899, Flora Snyder, daughter of Silas and Catherine Snyder, of Bucks county, Pennsylvania; Phebe Ellen, the widow of Charles Holcombe, Jr., resides with the subject of this sketch at Newtown. Charles Holcombe, Sr., died in Plumstead, August 7, 1881, aged eighty-two years.

OLIVER H. HOLCOMBE, of Wrightstown, is a worthy descendant of one of the oldest families in Bucks county. He is a son of John and Elizabeth (Hibbs) Holcombe, and was born in Upper Makefield township, Bucks

county, Pennsylvania, November 7, 1830.
The progenitors of the Holcombes of
Bucks county and of Hunterdon county,
New Jersey, were Jacob and John Holcombe, brothers, born in Triverton, Dev-
onshire, England, about 1680. George
Holcombe Larison, the historian of the
family, says that their father died when
they were quite young, but this does not
seem to be borne out by the records, as
Jacob Holcombe, while in middle age
and residing in Buckingham, requested
that a meeting of Buckingham Friends
might be held "at the home of his aged
parents." John and Jacob are supposed to be the sons of Richard Holcombe and Sarah Holme, daughter of
Thomas Holme, Penn's first surveyor-
general. The latter, in his will in 1694,
leaves a legacy "to the children of Richard Holcombe by my daughter Sarah."
Jacob Holcombe was one of the earliest
landholders in Buckingham, and died
there in 1748, leaving a son Thomas and
several daughters. His wife was Mary
Woolridge, whom he married at Falls
Meeting in 1712.

John Holcombe purchased in 1705 a
large tract of land on the Delaware in
New Jersey, including a large part of
the present city of Lambertville, and has
left numerous descendants of the name
in that vicinity. At the time of he purchase he was a resident of Abington,
Philadelphia county, and married at Abington Meeting of Friends, 4 mo. 28,
1707, Elizabeth Woolridge. He settled
in Amwell township, Hunterdon county,
New Jersey, where he later added to his
purchase of 1705 several other large purchases of lands, and owning at his death
in 1743 over one thousand acres of land
which he devised to his sons and grandsons. He was one of the judges of the
first court held in Hnuterdon. John
and Elizabeth (Woolridge) Holcombe
were the parents of six children: John,
who died a young man and unmarried;
Samuel, see forward; Richard, married
(first) Mary Harvey, and (second) Ann
Emley, and had one son and two daughters; Grace, married Philip Calvin; Mary,
married Samuel Furman, of Morris
county, New Jersey; and Julia Ann,
married Daniel Howell.

Samuel Holcombe, second son of John
and Elizabeth, born in New Jersey, 1711,
married Eleanor Barber, and they are
the ancestors of all the Holcombes of
Bucks county, as well as of Hunterdon
county, New Jersey. He was a member of Buckingham Friends Meeting,
and became a large landholder. He died
August 26, 1769. His wife Eleanor
survived him nearly a quarter of a century, dying June 2, 1793, aged about
ninety years. The children of Samuel
and Eleanor (Barber) Holcombe, were
nine in number: 1. John, born February
16, 1739, see forward; 2. Jacob, born
December 7, 1741, married Rachel,

daughter of John and Elizabeth Hyde,
and had eight children. 3. Phebe, born
October 23, 1743, married Henry Lott,
and had ten children, three of whom
died in infancy; 4. Samuel, born March
17, 1745, married first a widow Stephenson, nee Stillwell, and had two sons,
Samuel and George; married (second)
Sarah Emley, and had children: Mary,
Robert, Elisha, Atkinson, Thomas A.,
Solomon, Lewis and Hannah; he lived
and died in New Jersey near Mt. Airy.
5. George, born April 9, 1747, married
Achsah Knowles, and had five children:
Joseph, George, Achsah, John and Samuel. He was a soldier in the Revolution,
and rose to the rank of major. 6. Elijah,
born September 29, 1750, married Nancy
Brittain, and had eight children. He
and his family migrated to Zanesville,
Ohio, at an early date. He was also a
soldier in the Revolution. 7. Richard,
born December 30, 1752, married Hannah
Emley, and had seven children: Ann,
Emley, Lucilla, George, Elisha and Elinor. He was a revolutionary soldier.
His grandson, George B. Holcombe, was
sheriff of Hunterdon county, 1856-58.
8. Thomas, born November 19, 1754,
married (first) Leah Deremer, whose
only child died young. He married
(second) Mary T. Holcombe, and had
ten children, Richard, John, Abraham,
Leah, Elias, Thomas, Henry, Ralph,
Ann and Maria. 9. Elizabeth, born October 14, 1758, married John Bellis and
reared a family of ten children.

John Holcombe, eldest son of Samuel
and Elenor (Barber) Holcombe, born
February 16, 1739, married Mary Green,
daughter of Richard and Elizabeth
(Wolverton) Green. Mary was born in
Amwell township, June 26, 1741, and died
in Solebury township, Bucks county in
1829. John and Mary lived on the old
homestead near Lambertville, and reared
a family of nine children, several of
whom became residents of Bucks
county. John Holcombe moved to
Solebury in 1792, and died there in 1818.
The children were: 1. Elizabeth, died
unmarried in Solebury about 1855, at the
age of ninety years. 2. Samuel, see forward. 3. Richard, born 1767, married in
1792, Elizabeth Closson, see succeeding
sketch. 4. Elenor, married Asher Ely,
of Solebury, see sketch of William L.
Ely in this volume. 5. John, died in
Solebury in 1820; married Mary Pearson and had children: Pearson, Rhoda,
John, Hannah, Samuel, Mary, married
Jesse Walton, and Elizabeth, married
Thomas Paist. 6. Sarah, married Phineas
Walker, see sketch of William L. Walker
in this volume. 7. Margaret, never married, died in Solebury 1855. 8. Amaziah,
died young. 9. Daniel, died young.

Samuel Holcombe, eldest son of John
and Mary (Green) Holcombe, was born
in Amwell township, Hunterdon county,
New Jersey March 16, 1765. He married

November 9, 1797, Anna Amelia Van Horn, born January 25, 1775, daughter of —— and Sarah (Mode) Van Horn, and settled in Upper Makefield township, Bucks county, Pennsylvania, where he became a large landowner. Anna Amelia (Van Horn) Holcombe died March 12, 1833. He married (second) Elizabeth Furman, nee Wildman, who survived him. The ceremony was performed October 16, 1834. He died April 8, 1855. The children of Samuel and Anna Amelia (Van Horn) Holcombe are as follows: Sarah, born July 31, 1798, married Samuel Ross. Mary, born December 14, 1799, married Benjamin Beans. Elizabeth, born May 1, 1801, married William Hibbs. John, born December 4, 1802, see forward. Anna Amelia, born March 24, 1804, married David Phillips. Hannah, born April 6, 1806, married William Martindale. Samuel, born August 2, 1807, died unmarried, 1870. Phebe, born September 9, 1809, died March 11, 1831. Matilda, born April 25, 1811, married Carey Longshore. De Witt Clinton, born October 23, 1812, died unmarried, September 20, 1843. George, born May 31, 1815, married and had one son, Samuel, and three daughters; he died July 24, 1844. One child was born to Samuel and Elizabeth (Furman) Holcombe, Phebe W., born October 12, 1837, married Dr. Benjamin Collins. Samuel Holcombe was in early life a carpenter and cabinet maker, but later in life followed the life of a farmer.

John Holcombe, son of Samuel and Anna Amelia (Van Horn) Holcombe, was born 12 mo. 4, 1802, and died in Newtown 9 mo. 15, 1894, at the age of ninety-one years. He was a farmer in Upper Makefield until 1837, when he purchased a farm in Newtown township. He was a successful farmer and an active and prominent man in the community. He took an active part in the establishment of the public school system, and an active interest in all that pertained to the best interests of the community. He was a member of Wrightstown Friends' Meeting, and in politics was an ardent Whig, and later a Republican. His later years were spent in Newtown borough. He married Elizabeth Hibbs, who bore him five children of whom two survive: Oliver H., the subject of this sketch, and Hannah E., residing in Philadelphia.

Oliver H. Holcombe was born in Upper Makefield township, November 7, 1830. He acquired his education at the common schools and at a private school conducted by Jeremiah Hayhurst, at Kennett Square, Chester county, Pennsylvania. He married on March 22, 1855, Cynthia Scarborough, daughter of John and Hannah (Reeder) Scarborough, of Solebury, and began life as a farmer on a farm recently purchased by his father in Wrightstown township. A year later he removed to Newtown township on a farm purchased by his father across the road from the homestead, where he lived for five years, and then took charge of the homestead, where he lived for thirty-four years, having acquired the ownership of the homestead. In the spring of 1895 he removed to Newtown, and has since lived a retired life, purchasing his present residence in Pineville, and removing there in the spring of 1899. He has been a stockholder in the First National Bank of Newtown since its organization, and a member of the board of directors since 1899. He was one of the first to agitate the building of the Philadelphia & Newtown Railroad, spent much time and money to that end, and was elected one of the first directors of the completed road. He has served several years as a school director, and has filled other local positions. He has been for many years active in the cause of the Prohibition party; has been its candidate for congress and other offices; and in 1888 was a delegate to the national convention of the party in Indianapolis. Mrs. Holcombe has also been active in temperance work for many years, being the first president of the Bucks County Woman's Christian Temperance Union, which was organized in March, 1885, and under her efficient management about one thousand women were enrolled as members. For more than twenty-five years she has been a monthly contributor to the Home Department of the Farm Journal, of Philadelphia, under the pseudonym of "Mary Sidney," and her essays have been copied into many papers and attracted much attention. Mr. and Mrs. Holcombe are both members and regular attendants of Wrightstown Monthly Meeting of Friends, and for many years have been elders. They are the parents of two children: William P., now residing in New Hampshire; and Anna, wife of Edward R. Kirk, of Buckingham.

AMANDUS HARTZELL COPE, one of the progressive farmers of Richland Center, son of Jacob and Julia (Hartzell) Cope, was born April 17, 1852, on a farm then owned and operated by his father in Richland township, near Richlandtown. The property consisted of forty acres, and was located on Applebachville road, near the line of Haycock township. Jacob Cope (father), son of Jacob and Julia Cope, was born in Rockhill township, Bucks county. He attended the subscription and public schools of the neighborhood, after which he served an apprenticeship at the trade of cigarmaker, which he followed for some time, and later turned his attention to farming. He married Julia Hartzell, of Rockhill township, and had issue: Euphemia, who became the wife of Jacob Allum, a farmer; Maria, who became the wife of Jonas Suyden, and they reside in Philadelphia; Aaron, married Savilla Gangawere, and they reside in Haycock township; Eliza, widow of Jacob Fluck, and resides near Richlandtown; Jacob, deceased; William, married Amanda Mace, and they reside at Tylersport, Montgomery county, Pennsylvania; and Amandus Hartzell Cope.

In 1860, when Amandus H. Cope was eight years of age, his parents moved to Haycock township, near Tohickon creek, where they purchased a farm containing eighty-five acres, which later became the property of Peter Horn. The family resided thereon for the long period of twenty-eight years. After his marriage Amandus settled on his father's farm and succeeded the latter in managing the same on shares, which he continued to do until the death of his father in 1884, when the property was sold to a Mr. Gross. Amandus then moved to a place near Richlandtown, where he remained for one year, and in 1886 purchased a farm of twenty-two acres of improved land, situated on Mill near Third street, Quakertown, which was formerly the property of Henry Hager. He still resides on this property, which he operates as a general farm, and in addition to these duties he attends the Philadelphia market. He casts his vote for the candidates of the Democratic party, but owing to the demands made upon his time by his business takes no active part in local affairs. Mr. Cope enjoys the respect and esteem of a large circle of friends and acquaintances. November 6, 1875, Mr. Cope was united in marriage to Harriet Harding, who was born September 27, 1853, daughter of Reading and Emeline (Potts) Harding, farmers of Haycock township. Mr. and Mrs. Cope are members of the Reformed church at Richlandtown.

EDWARD H. TRAUCH. In Bedminster township there are few more popular men than Edward H. Trauch. Mr. Trauch is a grandson of Peter Trauch, for many years a prominent farmer of Williams township, and later of New Britain where he died.

William H. Trauch, son of Peter Trauch, mentioned above, was born in 1847, in Williams township, and at seventeen years of age became the teacher of a school in Tinicum township, working on a farm during the summer. At the end of two years he gave his attention entirely to farming, and after his marriage was employed for three years on the farm of his father-in-law, and then purchased his present home farm in Bedminster township, where he has since resided. For twelve years he has held the office of supervisor. He is a Democrat in politics, and belongs to the Lutheran church, being a member of the church council. He married Mary Jane, daughter of Elias Trauger, of Bedminster township, and of the twelve children born to them

ten are now living: Emma Laura, Ella Nora, Ira Elias, Minnie May, Clara, Edward H., mentioned at length hereinafter; William, Samuel, Susanna, and Mary.

Edward H. Trauch, son of William H. and Mary Jane (Trauger) Trauch, was born July 22, 1874, in Bedminster township, where he obtained his education in the common schools. At the age of nineteen he went to Keller's Church, where for two years he was employed as salesman. He then accepted a position with Lewis Keller, the proprietor of the extensive department of Bedminsterville, where he remained four years. In June, 1900, he purchased the bakery business of William Yost, of Bedminsterville, which he now so successfully conducts, the patronage having greatly increased under his management. He has filled various election offices, but is not an office seeker. He is a member of Maratina Castle, Knights of the Golden Eagle, and Ottsville Lodge, No. 32, Shield of Honor. He is a Democrat in politics, and belongs to the Lutheran church. Mr. Trauch married, November 20, 1897, Maggie, daughter of Titus Snyder, a prominent farmer of Bedminster township, and they have three children: Ildah, Elsie and Mary.

J. OSCAR DOAN. Several generations of the Doan family have been represented in Bucks county. The grandparents of J. Oscar Doan were Jonathan and Grace (Worthington) Doan, farming people of Buckingham township. The grandfather died when his son Wilson was but nine years of age, leaving a widow and ten children, only four of whom reached mature years. His widow continued to reside upon the home farm and there reared her family, continuing upon the old home property up to the time of her demise.

Wilson Doan, son of Jonathan and Grace Doan, was born in Buckingham township, October 20, 1823, and was carefully reared by his mother. He attended the public schools and being an apt student gained a very thorough common-school education, which enabled him to successfully engage in teaching for several years in the district schools. He followed that profession both prior and subsequent to his marriage, and gained such an excellent reputation for discipline that whenever there was an unmanageable school in the district he was sent to take charge and thereafter there was no trouble. He was married in 1845 and engaged in farming, leasing the Henry S. Knight farm in Buckingham township for five years. He afterward conducted a store in Cottageville for a shore time, and then engaged in teaching for several years, being identified with educational development of the county in this way for at least twenty years. He resided in Solebury township until his health became impaired, and in 1884 he purchased the home in Plumstead, the township where his daughter Elizabeth now resides and where he continued until his death, March 2, 1904. He was a member of the Friends' meeting, was a Republican in politics, and a man of sterling integrity, his life being imbued with high ideals and honorable principles. In 1845 he wedded Hannah Fenton, who was born in Cheltenham, Montgomery county, Pennsylvania, December 14, 1819, a daughter of William and Mary (Fenton) Fenton. Mrs. Hannah Doan died August 4, 1897. There had been born seven children of that marriage, of whom four are living: William F., Harry W., J. Oscar, and Elizabeth, who as stated occupies the home farm in Plumstead township.

J. Oscar Doan, son of Wilson and Hannah (Fenton) Doan, was born in Solebury township, October 26, 1854, and having acquired his education in the common schools worked with his father on the home farm during the periods of vacation and until his seventeenth year, when he started out in life on his own account as a farm hand. He was employed in this way for nine years, after which he spent two or three years at home. He was married April 17, 1884, to Miss Ida E. Thomas, a daughter of Newton R. and Margaret (Jamison) Thomas, both of whom died during the early girlhood of their daughter. Two children have been born of this union, Newton R. W. and Otis H. After his marriage Mr. Doan purchased a farm in the northwestern part of Solebury township, where he turned his attention to agricultural interests, and four years later removed to the Jacob Booz farm in Buckingham township, which he operated as a renter for eight years. In 1897 he purchased that property and still devotes his time and energies to its further development and improvement. He exercises his right of franchise in support of the Republican party, and he is a member of Pannaucussing Lodge, No. 221, K. P., of Carversville. The success which he has achieved has come as the direct result of his labors, and in his business career he has proved that a competence and an honored name may be won simultaneously.

JOSEPH M. LEWIS. Bucks county is ever mindful of the scions of her old families, watching with interest their progress and rejoicing in their prosperity. This she has not failed to do in the case of Joseph M. Lewis, of Lambertville, New Jersey. The founder of the Lewis family emigrated from Wales, and his son Ephraim was born in Bucks county. Ephraim Lewis was a volunteer in the war of 1812, serving in the Pennsylvania line and being stationed at Marcus Hook.

David M. Lewis, son of Ephraim Lewis, mentioned above, was born in Doylestown township, where he was brought up by an aunt, Mrs. Malsbury, attending the old Doylestown Academy. As a young man he went to New Hope, where he served a nine years' apprenticeship at the tailor's trade, after which he went to Davisville, where for a short time he carried on a tailoring business. He then removed to Lambertville, and was living there in 1841, when the sweeping away of the bridge by the flood brought such disaster to the place. At the end of a year he returned to New Hope and there conducted business for many years. During the Mexican war he was orderly sergeant of the Doylestown Greys, a company of the National Guard, and enlisted for the war, but the quota being full his services were not accepted. He was for a number of years a member of the I. O. O. F., but allowed his membership to lapse prior to his death. He was a Democrat in politics, and a member of the Methodist Episcopal church. He married Elizabeth Stackhouse, and one child was born to them; Joseph M., mentioned at length hereinafter. The death of Mr. Lewis occurred in New Hope, of which place he had been a resident of so many years.

Joseph M. Lewis, only child of David M. and Elizabeth (Stackhouse) Lewis, was born February 15, 1840, in Davisville, and in his sixteenth year went to Lambertville to learn the jeweler's trade. His five years' apprenticeship expired in February, 1861, and the following April witnessed the outbreak of the Civil war. Mr. Lewis was among those who responded to the first call for troops, two companies being raised in Lambertville. He joined and helped to drill Company E, commanded by Captain A. W. Angel. This company was attached to the Third New Jersey Regiment, Colonel Napton commanding, and formed part of the brigade commanded by Brigadier-General Runyon. Mr. Lewis was made drum major prior to leaving the state and served three months, his term expiring two days after the battle of Bull Run. The brigade was then resting at Fort Runyon after their retreat from Manassas. Mr Lewis then returned home, and six weeks later re-enlisted in the One Hundred and Fourth Pennsylvania Regiment, Colonel William W. H. Davis commanding. He was made a drummer in the band, serving all through the peninsula campaign, and remaining with the regiment until the passage of the act of congress disbanding all regiment bands, his discharge occurring August 11, 1862, at Harrison's Landing, Virginia. Mr. Lewis then returned home and accepted a position with a Doylestown jeweler, where he remained nine months, returning to Lambertville to accept a position in the store where he had served his apprenticeship. For one year he worked for his former employer, who then sold the business, Mr. Lewis entering the service of the new owner. At the end of three years Mr. Lewis purchased the business which he has conducted for the last thirty-six years, and is now the leading jeweler of Lambertville. He belongs to Angel Post, No. 20, G. A. R., of Lambertville, is a

Democrat in politics, and a member of the Presbyterian church. Mr. Lewis married December 9, 1868, Victoria R., daughter of Philip Harper Matthews, a lumber merchant of Lambertville, and they have one son, Frank B., who is in business with his father and married Jennie H., daughter of William Price, of New Hope. Mr. and Mrs. Lewis are the parents of one child, Florence Josephine.

CHARLES T. DAGER, proprietor of a hotel at Warminster, also identified with farming interests in the township of that name, was born at Baron Hill, Montgomery county, Pennsylvania, April 3, 1834. His grandfather, Frederick Dager, was a miller by trade and followed that pursuit throughout his entire life. He voted with the Democracy, but never aspired to office. During the revolutionary war he saved the life of an American officer who was being pursued by the British by hiding him in a chimney in the house at Marble Hall, Montgomery county. Frederick Dager died and was buried at Baron Hill. He and his wife were members of the Lutheran church at that place. Their children were: Philip, John, Henry, Charles, Martha, and Mrs. Frye.

Major John Dager, son of Frederick Dager, was born in Montgomery county, at Spring Mill, and in his youth assisted his father in the milling business, thus learning the trade in his younger days. After his marriage he settled upon the home farm, purchasing the property at Baron Hill, comprising twelve acres. There he conducted a hotel and upon his land raised much of the products needed for consumption by the guests of the house. He conducted the hotel altogether for forty-eight years, and was one of the best known citizens of that locality. He was largely instrumental in securing the postoffice at Baron Hill, and acted as postmaster when the office paid no salary. At the time of the building of the pike he strongly endorsed that movement, and in fact was an advocate of all progressive measures. In politics a Democrat, he was recognized as one of the leading supporters of the party in his locality and he filled a number of local offices, including that of school director and justice of the peace, occupying the latter position for many years. He was an enterprising and public-spirited citizen, a popular business man, and was widely known and highly respected. He was usually called Major Dager, having served his country as a major in the war of 1812. He was a devoted member of the Lutheran church, in which his wife was also identified. She bore the maiden name of Ann Freas, and was a daughter of Simon Freas, who belonged to one of the old families of Montgomery county. He engaged extensively in dealing in marble and was an enterprising farmer, recognized as one of the leading business men of his neighborhood. He held membership in the Lutheran church, and gave his political allegiance to the Democracy. His children were: Philip, who became editor of the Germantown Telegraph; Nicholas, a partner in the ownership of the paper; Charles, an extensive farmer, also a dealer in marble; Mrs. Ann Dager; Barbara, who became the wife of ————, a teacher in the high school of ————; and Henry, a merchant of Germantown. To Major and Mrs. Dager were born the following children: Margaret, wife of H. S. Hitner; Susanna, the wife of S. Struper; Mrs. Harriet Zimmerman; Mrs. Eliza Stifer; Mrs. Mary Lismyer; Mrs. Martha Richardson; Sarah and Anna, deceased; William, a farmer, and for many years overseer of the Lutheran church; Moulton R., a merchant; Charles Nicholas, who also follows merchandising; and Albert, a dealer in coal. The sons have become prominent and influential in business circles, and the daughters all married leading citizens of their respective communities.

Charles. T. Dager was born in the Baron Hill hotel, became familiar with the business of conducting a hotel in his youth, and throughout the greater part of his life has continued in that line of activity. For fourteen years he has been proprietor of the hotel at Warminster and is popular in this connection, having made an excellent record as a landlord. He remained under the parental roof until 1861, when he enlisted for three months service under General Hartranft. On the expiration of that period he received an honorable discharge, but in the following month he again enlisted, becoming one of the body guard of General Anderson's troop. He was assigned to the Army of the Cumberland and after reaching Ringgold, Georgia, was transferred to General Buell's body guard, serving in that capacity for more than three years or until the close of the war. He was then again honorably discharged and returned to his home with a most creditable military record, having displayed marked valor and loyalty in times of great danger. Mr. Dager was married at Chattanooga, Tennessee, during the period of the war, and after the cessation of hostilities he returned home bringing his bride to the north. He then located at the old homestead at Baron Hill and acted as barkeeper for his father. Later he followed the trade of brick mason, which he had learned in his youth. He conducted the business of contractor for a number of years, and at the same time assisted his father in the hotel business. Later he went to Marble Hall, where he took charge of a mining, marble and iron enterprise, continuing there for fifteen years, after which he again located at the Baron Hill Hotel, continuing in charge until April, 1890. He then bought the hotel and farm at Warminster, where he has since remained. He is a practical and successful hotel man, also active and energetic in his farming operations, and as the years have passed he has acquired considerable valuable farm property in Georgia and Tennessee and owns a number of farm mortgages. He has good, business discernment, has made creditable and judicious investment, and in guiding his business affairs has shown capability and sound sense. During the period of the civil war Mr. Dager married Miss Margaret Springer, who was born at Lookout Mountain, and was a daughter of Joel and Sarah (Lewis) Springer, the former a native of Pennsylvania. He went to the south, however, where he obtained a large plantation and became an extensive slave owner. Prior to the war of the rebellion he was one of the leading planters of his section of the country, and he remained and died upon the old homestead in Georgia. He was an earnest, Christian man. He was connected with the Whitesides family, who owned Lookout Mountain and were prominent people of his portion of the State. To Mr. and Mrs. Dager have been born five children: Henry, a farmer; Maggie, the wife of George Miller, who is engaged in the butchering business; Charles, who is engaged in the raising of vegetables which he sells in the Philadelphia market; Albert and Anna, both at home. Mrs. Dager is a member of the Baptist church. Mr. Dager votes with the Democracy and exercises considerable influence in the party councils. He served as a school director at Baron Hill for three years, was justice of the peace for three years and has also been supervisor of his township. He has never been a politician, however, in the sense of office seeking, his official positions being bestowed upon him by his fellow townsmen, who recognized his worth and ability. He is a member of the Lutheran church at Baron Hill, and has led an upright, honorable life. He has reared three sons who have never used intoxicants. His entire career has been characterized by fidelity to duty and straightforward dealing with his followmen, and during his long residence in this part of Pennsylvania has become widely and favorably known.

THE ROBERTS FAMILY. Robert Roberts, the progenitor of that branch of the Roberts family resident in Southampton, Bucks county, Pennsylvania, whose birth is supposed to have occurred in Montgomery county, near Willow Grove, about the year 1797, died in 1876. His wife, whose maiden name was Hannah Tyson, bore him the following children: Tacy, Mary, who became the wife of Ed. C. Walton and two children were born to them: John and Seth. Jonathan, who married (first) Martha Walton, of Montgomery county, who bore him two children: Edwin and Hannah: married (second) Mary N. Lawrence, who was born in Philadelphia, Pennsylvania, June 20, 1832, daughter of

George and Mary (Boss) Lawrence, and granddaughter of William and Mary (Weaver) Lawrence. George Lawrence was born April 25, 1798, and his wife Mary was born April 25, 1798, which was a most unusual incident. Jonathan and Mary N. Lawrence were the parents of one child, Jonathan Lawrence, born April 27, 1871, died April 26, 1879. Edwin, born April 9, 1851, in Montgomery county; in 1863 he accompanied his parents to Davisville, Southampton township, Bucks county, where his education was continued in the common schools. He began his career as a farmer, which vocation he followed for several years, or until his marriage with Annie E. Search. He then moved to the city of Philadelphia, where he engaged in the produce commission business, but after a residence of eleven years there returned to Bucks county, locating at Southampton, where his death occurred in the spring of 1898. Two children were born to Mr. and Mrs. Roberts, namely: Harry, born March 14, 1877, died December 23, 1885; and Harold S., born January 22, 1889.

Annie E. (Search) Roberts, widow of Edwin Roberts, traces her ancestry to one of three brothers—Charles, William and Lot Search—who came to this country during the eighteenth century and settled respectively in New Jersey, Pennsylvania and New York. Christopher Search, probably a son of Charles Search, a descendant of one of the three brothers aforementioned, was married twice. His first wife bore him six children, as follows: Samuel, who married Catherine Puff; William, Sarah, John, Charles, and James. His second wife, whose maiden name was Ann Miles, bore him eight children, namely: Miles, who died in infancy; George, who married Martha Owens and their family consisted of two children: Elizabeth and Celina; Jacob, mentioned hereinafter; Margaret, who became the wife of Elias Lefferts and they reared a family of eleven children: Ellen, Anna George, Rachel, Neismuth, Samuel, Sarah Lizetta, Jacob, Laura and Mary; Christopher, who married Margaret Fetter and they reared a family of seven children: Cornelia George, Newton, Casper, Margaret, Kattie and Weedie; Anthony, who married Eliz ———, and he with two of his son served in the Civil War, the latter bein killed; Ann, who became the wife of Caspe Fetter and mother of five children: George Christopher, Anna, Anthony, and one wh died in infancy; Griffith, who married Louisa Fetter and their family consisted o the following named children: Amy, Ida Cora, Louisa, Mary and Alice.

Jacob M. Search, son of Christopher an Ann (Miles) Search, was born at South ampton, Bucks county, Pennsylvania, December 7, 1810, on the old homestead farm now occupied by John Finney. His activ career was devoted to farming pursuit Although always intensely interested i politics he never held any public office othe than that of school director. He purchase the old homestead farm of one hundred, acres from his father, and a large portion of the present village of Southampton was built on this land. He married Nancy Corson, daughter of Richard and Elizabeth (Bennett) Corson, and their children were: Elwood, born September 22, 1838; Theodore, born March 20, 1841, married Anna White and by her had one daughter, Ida May, who married George Howard Cliff and has one child, Anna S.; Harry, born September 18, 1846, married Mary M. Lefferts and two children were born to them: Susannah, wife of Maurice Hartman, and they have one child, Vernon; and Theodore, unmarried; Erasmus, born March 7, 1851, married Mary Ella Warren, and three children were born to them: Pauline, who became the wife of William Benny, and they have one child, Doris; Pauline Benny died in March, 1905; Leroy, and Ethel; Anna E., born March 13, 1858, aforementioned as having become the wife of Edwin Roberts.

JOHN DAVIS SELLS, of Hatboro, Pennsylvania, was born at Dublin, Ohio, May 4, 1857, and is a son of Dr. Holmes and Amy (Davis) Sells. His paternal ancestors were political refugees from the provinces along the Rhine and came to this country in the early part of the eighteenth century, settling in Virginia about 1750. His great-great-grandfather was John Sells, and in about 1780 his son, John Sells, Jr., moved out to the Scioto valley, in what was then called Virginia, and settled at a point about twelve miles from where the city of Columbus now stands, in the state of Ohio, county of Franklin. At this place his grandfather Charles, his father Holmes Sells and himself were born.

Dr. Holmes Sells was born at Dublin, Ohio, March 29, 1826, and finished his medical studies in Philadelphia at Jefferson College. He married, June 12, 1850, Amy Hart Davis, born June 24, 1827, daughter of John and Amy (Hart) Davis, and sister of General W. W. H. Davis, and began the practice of his profession at Dublin, Ohio, from which point he removed with his family to Atlanta, Georgia, in 1859, where he was proprietor of a large drug store and practiced medicine for many years. They were residents of Atlanta during its bombardment by General Sherman in the fall of 1864 and lived for six weeks in their cellar. Several shells struck the house and the kitchen was entirely demolished, the cooking stove being the only article of furniture uninjured. In the beginning of the siege a shell burst on the bed from which Mrs. Sells had recently risen, and the concussion threw her through a partially opened door into the yard. Dr. Sells was almost financially ruined by the destruction of his property during the war, and though entirely loyal to the Union he received no remuneration therefor. The family remained in Atlanta until the death of Dr.

Sells in 1888. Mrs. Sells now resides with her sister at the old Davis homestead at Davisville. Dr. Holmes and Amy H. (Davis) Sells were the parents of two children: Charles Watts, born May 15, 1851, died September 9, 1862; and John Davis, the subject of this sketch. Charles Watts Sells had an extraordinary talent for music, and though dying at the early age of eleven years was quite a noted performer on the piano.

John Davis Sells was reared in Atlanta, Georgia. He entered Lehigh University, class of 1876, and finished his education at the University of Georgia, graduating in the class of 1876. He came north to live in 1877, and while residing at Davisville took up the study of law in the office of Hon. Harman Yerkes, at Doylestown, and was admitted to the Bucks county bar in June, 1882. In the fall of the same year he removed to Pottsville, Schuylkill county, Pennsylvania, and being admitted to the bar of that county practiced law there for ten years. In 1893 he went to Washington to fill a governmental position under President Cleveland, which he retained for two years. In 1895 he removed to Philadelphia and engaged in the iron and steel business, becoming associated with the Royersford Foundry and Machine Company, Inc., manufacturers of power transmission machinery, in which he has an interest, and is manager of the "power department" with offices at 43 North Seventh street. Mr. Sells resides with his family at Hatboro, Montgomery county Pennsylvania. He is a member of the Pennsylvania Society Sons of Revolution, and the Historical Society of Pennsylvania, the Trans-Atlantic Society, and is affiliated with the Masonic fraternity. He married, June 6, 1889, Ella Lane Schofield, daughter of Samuel Lane Schofield, of Scotch Irish ancestry, one of the pioneer civil engineers in locating the original surveys of several of the early railroads of Pennsylvania. His early ancestors settled in Philadelphia about 1745. On the maternal side Mrs. Sells is a great-great-granddaughter of Michael Kauffman, one of the original settlers of Lancaster county. Mr. and Mrs. Sells have one daughter, Elizabeth Davis Sells, a graduate of Hatboro high school, who now attends St. Mary's Hall, Burlington, New Jersey.

GEORGE McKINSTRY, one of the younger generation of farmers of Buckingham township, is a native of Plumstead township, though his paternal ancestors for three generations had been residents of Buckingham. He is a son of Oliver and Louisa (Miller) McKinstry, of Plumstead, both deceased, the former of Scotch-Irish and the latter of German descent.

Nathan McKinstry, the great-great-grandfather of the subject of this sketch was born in the year 1712 and came to this country in the "Scotch-Irish Invasion," as Secretary Logan termed the great influx of Ulster Scots about 1735. Whether accompanied by his parents is not known. Certain it is that he was accompanied by a sister Elenor, who married Hugh Young in 1737, and possibly by a younger brother Samuel who settled in Plumstead in 1761. Hugh Young purchased a tract of 195 acres in Wrightstown township, and in June, 1744, conveyed ninety-seven and one-half acres thereof to his brother-in-law, Nathan McKinstry. Here Nathan McKinstry and his wife Mary lived until 1753, when he sold his Wrightstown farm and purchased a tract of 202 acres in Buckingham (now Doylestown) township, one mile southeast of Doylestown, where he spent his remaining days, dying April 15, 1790, at the age of seventy-eight years. His wife Mary survived him several years. They were members of Neshaminy Presbyterian church, of which he was a trustee, and both are buried there. Their children were: Jane, born 1745, died July 15, 1797, married James Kerr; John, died 1791; Samuel, born 1748, died January 24, 1796; Henry, born 1750, died November 28, 1804; William; and Robert, born 1756, died July 25, 1834, married Mary Wier, sister to the grandmother of General U. S. Grant.

Samuel McKinstry, second son of Nathan and Mary, born in Wrightstown in 1748, died January 24, 1796, on the old homestead in Buckingham, which had been adjudged to him in 1791. His wife Mary survived him twenty-two years, dying April 4, 1818, at the age of sixty-four years. Samuel McKinstry had lived for a time prior to his father's death in Hilltown township, but his later days were spent on the homestead, where his father had built him a house. The children of Samuel and Mary McKinstry were: Nathan; James, Jane and Jesse, among whom the Buckingham plantation was divided in 1813. Nathan took the present farm of Frank Heaton, where he died in 1852; James the farm now owned by Amos Worthington, and Jane and Jesse thirty-four acres of the present Doan farm. James conveyed his farm to Jane in 1819, and she at her death in 1822 devised it to her brothers Nathan and Jesse.

Jesse McKinstry, youngest son of Samuel and Mary, born 1790, was the grandfather of the subject of this sketch. He was married prior to 1814 to Rachel Pierce and resided on the old homestead in Doylestown until April 1, 1837, having purchased the interest of his brother Nathan in the lower farm in 1827. In 1837 he sold the farm and after residing for one year in New Britain purchased a farm on the Durham road in Upper Buckingham which he sold a year later and removed to Pulmstead, where he died November 7, 1851. He was a member of Doylestown Presbyterian church, to which he left a legacy of forty dollars. His wife Rachel died July 22, 1869, at the age of sixty-eight years. Their children were: Harri-

son, born March 5, 1814, died May 20, 1876; Sophia; Jane; Nathan; Mary; Oliver; Alfred; Ezra; and John W., the latter dying in 1851, aged seventeen years.

Oliver McKinstry, father of the subject of this sketch, was born in Doylestown township, in 1822, and died in Plumstead township, August 2, 1902. His wife Louisa Miller was born in New Britain township, in 1827, and died in 1895. Oliver McKinstry on his marriage settled on a farm purchased for him by his father in 1846, and conveyed to him in 1850, and spent his whole life thereon, the farm being now occupied by his son Harry. Oliver and Louisa McKinstry were the parents of five children, four of whom survive, Harry, residing on the homestead; Nannie, wife of Frank L. Gordon, of Seattle, Washington; Ida, of Plumstead; and George.

George McKinstry was born and reared on the Plumstead farm and acquired his education at the public schools of that township and the Doylestown high school. He married in 1883 Mary R. Paist, daughter of James Monroe and Elizabeth (Conrad) Paist, of Buckingham, and for three years conducted the Cowdrick farm near Carversville. In 1886 he moved to a farm in Buckingham, purchased for him by his father, which he conducted for sixteen years. In 1901 he purchased his present home, a farm of sixty acres in Landisville, and removed there in the spring of 1904. To Mr. and Mrs. McKinstry have been born five children: Ethel, Bernice P., Clara F., Grace I., and Frances G., all of whom reside at home.

AMOS S. BERINGER, one of the prominent and active business men of the little borough of Silverdale, was born in Hilltown near the location of the present borough on October 22, 1868, and is a son of Amos and Sophia (Sheip) Beringer, both of German origin and descendants of early settlers in that locality.

Nicholas Beringer, the pioneer paternal ancestor of Amos S., came to Pennsylvania from Germany in the ship "Neptune," John Mason master, arriving in Philadelphia, September 24, 1754. He probably followed the trend of German emigration into Bucks by way of the present county of Montgomery. The first authentic record we have of him is in the list of non-associators of Hilltown township in 1775. On June 29, 1777, he purchased 140 acres of land in Hilltown of John Penn, the deed for which is still in the possession of the subject of this sketch as well as a large portion of the land therein represented. Nicholas Beringer died on the Hilltown plantation about October 1, 1783, and his wife Elizabeth died in March, 1808. They were the parents of three sons, John, Henry, and George, and three daughters, Elizabeth, wife of George Cramer, a cabinet maker of Hilltown; Catharine, wife of Amos

Miner, of Marlboro, Montgomery county; and Mary, wife of John Benner of Hilltown.

John Beringer, the eldest son of Nicholas and Elizabeth, purchased the homestead farm of his brothers and sisters and lived thereon during the active years of his life. In 1820 he and his wife Elizabeth conveyed it to their sons Henry and George. John, the father, lived to an advanced age, dying in December, 1842, his wife having died some years earlier. Their children were: John, Henry, and George; Henry died before his father, leaving a family.

George Beringer, son of John and Elizabeth, was born on the old homestead in Hilltown and lived there all his life. He purchased ninety-nine acres of it of his father in 1820, and in 1858 conveyed it to his son Amos Beringer, reserving for himself and wife the "new dwelling and garden" for their use during the remainder of their lives. He died in December, 1864. He married Catharine Nunamaker, daughter of Adam Nunamaker, of Rockhill, and granddaughter of Henry Nunamaker, who had purchased a tract of land in Rockhill and Hilltown in 1782 which descended to his son Adam in 1807. Adam died in 1742, leaving several children, among whom was Catharine, wife of George Beringer. George and Catharine (Nunamaker) Beringer were the parents of two children, Amos and Mary.

Amos N. Beringer, only son of George and Catharine, was born on the old homestead May 29, 1824, and lived there all his life, dying December 4, 1885. He purchased the homestead of his parents, April 21, 1858, and later acquired two lots in the village, now borough, of Silverdale, now occupied by the subject of this sketch. He was for many years a member of the school board of Hilltown and active in local affairs. He was twice married, first to Barbara Anglemoyer by whom he had two children, Ephraim and Mary, neither of whom survived him. He married (second) Sophia Sheip, of an old New Britain family, who survived him. Amos and Sophia (Sheip) Beringer were the parents of two children, Amos S. and Ellen. The family were members of the Lutheran church.

Amos S. Beringer, born on the old homestead which had been the home of his ancestors nearly a century, was educated in the public schools. His father dying when he was sixteen years of age, he at once assumed the superintendence of the farm which he has continued ever since and has never lived anywhere else. In 1893 he began pork butchering in connection with the conduct of his farm, which he has since continued with success, enlarging his business from year to year and marketing the product in Philadelphia. He has always taken an active interest in local affairs and has served in the town council of Silverdale since its organization, this being his third term. He is a member of the South Perkasie Lutheran church. Mr. Beringer mar-

ried on October 29, 1887, at Quakertown, Sophia Hedrick, daughter of Oliver and Mary (Fretz) Hedrick, who was one of twelve children and was born September 1, 1868. Her paternal grandparents were Henry and Elizabeth (Heistand) Hedrick, the latter being a daughter of David Heistand, born January 24, 1788, died July 17, 1860, by his wife Susan Kephard, born January 15, 1785, died January 23, 1851, daughter of Rev. John and Elizabeth (Fretz) Kephard; and the former, born July 10, 1751, being for many years minister of the Mennonite congregation at Doylestown.

FREDERICK R. VOID is engaged in general agricultural pursuits on the farm on which his birth occurred in Hilltown township, Bucks county, April 15, 1856. His father, Frederick Void, Sr., was born in Germany, in 1831, and was a noted musician, being able to play any musical instrument. He was a wheelwright by trade and followed that pursuit for many years. In 1844 he purchased a farm in Hilltown township and continued its cultivation and improvement up to the time of his death, which occurred in 1876. He was a Democrat in his political affiliation, was a member of the Reformed church, and lived a useful and upright life. He married Magdaline Roth, a daughter of Abram and Mary (Cramer) Roth, and they had two children, Charles R. and Frederick R. The former married Diana Housekeeper, a daughter of Samuel Housekeeper, and they have three children, Samuel, Harvey and Erasmus.

Having mastered the common branches of learning in the public schools of Hilltown township, Frederick R. Void worked with his father on the home farm, gaining practical knowledge of the best methods of cultivating the fields and caring for the stock. When he was married he began farming for himself and in 1884 purchased a farm adjoining his father's land, while in 1877 he bought the old homestead farm. He carries on general agricultural pursuits, having placed his land under a high state of cultivation, while neatness and thrift characterizes the entire place. Mr. Void is a member of the Reformed church of Hilltown, and is interested in the substantial improvement of his locality, giving his co-operation to many movements for the general good. He was married in April, 1881, to Miss Mary Alice Cope, who was born January 10, 1861, a daughter of Charles and Elizabeth (Kile) Cope. Her father was born October 23, 1814. His first wife was Elizabeth Hackman, a daughter of John and Catharine Hackman. She was born June 4, 1811, and by her marriage became the mother of four children, namely: Catharine, born April 3, 1844; Andrew J., born November 5, 1837, died at the age of one year and ten months; Malinda, born

March 6, 1839, died January 28, 1859; and Sarah B., born July 23, 1841. The mother of these children died March 22, 1853. Mr. Cope afterward married Elizabeth Kile, by whom he had three children: Charles, born December 17, 1856; Annie E., born September 30, 1857, died May 18, 1858; and Mary Alice. To Mr. and Mrs. Void have been born thirteen children, as follows: Bertha C., born July 14, 1882, died August 23, 1894; Charles C., born January 17, 1884; Elsie C., born June 12, 1885; Mable C., born October 9, 1887, died December 23, 1887; Edith C., born October 3, 1888; Wellington C., born December 8, 1889; Agnes C., born December 6, 1890; Della C., born August 1, 1893, died May 25, 1894; Harry C., born June 24, 1895; Edna C., born January 23, 1897, died September 14, 1897; Florence C., born December 7, 1898; Helen C., born October 19, 1903; and one that died in infancy.

DR. WILLIAM RIDGE COOPER, of Point Pleasant, Bucks county, Pennsylvania, was born at Point Pleasant, August 26, 1862, and is a son of the late Dr. Alfred M. and Elizabeth (Ridge) Cooper.

The great-great-grandfather of Dr. Alfred M. Cooper was a native of Stratford-on-Avon, England. William Cooper, the great-grandfather, settled in Tinicum township and his son, James Cooper, was born and reared there. William B. Cooper, son of James, was born in Tinicum, December 24, 1807, and came of English Quaker ancestry. He became an extensive land-owner in Tinicum township and died there December 12, 1854. He married Elizabeth Meyer, born May 9, 1807, died December 4, 1871, daughter of John Meyer, who was born June 23, 1773, and died September 9, 1823, by his wife Eve Fry, and granddaughter of Henry Meyer, who was born in Montgomery county, in 1750, married Susan Smith, and settled in Plumstead township, Bucks county. Henry Meyer, the father of the last named Henry, was a son of Hans Meyer and came to America with his parents at the age of one year about 1720. He inherited the homestead of his father, Hans Meyer, in Upper Salford, Montgomery county, and died there about 1800. His wife, Barbara Miller, came from Germany at the age of eighteen years, in 1738, and was a niece of Anna (Miller) Leisse, who married Jacob Stout, the pioneer ancestor of the Stout family in Bucks county. John Meyer, above mentioned, and his brother Henry followed teaming between Philadelphia and Pittsburg when much of the intervening country was a wilderness. On one of their trips John was taken sick and died and his brother Henry buried him in the wilderness. William B. and Elizabeth (Meyer) Cooper were the parents of eleven children: Lavina, born July 15, 1826, died December 24, 1893, married John H. Watson; Rebecca, who died young; Dr. Alfred

M.; Clara, living in Philadelphia unmarried; Rachel and Jane, who died young; Eve, who died in January, 1899; James B. born August 11, 1842, killed at a barn raising in Tinicum, October 5, 1875; Caroline, born January 14, 1845, married Eli Sigafoos, of Easton; Newton R., born August 26, 1848, died June 14, 1865; and Justus, born July 28, 1851.

Dr. Alfred M. Cooper, eldest son of William B. and Elizabeth (Meyer) Cooper, was born in Tinicum township, Bucks county, September 15, 1830, and was reared on a farm to the age of nineteen years. He received a good common school education and taught school for five years. At the age of twenty-three years he began the study of medicine and graduated at Jefferson Medical College, March 10, 1856. He located at Point Pleasant and began practice the same year, and was considered one of the leading physicians of Middle Bucks, being highly respected in the community for his many excellent qualities. He practiced at Point Pleasant until his death, September 15, 1898, after a continuous practice there for forty-two years. He was a member of the State Medical Society, the Bucks County Medical Society, the Lehigh Valley Medical Society, and the Hunterdon County (N. J.) Medical Society. He married, March 21, 1861, Elizabeth Ridge, daughter of William and Catharine (Wyker) Ridge, of Point Pleasant, and a descendant of Edward Marshall, the Walker of 1737. Dr. and Mrs. Cooper were members of the Baptist church of Point Pleasant, of which the former served as deacon and elder for many years. He also took an active interest in educational matters and served several years as school director. Dr. and Elizabeth (Ridge) Cooper were the parents of three children: Dr. William R., the subject of this sketch; J. Howard Cooper, M. D., now practicing medicine at Middle Bush, New Jersey; and Katherine E. C., wife of William S. Acuff, a lawyer of Ambler, Pennsylvania.

William R. Cooper was reared at Point Pleasant and attended public school there and later the First Pennsylvania State Normal school at Millersville, Pennsylvania. He studied medicine with his father for two years and then entered Jefferson Medical College, from which he was graduated April 2, 1885, and began to practice the same year as an assistant to his father. Five years later he established an office of his own. On the death of his father he removed to the old homestead, in the spring of 1899, where he has since resided and continued the practice of his profession, retaining practically all the practice of his honored father. He is a member of the American Medical Association, the State Medical Society, the Bucks County Medical Society, and the Lehigh Valley Medical Association. He is a member of the Point Pleasant Baptist church, of which he is a trustee. Dr. Cooper married, March 20, 1890, Mary Smith Shaddinger, daughter of

Andrew and Martha (Smith) Shaddinger, of Point Pleasant, and they are the parents of two children, Lloyd Napier, and Dorothy S.

WILLIAM H. MURRAY, one, if not the oldest resident of New Hope, Pennsylvania, at the time of his death, was born in the city of Philadelphia, Pennsylvania, January 31, 1817, and died in New Hope, Pennsylvania, November 23, 1904, after an almost continuous residence of nearly eighty-eight years. He was one of thirteen children born to Joseph D. and Margaret M. (Sharp) Murray, four of whom still survive. Thomas S., a resident of Trenton, New Jersey; Frances, wife of James E. Darrow, Trenton, New Jersey; Anna, widow of Charles E. Aaron, of Norristown, Pennsylvania; and J. Howard Murray, of Trenton, New Jersey. Joseph D. Murray (father) was born in Edenton, North Carolina, November 7, 1788. His grandfather emigrated from Scotland with a colony that settled on the Roanoke river, naming the settlement Scotland Neck. His parents settled in Edenton. His mother dying in his infancy, he was left an orphan at the age of seven years by the death of his father, and came under the care of his uncle Henry. After his uncle's death, and at the age of eighteen years he came to Philadelphia, engaging in the dry goods business. In the spring of 1817 when his son William was but two weeks old he removed to New Hope, Pennsylvania, where he engaged in general merchandising. He purchased the house in which his son so long resided (a portion of the residence being built later), and in two rooms of this house conducted a successful business. After engaging several years in mercantile pursuits he disposed of the same, and then turned his attention to the lumber business, from which he derived a goodly income.

At the age of fifteen years, after completing a common school education with two years at a private school at Burlington, New Jersey, William H. Murray accepted a position in an engineer corps engaged in laying out and building the Beaver Meadow Railroad above Mauch Chunk, Pennsylvania, with Ario Pardee at head of corps. His compensation at first was $14 per month, which was later advanced until it reached $4 per day, and at finishing of road was made superintendent of same at nineteen years of age. Subsequently he engaged in the lumber business with his father In 1838 and '39 he was in the silk business, hatching out the eggs and carrying it on in its different branches to the finished product. This was considered at the time as a business with a bright future. In 1840 Mr. Murray engaged in mercantile pursuits, but at the expira-

tion of six years he disposed of same to his brother Thomas. In 1848 he joined in partnership with A. J. Beaumont and Samuel Sutton in the plow business, continuing until 1852. In 1853 and '54 he was engaged with his brother Thomas in building a portion of the Flemington railroad. In 1858 and '59 he was in the soap and candle business bought of Charles B. Knowles. In April, 1859, he again became interested in the agricultural implement business, and for the next ten years manufactured the same. When the civil war broke out Mr. Murray told his employees to offer their services to their country if they so wished and he would take care of their families as far as he was able. He called upon the burgess and prominent citizens in order to secure funds to raise a company, was successful therein and he assisted in putting in the crops for the men who went to the front. In 1871 he was engaged in the lumber business with his brother-in-law, James E. Darrow, Trenton, New Jersey, for four years. In 1877 he engaged in the grocery business, continuing until 1896 when he retired from active pursuits and lived a retired life. He was a consistent member of the Baptist church for many years, and an earnest advocate of Republican principles.

CHARLES EDWARD DURNER, a prominent factor in commercial circles in Bucks county, Pennsylvania, was born on Front street, Quakertown, the son of Charles Frederick and Mary Jane (Speaker) Durner, and belongs to a family distinguished for five generations as organ builders. Charles Edward Durner is descended from Conrad Durner and his wife, Rosina Gauibier, of Wurtemberg, Germany. Their son, Christian Durner, (grandfather of Charles Edward Durner) was born 1810, and died 1879. He followed the trade of organ building, as did his ancestors, and emigrated to America, settling in Zion Hill. He married Catherine Goll and had a son, Charles Frederick.

Charles Frederick Durner, father of Charles E. Durner, was the son of Christian and Catherine (Goll) Durner, and was born April 3, 1838, in Wurtemberg, Germany. He attended the state schools until he was fourteen years of age, when he commenced a term of apprenticeship to learn the trade of organ-building, serving five years. He then went to Lyons and Grenoble, France, at these places working as journeyman and tradesman for about five months. The experience thus gained proved of no little value to him in later years. In 1859 he emigrated to this country, settling at Zion's Hill. Here he entered into business for himself, but met with opposition at first, owing to the fact that the trade of organ-builder was not a popular one with the people of this country at that time, who considered that time wasted that was spent in "producing sounds" from an instrument. However, Mr. Durner persevered in his work and has been attended with great success, as is demonstrated by the large and well-equipped factory in Quakertown, to which place he removed his business in 1861. The first organ Mr. Durner built was valued at seven hundred and fifty dollars, the building of which occupied Mr. Durner for nearly a year, the compensation he received being the munificent sum of about fifty cents per day. His means being limited, he began with foot-power, which was superceded by steam as his business developed, and he is now at the head of one of the largest and most completely equipped organ factories in Pennsylvania. In 1876 he built an organ for the Centennial exposition at Philadelphia, which won for him the highest honors. Though small in size, (compared with many others on exhibition) it was considered in volume and sweetness of tone and perfection of mechanism superior to many other organs on exhibition, the production of more pretentious establishments. His instruments also received the first premium at the State fair in 1878. Mr. Durner's business has extended over the greater part of eastern Pennsylvania, and his handiwork is highly appreciated wherever seen. Mr. Durner's political affiliations are with the Democratic party, and while he takes much interest in local affairs, he has little to do with politics, beyond the influence of his opinion as expressed in his vote. He is a member of St. John's Lutheran church, and is especially interested in religious work, and was a trustee for many years.

In 1862 Mr. Durner was united in marriage to Miss Mary Jane Speaker, daughter of William and Lydia (Poorman) Speaker, of Center county, Pennsylvania. Immediately after his marriage Mr. Durner and his wife removed to Quakertown, settling in the house where they now reside. The following named children were born to them: Charles Edward, September 1, 1863, spoken of at length hereinafter; 2. Anna Elizabeth, born January 5, 1866, married Calvin F. Heckler, lawyer, son of John and Victoria (Fluck) Heckler, farmers of Hilltown township, Bucks county, Pennsylvania. 3. Mary Katherine, unmarried, and lives at home. Mrs. Durner died January 5, 1893, in the seventy-first year of her age.

CHARLES EDWARD DURNER, eldest child of Charles Frederick and Mary Jane (Speaker) Durner, attended the common schools of his native place until his sixteenth year. He then devoted himself to learning the trade of organ-building with his father, with whom he is still engaged at the organ factory in Quakertown, on the corner of Front and Juniper streets, one of the largest and most prosperous of its kind in that section of the country. Mr. Durner and his father have worked themselves up to a very high place in the world of business, and theirs is an example of what perseverance, indomitable will and unfailing energy can accomplish in the way of assisting men to attain the highest success. In political affairs, Mr. Charles E. Durner helps support the Democratic party, and although he never aspired to public office, takes a lively interest in the welfare of that organization. He is a member of St. John's Lutheran church, in the affairs of which he has always taken an active part. He was a member of the church council for fourteen years, and for a period of thirteen years was secretary of that body.

June 17, 1889, Charles Edward Durner was united in marriage to Miss Emma Jane Fluck, daughter of William Benjamin and Catherine (Hager) Fluck, of Quakertown. She is a descendant of an old German family who emigrated to this country under Richard and Thomas Penn, settling in Bucks county, Pennsylvania. After their marriage, Mr. and Mrs. Durner settled in Juniper and Third streets, in a house that they had had erected previous to their marriage. The following named children were born to them: Harold Frederick, born October 25, 1890, lives at home and attends the Quakertown schools; and Laura Catherine, born March 22, 1893, also lives at home, attending school in Quakertown.

CALVIN F. HECKLER. The early ancestors of Calvin F. Heckler, both direct and collateral, settled in the southeastern counties of Pennsylvania more than one hundred and fifty years ago. Mr. Heckler is a descendant of George Heckler, a Redemptioner, who arrived in Philadelphia on the ship "Neptune," September 30, 1754. He was purchased by John Steiner of North Coventry township, Chester county, near Pottstown. George Heckler was the son of Michael Heckler, and was born in 1736 in the province of Lower Alsace, on the Rhine. He was obliged to work on a farm for three years in order to redeem his passage, and afterwards married Christiana Freed, daughter of Peter Freed, of Lower Salford township, Montgomery county. He died August 28, 1816, aged eighty years, and by his thrift and industry had acquired considerable property. At the beginning of the American Revolution George Heckler bought a two hundred acre farm on or near the site of the Mennonite meeting house at Blooming Glen, in Hilltown township, Bucks county. He rendered assistance to the patriots when the Continental army was in and around Philadelphia. In 1774, according to a tax duplicate record, he was rated among the list of taxables of Hilltown township. The European branch of the family fought alternately for and against Napoleon, according to the fate of the Alsace and Loraine provinces as determined by the fortunes of the Napoleonic wars.

Samuel (Detweiler) Heckler, grandson of George Heckler mentioned above, whose father's name was also George, was born in Lower Salford township, Montgomery county, in 1803. After his marriage he settled in New Britain township, near the village of Greer's Corner, where he resided for six years. He then purchased a farm of about one hundred and twenty acres in the western part of Hilltown township, where he resided until his death, which occurred in the spring of 1884, at the age of eighty-one years. He was a lifelong farmer, disposing of his produce in the Philadelphia markets. He was very successful, reared a family of twelve children, and accumulated considerable property. In religious belief he was a liberal Mennonite, and belonged to the church of that sect at Line Lexington, Bucks county, Pennsylvania. In politics he was affiliated with the Whigs, and later with the Republicans. He married, in 1825, Anna Rosenberger, of the vicinity of Norristown, Montgomery county. Their children were as follows:

1. Anna Eliza, unmarried, died at the age of twenty-two years.

2. George, unmarried, died in 1859, at the age of twenty-nine years.

3. Elias, married Rebecca Gerhart, of Hilltown township, and died in 1900.

4. Hester Ann, deceased, became the wife of George W. Magargal, of Elkins Park, Montgomery county.

5. David R., married Amanda Kimbel, of Buckingham township, in 1862, and is now a prosperous farmer in West Bedminster township, Bucks county.

6. Jacob R., married Lydia Baringer, of Hilltown township, and is now a retired resident of Perkasie, Pennsylvania.

7. Aaron R., married Sophia Rosenberger, of Hatfield, Pennsylvania, and is one of the substantial farmers of that township.

8. Samuel, died in infancy.

9. John R., mentioned at length hereafter.

10. Samuel R., having served throughout the great civil war as a volunteer, married Rebecca Kimbel, of Buckingham, and is now a retired farmer living near Lansdale, Pennsylvania.

11. Amanda, the widow of Charles Massinger, deceased, of Chalfont.

12. Franklin R., deceased, married Margaret, daughter of Christian Moyer, of Hilltown.

John R. Heckler, son of Samuel Detweiler and Anna (Rosenberger) Heckler, was born November 3, 1840, on the homestead in Hilltown township. His boyhood was passed in rendering assistance on the farm, and at the same time attending the subscription and free schools. He taught a public school in Monroe county, Pennsylvania, and afterwards at Fluck's school house, in Hilltown township for two years. He was for some years afterward a tenant-farmer, but in 1885 purchased one of his father's farms, where he lived until 1892, when he moved to Perkasie, Pennsylvania. John R. Heckler married, in 1861, Victoria S. (Stout), daughter of Tobias and Anna (Stout) Fluck of Hilltown and the following children were born to them:

1. Calvin F. (christened Samuel Calvin), mentioned at length hereafter.

2. Allen Henry, born August 26, 1866, married in 1891 to Elizabeth, daughter of John D. Hunsberger, of Souderton, one child, Sallie Lorene, being born in 1892. Mrs. Heckler's death occurred shortly afterwards. Mr. Heckler married again, in 1894, Kate Abele, of the city of Philadelphia, where he now resides. Since 1888 he has been a foreman of carpenters in the service of the Philadelphia and Reading Railroad Company. Their children are: Calvin F., Jr., deceased; Henry Frederick, and Ernest Abele.

Nari Franklin, the third son of John R. Heckler, was born February 4, 1873, in Hilltown, Bucks county, Pennsylvania, and attended the common schools and the Sellersville high school. In July, 1888, he became a telegraphic student with the Philadelphia and Reading Railroad Company at Souderton, Pennsylvania, and afterwards served as a telegraph operator of the Philadelphia and New York divisions until October 24, 1895, when he resigned to enter the service of the American Printing Company, of New York City. On March 30, 1896, he was employed by the Union League of Philadelphia, as a stenographer, and was gradually promoted until he was appointed superintendent of that famous organization on March 20, 1900, which position he still retains. He is an active member of the Baptist church, and was married to Alberta Lorene, daughter of John G. Fritz, of Lafayette, Montgomery county, and has one child, John Franklin, who was born July 12, 1896.

Calvin F. Heckler, son of John R., and Victoria Stout (Fluck) Heckler, was born on the Heckler homestead in Hilltown township, Bucks county, June 12, 1864. He received his preliminary education in the common schools of the township, afterward attending the Sellersville high school and also the normal school at Millersville, Pennsylvania. He worked on the farm during the summer, taught school during the winter in Hilltown and Bedminster townships, saved his money, and worked his way through the University of Pennsylvania, graduating with high honors in the law department of that institution in 1887. He registered as a law student with Hon. Henry M. Hoyt, former governor of Pennsylvania, with whom he served three years, and on whose motion he was admitted to practice in all the county courts. He was afterward admitted to the Pennsylvania supreme court and the United States courts. He further supplemented his legal attainments by afterwards associating himself with the law firm of Arundel & Moon (Congressman Reuben O. Moon of Philadelphia) until he took offices for himself in the Pennsylvania Building at Fifteenth and Chestnut streets, Philadelphia, where he is favored with a large clientage. He has held various positions of trust, and since February, 1904, is serving as a member of the borough council. His political support is always freely given to the Republican party, and he has actively participated in every state and national campaign since 1884. Mr. Heckler has traveled extensively in the United States and many of the provinces of Canada. He is a member of the German Reformed church, to which his parents also belong. Mr. Heckler is past master, by merit, of the Quakertown Lodge, No. 512, F. and A. M., and member of the Philadelphia Sovereign Consistory, S. P. R. S. 32d degree. He also belongs to numerous other fraternal organizations. Mr. Heckler married, 1892, Anna Elizabeth Durner, who for ten years prior was a successful teacher in the public schools of Quakertown. She is an active member of the Lutheran church and other auxiliary organizations, and is devoted to all the interests and duties of her home and family. Mrs. Heckler belongs to a family distinguished for five generations as church-organ builders. She is a daughter of Charles F. and Mary J. (Speaker) Durner, of Quakertown, Pennsylvania.

MILTON ALTHOUSE BIEHN, of West Chester, Pennsylvania, was born June 10, 1851, at Bunker Hill, now Rich Hill, in Rockhill township, Bucks county, Pennsylvania, a son of Michael Martin and Catharine (Althouse) Biehn, and grandson of Abram and Mary (Martin) Biehn.

Michael Martin Biehn (father) was born in Rockhill township, Bucks county, Pennsylvania, October 3, 1810. His ancestors were among the German emigrants who came to this country under Thomas and Richard Penn and took up a considerable tract of land. They followed farming and the weaving of cloth

and carpets. On June 10, 1838, Mr. Biehn married Catharine Althouse, daughter of Daniel and Elizabeth (Wert) Althouse, of Richland township, farmers, and settled at Bunker Hill. Their children are: Maria, born April 13, 1840, married, September 10, 1859, Tobias Hinkle, of Bunker, or Rich Hill, a full account of whom appears in the sketch of Harry Hinkle; Elizabeth, born March 8, 1847, resides with her sister, Mrs. Maria Hinkle, at Quakertown; and Milton Althouse, mentioned hereinafter.

Milton Althouse Biehn attended the Rock Ridge public school until his fourteenth year, after which he was apprenticed to learn the boot and shoe making with his brother-in-law, Tobias Hinkle, with whom he continued as journeyman or tradesman for several years thereafter. In 1871 he moved to Quakertown, Pennsylvania, in company with Tobias Hinkle, in whose service he continued there and finally formed a copartnership with him in a boot and shoe store on Front street. In 1874 Mr. Biehn erected the storehouse now occupied by Harry Wilson Hinkle, son of Tobias Hinkle, and conducted business under the title of Hinkle & Biehn, this connection continuing until the retirement of Tobias Hinkle on account of failing health, when he was succeeded by his sons Harry W. and Nelson B. Hinkle, and this partnership was continued until 1892. In 1893 Mr. Biehn moved to West Chester, Chester county, and established a boot and shoe store in that town. Mr. Biehn has been remarkably successful in his business ventures, which is owing largely to his close study of trade conditions and the needs of his customers. His store is located at No. 33 West Gay street, this being the first one he established, but in 1904 he established another at the corner of Gay and Church streets, which is managed by his son, Harry Biehn. Mr. Biehn and his family are members of the West Chester Methodist Episcopal church, in the affairs of which Mr. Biehn is much interested, serving as class leader, and for nine years assistant superintendent of the Sunday school connected therewith. He is a trustee of the Young Men's Christian Association of West Chester, in which position his services are highly appreciated. He was formerly an adherent of the Republican party, but differing from them on several issues, particularly the liquor question, he thought best to cast his vote with the party whose principles were more closely allied with his own, the Prohibition party. On December 11, 1877, Mr. Biehn was married to Sarah Edwards, daughter of Benjamin Roberts and Lydia (Bartholomew) Edwards, of Quakertown, a family descended from the early and substantial settlers of Bucks county. The issue of this marriage was: 1. Nellie E., born September

18, 1878, attended the Quakertown pub-, lic schools, the West Chester high school, from which she was graduated in the class of 1896; Philadelphia Collegiate Institute, from which she was graduated in the class of 1897; and the Woman's College, at Baltimore, Maryland, from which she was graduated in the class of 1901. She is now (1905) a teacher in the department of mathematics at the West Chester high school; she resides at home. 2. Harry E., born May 24, 1880, attended the Quakertown public schools, West Chester public schools, Williamson Trade school, Delaware county, and State Normal school, at West Chester. He entered his father's boot and shoe store, and is now manager of the new store established by his father in the fall of 1904 at West Chester. 3. Grace E., born October 14, 1886, died July 1, 1887.

Mrs. Biehn traces her ancestry to Hugh Edwards, of Wales, who migrated to this country under William Penn and settled first in the southern part of Bucks county, Pennsylvania. He resided for a time in the vicinity of Penlyn, Gwynedd township, now in Montgomery county. He was a man of considerable force of character, was a member of the Society of Friends and devoted considerable time to preaching. During the early part of the eighteenth century he settled in that part of Bucks county now occupied by Milford and Richland townships. William Edwards, son of Hugh Edwards, married Martha ———, and among their children was a son, William Edwards, born May 13, 1746, near Trumbauersville, Milford township, Bucks county; he was a farmer by occupation. He married Maribah Gaskill, daughter of Samuel and Margaret Gaskill and had issue: Margaret and Amos. Amos Edwards was born in Richland township, April 10, 1786, married Abigail Roberts, daughter of Abel and Margaret Roberts, and their children were: Eveline, born May 18, 1821, married Milton Johnson, a farmer, of Richland township; and Benjamin R., born January 1, 1824. Benjamin R. Edwards, father of Mrs. Biehn, was born as above stated in Richland township on a farm containing forty acres then owned and operated by his parents. He attended the subscription schools of his township, also the school attached to Richland Monthly Meeting of the Society of Friends, and among the teachers at the latter school were John Ball and Hannah Foulke, prominent educators of that day and place. Leaving school at the age of nineteen years, he for a time conducted a subscription school of his own and also assisted on the home farm. At the age of twenty-five years, he went to Milford township and there learned the milling trade with Daniel Heist, who conducted a grist mill

at Swamp creek. Settling at Milford Square, he conducted for a time a mill for grinding feeds, but in 1856 disposed of his business and moved to Quakertown where he conducted a flour and feed store until 1899, in which year he retired from active business. He is a birthright member of Richland Monthly Meeting of Friends, of Quakertown, and in politics is a Republican, taking an active interest in the success of that party. On November 13, 1853, Mr. Edwards married Lydia Bartholomew, daughter of Henry and Ann (Bleam) Bartholomew, farmers of Milford township. Their children are: Ellen R., born July 19, 1856, became the wife of George T. Hersh, of Allentown. Henry, born February 13, 1858, married Hermina Brown, of Rockhill township, and they reside in Quakertown. Sarah Roberts, born May 20, 1860, became the wife of Milton A. Biehn, as afore mentioned. Amos, born March 27, 1870, is unmarried and resides at home.

JOHN B. HERITAGE. The Heritage family is of English ancestry and was founded in America by two brothers, one of whom settled in New Jersey and the other in Bustleton, Philadelphia, Pennsylvania being among the first settlers in that village. John F. Heritage, grandfather of John B. Heritage, was born in Bustleton, Philadelphia. He served his country in the war of 1812 and in his home community was regarded as a representative citizen. He was a tailor by trade, and while carrying on that business for many years also conducted agricultural pursuits. In politics he was a Democrat. He married Ann Fetters, a native of Montgomery county, and their children were: John F.; Joseph; George; Samuel, who died at the age of thirty years; Sarah, the wife of D. Test; and two daughters who died in early womanhood.

John F. Heritage, Jr., son of John F. and Ann (Fetters) Heritage, was born in Philadelphia county, and in his youth learned the trade of tailor under the direction of his father, whom he also assisted in the operation of the home farm up to the time of his marriage, when he settled upon another farm and in connection with its cultivation worked at his trade. He thus carried forward the business that his father had inaugurated, but upon a more extensive scale. Interested in military affairs, he became a captain of a militia company which was called to active duty in Philadelphia at the time of the riots there. In politics he was a Democrat. Purchasing his father's homestead at Bustleton he therein spent the evening of life, dying at the ripe old age of seventy-five years. He was a man of good physique, large and well proportioned, of a social nature, enjoying the companionship of his friends, while to the poor and needy he was charitable and benevolent. His integrity and honor were above reproach, and he was a consistent and worthy member of the Pennypack church for thirty or forty years, regularly attending its services and contributing liberally to its support. His wife died about five or six years prior to his demise. She bore the maiden name of Ann Benner and was a daughter of John Benner, who died during her early girlhood, leaving two daughters, the sister of Mrs. Heritage being Mrs. Hannah Campbell. Her maternal grandfather was Joseph Durman, who was a captain of a company in the war of the revolution, defending the cause of the colonies. When at home on a furlough he was taken from his bed by the English and sent to an English prison, but later was exchanged and rejoined the American forces, continuing to serve with the continental troops until independence was achieved. Following the establishment of the republic he settled in Philadelphia county, where he followed farming and spent his remaining days. His farm remained in possession of the family for many years. Seven children were born of the marriage of John F. Heritage and Ann Benner as follows: Anna, wife of George Brooks; Joseph, a carriage and coach manufacturer; Samuel, who is connected with his brother Joseph in business; John B.; George, a farmer; Mary A., who died unmarried; and Emma C., who died at the age of thirty-five years.

John B. Heritage was born near Bustleton in Philadelphia county, Pennsylvania, July 23, 1835. In the public schools he acquired his education, while upon the home farm he was reared, early becoming familiar with the duties and labors that fall to the lot of the agriculturist. Thinking that he would find an industrial pursuit more congenial he learned the carriage painting trade, which he followed for a number of years, but his health prevented his continuance in that line of activity and he returned to agricultural life about three years after his marriage. He rented a farm and was engaged in its cultivation when he was drafted for service in the rebellion, but he hired a substitute and continued his farming operations in Montgomery county. In 1866 he purchased the farm in Bucks county upon which he now resides, its former owner having been Morris Jarrett. Here he carries on general agricultural pursuits, and also attends the city market. His business affairs are capably managed and are bringing to him a good financial return. He has never aspired to public office, yet his fellow townsmen elected him to the position of supervisor. In politics he is a Democrat. In 1860 Mr. Heritage married Miss Mary L. Harris, who was born in Bustleton, January 13, 1836, and who has been to him a faithful and devoted wife. She is a daughter of Theophilus and Ellen (Merritt) Harris, the former a native of Virginia, and the latter of Bucks county. Her grandfather, Theophilus Harris, was of Welsh descent and was a leading divine of the Primitive Baptist church. On leaving Virginia he removed to Bustleton, Pennsylvania, where he engaged in church work and also farming. He was likewise connected with the cloth factory, and was prominent in local affairs in his community as well as in the church. His first wife bore the maiden name of Mary Long Harris and was of English descent. She died in Virginia, and after his removal to Pennsylvana he married a daughter of Dr. Jones, of a prominent Baptist family. By the first marriage there was one son, Theophilus Harris. By the second marriage the children were: Mrs. Sarah Griffith; Mrs. Martha Chilton; Mrs. Mary Bazier; and Mrs. Ann Willstack, whose husband was a wealthy resident of Philadelphia, and he and his wife donated millions of dollars to the city. To Mr. and Mrs. Heritage have been born four children: Charles E., a farmer; Mrs. Mary E. Schlotzhaur; John, a farmer; William C., who is operating the old homestead and who married Sallie Fenton, by whom he has one child, Hannah May. Both Mr. and Mrs. Heritage are members of the Baptist church.

Theophilus Harris, father of Mrs. Heritage, was a highly educated man who assisted his father in business, acting as bookkeeper in the factory and supervising other business enterprises. Later he engaged in farming, giving to the cultivation of the soil his entire attention, and in the evening of life retired from active business pursuits, his children conducting the farm. In politics he was a Democrat, and he supported the Baptist church, although he was not a member. His wife died in 1858, and his death occurred in 1865. Their children were: Mary L.; Theophilus, of Philadelphia; Mrs. Christiana Clayton, who died leaving three children; Thomas, of Philadelphia; and Ellen, wife of George W. Heritage.

PATRICK BREEN, who following the occupation of farming in Warwick township, has also been active and influential in political circles, was born in county Tipperary, Ireland, December 26, 1830, his parents being James and Mary (Hays) Breen, both of whom are natives of Ireland, where their marriage was celebrated. Mrs. Breen was of a distinguished family, one of her great uncles being a general in the English army. The paternal grandfather, John

Breen, was a resident of Ireland and spent his entire life there. His only child was James Breen, who following his marriage settled upon a farm in Ireland, and all of his children were born in that country. In 1849 he emigrated to America, and the following year was joined by his family. He went first to New Jersey, but soon afterward removed to Bucks county, Pennsylvania, and located in Northampton township. He was there employed as a laborer and did some contracting on the turnpike. Later he purchased a small farm in Wrightstown township, and subsequently sold that property and bought a tract of land in Northampton township. His wife died in Northampton township in 1858, and he afterward married again. In his old age he and his second wife made their home with his son, Patrick, and he here died in 1881. He was a stanch Democrat in his political views, but never an aspirant for office. Both he and the mother of Patrick Breen were Catholics in religious faith. They had five children: Patrick; Johanna, who since 1861 has been in the convent known as Mount Hope Retreat near Baltimore, Maryland; Margaret, the wife of Patrick McNanaman; William, a prominent farmer, who died at Spring House; and Elizabeth, who became the wife of A. Colligan, of Jersey City, New Jersey, but both have passed away.

Patrick Breen pursued his education in subscription schools of his native land, and when nineteen years of age crossed the Atlantic to the new world. For four years he was employed as a laborer, and then rented a farm, remaining thereon for two years after his marriage, when in 1856 he purchased the farm upon which he now resides known as the Thomas Helm farm. It was then but partly improved, but he has erected a large commodious frame residence, a substantial barn and other necessary outbuildings for the shelter of grain and stock and has added all of the modern equipments, keeping his place in an excellent state of cultivation. He follows general farming and markets his products at Philadelphia. He also raises some stock, keeping a herd of good cows and selling the milk at the creamery. He has always been a practical and successful farmer, and is a stockholder in the Creamery Company.

In January, 1853, Mr. Breen was united in marriage to Miss Catherine Maher, who was born in Ireland, a daughter of Mr. and Mrs. Thomas Maher, who spent their entire lives in that country. Mrs. Breen was reared by an aunt, as was her brother, Timothy Maher, who came with her to America and who was later known as a leading agriculturist of his community. He died and was buried in Doylestown. In the

family of Mr. and Mrs. Breen were nine children, of whom six died in childhood, including Lizzie, who passed away at the age of thirteen. The others are: William, who followed the butchering business; Thomas, who was a painter by trade and possessed considerable artistic skill; and James, a butcher. The last named is the only one now living. Mrs. Catherine Breen departed this life in July, 1879, in the faith of the Catholic church. On the 24th of November, 1881, Mr. Breen was married to Miss Annie Brahan, who was born in Ireland, July, 1846, a daughter of Michael and Mary Brahan, also natives of that country whence they came to America in 1849, settling in Bucks county. Her father was an industrious man and hard worker. He voted with the Democracy, and both he and his wife were of the Catholic faith. He died in 1903 at the age of eighty years, while his wife's death occurred in 1882, when she was seventy-five years of age. Their children were Annie; Kate, deceased; Maria, deceased, who was the wife of William J. Brennan; Bridget, deceased. Mr. and Mrs. Breen had one son, John, who was born January 15, 1892, and died April 14, 1892.

Mr. Breen gave his early political support to the Democracy, but at the opening of the rebellion, he became a champion of Republican principles. He is thoroughly informed on all questions pertaining to the history of the world. He has always taken an active interest in politics, has been judge of elections, and in 1892 was chosen to fill the position of clerk of quarter sessions in Bucks county, serving for three years in a manner creditable to himself and satisfactory to his constituents. In 1879 he was appointed by the legislature to the position of engineer for the capitol at Harrisburg, and acted in that capacity for two years. He has a wide and favorable acquaintance in the county in which he has lived from early manhood to the present.

O. JAMES JOHNSON, a well known resident of Haycock township, Bucks county, Pennsylvania, son of Charles and Esther (Strawn) Johnson, was born January 10, 1838, on the homestead farm now owned and occupied by his brother, H. Watson Johnson, in the northern part of Richland township, and which farm is part of the tract of land acquired by Casper Johnson (1), from Richard and Thomas Penn in the early part of the eighteenth century. Casper Johnson (2), son of Casper Johnson, the immigrant, was the father of Charles Johnson, who in turn was the father of O. James Johnson.

Charles Johnson (father) was born on the homestead farm. He attended the subscription schools of the neighborhood, and his active career was devoted to farming. He was one of the public-spirited and influential men of the community, and highly esteemed for his integrity and enterprise. He was an advocate of the principles of the Whig party, to which organization he gave his allegiance. He was united in marriage to Esther Strawn, daughter of Abel and Elizabeth Strawn, of Quakertown, and their children were: H. Watson, a sketch of whom appears elsewhere in this work; Mary Ann, wife of Aaron Walp, of Quakertown; Oliver James, mentioned hereinafter; and Anna Maria, wife of Louis N. Shelly, of Quakertown.

After attending the public schools of Richland township until his seventeenth year, O. James Johnson assisted at farming with his father until his marriage in the year 1867. Shortly afterward he settled on a farm near California station, in Richland township, where he remained for one year, after which he removed to the farm of his father-in-law, Abram Stover, at Tohickon, in Haycock township, where he remained until the spring of 1883, when he moved to where he now resides. This farm which contains eighty-seven acres of arable land, he purchased in 1882 from Charles McCarthy, and he greatly improved the same by erecting an entire new set of buildings which added greatly to its appearance. He conducted this as a dairy and general farm until 1900, when he retired from active work and was succeeded by his eldest son, Elmer Johnson, to whom he rented the farm and stock. Since that year Mr. Johnson has led the quiet life of a country gentleman, enjoying to the full the consciousness of a life well spent. He takes little interest in public affairs. He is a Republican in politics, and while he ardently believes in the principles of that party has taken only nominal interest in its work, and beyond serving two terms as a school director has never aspired to or held any other office of a political nature.

Mr. Johnson married January 19, 1867, Anna Maria Stover, daughter of Abram and Sarah (Fulmer) Stover, farmers, of Haycock township, Bucks county, Pennsylvania. Their children are as follows: Elmer, born April 16, 1868, married November 10, 1894, Emma Afflerbach, daughter of John and Abbie (Fulmer) Afflerbach, farmers of Haycock township. Mr. and Mrs. Elmer Johnson reside on a farm, and their children are: Abbie Laura, died in infancy; Anna Maria, and Clarence Wilmer. Mr. and Mrs. Johnson belong to the Reformed church at Kellers Church, Pennsylvania. Laura, born August 12, 1869, married, December 12, 1892, Stover Detweiler, son of John and Lavina Detweiler, of Haycock township; he is a miller by trade. and resides in East Rockhill township, near Thatcher Post Office, Pennsylvania, and their children are: Mabel, died in infancy; Laura Grace, Blanche, died in infancy; and Earl. Mr. and Mrs. Detweiler are members of Kellers Reformed church. Louis, born

May 9, 1871, married, February 19, 1896, Annie Frankenfield, daughter of Abel and Cathrine (Hager) Frankenfield, farmers of Haycock township. They reside at Haycock Run, where Mr. Johnson is engaged at farming; their children are: Elsie, James Freeman and Ruth. Mr. and Mrs. Johnson belong to the Lutheran church at Kellers Church, Pennsylvania. Harry, born November 12, 1872, died October 5, 1873. Minnie, born November 2, 1874, married February 20, 1897, Isaac Ruth, son of David and Mary (McElroy) Ruth, farmers of Springfield township. They reside at Pleasant Valley, Springfield township, where Mr. Ruth is engaged in farming. Mr. and Mrs. Ruth are both members of the Lutheran church of Springfield township, Pennsylvania. Their children are: Florence Pearl, and Harry Watson, died in infancy. Elmira, born October 31, 1876, married, November 28, 1898, Edwin Lewis, son of Jesse and Elizabeth (Lutz) Lewis, of Haycock township; they reside at Lansdale, Pennsylvania, where Mr. Lewis is engaged in the livery business. Mr. Lewis is a member of the Lutheran church at Kellers Church, Pennsylvania, and Mrs. Lewis is a member of the Reformed church of the same place. Their children are: Esther Elizabeth, Richard, died in infancy; Evelyn Myrtle, died in infancy; and Edith Margaret. Freeman, born April 3, 1880, unmarried, is employed on the home farm with his brother, Elmer Johnson. He also is a member of the Reformed church at Kellers Church. Warren, born October 16, 1881, unmarried, resides at Fairview, near Quakertown; he is a blacksmith by trade. Stover, born May 21, 1887, unmarried, resides on the homestead farm, and is a member of the Reformed church of Kellers Church.

JOEL M. MASON has spent his entire life in Falls township, his birth occurring within its borders on May 1 1850. Several generations of the family have been represented here. His paternal grandfather, Ernest Mason, lived and died in Bucks county and was identified with its agricultural interests. He married Hannah Hart and they had five children: Daniel; Joel; Edmond; Ruth, wife of Walter Collas; and Ernest, who was drowned when a child.

Joel Mason, son of Ernest Mason, was born in Falls township, in 1883. In early life he began farming and afterward in connection with the tilling of the soil took contracts to make excavations. In politics he is a stanch Democrat, active in the interest of the party and doing all in his power to promote its growth and insure its success, yet never seeking political preferment for himself. For some years he was the supervisor of the Delaware Navigation Company on its canal. He married Miss Anna Feir, of New Jersey, and they had five children

Rebecca, wife of Samuel Burk, of Montgomery county, Pennsylvania; Annie, who became the wife of Charles Schaffer and after his death married Jacob Painter; Joel M.; Matilda, wife of George Harry; and Edmond, of Morrisville, Pennsylvania.

Joel M. Mason, the elder son of Joel Mason, pursued his education in the Friends' school at Falsington and in the public schools at Morrisville, Pennsylvania. When he was about twenty-two years of age he began farming for himself in Lower Makefield, where he remained for two years. He then returned to the old homestead farm in Falls township, where he was born and continued its cultivation until 1886, when he removed to Morrisville. There he engaged in the stock business and also continued his farming operations, and he is now well known as a stockdealer of that town, making extensive purchases and shipments so that his annual sales reach a large figure. Mr. Mason has been prominent in public affairs, and is a stalwart advocate of the Democracy. He has been elected three times as a member of the council of Morrisville, and was street commissioner for one year. He was also appointed fish and game warden of Bucks county in 1899 for a term of three years, and the capable manner in which he has discharged his business duties has fully justified the confidence reposed in him by his fellow citizens. Mr. Mason married Miss Annie Crosslie, a daughter of Thomas and Elizabeth Crosslie. They are the parents of five children: Edmond, who is engaged in the ice business; Annie, the wife of Henry Ort; Joel, who deals in coal and lumber; Charles, who is connected with the Wright Publishing Company; and William, a motorman. After the death of his first wife, Mr. Mason wedded Mrs. Jennie T. Moorehouse, nee Tice, and there is one child by this marriage, Jennie L. Mason.

MARTIN H. SMITH, an esteemed and honored citizen of Dovlestown township, Bucks county, Pennsylvania, was born October 16, 1838, a son of John D. and Mary M. (Hevener) Smith, and grandson of George and Susanna (Deaterly) Smith. George Smith (grandfather) was a lifelong resident of Bucks county, where he followed farming and teaming, and, being a man of energy, industry and perseverance, achieved a fair degree of success. By his marriage to Susanna Deaterly, eleven children were born, as follows: Joseph; Mary, who became the wife of Philip Swartley; Sarah, who became the wife of Martin Loux; Henry; Catherine, who became the wife of Henry Treisbach; Elizabeth, who became the wife of John Fox; John D., mentioned hereinafter; Susanna, who be-

came the wife of Peter Frick; Nancy, who became the wife of Eli Ruth; George; and Lydia, who died in childhood. George Smith was buried in the Mennonite churchyard at Deep Run.

John D. Smith (father) was born in Plumstead township, Bucks county, September 29, 1812. In early life he learned the blacksmith trade, but after his marriage commenced farming, giving his entire attention to that pursuit until compelled to retire on account of infirmities due to old age. He was one of the first school directors of Bedminster township, his incumbency of the office being noted for integrity and efficiency. He was a member of the German Reformed church, and his political support was given to the Republican party. He married Mary M. Hevener, daughter of Abraham and Elizabeth Hevener, and their family consisted of nine children, one of whom died in infancy. The surviving members of the family are: Martin H., whose name heads this review, born October 16, 1838; Frances, born September 2? 1840, married Sarah Snyder, and their children are: Martha, Mary, Ellen, deceased; Amanda, wife of James High; Clara, wife of Jacob Beerley, and John. Mary Ann, born November 11, 1843, widow of Henry Kile. Ephraim and Oliver (twins), born September 25, 1845; Oliver married Mary Ann Myers, daughter of Christian B. and Sarah Landis Myers, and they are the parents of one child, Emily, wife of Isaac Long. Susanna, born June 19, 1850. George, born October 22, 1853, married and has two children: Catherine and George, Jr., Reed, born February 16, 1856, now deceased.

FRANCIS M. PHILLIPS, who was born in Warminster township, Bucks county, where he yet follows the occupation of farmer, is a son of Horace G. and Caroline (Matlack) Phillips, the former of Bucks county and the latter of Philadelphia county. The paternal grandfather, Horace Phillips, was a native of New Jersey and in early life settled in Bucks county, where he followed the occupation of farming. He also carried on shoemaking for some time, but subsequently devoted his undivided attention to agricultural pursuits. In politics he was a Democrat, but never aspired to office, and he belonged to the Presbyterian church. He died in Hartsville, Pennsylvania. In his family were the following named children: Hannah, the wife of B. T. Jamison; Caroline; David S., a business man of Philadelphia; and Horace G.

Horace G. Phillips, father of Francis M. Phillips, always followed the occupation of farming and at the time of his marriage rented a tract of land. Later he became owner of a farm and continued to engage in general agricultural pursuits and in marketing until his demise. He voted with the Democracy, served as school director and filled some minor township offices. In the Presbyterian church he held membership, served as one of its elders and took an active interests in its work. He married Caroline Matlack, a daughter of Francis E. and Mary (Titus) Matlack, the latter a native of Doylestown, Pennsylvania, while Mr. Matlack was born in Philadelphia and was a son of Abram and Elizabeth (Elliott) Matlack. Abram Matlack was a native of Petersburg, Pennsylvania, and when a young man removed to Philadelphia, where he followed the wheelwright's trade for a number of years. Subsequently he returned to Petersburg, where his remaining days were passed. Francis E. Matlack was born in Philadelphia and spent his entire life in this state. He pursued his education in his native city, and later engaged in the conduct of a boot and shoe factory for many years. In 1866 he retired from that business and purchased a farm in Warminster township, carrying on general agricultural pursuits until his demise, which occurred December 1, 1890. In politics he was a Whig and afterward a Republican, but he never aspired to public office. He was a consistent and worthy member of the Presbyterian church, contributed generously to its support, aided actively in its work and served as one of its trustees. He died December 1, 1890, while his wife passed away in 1881. She was the daughter of Joel and Hannah (Thompson) Titus, both natives of Bucks county, and descended from old colonial families. The children of Mr. and Mrs. Titus were: Joseph; John; Samuel; Elizabeth; Griffith; Susan, who became the wife of J. Manahon; Lucy A.; and Mary, the wife of F. Matlack. The children of Francis Matlack are: Mary E., and Caroline, the latter the wife of Horace G. Phillips. Following their marriage Mr. and Mrs. Horace G. Phillips resided upon a farm in Bucks county and here his death occurred January 28, 1904, while his wife passed away July 25, 1902. They were the parents of seven children: Francis M.; Emily, the wife of H. Haldeman; Mary, the wife of C. Sprogell; Elizabeth, the wife of W. McDaniel; Rachel, the wife of H. Barton, an architect in the employ of the government at Washington, D. C.; Caroline, the wife of W. Vanartsdalen; and Ella G.

Francis M. Phillips was born and reared in Warminster township, early becoming familiar with agricultural pursuits and throughout his entire life he has engaged in the tilling of the soil. He acquired his education in the common schools, and remained at home until after his marriage, bringing his bride to the old homestead farm, where he yet resides. He inherited the Matlack homestead and expects always to make it his place of residence. On February 1, 1900, Mr. Phillips was married to Miss Florence E. Watson, who was born in Bucks county, January 1, 1877. Her paternal grandfather, Howard Watson was

born at Edgewood, Bucks county, March 10, 1822, and learned the blacksmith's trade, which he followed throughout his active business career, but in his later years lived retired. After his marriage he settled at Horsham, where he conducted a smithy for a number of years, but is now living retired in Byberry. He married Catherine L. Doron, who was born in June, 1826, and was reared at Hatboro Mill. They resided for forty-nine years at the Horsham homestead, having there a small tract of land and a commodious home. They were members of the Horsham meeting, and Mr. Watson was a Republican in his political affiliation. Their children were: Elwood, a steamboat clerk and business man; B. Frank; Enos, a farmer of Horsham; Howard, engaged in the insurance business; and Adele, wife of H. Jenks. B. Frank Watson was born at Horsham and learned the blacksmith's trade with his father. He remained at home until his marriage and then settled upon a rented farm, where he lived for a year. He afterward located upon the homestead now occupied by Francis M. Phillips, and here he carried on agricultural pursuits throughout his remaining days, passing away February 28, 1898. He followed general farming and also raised some stock, and was practical and successful in his business methods. In politics he was a Republican, and fraternally was connected with the Knights of Pythias. His wife died in 1897. She lost her parents during her early girlhood and was reared by her grandparents, who were prominent farming people and were highly respected throughout the community in which they lived. Mrs. Watson was an only child. By her marriage she became the mother of four children: Florence E., now Mrs. Phillips; Herbert; Claude L.; and Leila H. Both Mr. and Mrs. Phillips hold membership in the Hartsville Presbyterian church. They are widely known in Bucks county, representing old families of Pennsylvania, and Mr. Phillips is regarded as one of the progressive agriculturists of his community.

ELMER E. ALTHOUSE, editor and proprietor of the "Sellersville Herald," was born in Sellersville, Bucks county, Pennsylvania, December 12, 1874, and is a son of Milton D. and Elizabeth (Nace) Althouse. The pioneer ancestor of the subject of this sketch was Arndt (Andrew) Althouse, who emigrated from Germany in the ship "Fane" arriving in Philadelphia on October 17, 1749. He located on the Tohickon, near Church Hill, in Haycock township. He and his wife Anna Maria were members of Tohickon Reformed church at Church Hill, and their son Daniel was baptised there March 4, 1753.

Daniel Althouse was a farmer in Haycock township until 1785, when he located in Bedminster township, where he died in 1795. He was twice married and left the following children: Maria, Frederick, Abraham, Conrad, Michael, Jacob and Rebecca by the first wife, and Isaac, Elizabeth, Daniel, Martin, and George by the second wife.

Frederick Althouse, born in Haycock in 1783, on attaining manhood located in Rockhill township, where he purchased twenty-three acres of land in 1818. In 1824 he purchased of Andrew Schlichter a farm of eighty-seven acres on the Bethlehem road, near Sellersville, and lived there the remainder of his life, dying January 26, 1852. He married Susanna Schlichter, of Rockhill township, and had nine children who survived him, viz: Thomas, Elias, Daniel, James, Andrew, Elizabeth, wife of Enos Sellers; Hannah, wife of Isaac Barndt; Mary, wife of Noah Weisel, and Abigail.

Elias Althouse, second son of Frederick and Susanna (Schlichter) Althouse, was born and reared in Rockhill township. He was born August 5, 1814, and died in July, 1869. At the death of his father he accepted a portion of the homestead and it was adjudged to him by the orphans' court, and part of his allotment was a small lot included in the present limits of Sellersville borough. He was a tailor by trade, and probably lived on this lot and followed his calling. He moved back to Rockhill in 1856, and lived there until his death in 1869. He married Maria Dietz, daughter of Abraham Dietz, of Rockhill, and they were the parents of nine children, viz: Milton D.; Susanna, wife of Thomas R. Leister; Elizabeth, wife of Peter R. Ziegenfuss; Henry; John; Thomas; William; Amos; and Emma, wife of Charles Himmelwright.

Milton D. Althouse was born in Rockhill township, January 6, 1841, and was reared and educated in Sellersville. He learned the trade of a cigar maker when a boy, and worked at that trade for twenty-five years. He at one time owned and conducted a cigar factory in Sellersville. He has always taken an active interest in the affairs of the town, and has filled a number of local offices, serving as school director and member of borough council for several terms. In politics he is an ardent Republican, and for many years took an active part in the councils of the party. He was elected to the office of recorder of deeds of Bucks county in 1884, and served one term of three years. He has also filled the position of transcribing clerk in the recorder's office. In 1889 he was appointed postmaster of Sellersville by President Harrison, and filled that position for four years. Since July, 1903, he has had charge of the rural free delivery on the Sellersville mail route. He and his family are members of the Reformed church at Schlichtersville, of which he has been an elder for

twenty-two years, and deacon for eight years. He also filled the position of trustee and treasurer of the church. He is a member of the Knights of the Golden Eagle and Patriotic Order Sons of America. He married, October 15, 1863, Elizabeth Nace, and they have been the parents of four children, of whom only Elmer E., the subject of this sketch, survives.

Elmer E. Althouse was born in 1874, and was reared in Sellersville. He graduated from the Sellersville high school in 1891, and from Pierce's Business College, Philadelphia, in 1892. He entered the law department of the University of Pennsylvania and graduated in 1896. He, however, had a taste for journalism, having been correspondent for Philadelphia and Doylestown papers for some years, and in 1897 started the "Sellersville Herald" in partnership with C. R. Addison. During the first year he purchased his partner's interest, and has since conducted the paper alone, which now has the largest subscription of any weekly paper in upper Bucks. He is also connected with the "Emaus Herald," published at Emaus, Lehigh county, Pennsylvania. The "Herald" is a popular weekly local paper and exercises a potent influence toward the improvement and development of the town of Sellersville and vicinity. Mr. Althouse is deeply interested in the affairs of his native town, and has filled a number of local positions; he is now serving as borough auditor.

He is a member of McCalla Lodge, No. 596, F. and A. M., and Sellersville Lodge, No. 658, I. O. O. F. Mr. Althouse married June 30, 1807, Margaret G. Leinbach, daughter of Rev. Samuel A., and Margaret (Everhart) Leinbach, and they are the parents of two children—Samuel L., born October 12, 1899; and Mary Elizabeth, born March 23, 1905. The family are members of St. Paul's Reformed church, Sellersville.

HENRY KEMMERER KLINE, residing at Quakertown, Bucks county, Pennsylvania, is a representative of an old family of German extraction. His ancestor, Isaac Kline, came from Germany and settled in Bucks county prior to the Revolutionary war. By his wife Barbara, Isaac Kline was father of a son George, born August 17, 1788, who married Susanna Hembach, born November 16, 1803. George and Susanna (Hembach) Kline were the parents of the following named children: 1. Solomon, born February 12, 1826; died July, 1904; he married Sarah Keppler, and resided in Easton. 2. Mary, married M. Erdman. 3. Isaac, born 1828; married Emeline Kneedler, of Kneedler's Corner, Gwynedd township, and lived in Bethlehem. 4. Sarah, born April 12, 1834, married Joseph Himevelt, and lived in Philadelphia. 5. Susanna, born September 3, 1835, married Louis Kehl, of Montgomery county. 6. George, to be further mentioned hereinafter. 7. An infant. The father of this family died February 3, 1838, and his wife survived him many years, dying January 14, 1875.

George Hembach Kline, son of George and Susanna (Hembach) Kline, was born January 13, 1837, on a farm then owned and cultivated by his father, at Hembach, Lower Milford township, Lehigh county. He attended the subscription school of Samuel Crawford, at Swamp Church, and also for two years the public schools, which were then first opened. He then went to Plymouth Meeting, Montgomery county, where he remained until his sixteenth year, working on a farm and attending the Friends' school. He was then apprenticed to Jacob Harley, a harness maker at Zion Hill, Lehigh county, and who was father of Jonas Harley, proprietor of a harness manufactory at Quakertown. Here George Kline remained one year, when he went to Quakertown, where he entered the employ of Louis P. Jacoby. In the course of a few years he established a shop on his own account at Riegelsville, Durham township. In 1859 he located in Quakertown, where he purchased the business of his former employer, Louis Jacoby. He conducted his establishment profitably until the second year of the civil war, when (October 1, 1862) he enlisted in Company H, Fifteenth Regiment Pennsylvania Cavalry, Colonel William J. Palmer commanding. He was detailed for special duty as saddler, and in August, 1863, was promoted to sergeant, which rank he held until he was honorably discharged from the service of the United States after the collapse of the rebellion, in June, 1865. He participated in some of the most stirring campaigns of the great conflict, and among the notable battles in which he bore a part was the sanguinary struggle at Chickamauga, Tennessee. After returning from his army service, Mr. Kline resumed his business, which he has successfully conducted to the present time. He has always taken an active part in community affairs, and enjoys the respect and confidence of his neighbors in high degree. During President Cleveland's first administration he filled a full term of four years as postmaster, discharging the duties of the position with ability and integrity. In politics he is a stanch Democrat. With his family he holds membership in St. John's Lutheran Church, in which he has served as deacon, and has otherwise been active in church work.

In 1857, while residing in Riegelsville, Mr. Kline married Elmina, daughter of Henry and Lydia (Bartholomew) Kemmerer, and of this union were born the following children: 1. Henry Kemmerer, to be further mentioned; 2. Emma B., who became the wife of Harry Y. Jacoby, son of Simon Jacoby, of Sellersville, Bucks county; 3. Susan B., who became the wife of Andrew Snovel, of Hatfield, Montgomery county; 4. William K.

Henry Kemmerer Kline, eldest child of George H. Elmina (Kemmerer) Kline, was born June 4, 1862. He attended the common schools and the high school until reaching his sixteenth year, after which he worked for J. S. Harley. He became assistant postmaster to his father, acting in that capacity for four years. During the second Cleveland administration and that of President Harrison he was assistant postmaster to Edward Ochs, and after the death of Mr. Ochs, with Dr. Joseph Thomas. For two years and a half he was assistant to Mahlon Detweiler, after which he was employed for six months by Mrs. Clymer. Since October, 1903, he has been engaged in stovemounting. He has been active in public affairs, and for four years served as clerk of the council, and is now a member of the school board and clerk of the election board. In politics he is a Democrat. He and his wife are members of St. John's Lutheran Church, in which for many years he has served as deacon and secretary of the Sunday school. Mr. Kline married, December 26, 1891, Emma Matilda, daughter of Til and Amelia (Mint) Osnean, of Quakertown, formerly of Allentown, and they have three children: J. Robert, Herman Otto and Lillian Naomi. All these children attend school and J. Robert is studying music.

JOSHUA TOMLINSON, honored as the oldest living resident of Langhorne, of which city he is a native, and the only surviving charter member of the Lodge of Odd Fellows in that village, is a representative of ancestry who settled in Pennsylvania in the colonial days, shortly before the Revolution. The founders of the American branch of the family came from England and settled in Philadelphia and Bucks counties. They were farmers by occupation, and Friends in religion.

Mr. Tomlinson was born March 24, 1822, in Middletown township, son of Aaron and Jane (Headley) Tomlinson; grandson of William and Rachel (Everett) Tomlinson; and great-grandson of Richard Tomlinson. He was educated at the Friends' school and the Belleview school in Langhorne, that last named being then under the charge of William Mann, one of the most capable

teachers of that day. Young Tomlinson labored upon the paternal farm until he was seventeen, and at that early age entered upon an apprenticeship to the coachmaker's trade in a shop which his father conducted in connection with his farming labors. He was so employed for four years, and at the expiration of that time, his father retiring, he succeeded to the management. He conducted the business with much success until 1849, when he sold it and went to Maryland, where he cultivated a plantation for a couple of years. In 1851 he returned to Middletown and resumed his coachmaking business, in which he successfully continued until 1875, when he retired to a finely improved and highly productive farm which he had previously purchased, and where he made his home for thirteen years. He then made a final removal to Langhorne, where he has since resided, occupying a beautiful and comfortable home where he enjoys that well merited ease and contentment which should properly crown so active and well spent a life. He enjoys the esteem and confidence of the community, to whose prosperity and advancement he has materially contributed, and among whom he is held in peculiar regard as the oldest citizen. He is the oldest surviving member of and the only charter member now living of Orionto Lodge, No. 177, I. O. O. F., organized in May, 1846, and of which he has been an active and contributing member continuously down to the present time, a period of forty-eight years. He was for five years a justice of the peace, and for many years was a member and secretary of the old Attleboro Fire Company. In religion he is a Friend, and in politics a staunch Republican, having affiliated with the party when it organized in 1856 for its noble purpose of staying the aggressions of slaveholders and the prostitution of free soil to human slavery, a crime against humanity and a sin against God. Mr. Tomlinson married, July 4, 1847, Miss Lydia Ann Noble, of Philadelphia, daughter of Edward and Elizabeth (Tiller) Noble. Of this union were born three children, all of whom were educated in the Friends' and public schools of Langhorne. They were: 1. Edward Hicks, born May 11, 1848, he married Annie Reigan, and they became the parents of the following children— Florence May, born 1874; Joshua Noble, who married in 1904, Elizabeth Griffith; Estelle, Clarence L., and one who died in infancy. Florence May was married to Ervin Fisher, of Philadelphia, and they became the parents of two children: Nevin and Oswald Fisher. Elizabeth Jane, born September 29, 1850. Frederick Noble, born June 17, 1855, never married. Mrs. Tomlinson, mother of this family, passed away January 28,

1902, leaving to her mourning husband and children the tender memories of a beautiful spirit which shed the light of love upon all who came into companionship with her.

GEORGE TOMLINSON, son of Aaron and Jane (Headley) Tomlinson, and grandson of William and Rachel (Everett) Tomlinson, mentioned in the preceding sketch, was born in Middletown, February 15, 1840, and was educated at the public and Friends' schools of Langhorne. He remained on the farm with his parents until twenty years of age. In 1861 he responded to the call of his country by enlisting in Company F, One Hundred and Fourth Regiment Pennsylvania Volunteers under Captain Alfred Marple, and that veteran of two wars, Colonel (now General) W. W. H. Davis, and participated with his regiment in the bloody battles of Fair Oaks, the Seven Days Fight, Malvern Hill, as well as in a number of other engagements and skirmishes. On account of ill health he was honorably discharged on October 3, 1862, after having been confined for some time to the military hospital on David's Island, New York. He returned home, and after careful nursing regained to some extent his normal health, though he never fully recovered from the results of the campaign of hardships in the Virginia swamps. As soon as sufficiently recovered he resumed the vocation of a farmer, which he followed until 1883 when, having purchased a house on Green street, Langhorne, he retired to that borough, where he has since resided, having built his present residence in 1891. He has always taken an active interest in the affairs of the town, and is a member of Sergeant Hugh A. Martindale Post, G. A. R., No. 366, and of Orionto Lodge, No. 177, I. O. O. F. He was reared in the faith of the Society of Friends, of which his ancestors have been members for many generations. In politics he is a Republican, and has always taken an active interest in the success of his party. He married, December 21, 1865, Annie Strouse, daughter of Samuel and Susan (Lutz) Strouse, of Langhorne.

EDWARD A. IVINS, of Falls township, a representative of one of the old and honored families of Bucks county, may be properly mentioned among the citizens who are contributing their quota toward the development of the agricultural interests of the community. He is a native of Penns Manor, the date of his birth being February 11, 1858.

Aaron Ivins, grandfather of Edward A. Ivins, resided at Penns Manor, Falls township, where he successfully conducted agricultural pursuits for a number of years. He married Hope Aaronson, and they were the parents of three children: Edward A.,

Aaron R., and Stephen Woolston. His second wife, whose maiden name was Hannah Eastburn, bore him two children, one of whom died in childhood, the other being William Henry Ivins, of Langhorne, Pennsylvania.

Edward A. Ivins, eldest son of Aaron and Hope (Aaronson) Ivins, was born in Penns Manor, July 30, 1828. The occupation to which he was reared he made his life work, being accounted one of the practical and progressive farmers of his locality. He enjoyed the confidence of the entire community, and was thoroughly trustworthy in all the relations of life. He was united in marriage to Anna Brown, who was born in Penns Manor, May 23, 1830, a daughter of Moses and Ann (Harvey) Brown, lifelong residents of Penns Manor. Moses Brown was born in 1792, was a farmer by occupation, and died May 16, 1874, aged eighty-eight years. His wife, Ann (Harvey) Brown was born in 1794, and died January 10, 1852, at the age of fifty-eight years. They were the parents of five children: Alice, who died in infancy; Elizabeth, who became the wife of Thomas Headley, and died at the age of eighty-five years; Sarah, born 1820, died at the age of twenty-one years; Mary, born 1825, died in 1871; and Anna, aforementioned as the wife of Edward A. Ivins. The family on both sides were members of the Friends Society. The children born to Edward A. and Anna B. Ivins were as follows: Annie, who died unmarried; De Witt Clinton, a resident of Plainfield, New Jersey; Edward A., mentioned hereinafter; M. Harvey, a resident of Langhorne, Bucks county, and William Henry, deceased. Edward A. Ivins, father of these children, died at Penns Manor, August 12, 1900.

Edward A. Ivins, second son of Edward A. and Anna (Brown) Ivins, entered the public schools of Penns Manor at the usual age, and after studying for some time became a student in the Friends Central School, of Philadelphia, conducted by Aaron B. Ivins, a relative. When he had completed his course of study he entered the employ of the Philadelphia and Reading Railroad Company as clerk in the counting department, and remained there for eighteen years, this fact being ample proof that he was one of its most trusted and capable employes, discharging the duties assigned to him in a conscientious and painstaking manner. In June, 1900, prior to the death of his father, he returned to the old homestead and assumed its management, and since then has given his attention exclusively to the same, his energy and enterprise being resultant factors in making this one of the fine farming properties of the locality, having thereon all the improvements usually found upon the estate of a careful, energetic and progressive farmer.

Edward A. Ivins married Mary L. Thomas, who was born January 8, 1863, a daughter of Jonathan and Mary Ann (Knight) Thomas, deceased, who were well known residents of Bensalem township, and the parents of eleven children, among whom were the following: Ellwood, Carrie, wife of J. J. Broadhurst, of Langhorne; Howard, Reese, Henry, Russell, Mary, wife of Edward A. Ivins; Franklin, and Clinton Thomas; they also had a step-daughter, Ellen Thomas. One child was the issue of the marriage of Edward A. and Mary L. Ivins, A. Russell Thomas Ivins, born January 19, 1892.

SAMUEL J. GARNER, of Hatboro, Montgomery county, Pennsylvania, was born in Philadelphia, of Bucks county parents, May 2, 1852, but for the last thirty years has been one of the leading citizens of the thriving borough, just over Bucks county's southwestern line.

The family of Garner is of German origin, and descended from Hans (John) Garner, who came to Bucks county about the middle of the eighteenth century and settled in New Britain township, near the present village of Colmar on the county line. Samuel Garner, son of John, the pioneer, was reared in New Britain township, Bucks county, and became a prominent man and a large landowner there and in Warrington. He reared a large family of children, among whom was Samuel, the grandfather of the subject of this sketch. By a later division of the township most of the land of Samuel Garner, Sr., in New Britain township, was incorporated into the township of Warrington and is still owned and occupied by his descendants.

Samuel Garner (2) was born in New Britain township, Bucks county in 1798, and, inheriting a portion of his father's real estate, followed the life of a farmer there and in Warrington during the active years of his life, removing late in life to Doylestown where he died about 1877. He took an active interest in the affairs of his locality, filled a number of local positions, and was a soldier in the Mexican war. He married Mary A. Snare whose father was for several years proprietor of the old historic Green Tree Tavern on the county line in Warrington township. On the maternal side she was descended from the Polks and other prominent Scotch-Irish families of Neshaminy colony in Warwick and Warrington.

Samuel S. Garner, son of Samuel and Mary A. (Snare) Garner, was born in Warrington township, Bucks county, in March, 1828, and lived there until the age of eighteen years, when he went to Philadelphia and learned the trade of a bricklayer, and resided there the greater part of his life. He married a widow Ray, whose maiden name was Elizabeth Carr. He died in 1890.

Samuel J. Garner, the son of Samuel S. and Elizabeth (Carr) Garner, born in Philadelphia, May 2, 1852, attended school

in Philadelphia and in Doylestown township, Bucks county, where a portion of his boyhood was spent. He later learned the jewelry trade, and in 1872 located in Hatboro and opened a jewelry store, later opening a clothing and a more general merchandise store. He conducted both businesses for ten or twelve years, and then engaged in the real estate business, which he has since followed with success. In politics Mr. Garner is a Republican, but he has never aspired to public office. He has served many years on the local school board, of which he is president, and has always taken an active interest in educational matters. He has also served for several years as a member of borough council, and taken a leading part in all that pertained to the best interests of the borough. He is one of the directors of the Bucks County Trust Company, and interested in a number of Bucks county's local enterprises.

He married Fannie H. Wilson, daughter of Silas Wilson, a well known dry goods merchant of Philadelphia, and they are the parents of five children: Howard W., a graduate of the University of Pennsylvania, and now studying in Paris; Marion, residing at home; Samuel Carl, in the brokerage business in Philadelphia; and Ralph and Florence, who are attending the public school.

FRANKLIN GILKESON. The late Benjamin F. Gilkeson, for many years one of the leading attorneys of the Bucks county bar, and prominently identified with the political affairs of his native county, was born in Bristol, Bucks county, August 23, 1842, and spent his whole life there.

His father, Andrew W. Gilkeson, Esq., was born in Montgomery county, but was of Bucks county ancestors, and spent most of his life in this county. His father, also named Andrew, was a lieutenant-colonel in the war of 1812, and prominently identified with the volunteer militia in the years immediately following the second war with Great Britain, and the family were among the early settlers of Pennsylvania. Andrew W. Gilkeson was a prominent attorney, being admitted to the Bucks county bar April 29, 1840, and practicing for many years at Bristol. He took an active interest in the affairs of the county, and filled the office of prothonotary of the county for the term of 1854-7. He married Margaret M. Kinsey, of that borough, whose ancestors had been among the early English settlers in Bucks county, her great-great-grandfather, Samuel Kinsey, having settled in Bristol township in 1728. Andrew and Margaret M. (Kinsey) Gilkeson were the parents of four children, of whom Benjamin Franklin was the eldest, and the late A. Weir Gilkeson, also a prominent attorney of Bristol, was the youngest.

Benjamin F. Gilkeson was educated in the graded schools of Bristol and at the academy at Hartsville. He studied law with the late Anthony Swain, of Bristol, and was admitted to the bar February 2, 1864, and at once engaged in practice at Bristol. Possessed of more than ordinary ability in the line of his profession, an earnest and careful student, his unflagging energy and indomitable will soon brought him to the front, and for twenty-five years prior to his death he was the leader of the Bucks county bar, and represented vast corporate interests both in the county and elsewhere. Soon after his admission to the bar he launched into the political arena, and was a prominent figure in the political councils of the county and state for many years. Reared in the Democratic faith, he was an early convert to the principles of the Republican party, and was for several years a colleague of Hon. Caleb N. Taylor, at that period a potent political factor in Bucks county and twice her representative in congress. Taylor and Gilkeson later became estranged, and the rising young attorney became the recognized leader of his party in the county, and held that position in local and state politics for many years. He served as the representative of his county in many state, national and congressional conventions, and also in the state committee, of which he was for some years chairman. He was intimately associated with the leading statesmen and politicians of his day, serving in the cabinet of Governor Daniel H. Hastings as commissioner of banking, and taking an active part in state affairs for many years. He was second comptroller of the United States Treasury during the administration of President Harrison, and made an excellent record. He was prominent in the Masonic fraternity, and served as district deputy grand master for Bucks and Montgomery counties. He was one of the trustees of the State Lunatic Asylum at Norristown, and held many other positions of trust and honor.

Mr. Gilkeson was twice married; first in 1870, to Charlotte B. Jones, daughter of George B. Jones, of Pittsburg. She died in 1872, and he married (second) in 1874 Helen E. Pike, daughter of Samuel Pike of Bristol, and they were the parents of three children: Franklin, a member of the Bucks county bar, and of the firm of Gilkeson & Janes, and two daughters, Helen and Ethel.

HARRISON C. STOUT. Among the useful and respected citizens of Bucks county must be numbered Harrison C. Stout, of Quakertown. He is a grandson of Jacob and Lydia (Barndt) Stout, whose son, Abraham Barnard, in youth assisted his father on the farm and afterward learned the cabinet maker's trade. In politics he was a Whig, and in religion a member of the German Reformed church. He married Lydia Cressman, and they were the parents of one son; Harrison C., mentioned at length hereinafter. The death of Mr. Stout occurred in 1841.

Harrison C. Stout, son of Abraham Barnard and Lydia (Cressman) Stout, was born October 3, 1836, at Sellersville, Rockhill township, and was the only child of his parents. While he was still an infant the family moved to Milford township and settled in what is now Rosedale. After the death of his father his mother moved to Sellersville, and it was there that Harrison C. spent his boyhood. At the end of eight years he went to live with his uncle, Jacob Stout, and in 1851 moved to Doylestown, where he was employed on the "Bucks County Express," a German newspaper. After a few months he was obliged to abandon this work on account of failing sight, and took a position with Dr. W. S. Hendrick, with whom he remained for one year. He then went to Hagersville in order to learn the carpenter's trade with Elias Rosenberg, and after applying himself to that calling for two years and a half migrated to Stirling, Illinois. Thence he proceeded to Missouri, and extended his wanderings as far south as Fort Scott, Kansas. In the spring of 1859 he returned to Pennsylvania and settled with his uncle Jacob at Bridgetown, where for some time he worked at his trade. In 1863 he moved to Philadelphia, where for a short time he was employed as railroad carpenter, afterward applying himself to general carpentry. He then became foreman in the furniture factory of Ebert, Sleifer & Hall, a position which he held for eight years. In 1870 he moved to Sellersville, where he followed his trade until 1875, in which year he established himself as a manufacturer of cigar boxes. In 1890 he settled in Quakertown, building the plant which he now operates, and in which he employs a large number of hands. He is actively interested in local affairs, and during his residence in Sellersville served as chief burgess. Since coming to Quakertown he has been for three years a member of the council, and has also served as chairman of the electric light committee and of the fire department. He has been prominently identified with fire departments in various places for about fifty-three years. He was one of the organizers of the fire department at Sellersville, Bucks county, and was its first chief. In 1892 he organized the Quakertown fire department, and has been chief ever since. He had a wide reputation as a fireman, and has in many instances risked his own life to save others from being consumed by the flames. Politically he is a Republican, and is active in the interests of the organization. He is a member of the First Reformed church, in which he has held the office of trustee and since 1889 has served continuously as elder.

Mr. Stout married, October 18, 1860, Mary Ann Nace, and they have one son. Edward Newton, born March 30, 1863, and lives in Philadelphia, where he is employed as an engineer in Cramp's shipyard. He

married in 1882, Susan, daughter of Jesse and Eliza (Nace) Nace, of Sellersville, and their family consists of the following children: Minnie, died in 1891; Harrison Stephen, born September 20, 1885, and lives with his grandfather in Quakertown; William, born June 30, 1891, and is at home with his parents in Philadelphia; and Charles, deceased. Mrs. Stout is a granddaughter of Adolf and Annie (Weitzel) Nace, whose son Isaac was born July ?, 1810, and was a lifelong farmer. He lived at one time in Montgomery county, and later took up his abode in Haycock township. He married in 1835, Anna, daughter of John and Mary (Zellers) Berger, and they were the parents of the following children: 1. William, born January 21, 1837, married, January 1, 1860, Lisetta Seems, and lives at Siegfried, Lehigh county. 2. Mary Ann, born February 8, 1839, became the wife of Harrison C. Stout, as mentioned above. 3. Henry, born October 25, 1841, is unmarried and makes his home with his sister. 4. Eliza, born February 21, 1843, resides in Philadelphia. 5. Isaac, born February, 1846, married Elizabeth Monroe, of Philadelphia, and died in 1889. 6. Sarah, married a Mr. Obiedenn, of Philadelphia. 7. Isaac, born July 3, 1855, died in 1899. Mr. Nace, the father, passed the greater part of his life in New Britain township, but at the time of his death was a resident of Silverdale, Hilltown township.

WILLIAM SCOTT is the owner of a good farm about a mile distant from Yardley. It was in the vicinity of this borough that he was born, on the 16th of December, 1864. His father, Thomas Scott, emigrated from his native country, Ireland, to America in 1857, when nineteen years of age, and settled in Chester county, Pennsylvania, where he worked on a farm for about three years. He then removed to Penns Manor, Bucks county, where he entered the employ of Arthur Collins, in whose service he remained for some time. He then began farming on his own account, and has since given his undivided attention to agricultural pursuits. He is a member of the Presbyterian church of Morrisville, and a respected and worthy citizen of his community. He married Miss Cecelia Moran, a daughter of William and Margaret Moran, of Chester county, Pennsylvania, and they had four children, one of whom died in childhood, the others being William Robert, a resident farmer of Lower Makefield township; and Mary, at home.

At the usual age, William Scott entered the public schools, his time being passed in a manner similar to that of most farm lads of the period. He continued to assist his father in the cultivation of the home place until eighteen years of age, when he went to New York city, believing that he would prefer commercial life. He then entered the employ of T. G. Patterson,

Thomas. K. Gumpper

manufacturer of packing boxes, with whom he continued for twelve years. On the expiration of that period he returned to Chester county, Pennsylvania, where he had charge of a farm for William J. Moran for two years, and then returned to Bucks county, where he purchased the farm upon which he now resides, about one mile distant from Yardley, and has since given his entire attention to agricultural pursuits. In politics he is a Democrat, but has never sought or desired public office, preferring to devote his attention to his business affairs, in which he is now meeting with creditable and gratifying success. Mr. Scott married Miss Margaret Irwin, and they have two children: Edith G., born February 4, 1901; and Florence, born July 17, 1902.